CELEBRATING CANADA

Volume 1

Holidays, National Days, and the Crafting of Identities

Holidays are a key to helping us understand the transformation of national, regional, community, and ethnic identities. In *Celebrating Canada*, Matthew Hayday and Raymond Blake situate Canada in an international context as they examine the history and evolution of our national and provincial holidays and annual celebrations.

The contributors to this volume examine such holidays as Dominion Day, Victoria Day, Quebec's Fête Nationale, and Canadian Thanksgiving, among many others. They also discuss how Canadians celebrate the national days of other countries (such as the Fourth of July) and how Dominion Day was observed in the United Kingdom. Drawing heavily on primary sources, as well as theories of nationalism, identities, and invented traditions, the essays in this collection demonstrate that national days and holidays provide rich ground for analysing Canada's social, cultural, and political development.

MATTHEW HAYDAY is an associate professor in the Department of History at the University of Guelph.

RAYMOND B. BLAKE is a professor in the Department of History at the University of Regina.

Celebrating Canada

Volume 1

Holidays, National Days, and the Crafting of Identities

Edited by Matthew Hayday and
Raymond B. Blake

UNIVERSITY OF TORONTO PRESS
Toronto Buffalo London

© University of Toronto Press 2016
Toronto Buffalo London
www.utppublishing.com
Printed in Canada

ISBN 978-1-4426-4980-4 (cloth)   ISBN 978-1-4426-2713-0 (paper)

Library and Archives Canada Cataloguing in Publication

Celebrating Canada. Volume 1, Holidays, national days, and the crafting of identities / edited by Matthew Hayday and Raymond B. Blake.

Includes bibliographical references.
ISBN 978-1-4426-4980-4 (hardback)   ISBN 978-1-4426-2713-0 (paperback)

1. Holidays – Canada.   2. Canada – Social life and customs.   3. National characteristics, Canadian.   4. Nationalism – Canada.   I. Hayday, Matthew, 1977–, editor   II. Blake, Raymond B. (Raymond Benjamin), editor   III. Title: Holidays, national days, and the crafting of identities.

GT4813.A2C434   2016   394.26971   C2016-905760-7

This book has been published with the help of a grant from the Federation for the Humanities and Social Sciences, through the Awards to Scholarly Publications Program, using funds provided by the Social Sciences and Humanities Research Council of Canada.

University of Toronto Press acknowledges the financial assistance to its publishing program of the Canada Council for the Arts and the Ontario Arts Council, an agency of the Government of Ontario.

Canada Council   Conseil des Arts
for the Arts   du Canada

ONTARIO ARTS COUNCIL
CONSEIL DES ARTS DE L'ONTARIO
an Ontario government agency
un organisme du gouvernement de l'Ontario

Funded by the   Financé par le
Government   gouvernement
of Canada   du Canada   Canadä

Contents

Acknowledgments

Writing a book is always a complex and involved process, often an enjoyable one, but definitely one that involves collaboration with and help from numerous people.

This volume took shape largely at a workshop that took place in the fall of 2014 at the Canadian Museum of History, supported by a Social Sciences and Humanities Research Council of Canada Connections Grant. Our research assistant, Ted Cogan, did an excellent job coordinating logistics for this workshop both before and after and handled our website. We would like to thank Maureen Ward, Lisa Leblanc, Shainna Laviolette, Forrest Pass, and James Trepanier from the Canadian Museum of History for all of their help in making that workshop come together and for the museum's sponsorship of the event. Mark Kristmanson, Robert Talbot, Marc-André Gagnon, and Yves Frenette participated in our public roundtable discussion, which gave participants some initial food for thought. Sean Graham, from ActiveHistory.ca, recorded an interesting set of podcasts for the History Slam series with workshop participants in connection with this project.

In addition to all of the contributors to this volume, we would like to thank the following people who also participated in the Celebrating Canada workshop and contributed to the improvement of the draft chapters that were discussed there: Meaghan Beaton, Lee Blanding, Denis Bourque, Lynn Caldwell, Caroline-Isabelle Caron, Helen Davies, Brandon Dimmel, Bonnie Huskins, Darryl Leroux, Christopher Los, Greg Marquis, Matthew McRae, Del Muise, Ryan O'Connor, Cristina Ogden, Peter Price, Chantal Richard, Ron Roy, Robyn Schwarz, Lindsay Thistle, and Anne Trépanier. Additional financial support for this project came from the Dean's Office of the College of Arts and the History Department at the University of Guelph.

We would like to thank the two anonymous readers whose suggestions made this volume stronger. We are also grateful to the entire team at the University of Toronto Press for their work on this volume, in particular Len Husband, who worked closely with us through the whole development process; Barbara Tessman, for her careful work copy-editing the manuscript; and Frances Mundy, who oversaw the production process.

Finally, on a personal note, Matthew Hayday would like to thank his husband, Matthew Kayahara, both for his support and encouragement over the years of working on this project and also for the fond memories of walking home, drenched to the bone, in the torrential rain that turned Elgin Street into a virtual river after the Canada Day concert on Parliament Hill in 1999. Raymond Blake wishes to thank his family, Wanda, Robert, and Ben, who have spent several vacations in small-town Canada while he laboured away in local archives in British Columbia, Alberta, and Nova Scotia. They thoroughly enjoyed Canada Day on Parliament Hill in 2005 as part of their drive from Regina, Saskatchewan to Hermitage, Newfoundland, where they also participated in Hermitage Day celebrations. Canada Day celebrations have become an annual event in their home, though the nature of those celebrations have changed as they are now young adults.

CELEBRATING CANADA

Volume 1

Holidays, National Days, and the Crafting of Identities

Introduction: Nationalism, Identity, and Community in Canada's Holidays

MATTHEW HAYDAY AND RAYMOND B. BLAKE

This book considers the role that holidays and annual celebrations have played in the construction of national, regional, provincial, and community identities in Canada. It is, therefore, appropriate to begin with a couple of personal histories of how Canada's national days have been experienced by the editors of this collection.

Matthew Hayday, raised in the Toronto suburb of North York in the 1980s, remembers the Canada Days of his childhood as an occasion to go and watch fireworks, whether the massive displays at Ontario Place or Canada's Wonderland, or the smaller ones set off by neighbours in the local park. When he was a child, this holiday was on par with Victoria Day in terms of the scale of the firework displays, and he has no memories of attending any particularly patriotic events. It was not until he was a graduate student at the University of Ottawa in the late 1990s that he first experienced the massive, patriotic Canada Day festivities in the nation's capital. The entire downtown was closed to vehicular traffic to accommodate the huge crowds that swelled the Parliament Hill area to see the formal ceremonies, attend the concerts, and watch the fireworks. Now a resident of Guelph, Ontario, Matthew hosts an annual barbecue at his house on Canada Day, serving suitably Canadian food like Nanaimo bars and apple-and-maple sausages. On July 1st, he flies the Canadian flag that he received from the Department of Canadian Heritage in 1996 in honour of National Flag of Canada Day.

For Raymond Blake, raised in rural Newfoundland and Labrador during the 1960s, one might have expected memories of how the Battle of Beaumont-Hamel was commemorated on July 1st. This event, on the first day of the Battle of the Somme in 1916, marked a devastating loss for the Newfoundland Regiment and makes the anniversary of Confederation today a more sombre event in the province. But Raymond has few strong memories of the Dominion Days of his childhood or even of the commemoration of Beaumont-Hamel, remembering them as fairly low-key events, even during his university days in St. John's. It is Empire Day that stands out much more strongly in his memory as the occasion for picnics and waving the Union Jack.

For the co-editors of this volume, then, three of Canada's national holidays are part of their memories, although in rather different ways, and weighted differently in their importance. As the chapters in this volume will attest, this variability in how holidays are celebrated and in the importance attached to them by Canadians is not surprising. Flexibility, it seems, has been key to establishing the traditions around annual celebrations of national days in Canada and to providing various ways for Canadians, with their diverse identities, to find meaning in these holidays. Indeed, the question of defining Canadian identity itself has proven to be tricky indeed.

It might seem trite to answer the question, "What does it mean to be Canadian?" with a glib "Not to be American." And yet, many Canadians, when posed with this question, will start by rattling off elements of their identity in opposition to this American "other." This is particularly true in English-speaking Canada, where there is no language difference from our neighbour to the south. But the issue of identity is not much simpler in French-speaking Canada, where the traditional markers of identity oriented around a Roman Catholic faith and a common ethnic background have declined in salience (or at least become more problematic with respect to political correctness). In both linguistic communities, many give serious thought before they begin to respond seriously to this question.

From an academic perspective, the fact that Canadian identity is hard to define is a goldmine that has given rise to a wealth of scholarly work. The ongoing process of defining "Canadian-ness" (along with all of Canada's various subnational identities) has a rich history. There tends to be particular interest, both in Canada and other countries, of using major landmark anniversaries to assess the state of the nation – the nature of its history, the lay of the land at present, and the possibilities for the future. With the 150th anniversary of Confederation – the political act that gave birth to the Dominion of Canada – being observed in 2017, the time seemed right for such an evaluation of how Canadians have defined and celebrated themselves. The authors represented in this collection came together at the

"Celebrating Canada" workshop in Ottawa in the fall of 2014 to share their research, explore connections and common themes in their work, and enhance their understanding of the bigger picture of Canada's cultures of celebration and commemoration.

The essays in this volume focus on the particular ways in which Canadians, throughout their history, have observed their national days and other significant holidays. They inquire into the whys, whos, and hows related to the organization of these annual celebrations. They probe what these celebrations and holidays say about the nation(s) observing them, and trace how these events have changed over time. These celebrations, combined with commemorations held to mark major anniversaries of landmark events in Canada's development, have played major roles throughout Canada's history to forge, foster, and modify its identities.

The National Days: The Scaffolding of Nationalism

In his work on national symbols, Michael Geisler argues that "national holidays, more often than not, are relatively weak and extremely unstable signifiers of national identity,"[1] noting that they fail to appear alongside such symbols as flags, emblems, currencies, and even national monuments in Anthony Smith's work on nationalism. Unlike these symbols, which make up a large part of the repertoire of "banal nationalism" analysed by Michael Billig,[2] national days cannot pass unnoticed. Since they each occur only once a year, national holidays do not fade into the background and become part of what people internalize subliminally as their national identities. Their rare occurrence – when compared to repeated use of flags, anthems, or money bearing national symbols – means that they are more visible (when they are indeed celebrated), and thus they "reveal the scaffolding of the nationalist construction."[3] Although this may make national holidays less than ideal as a vehicle for studying national symbols, it makes them perfect for our objectives. For it is this "scaffolding" that interests us – the who, the what, the why, and the how related to the construction, portrayal, and contestation of Canada's various national and subnational identities throughout the country's history.

The study of national days, while no longer in its infancy, is still a developing field. It owes much to the pioneering concepts and terminology developed by Benedict Anderson and Eric Hobsbawm, scholars of nationalism who, respectively, coined the concepts of "imagined communities" and "invented traditions." Anderson observes that there is nothing inevitable or particularly organic about nations. The vast majority of inhabitants of a given political state will never meet or encounter each other, and yet there are nonetheless processes that lead these people to think that they have much in common with each other – enough to die for their country in times of war.[4] Although nations may be communities of the mind, and thus "imagined," as opposed to having a physical reality, they are nonetheless very real in the minds of those who believe in them. Anderson explored many factors that contributed to the formation of these imagined communities and to the spread of the concept of nationhood worldwide. A shared national mass media for instance – or "print capitalism," to use Anderson's term – may reinforce a sense of nationhood by defining the "foreign" and the "national" in terms of how events are reported. And the idea of a widely printed newspaper, commonly being read by individuals across the country, using a shared and fixed language, was itself a shared experience of the national community.[5]

Often the tools used to either create or reinforce a sense of common national identity were deliberately fostered by the state. Eric Hobsbawm argues that many so-called "traditions" within national communities are "quite recent in origins and sometimes invented."[6] These "invented traditions" are "sets of practices, normally governed by overtly or tacitly accepted rules and of a ritual or symbolic nature, which seek to inculcate certain values and norms of behaviour by repetition, which automatically implies continuity with the past. In fact, where possible, they normally attempt to establish continuity with a suitable historic past."[7] Hobsbawm further notes that although this process of inventing traditions has cropped up throughout history, it occurs more frequently in periods when there has been a rapid transformation of society that challenges or destroys old social patterns or traditions, and when old traditions are no longer sufficiently adaptable or flexible to accommodate the new order.[8] They are often, therefore, a key tool in the *re-invention* or reformulation of the national community. Sometimes these new traditions can be grafted onto old ones, or can borrow tools from common rituals and symbolic practices. Other times, they require innovation and originality.[9]

Since the advent of the industrial revolution, these traditions, according to Hobsbawm, have belonged to three overlapping types: "a) those establishing or symbolizing social cohesion or the membership of groups, real or artificial communities, b) those establishing or legitimizing institutions, status or relations of authority, and c) those whose main purpose was socialization, the inculcation of beliefs, value systems and conventions of behaviour."[10] National public holidays, as one of the forms of invented traditions,[11] fit into all three types. And yet, these "invented traditions" would neither come into existence nor establish themselves if they could not acquire significant social and political functions. There are therefore, arguably, limitations to how manipulable they are. Moreover, the tastes and fashions of what will become popular with the masses can be "created" only within certain limits.[12] In other words, state authorities cannot simply dictate that a tradition will come into being and become popular with the citizenry – the idea must tap into some type of need, and resonate with the population. It is the task of the historian (and scholars in related fields) to determine why and how such traditions, including national holidays, come into being and why they succeed or fail.

In the introduction to her 2004 edited collection, *National Days, National Ways,* communications scholar Linda K. Fuller observed that national days "bespeak the ways a country operates. How those holidays are experienced by the public, and how those nations are viewed by the wider world, become pivotal. National images, we learn, can help form attitudes and affect behaviours. National days encourage that image making."[13] Focused on discourse analysis and the media as a tool for shaping national identity, the essays in Fuller's collection considered historical, political, and religious celebrations from around the world, primarily with a present-day orientation. The essay on Canada by Derek Foster considered the competitive celebrations of Canada Day (1 July) and Quebec's Fête nationale (24 June) in the 1990s (with the then-recent addition of National Aboriginal Day on 21 June). Foster also noted that Canada Day had become an opportunity for Canadians to engage in a "moment of the carnivalesque, a rupture in the usual state of being,"[14] as they celebrated their country with vigour, in contrast to their normal state of comparative sobriety. In the 1990s, Canada Day celebrations tended to be celebrations "of the people" rather than of history, current events, or hopes for the future, an emphasis he attributed to the divided nature of the Canadian nation and to the goal of inclusivity in the celebrations.[15] However, that chapter, like most in the collection, said little about the origins of these national days or about how their celebration and observance had shifted over time. Fuller noted the relative paucity of systematic studies of national days and their symbolic content, and expressed hope that her collection would launch further explorations.

Sociologist David McCrone and cultural policy professor Gayle McPherson further advanced the discussion of national days in their 2009 volume *National Days: Constructing and Mobilising National Identity*, which included contributions about twelve different national days, but, alas, no Canadian examples. These case studies, spanning four continents, demonstrated the extremely variable experiences of national days. Indeed, McCrone and McPherson noted that the sole commonality of these national days was that all were "key markers in national biography."[16] Not all of the nations and subnational groups studied in their collection even observed their national days. Of those that did, the ways in which they did so, the degrees of state support and organization, and the forms of celebration varied widely. There was certainly no inevitability that a national day would be celebrated or what form such a day might take. Rather, McCrone and McPherson observed that "national days come to be through some complex cultural and social struggles... We learn much about the structuring of power by the way national days are, or are not, done." Moreover, "what they are, how they are celebrated, and by whom reveals much about the societies in which they occur."[17]

McCrone and McPherson's collection (which they acknowledged was only the beginning of understanding national days[18]) pointed to the need to consider the social and economic interests served by these celebrations, and their changing meanings. Even the date chosen was of great importance because of how it defined the "we" of the nation.[19] Even in countries with well-known and seemingly well-established and entrenched national days, the initial establishment of these holidays was a contested, political act, as Christian Amalvi notes in his chapter on Bastille Day in Pierre Nora's classic *Lieux de Mémoire*, and as Len Travers has similarly observed about Independence Day in the United States in *Celebrating the Fourth*.[20] In England, the national day – St George's Day – is not routinely observed. And yet in the broader context of the British Isles, both St Andrew's Day and St Patrick's Day are significant events. This dynamic in the United Kingdom highlights a few key aspects of the study of national days, as there are competing national days in many countries, commemorating political and cultural events "which remain contested and problematic."[21] Moreover, it is common to have a disjuncture between the "nation" and the "state" in countries such as the United Kingdom and Spain – and, indeed,

Canada – which gives rise to tensions between sub-state national "fêtes" and state-ordained holidays. In other cases, national days are deliberately *not* celebrated because of how problematic they are to one group or another. With all of this variability and conflict, McCrone and McPherson aptly observe, "one might even say that their [national days'] significance lies in being markers of conflict and contestation."[22] They are "subject to competition and conflict; to invention and reinvention; to remembering and forgetting." As such, these days provide an opportunity to analyse what they "tell us about who people think they are, who others think they are ... and how national identities are made, unmade and remade."[23]

Considering the Canadian Context

These ideas provide us with a fruitful launching point for an in-depth consideration of the Canadian context for national days and holidays. The Canadian calendar is a rather busy one, with a mix of different types of national, regional, subnational, imperial, and religious holidays – along with the feast days of other nations and their patron saints – all contributing to the fostering of Canada's various national identities. The importance of these various holidays has waxed and waned over the past two centuries, and the forms of their observance have radically changed over time. As Matthew Hayday's work on the history of Dominion Day and Canada Day shows, Canada's federal governments did not feel a particular need to sponsor celebrations of the "national day" until the 1950s. Once this attitude changed, these celebrations went through successive waves of redefinition and adaptation of both form and content, according to the political needs and cultural conceptions of the country's governments.[24] Moreover, as Raymond Blake's work has demonstrated, even the name of Canada's national day was highly contentious; it took over thirty-five years for the government to officially change "Dominion Day" to "Canada Day."[25] In this volume, chapters by Forrest Pass; Mike Benbough-Jackson; Lianbi Zhu and Timothy Baycroft; Stuart Ward; Matthew Hayday; and Raymond Blake and Bailey Antonishyn analyse how the celebration of Canada's national day has undergone substantial transformation and has been a site of contestation of Canadian national identity throughout the country's 150 years of existence.

The Canadian context is complicated by the existence of multiple "national" communities co-existing within one country. This has given rise, in turn, to competing national holidays. French Canada's national holiday (June 24th) has undergone a transformation comparable to that of the Dominion Day–Canada Day trajectory. As cultural and religious studies scholars including Eva-Marie Kröller, Katia Malausséna, Donald Luc Boivert, and Amie Gérin have shown, the nationalist, but highly religious, Saint-Jean-Baptiste Day morphed from a celebration laden with religious iconography and messages of survival and cultural preservation to become Quebec's Fête nationale in the 1970s, with more modern, nationalistic overtones.[26] As Marc-André Gagnon's chapter in this volume shows, the early years of the Fête nationale period were also the subject of political controversy, as the government of Quebec and the major nationalist organizations sought to control the day and invest it with particular messaging. Outside of Quebec, June 24th has continued along a more traditionalist path in francophone Ontario and other French-Canadian communities.[27] In Acadia, le 15 août celebrations that were initially timed to coincide with the Catholic feast of the Assumption have also assumed increased importance for nationalist organizations seeking to advance political agendas, as Michael Poplyansky's chapter informs us. More recently, efforts to promote and celebrate a National Aboriginal Day on June 21st have added to the density of national holidays in Canada's summer calendar.

Other holidays, even those that are not explicitly "national" days, have certainly contributed to the definition of Canadian identity. In one of the earliest published academic studies of a holiday in Canada, Robert Stamp considered how Empire Day was used in Ontario schools to foster particular conceptions of the role of the British Empire in Canadian life, equating Canadian nationalism and British imperialism.[28] Empire Day, unlike Victoria Day, which occurs in the same month, was explicitly not a day off from work or school but was intended to be an opportunity for school-based activities to inculcate specific values in Canadian schoolchildren. As the chapters in this volume by Marcel Martel, Allison Marie Ward, Joel Belliveau, and Brittney Anne Bos demonstrate, the meaning of Empire Day changed over time, as organizers attempted to keep it relevant and to appeal to an increasingly diverse population. They did not always succeed, and the holiday fell out of favour, first in French Canada in the context of the First World War conscription crisis, and then throughout the Commonwealth by the decolonization era of the 1950s.

As much of the scholarly literature on celebrations and holidays shows, the long-term success of a holiday may well be determined by its capacity for flexible interpretation, inclusiveness, and change over time. Craig Heron and Steve Penfold's history of Labour Day, which became a statutory national holiday in 1894, provides an excellent example of a holiday that went through many waves of reinvention as social groups reshaped the day and made it their own, with competing appeals of various activities that took place on this day. Labour Day was always a combination of, and competition between, the priorities of workers' movements and of wider communities; there was never "a singular notion of the holiday's meaning."[29] Tensions between different organizers' visions, and between the desires of organizers and participants as to how these days should be observed and celebrated, are a constant thread throughout the literature on holidays and national days.

One might even argue that creative tensions and contestations help to keep holidays alive and relevant. As Jonathan Vance noted in his analysis of Armistice Day (which became a national holiday paired with Thanksgiving Day in 1921), a reaction against pacifist groups that wanted the holiday scrapped for its perpetuation of militarism led to a revitalization and reinvigoration of the observance of that holiday in the late 1920s.[30] This challenge to the meaning of the memory of the war led veterans groups to recommit to the holiday and reinvigorate its observance throughout the 1930s. Ultimately, the day was rebranded as Remembrance Day and officially separated from Thanksgiving, as Teresa Iacobelli's chapter details.[31]

At a broader level, our understanding of these holidays is informed by the century and a half of efforts since Confederation to determine what exactly Canadian culture is, or should be. Although Father of Confederation George-Étienne Cartier had a vision of a common Canadian political identity that could encompass multiple cultures and nations, there have nonetheless been many efforts to try to shape a common Canadian culture, originating largely within the dominant English-speaking community (although there is certainly a long-running "deux nations" tradition that many trace to Henri Bourassa in the late nineteenth century). As Carl Berger observed in his classic work *The Sense of Power*, in the late nineteenth and early twentieth centuries, many English-speaking Canadians viewed partnership in the British Empire as an avenue to national greatness, and British values as the bedrock of Canadian cultural identity.[32] Then, over the course of the first four decades of the twentieth century, war, immigration, and changing trading patterns and mass media influences all combined to challenge this British-centric conception of Canadian identity. The rising stature of the

United States in international affairs and the impact of its mass media in Canada provided an alternative identity model – embraced by some, but feared by others.

The years following the Second World War witnessed a much broader set of projects related to the definition of cultural identity. Between 1945 and 1971, Canada established its own citizenship law, which created a Canadian citizenship separate from that of the British subject; it launched a series of royal commissions on issues related to culture, the arts, broadcasting, and the mass media; it adopted a new flag; and it instituted new public policies on official languages and multiculturalism. With the establishment of new policies to promote Canadian content in the mass media, publishing, and universities as well as on the airwaves, the Canadian government was definitely "in the business" of culture and identity in these decades. However, the precise contours of what that identity should be, and how it would express itself, were certainly up for debate and contestation. The English-speaking side was pulled in different directions by the twin attractors of Britain (not yet completely faded) and the United States (on the ascendancy); French Canada continued to be a sizeable and influential national presence; and both multicultural and First Nations communities increasingly staked claims to roles in defining the national imaginary.[33] All of these factors came into play in shaping the national days observed in this period.

José Igartua has argued that by the start of the 1970s, a new Canadian identity had emerged that had shed much of its British trappings and had embraced a new, bilingual, multicultural model. There is certainly evidence that "official" Ottawa-led culture had moved in this direction, although C.P. Champion has contended that many of the new Canadian symbols of the Pearson era remained rooted in British traditions, and Bryan Palmer contends that a new identity model had failed to firmly coalesce. While the revised Canadian identity described by Igartua may have dominated much of the official, elite, and mass media discourse about the nation, not all accepted this transition without question. Indeed, as Eva Mackey noted in her study of Canada's 125th anniversary celebrations in 1992, there were many "ordinary," undifferentiated, white Canadians who did not identify with the multicultural Canadian mosaic and, indeed, felt marginalized by it. Many of these "Canadian-Canadians" were hostile to the rejection of the British traditions with which they at least nominally identified.[34] This same cohort felt that, along with its Britishness, Canada had shed its connection to, and pride in, its military heritage. The merger of the three branches of the armed forces under the government of Pierre Trudeau was a particular sore spot. More recently, as Ian McKay and Jamie Swift have argued, these Canadians, along with allies in the government of Stephen Harper, attempted to foster a more militaristic version of Canada's history and identity.[35] This "Warrior Nation" persona contrasts starkly with the peacekeeping-oriented version that accompanied the redefinition of Canada during the 1960s.

Towards an Understanding of Canada's Cultures of Celebration and Holiday Practices

The essays in this collection analyse the evolution of Canadian holidays and the forms of identity Canadians attempted to articulate around them from the 1840s to the present day. Although covering over a century and a half of history, and events that range from the local to the national, from British Columbia to Nova Scotia, there is nonetheless a great deal of commonality to the issues and themes that they address. All are concerned, to various degrees, with the central issue of identity and the symbolic practices that shape it. While some chapters are more explicitly concerned with local, community, or provincial identities than national ones, in most cases these are local identities that are being defined in relation to, or in competition with, a broader national or international context. Several chapters explicitly speak to the international dimensions of Canada's celebratory practices in its national holidays, as governments, organizers, and citizens attempted to define how the country of Canada would relate to, draw inspiration from, or react against its "parent" countries of Britain and France, or its neighbour the United States. Many authors also speak to how Canada's religious identities, primarily those of the Protestant and Catholic traditions, informed the way its national communities performed their identities on these holidays and how the role of religion, broadly speaking, has declined over time.

One of the strengths of the approach taken in the chapters in this collection is that it allows for the consideration of the evolution of these holidays and the construction of national identity over time, rather than capturing only a single moment in time. This enables the authors to consider how these celebrations and observances have changed to suit new demands, or have failed to change and declined in relevance. Of the holidays discussed in this volume, those that have persisted over time have often done so because their organizers allowed for flexibility in how they were observed and what meanings they could convey. In many cases, participants insisted on this flexibility to celebrate in the ways they wanted. This also allowed for multiple forms of participation by Canadians. Indeed, as will be clear in many of the chapters, the meaning of what a "holiday" should be, and how it might be observed, could vary greatly at the individual level. Participation could range from participating in a parade or public ceremony to being a live spectator at such an event. After the 1950s, it might have involved watching an organized spectacle on television. Or Canadians might have marked the holiday in their own fashion by taking the day off to go to the beach or organizing a family barbecue. It is often difficult to trace how Canadians who engaged in some of the more "passive" forms of observance might have derived meaning from these holidays, but it would be a mistake to assume that they did not find their own meaning and significance in these personal rituals or that they considered these holidays to be irrelevant to their own lives. However, while flexibility of observance could be a strength for many holidays, there were limits. If a holiday's meaning lost its relevance for its intended audience, or it could not reinvent itself to regain significance, it could fade away, as was the fate of Empire Day. There were limits to the elasticity of what some holidays could mean, and sometimes a renaming was needed (or perceived to be so) to regain traction with the people.

Reinvention, whether of identities or of the celebrations helping to define these identities, is a recurrent trope throughout the chapters in this volume. The identities of Canadians, Quebeckers, Acadians, British Columbians, and so forth were not static, nor were the means by which they were celebrated and marked. Nor were these identities monolithic, and one of the most interesting dimensions of these celebrations is the contestation between competing conceptions of what these identities were, and what they should be. This even manifested in competing festivals, events, and holidays on days either proximate or overlapping on the calendar. As McCrone and McPherson observe, "national days ... can be contested, argued, even fought over, claimed and disclaimed, reinvented as well as fall into abeyance."[36]

Not all holidays are born equal, nor do they enjoy the same official status. Moreover, the purpose of the holiday will inform its rites and its structure. Within this volume, there is a mix of holidays that are "official" statutory days when citizens do not have to work, and others that, while marked on the calendar as holidays, do not absolve

Canadians from school or work. As the authors in this volume note, this variation is often deliberate, as the actors who instigated or shaped the holiday often wanted to emphasize certain types of observances or rituals. Empire Day, for example, had an explicit educational focus and thus observing it with classroom-based activities on a school day was important. Many did not want Remembrance Day to be a holiday, in the "day-off" sense of the term, because the significance of the moment of silence was heightened by it being a deliberate break in the workday. The timing of holidays within the calendar, and indeed within the week, was also contested. There were economic considerations that fed into debates over whether workers should be given certain days off and also over whether holidays should be fixed to a specific calendar date or should "float" to permit the creation of long weekends. Long weekends could benefit tourism-based industries yet detract from active participation at ceremonial events. These debates were usually mediated through the state. Federal, provincial, and municipal actors are central to the dramas that played out over which holidays would be given official status, how that status would be manifested, and the degree to which the state would regulate or fund activities organized by third-party organizers or manage these holiday celebrations directly.

Each of the holidays discussed in this book considers identities, nations, and communities to varying degrees, and how these are expressed and celebrated. The manner in which these holidays orient their messaging and conceptualization of identities to the past, the present, and the future can be complex and fascinating. At different points in the history of these holidays, any of these points in time could be divisive or unifying – or both. History was not always a rallying point for the community or nation, the present could be a time of active conflict, and/or the future could be uncertain. When considering how visions of the past, present, and future enter into the identities being celebrated and constructed in these holidays, then, we must also consider the silences – what is being overlooked, deliberately and communally forgotten, or elided. For these silences also tell us much about the nationalisms, identities, and community values that were being articulated in these events. Our chronicle of Canadian celebrations begins in the decades prior to Confederation, when Canada had no national day of its own to celebrate or commemorate. But its major urban centers were already diverse places where a variety of different ethnic and religious groups lived side by side. These communities sought to maintain their own cultures while also demonstrating that they could participate in, and shape, a common civic culture. As Gillian Leitch demonstrates in her chapter about parades in the streets of Montreal on national days and religious holidays in the mid-nineteenth century, a wide array of different ethnic groups – including the English, Irish, Scots, French Canadians, and Germans – sought to celebrate national days from their countries of origin, and yet demonstrate their commitment to a unified civic identity. Their annual parades employed a common repertoire of symbols and performance structures that allowed them to both highlight their own distinctiveness and show that they were invested in the city as members of the broader British Empire. The various ethnic communities of Montreal initially participated in each other's national day parades, and later were eager spectators at these annual events. Roman Catholics, the largest population in Canada East/Quebec, engaged in peaceful religious processions on major feast days, largely without provoking disturbances. Groups that might have provoked discord (or riots), such as the Orange Order, were not tolerated in the streets and were denied permission to parade. Ethnic identities, and the celebration of national and community difference, were tolerated as long as they were celebrated in a harmonious, unified approach that respected the broader civic community.

While Catholics in Montreal, a minority group in the broader national Canadian community at Confederation, used their processions at least partly to assert their right to participation in the public sphere, Protestant clergymen in Ontario were similarly making use of feast days to try to shape Canada's emergent identity. First declared as a holiday in 1859 by the governor general, Canadian Thanksgiving demonstrates the complex relationship between the state and religious authorities in shaping the observance and meaning of such a holiday. As Peter Stevens argues, Thanksgiving was initially explicitly Protestant in origin, and clergymen sought to use this religious holiday to promote a vision of Canada as a chosen people, superior to both the United States and Catholic nations. Over time, as these religious leaders campaigned to have the state declare Thanksgiving a public holiday, they lost control over both the form of Thanksgiving observances and, indeed, the specific timing of the holiday. Over the late nineteenth and early twentieth century, the holiday took on both imperialist and secular harvest-festival trappings. While these popularized Canadian Thanksgiving and even opened it up to Catholics, it signalled a loss of control by religious leaders. Of course, Thanksgiving was also a quintessentially American holiday in the minds of many, and asserting the particular

Canadian-British spin on the day was a challenge. As both Leitch and Stevens demonstrate, the religious divisions in the Canadian population did not result in a secularized approach to the construction of Canada's identity. Rather, both Catholics and Protestants sought to assert a visible presence, and if possible a guiding hand, in Canada's celebratory culture of the nineteenth century.

Chapters 3–6 consider the important role played by Great Britain, the British monarchy, and the wider British Empire (and then the Commonwealth) in shaping Canadian identity and the dominion's holidays at the turn of the twentieth century, and then through the following five decades. Conceptions of empire, and the potential role that a mature and developed Canadian state could play in its activities, constituted an important strand of British-Canadian nationalism in the late nineteenth and early twentieth century. This was clearly manifested in the types of holidays that English-speaking Canadians sought to create and celebrate towards the end of Queen Victoria's reign. While Gillian Leitch's chapter notes that celebrations of the Queen's Birthday were commonplace throughout the empire (including Montreal), the celebration of Victoria's Diamond Jubilee in 1897 was the impetus for additional celebrations of the queen and the wider British Empire.

Chris Tait's chapter considers the parliamentary efforts to make the 24th of May, Victoria's birthday, a national holiday in Canada. These efforts, finally successful in 1901, made Victoria Day a perpetual holiday in Canada. Ultimately, it became a unique celebration in the British Commonwealth, as other countries moved their queen's (or king's) birthday celebrations with each subsequent monarch. Tait considers the regional popularity of Victoria's birthday, and how religious, commercial, and seasonal factors all shaped the debates over whether Canada should create a holiday in May to honour the monarch who was in power from the Union period to the end of the century. Tait argues that the ultimate acceptance of the holiday by the Laurier government, but with the name of "Victoria Day" rather than "Queen Victoria Day," was done partially to appease anti-imperialist French-Canadian sentiment. This lack of an explicit element of royalism and imperialism in the name has perhaps contributed to the holiday's longevity. For a wider swathe of the population, it seemed more acceptable to honour Victoria herself, rather than the role of the monarch, with a permanent place on Canada's festive calendar.

While Victoria Day has endured to the present (albeit largely as an occasion for fireworks and "two-fours" at the cottage) in English-speaking

Canada (unlike in Quebec, where the competing holidays of the Fête de Dollard and then the Journée nationale des patriotes were observed on the same weekend), the same was not true of the accompanying day for educational activities and celebration of the British world. Empire Day, which was not a holiday in the sense of being a day off from work, had variable durability in Canada and the rest of the empire, as the three chapters by Marcel Martel, Allison Marie Ward, Joel Belliveau, and Brittney Anne Bos demonstrate. Created initially in Ontario in 1898 at the instigation of Clementina Fessenden Trenholme, Empire Day ultimately spread to the rest of Canada through the efforts of its imperialist backers as a day to celebrate British values and imperialism. A proto-national holiday, it mixed elements of the monarch's birthday with those of a national day. Over the course of the first half of the twentieth century, the themes emphasized on the day and the manner of its celebration evolved in an effort to maintain public interest and its relevance. Martel and Belliveau argue that French-Canadian communities initially gave the observance of Empire Day a chance, attempting to stress the openness of British democratic values and liberties and the place French Canada could have within the empire. However, the conscription crisis of the First World War brought an end to such openness, as nationalist organizations increasingly opted to celebrate the colonial-era hero Dollard des Ormeaux on the same weekend – a deliberate counter-celebration and act of resistance to Empire Day's imperial narrative.

Even in Hamilton, Ontario, the birthplace whence Empire Day spread throughout Canada and then to Australia and the United Kingdom, the celebration of this day ultimately faded. As Bos and Ward discuss, local celebrations endured for a few decades, able to maintain public interest through the flexibility organizers showed in stressing different aspects of the empire, including opportunities for immigrants and the global merits of British democratic values. Diversity was a key trope that helped Empire Day endure until after the Second World War. However, with the collapse of the empire itself, and its replacement by the British Commonwealth, Empire Day was an anachronism by the 1950s, and it faded from observance. Flexibility of meaning could help the holiday endure only as long as some importance was attached to its key referent and the population was willing to engage in its observance.

Bos and Ward observe that militarism and youth were key elements of Empire Day activities of the 1920s. The place of the military and Canada's wartime sacrifices were central to the efforts to create another holiday – or perhaps day of observance might be the better term – to mark the end of the First World War and honour Canada's war dead. Teresa Iacobelli's chapter considers the debates around Armistice Day and Remembrance Day and how the date and nature of an annual commemoration of the end of the war were constructed. Initially linked with Canadian Thanksgiving, which was moved to 11 November for several years after the end of the war, the day was called Armistice Day for the next decade. The ten-year anniversary of the war, combined with efforts by the Royal Canadian Legion, prompted a re-examination of the holiday, which was renamed Remembrance Day to shift the focus to the ordinary men and women who served in the war rather than the political act of the armistice. Iacobelli traces the heated debates around when and how Remembrance Day would be observed, and analyses the interests, including those of business, veterans, and national myth–makers, that shaped the interpretations, forms of observance, and legal status of the day. Remembrance Day exemplifies the distinction between holidays as celebrations/days off and those that followed a more commemorative, educational, and solemn model of observance.

Canada's "national" day, July 1st, marks the anniversary of Confederation in 1867. Initially called Dominion Day, it was renamed Canada Day in 1982. Although it marks an important stage in the political transformation of Canada from colony to country, July 1st is of variable significance across the provinces, as some joined Canada on different dates. In Newfoundland (which did not become a province until 1949), the day is one of mourning in honour of those killed in the Battle of Beaumont-Hamel during the First World War. As the six chapters in this volume that deal with Dominion Day / Canada Day attest, its observance and celebration have been varied and complex indeed.

Our examination of Dominion Day begins in a province that was not an initial party to Confederation. As Forrest Pass argues in his chapter on how the day was observed in British Columbia, Dominion Day's flexibility to accommodate multiple forms of observance and meaning was one of its key strengths. British Columbians used the day not only to celebrate their regional identities within Confederation but also to challenge federal policies and approaches to nationhood that they found exclusionary. British Columbians could redefine the meaning of Dominion Day because they viewed Canada's national identity as a participatory process rather than a received ideology. As Pass compellingly describes, this held true as well for often-marginalized ethnic communities and Indigenous peoples within the province. Aboriginal communities actively participated in the province's Dominion Day events, both to assert their identities and to contest assimilationist policies, although many white organizers viewed their participation as a (welcome) sign of assimilation. Chinese and Japanese Canadians also organized floats in British Columbia's Dominion Day parades to stress their role in the building of the province, although in later decades, as Lianbi Zhu and Timothy Baycroft's chapter shows, the Chinese would adopt a different approach to contest Canada's exclusionary immigration policies.

Pass's analysis of Dominion Day celebrations demonstrates how the tradition of celebrating American Independence Day, which fell just three days later, had been ingrained in the colony before it became a province. In the early decades following 1871, when British Columbia joined Confederation, there was a certain degree of overlap of the holidays and appropriation of key themes, such as 1 July being British Columbia's "Independence Day," with many seeing revolutionary aspects in the political transformation from colony to province. The proximity of these two North American national days invited comparisons, which played out in interesting ways among expatriate communities, as Mike Benbough-Jackson notes in his chapter about how Dominion Day was observed in the "mother country" in the first two decades of the twentieth century. Benbough-Jackson shows that it is not just the inhabitants of the nation who contribute to its imagining, but outsiders as well, particularly when there is a shared cultural heritage. His chapter moves off the wartime battlefield, so often asserted of late as the place where Canada was "forged as a nation," and argues that there were processes of identity formation and the adoption of symbols and identity tropes ongoing in the first two decades of the twentieth century among Canadians living in Britain. On British soil, Canadians used their national day to perform their identities, and this played out in various ways that asserted their North American roots. In addition to displays of Canadian flags (of the Red Ensign variety), performances of patriotic songs, and other symbolic elements, a vigorous, masculine, northern identity was performed in sporting and lumberjack contests. Themes of the north and nature played out in a variety of ways, marking the Canadians as distinct both from the Britons with whom they were living and the Americans who marked their Independence Day three days later.

Lianbi Zhu and Timothy Baycroft's chapter provides a fascinating look at how British Columbia's Chinese community contested

Dominion Day in the years following the passage of the Chinese Exclusion Act. Although China's diplomatic envoys to Canada refused to protest this legislation, leaders of British Columbia's Chinese community created a politically pointed celebration, Chinese Humiliation Day, which was observed on Dominion Day. Members of Vancouver and Victoria's Chinese communities were urged to wear badges, hang banners in windows, and fly flags at half mast to mark the humiliation of Canada's exclusionary policies towards the Chinese. Yet there were internal tensions within the community, because the Chinese both wanted to ensure that these policies were changed and also sought full participation in Canadian society. They thus debated whether abstaining from Dominion Day involvement and instead promoting their own day in protest was the best way to reach their goals.

Although the Canadian government organized elaborate festivities for the Diamond Jubilee of Confederation in 1927, as work by Robert Cupido and Jane Nicholas has discussed,[37] Ottawa otherwise took a hands-off approach to the observance of Dominion Day for many decades, leaving the organization of festivities to local communities. This changed in the 1950s. Matthew Hayday's chapter traces the evolution of federally sponsored events on Dominion Day and Canada Day from the Diefenbaker years through to their assumption of a standardized form in the late 1980s and early 1990s. Hayday shows how a succession of governments and their key policy makers attempted to use the national day to craft a national narrative of Canadian identity and how that narrative changed from British-centric to one that was bilingual, multicultural, populist, and inclusive of Aboriginal peoples. Yet organizers struggled mightily to establish a tradition that would gain widespread acceptance from Canadians while not simply mimicking the U.S. model of nationalism and celebration that marked their national day.

The name of Canada's national day was problematic in many ways, with many Canadians, for various reasons, thinking that the term *Dominion* implied subordination to Britain, or at least an overly British orientation to the day. As Raymond Blake and Bailey Antonishyn's chapter shows, this was the belief of the government of Pierre Elliott Trudeau. That government was engaged in a project of reconstructing Canada's national identity through national bilingualism, constitutional patriation, cultural pluralism, and entrenched human rights, in an effort to return to George-Étienne Cartier's vision of a Canadian identity rooted in diversity, but updated to the modern reality of the 1970s and 1980s. Trudeau's annual speeches on 1 July exhorted

Canadians to embrace this new approach to Canadian identity. Meanwhile, he and his ministers carefully avoided use of the term Dominion Day, instead using variants of "Canada's national day" and "Canada's birthday" before finally succeeding in having the name itself changed in 1982 to Canada Day. This change of name and identity formation was tied to larger questions about how large a role history and heritage should have in shaping Canada's national identity and symbols. Blake and Antonishyn argue that Trudeau thought history and heritage should play a limited role in the future shaping of Canada's identity – Canada should, he felt, understand its past, but neither be chained to it nor worship it.

The "de-dominionization" of Canada's national day had a broader international context, as Stuart Ward's chapter shows. Throughout the Commonwealth, settler states were simultaneously re-evaluating and recasting their identities and celebratory practices. Although Canada, Australia, New Zealand, and the white rebel enclave that declared independence in Rhodesia in the 1960s were seemingly unaware of how their fellow Commonwealth members were reinventing their national days and practices, all four were struggling to adjust to a post-imperial world. This shift posed similar challenges in each state, despite wildly different political contexts. Ward discusses three parallels to Canada's Dominion Day experience: the effort to upgrade Australia Day to the status of a "truly national" day; the attempts to modify Waitangi Day and make it a national holiday in New Zealand; and the search for an alternative to the Queen's Birthday as a national day in Rhodesia. He notes that the renewal of civic nationalism was not driven by "particularly coherent or consensual ideas about what the emergent nation-in-waiting should be"; rather, in each case there was the sense that civic cultural traditions required reinvention in a post-empire world. The official attempts by governments to create these new traditions "met deep pockets of resistance from conservative elements" within each national community. This has resulted in an enduring sense of doubt and discord about the precise meaning and purpose of the national holidays, and never-ending debates about the appropriate rituals of national observance. In each case, a certain degree of leaving the past behind was key to the approach of those seeking new national observances, and yet this was itself the cause of deep national divisions. In the Canadian context, at least, the national day did survive its renaming and reinvention (although pockets of Dominion Day diehards still exist). The capacity of Canada's national holiday for contestation and reinvention is perhaps reflective of the country itself, which has shown remarkable resiliency despite its internal turmoil.

"Canada," of course, is not the only "nation" on the northern half of the North American continent, and an entirely different set of national traditions, holidays, and observances existed in Québécois, Acadian, and other French-Canadian communities. For French Canada, including Quebec, the feast day of their patron saint, John the Baptist, or Saint-Jean-Baptiste, on 24 June, just a week before Dominion Day, had served as the national holiday since at least the middle of the nineteenth century. For most of the first century following Confederation, Saint-Jean-Baptiste Day observances were normally organized by the local Société Saint-Jean-Baptiste and were explicitly and overwhelmingly Roman Catholic in their orientation, featuring the image of the child John and his lamb. As cultural studies of the evolution of this holiday have discussed, in the 1960s the iconography of John the Baptist was radically updated, projecting an older, stronger, more vigorous figure, and the peaceful religious processions gave way to more nationalist demonstrations. Ultimately, in the late 1960s, the day was marked by riots. Indeed, the image of Prime Minister Trudeau defiantly refusing to move from the Montreal reviewing pavilion as separatist rioters pelted the stand with bottles was one of the defining images of the 1968 federal election.

By the late 1960s and 1970s, Quebec's identity was undergoing a dramatic transition, as the Quiet Revolution ushered in a secular, modern version of what it meant to be Québécois (and indeed a provincial/national identity less connected with the French-Canadian and Acadian minority communities elsewhere in Canada). As Marc-André Gagnon's chapter demonstrates, the Quebec government took an active interest in Saint-Jean-Baptiste Day as a vehicle to promote its vision of Québécois nationalism. His chapter traces the evolution of the politics of June 24th under the Parti québécois (PQ) government of René Lévesque, a period in which the day was renamed la Fête nationale and made a statutory holiday. Gagnon traces the dynamics of the PQ government's attempt to create structures for the celebration of the day and to craft messaging about an inclusive Quebec nationalism. This effort was complicated by the dynamic between the PQ government and its supporters among the nationalist organizers, particularly the Mouvement national des Québécois (MNQ) – the successor organization to the provincial federation of the Sociétés Saint-Jean-Baptiste that had borne responsibility for organizing the June 24th festivities. As Gagnon demonstrates, these years were marked by efforts to counter the federal government's Canada Day brand of nationalism and struggles around organization and financial management. The two "national" days were in a virtual cold war with each other, and yet each tried to avoid direct reference to the other as they used variants of the same repertoire of celebratory practices.

As Saint-Jean-Baptiste Day was secularized into the Fête nationale, so too was there a challenge to the original, Catholic formulation of the Acadian national day, le 15 août. The feast day of the Assumption had been deliberately chosen by Acadian leaders in the late nineteenth century as the national day. As Michael Poplyansky's chapter shows, le 15 août was rooted in traditional Acadian nationalism, which made it – like other Acadian symbols, including the Stella Maris flag – the target of neo-nationalists seeking to reinvent Acadia and francophone New Brunswick in the 1960s. But the power and tradition of the established holiday proved potent. Thus, over the course of the 1960s to the 1980s, the moderate nationalists of the Société des Acadiens du Nouveau-Brunswick and the radicals of the Parti acadien both ended up embracing the holiday and attempting to use it to advance their respective political projects and visions for the future of the Acadian nation. The day could serve as a rallying point for pride in what Acadians had accomplished in transforming the New Brunswick state by gaining equal institutions, or a rallying point symbolizing the unfinished business of creating an Acadian province. Repurposing the holiday (which never lost its traditional religious elements to the same extent as Saint-Jean-Baptiste Day had in Quebec) proved to be a more viable and productive approach than rejecting it, and linking themselves to the holiday was a way for nationalist organizations to legitimize themselves and their political agendas in the eyes of their fellow citizens.

Canada's governments continue to invent new holidays and attempt to imbue them with particular visions of the country's identity. In the final chapter of this collection, Richard Nimijean and Pauline Rankin consider the curious case of National Flag of Canada Day. Inaugurated in 1996, it is observed on 15 February, the anniversary of the first hoisting of the Maple Leaf flag in 1965. Nimijean and Rankin consider the strategic role of holidays as part of a broader policy of nation branding and efforts to mould the nation's political culture, comparing the observances of Flag Day under the Liberal and Conservative governments that have held office since its inauguration. National Flag of Canada

Day is not a statutory holiday, although in some years it overlaps with provincial holidays such as Family Day in Alberta, Saskatchewan, and Ontario and Manitoba's Riel Day, which are celebrated on the third Monday of February. Nimijean and Rankin observe that there have been overtly political dimensions to how governments have attempted to use this day, whether it be the Chrétien government's efforts to use it to promote Canadian symbols in Quebec after the 1995 referendum or Stephen Harper's attempts to link the Canadian flag to a more militaristic branding of Canadian identity. While many Canadians do not observe this "holiday," which has failed thus far to gain massive public traction, the authors caution us not to dismiss its significance. As they note, Flag Day is "best understood as a symbolic form of celebration created to operate on multiple levels related to identity, values, culture, partisan politics, and even leadership, not simply as a perfunctory and somewhat muted day of commemoration."

Holidays are celebrated and observed within broader political cultures and complex public policy frameworks, and we can learn much about the politics of national identity from how they are, or are not, celebrated. Canada's identities have transformed dramatically in the century and a half since Confederation, and it is our hope that the essays in this volume will shed a great deal of light on how its array of national holidays have contributed to that process. While organizers, participants, and observers were celebrating Canada, Quebec, Acadia, the British Empire, and a host of other ethnic, religious, and provincial identities, they were also constructing, shaping, and changing these same identities. These dynamic, politicized, and contested processes continue to the present day, and much can be learned about how this occurs through understanding what has happened in the past. For this, we now turn to the detailed examinations of these holidays.

NOTES

1 Michael Geisler, "The Calendar Conundrum: National Days as Unstable Signifiers," in *National Days: Constructing and Mobilising National Identity*, ed. David McCrone and Gayle McPherson (Houndmills, UK: Palgrave Macmillan, 2009), 14.
2 Michael Billig, *Banal Nationalism* (London: Sage, 1995).
3 Geisler, "The Calendar Conundrum," 17.

4 Benedict Anderson, *Imagined Communities: Reflections on the Origins and Spread of Nationalism* (London: Verso, 1983, 2006), 6.

5 Ibid., 43–5.

6 Eric Hobsbawm, "Introduction," in *The Invention of Tradition*, ed. Eric Hobsbawm and Terence Ranger (Cambridge: Cambridge University Press, 1983), 1.

7 Ibid., 1.

8 Ibid., 2–3.

9 Ibid., 6.

10 Ibid., 9.

11 Eric Hobsbawm, "Mass-Producing Traditions: Europe, 1870–1914," in *The Invention of Tradition*, ed. Hobsbawm and Ranger, 263.

12 Ibid., 307.

13 Linda Fuller, "Introduction," in *National Days, National Ways: Historical, Political and Religious Celebrations around the World*, ed. Linda Fuller (Westport, CT: Praeger, 2004), 3.

14 Derek Foster, "Canadian Days, Non-Canadian Ways" in *National Days, National Ways*, ed. Fuller, 47.

15 Ibid., 49.

16 David McCrone and Gayle McPherson, "Conclusion," in *National Days*, ed. McCrone and McPherson, 213.

17 Ibid., 218.

18 Ibid., 220. The journal *Nations and Nationalism* recently dedicated a special issue to the study of national days in Africa. *Nations and Nationalism* 19, no. 2 (2013): 203–408.

19 McCrone and McPherson, "Conclusion," 214.

20 Len Travers, *Celebrating the Fourth: Independence Day and the Rites of Nationalism in the Early Republic* (Amherst: University of Massachusetts Press, 1997). Christian Amalvi, "Bastille Day: From Dies Irae to Holiday," in *Realms of Memory: The Construction of the French Past*, vol. 3, *Symbols*, directed by Pierre Nora, English-language edition ed. Lawrence D. Kritzman (New York: Columbia University Press, 1998), 117–159. Hobsbawm also points to both days as invented traditions: Hobsbawm, "Mass-Producing Traditions," 271, 279.

21 David McCrone and Gayle McPherson, "Introduction," in *National Days*, ed. McCrone and McPherson, 1.

22 Ibid., 6.

23 Ibid., 8.

24 Matthew Hayday, "Fireworks, Folk-dancing, and Fostering a National Identity: The Politics of Canada Day," *Canadian Historical Review* 91, no. 2

(June 2010): 287–314; Hayday, "Variety Show as National Identity: CBC Television and Dominion Day Celebrations, 1958–1980," in *Communicating in Canada's Past: Essays in Media History*, ed. Gene Allen and Daniel Robinson (Toronto: University of Toronto Press, 2009), 168–93; Hayday, "La francophonie canadienne, le bilinguisme et l'identité canadienne dans les célébrations de la fête du Canada," in *Entre lieux et mémoire: L'inscription de la francophonie canadienne dans la durée*, ed. Anne Gilbert, Michel Bock, and Joseph-Yvon Thériault (Ottawa: Presses de l'Université d'Ottawa, 2009), 93–115.

25 Raymond B. Blake, "From Dominion Day to Canada Day, 1946–1982: History, Heritage and National Identity," *Asian Journal of Canadian Studies* 17, no. 2 (winter 2011): 1–32.

26 Donald Luc Boisvert, "Religion and Nationalism in Quebec: The Saint-Jean-Baptiste Celebrations in Sociological Perspective," (PhD diss., University of Ottawa, 1990); Eva-Marie Kröller, "Le Mouton de Troie: Changes in Quebec Cultural Symbolism," *American Review of Canadian Studies* 27, no. 4 (1997): 523–44; Katia Malausséna, "Commémoration et lien territorial: L'Angleterre et le Québec en comparaison," *Recherches sociographiques* 43, no. 1 (2002): 79–110. Amie Gérin, "Les espaces multiples de la fête: la Saint-Jean-Baptiste 1968 à Montréal," *British Journal of Canadian Studies* 27, no. 1 (2014): 1–20.

27 June 24 is celebrated with a public holiday in Newfoundland and Labrador to commemorate John Cabot's discovery of Newfoundland on the Feast Day of St John the Baptist.

28 Robert M. Stamp, "Empire Day in the Schools of Ontario: The Training of Young Imperialists," *Journal of Canadian Studies* 8, no 3 (1973): 32–42.

29 Craig Heron and Steve Penfold, *The Worker's Festival: A History of Labour Day* (Toronto: University of Toronto Press, 2005), xiii–xiv. Jacques Rouillard has undertaken a comparable study of the rising observance, and then ultimate collapse in the observance, of Labour Day in Montreal after the Second World War. See Jacques Rouillard, "La fête du Travail à Montréal le premier lundi de septembre: symbole de l'affirmation de la class ouvrière dans l'espace public (1886–1952)," *Revue d'histoire de l'Amérique française* 64, no. 2 (2010): 33–73.

30 Jonathan Vance, *Death So Noble: Memory, Meaning and the First World War* (Vancouver: UBC Press, 1997), 214.

31 Ibid., 211–19.

32 Carl Berger, *The Sense of Power: Studies in the Ideas of Canadian Imperialism, 1867–1914* (Toronto: University of Toronto Press, 1970).

33 The literature on postwar Canadian culture and identity continues to expand rapidly. Some of the key elements of these changes, and debates

over which conception of Canada was dominant, can be found in: José Igartua, *The Other Quiet Revolution: National Identities in English Canada, 1945–1971* (Vancouver: UBC Press, 2006); Bryan Palmer, *Canada's 1960s: The Ironies of Identity in a Rebellious Era* (Toronto: University of Toronto Press, 2009); Len Kuffert, *A Great Duty: Canadian Responses to Modern Life and Mass Culture, 1939–1967* (Montreal: McGill-Queen's University Press, 2003); Ryan Edwardson, *Canadian Content: Culture and the Quest for Nationhood* (Toronto: University of Toronto Press, 2008); Paul Litt, *The Muses, the Masses, and the Massey Commission* (Toronto: University of Toronto Press, 1992); Gary Miedema, *For Canada's Sake: Public Religion, Centennial Celebrations, and the Re-making of Canada in the 1960s* (Montreal: McGill-Queen's University Press, 2005); C.P. Champion, *The Strange Demise of British Canada: The Liberals and Canadian Nationalism, 1964–68* (Montreal: McGill-Queen's University Press, 2010); Phillip Buckner, ed., *Canada and the British Empire* (Oxford: Oxford University Press, 2008).

34 Eva Mackey, *The House of Difference: Cultural Politics and National Identity in Canada* (Toronto: University of Toronto Press, 2002), 19–22.

35 Ian McKay and Jamie Swift, *Warrior Nation: Rebranding Canada in an Age of Anxiety* (Toronto: Between the Lines, 2012).

36 McCrone and McPherson, "Introduction," 3.

37 Jane Nicholas, "Gendering the Jubilee: Gender and Modernity in the Diamond Jubilee of Confederation Celebrations, 1927," *Canadian Historical Review* 90, no. 2 (June 2009), 247–74; Robert Cupido, "The Medium, the Message and the Modern: The Jubilee Broadcast of 1927," *International Journal of Canadian Studies* 26 (fall 2002): 101–23; Cupido, "'The Puerlities of the National Complex': English Canada, the Empire and the Diamond Jubilee of Confederation," in *Beyond National Dreams: Essays on Canadian Citizenship and Nationalism*, ed. Andrew Nurse and Raymond B. Blake (Markham, ON: Fitzhenry & Whiteside, 2009), 81–110; Cupido, "Appropriating the Past: Pageants, Politics, and the Diamond Jubilee of Confederation," *Journal of the Canadian Historical Association* 9, no. 1 (1998): 155–86.

1 Claiming the Streets: Negotiating National Identities in Montreal's Parades, 1840–1880

GILLIAN I. LEITCH

Introduction

Throughout the nineteenth century, Montreal's streets served as a stage for the expression of various national and socio-economic identities. Identity in Montreal was shaped by the city's particular circumstances and the relative power various national and religious groups held within society. The period between 1840 and 1880 was significant as it was marked by an increasing population, immigration from Europe and from the rural hinterland, rapid industrialization, and political change, notably with Confederation in 1867. This period also saw the city's ethnic balance shift from a majority anglophone population (made up mostly of those of British origins) to francophone or French Canadian.

Montreal's streets, and the demonstrations in them, were indicators of the presence of many national identities. The streets acted as a stage for the various national, religious, and associational groups to act out their identity while proving their belonging to Montreal and the larger society. Montreal's voluntary societies appropriated not only the actual streets where they marched but the buildings around them, which were decorated symbolically, and they constructed arches along the route, expressing and claiming their right to occupy the public space. The groups who used the streets successfully, and with little controversy, did so by using a performance language that was non-threatening and familiar and by displaying symbols that tied all of the groups together. Who was able to march and how they were received by society at large were key to understanding the identities present. The parades were both unique and similar.

The newspapers of the day referred to Montreal as a place of mixed communities, and it was this awareness of difference that led to the establishment of norms that could be used to express these different identities and allow the groups to function together. Through these public displays of identity, Montrealers created a larger identity rooted in the political and social reality of the city. They were all a part of the city as members of the empire, and invested in the symbols of the state to demonstrate their belonging to it, while maintaining other identities. These demonstrations of national identity, when performed according to "tradition," were supported, and the streets were considered safe and acceptable spaces for the expression of identity. These parades were "a part of institutionalized boundary maintenance between Montreal's cultural communities."[1]

The city's newspapers were the voice of the public and reflected the various views and groups represented at an event. They were responsible, to a certain degree, for informing the public of upcoming events, reporting on their outcomes, and criticizing groups when they acted contrary to perceived social conventions. There were a number of different English-language papers in Montreal during this period, and they were, where copies existed, consulted for this chapter.[2] Some French-language papers were also consulted, but there was very little reporting on events in the English language communities, apart from the Irish, in their pages. The perspective of identity, while limited by the English-language sources, is still fairly broad, representing many of the communities who were claiming Montreal's streets.

Introduction

As illustrated in chart 1.1, Montreal's population came from a number of different origins.[3] French Canadians as a group were the majority after 1861, but the British (Canadian- and British-born) came very close in numbers. Montreal was a city in a state of growth all through the period under study. That growth was most rapid between 1852 and 1860, and after 1870 until around 1890.[4] People were moving into Montreal from the rural hinterland and from overseas to serve the city's rapidly industrializing economy. This enormous growth was followed by a movement of the middle class and the elite population towards the suburbs while the city centre became an area of business.[5] While some parts of the city could be said to contain areas where one group dominated, such as the Irish in Griffintown, there was, in general, "an absence of high levels of ethnic residential segregation."[6]

Chart 1.1 Montreal's Population by Ethnicity and Place of Birth, 1871.

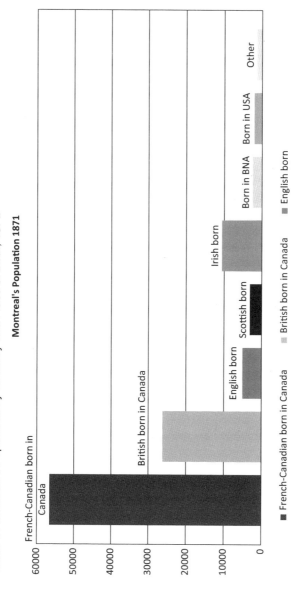

Montreal's Population 1871

The period of study for this chapter begins in 1840, when the provinces of Upper and Lower Canada were united politically. Already by this time, the city of Montreal had a highly developed associational life. The people of Montreal had organized themselves into various groups that catered to the provision of charitable services, cultural enrichment, and the fostering of religious and national identities. Tied to these voluntary associations and institutions were rituals of membership, formal occasions when groups gathered to affirm their identity, and public demonstrations of their belonging to their groups and to society as a whole. In Montreal this translated into meetings, dinners, balls, and parades. A number of these groups appropriated established holidays for their particular use. For instance, the St Andrew's Society used St Andrew's Day to celebrate Scottish identity, while the masons chose the feast of St John the Evangelist for their annual day. The principal days under discussion in this chapter will be: St Andrew's Day (30 November – Scots); St George's Day (23 April – English); St Patrick's Day (17 March – Irish); Orangemen's Day (12 July – Irish); Saint-Jean-Baptiste Day (24 June – French Canadians); the Queen's Birthday (24 May); and the anniversary of the Battle of Waterloo (18 June). Many of these groups, even if they were generally more private in their day-to-day operations, would use their day to express their distinctiveness and to do so in a public manner. "By occupying public space, marchers made a clear and direct claim to public attention"[7] and were situating themselves within Montreal's society. In this chapter, those holidays which were celebrated outdoors, in the streets and public squares will be examined.

Celebrations are deliberate and serve those who create them. They reinforce, through their performance, a sense of belonging to a shared past, a sense of belonging to a particular group, and a sense of cohesion.[8] Holidays or days of commemoration are chosen because they are considered traditional in their group, but tradition is a flexible concept. Events can be more modern than claimed, or completely invented, as "responses to novel situations which establish their own past by quasi-obligatory repetition."[9] The celebration of days aligned to specific identities, established or created to suit the needs of various groups, echoes through this volume with the celebrations of Empire Day, le 15 août, and Saint-Jean-Baptiste Day.

The streets should be understood as stages for the performance of identity and places of encounter. Mary P. Ryan, in *Civil Wars*, observes that it was "the humble streets that brought most city people together on a daily basis."[10] Here was where the citizens of all origins, faiths, and social positions ultimately walked. Identities were both performed and negotiated in the public space, which was controlled not only by the state (municipality) with regulations but also by the court of public opinion. The public, through newspapers and their own physical presence, showed their approval or disapproval of events and groups within this space. Such responses could include negative or positive accounts in the city's newspapers before and after the event; official action on the part of the municipality, specifically calling in the police or army to prevent or limit the presence in the streets; or lastly, crowd action (that is, riots) that restrained or forcefully removed the actors from the streets.

National Identity

In the years leading up to the Rebellions of 1837–38, Montrealers began to organize themselves along national lines. This started in 1834 with the creation of the St Patrick's Society. It was organized by a group of more conservatively minded Irishmen who were opposed to the way another group had celebrated that year's St Patrick's Day, and decided to ensure that Irish identity was framed in a manner that suited them. In June 1834, Reformers created Aide-toi et le ciel t'aidera (which later became the Société Saint-Jean-Baptiste), adopting Saint-Jean-Baptiste Day as a "national" day, along the same lines as St Patrick's Day.[11] The conservatively oriented St George's Society, St Andrew's Society, and the German Society formed in 1835. Each of these societies chose a saint's day on which to commemorate its "national" identity and host a number of events.[12] The saint's day started with a parade and a church service and ended in the evening with a dinner. Membership in these societies was exclusively male up until the 1880s. The national identities expressed in the public sphere were a masculine identity. Women were able to participate only as spectators.

In the period prior to 1840, each group, with the exception of the forerunner of the Société Saint-Jean-Baptiste, held a parade in the "principal streets." These parades were distinguished by the length and placement of their route, the number of participants, and the number of spectators. All were colourful, noisy, and disruptive. Parades occurred with the approval, implicit or explicit, of the community. Thus, the "national" parade, even though it represented only a portion of that community, had to function in accordance with norms of the larger society in order for its presence to be tolerated. One way of achieving this acceptance was through the use of common forms and symbols. The parades of the nineteenth century tended to follow a particular pattern, with participants marching in a clear and established order, often using banners and flags allied with the saints of the day but also with national heroes and emblems, and incorporating a military band and symbols of the larger society, such as imperial and British flags. In the 1830s, sister societies participated in each other's parades. In 1835, the St Patrick's, St George's, St Andrew's, and German societies met together to agree to an order of procession for each parade: the association celebrating their day would march first, with the other groups following according to the date of their own national days.[13] Marching together was the most obvious way to show approval for the community and its celebration, but there was also a larger societal approval for the identities and ideas being expressed on the streets.

In the 1840s, the parades had become a customary occurrence, and the need for other groups to sanction the parade with their presence in the ranks had ceased. Instead, the sister societies began to position themselves on the sidelines as spectators, but their approval was still implicitly required, and noted. For example, in the account of the St Andrew's parade in 1840, the *Gazette* wrote, "At the different places where the banners of the St George, German and St Patrick's Societies were exhibited in honor of the day, three cheers were given by the members of the St Andrew's Society, and opposite the residence of the Governor General, three cheers and one cheer more were enthusiastically given."[14] The German Society ceased organizing parades in the early 1840s and left their celebrations of the national day to more private dinners held in the city's hotels. But as the Germans left the public space, the Société Saint-Jean-Baptiste incorporated parades into its annual commemorations, beginning in 1842.[15] The parade was a way for this group to legitimize its presence in a post-rebellion Montreal. Its utilization of familiar forms and clearly recognizable symbols enabled it to succeed in the larger society. For example, the parade in 1846 was described in a positive light by the *Transcript*:

> The procession in the morning was the largest and – of the kind – the most striking we have ever seen in Canada. It demonstrated the national zeal of the French Canadian population and enlisted participators of all ranks and all ages in its cause. We should suppose that there must have been between 4000 and 5000 young and old, in it; including, however, a number of Irish, who in honour of St Jean Baptiste, turned out on the occasion.[16]

Most of the descriptions of the various national parades stress the respectable nature of the participants and of the group. The celebrating groups were characterized in the English-language press, regardless of their political leanings, as well-mannered, orderly, and distinctive. Order was an important aspect of these demonstrations – they were not unruly, violent, or excessively disruptive. Good conduct translated to respectability. National pride, when presented in a respectable manner, was acceptable. The fact that these national celebrations were either preceded or followed by a church service no doubt supported an impression of respectability and enhanced their acceptability. These celebrations were not offensive to the public; rather they were welcomed and often cheered by the audience in the streets. As Horner states, parades and processions were demonstrations of order and were a means to "draw the popular classes into a shared project of ordering the urban landscape."[17] Parades were seen as positive expressions of identity inclusive and were welcome sources of public entertainment.

That is not to say that these parades were simple marches through the streets, with the men merely quietly going along, some with flags or banners. The elements of order, discipline, and spectacle were interwoven: "We have seldom seen so gratifying a ceremony in this city, not so much owing to the pomp and glitter of the paraphernalia (though there was plenty enough of these too), but from the air of respectability and sturdy independence of the main actors in the scene."[18] Heron and Penfold state that this "litany of compliments for ordered presentations is a testimony to the civic boosterism of Victorian newspapers, as well as to the dominance of the respectable, militia style of parading."[19] Respectable though, was not boring, and could accommodate fancy banners, horses, flags, costumes, and flash. The visual impact of so many men[20] was clearly as important to the success of the event, as the numbers present.

The marching orders for the 1848 St Patrick's Day Parade, published the day prior in the *Transcript*, provide an excellent example of the type of show provided by these events:

[Irish Harp picture with "Erin go Bragh"]
Two stewards with wands
Supporter with spear} Union Jack {Supporter with Spear
Band
John McDonnell, Grand Marshal, on horseback
Supporter} Blue Banner of the Cross {Supporter

Two deputy marshals
Sup.} Original Harp Banner { Sup.
Members four abreast
Two stewards with wands
Sup.} Green Medal Banner {Sup.
Members four abreast
Two stewards with wands
Sup.} Ladies Crimson Tree Banner {Sup.
Members four abreast
Two stewards with wands
Sup.} Father Mathew's Banner {Sup.
Two deputy marshals
Supporter with spear} Banner of St. Patrick { Supporter with spear
Two stewards with wands
Two and two} Committee { Two and two
Two stewards
Honorary members
Secretaries
Treasurers
Past presidents and Vice-presidents
Supporter with spear} Grand Banner {Supporter with spear
Stewards} Presidents { Stewards
Five stewards[21]

The parade represented a given organization's power, popularity, and prestige. The marchers were ordered by rank and were accompanied by colourful banners that were highly symbolic. The societies made the purchase of these visual accessories a high priority. For example the St Andrew's Society, on its second meeting after forming, resolved to purchase five transparencies (images printed on glass and lit from behind for effect), of Sir William Wallace, John Knox, Sir Walter Scott, Robert Burns, and a Highland chief in full costume); two flags (the Royal Arms of Scotland and the Royal Standard of Scotland); and two banners (a Caledonian and an Ancient Caledonian).[22] A St Andrew's Society banner was also sewn by the "ladies" (wives and daughters of the members) for their first parade.[23] According to descriptions in newspapers, every parade, regardless of the group it represented, included the Union Jack. The societies understood the importance of the impressions they conveyed during their parades, and they undertook to ensure that the presentation was as spectacular as possible and used symbols that could be understood by the public. The overall impact on the spectator was intended to be impressive.

The visual experience extended beyond the impressions made by the marchers themselves. The streets and even the spectators were decorated to honour those marching. It is not always clear from the parade accounts whether or not the organizing societies were responsible for all of the decoration on the streets. The following description the of Saint-Jean-Baptiste parade leads the reader to believe that the home-owners contributed to the event by decorating themselves and their homes with the appropriate symbols:

> Flags floated on every roof and from every window, tiny bunting swung in the mild June air in many coloured festoons over the crowded streets. The sidewalks were gay and green with maple trees, and thronged with spectators in festive attire, many of them disappearing behind white badges blazoned with our national emblem and enemy the beaver, with a dressing of maple leaves, or sinking under the weight of a collar gorgeous with the same.[24]

These events also had an auditory impact. Not only would the sheer presence of many people marching and the crowds watching create a lot of noise, but there were also the military bands and personnel who were co-opted into marching with the various national societies. Occasionally the marching regiments would be composed of those of the same origin as the society marching, such as when a Highland Regiment would march with the St Andrew's Society,[25] or an English-based regiment with the St George's Society. This was, however, not always the case, and depended entirely on which British regiment was stationed in Montreal at the time. At no time were the regiments French Canadian, although the Saint-Jean-Baptiste parades always included a band, usually a military one.

The presence of these military bands and other military personnel could be understood in a number of ways. At the most basic, these military men were an impressive sight with their uniforms, weapons, and instruments. The addition of music was always appreciated for its entertainment value, and specific national airs roused the audience. However, these were military bands and, as such, were representatives of the state. Their presence was both a symbolic connection to the state and a sign of state consent, and thus these bands lent an air of credibility to the occasion. The presence of these and other symbols of state, such as flags and banners that reflected the connection to the empire and the queen, meant that the display of a particular national identity was combined with that of an imperial – that is, British – one. Such displays were tangible expressions of a local British identity and underlined the public perception of loyalty. This demonstration of loyalty was further reinforced by the presence of a state official or the inclusion of a building that represented the state. For example, in 1848, the St Patrick's Parade included a march past the governor general, who acknowledged the marchers as they saluted him.[26]

The route for national parades was specifically designed to take in the most important of the city's landmarks. It always included the offices of the other national societies and governmental buildings. In 1846, for example, the St Patrick's parade started at the Recollet Church on Notre Dame and proceeded down the street to Notre Dame Church, where the religious service was held. Following the service, the parade reformed and marched further along Notre Dame Street to Dalhousie Square, returning to the society's offices via St Paul Street.[27] In 1848, representatives of the St George's Society marched from their offices at the Clifton Hotel, past Rasco's Hotel, to Jacques Cartier Square into Notre Dame Street to St George's Chapel for their religious services. The procession reformed afterwards and went through Great St James Street to Government House, after which the parade broke up.[28] These were long routes that crossed the centre of town, using the main thoroughfares and passing in front of important institutions and through public squares. The groups marching were claiming the most important parts of the city as their own, at least for the day.

The public face of the national societies was largely associated with the celebration of their national days. The days' events, dinners, services, and parades were their moment to shine, but they also served as fundraisers for their other activities, including charitable work. The original saints' societies thus had much to protect in relation to the days associated with their names. The growth of Montreal's population presented a challenge to their hegemony, specifically when other associations were formed that claimed to represent the same national identity. If the national days were intended to celebrate all Scots, Irish, or English, then these new groups had to somehow be accommodated within the existing structure of celebrations, or the societies risked losing their pre-eminent position.

The Scots societies developed a policy of inclusion, and when the Thistle Society and Caledonian Society were founded in the 1850s they were invited to join the St Andrew's Society in the march to and from the church. The same was true for the English St George's Society when the English Workingman's Benefit Society formed in 1864 and the Sons of England at the end of that decade. By being included, and by including others who identified similarly, the societies were reinforcing the importance of their identity and their specific groups to the public. The societies (both those named for saints and others) advertised in the city's English-language papers to invite all to march in their processions, and they often included space for those not affiliated with any specific society. The aim was to create a sense of unity among related groups, with the inclusion of those who shared the national, if not the specific associational, identity.

The form and basic function of the parades remained stable throughout this period, but as Montreal was growing and its public changing, the groups did change the role of parades in relation to their other celebrations. While their parades had become more inclusive, from the 1860s onwards the St George's Society and the St Andrew's Society scaled back their length. In the two decades prior, they had taken the opportunity to honour their day in a procession to the church of choice for the service and then as a group through the principal streets. The routes, when detailed in the newspapers, were fairly long. But through the following decades they gradually became shorter and by the end of the period were restricted to a march from the societies' offices to the church before the service. The church service continued to be well attended. By the 1870s, male-only dinners had become balls, which, of course, included the participation of women. By 1900 neither the St Andrew's nor St George's group marched on its saint's day.

The St Patrick's Society included other Irish groups much earlier than the Scots or the English integrated their compatriots. In 1840, the Irish Catholic Temperance Association had been formed and had immediately been incorporated into the parade. The Recollet Church's Christian Doctrine Association also joined in the parade in the 1840s.[29] The St Patrick's Society was at this time non-denominational, so both Catholics and Protestants were represented in the parade. However, a number of factors – including the impact of the Ultramontane movement, the development of an Irish-Catholic community centred on the church, and the influence of Father Dowd, the priest at St Patrick's Church – led to the splintering of the St Patrick's Society in 1856.[30] The Irish Protestant Benevolent Society was formed, and the St Patrick's Society became exclusively Catholic. The parades took on a stronger

Catholic nature, and the Protestants were relegated to the organizational sidelines. Yet St Patrick's Day was still thought to represent all
Irish in Montreal, and the Protestant Benevolent Society held annual
dinners in honour of the saint on that day. At the same time, the Société
Saint-Jean Baptiste was likewise re-orienting itself around the Catholic
Church, and its parades also reflected this change.[31] Both the St Patrick's Society and the Société Saint-Jean Baptiste continued to inhabit
large portions of the principal streets during the period, and, unlike
the Scots and British groups, even expanded their marching territory to
include parts of the city's suburbs.

Other Identities

By virtue of their annual nature and the number of parades held, the
national days were the most visible expression of identities on Montreal's
streets. They were not, however, the only ones. Different groups, from
religious groups and voluntary associations to the military, laid claim
to the streets. The influences of the saints' celebrations were evident in
terms of how other groups chose to present themselves to the public.

While the parades of the Société Saint-Jean-Baptiste and the St Patrick's Society were becoming increasingly religious in nature, they
were not perceived as exclusively religious parades. Rather, they were
viewed as celebrations of a national identity, which had an obvious religious component. But the public space was open to religious processions as well – most often, to Catholic processions. For example, the
Feast of Corpus Christi, which occurs sixty days following Easter, traditionally included a procession through the streets with the Blessed
Sacrament. The majority of Montreal's population was Catholic, so
most were not only familiar with these practices, but were also participants. In the city's English-language papers "Fête-Dieu" was always
commented on, and there were rarely instances of disapproval of this
use of the public space.[32] This was in stark contrast to Toronto's Corpus
Christi parades, which were often marked by episodes of violence and
were frequently attacked in the city's papers.[33]

In Montreal, the principal celebration for Fête-Dieu was organized by
the bishop and was held either at Notre-Dame or at his cathedral. The
following account from 1841 stands as a typical description of the parade:

> The procession was remarkable for that imposing solemnity with which
> the Catholics so well understand how to invest their religious ceremonies,

and the canopy covering the Host was of unusual splendour. A detachment of the 7th Hussars preceded the numerous priests, nuns and scholars of the several religious establishments, in rear of whom, and immediately preceding the Host were those who carried baskets of flowers and strewed them in the air, and those who carried Censers. Immediately after the Host followed the members of the Bar, which body succeeded by the Band of the 23rd Regiment, playing most beautifully, as if inspired by the solemnity of the occasion. Grenadiers of the 23rd, each with his musket and fixed bayonet, marched at intervals of about ten paces on each side, thus protecting the flanks of the procession from any pressure by the assembled crowd. A great many of the Police were also in attendance, but we are happy to say that nothing could exceed the decorum and respect universally displayed.[34]

As with the national parades described in earlier in this chapter, press described the Fête-Dieu parade with reference to colour, spectacle, and respectability. Such religious parades were treated by the public, and in the press, in the same manner as the national parades – that is, as legitimate occupiers of public space. And the parades were organized in such a way as to ensure such acceptance. They included many of the same elements as the national parades, members (priests, nuns, lay members of church societies) marching in an orderly manner, with music provided by a military band, and accompanied by a military guard of honour. The performance was the same, even if the message was slightly different. Symbols, including the Host and censers, were understood by those involved. The streets were gaily decorated, and there was an enthusiastic crowd.

The military acted as a guard, providing a buffer between participants and audience, but also signified tacit approval. Press accounts never questioned the right of the Catholic Church to appropriate the street; rather they confirmed that right and congratulated the church's use of the space. Religious identity was understood and accepted when it was presented in the same manner as other identities in Montreal.

The streets also acted as a stage for a number of different voluntary associations that had sprung up in Montreal by mid-century. At certain points, many of these societies laid claim to the streets to assert their presence and legitimize their identity. Sports clubs and groups such as the Odd Fellows took to the streets occasionally. And their right to do so was generally not questioned, although there could be confusion as to the message they were sending spectators. For example, when the cornerstone to the new Masonic Hall was laid in 1846, the parade to the site was framed in the same light as others, with a respectable march of around 250 members to the building, with banners, music, and the usual accoutrements. However, the reporter was puzzled by the symbols displayed, and struggled to find meaning in them: "An intelligent friend was endeavouring to give us an inkling of the signification of the different symbols as the passed by, – like the man in the Farce, it became a confused mass – and we recollected nothing at all."[35] The public display of these mysterious and exclusive symbols served the Masons well, reinforcing their elite image

Funeral processions were also a common feature of Montreal street life. Most voluntary associations organized processions for their members' funerals. Ads were frequently placed in the newspapers calling members to assemble and march in procession for the dearly departed. This ad for the Independent Order of Odd Fellows in 1846 is one example:

> Notice – the members of the Loyal Victoria Lodge, MU, are requested to attend the funeral of their late Brother Andrew Connell, this day (Saturday), the 16th instant, at three o'clock in the afternoon, at which hour the hearse (from his late residence in the country) will be at the head of the main street, St Lawrence Suburbs, from thence to the old burying ground. The members of the other lodges of the Manchester Unity are respectfully invited to attend.[36]

Similar advertisements appeared for various national societies and for the Freemasons. The processions were not nearly as elaborate as the more festive parades, and appear not to have involved any bands or banners, but would have been impressive nonetheless in their solemnity. They certainly demonstrated to the public the solidarity and respectability of a group.

State funerals stand apart from these simpler processions, and in Montreal during this period no funeral was more impressive or more widely attended than that of Thomas D'Arcy McGee. His funeral involved a procession from his home on St Catherine Street, through the major streets to St Patrick's Church, where a service was held. Then the procession made its way to Notre-Dame Church before it turned up the mountain to the Côte des Neiges Cemetery. Private homes and businesses along the route had draped their properties in black crepe. The procession included all of the city's national societies, along with

1.1 Funeral of Thomas D'Arcy McGee, 13 April 1868, photographed by James Inglis, Library and Archives Canada, C-083423.

the clergy, members of Parliament, judges, police, and members of various associations.[37] Photographs of the event show the streets packed with people, and *La Minerve* reported that about 10,000 people had assembled around St Patrick's Church.[38]

The funeral used the same forms that the national societies did in their own parades: the funeral procession took over the most important Montreal streets, and the participants marched according to a pre-established order. The participation of the city's national societies marked their respect for McGee,[39] but it also their reflected their identification with Montreal and Canada, even though they used their specific national identities to express this.

State Identities

In all of the preceding types of parades, references to the state were made as a part of the representations of other identities. The state lent its presence while honouring these non-governmental identities. These groups combined the symbols of their specific identities with those of the state to display their belonging to Montreal and to the empire of which it was a part. But there were also more state-centred events that were celebrated in the city's public spaces.

The most obvious of these types of events was the celebration of the Queen's Birthday on 24 May, although Victoria Day, as Chris Tait's chapter discusses, would not become a legal holiday until 1901. Even before its status became official, this day was typically observed as a holiday, and most businesses were closed. Generally, the birthday celebrations appear to have been organized by the garrison in Montreal. Most years the day was celebrated with a march of the troops to an open space, sometimes the Place d'Armes, other times the grounds near the old race course. The troops were paraded on the field, guns were fired (a *feu de joie*),[40] and then the soldiers returned to barracks. The events attracted spectators, although it is unclear whether they were attending to honour the queen or to witness the gunfire – both had their appeal. In this way, the state asserted its control over the public space, but with the cooperation of the public, who viewed the display as an entertainment.

The celebration of the Queen's Birthday was both a patriotic event and an opportunity for the military to present themselves in a good light. They attempted to add to this lustre in the 1840s with the celebration of the anniversary of the Battle of Waterloo. Apparently though, such a commemoration was not considered politically acceptable, and

Governor General Lord Elgin cancelled it in 1849.[41] An account of that year's commemoration gave no hint of political difficulties and stated that the celebration was a popular event. However, a survey of newspapers for the period does not reveal many instances of its public celebration or of any obvious popularity among the public. Calls to tradition then, even by groups in clear positions of power, did not automatically endow proposed events with public approval.

In June 1867, some of Montreal's population decided to celebrate the coming of Confederation. A fireworks display was organized and the newspapers called on the public to decorate their homes and light them up so "there will be enough to make a walk through the streets on Monday evening more than usually interesting."[42] This was a passive form of parading, with the buildings, rather than a group of citizens, as the show. And while the newspapers were enthusiastic about the celebration, it is obvious by their continued calls for the public to decorate that this was not an entirely successful endeavour. Subsequently, there would be little commemoration of 1 July in the city.[43] Montrealers were more invested in celebrating their current calendar of events than adding a new one.

While parading in Montreal generally occurred on dates that had particular associations with identity, other opportunities were also taken to demonstrate in public. Regal and vice-regal visits were a special opportunity for Montreal and its civic authorities to demonstrate their loyalty and respectability to representatives of the empire. Here the state was the focus of the celebrations. The visit of the Prince of Wales in 1860 was one moment when the city as a corporate body, along with its most prominent members, was able to welcome their sovereign's son and demonstrate both its prosperity and loyalty. Montreal put on quite a show, and the prince's week-long stay gave both city and heir a chance to be seen. Processions were an integral part of the visit. As Ian Radforth stated, "the Procession not only put the prince on display for the enjoyment of the spectators; it put the city on display for the appreciation of the prince and his suite."[44] Arches were erected along the routes, and the buildings clad in flags and bunting. Although the pomp was largely for the benefit of the prince and his entourage, Montrealers saw themselves, at least in part, represented in these displays.

Vice-regal visits likewise were opportunities for civic authorities and for Montreal's voluntary societies to greet the state representatives to the city and to demonstrate their role and identities within it. And they were far more frequent than royal visits. The arrival of the governor general was an important occasion, both when the city acted as the capital (1844–49) and when it was not, and the route was decorated for the ceremonial procession from the port into the city. Not only was the city's corporation and military mobilized for such an event, but Montreal's national societies were invited to assist. In 1840 the St Andrew's, St Patrick's, St George's, and German societies escorted the governor general from the port into the city and on to Government House.[45] Over the course of this period, these occasions became increasingly elaborate. In 1844, the national societies were joined by the military, the Société Saint-Jean-Baptiste, and the Odd Fellows.[46]

The construction of triumphal arches along the processional route was perhaps the grandest expression of identities. They were constructed for these state visits as ways of showing loyalty and expressing a specific identity. Some, such as those erected by businesses,[47] were essentially advertising, but others were constructed by national societies. The *Canadian Illustrated News* contains an illustration of an arch constructed for the visit of the governor general to Montreal in 1878 (see figure 1.2). Because it was used to greet a governor general who was a Scottish lord, the Marquis of Lorne, the Scottish arch was no doubt the grandest of those constructed on this occasion (and no doubt why it was chosen for publication). The arch's use of symbols such as the British and Canadian flags, along with symbols closely associated with Scottish identity, such as the Cross of St Andrew and the piper on the parapet, make it a striking representation of local identity. For societies like St George's and St Andrew's, which were moving away from activities such as processions, the financial investment in an arch was likely ideal. They were able to display the symbols and flags that had featured in their parades, but the visual impact lasted longer. Moreover, by the time of Lorne's visit, the press tended to focus more on these constructions than on any accompanying procession. Finally, for this vice-regal visit, the city made a point of illuminating various buildings. The government buildings had an "illuminated coat of arms, fifteen feet high, a shield enclosing an archer surmounted by a crown."[48]

Conflicting Identities on the Streets

The previous parts of this chapter have discussed those parades and processions that occurred without incident. They were moments of relative social harmony, where the expressions of particular identities were generally uncontested. They were, in a sense, sanctioned by the

1.2 The Vice-Regal Reception – The Arch of the Scottish Societies at Montreal, 1878. *Canadian Illustrated News* 18, no. 24, 14 December 1878, 372.

state and society as a result of their adhesion to strict standards related to display, behaviour, and methods of expression, which demonstrated respectability and loyalty. But not all processions or gatherings in the streets observed these standards or were as well received.

Considerable violence occurred in the streets of Montreal in the period under discussion; several events brought about much scrutiny and social unrest. In 1849, after the passage of the Rebellion Losses Bill, the streets around the Ste Anne's Market building erupted into violence, and the building was vandalized and then burnt to the ground. The governor general was attacked while leaving the building, and mobs continued to attack places associated with support for the bill, including the offices of the *Pilot* newspaper. Likewise, in June 1853, Irish Catholics attacked the Zion Church, which was hosting a speech by anti-Catholic activist Alessandro Gavazzi. The police protected the building, firing on those outside to prevent their entry. The streets became battlegrounds over differing values or the site for reactions to events that occurred outside the public's gaze. Unlike the groups discussed above, protestors used public space to display disapproval.

Events to mark Orangeman's Day (12 July) provide another example of the contested use of public space. As demonstrated by Houston and Smyth, the Orange Order never held the high position or large membership numbers in Quebec as it did in Ontario.[49] Nevertheless, Montreal had a few Orange Lodges, and their members sought to march in the streets, as the other national societies did. Because Montreal was largely Catholic, the appeal of the Orange Order was limited, as was the celebration of the Orange anniversary. The city's inhabitants would have balked at Orange symbols. This was particularly true of Irish Catholics, who understood better than others their cultural and social implications. It should be noted that the city's English-language newspapers, although run in the main by Protestants, were also against displays of anti-Catholic sentiment. For many, such a response reflected more an abhorrence of the violence inherent in displays of Orange sympathies than respect for Catholics. Early accounts of Orange celebrations indicate that they were small scale, with descriptions of men walking around town on the day with orange lilies. The Orange Lodges were in the 1840s and 1850s more discreet in their operations, and so there was no formal organization attached to these demonstrations, just the actions of a small group of individuals. Even so, this was provocative behaviour, "for every one knows that they act on the ignorant among Irish Catholics like a red flag to a bull."[50]

By the 1870s, Orange Lodges started to press for the celebration of their day with a march, causing a great deal of controversy in Montreal. The ability of the lodges in other parts of Canada to parade as they pleased acted as a spur for those in Montreal to have equal access to such a mode of expression. Some Montrealers felt that this was an issue of discrimination, viewing the Orange parades in the same light as those, whether religious or national, that were regular features of Montreal's street life: "If a mixed community of Catholics persist in walking in honor of their religious saints, they cannot expect Protestants not to walk in honor of their political saint."[51] Many called for the cessation of all parades or the acceptance of all parades.

Opposition to the Orange parades centred on the anti-Catholic sentiment of the Orange Order. As expressed by both sides in the debate about Orange processions was the principle that Montreal was a "mixed community"[52] and the belief that there was an entente cordial whereby the display of specific identities, be they religious or national, was to be discouraged or forbidden when it triggered violence.[53] The celebrations of 12 July by the Orange Order were not tolerated because of the violence that accompanied them. One commentator suggested that, for St Patrick's Day, "their programme should be altered as follows: No religious emblems or banners of saints, martyrs, or patriots to be carried in the ranks, but the grand old flag or banner of Great Britain and Ireland. The music for the occasion should be selected so as to be agreeable to all denominations."[54] This would eliminate the need for Orange parades, on the assumption that all aspects of Irish identity were expressed on St Patrick's Day.

In 1877, the Orange Order made plans to celebrate Orangeman's Day with a parade in the city's streets. City officials were against the idea of a parade and urged the Orange Lodges to restrict their celebrations to their meeting houses and homes.[55] However, the Orangemen were adamant that they had the same right as other groups to parade in the streets. In last minute negotiations on the evening of 11 July, the Orange Order was convinced by a deputation representing the city corporation and the other national societies to cancel its procession. As the *Daily Star* reported, the Orangemen "have listened to the voice of reason, and resolved to act as good citizens, to refrain from anything that would look like a challenge to those who oppose their existence, and to conduct their celebration, in short as becomes peaceable and respectable members of a community, respecting the feelings and prejudices of their fellows of different faith or opinion."[56]

Yet this agreement did not mean that no violence occurred. Accounts in the papers vary as to the causes, with some blaming Catholics, and others Orangemen, for the violence that occurred and that resulted in the death of an Orangeman, Thomas Hackett. The parade that was cancelled was soon re-created in the funeral procession for Hackett, which included the participation of the national societies in the city, the Prince of Wales Regiment, and several marching bands.[57] The next year, the city called on the federal government to send troops to the city to keep the peace on Orangeman's Day.[58] Although the violence of the preceding year was avoided, the day saw a few demonstrations by Orangemen around their hall on Fortification Lane, which were later illustrated to dramatic effect in the *Canadian Illustrated News*.[59]

Conclusion

Between 1840 and 1880, Montreal's streets were the stage for the performance of a variety of identities based on national or ethnic origin, religious faith, or social or political interest. By marching in the streets, these groups were exposing themselves to their fellow Montrealers. This performance of identity and its reception constituted a form of negotiation. When displays ran counter to what was considered proper or acceptable, there was the possibility of disruption or, in extreme cases, violence.

The utilization of established forms of parading was a key component in ensuring community acceptance. These parades were presented to a general public in the same manner as every other parade presented. The audience could expect to see banners and flags, some relating to the specific group on parade, others that spoke to the place they lived, and many representing the state. The flag of Ireland, the harp, the thistle, the flag of St George, or the Host could be understood and appreciated, or at least tolerated, when placed next to a military band, a royal standard, the Union Jack, or the Red Ensign.

Montreal was a mixed community, as its papers proclaimed, and its overall identity was reflected in the expression of multiple identities within its boundaries. When positioned to demonstrate their identities to visitors such as representatives of the Crown, Montrealers embraced the idea of the state and their loyalty to it. While this was undeniably a British identity, as the state system was part of the British Empire, it was also Irish, Scottish, French Canadian, English, Catholic, and more. All these were presented together as a local identity, the various parts constituting the larger whole.

NOTES

1 Sherry Olson, "A Profusion of Light in Nineteenth-Century Montreal," in *Espaces et culture / Space and Culture*, ed. S. Courville and N. Seguin (Sainte-Foy: Presses Université Laval, 1995) as cited in Rosalyn Trigger, "The Role of the Parish in Fostering Irish-Catholic Identity in Nineteenth-Century Montreal" (master's thesis, McGill University, 1997), 26.

2 *Montreal Gazette, Montreal Standard, Montreal Daily Star, Montreal Morning Courier, Montreal Transcript, Montreal Herald, Canadian Illustrated News, Montreal Witness,* and *Pilot and Evening Journal of Commerce.*

3 Jean-Claude Robert, "Montréal, 1821–1871: Aspects de l'urbanisation" (PhD diss., École des Hautes Études en Sciences Sociales, Université de Paris I, 1977), 106.

4 Jean-Claude Robert, *Atlas historique de Montréal* (Montreal: Art Global / Éditions Libre Expression, 1994), 110.

5 Ibid., 110–11.

6 Trigger, "The Role of the Parish," 4.

7 Craig Heron and Steve Penfold, *The Worker's Festival: A History of Labour Day in Canada* (Toronto: University of Toronto Press, 2005), 7.

8 Geneviève Fabre, "Lieu de fête et de commémoration," *Revue française d'études américaines* 51 (February 1992): 7.

9 Eric Hobsbawm, "Introduction: Inventing Traditions," in *The Invention of Tradition*, ed. Eric Hobsbawm and Terence Ranger (Cambridge: Cambridge University Press, 2000), 1–2.

10 Mary P. Ryan, *Civic Wars: Democracy and Public Life in the American City during the Nineteenth Century* (Berkeley: University of California Press, 1997), 38.

11 Robert Rumilly, *Histoire de la Société Saint-Jean-Baptiste de Montréal: des Patriotes au fleurdelisé 1834–1948* (Montreal: Les Éditions de l'Aurore, 1975), 16–17.

12 The German Society intended to honour a specific saint but could not decide on a saint who suited the varied Germanic identities that their members represented. They instead chose 1 August, the anniversary of the Hanover Succession.

13 *A Summary of the First Fifty Years: Transactions of the St Andrew's Society of Montreal* (Montreal: McQueen and Corneil, 1886), 8.

14 *Montreal Morning Courier*, 2 December 1840.

15 *Montreal Gazette*, 27 June 1842.

16 *Montreal Transcript and Commercial Advertiser*, 25 June 1846.

17 Dan Horner, "Taking to the Streets: Crowds, Politics and Identity in Mid-Nineteenth-Century Montreal" (PhD diss., York University, 2010), 27.

18 *Montreal Gazette*, 17 March 1842.

19 Heron and Penfold, *The Worker's Festival*, 16.

20 The masculine nature of parading was common in this period for Canada, where the public sphere was considered the dominion of men. Ibid., 16.

21 The curly brackets denote space between people marching abreast in the procession. *Montreal Transcript and Commercial Advertiser,* 16 March 1848.

22 *A Summary of the First Fifty Years*, 7.

23 Ibid.

24 *Montreal Gazette*, 25 June 1868, 2.

25 The St Andrew's Society was always able to secure the services of a military piper for its events, which would indicate that there was usually a piper, regardless of which regiment was stationed in Montreal.

26 *Montreal Gazette*, 20 March 1848.

27 Ibid., 18 March 1846.

28 Ibid., 24 April 1848.

29 See ibid., 16 March 1843, for an example of the order of procession for the parade.

30 Kevin James, "The Saint Patrick's Society of Montreal: Ethno-Religious Realignment in a Nineteenth-Century National Society" (master's thesis, McGill University, 1997), 68.

31 Robert Rumilly, *Histoire de la Société Saint-Jean-Baptiste de Montréal: des patriotes au fleurdelisé, 1834–1948* (Montreal: Les Éditions de l'Aurore, 1975), 68.

32 For a discussion on the opposition to the Fête-Dieu in Montreal, which peaked around 1844, see Horner, "Taking to the Streets," 169–72. It should be noted that the processions were almost always referred by their French name, and not as Corpus Christi.

33 Ian Radforth, "Collective Rights, Liberal Discourse, and Public Order: The Clash over Catholic Processions in Mid-Victorian Toronto," *Canadian Historical Review* 95, no. 4 (December 2014): 512.

34 *Montreal Transcript*, 15 July 1841.

35 *Montreal Morning Courier*, 2 October 1846.

36 *Montreal Transcript and Commercial Advertiser*, 16 May 1846.

37 *La Minerve*, 13 April 1868, 2.

38 Ibid., 14 April 1868, 2.

39 As stated by the St. Andrew's Society in their minutes: "That in order to show the appreciation by this Society of Mr. McGee's worth as a public man and a statesman and their gratitude for the sympathy and assistance he extended to it on so many occasions it is resolved that this Society do attend his funeral in a body wearing suitable mourning badges."

Minute Book of the St. Andrew's Society, 13 April 1868, Archives of the St. Andrew's Society of Montreal.

40 *Montreal Transcript*, 26 May 1840.

41 *Montreal Gazette*, 20 June 1849.

42 Ibid., 29 June 1867, 2.

43 It was in 1879 that Dominion Day became an official national holiday. Matthew Hayday, "Fireworks, Folk-dancing, and Fostering a National Identity: The Politics of Canada Day," *Canadian Historical Review* 91, no. 2 (June 2010): 289.

44 Ian Radforth, *Royal Spectacle: The 1860 Visit of the Prince of Wales to Canada and the United States* (Toronto: University of Toronto Press, 2004), 110.

45 *Montreal Gazette*, 22 September 1840.

46 *Montreal Transcript and Commercial Advertiser*, 25 June 1844.

47 The Turnpike Company had erected an arch in honour of the visit. *Montreal Transcript and Commercial Advertiser*, 25 June 1844.

48 *Montreal Daily Star,* 28 November 1878, 1.

49 Cecil J. Houston and William J. Smyth, *The Sash Canada Wore: A Historical Geography of the Orange Order in Canada* (Toronto: University of Toronto Press, 1980), 49–50.

50 *Montreal Morning Courier*, 13 July 1849.

51 *Montreal Herald*, 15 August 1871, 1.

52 Ibid., 15 August 1871, 1.

53 Ibid.

54 *Montreal Daily Star*, 10 March 1877, 3.

55 Ibid., 5 July 1877, 2.

56 Ibid., 11 July 1877, 2.

57 Brian Young, *Respectable Burial: Montreal's Mount Royal Cemetery* (Montreal and Kingston: McGill-Queen's University Press, 2003), 74.

58 *Montreal Daily Star,* 8 July 1878, 3.

59 *Canadian Illustrated News*, vol. 18, no. 4, 27 July 1878, 56–7.

2 "Righteousness Exalteth the Nation": Religion, Nationalism, and Thanksgiving Day in Ontario, 1859–1914

PETER A. STEVENS

In the United States of America, few annual events stir the national imagination as thoroughly as Thanksgiving Day. The holiday's rituals and symbols harken back to the nation's founding fathers, evoking images of pilgrims landing at Plymouth Rock and sharing a harvest feast with the surrounding Native peoples in 1621. The myth of this first Thanksgiving, which is a staple in the education of every American schoolchild, informs U.S. citizens that their country is a land of opportunity and new beginnings, a place of piety, abundance, and inclusivity. Other Thanksgiving customs uphold family, consumerism, and competition as core American values. The holiday is a favourite occasion for get-togethers with friends and relatives, with festivities revolving around turkey dinners, Santa Claus parades, and football games, all unfolding against the backdrop of autumn leaves and newly gathered crops. Scholars have parsed American Thanksgiving in considerable detail, and there is a lively debate over which Thanksgiving traditions are rooted in historical fact and which are based in fiction. What is beyond dispute, however, is the overtly nationalistic character of the day.[1]

In the Canadian context, by contrast, Thanksgiving Day is surrounded by ambiguity. Media reports regularly express doubts about the meaning and purpose of the holiday, while Canadians themselves often seem unsure about how *their* Thanksgiving differs from the American one, and why the two holidays do not share the same date.[2] Thus far, scholars have offered few answers to these questions, as academic treatments of Canadian Thanksgiving are scarce, speculative, and limited in their analysis. Significantly, these works downplay the holiday's importance as a patriotic celebration, making only passing reference to a "subtle influence of Canadian nationalism" that is evident on Thanksgiving Day.[3] This chapter cannot relate the entire the history of Canadian Thanksgiving, but it does take up the beginning of the story by examining the origins of the holiday in late-nineteenth-century Ontario. In doing so, it reveals that Canadian Thanksgiving initially had a nationalistic focus that it since has largely lost. In the minds of the men who first developed the holiday, Thanksgiving was intended to be a day for celebrating Canada.

The existing literature on national public holidays in North America raises several points that help to illuminate the specific history of Thanksgiving Day in Canada.[4] First, while public holidays often appear to be age-old celebrations that emerged organically out of the national fabric, they are actually examples of invented traditions. According to Eric Hobsbawm, an invented tradition is "a set of practices, normally governed by overtly or tacitly accepted rules and of a ritual or symbolic nature, which seek to inculcate certain values and norms of behaviour by repetition, which automatically implies continuity with the past."[5] Holidays, as annual events that are steeped in ritual, constitute a powerful form of invented tradition, for while they seem to be neutral and apolitical, they are actually compelling advertisements for the world views of those who shape and promote them.

Second, public holidays often serve as important tools of nation building. Holiday customs and iconography give members of a population a sense of a shared past and subtly inform them about who they are as a people. By reinforcing messages about common values and experiences, holidays thus encourage individual citizens to imagine themselves as being members of the same political community, or nation.[6] This is not to suggest that the meanings of holidays are static, however. Because holidays are such potent expressions of national beliefs, ambitions, and identity, they become temporal battlegrounds in the cultural contests between different interest groups. Holidays are contested terrain, and their meanings can change over time as they are controlled and influenced by groups that have competing visions for the nation.

Where Canadian Thanksgiving is concerned, the figures who were most responsible for establishing the celebration on an annual basis were Protestant clergymen in Ontario. Their interest in the holiday was primarily a response to two great challenges that faced them, as Canadian church leaders, beginning in the second half of the nineteenth century. Particularly after Confederation, ministers felt a moral and historical obligation to chart Canada's course. At the very moment that preachers most sensed a call to lead their country, however, global intellectual developments issued challenges to Christianity so fundamental that they threatened to dissolve many Christians' faith. The American Thanksgiving holiday revealed to church leaders a means by which they could restore Canadians' confidence in Christianity and secure their own positions at the helm of the young country.

Ontario clergymen did not simply duplicate the American Thanksgiving festival, which by the 1860s had evolved into a national public holiday.[7] Rather, they recast Thanksgiving as a predominantly religious event and naturalized the holiday by steeping it in Canadian nationalism. Ontarians responded positively to this mix of Protestantism and patriotism, and ministers successfully instituted Thanksgiving as an annual holiday in Ontario. Once Thanksgiving became a yearly event, however, other cultural interest groups increasingly challenged Protestants' holiday hegemony. As a result of these challenges, the Thanksgiving that Ontarians marked on the eve of the Great War was little like the holiday that clergymen had established several decades earlier. Yet, one aspect of the holiday remained unchanged: its nationalist content. Although Thanksgiving acquired many new meanings and customs, it remained throughout the Victorian period a day for Ontarians to celebrate their status as Canadians.

The early history of Thanksgiving Day in Ontario contributes to discussions of religion in late-nineteenth-century Canada by highlighting the prominent but waning influence of Protestant church leaders within the public sphere. It also complicates our understanding of Canadian patriotism during this critical period in the country's history. In particular, the origins of Canadian Thanksgiving demonstrate the complex and sometimes contradictory ways that citizens of the new dominion sought to define themselves in relation to both Great Britain and the United States. In this respect, Thanksgiving Day had much in common with Dominion Day, Empire Day, and other public celebrations of the era, which likewise sought to define Canadian identity in reference to both Britain and the United States (as discussed in the chapters in this volume by Marcel Martel, Joel Belliveau, Brittney Anne Bos, Allison Marie Ward, Forrest Pass, and Mike Benbough-Jackson).

Protestant Authority in Context

The advent of Thanksgiving Day in Ontario was closely related to broader developments within Canada's Protestant community. The first half of the nineteenth century had been a period of great activity for Protestant churches in what is now Ontario. The various denominations gradually gained autonomy from their parent organizations in Britain and built new churches and local organizational structures to accommodate waves of new immigrants. Churches formed Sunday schools for children, created Christian reading-rooms and libraries, and asserted their authority over higher education by founding numerous denominational colleges and universities. By the middle of the nineteenth century, these initiatives had injected the power of organized religion into virtually all aspects of Canadian life and had established Protestant officials as leading authorities on all of the major questions that faced the Canadian public.[8]

Protestant influence within Canada became even more crucial with the prospect, and then the reality, of Confederation. In the view of church leaders, Canada, with its abundant territory and resources, was clearly a promised land, and Canadians were a chosen people who would lead civilization's march towards Christian perfection. This glorious destiny would not be fulfilled, however, if the new country ceased to take its direction and inspiration from God. Accordingly, Protestant leaders felt a tremendous responsibility to chart the country's course. If businessmen, politicians, and other civic leaders conducted their affairs in accordance with Christian principles, they would bring peace and prosperity to the country, and they would also move the Canadian people closer to moral perfection. Thus, to Protestant ministers in late-nineteenth-century Ontario, making good Canadians and making good Christians were one and the same.[9]

In contemplating the character and destiny of the Canadian people, Protestant thinkers formed an integral part of the Canadian imperialist movement, a loose alliance of nationalists that Carl Berger has examined at length. Collectively, this mix of churchmen, academics, and public intellectuals espoused a form of citizenship that centred on Canada's connection with Britain. Convinced that Anglo-Saxons were innately superior to all other races, these Canadians viewed British imperialism as a progressive, civilizing force. They thus revered Canada's inherited political institutions and called for the creation in Canada of British-style caste and education systems. Furthermore, Canadian imperialists envisioned a reconfigured empire in which Canada enjoyed power equal to or even greater than that of Britain. History demonstrated that Canadians were a loyal, law-abiding people, and the country's northern climate dictated that Canadians be strong, hardy, and determined – superior as a people to even Americans and Britons. Protestant clergymen simultaneously drew from and contributed to this conception of Canadian imperialism when expressing their vision of Canada's Christian destiny.[10]

In and of itself, the project of directing and enlightening Canadian society was no small undertaking for Protestants in the years following Confederation. But the churches' mission was further complicated by the intellectual ferment that was then challenging Christianity. In 1859, Charles Darwin published *On the Origin of Species*, a work that rejected the biblical account of creation. Darwin argued that all life forms – humankind included – were composed of the same matter and had evolved into different species through a process of natural selection. This theory of evolution contradicted Christianity in several ways: not only did it suggest that the earth was far older than Christian sources indicated, but it also attributed human existence to something other than divine intervention. Darwin's theory cast science and Christianity as incompatible paradigms of truth and shook the very foundations of the Protestant faith.[11]

By the 1870s, Christianity was also under threat from higher criticism, a new scholarly approach that treated the Bible as an historical document. Linguists, archaeologists, and other social scientists subjected the Holy Book to unprecedented scrutiny and raised doubts regarding its meaning, authenticity, and authorship. This new scholarship had profound implications for Christians around the world: whereas believers had long assumed that scripture was unambiguous in meaning, higher criticism insisted that it was open to multiple interpretations. Thus, the Bible was not the untainted Word of God but was instead a mélange of imperfect stories to be read and analysed like any other text. Christians could no longer confidently seek solace in the Bible, for they could find therein only highly subjective answers. Much like *On the Origin of Species*, then, higher criticism raised objections that struck at the centre of Christianity.[12]

In Canada as abroad, higher criticism and Darwinian science created "a crisis of belief" among Christians.[13] Although membership in Canada's churches remained high throughout the Victorian era,[14] ministers observed growing religious uncertainty among their parishioners, and they addressed these doubts by striving to reconcile Christianity with the theory of evolution and the insights of higher criticism. By projecting divine sanction onto Darwin's theories, preachers insisted that God was indeed the supreme architect of the universe and that evolution was possible only because He had willed it. Similarly, theologians explained that the new biblical criticism would eventually improve humankind's understanding of God's intentions, thus strengthening, not weakening, Christianity. Far from being detrimental to Christianity, these thinkers argued, the new intellectual developments would ensure the future of the religion.[15]

Preachers' attempts to demonstrate the supremacy of Christianity marked a departure from traditional Christian thought, for they downplayed God's role as a miracle worker and emphasized His hand in everyday human affairs. The result was what came to be known as the "social gospel." If, as theologians now maintained, God's immanence was paramount, then it behoved Christians to likewise focus their attentions on the world around them. While promises of spiritual transcendence and eternal life remained central to Protestantism, social salvation became a prerequisite for individual salvation. In Ontario as elsewhere, the social gospel inspired Protestants to work, as Christians, towards the regeneration of society, and they threw themselves into a wide range of projects, including charities, urban moral crusades, the temperance movement, and campaigns for government-led social reforms. In the long term, the net effect of the social gospel was to gradually undermine the authority of the church, for it transferred Christians' attention from supernatural matters to more secular issues. In the short term, however, this new focus on worldly concerns fit nicely with church leaders' determination to set the course for the fledgling Canadian nation, a mission in which a new Thanksgiving holiday played no small part.[16]

A Solemn and Pious Occasion

Though Thanksgiving Day did not become an annual event in Ontario until the 1870s, Protestant officials set the tone for the holiday during the years immediately preceding Confederation. In 1859, the governor general of the Province of Canada proclaimed that Thursday November 3rd would be "a General Holiday and Day of Thanksgiving to Almighty God" in honour of "the blessings of an abundant harvest … [and] Peace and Plenty now enjoyed by Our people."[17] Reaction to the declaration was mixed. Some Protestant groups objected to the announcement, arguing that a government-declared Day of Thanksgiving voided the necessary separation of church and state. Thus in Toronto, the United Presbyterian presbytery announced that "they hold it an important Christian duty to obey magistrates, yet they cannot recognize the right of civil rulers to interfere in matters of religion." A more typical response came from Reverend John Jennings, of Toronto's Bay Street Presbyterian Church, who noted that he "was a party in asking the Government to appoint such a day" and explained that a proclamation from the governor general was the only practicable means by which all Canadians could unite in appreciation of God's blessings.[18] Though this would not be the last time that the relationship between state and religion became an issue on Thanksgiving Day, the Toronto presbytery ultimately agreed to mark the holiday. According to the *Toronto Globe*, Canada's first Thanksgiving was a solemn and pious occasion, with businesses and public offices closing for the day, and the churches being "attended by larger numbers than generally gather together upon the Sabbath."[19]

In the churches, ministers treated their swollen holiday congregations to sermons that were equal parts theology and nationalism – a blend that would characterize Ontario Thanksgiving discourses for many decades to come. Significantly, though, ministers presented an unfocused form of Canadian nationalism that featured a measured allegiance to both Great Britain and the United States. The Canada–U.S. Reciprocity Treaty, signed in 1854, was shifting Canada's economic focus from Britain to America,[20] while Thanksgiving Day itself was proof that North American economic integration had cultural parallels. At a time when Canada's national ties were in limbo, ministers seemed unsure as to where their loyalties lay. Thus, at Toronto's Second Congregational Church, Reverend F.H. Marling noted that "we were, as a nation, highly favoured of God [what with] our geographical position, whence every part of the world was so easily accessible; [and] our alliance by blood, language, government, literature and commerce, with the two foremost nations, in regards to knowledge, liberty, and religion, of the earth."[21] Long before Ontarians celebrated their first Thanksgiving, American preachers had identified the holiday as a time to deliver nationalist sermons.[22] Ministers such as Marling continued this tradition as part of Canada's first Thanksgiving services, but notably, they portrayed the Canada of 1859 as very much a nation in between.

Despite the general enthusiasm with which Canadians greeted their first Thanksgiving Day, the holiday's status as an annual affair was far from secure (see table 2.1). In 1860, the Canadian government declared a day of Thanksgiving for 6 December, and once again, holiday crowds packed churches around the province, with the *Ottawa Citizen* reporting

Table 2.1 Days of Thanksgiving Declared in Recognition of the Harvest, 1859–1913

Year	Date	Day	Year	Date	Day
1859	3 November	Thursday	1889	7 November	Thursday
1860	6 December	Thursday	1890	6 November	Thursday
			1891	12 November	Thursday
1862	4 December	Thursday	1892	10 November	Thursday
1863	11 November	Wednesday	1893	23 November	Thursday
			1894	22 November	Thursday
1865	18 October	Wednesday	1895	21 November	Thursday
			1896	26 November	Thursday
1871	16 November	Thursday*	1897	25 November	Thursday
1872	14 November	Thursday*	1898	24 November	Thursday
1872	6 November	Thursday*	1899	19 October	Thursday
1874	29 October	Thursday*	1900	18 October	Thursday
1875	28 October	Thursday*	1901	28 November	Thursday
1876	2 November	Thursday*	1902	16 October	Thursday
1877	22 November	Thursday*	1903	15 October	Thursday
1878	4 December	Wednesday*	1904	17 November	Thursday
1879	6 November	Thursday	1905	26 October	Thursday
1880	3 November	Wednesday	1906	18 October	Thursday
1881	20 October	Thursday	1907	31 October	Thursday
1882	9 November	Thursday	1908	9 November	Monday
1883	8 November	Thursday	1909	25 October	Monday
1884	6 November	Thursday	1910	31 October	Monday
1885	7 November	Saturday	1911	30 October	Monday
1886	18 November	Thursday	1912	28 October	Monday
1887	17 November	Thursday	1913	20 October	Monday
1888	15 November	Thursday			

An asterisk denotes Days of Thanksgiving proclaimed by the province of Ontario; all other Days of Thanksgiving were proclaimed by the government of Canada.
Source: Canada, Parliament, *The Canada Gazette* (Montreal, Toronto, and Ottawa: Queen's Printer), 1859–1913; Ontario. Parliament, *The Ontario Gazette*, (Toronto: Queen's Printer), 1871–1878.

that "the day was marked by becoming seriousness."[23] In 1861, however, the government did not proclaim a Day of Thanksgiving, and when it did appoint a holiday again in each of the following two years, several religious organizations once again protested that the state was interfering with matters that were more properly the responsibility of the church.[24] This controversy, together with the holiday's irregularity, indicated that sizeable portions of the population were uncomfortable with the existing constitution of Thanksgiving Day.

The squabbles between Christian groups were significant for, until the mid-1870s, the Ontario Thanksgiving, unlike the American festival, was almost exclusively a religious holiday. In the United States, pilgrim imagery and turkey dinners were essential parts of Thanksgiving; in Ontario, by contrast, clergymen promoted the holiday as, quite simply, a day for giving thanks to God. The pilgrims and the Thanksgiving myth, though fascinating, were the particular cultural inheritance of Americans, not Canadians. Thus, while Ontario preachers did occasionally refer to the New England pilgrims, they generally rejected the American model of romantic, pseudo-historical Thanksgiving sermons. Whereas American clergymen looked to the past for inspiration on Thanksgiving Day, Canadian ministers looked more to the future.

During the early 1860s, the American Civil War and increased tension between Britain and the United States led preachers to reconsider Canada's relationship with its neighbour to the south. What resulted in Ontario Thanksgiving sermons was not anti-Americanism per se, but rather a conviction that, in the eyes of God, the Canadian nation was superior to even the American one. The stain of slavery, Canadian preachers argued, would forever mar the American nation, and since, they mistakenly asserted, Canadians had avoided this stain altogether, they were naturally the greater of the two peoples.[25] "You are better off in some respects than the highly-favoured land adjoining," the Reverend Dr Caldicott informed Toronto Baptists in 1860. "The slave-power has been the curse of that beautiful and otherwise blessed country… No person who touches this soil, no matter what be the colour of his skin, can be a slave."[26] In 1862, as the American Civil War raged, Congregational minister F.H. Marling explained, "God is teaching us by contrast how favoured is our lot."[27] Even after the war had ended, Canadian preachers remained wary of Americans: in 1865, Toronto Methodist minister Reverend Pollard noted, "Forming, as we do, an integral part of the British Empire, we have, though often menaced by the press and politicians in the neighbouring republic, been preserved in peace by the providence of God."[28] Events in the United States thus brought focus to the nationalism of Ontario Thanksgiving discourses. While clergymen continued to describe Canadians and Americans as members of the same race, they increasingly spoke of a Canadian people that was different from, and ultimately superior to, the American people.

Two 1860s Thanksgiving sermons warrant particular attention, for they foreshadowed the tone of post-Confederation Thanksgiving addresses. The first, an 1865 speech by the Toronto Anglican Henry

Scadding, exemplifies the Protestant response to the Christian crisis of belief; the second, an 1866 sermon by Hamilton Presbyterian David Inglis, reveals the Protestant recipe for creating an exemplary Christian nation in Canada. Together, these sermons encapsulate the central ideas, concerns, and assumptions that governed Protestants' approach to Thanksgiving Day for the duration of the Victorian period.

The urgency of reconciling Christianity and Darwinian science formed the explicit subject of "Christian Pantheism," the sermon that the Reverend Dr Scadding delivered at the Church of the Holy Trinity, Toronto, on Thanksgiving Day, 1865. "The dissociation of the certain truths of science and the distinctive truths of religious faith has, without doubt, occasioned much harm in the world, by giving rise to an appearance of antagonism between the two sets of truths," Scadding explained. "It would be better if a clear view were properly established of the mutual light and help which the one can afford to the other."[29] Thanksgiving Day, as a religious celebration of the harvest, was a fitting occasion for Scadding to begin this all-important task.

The workings of nature, Scadding reasoned, were just as miraculous as the feeding of the multitudes and other biblical events; as such, they demonstrated the presence "of God in common objects – in the familiar things and beings of earth and water and sky around us."[30] In order to fully comprehend God's immanence, however, Canada's schools must "embrace, as necessary instruments of training and just human development, departments of science." Such features, Scadding argued, were essential to a modern educational system and, "while they are indispensable for the due understanding and effective use of earth and the things of earth, [they] lead likewise, under wise direction, to a real acquaintance with God."[31] By embracing Christian pantheism, Scadding suggested, Canadians would gain an appreciation of their myriad blessings as well as their Christian destiny. Thanksgiving, then, was a time for Ontarians to consider their nation's future.

Canada's Christian destiny was also the central theme in David Inglis's 1866 Thanksgiving Day sermon, "Righteousness Exalteth a Nation." While the government didn't declare a public holiday that year, Inglis's Hamilton church decided to hold its own Day of Thanksgiving. Scripture reveals that sin is "a source of weakness which, if preserved in, must ultimately lead to the decline and fall of the mightiest people," the pastor explained. But if Canadians persisted in living upright, moral lives, he argued, they would continue to receive the "Holy favours that distinguished them from other nations." Their British inheritance, for example, set Canadians apart from inferior, Catholic peoples, for "while the Protestant nations have risen in spite of trial, the Popish nations have sunk by a slow process of moral decay into imbecility and distress."[32] Likewise, righteousness exalted Canadians to a position loftier than that of Americans:

> It is argued that we are powerless to defend ourselves against the forces which the United States could pour in upon us from every direction… But should war be forced upon us, in our defence and in a righteous cause, who will say that we cannot maintain our own…? The sooner our neighbors realize that we value our present political institutions, and above all, our connection with the British throne, and that we will defend these to the utmost, the better it will be for the cause of peace on this continent.[33]

Inglis may have been remarkable for his confidence in Canadian military prowess, but his suspicion of Americans was typical of Ontario Thanksgiving sermons. Protestant leaders increasingly viewed Canadians as a unique, chosen people, and Inglis's notion of Canadian righteousness would become a very popular one after Confederation.

Inglis himself recognized that the proposed union of British North America, then under discussion at the London Conference in England, would bring some unique challenges and opportunities to Canadian Christians. "In the good Providence of God our lot has been cast here," he pronounced, "and at this time we are called to do our part in building up what may be regarded as a new nation. A high responsibility devolves upon us. What is to be our national character? On what do we rest as our security for national permanence and prosperity?" According to Inglis, so long as Canadians embraced "earnest, practical religion" and "let upright, high-resolved moral principle guide [their] every transaction," then their prosperity, safety, and Christian destiny would be secure: "If we possess and maintain that righteousness which exalteth a nation, then no power shall be suffered to prevail against us."[34]

Together, Scadding's and Inglis's sermons capture the beliefs and concerns that girded nineteenth-century Protestants' interest in Thanksgiving Day. Dr Scadding's discourse embodied the new theology that Protestants embraced in response to the global crisis of belief. In speaking on the relationship between nature and religion, Scadding clearly identified Thanksgiving Day as a time to reassure unsettled Christians and to defend the authority of Canadian churches. Reverend Inglis's sermon anticipated several of the arguments that Canadian imperialists would advance in the first half-century following Confederation. Further, by stressing Canadians' Christian destiny and by repeating the adage "righteousness exalteth a nation," Inglis emphasized the important role that Protestant leaders were to play in the making of a Canadian nation. These sermons by Inglis and Scadding, then, demonstrate the links between Confederation, the Christian crisis of belief, and Protestant leaders' commitment to Thanksgiving Day. The themes and opinions that they exhibited would be echoed in Canadian Thanksgiving sermons for decades to come.

A Protestant Holy Day?

On Thanksgiving Day 1859, Reverend Scott of the Richmond Street Wesleyan Methodist Church in Toronto hinted at the initiative that Ontario Protestants were willing to take in connection with Thanksgiving. "If there had been no recognition by Government of this goodness," he surmised, "the Church would have taken the matter into her own hands, and would have called upon Christians of all denominations to thank God for the bountiful harvest he had bestowed."[35] The controversy over church-state relations suggests that Protestants would not likely have reached unanimity on the issue of Thanksgiving. Still, when state officials failed to declare a Thanksgiving holiday in the years 1866–70, they unwittingly forged a consensus among Ontario denominations. Some Ontario churches, such as Inglis's congregation in Hamilton, held their own Days of Thanksgiving during these non-holiday years; nevertheless, by 1871, the government's indifference galvanized Protestants into action. Reverend Scott's comments proved to be accurate after all.

Toronto Anglican officials took the lead in trying to revive Thanksgiving Day, and they soon reached an agreement with their colleagues from other denominations that Thursday 16 November would be an appropriate day for the holiday. The Anglicans even invited the Roman Catholic Church to join their campaign – no small concession during an era of bitter sectarian feuding – although there is no evidence that Catholics were receptive to this invitation.[36] Having decided upon a suitable date, the churchmen petitioned government officials to declare a public holiday, which "would enable clerks and foot officials to close their office, and attend their different places of worship." By early November, the lieutenant governor of Ontario had agreed to declare a holiday for the Day of Thanksgiving organized by the churches. Christian ministers, despite their denominational differences, had joined together and brought Thanksgiving Day back to Ontario.[37]

Despite this initial success, Protestant leaders soon learned that their influence over Thanksgiving Day was not absolute. In 1872, the lieutenant governor once again agreed to declare a public holiday for a date selected by the churches. The following year, however, he ignored the date suggested by church representatives and instead appointed Thanksgiving Day for a later date – one that was more convenient for business interests. The result was not only widespread confusion as to the actual date of Thanksgiving Day, but also outrage from church officials. The *Canadian Independent*, the voice of the Canadian Congregationalist Church, fumed, "Our commercial men are to be pitied, for either they have not during the year received blessings sufficient to warrant the sacrifice of a day's profits, or having received them they will not take the trouble to make the acknowledgement... What do they expect their thanksgiving will be worth when it is because they have nothing else to do!"[38] The lieutenant governor, by choosing his own date for Thanksgiving, undercut the authority of Protestant church leaders and called into question the religious focus that had hitherto defined the holiday.

Thus sidelined, Ontario clergymen struggled to maintain control over Thanksgiving Day. In 1873, the confusion over the holiday's date led to poor attendance at church services and more business activity than on previous Thanksgiving Days. In the view of the *Toronto Globe*, these developments reduced the holiday to a "mere sham," and the paper called on Ontarians to decide whether the holiday was even worth having, and if so, what its form and purpose should be.[39] The next few years brought little clarity, however, as the various Protestant denominations each appointed their own separate days of thanksgiving, resulting in further public turmoil. Finally, in 1877, the Methodist *Christian Journal* reported that "the Churches of Canada accept the day appointed by the civil authorities for the purpose of public thanksgiving to Almighty God, for the blessing of a bountiful harvest." Having formerly been instrumental in establishing Thanksgiving Day and determining its date, Ontario Protestant leaders now found themselves acquiescing to a date dictated by provincial authorities.[40]

For chastened clergymen, the only source of consolation lay in asserting their influence over Thanksgiving Day at the federal level. Though individual provinces had occasionally declared days of thanksgiving, not since before Confederation had all of Canada celebrated the holiday on the same day. In June 1877, however, the Presbyterian Church in Canada lobbied the governor general to appoint an annual national Thanksgiving Day. While the governor general did not himself issue a declaration that year, he did convince the various lieutenant governors to proclaim coinciding provincial holidays. In 1878, he agreed to the Presbyterians' request and declared a national Day of Thanksgiving for 4 December. Thereafter, Thanksgiving Day would be the responsibility of the federal government, and all regions of Canada would celebrate the autumn festival on the same day (see table 2.1).[41]

Disputes regarding the date and guardianship of Thanksgiving Day may have eroded holiday church attendance, but they brought little change to the content of preachers' sermons, which invariably revolved around the harvest. At a time when agriculture formed the backbone of the Canadian economy, ministers interpreted abundant crops as evidence of God's immanence and a measure of Canadians' piety. The harvest also provided an evocative metaphor for the country's other gifts from God. "It was most appropriate to speak of the great blessings of a plentiful harvest," explained one speaker in 1873, "for where the pursuits of agriculture prosper, commerce and mechanical arts, and the commonest labourer are all joined in its success, and so the blessing reaches everywhere." Such blessings, preachers argued, were "assuredly a reward of a nation's holiness," and a sign that Canadians were a chosen people.[42]

Nor, according to Thanksgiving discourses, was economic abundance the only indicator that Canada was predestined for national greatness; equally significant were the country's connections to Great Britain, and the superior racial and religious composition of Canada's population. As Toronto Anglican Reverend Canon Dumoulin asserted in 1892, "One of the many cases for thanksgiving at this time was that this great North American continent had been opened up to civilization, and that it had become Anglo-Saxon in tone and spirit and constitution, instead of Spanish or French as had at one time threatened."[43] Yet, while Canadians apparently shared the same ethnic backgrounds as Americans, they departed from their neighbours in their "growing attachment to British institutions and British rule."[44] Thanksgiving sermons routinely glorified the British Empire and applauded Canada's retention of the British system of parliamentary democracy, which they hailed as the world's best system of government.[45] Finally, clerics used Thanksgiving Day as an opportunity to take rhetorical jabs at the Roman Catholic Church. "Moral and intellectual progress was made in the same ratio as the family Bible was studied and its precepts followed," reasoned a Toronto Methodist in 1892. "That was the difference to-day between Ontario and the adjoining Province of Quebec, where superstition had still a home."[46] In defining Canada in terms of its British heritage, its Anglo-Saxon lineage, and its Protestant allegiance, Thanksgiving Day sermons fit firmly within the tradition of the Canadian imperialist movement.

Ontario churchmen also echoed Canadian imperialists through their depictions of Canada's glorious national future. Some, such as Ottawa Congregational minister William MacIntosh, emphasized Canada's unique role as an intermediary between Great Britain and the United States: "Instead of being a cause of friction between the motherland and the republic to the south, we are really the solder that will cement into one the great Anglo-Saxon race."[47] Others had even grander visions for Canadians, maintaining that they were destined to create a Christian society that would serve as a model for all of humankind. In 1907, at Ottawa's Dominion Methodist Church, the Reverend Dr Henderson compared Canada to the biblical promised land of Canaan and argued that "Canada is the great world center of attraction to the population of the globe."[48] Another year, the Ottawa Presbyterian Reverend W.T. Herridge struck a similar note, observing, "We are Canadians, and as Canadians we believe that we too have a destiny. We too, desire to carry forward unsullied the banner of our national birthright, and to win for ourselves an honourable place among the nations of the earth... But in order to do so we must be Christian patriots, and we must enthrone character above all questions of selfish expediency." Canadians were a chosen people, men like Herridge argued, but they would fulfil their national destiny only if they remained faithful to God, embraced the social gospel, and governed their society according to Christian principles.[49]

Ontario Protestant leaders viewed Thanksgiving Day as a time for religion, but they also recognized it as a festive occasion. Accordingly, they reinforced the nationalist messages of their sermons by instituting a range of holiday customs that emphasized the social aspects of Christianity and elevated Thanksgiving Day programs above the routine of ordinary Sunday church services. Thanksgiving, as a holiday in recognition of national blessings, invited Christians to look beyond their own parish and to consider the broader community of which they were a part. In keeping with this theme, many churches took to holding joint services with other congregations. In 1873, for example, Presbyterian, Methodist, and Baptist churches in St Catharines held a single,

2.1 Union Jacks join symbols of the fall harvest to complete the decorations for a Harvest Home celebration at St Andrew-by-the-Lake Anglican Church, Centre Island, Toronto. "Interior of St Andrew-by-the-Lake Harvest Home Service. Rt. Rev. W.D. Reeve ca. 1924." St Andrew-by-the-Lake papers, Anglican Church of Canada Diocese of Toronto Archives.

interdenominational service; three years later, all five of Toronto's Congregational churches united to mark the holiday as one.[50] Thanksgiving was thus a time for unity, and a time for Canadians to strengthen their communities by discounting their differences and celebrating their common blessings.

Many Ontario churches adopted aspects of the Harvest Home festival, an Anglican celebration that was popular in Great Britain.

Encouraged by Anglican publications such as the *Canadian Churchman*, Ontario Protestants decorated their church sanctuaries with flowers, produce, corn stalks, and other symbols of the harvest (see figure 2.1). They also relaxed their liturgies, sometimes substituting cantatas for formal sermons, and replacing hymns with "God Save the Queen" and other secular, nationalist songs. Thanksgiving also became a popular time for promoting fellowship, with churches incorporating concerts, parades, sporting events, and community dinners into their holiday celebrations. By borrowing these features of the Harvest Home festival, Protestants transformed their Thanksgiving Day celebrations from mere church services into elaborate public spectacles that reached out to the entire community. These more secular activities increased the stature of the autumn holiday while upholding the themes that were so central to preachers' Thanksgiving sermons – the harvest, nation building, and British imperialism.[51]

Towards a Secular Holiday

Protestant leaders in Ontario continued to shape Canadian Thanksgiving into the early twentieth century, but once the holiday became an annual institution, they progressively faced challenges from other cultural authorities. Over time, business interests, American Thanksgiving customs, and the Canadian armed forces all came to exert their influence over the autumn harvest festival, divesting it of most of its religious associations. (Indeed, a broad and flexible approach to public celebrations would later prove to be key to Canadians' acceptance of other national holidays and commemorative events, as Forrest Pass and Matthew Hayday demonstrate in their respective chapters about Dominion Day and Canada Day.) Yet if Ontarians' priorities on Thanksgiving Day were changing, much of the responsibility lay with Protestant churches themselves, whose original conception of the holiday had proved to be too narrow to be embraced by Canada's increasingly diverse population.

In many respects, churches' own practices contributed to Ontarians' weakening interest in the religious elements of Thanksgiving. For example, because Thanksgiving was devoted to celebrating the harvest, the holiday necessarily highlighted the profane. Sermons usually stressed that the harvest derived from God's power but, to many Ontario Christians, an impressive yield demonstrated the capabilities of not the Lord, but the farmer. Although preachers typically reminded listeners that God's spiritual gifts were far more important than His temporal blessings, the overall effect of Thanksgiving sermons was to turn Protestants' attention from personal religious salvation to more worldly considerations.[52] The same could be said of the concerts, floral displays, and social functions that had gradually become integral to many churches' Thanksgiving celebrations. These events blurred the distinction between worship and entertainment, transforming Thanksgiving services into Thanksgiving shows. Along the way, the holiday's emphasis shifted from the sacred to the secular.[53]

The content of Thanksgiving church services also would have been unappetizing to working-class Ontarians. Although church leaders painted pictures of Canadians' material abundance, labourers received but a small share of this wealth. In an era when Ontario workers were organizing to combat the inequalities of industrial capitalism,[54] they would have had little time for the middle-class assumptions and classical liberal values that infused many Thanksgiving sermons. Preachers dismissed critics of the socio-economic status quo as "grumblers" and "grouches," and argued that the obstacles to individual prosperity were not structural problems, but the absence of good habits, "industry and self-reliance."[55] This diagnosis would have confounded working-class Ontarians, whose own lives proved that virtue did not necessarily lead to a comfortable existence. Hence, on Thanksgiving of 1886, when a Toronto Congregational minister eulogised Canada's great wealth, and claimed that "wages are higher in Ontario than in any State or country in the world," workers in the audience interrupted his sermon to protest his remarks.[56] Most disenchanted workers simply stopped attending holiday church services. If preachers were going to devote Thanksgiving sermons to the defence of a middle-class view of society, then working-class Ontarians might just as well stay away.

One alternative to church services was the New England model of elaborate family Thanksgiving dinners, which became increasingly common in Ontario during the latter decades of the nineteenth century.[57] The chief promoters of this development were members of the popular press, which had long provided Canadians with descriptions of American holiday traditions. "Thanksgiving dinner will be the grand social event of the day, or should be, if old customs are to be honored," the London Free Press instructed readers in 1874. "Every family circle that can be should be complete at that meal, which should consist of a thoroughly substantial bill of fare, as elaborately prepared and served as circumstances will admit of. Turkey is the chief viand, and should be roasted to a turn, and flanked with all the seasonable side-dishes, filled with steaming contents."[58] In subsequent years, other newspapers offered similar advice, and by the mid-1880s, Thanksgiving, in Canada as in the United States, was, as the *Toronto Globe* later remarked, a "Bad Time for Turkeys."[59] The growing popularity of family Thanksgiving get-togethers opened up new profit opportunities for businesses. Railway companies encouraged holiday travel by offering return tickets at cut rates,[60] while department stores tried to increase sales by marketing all manner of products as essential holiday items. In 1898, for instance, the Simpson department store advertised "Furs for Thanksgiving," "Jackets at Thanksgiving Prices," "Groceries for Thanksgiving," and even a "Thanksgiving Parlor Suite." Thanksgiving Day in Ontario was steadily becoming a time for not religion, but consumption.[61]

Significantly, the rising popularity of Thanksgiving dinners opened the harvest festival up to those Ontarians who were excluded by the brand of Canadian nationalism that infused Protestant versions of the holiday. Thus, while Catholics had been marginalized by the sectarian bias of holiday church services, they saw no harm in adopting secular Thanksgiving customs, such as turkey dinners. In 1910, for example, Thanksgiving Day landed on the eve of All Saints', which is a Catholic fast day. Roman Catholics, feeling robbed of their turkey dinners, berated the Canadian government for selecting a day for Thanksgiving that conflicted with the Catholic calendar.[62] This episode is instructive, for it reveals that, although Protestant assumptions continued to guide the government's handling of Thanksgiving Day, Catholics were adapting the holiday to suit their own lifestyles and belief system.

By the final two decades of the nineteenth century, Protestant churches were also facing competition from a wide range of commercial amusements and other community events. In cities, the Thanksgiving holiday provided workers with a rare chance to engage in modern leisure activities. While some people attended theatres to watch plays, operas, and choral performances, others flocked to events of a more carnivalesque nature. In 1882, for instance, Toronto promoters hosted a Thanksgiving menagerie that included performing elephants, a fire-walking demonstration, foot races for schoolchildren, and a fireworks display. In other years, ventriloquists, comedians, agricultural exhibitions, and similar curiosities vied for Torontonians' holiday dollars.[63]

By the 1880s, sports-minded Ontarians also found plenty to do on Thanksgiving Day. Spectator sports became exceedingly popular, as bicycle races, horse races, and especially football matches attracted large holiday crowds. The custom of Thanksgiving football games, which began in New York in 1876, represented yet another American practice that Canadians grafted onto their own holiday. In Canada as in the United States, football was intimately associated with notions of national pride, for the virtues that made a football team success-ful – teamwork and individual performance, ingenuity, persever-ance, physical strength – were the same qualities that would make a nation successful. No matter which team Ontarians supported, they were learning and endorsing the values that would lead to a prosper-ous Canada. Thus even at parks and stadiums, Thanksgiving activities could be saturated with nationalist messages.[64]

The holiday was also a time for workers themselves to enjoy some outdoor recreation and relaxation. On most Thanksgivings, though, the cold November weather restricted athletes to their local ice and roller rinks. Beginning in 1899, however, the government usually scheduled Thanksgiving for mid-to-late October, a change that often enabled Ontarians to spend their holiday outdoors. In 1900, when 19 October was Thanksgiving Day, the *Toronto Globe* mused, "the action of the Gov-ernment in advancing the date of the holiday to a day on which it could be enjoyed in the open air must have been appreciated all over this country... [It] was probably the first Thanksgiving in many a year that the parks were crowded." With the harvest festival falling in October, workers were able, more than ever, to spend the day playing sports, entering turkey shooting competitions at local taverns, or simply stroll-ing through town. In 1913, the *Globe* reported, "thousands of Italians, Greeks, Macedonians and others, having their feet off the treadmill for a few hours, simply wandered aimlessly about or feasted their eyes on the shop windows." For these non-British working-class immigrants, Thanksgiving Day represented a welcome opportunity to partake of modern urban delights.[65]

Thanksgiving also emerged as an important recreation day for Ontar-io's more affluent citizens. For many respectable gentlemen, the holiday provided an opportunity for courting or for hunting excursions. Others spent the day at the curling rink, or, in years when weather permitted, at the cricket pitch or the golf course. Private clubs and associations also sponsored holiday events: at the annual Thanksgiving concert of the Toronto St George's Society, revellers typically enjoyed songs such as "Rule Britannia" and "Hurray for Merry England." The Canadian imperialism that characterized church services also, it seems, found expression at some respectable secular Thanksgiving events.[66]

By the start of the Great War, the secular event that most challenged Protestant churches for Thanksgiving audiences was the annual sham battle staged in Toronto by the Canadian military. Military manoeuvres had been a part of Thanksgiving in Ontario since 1879, when the Queen's Own Rifles assembled for inspection at the Toronto armoury. The holiday military display quickly grew in popularity, and in 1888, the Queen's Own joined with the 10th Royal Grenadiers to stage the "Battle of High Park," which attracted more than ten thousand spectators. Over the next fifteen years, the spectacle was repeated on an even grander scale, eventually growing to involve a half dozen regiments, including several from Hamilton, whose travel expenses were absorbed by Toronto city council.[67] Much like Thanksgiving church sermons, the sham battle was consistent with the doctrines of Canadian imperialists, for whom British military traditions and a healthy martial spirit were essential components of Canadian nationalism.[68] Despite these parallels, however, the military manoeuvres received harsh criticism from Protestant clergymen. In 1892, for example, Reverend Frizzell of the Leslieville Presbyterian Church blasted "the apparent inconsistency of the Governor-General in setting apart a day for national thanksgiving and at the same time calling out the militia to take part in a sham battle which prevented many from attending church."[69] Such protests were in vain, however: by 1900, the *Toronto Globe*, after running through a menu of that year's Thanksgiving activities, matter-of-factly concluded that "most important, of course, will be the sham fight."[70]

The swarms of military enthusiasts and pleasure-seekers changed Thanksgiving from a primarily private to an ever-more-public holiday, but they did not transform the harvest festival into a day of lawlessness. As the *Toronto Globe* reported following Thanksgiving Day, 1903, "A noticeable feature of the day was the excellent behavior of the crowds everywhere, and the practically entire absence of drunkenness."[71] Even so, the increasingly secular nature of the holiday devastated many Protestants. In 1882, the newsletter of a Toronto Anglican parish complained that "there were many who observed Thanksgiving Day as a holiday and not as a day of thanksgiving."[72] Similarly, in an 1896 letter to the *Globe*, one O.G. Langford lamented that "in the country thousands go shooting; in towns and villages many drink and carouse… A few, a very few, regard the day as sacred, and turn their thoughts upward to the Great Father."[73]

Finally, in 1908, Protestant churches lost what little remaining influence they still had over Thanksgiving. Throughout the Victorian period, the governments of Ontario and Canada had unfailingly scheduled Thanksgiving Day for a Thursday, or occasionally a Wednesday (see table 2.1).[74] As early as 1898, however, railway companies and prominent newspapers began to argue that the Thanksgiving holiday should be permanently moved to a Monday, thus creating a fall long weekend.[75] Church officials condemned such proposals, declaring that "in the interests of public morality it is undesirable that the National Thanksgiving Day should be changed from Thursday to Monday."[76] In 1908, however, the transportation companies emerged victorious, as the federal government appointed Thanksgiving Day for the 9th of November, a Monday.[77] The results, in the years that followed, were predictable. For the railway companies, the new Thanksgiving long weekend quickly became one of the busiest times of the year, with each year bringing record numbers of holiday travellers.[78] For the churches, however, the change was disastrous. By 1911, the *Toronto Globe* reported that few Toronto churches had even held services on Thanksgiving Day, because the holiday was too near Sunday. Just two years later, the *Globe* reported not a single Thanksgiving Day church service. The transformation of Thanksgiving from holy day to holiday was complete.[79]

Conclusion

Popular opinion holds that, until well into the twentieth century, Canadians took their institutional and cultural leads from the "mother country," Great Britain. Historians have often endorsed this view, citing John A. Macdonald's 1891 election avowal, "A British subject I was born – a British subject I will die."[80] The early history of Thanksgiving Day in Ontario does not exactly refute the claim that Canadians were a British-oriented people throughout the Victorian period; it does reveal, however, that Canadians' loyalty to Britain was far from straightforward. Ontarians sometimes expressed their faithfulness in complex and seemingly contradictory ways. While the content of Ontario Thanksgiving celebrations expressed Canadians' allegiance to Britain, the form of these celebrations revealed Canadians' attachment to America. The Thanksgiving holiday was one way in which Canadians attempted to define themselves vis-à-vis both their position in the British Empire and their proximity to the United States.

Protestant leaders, more than any other group, were responsible for establishing Thanksgiving Day in nineteenth-century Ontario. At a time when Canadians were searching for an identity, and Christians were questioning their faith, clergymen crafted a holiday that addressed both of these issues. Canada's bountiful harvest demonstrated not only that God was a presence in the material world, but also that Canadians were a chosen people. Protestant pastors combined this evidence with aspects of the American Thanksgiving and formed a Canadian harvest holiday that was at once religious and nationalist in nature. From their perspective, Thanksgiving was a sacred day, a time for Canadians, as a nation, to publicly celebrate the numerous gifts that God had granted them, and learn how they could fulfil the great national destiny that He had reserved for them. To Ontario Protestant leaders, then, Thanksgiving was not simply about making Canadians. Rather, it was about nurturing the eventual custodians of all humanity.

Despite having founded Thanksgiving Day in Canada, Ontario clergymen were unable to retain control over the holiday in the long term. In an effort to attract worshipers, Protestant churches borrowed from the Anglican Harvest Home tradition to produce Thanksgiving events that were more shows than services. Such spectacles associated Thanksgiving with entertainment, thereby creating an audience-in-waiting for the commercial amusement operators who soon began to tempt holiday crowds. By the turn of the century, church services faced competition from a wide range of secular holiday events, including family get-togethers and turkey dinners, public entertainment and sporting events, and the Canadian military's sham battle. Business interests also exerted their influence, and in 1908, railway companies effectively ended the churches' Thanksgiving hegemony by successfully lobbying the government to move the holiday from mid-week to a Monday.

While Protestant leaders bemoaned the secularization of Thanksgiving, they themselves had inadvertently encouraged this process. Their conception of the holiday – like their vision for the country that it celebrated – excluded large segments of Canada's increasingly diverse population. Too often, the message contained in holiday church sermons was a hostile one for Catholics, for working-class people, and for non-British immigrants. These allegedly "other" people certainly thought themselves to be Canadians, and they defied those authorities who told them otherwise. By dismissing the Protestant form of Thanksgiving and embracing alternative versions of the holiday, these individuals rejected ministers' definition of "Canadian" and suggested their own, more inclusive definitions.

The passing of the church-oriented Thanksgiving did not mean that the holiday lost its nationalist flavour. The Canadian imperialist sentiments that had once been such important parts of preachers' sermons found new expression in many secular Thanksgiving events. Football matches, St George's Society functions, and most vividly, the sham battle were just some of the activities that continued the tradition of Ontario Thanksgiving nationalism. The patriotic associations of Thanksgiving Day would be further reinforced after the Great War, when the holiday was changed to coincide with Armistice Day, although this arrangement proved awkward, as Teresa Iacobelli's chapter demonstrates.[81] Turn-of-the-century Protestants may have lost control of Thanksgiving Day in Ontario, but their nineteenth-century predecessors had left an indelible mark on the holiday.

NOTES

1 Recent works include Laurie Collier Hillstrom, *Thanksgiving: The American Holiday* (Detroit: Omnigraphics, 2011); James W. Baker, *Thanksgiving: The Biography of an American Holiday* (Durham: University of New Hampshire Press, 2009); Tuğçe Kurtiş, Glenn Adams, and Michael Yellow Bird, "Generosity of Genocide? Identity Implications of Silence in American Thanksgiving Commemorations," *Memory* 18, no. 2 (2010): 208–24; Amy Adamczyk, "On Thanksgiving and Collective Memory: Constructing the American Tradition," *Journal of Historical Sociology* 15, no. 3 (September 2002): 343–65; Elizabeth Pleck, "The Making of the Domestic Occasion: The History of Thanksgiving in the United States," *Journal of Social History* 32, no. 4 (summer 1999): 773–89.
2 In Canada, the media often marks Thanksgiving Day by running stories about explorer Martin Frobisher, who staged a ceremony of thanksgiving upon landing at Baffin Island in 1578 – proof, they claim, that the first Thanksgiving was actually Canadian, not American. Despite such arguments, there is no evidence that connects the modern Canadian Thanksgiving to Frobisher's sixteenth-century celebration. For example, see *Toronto Sun*, 5 October 2010; *Toronto Star*, 7 October 2012.
3 A.D. "Tony" Doerksen, "The History of Thanksgiving," *Manitoba Pageant* 20, 1 (Autumn 1975): 1–8; Andrew Smith and Shelley Boyd, "Talking Turkey: Thanksgiving in Canada and the United States," in *What's to Eat? Entrées in Canadian Food History*, ed. Nathalie Cooke (Montreal: McGill-Queen's University Press, 2009), 116–44 (quotation at 128).

4 Craig Heron and Steve Penfold, *The Worker's Festival: A History of Labour Day in Canada* (Toronto: University of Toronto Press, 2005; Nicholas Rogers, *Halloween: From Pagan Ritual to Party Night* (New York: Oxford University Press, 2002); Karal Ann Marling, *Merry Christmas! Celebrating America's Greatest Holiday* (Cambridge, MA: Harvard University Press, 2000); Ellen M. Litwicki, *America's Public Holidays, 1865–1920* (Washington, DC: Smithsonian Institution Press, 2000); Stephen Nissenbaum, *The Battle for Christmas* (New York: Alfred A. Knopf, 1996); Penne L. Restad, *Christmas in America: A History* (New York: Oxford University Press, 1995); Leigh Eric Schmidt, *Consumer Rites: The Buying and Selling of American Holidays* (Princeton, NJ: Princeton University Press, 1995); Jack Santino, *All Around the Year: Holidays and Celebrations in American Life* (Urbana and Chicago: University of Illinois Press, 1994); William B. Waits, *The Modern Christmas in America: A Cultural History of Gift Giving* (New York and London: New York University Press, 1993); Tom Flynn, *The Trouble with Christmas* (Buffalo: Prometheus Books, 1993).

5 Eric Hobsbawm, "Introduction: Inventing Traditions," in *The Invention of Tradition*, ed. Eric Hobsbawm and Terence Ranger (Cambridge: Cambridge University Press, 1983), 1–14.

6 Benedict Anderson, *Imagined Communities: Reflections on the Origin and Spread of Nationalism* (New York: Verso, 1983); Michael Kammen, *Mystic Chords of Memory: The Transformation of Tradition in American Culture* (New York: Vintage Books, 1991).

7 Baker, *Thanksgiving*, chap. 4.

8 Terrence Murphy, "The English-Speaking Colonies to 1854," in *A Concise History of Christianity in Canada*, ed. Terrence Murphy and Roberto Perin (Toronto: Oxford University Press, 1996), 108–89; Brian Clarke, "English-Speaking Canada from 1854," in ibid., 325.

9 William Westfall, *Two Worlds: The Protestant Culture of Nineteenth-Century Ontario* (Montreal: McGill-Queen's University Press, 1989), 3–18; Phyllis D. Airhart, "Ordering a New Nation and Reordering Protestantism, 1867–1914," in *The Canadian Protestant Experience, 1760–1990*, ed. George A. Rawlyk (Montreal: McGill-Queen's University Press, 1990), 98–106; Carl Berger, *The Sense of Power: Studies in the Ideas of Canadian Imperialism, 1867–1914* (Toronto: University of Toronto Press, 1970), 217–32.

10 Berger, *Sense of Power*, chaps 1, 3–5.

11 Airhart, "Ordering a New Nation," 111–12; Clarke, "English-Speaking Canada," 315–22; John Webster Grant, *The Church in the Canadian Era* (Burlington, ON: Welch Publishing, 1988), 11 and 60–63; David B. Marshall, *Secularizing the Faith: Canadian Protestant Clergy and the Crisis of Belief,*

1850–1940 (Toronto: University of Toronto Press, 1992), 45–7 and 53–4; Ramsay Cook, *The Regenerators: Social Criticism in Late Victorian English Canada* (Toronto: University of Toronto Press, 1985), 7–16.

12 Cook, *Regenerators*, 16–23; Marshall, *Secularizing the Faith*, 45–46; Grant, *Church in the Canadian Era*, 60–63; Clarke, "English-Speaking Canada," 315–22; Airhart, "Ordering a New Nation," 111–12.

13 Cook, *Regenerators*, 8.

14 Census figures indicate that between 1851 and 1911, between 85 and 97 per cent of the Canadian population were members of the leading Christian denominations. Clarke, "English-Speaking Canada," 262.

15 Cook, *Regenerators*, 7–25; Marshall, *Secularizing the Faith*, 49–71; Clarke, "English-Speaking Canada," 315–22.

16 Cook, *Regenerators*, chaps 10 and 12; Marshall, *Secularizing the Faith*, 49–71 and 249–56; Richard Allen, *The Social Passion: Religion and Social Reform in Canada, 1914–28* (Toronto: University of Toronto Press, 1973).

17 Canada, Parliament, *The Canada Gazette* (Montreal: Queen's Printer, 1859), 2305.

18 *Toronto Globe* (hereafter *TG*), 2 November 1859.

19 Ibid., 4 November 1859.

20 Kenneth Norrie, Douglas Owram, and J.C. Herbert Emery, *A History of the Canadian Economy*, 4th ed. (Toronto: Thomson Nelson, 2007), 150–55.

21 *TG*, 4 November 1859.

22 Baker, *Thanksgiving*, chap. 2.

23 *Ottawa Citizen* (hereafter *OC*), 7 December 1860; *TG*, 7 December 1860. If Ontario Protestants once again lobbied for a Thanksgiving Day in 1860, their correspondence with the government no longer remains.

24 *Canadian Independent* 9, no. 4 (November 1862); *TG*, 5 December 1862, 11 November 1863.

25 In fact, slavery *had* existed in Canada. See Robin W. Winks, *The Blacks in Canada: A History*, 2nd ed. (Montreal: McGill-Queen's University Press, 1997), chap. 2.

26 *TG*, 7 December 1860.

27 Ibid., 5 December 1862.

28 Ibid., 19 October 1865.

29 Henry Scadding, *Christian Pantheism: An Address on Thanksgiving Day, 1865* (Toronto: Rollo and Adam, 1865), 4.

30 Ibid., 3–5.

31 Ibid., 6.

32 David Inglis, *Righteousness Exalteth a Nation: A Thanksgiving Sermon* (Hamilton: Spectator Steam Press, 1866), 5.

33 Ibid., 11–12.

34 Ibid., 10, 12–13.

35 *TG*, 4 November 1859.

36 *Christian Journal*, 10 November 1871; Charles J.S. Bethune and George Hopkins to Archbishop Lynch, 14 August 1871, Archives of the Roman Catholic Archdiocese of Toronto, Call number L AH22.13. The Roman Catholic Archives incorrectly attributes the letter to the year 1877; dates in the text clearly indicate that it was written in 1871. There is no record of the Catholics' response to this correspondence.

37 Council Minutes, 1871, 173, 174 and 179, City of Toronto Archives; Stephen Radcliff, to E.G. Curtis, 8 November 1871, and Curtis to Radcliff, 10 November 1871, Archives of Ontario (hereafter AO), Records of the Lieutenant-Governor's Office, Series 2, file 129A; James Lyster to the Lieutenant-Governor, 9 November 1871 (quotation), Lyster to E.G. Curtis, 9 November 1871, and Curtis to Lyster, 10 November 1871, AO, Records of the Lieutenant-Governor's Office, Series 2, file 130.

38 *Canadian Independent* 19, no. 5 (November 1872); 20, no. 5 (November 1873); *London Free Press* (hereinafter *LFP*), 5 November 1873.

39 *TG*, 7 November 1873; 6 November 1873 (quotation).

40 *LFP*, 29 October 1874; *TG*, 2 November 1876; *Christian Journal*, 9 November 1877. Though the lieutenant-governor proclaimed the annual Days of Thanksgiving, the dates for the holidays actually were selected by the lieutenant-governor-in-council and recommended to His Excellency through orders-in-council. See Communication of Order-in-Council from Ontario Provincial Secretary to the Lieutenant-Governor, 19 September 1877, AO, RG 8–1, Records of the Department of the Provincial Secretary, Series 1–1-D, file 1412/1877.

41 *LFP*, 21 November 1877; *Presbyterian Record*, November 1877 and October 1879; *Acts and Proceedings*, Third General Assembly, Halifax, 1877, 30–1 and 35; *Acts and Proceedings*, Fourth General Assembly, Hamilton, 1878, 13, Presbyterian Church in Canada Archives; Federal Secretary of State to Provincial Secretary of Ontario, 30 September 1879, AO, RG 8–1, Records of the Department of the Provincial Secretary, Series 1–1-D, file 1414/1879; Provincial Secretary of Ontario to Secretary of State, 19 October 1879, AO, RG 8–1, Records of the Department of the Provincial Secretary, Series 1–1-D, file 1558/1879. The holiday continued to be announced by a special declaration each year up until 1957, when Parliament permanently fixed Canadian Thanksgiving on the second Monday of October. Smith and Boyd, "Talking Turkey," 129.

42 *TG*, 7 November 1873, 23 November 1877.

43 Ibid., 11 November 1892.

44 Ibid., 30 October 1974.

45 Ibid., 11 November 1892, 29 November 1901.

46 Ibid., 19 November 1886, 11 November 1892 (quotation).

47 *OC*, November 26, 1897.

48 Ibid., 1 November 1907.

49 Ibid., 11 November 1892.

50 *TG*, 1 November 1876, 6 November 1873, 23 November 1877; *Canadian Independent* 12, 4 (October 1865).

51 *Canadian Churchman*, 4 November 1864, 3 November 1869; *Dominion Churchman*, 14 September 1876, 19 October 1876; *Canada Christian Advocate*, 6 November 1972; *TG*, 23 November 1877, 2 November 1880, 4 November 1880; 22 November 1894; *LFP*, 18 October 1913; *OC*, 27 October 1905.

52 *TG*, 7 December 1860, 3 November 1876; *Christian Journal*, 20 November 1863; *Canadian Independent* 19, no. 6 (December 1872).

53 Here my analysis follows that of religious scholars who argue that social gospellers, while seeking to defend their churches against powerful secular and commercial interests, inadvertently ushered in and legitimated those same forces. See, for example, Cook, *Regenerators*, 228–32; Marshall, *Secularizing the Faith*, 249–52; Susan Curtis, *A Consuming Faith: The Social Gospel and Modern American Culture* (Baltimore and London: Johns Hopkins University Press, 1991). On criticisms of this "secularization thesis," see Marguerite Van Die, "Protestants, the Liberal State, and the Practice of Politics: Revisiting R.J. Fleming and the 1890s Toronto Streetcar Controversy," *Journal of the Canadian Historical Association*, new series 24, no. 1 (2013): 89–129, nn 3–4.

54 Gregory S. Kealey, *Toronto Workers Respond to Industrial Capitalism, 1867–1892* (Toronto: University of Toronto Press, 1980).

55 *TG*, 5 December 1878, 4 November 1880, 28 October 1912; James Little, *Our Thanksgiving: Its Objects and Motives* (Toronto: Presbyterian Printing Office, 1881), 17.

56 *TG*, 19 November 1886.

57 Smith and Boyd, "Talking Turkey."

58 *LFP*, 28 October 1874.

59 *TG*, 19 October 1900.

60 *LFP*, 21 November 1877; *Hamilton Spectator*, 11 October 1900.

61 *TG*, 22 November 1898.

62 *LFP*, 29 October 1910; *TG*, 1 November 1910; *OC*, 28 October 1910.

63 *LFP*, 4 December 1878; *TG*, 10 November 1882; 11 November 1892, 19 October 1906.

64 *TG*, 4 November 1880, 18 November 1890, 27 November 1896; *OC*, 10 November 1882. 25 November 1898, 16 October 1903, 29 October 1912;

Stephen W. Pope, "God, Games and National Glory: Thanksgiving and the Ritual of Sport in American Culture, 1876–1926," *International Journal of Sport* 10, no. 2 (August 1993): 242–9; Eric Hobsbawm, "Mass-Producing Traditions: Europe, 1870–1914," in Hobsbawm and Ranger, *Invention of Tradition*, 263–307.

65 *LFP*, 4 December 1878; *TG*, 19 October 1900; 27 October 1905; 21 October 1913.

66 *OC*, 17 October 1900, 16 October 1903, 29 October 1912; *TG*, 4 November 1880; 7 November 1884, 29 November 1901; 29 October 1912 (quotation).

67 *TG*, 6 November 1879, 16 November 1888, 27 October 1905, 31 October 1910, 21 October 1913; Council Minutes, 1896, 268 and 271; 1897, 247; 1898, 228 and 714; 1899, 233 and 247; 1903, 223, 234, and 235; 1905, 245, City of Toronto Archives.

68 Berger, *Sense of Power*, 233–58.

69 *TG*, 11 November 1892.

70 Ibid., 18 October 1900.

71 Ibid., 16 October 1903; *OC*, 1 November 1910; *LFP*, 1 November 1907.

72 *Parish Church Work* 2, no. 11 (November 1882).

73 *TG*, 26 November 1896.

74 The preference for holding Thanksgiving Day on a Thursday apparently followed the American precedent, which in turn derived from the New England tradition of holding weekday church gatherings on Thursday afternoons. Edwin T. Greninger, "Thanksgiving: An American Holiday," *Social Science* 54, no. 1 (winter 1979): 3–15.

75 *LFP*, 24 November 1898.

76 Albert Carman to S.D. Chown, 13 September 1905, and attached, unidentified newspaper clipping, United Church of Canada Archives, Albert Carman Papers, 86.003C, Box 26, file 148.

77 *OC*, 28 October 1910.

78 Ibid., 29 October 1912; *LFP*, 21 October 1913; *TG*, 31 October 1911, 29 October 1912.

79 *TG*, 31 October 1911, 29 October 1912, 21 October 1913.

80 R. Douglas Francis, Richard Jones, and Donald B. Smith, *Destinies: Canadian History since Confederation*, 2nd ed. (Toronto: Holt, Rinehart and Winston, 1992), 104.

81 The dissonance between giving thanks while also remembering the war dead ultimately led to the separation of the two holidays in 1931. Smith and Boyd, "Talking Turkey," 129; Jonathan F. Vance, *Death So Noble: Memory, Meaning, and the First World War* (Vancouver: UBC Press, 1997), 211–21.

3 The Politics of Holiday Making: Legislating Victoria Day as a Perpetual Holiday in Canada, 1897–1901

CHRIS TAIT

It has become a cliché among those writing about the observance of Victoria Day in Canada to remark that modern customs associated with the long weekend in late May, such as gardening, opening the cottage, or drinking beer at backyard barbecues, have little or nothing to do with Queen Victoria, stereotypically portrayed as a round old woman dressed in black who is "not amused." While it is sometimes noted that Canada made the Queen's Birthday a perpetual holiday after she died in 1901, this fact has elicited little attention from scholars, who perhaps assume that this was simply a natural and automatic response from a semi-colonial society that was still very much attached to the "mother country" at the time. On the surface, this appears to be the case, but such a conclusion ignores the fact that Canada was unique within the empire in 1901 in its strong desire to continue the traditions of the 24th of May, and moreover that the Liberal government of Sir Wilfrid Laurier (in office from 1896 to 1911), along with a number of other political and business figures, did not share the enthusiasm of the general public and had successfully scuppered a bill to make the holiday permanent in 1897, the year of the queen's Diamond Jubilee.

When compared to other policy decisions by the government of Canada in the last years of Victoria's reign, such as the 1897 preferential tariff on British imports to Canada or sending Canadian volunteers to fight against the Boers in South Africa between 1899 and 1902, a law to retain an existing holiday hardly seems to have been a grand sacrifice in favour of imperialism or a great imposition on the economy. In this respect, it is not surprising that it has been overlooked or ignored in virtually all of the scholarship on the early Laurier period. Still, the perpetuation of the 24th of May as a Canadian custom was neither inevitable nor uncontested. The public and private discussions between 1897 and 1901 that led to the establishment of the permanent statutory holiday were far from a simple debate on the merits of commemorating the life and career of the queen. Indeed, while it was Victoria's death that reopened the debate, there were few who framed the question in terms of whether or not the queen deserved to be honoured. Arguments about the respective rights of business and labour, the nature of Canada's relationships to the British Empire and the United States, respect for popular custom and religion, and even the weather, all contributed to the deliberations. Moreover, the decision was made against the backdrop of Canadian participation in the British war in South Africa, a conflict that created a serious rift between English and French Canada and made the prime minister ever more wary of imperial causes. In the end, Laurier's resistance to the glorification of Queen Victoria as an icon of British imperialism in Canada was unintentionally farsighted. In attempting to prevent the holiday from becoming a divisive political issue, he helped to dampen its imperialist tone enough that the 24th of May could be vested instead with meanings particular to Canada, which helps to explain its persistence in this country while the date has been all but forgotten elsewhere.

Royal anniversaries, including birthdays of various members of the French and British royal families, along with accession and coronation dates of the reigning sovereign, have been commemorated in various parts of Canada at least since the eighteenth century. Long before such holidays were enshrined in law, they were marked by official ceremonies such as governor's levees and military reviews, and popular customs such as banquets, balls, and sporting events. The fact that there was little or no formal legislation relating to the observance of various kings' and queens' birthdays before the middle of the nineteenth century does not mean that pre-Confederation Canadians did not celebrate those occasions, as some have suggested.[1] Nor does the fact that Victoria Day is the only royal anniversary still listed as a statutory holiday mean that it is the only one that was ever observed. Many different days have been formally marked for royal birthdays over the centuries, and some, like George III's birthday on 4 June, continued to be observed in one form or another for decades after the death of the monarch.[2] The decision to perpetuate Victoria's birthday as a statutory holiday after her death in 1901 was certainly guided by loyalty and sentiment, but it was also made in the context of an industrializing, urbanizing, northern-climed country with a population that wanted to

3.1 Canadians gathering on Parliament Hill, Ottawa, for celebrations of Queen Victoria's Diamond Jubilee in 1897. William James Topley/Library and Archives Canada/PA-009636.

get out of the factories and the cities in the warmth of late spring. Had legislators in British North America in 1820 concerned themselves with regulating the leisure time of the average person, then 4 June might also have become a permanent holiday in Canada, given the outpouring of colonial affection for George III when he died in that year.

During the nineteenth century, the monarch's birthday faced some competition, in terms of emotional commitment, from the feast of Saint-Jean-Baptiste in Lower Canada/Quebec and from Dominion Day in most provinces after Confederation, but it was common for many people to celebrate more than one of these national rituals every year. As the florid rhetoric of one of Laurier's predecessors, the Scottish-born Sir John A. Macdonald ("A British subject I was born – a British subject I will die"), and the French-Canadian Laurier himself ("It would be the proudest moment of my life if I could see a Canadian of French descent ... in the parliament of Great Britain"), made clear, being a Canadian and a British subject were not mutually exclusive identities.[3] In English Canada in the 1890s, moreover, some still placed greater emphasis on their loyalty to Queen Victoria than on the commemoration of the British North America Act. In 1897, the town of Perth, Ontario, opted not to organize any public celebrations of Dominion Day, having exerted so much energy to mark the Diamond Jubilee a week before.[4]

The jubilee was the highlight of 1897 for most Canadians. In the months leading up to 22 June, which marked sixty years since the queen's accession, major celebrations were organized across the country, featuring parades, sports, feasts, and a proliferation of literary works and souvenirs of varying quality. In this atmosphere of ecstatic imperialism, the Conservative senator William J. Macdonald of British Columbia was inspired to present a bill to fix the Queen's Birthday as a permanent holiday for posterity, a tribute that he hoped would be "as lasting as bronze or marble."[5] He expected his bill would receive bipartisan support, and he had a Liberal colleague from Ontario, David Mills, to second it. Macdonald bothered to contact Laurier about the bill only some two weeks after its first reading in the Senate. Perhaps encouraged by Mills's cooperation, Macdonald trusted it would have the prime minister's approval.[6]

Indeed, Macdonald seems to have believed that this issue was not a matter of party or ethnic politics. In his speech during second reading, he referred to the joint destiny of the "Anglo-Saxon and Anglo-Norman race," a common rhetorical device for those who wished to paper over cultural differences between anglophone and francophone Canadians.[7] In outward appearance, the bill drew support from a wide cross-section of Canadian society. It had been introduced by a western Conservative and seconded by an Ontario Liberal in the Senate, and when subsequently introduced in the Commons, it was sponsored by two Quebec francophone members, the Liberal Henri-Gustave Joly de Lotbinière and the Conservative Alfonse Caron.

But this picture of harmony is deceptive. None of these men appear to have been acting on behalf of their parties, or with the full support of their leaders. The government and opposition leaders in the Senate, Oliver Mowat and Mackenzie Bowell, respectively, did not speak during the debates in that chamber, although they were present. Party unity counted for nothing; there were Liberals and Conservatives (including Liberal-Conservatives) on both sides on the question, and members did not hesitate to argue with their own caucus colleagues. In the Commons, Conservative leader Charles Tupper twice asked the government to place the bill on the Government Orders, but he did not press the case as insistently as the party later would in 1901.[8] Laurier did not engage in the discussion at all, and his House leader, Richard Cartwright, evidently felt no obligation to deal with Macdonald's proposal. When one Conservative member pressed him on the status of the bill, Cartwright replied testily, "the Government are not going to be dictated to as to the way in which they carry on their business."[9]

In the Senate, those who spoke in opposition to the holiday bill went out of their way to stress that they had no objections to commemorating the queen herself, who all agreed was beyond reproach. Instead, the two main counter-arguments were religious and economic. Two Catholic senators from New Brunswick, the Acadian Pascal Poirier and the Irish-born James Dever, stated that the perpetual glorification of a living person sat uneasily with their faith. In Dever's view it was "profanity, bordering on idolatry." Poirier declared he would not vote for "a motion that would make our gracious and beloved Queen a goddess."[10] An Irish Catholic and a French Canadian openly opposing, on religious grounds, a motion with such symbolic significance for Canada's British identity might have been expected to provoke an Anglo-Saxon Protestant backlash, but it did not. This silence could be interpreted as a sign of increasing tolerance and accommodation of minority groups in Canadian society; more likely, however, it was an indication of the fact that most people were not particularly excited about the issue.

A more common objection (and one that would be raised in numerous debates over the establishment of Canadian statutory holidays in the nineteenth and twentieth centuries, including Thanksgiving and Remembrance Day, as discussed in the chapters by Peter Stevens and Teresa Iacobelli) was based on the principle of laissez-faire. At least four of the senators opposing the bill had extensive business interests as merchants or manufacturers. Not surprisingly, they argued that adding another holiday would be disruptive to the economy, but they wisely avoided trying to evoke much pity for the comfortable capitalist and instead focused their concern on the working class. Samuel Prowse, a PEI manufacturer and merchant, invoked "the great struggle that the labouring classes from this time will experience in making a living for themselves" and decried the loss of a day's wage to enforced idleness. James Lougheed of the Northwest Territories observed that "it is very well for hon. gentlemen not actively engaged in business pursuits, and who do not come in direct contact with ... business life, to move that a day be set apart and that business be tied up for twenty-four hours each year in perpetuity."[11] His remarks barely concealed his contempt for those who had drawn on the public purse for most of their lives, but in truth most of the proponents of the holiday had done so, as politicians, patronage appointees, and military officers.

In response, Mills argued for the benefits to body and mind from recreation and patriotic community events, reminding his colleagues that there was more to life than earning a living. Charles Boulton of Manitoba added that a public holiday did not prevent people from doing household chores or gardening and that families would benefit from spending time together. Alexander Vidal of Ontario suggested that if the holiday, which had already been observed for decades, had been such an imposition on the masses, then surely some member of Parliament would have raised the issue on behalf of his constituents, or citizens would have sent petitions, but neither had occurred. "And so," he concluded, "we have a clear indication of the public approval of the observance of the holiday whatever inconveniences may attach to it."[12] Most senators agreed, and the bill passed third reading on 3 May 1897.

Some caveats are in order here. The Senate passed the bill without division, suggesting that members did not feel it was controversial or close enough to require a roll call. Moreover, in one of its reports on the debate, the *Montreal Star* remarked that the Senate was less busy than usual at that time of year.[13] Thus the lengthy exchanges do not necessarily signify a major rift in public opinion; the holiday may simply have been the most interesting subject that the Senate could find to talk about.

Nevertheless, most of the arguments that were deployed in discussions both for and against the holiday did appear elsewhere in 1897 and again in 1901. The Senate debate was thus an opportunity for opposing views on the issue to confront each other directly. Most major newspapers reported on the discussion as part of their parliamentary coverage, so it may have had some influence on public opinion. Although the debate proved fruitless in the short term, it was the only time that a parliamentary body gave the matter a thorough public airing, and it provides ample evidence of the complexity of the holiday question for many contemporaries. Finally, the regional distribution of the debaters is intriguing: five Ontario senators, representing both parties, spoke for the bill, while all four of the Maritime speakers were opposed, and no representative of Quebec, francophone or anglophone, offered any view at all. This is hardly a scientific sample of public opinion inside or outside the Senate, but it certainly suggests that the 24th of May was more significant in Ontario than elsewhere.

While no Quebec senator entered the fray, a major newspaper in that province did. Macdonald's bill met with derision in Montreal's influential Liberal daily *La Presse*. The paper's political correspondent in Ottawa dismissed the idea as "a Senate fad that interests no-one… It would be better to drop it." The writer agreed with many of the objections to the holiday that had been raised in the Senate, not least of which was the imposition on workers' wages. In an age that had seen numerous traditional observances set aside in the interests of industrial productivity, establishing a new one "for purely sentimental reasons" was a step backward.[14] After the bill passed third reading in the upper chamber, *La Presse* asked whether the Commons could possibly allow such a "ridiculous loyalist fantasy" to become law.[15]

After the Senate's passionate and wide-ranging debate on the holiday, the bill was sent down to the Commons, where it languished as a private member's bill. As mentioned earlier, Tupper tried sporadically to get the ministry to support it, but to no avail. Without government backing, the bill failed to reach a second reading in the Commons before Parliament was prorogued on 29 June 1897, and it thus expired. But whatever indignation or suspicions of Liberal disloyalty this failure may have prompted, these were overwhelmed by the enthusiastic celebrations of the queen's Diamond Jubilee on 22 June and by the reports of Laurier's virtuoso performances during visits to Britain and France.[16] Indeed, there was so much anticipation of Jubilee Day that in Winnipeg the *Manitoba Free Press* noted on 25 May that the event "cast its shadow before and detracted somewhat from the enthusiasm with which loyal Winnipeggers generally celebrate the birthday of her gracious majesty Queen Victoria."[17] The *Montreal Star* agreed that "the real Jubilation comes in June."[18]

Still, the failure to transform the twenty-fourth of May into a permanent celebration of Canadian loyalty to the empire in the jubilee year must have been a great disappointment for many. In 1898, Clementina Fessenden Trenholme, a member of the Wentworth Historical Society in Ontario, began to lobby for the creation of a new annual observance to complement the Queen's Birthday, which would come to be known as Empire Day. The evolution of Empire Day and the activities associated with it are explored in greater detail in chapters by Marcel Martel, Joel Belliveau, Brittney Bos, and Allison Ward, so for the purposes of this discussion of Victoria Day, a brief overview will suffice. As promoted by Trenholme, Empire Day would not be a general holiday but rather would provide the opportunity to implement a special program of patriotic activities and lessons for schools and other civic institutions, teaching children to love and serve both Canada and the British Empire. It would be held each year on the last day of school prior to the holiday, normally 23 May. It could be implemented easily at the school and board level and would not need to be legislated into existence. Nevertheless, Trenholme gained some key political allies, including George Ross, the Ontario minister of education. Ross was a genuine imperialist, but he also saw the idea as a popular cause that could put him in the premier's office. Through his vigorous advocacy, Empire Day was adopted as a school event in a number of provinces, including Ontario, Nova Scotia, and Quebec (at least by the Protestant schools).[19] The Queen's Birthday was thus prefaced by nationalist and imperialist messages more explicit than the occasion had seen in the past.

Such emphatic associations between imperialism and the 24th of May were politically problematic for Laurier. In 1899, he attended the celebration of the Queen's Birthday in Montreal, along with the governor general, Lord Minto, and numerous federal and provincial politicians. Imperial feeling was clearly in evidence, with military parades, speeches about the "British mission," and a concert, given by the Protestant School Commission, that included "Rule Britannia" and "Here's a Health unto Her Majesty" along with the more Canadian "The Land of the Maple."[20] Only months later, when Britain went to war with the Boer republics in South Africa, many English Canadians (particularly in Ontario and Montreal) wrapped themselves in the flag and demanded that Laurier's government provide men and material support for the cause. Thousands volunteered to serve. A newly founded women's organization, the Daughters of the Empire Federation (later the Imperial Order Daughters of the Empire), included among its aims promoting the imperial credo among youth through Empire Day activities, as well as sending donated supplies to the troops overseas and ensuring that the fallen were properly commemorated.[21] English Canada was clearly willing to back the imperialist rhetoric of 23 and 24 May with concrete action.

Meanwhile, French Canada was almost uniformly against any Canadian participation in South Africa, and *La Presse*, which had heaped scorn on the Victoria Day bill in 1897, now became one of the leading voices in opposition to the war and the government's contribution to it. In the end, Laurier compromised by allowing volunteers outfitted by the Canadian government to go to South Africa to fight as part of the British army. To gain the acquiescence of the francophone portion of his caucus, he declared that this would not constitute a precedent for future wars. But he had nevertheless alienated some of his base in Quebec: the clearest demonstration of this was the resignation of Henri Bourassa, who left the Liberal caucus to run as an independent and became a permanent thorn in the side of Laurier's government.[22]

At the same time, not all English Canadians were mollified by Laurier's compromise. Excessive zeal and drink during celebrations of the victories at Ladysmith and Paardeberg prompted some McGill students to attack the offices of the leading francophone anti-war papers and the Université Laval de Montréal in March 1900. Demonstrations by Laval students provoked a violent confrontation between the two groups and brought about the intervention of the police and other residents of the city.[23]

All of these considerations, as well as a possible election in the near future, must have been on Laurier's mind in the spring of 1900, when his political ally John Willison, editor of the *Globe*, invited him to celebrate the Queen's Birthday in Toronto. Laurier saw how doing so could boost his political fortunes in Ontario and agreed that "it would be a good idea." However, he declined the offer in order to spend time "among my fellow countrymen of French origin in Quebec," as "there is a constant report amongst them that I neglect them to attend only to the English electors."[24]

The general election that followed was further proof of the cultural divide. In November 1900, the Liberals won a second consecutive term in power, with a slightly larger majority than before. But the regional locus of that majority had shifted from the previous general election in 1896. While Laurier's deft compromise on the South African issue had probably saved his government, the balance of power between Ontario and Quebec in his party was thrown off, with the latter dominant. The Conservative opposition, meanwhile, had gained seats in Ontario while conceding in Quebec. The Liberals' advantage in Quebec, and in Parliament, might hold only as long as they continued to handle nationalist and anti-imperialist sensibilities with great care. Despite his overall gains, Laurier confessed himself "much disappointed with the result in Ontario."[25] As Réal Bélanger notes, after the compromises that Laurier had made on the Manitoba schools question in 1896, the preferential tariff on imperial goods in 1897, and the commitment of troops to South

Africa in 1899, all of which had run counter to his personal instincts, Ontario voters had still turned their backs on him.[26] Perhaps he was tempted to ignore further pro-British demands from the province for a while. But in a few months, Ontario would be testing the prime minister's commitment to imperialism yet again.

On 22 January 1901, Queen Victoria died. Canadians' shock at this event quickly gave way to hagiographic eulogies and self-congratulatory historical surveys. Politicians trumpeted the political and constitutional maturity of the dominion, looking back at the achievements of responsible government, Confederation, and territorial and demographic expansion. Businessmen lauded the relentless growth of industry and trade. Preachers and social reformers hailed the improvements in morality, propriety, and hygiene. Nearly all agreed that the Victorian era – for even those who lived in it already considered it a distinct period in human history – was marked by unparalleled progress. The *Manitoba Free Press* described it as "a golden period" that was "filled with numberless eminent names in every department of human thought and achievement."[27] The *Toronto World* was even more hyperbolic: "The Victorian era is the greatest epoch in the world's history. It has done more for the betterment of the human race than all the other eras of English history rolled into one."[28]

The late Victorian era was characterized by such triumphal and self-satisfied pronouncements – one is reminded of Laurier's "Canada shall fill the twentieth century" speech – even though they often masked serious insecurity about the present and the future. When Queen Victoria died, imperial forces, including the Canadian volunteers, were still mired in the South African conflict. What should have been a mere exercise in frontier pacification had become instead a difficult counter-insurgency campaign and a political and diplomatic controversy the world over. The war remained unpopular in Quebec, where the Montreal journal *L'Avenir* boldly declared in its announcement of the queen's demise, "we reserve our tears for other sorrows ... and we will sooner weep for the death of the Boer people that the mercenaries of Queen Victoria tried to eliminate down to their roots."[29] *La Patrie* mourned the queen, but also asked "why must war, crazy war, have poisoned her last years [and] shortened her life?"[30]

It was in this context that the discussion of the most fitting ways to commemorate Queen Victoria took place in Canada. There were, of course, the immediate and ephemeral gestures, differing little from those of the Diamond Jubilee: the newspaper editorials and special

3.2 Parliament Hill, Ottawa, draped in mourning for Queen Victoria, March 1901. William James Topley/Library and Archives Canada/PA-008988.

editions, political speeches, sermons, and hurriedly reissued biographies, portraits, and prints. There was an official period of mourning. Then there were the more permanent tributes: within a few years, new statues of the queen adorned Ottawa, Toronto, Hamilton, and Winnipeg, numerous parks and streets were named after her, and eventually the Victoria Memorial Museum Building (now home to the Canadian Museum of Nature) was constructed in the capital.

All of these were largely static forms of memory. They were reminders of the past, but ones that might someday become marginalized by a society that could embrace other values and symbols. A yearly day of celebration, however, promised to keep Victoria in the hearts and minds of future generations. As Jonathan Vance writes of the memory of the First World War, "there remained the possibility that some townsfolk might pass [a memorial] by without pausing to ponder its significance," but "an annual observance ... could ensure that the lessons of the war remained at the forefront of the public's consciousness." So began the tradition of Remembrance Day.[31] In 1901, the feeling was very much the same with respect to the queen. A *Toronto Globe* editorial asserted that "we can think of no more practical way of preventing its measurable obliteration than by setting aside a general holiday dedicated to her name... A time might come when the name so familiar to us would have become but a vague gem on the bead-roll of Sovereigns. While Victoria Day lasts this can hardly be."[32]

In contrast to the establishment of Armistice/Remembrance Day after the First World War, however, celebrating and remembering Victoria on her birthday was not a matter of inventing a new ritual, since marking each sovereign's birthday had been a colonial practice for over a century. But the observance of the 24th of May in particular had become so widespread and so deeply stamped on the Canadian consciousness that it could not simply be abandoned in favour of the new king's birthday. Edward VII had visited parts of Canada in 1860 as a young man – something the queen never did – but he was always in his mother's shadow. At the time of that tour, a Prince Edward Island poet wrote, "We love him for his mother's sake, / Because we love our Queen."[33]

Another problem for Edward VII's public image was that his birthday was on 9 November. Edward Horsey, the Liberal member of Parliament for North Grey who in 1901 proposed the bill to make Victoria Day a perpetual holiday, observed that "from the very nature of things, the 9th of November can never take the place of the 24th of May in the hearts of the people of Canada. The season is not so favourable for all of the outdoor pastimes with which tradition in this country has associated the Queen's birthday." In 1902, Canada officially designated 24 May as the day to mark the king's birthday as well, a reasonable decision considering all of the factors listed above.

Victoria had a grip on the public imagination that went beyond mere political allegiance and personal admiration to something approaching religious veneration. A resident of Digby, Nova Scotia, told the *Halifax Chronicle* that he supported the perpetual observance of 24 May because "other Saint's [sic] days are observed as holidays in the Dominion, why not this one?"[34] Observing the Queen's Birthday after her death was a form of public memory, but it was also a symbol of continuity with an idealized past that seemed to be intimately connected with her life. Surveying Victoria's reign, Canadians could find reassuring examples of progress and achievement to convince themselves that their present challenges could also be overcome. As Sir George Parkin of Upper Canada College argued, "All the past of a nation goes to mould its future, and so it is the part of wisdom for a people to make much of its noblest traditions. The popular determination to keep Victoria Day springs from a wish to cling to a high ideal of sovereignty and of national life."[35]

Although there was support from all corners of the country for making the 24th of May a perpetual holiday, the greatest enthusiasm was, unsurprisingly, in Ontario. The Conservative *Mail and Empire* of Toronto seized on the idea immediately following news of the queen's demise, and from late January onward the paper repeatedly took credit for the whole movement to establish the holiday.[36] Never mind that the proposal was at least four years old, or that many other newspaper editors, politicians, and ordinary people were clamouring for it at the same time with no prompting from the *Mail and Empire*. The city councils of both Toronto and Hamilton petitioned the dominion government in favour of the event.[37] Supporters wrote letters to their local paper, to government officials, and directly to Laurier.

Laurier's manner in dealing with the issue in Parliament was curt and unenthusiastic, even allowing for the dry style of the official record. When the Conservative Frank C. Bruce of Hamilton asked the prime minister if the government intended to perpetuate the holiday, Laurier said tersely that it did not.[38] When fellow Conservative William Maclean of East York, Ontario, raised the question again two months later, Laurier replied only that "there is a Bill before the House." This was true, but misleading, since it had been presented as a private member's bill by the Liberal backbencher Horsey and, as in 1897, there was little chance of it passing unless the Liberals placed it on the Government Orders. Knowing this, Maclean persisted, asking again if the government would support the bill. All Laurier would say was that the public would know the government's plan "in due time." After another week of official silence on the question, Maclean resumed his hounding of Laurier. On 23 April, Laurier promised to present his decision six days later.[39]

In his correspondence and public remarks, Laurier never gave a clear reason for his resistance to a perpetual holiday on 24 May. Indeed, as indicated above, he went out of his way not to be drawn into any discussion of the matter. As R. Craig Brown and Ramsay Cook have noted, this was to some extent Laurier's standard approach to thorny issues: "to temporize, to blunt divisive issues, might not be heroic, but it could ensure peace – and power."[40] Senator Macdonald, Lord Minto, and others complained vaguely that Laurier was influenced by anti-imperial elements, but they did not or could not identify and such specific individuals or groups.[41]

One obvious explanation for Laurier's reluctance to support the perpetual holiday was that it could alienate Quebec from the Liberal government. The ongoing war in South Africa had already led to the disaffection of his Quebec lieutenant Joseph-Israel Tarte, the hostility of Bourassa, and heavy criticism in the editorial pages of *La Presse*, *La Patrie*, and other Liberal-leaning papers in the province. From this angle, creating a special holiday to commemorate the dead British queen was a dangerous ploy. If *La Presse* was speaking for a sizeable constituency in French Canada when it decried the 1897 bill, then Laurier's endorsement of the perpetual holiday could undermine his credibility as a brake on English-Canadian jingoism. Laurier knew that the occasion was usually laden with imperialist messages. What if it led to violence similar to the student riots in Montreal in 1900? Perhaps, like the British Liberal Party in the years before the Great War, he suspected that such a holiday would benefit only the Conservatives politically, even if his government enacted it.[42] On the other hand, allowing the Conservatives to claim the issue as their own could lead to further losses in Ontario in the long run.

Fortunately for Laurier, the opposition in Quebec to commemorating the queen was not as vociferous in 1901 as it had been in the past. While *L'Avenir* shed more tears for the Boers than for Queen Victoria, most journals in the province were respectful of the monarchy. *La Presse* may have opposed the idea of a perpetual holiday in 1897, but it gave ample coverage to celebrations of the Queen's Birthday, and its coverage of her illness and death, while lacking the hagiographic tone of some Ontario papers, was as detailed and reverent as almost any other Canadian news outlet. Moreover, the paper's coverage of the 1901 holiday bill was largely restricted to reports on the discussions in Parliament, and it offered no editorial opinion of its own. Whether this marked a real change in attitude is difficult to determine, but at the very least it is likely that the editors of *La Presse* were by that time far more concerned with the war than with picking a fight over a well-established holiday.

La Patrie, meanwhile, declared its support for the bill once it had passed, although it did not take a public position during the debate.[43]

Laurier also had to consider the interests of the business community. In 1901 the Council of the Quebec Board of Trade, a group composed of both francophone and anglophone businessmen and professionals, wrote to Laurier to express the same economic concerns that Lougheed and others had in 1897. While declaring themselves "in full sympathy with the sentiment which prompts the proposal," the council members did not wish to see commerce further hindered by such annual disruptions. They bemoaned what they saw as an excessive number of holidays already on the calendar, such that they could not realistically observe all of them and still conduct their business. As such, they proposed that one or more existing holidays should be dropped if Victoria Day were to be adopted.[44]

Yet few other Canadian businesses expressed such opposition to the expansion of the holiday calendar. The manager of the Bank of Ottawa wrote to the Department of Justice to point out that the original wording of the bill did not clearly apply to banks. He wished to broaden it so that bankers could join their fellow citizens in celebration.[45] Reginald Kennedy, the president of the *Hamilton Times*, inquired with some urgency about the status of the Victoria Day measure in April 1901 because his railway and other business clients needed to arrange their holiday-related advertisements.[46] Since the middle of the nineteenth century, the rail and steamship operators had organized special excursions for the major holidays, bringing country folk to the larger towns to see the military spectacles and fireworks, and taking city dwellers out to enjoy nature. Another holiday meant more, rather than less, productivity and profit for them. Other businesses also stood to gain from such special occasions. One bookstore in Toronto hawked discounted novels and special souvenir portraits of the queen in the days leading up to the holiday.[47] In the House of Commons, William Maclean pressured the government to commit to the bill in the interests of the public and of business, adding that he knew of a firm that had ordered $65,000 worth of fireworks for the event.[48]

Laurier even tried to use imperial unity as an excuse for inaction. This was ironic, given his negative views on imperial federation and his continued insistence since 1897 that Canada should be able to decide for itself the extent of its commitment to imperial causes. He told one supporter of the holiday that the idea was "engaging the attention of public men at this moment, not only in Canada, but in England and in some other colonies" and as such "it would be preferable to have some joint action on the subject."[49] The flimsiness of this argument was revealed the following month, when Premier John Gordon Sprigg of Cape Colony sent an enthusiastic telegram proposing that if Canada, Cape Colony, and Australia could all agree on the matter, together they could surely persuade London to act. Laurier immediately replied with "Government thinks better leave question to be primarily dealt by Imperial authorities."[50] Now it seemed it was no longer a question of joint imperial concern – it was a purely British decision. Was Laurier thus prepared to accept the decision from London as the last word? He never had to face this dilemma directly. As it turned out, public opinion in Canada was more insistent on the point than in Britain. The British campaign spearheaded by the Earl of Meath to mark Victoria's birthday as a permanent bank holiday there drew on the Canadian act as a precedent, rather than the other way around.[51]

Indeed, although the custom of celebrating the monarch's birthday had originally arrived in the colonies with patriotic Britons, by the end of the nineteenth century the transplanted practice seemed to have been more important in colonial culture than back home. Edward Horsey observed that, "in this country the day has always been kept as a holiday by the whole people in a way entirely unknown in England where it was simply a formal holiday observed by public institutions only." For this reason, he felt that the imperial authorities did not need to be consulted on its perpetuation.[52] The novelist Sara Jeannette Duncan opened her 1904 novel, *The Imperialist*, with a lengthy and vivid description of a typical Canadian observance of the 24th of May, which she playfully compared with the more muted version in Britain: "Travelled persons, who had spent the anniversary there, were apt to come back with a poor opinion of its celebration in 'the old country' – a pleasant relish to the more than ever appreciated advantages of the new, the advantages that came out so by contrast... A 'Bank' holiday, indeed! Here it was a real holiday, that woke you up with bells and cannon."[53] The *British Empire Review*, which strongly advocated for an empire-wide commemoration of the queen, admitted that the traditional observance of Whitsuntide took precedence over the queen's birthday in Britain and would not be easily dislodged from the popular festive calendar.[54] Even at the highest levels, the 24th of May was treated differently in Britain and Canada. Motions to adjourn for the Queen's Birthday were essentially unchallenged in the North American colonial legislatures from the 1840s onward. In 1900, a similar motion in the British House of Commons "to enable members to join in the commemoration of Her Majesty's birthday" only narrowly passed, with 106 in favour and 100 opposed.[55]

Australia's intervention in the pan-imperial discussion, had it come, would hardly have changed Laurier's mind. There was sufficient opposition to the idea from labour and Irish interests in Australia that – with the exception of the state of Queensland, which continued to mark the 24th of May as a holiday from 1901 – it would take until 1905 merely to establish a half-holiday for schools only. This "Empire Day" was modelled more on Trenholme's educational program in Ontario than on the public holiday for all that the Canadian Parliament created. Even then, hostility to the imperialist message of the celebration persisted through the early decades of the twentieth century.[56] One might add a geographical consideration here: for the Antipodes, 24 May is not the prelude to summer that it is in Canada. So, for a variety of reasons, Canada and Australia diverged in their manners of paying tribute to Queen Victoria.

Another factor unique to Canada was the proximity to the United States. As Norman Penlington, Carl Berger, and others have pointed out in their studies of the political atmosphere in this period, Canadian views of imperialism and imperial unity were inescapably coloured by the dominion's relationship with the neighbouring republic. For some, old ideas about the Loyalist rejection of the American experiment still carried water. For others, British military and diplomatic might were the chief guarantors of Canadian autonomy.[57] The indignant responses from across the country in 1901 to a proposal from Boston to erect a memorial to General Richard Montgomery on the spot where he died leading the American assault on Quebec in 1775 showed that the old wounds had not completely healed.[58]

Supporters of Victoria Day played up its value as a symbol of these beliefs. Charles Boulton contrasted the values of Independence Day in the United States, "ushered into that great country in the midst of war, bloodshed and revolution," with the peaceful message of Victoria Day, which "announces to the world ... that we respect our sovereign and desire to perpetuate the system of government under which we live."[59] It is telling that Boulton chose the Queen's Birthday, rather than Dominion Day, as the primary holiday for expressing Canadian identity at that time. (Although, as noted in the chapters by Forrest Pass, Mike Benbough-Jackson, and Matthew Hayday in this volume, comparisons between the values and identity expressed by Dominion Day and those of the U.S. holiday also have a long history.)

The birthday of George Washington, officially marked in the United States since 1870, was also cited as a precedent. W.N. Hossie of Brantford, Ontario, told Laurier in 1901 he would be "grieved to have given up the 24th of May, while Washington and Lincoln's Birthdays are still observed and honoured."[60] The comparison with Washington was in many ways an apt one. Washington was supposed to embody the ideals of the American republic, as a soldier, statesman, and gentleman. Canadians had projected many of their political, moral, and social values onto the queen, as the jubilees and the period surrounding her death had so clearly demonstrated.

Given the intensity of pro-British sentiment in English Canada, which had been elevated by the war in South Africa, Laurier had to address the issue directly. Thus, on 29 April 1901 – less than a month before the holiday would be marked – the prime minister told the Commons that "it is the general, if not the unanimous, desire of the people of Canada that the 24th of May, which has been celebrated as a national holiday, should continue to be so celebrated," and he was therefore moving to have the bill placed on the list of Government Orders.[61] During the debate on 2 May, there were some last-minute disagreements about the official name for the day – some members proposed to leave it as "the Queen's Birthday" or to call it "Queen Victoria Day," but Laurier insisted that "Victoria Day is quite enough."[62] The bill then passed third reading in the House of Commons.

The Senate, which had seen considerable debate on the issue in 1897, opted in May 1901 not to deliberate on a bill that was clearly favoured by public opinion and the Commons. In fact, the normal rules of procedure were suspended, and the bill was passed through its second and third readings simultaneously. Only a handful of senators spoke during the debate, most of whom had participated in the 1897 exchange. David Mills reiterated the popularity of the queen and the day in her memory. William Macdonald complained that the bill would have passed the first time but for "some pressure" from unspecified quarters; he was nonetheless pleased to see it implemented. One senator hoped that the Red Chamber would be unanimous in its support, but Samuel Prowse repeated his objections to forcing workers to forgo a day's wages and businesses to close up shop, which elicited agreement from Pascal Poirier.[63] But, as in 1897, these arguments fell largely on deaf ears, and the bill passed without division.

Despite the Senate's uncharacteristic haste, the bill was still not in force. In order to take effect, it had to receive the governor general's signature, which would occur at the end of the session. As late as 14 May, the date that Parliament would be prorogued was still not known to the public, and the *Globe* fretted that, if the session lasted past the 24th, there would be no official holiday. Still, the paper presumed that the public would celebrate it anyhow.[64] As it happened, the legislature sat until 23 May, so the act received royal assent one day before the event. In Minto's brief speech to Parliament at the end of the session, the first piece of legislation he mentioned was the holiday act, which he called "a worthy tribute" to the late queen.[65] What had begun as a private member's bill facing tacit hostility and outward indifference from the government majority was now being hailed as a showpiece of the session. How much credit the Liberal government could really take for this was debatable; the *Montreal Gazette* declared in a headline that "Laurier bow[ed] to the public will."[66]

Even if the federal legislation had failed again in 1901, some in Ontario were not prepared to abandon the holiday lightly. A Liberal appointee in Lindsay warned the prime minister that his neighbours were planning to take the day off, regardless of the law. He begged the prime minister to spare a thought for the poor civil servants who would have to stay in their offices while everyone else celebrated, and he also hinted that at least one local Conservative was prepared to switch parties if the holiday was preserved. [67]

For her part, Clementina Fessenden Trenholme was determined that Empire Day should not be affected by the retention or cessation of the celebration of Victoria's birthday. In a letter to the *Globe*, she proposed if the 24th of May became a perpetual holiday, then Empire Day, "this child of the empire," should continue to serve its original, auxiliary purpose. If not, then Empire Day should be renamed "Victoria Empire Day" and incorporate elements of both celebrations.[68] As the school-related activities of Empire Day were arranged at the local and provincial rather than the federal level, the Liberal government in Ottawa would not be able to erase all traces of the tradition even if it wanted to.

The Ontario government was more than happy to take up the cause of Victoria Day. By 1901, the premier was none other than George Ross, the former minister of education who had championed Trenholme's original proposal for Empire Day. The province ensured that the Queen's Birthday would continue regardless of Ottawa's decision. On 22 May 1901, the lieutenant governor proclaimed the day a holiday for all provincial public offices. In part, this was a matter of constitutional necessity, as the federal government's legislation applied only to its own offices and services. But there was also some uncertainty about whether the federal bill would in fact receive the vice-regal signature in time for the holiday to be observed.[69] Loyal Ontario would not leave this to chance.

During the debates over the perpetuation of Queen Victoria's birthday in 1897 and 1901, Laurier found himself in the all-too-familiar position of having to conciliate disparate interests: English and French, nationalist and imperialist, laissez-faire and interventionist. Having seen how celebrations of imperial symbols and events could fuel demands for concrete action and, in at least one instance, could lead to violence between English and French Canadians, he was probably loath to encourage an event fraught with political baggage.

Laurier's attempt to blunt the imperialist edge of the holiday, by ensuring that it would be known as "Victoria Day" rather than "the Queen's Birthday," "Queen Victoria Day," "Victorian Empire Day," or any of the other proposed variations, may have contributed to its long-term survival and gradual transformation into the politically toothless occasion it is today, at least outside of Quebec. The formal title of the day had no explicit associations with royalism or imperialism, although clearly these were implicit and well understood at the time. The *Montreal Star* called it "a day inseparably identified with the growth of the vast aggregation of kingdoms known as the British Empire."[70] The *Manitoba Free Press* declared that "every Canadian boy, as he cheers for the flag and for the King today, gives an earnest [sic] of the continued solidarity of Canadian loyalty to imperial unity in the time to come." In Calgary, 24 May 1901 included a ceremony honouring veterans returning from South Africa.[71]

But Victoria Day did not *need* to be anything more than a day to remember the life of a particular individual who was widely respected for her personal values and political restraint. This was something that even anti-imperialists and republicans conceded. Newspapers such as *La Presse* and Goldwin Smith's *Weekly Sun*, which had strongly opposed Canada's participation in the South African War, could at least agree that the queen was an admirable figure in her own right.[72] John B. Silcox, a Congregational minister in Winnipeg who had previously lived in the United States, declared his preference for a republican government, yet admitted that "the thought of this great and good woman who ruled the British empire restrained me" from becoming an American citizen.[73] Canadian Irish Catholics, traditionally not inclined towards royalism or imperialism, had by 1901 generally embraced Queen Victoria as a symbol of their political liberty (in Canada, if not in Ireland itself) and of idealized womanhood and motherhood.[74] Likewise, *La Patrie* supported the holiday, but because it was a tribute to a fine woman and because it was during her reign that French Canadians gained true political freedom.[75]

It should be remembered, however, that these were not the voices calling for the perpetual holiday; they merely acquiesced in its passage because they could interpret it as something other than an imperial festival. Even that acquiescence did not last forever, as later chapters in this volume will make clear. As Joel Belliveau and Marcel Martel explain in their chapter on Empire Day, by the end of the First World War there was a strong reaction in francophone Quebec against British imperialism and its cultural offshoots in English Canada, so in that province the celebration of the French Catholic "martyr" Adam Dollard des Ormeaux was timed to coincide with, and thereby supersede, Victoria Day and Empire Day. In 2003, Quebec's provincial government made its symbolic opposition to Queen Victoria even more blatant by declaring 24 May a day to honour the "Patriotes" who rebelled against British rule in Lower Canada in 1837, the year that Victoria became queen.

That said, for many Canadians in 1901, apolitical merrymaking was just as significant a part of the day as it had always been. Newspapers, such as the *Manitoba Free Press* and the *Montreal Star*, that stressed the utility of Victoria Day to reinforce imperial unity nevertheless ran numerous stories and advertisements suggesting pleasant diversions such as picnics and sporting events.[76] Rail and steamship lines across much of the country promoted holiday trips to the Pan-American Exposition in Buffalo, New York.[77] And old habits, such as drinking and setting off fireworks, died hard. The *Mail and Empire* noted in its holiday news that one young man in Toronto blew his hand off with a firecracker and another man was arrested for smashing windows after a night of carousing.[78]

The ability of the holiday to carry such different meanings for those who observe it – something that was evident even in the period discussed here – has no doubt contributed to its longevity in Canada. Elsewhere in the British world, the school-centred Empire Day on 24 May became Commonwealth Day in 1958 and faded into near irrelevance.[79] Newly independent states in Africa, Asia, and the Caribbean had no use for a holiday and a message that dated from the era of Rudyard Kipling and Joseph Chamberlain. Although it still exists, Commonwealth Day has moved to mid-March, and it is not a statutory holiday in Britain, Canada, or elsewhere. As Britain, Australia, and New Zealand observe the present queen's official birthday in June, the annual commemoration of Victoria in those countries has effectively ended.

In Canada, too, Empire Day is gone; the event's decline in its birthplace, Hamilton, Ontario, is traced in Brittney Bos and Allison Ward's chapter in this volume. But Empire Day had always been the opening act before the main event. The link between Victoria Day and the imperialist sentiment in English Canada that pressed Laurier to make it a perpetual holiday is now largely forgotten. In 1952, the Liberal government of Prime Minister Louis St Laurent further loosened the association between the queen and the holiday by making the date variable; it would thereafter fall on the last Monday before 25 May each year, thus ensuring that most Canadians would have an annual long weekend to look forward to as the weather grew milder.[80] If the historically inclined attempted to explain the holiday's continuation, they usually thought exclusively about the queen's place in Canadian history. The *Globe and Mail*'s editorial for Victoria Day in 1952 called it "a custom peculiar to Canada. It is a symbol of a deep and loyal Canadian response to a very remarkable human being ... who will be permanently and irrevocably associated with the founding of this nation."[81] Four decades later, John Aimers of the Monarchist League echoed this belief in his explanation for the persistence of the holiday: "Victoria was on the throne at the time of Confederation and conferred the title of Dominion on us... So she remains significant to Canada."[82] William Macdonald, Edward Horsey, and others who promoted Victoria Day did acknowledge this point, but it was only a small part of their overall case in favour of the holiday. They spoke from the conviction that Canada was a British country (albeit a largely self-governing one) with British values. Ironically, a holiday that was intended to show Canadian solidarity with the British throne and empire is now an eccentric anachronism that differentiates Canada from Britain and every other member of the Commonwealth.

NOTES

1 Editorial, "A Canadian Tradition," *Globe and Mail*, 24 May 1952; Editorial, "Canada's Monarchy," *Globe and Mail*, 23 May 1994; "Victoria Day," Department of Canadian Heritage, accessed 22 December 2014, http:// canada.pch.gc.ca/eng/1455132650913.

2 In 1843, one Canadian farmer still described the fourth of June as "a holiday, which I have always kept in commemoration of the birth of good King George III, of blessed memory." It was also the day designated for the annual militia muster in most provinces into the 1850s. See Catharine Parr Traill, *The Canadian Settlers' Guide* (London: Edward Stanford, 1860), 184.

3 Desmond Morton and Morton Weinfeld, *Who Speaks for Canada? Words That Shape a Country* (Toronto: McClelland and Stewart, 1998), 46; Robert Craig Brown and Ramsay Cook, *Canada, 1896–1921: A Nation Transformed* (Toronto: McClelland and Stewart, 1974), 32.

4 *Perth Courier*, July 2, 1897.

5 Canada, *Senate Debates*, 30 April 1897, 239.

6 W.J. Macdonald to Laurier, 17 April 1897, Library and Archives Canada (hereafter LAC), MG26-G, Sir Wilfrid Laurier fonds, vol. 43, file 13992.

7 Canada, *Senate Debates*, 30 April 1897, 241.

8 Canada, *House of Commons Debates*, 8 June 1897, 3583 and 17 June 1897, 4373.

9 Ibid., 8 June 1897, 3583; 17 June 1897, 4373; 18 June 1897, 4499–500.

10 Canada, *Senate Debates*, 30 April 1897, 252, 254.

11 Ibid., 242, 247, 250.

12 Ibid., 242, 254, 259.

13 *Montreal Star*, 4 May 1897.

14 *La Presse* (Montreal), 3 May 1897 ("pour des motifs purement sentimentaux").

15 Ibid., 4 May 1897 ("ridicule fantaisie loyaliste").

16 Norman Penlington, *Canada and Imperialism, 1896–1899* (Toronto: University of Toronto Press, 1965), 54–57.

17 *Manitoba Free Press*, 25 May 1897. The jubilee also proved to be a significant distraction in Lanark, Ontario, where the Queen's Birthday was "scarcely observed" that year. The same week, a town meeting voted to organize a "grand picnic" for 22 June. *Perth Courier*, 21 and 28 May 1897.

18 *Montreal Star*, 25 May 1897.

19 Robert Stamp, "Empire Day in the Schools of Ontario," *Journal of Canadian Studies* 8, no. 3 (August 1973): 34.

20 Carman Miller, *Painting the Map Red: Canada and the South African War, 1899–1902* (Ottawa: Canadian War Museum, 1993), 7.

21 Circular letter from Margaret Polson Murray, LAC, MG28 I17, Imperial Order Daughters of the Empire (hereafter IODE) fonds, vol. 15, file 2, 8.

22 For more on the war in South Africa and the variety of responses it prompted in Canada, see Miller, *Painting the Map Red*.

23 Ibid., 443–4.

24 Laurier to Willison, 5 May 1900, LAC, MG30-D29, Sir John Willison Fonds, volume 24, folder 179c, 17947.
25 Laurier to Willison, 12 November 1900, ibid., 17950.
26 Réal Bélanger, *Wilfrid Laurier: Quand la passion devient la politique* (Quebec: Presses de l'Université Laval, 1986), 248.
27 *Manitoba Free Press*, 23 January 1901.
28 *Toronto World*, 23 January 1901.
29 *L'Avenir* (Montreal), 27 January 1901 ("Nous reservons nos larmes pour d'autres douleurs ... et nous pleurerons plutôt la mort du peuple boer dont les mercenaires de la reine Victoria ont entrepris de couper l'existence jusque dans ses racines.").
30 *La Patrie* (Montreal), 22 January 1901, late edition ("Pourquoi faut-il que la guerre, la guerre démente, ait empoisonné ses derniers ans, ait abrégé sa vie?").
31 Jonathan Vance, *Death So Noble: Memory, Meaning, and the First World War* (Vancouver: UBC Press, 1997), 210.
32 *Toronto Globe*, 24 May 1901.
33 *Charlottetown Islander*, 31 August 1860.
34 *Halifax Chronicle*, 8 February 1901.
35 *Toronto World*, 25 May 1901.
36 *Mail and Empire*, 23 and 31 January and 4 May 1901.
37 LAC, RG2, Privy Council Office fonds, Series A-1-d, 1901–0524 and 1901–0672.
38 Canada, *House of Commons Debates*, 25 February 1901, 333.
39 Ibid., 18 April 1901, 3271.
40 Brown and Cook, *Canada, 1896–1921*, 8.
41 See, for example, Macdonald's remarks to the Senate, *Debates*, 8 May 1901, 324, and Minto's letter to George Parkin, 26 September 1904, in *Lord Minto's Canadian Papers: A Selection of the Public and Private Papers of the Fourth Earl of Minto, 1898–1904*, vol. 2, ed. Paul Stevens and John T. Saywell (Toronto: Champlain Society, 1983), 540.
42 Jim English, "Empire Day in Britain, 1904–1958," *Historical Journal* 49, no. 1 (2006): 259.
43 *La Patrie* (Montreal), 24 May 1901.
44 Quebec Board of Trade to Laurier, 14 April 1901, LAC, Laurier fonds, vol. 194, 55579–80,
45 George Burn to E.L. Newcombe (deputy minister of justice), 14 March 1901, LAC, Department of Justice fonds, RG13, vol. 118, file 1901–279.
46 Reginald Kennedy to Laurier, 26 April 1901, LAC, Laurier fonds, vol. 195, 55727.
47 *Toronto Globe*, 22 May 1901.

48 Canada, *House of Commons Debates*, 18 April 1901, 271.
49 Laurier to Elizabeth O'Brien, 2 February 1901, LAC, Laurier fonds, vol. 186, 53130.
50 Laurier to Premier of Cape Colony, 30 March 1901, LAC, Laurier fonds, vol. 753, part 1, 215373.
51 Maurice French, "The Ambiguity of Empire Day in New South Wales, 1901–21: Imperial Consensus or National Division," *Australian Journal of Politics and History* 24, no. 1 (1978): 62; English, "Empire Day in Britain," 248. Lord Meath and his Empire Day campaign are discussed further in chapter 4.
52 Canada, *House of Commons Debates*, 13 March 1901, 1434.
53 Sara Jeannette Duncan, *The Imperialist* (Toronto: McClelland and Stewart, 1990), 9.
54 *British Empire Review* 2, no. 9 (March 1901): 173; ibid., 3, no, 2 (August 1901): 21. Others in Britain raised the same objection: see, for example, the letter from Howard Ruff of the Royal Society of St George in the *Times* (London), 17 May 1904.
55 *Times* (London), 24 May 1900.
56 French, "The Ambiguity of Empire Day," 63–8.
57 Penlington, *Canada and Imperialism*, 213; Carl Berger, *The Sense of Power: Studies in the Ideas of Canadian Imperialism, 1867–1914* (Toronto: University of Toronto Press, 1970), 174–6; Brown and Cook, *Canada, 1896–1921*, 28–9.
58 *Montreal Star*, 25 May 1901; Minutes of Ontario Auxiliary, 10 April 1901, LAC, IODE fonds, vol. 15, file 3, 47; Canada, *House of Commons Debates*, 15 May 1901, 5211.
59 Canada, *Senate Debates*, 3 May 1897, 259–60.
60 W.N. Hossie to Laurier, 4 May 1901, LAC, Laurier fonds, vol. 196, 56000–1.
61 Canada, *House of Commons Debates*, 29 April 1901, 3983.
62 Ibid., 2 May 1901, 4255.
63 Canada, *Senate Debates*, 8 May 1901, 341–3.
64 *Toronto Globe*, 14 May 1901.
65 Canada, *House of Commons Debates*, 23 May 1901, 5976.
66 *Montreal Star*, 30 April 1901.
67 C.D. Barr to Laurier, 17 May 1901, LAC, Laurier fonds, vol. 197, 56309.
68 *Globe*, 2 March 1901.
69 Ibid., 23 May 1901.
70 *Montreal Star*, 23 May 1901.
71 *Manitoba Free Press*, 24 and 25 May 1901.
72 *La Presse* (Montreal), 22 January 1901; *Weekly Sun* editorial reprinted in *Toronto World*, 24 January 1901.

73 *Manitoba Free Press*, 29 January 1901.

74 Mark McGowan, *The Waning of the Green: Catholics, the Irish, and Identity in Toronto, 1887–1922* (Montreal: McGill-Queen's University Press, 1999), 202–9.

75 *La Patrie* (Montreal), 24 May 1901.

76 *Manitoba Free Press*, 24 May 1901; *Montreal Star*, 22 May 1901.

77 *Manitoba Free Press*, 4 May 1901.

78 *Toronto Globe*, 17 August 1901.

79 English, "Empire Day in Britain," 274; K.S. Inglis, "Australia Day," *Historical Studies* 13, no. 49 (1967): 20.

80 José E. Igartua, *The Other Quiet Revolution: National Identities in English Canada, 1945–71* (Vancouver: UBC Press, 2006), 107–9.

81 Editorial, *Toronto Globe and Mail*, 24 May 1952.

82 "Victoria's Holiday," *Toronto Star*, 19 May 1997.

4 Promoting a "Sound Patriotic Feeling" in Canada through Empire Day, 1899–1957

MARCEL MARTEL, ALLISON MARIE WARD,
JOEL BELLIVEAU, AND BRITTNEY ANNE BOS

In 1929, the national president of the Imperial Order Daughters of the Empire, J.A. Stewart, trumpeted the success of Empire Day. In her celebratory message to teachers of Ontario, she alluded to the fact that Empire Day had been celebrated the day before Victoria Day every year since its inception in 1899 and had spread everywhere in the country and the empire. She stated:

> So, we Canadians are proud to be also British subjects, serving a British king, under British modes of government, which are the freest in the world. And in common with Australia, New Zealand, South Africa, Newfoundland, India, and all the other far flung lands that own the British flag, we have been doing our part in the building of the British Empire, of which we are the oldest and largest Dominion.[1]

The challenges that remained, according to Stewart, were to improve the celebration's format, to diversify its activities, and to convince as many pupils as possible to take part in it. Ontario's Department of Education, which organized this celebration in the province, was also of the opinion that the project had succeeded in promoting a "sound patriotic feeling."[2] Empire Day had been a means to put forward and promote a strong national identity for Canadians. This identity, however, was rooted in a particular relationship to the empire. Its narrative was simple: Canada was the largest, oldest, and most important of the dominions of the world's greatest empire. The idea of racial and cultural diversity was present in the identity that was put forward, but it was most often used to characterize the empire as a whole, rather than Canada. On this front, Canadian nationalists mostly used Empire Day as a space to promote the Anglo-Saxon "race" and its triumphs.

In his article on Dominion Day, Matthew Hayday observes that the state did not organize national festivities before 1 July 1958, with the exception of the celebration of the sixtieth anniversary of Confederation in 1927.[3] However, this does not necessarily mean that Canada did not partake in state nationalism until this late period. Indeed, the state, notably the provinces, did organize other kinds of celebrations promoting Canadian identity and national belonging. Empire Day, a citizen's initiative that was used by the state to promote a national vision and create a common identitary reference for everyone, is a prime example. We would argue that Empire Day, coupled as it was with Victoria Day, represents a sort of proto-national holiday for Canada. This interpretation both "normalizes" Canada's experience and helps us make sense of it by situating the creation of Empire Day within an international trend.

National holidays are not as old a tradition as most believe. Although it has been a long-standing tradition, in many countries, to celebrate the sovereign's birthday or the anniversary of a cultural group's patron saint, proper "national holidays" first appeared in the late nineteenth century. To cite two prime examples, it was only in 1870 that the Fourth of July was proclaimed Independence Day by the U.S. Congress, and in 1880 that Bastille Day was named a national holiday in France.[4] At the turn of the twentieth century, Canada, in effect, blended these two types of celebrations, creating a hybrid that combined elements of modern national holidays and of more traditional monarchic celebrations. It achieved this by making its *founding* monarch's birthday into a permanent holiday (rather than choosing to continue celebrating the *current* monarch, as discussed in the previous chapter by Chris Tait) and by creating a civic sidekick to it: Empire Day.

By targeting students in elementary and high schools, the promoters of Empire Day hoped to plant seeds that would last forever, fostering national *and* imperial unity. Studying these early Canadian efforts at nation building is an effective means to better understand the evolution of political and cultural identities during the first half of the twentieth century. This chapter first explores the origins of Empire Day, then turns to its implementation in the country until 1957. Despite attempts to update Empire Day, and to keep it timely – with emphasis on the war effort during the world wars, on the monarchy at the time of Elizabeth II's coronation in 1952, and on the new discourse associated with the creation of the "Commonwealth" – the goal of creating a common Canadian identity based on imperial ties ultimately failed. Despite this failure, the study of Empire Day opens a unique window for the study of Canada's evolving sense of self during the first half of the twentieth century and of how references to Britain ceased to be a rallying point in the 1950s.

Empire Day: Origins and Context

Empire Day, falling on the last school day before 24 May, grew out of Victoria Day and the ways in which the queen's birthday was celebrated in colonial Upper Canada and the post-Confederation dominion. Victoria Day, in its early iterations, had been celebrated locally on 24 May since the queen's coronation, and her birthday had been declared an official holiday in 1845.[5] These celebrations were locally organized and were largely opportunities for communities to come together in fun and festivities. The tradition of celebrating the queen's birthday continued after her death and has persisted to the present day, though its monarchical significance has long been abandoned in favour of cottage trips and barbeques.

At the end of the nineteenth century, some Canadians were concerned that celebrations for the queen's birthday did not demonstrate the serious tone that a holiday recognizing the greatness of Queen Victoria deserved. It is in this context that the idea of setting a time during the year for Canadians, and in particular young students, to celebrate their identity and notably their belonging to the British Empire began to gain traction. Empire Day was first and foremost the result of a citizen's initiative, suggested by Clementina Fessenden Trenholme. A resident of the Niagara region, where she was an active contributor to local publications, Trenholme was concerned by the lack of enthusiasm for Canada's British connection and "viewed non-British immigration and lingering continentalist ideas as threats that had to be averted."[6] Her social activism led her to join the League of the Empire and to become secretary of the Wentworth Historical Society. She capitalized on Queen Victoria's Diamond Jubilee to promote the British link as a fundamental component of Canadian identity and nationhood.

Trenholme felt especially passionate about preserving and teaching Canada's imperial ties and heritage. She was fiercely patriotic and openly promoted the ideal of Canada as a cherished outpost of the British Empire, tied together by a common ancestry and values. Following her husband's death in 1896, she moved to Hamilton and launched a zealous and ultimately successful campaign for Empire

4.1 Clementina Fessenden Trenholme's Gravestone. Photograph by
Allison Ward.

Day. She believed that the time had come to organize activities targeting young people, as the goal was to promote nationalism over the long
term. "Impressed by the inspirational effect of a patriotic oration on her
small grand-daughter" when bestowed with a maple leaf badge at her
husband's funeral,[7] Trenholme became highly motivated and engaged
in her endeavour. She called for "the endorsation of a movement looking towards the formation of a national patriotic scheme of education,"
focused especially on "a day of special exercises," intended to "inculcate patriotic sentiment" in students at all levels.[8] Hamilton was also
the site of the founding of the Canadian Club and the Women's Canadian Club in the last decade of the nineteenth century, and the city was
deeply enmeshed in patriotic organizations by the turn of the century.[9]
Its citizenship initiatives had many supporters from old, established

Loyalist families but also included the youngest and most recent immigrants in the city's schools.

Believing that her initiative was appropriate and timely, Trenholme wrote to various magazines to publicize her idea. However, she was more successful at convincing school boards to invest resources in the celebration of national belonging and the promotion of civic education.[10] In her writing campaign, she also targeted provincial and federal politicians. She wrote to Prime Minister Wilfrid Laurier, asking him to decree a day dedicated to the celebration of the British Empire in schools. Laurier rejected the idea, pointing out that education was a provincial jurisdiction.[11] She then discovered a strong ally: Ontario's minister of education and future premier, George W. Ross. In an 1897 letter to Ross, she described her plan to mobilize schools, as these institutions provided a fertile ground for instilling a passion for Canada and the empire in young people. Ross liked the proposal: he himself had been searching for a means of promoting nationalism and civic education. A proposal of his to develop a Canadian history textbook and dedicate more time to teaching Canadian history in schools had met with criticism from people who believed that an understanding Canadian history had to be underpinned by the study of British history as well. Although he also contemplated the possibility of celebrating the flag, the idea was a non-starter, particularly as there was not yet an official Canadian flag.[12] Moreover, Americans had a similar flag celebration and, in the nationalist context of the late nineteenth century, Canada had to assert itself and differentiate itself from the United States. Thus, Ross chose Empire Day as a way to reassure those people who were already critical of him. The celebration would distance Canada from the United States while highlighting one of the hallmarks of Canada: its membership in the British Empire. Through Empire Day, young Canadians would not only better appreciate the dominion, they would also develop an international awareness arising from their membership in the worldwide community that constituted the empire. Empire Day would expand horizons, create a dialogue with other parts of the world that were under the British flag, and convey a sense that Canada had relationships beyond its borders and a unique role within the empire.

This way of characterizing membership in the empire recalls Carl Berger's thesis according to which British imperialistic fervour constituted, ironically, Canada's first type of national identity.[13] The creation of Empire Day, of course, was not a random occurrence. Rather, it was the product of a particular context: the "nationalization" of British

Canadian identity or, in other words, the advent of contemporary nationalism in the dominion. And with this nationalism came a new definition of Canada.

By the turn of the century, the Canada imagined at the time of Confederation was disappearing. That Canada had been a pragmatic project, based on economic goals common to the various regions of the country. As J.R. Miller has observed, "the unity that Confederation was to produce was union at the political level, not cultural."[14] Confederation had been imagined – much like the British Empire, it should be said – as an entity in which different "nationalities" could co-exist and cooperate, united by the Crown. It was a community of communities. However, this vision of Canada was strongly challenged in the 1880s. In the context of European imperialism, there arose a vision of Canada that would be and should be British not only politically, but also culturally. This vision was due to "the influence in Canada of radically new theories of national unity that focused upon language and culture, rather than economic cooperation, as essential criteria for unification... In English Canada, many people had ... by the 1890's rejected the pursuit of unity in diversity."[15]

This new definition of Canada – or rather, of what Canada should be – was spawned in part by the economic and political troubles of the 1870s and 1880s. As Carl Berger has convincingly shown, Canada found itself in an identity crisis of sorts at this juncture: "The cumulative impact of the long depression [of the 1870s], the failure of Macdonald's National Policy to generate prosperity and economic integration, and the cultural crisis that followed the execution of Louis Riel, produced a widespread feeling of pessimism about Canada's future."[16]

As in any time of crisis, many different paths forward were suggested. One such program was continentalism, advocating some kind of union with the United States. This was crystallized in Goldwin Smith's 1891 manifesto *Canada and the Canadian Question*. Despite the troubles of the times, however, this annexationist option was not embraced by masses of English-speaking Canadians; rather they migrated towards a reaffirmation of the British connection. Many who opposed Smith's vision "believed that Canada could grow and survive only if it held fast to the imperial connection."[17]

This emergent imperialist movement, at first defensive, became "more impatient, assertive and bellicose" during the 1890s.[18] Unlike continentalism, it inspired a flurry of activity in civil society and in the media; the period saw the creation of multiple organizations, some radical, some moderate and respectable, but all affirming Canada's British nature and its allegiance to the empire. The most influential, and one of the most moderate, was undoubtedly the Imperial Federation League. Created in London, England, in 1884, it quickly opened chapters in Canada and claimed one in four Canadian parliamentarians as members by 1889. On the more radical end of the spectrum, the Equal Rights Association created by D'Alton McCarthy in 1889 and a review called the *Anglo Saxon*, created in 1887, were more strident in their imperialist promotion. As the Boer Wars began, the experience of imperialism became, for many English Canadians, "invested with all the enthusiasm of nationalism."[19]

Empire Day in Action: The Promoters at Work

It is in this unruly context, then, that Empire Day was created, with the explicit aim of promoting "civic spirit" and "sound patriotic feeling."[20] Ross took the initiative. First, he wanted Empire Day to be celebrated across the country. In this, he obtained the support of the Dominion Education Association, which endorsed his proposal at its meeting in Halifax in August 1898. At that meeting, Ross proposed "the selection of some day during the School year to be devoted to exercises of a patriotic character, and ... recommended the 23rd of May to be set apart for that purpose, naming it 'Empire Day.'"[21] Needing those who shared his views on Canadian identity to rally around the proposal and engage schools in its implementation, he found an enthusiastic ally in Clementina Trenholme. She pressed school boards to join this initiative, though she became saddened by the lack of official recognition for her critical role in the development and promotion of the day.[22] She campaigned hard to receive proper acknowledgment of her leadership role, publishing *The Genesis of Empire Day* in 1910.[23] Her son tried again, several years later, hoping to resurrect her importance in public memory.[24]

The first Empire Day was celebrated on 22 May 1898 in Dundas, an Ontario town just west of Hamilton, the city where Trenholme had first pitched the idea.[25] Empire Day rapidly grew in popularity, at least according to documents prepared annually for schools by the Ontario Ministry of Education. Within a year, Ontario, Quebec, and Nova Scotia each organized a day dedicated to the empire to be observed in schools. In Quebec, the province's Protestant Committee of Public Instruction was in charge of its promotion. This nationalist fervour attracted other departments of education, and by 1900 all Canadian provinces had organized Empire Day events and activities.[26]

Flushed with their pan-Canadian success, the Ontario officials who prepared the annual Empire Day booklet of activities looked to turn this celebration into an event celebrated throughout the empire. In this task, Canadian promoters counted on the dedication and enthusiasm of Reginald Brabazon, the twelfth Earl of Meath, who was to play a crucial role in the dissemination of this idea. After a career as a diplomat, he pursued a new venture by espousing philanthropic activities, targeting youth in particular. Disturbed by the South African War, Brabazon looked at ways to develop "a sense of collective identity and imperial responsibility among young empire citizens."[27] He thought that the Canadian initiative was worth celebrating throughout the empire. Thus, at the 1902 Imperial Conference, he promoted the idea of an "Imperial Empire Day."[28] Britain, Australia, and New Zealand were the first to implement this idea, followed by India and South Africa. King Edward helped the promoters of Empire Day in 1903 by decreeing that a day celebrating the empire had to be chosen.[29] Proponents of Empire Day, at least those in Ontario, saw this success as a validation for their goal of creating an imagined community. Young people, whether in Sudbury, Cornwall, or Toronto, took part in activities similar to those taking place not only in other parts of the country but also in other British colonies. The boundaries of this imagined community were thus international, despite the initial intent of the project to foster a national identity.

Ontario's Empire Day promoters suggested that the event should be used to "make Canadian patriotism intelligent, comprehensive and strong."[30] To achieve this objective, the Department of Education prepared an annual booklet, first for school inspectors and later for teachers, that detailed how the day should be organized and what would be appropriate activities. In the first such document distributed by the Department of Education in March 1899, its author provided a broad goal: attention should be paid to "the study of the history of Canada in its relation to the British Empire and to such other exercises as might tend to increase the interest of the pupils in the history of their own country and strengthen their attachment to the Empire to which they belong."[31]

At first, the annual "booklet" was but a single page. Although its size increased from 1899 to 1956, the two types of suggested activities did not change substantially. First, teachers would prepare lectures on the British Empire, the "relationship of Canada to the Empire," the "unity of Empire and its advantage," and the privileges that Canadians – as British subjects until 1947 – had as a result of their membership in the empire. During the second part of the day, students would recite poems, read excerpts from relevant readings, and sing "appropriate" songs, such as "Rule Britannia," "Land of Hope and Glory," or "The Maple Leaf Forever." For the afternoon performance, the audience would optimally include school councillors, church representatives, and other prominent members of the community. Schools were also actively encouraged to fly the British flag or the Canadian Ensign. In the second decade of the century, the Ontario Department of Education would provide a Union Jack to those schools in the province that did not have one. Similar sets of activities – history lessons and songs – were organized in both Australia and Britain.[32]

Of course, ultimately, the success of Empire Day in Ontario and elsewhere in the country relied upon the enthusiasm and dedication of teachers. While the province could designate a day for patriotic celebration and education, its execution relied upon the work of teachers. If persuasion was not enough, the annual document prepared by the Department of Education reminded teachers of their obligations with respect to the day: "Empire Day, the last school day before the 24th of May, shall be duly celebrated in every school; the forenoon being devoted to a study of the greatness of the British Empire, and the afternoon to public addresses, recitations, music, etc., of a Patriotic Character (Regulations 8, 2)."[33]

The Consolidation and Evolution of a Celebration

Because Empire Day had civic goals, promoters incorporated world events to make it – and later try to keep it – relevant. In 1902, they included references to the coronation of Edward VII, as it was an appropriate occasion for increasing the "love for British institutions."[34] However, the emphasis remained on the importance of British heritage and lineage to the future of Ontario pupils. "A national holiday," Ontario curriculum documents advised, in 1910,

> should be used by the teacher for impressing upon the minds of his pupils such facts and circumstances as would foster a national spirit... The relations of Canada with the Empire, politically and historically, should be considered. Though far removed from the capital, and although in many respects differing in our habits, laws, and modes of thought from our kinsmen in the British Isles, yet we are of the same race, and equally interested in the prosperity and honour of the Empire.[35]

References to kinship and a shared racial heritage were deliberately chosen as reflections on the nature of Canadian settlement up to that point. In this early decade, such references were easily sold to parents, most of whom shared this British heritage and often its attached values. Suggested lessons emphasized this grand heritage and suggested reflection on questions such as the following: "Is it True That 'The Sun Never Sets on the British Empire'?"; "What are Some of the Great Empire Years in History in the Last Century?"; "Is Britain Still 'Mistress of the Seas?"; and "What is 'the Mother of Parliaments'?"[36] In schools these lessons were to be presented over a full day of programming that included psalms, secular readings, skits, drills, flag displays, and similarly solemn reflections on the empire and students' knowledge of its values and their responsibilities in relation to it.

When the First World War broke out, Empire Day instruction took on a decidedly militarized tone. Curriculum programming focused heavily on great generals, great battles, and brave Canadian soldiers fighting for the motherland. "As Canada's part in the Great War has now become a momentous and brilliant chapter in the History of Empire," it merited students' attention.[37] In 1918, the instruction built up the nation-building myths of Canada's First World War experience, calling it a moment of a "New National Consciousness," yet it attributed the country's successes largely to supposedly unique British traits like bravery, ingenuity, and perseverance.[38] It also firmly restated the idea that Canadians were all British and tied to the motherland, especially in these times of conflict.

During the fiftieth and sixtieth anniversaries of Confederation, in 1917 and 1927, booklets for Empire Day contained a historical account of the first years of Confederation. The historical narrative focused on the harmonious and progressive development of Canada. Although, in 1917, the Great War may have created a context in which promoters felt they needed to emphasize unity over tension, the continuation of this narrative in 1927 suggests that the festive nature of the Confederation celebrations might themselves have served as inspiration.

When Britain reorganized its relations with the dominions, the 1928 Empire Day booklet declared that these changes should not be feared. On the contrary, this reorganization was part of the empire's historical evolution and proof of its ability to adapt to new political realities. The booklet stated, "The proud and entrancing story of our Empire's progress and resources should be heard in every family circle, studied in every school and repeated on the platform, in the pulpit, and in the press."[39] In the 1950s, booklets featured the coronation of a new monarch, Elizabeth II, her family, and her dedication to the empire.

Empire Day and "Internal Others": French-Speaking People, Ethnic Communities, and Aboriginal Peoples

Although these early celebrations fulfilled Clementina Trenholme's aspirations for a day of reflection and education, great challenges to Empire Day's success would arise in subsequent decades. As immigration from countries that did not share this British heritage increased, boards of education and devotees of the empire were confronted with the challenge of transforming an explicitly British observation into an educational opportunity for the improvement of all.

In the latter part of the 1920s, changes began to creep slowly into the day's curriculum and promotional material. The 1928 curriculum documents encouraged teachers to observe Empire Day as a celebration of both Canada and the empire.[40] Although promotional material from the 1920s through to the 1950s still alluded to British heritage and stock, it made explicit references to French Canadians and immigrants and spoke more of good behaviour than a single preferred heritage.[41] This message of inclusion suggested that immigrants and members of cultural minority groups could overcome their former ethnic identities and, through working together, could become good citizens of the British Empire. As the cover of the 1931 Empire Day program (see figure 4.2) so vividly suggested, striving to be a good citizen of the British Empire had become a global rather than national pursuit. Somewhat more inclusive lessons and stories, accompanied by instructive examples, became common features in Empire Day teaching aids.

Still, all in all, there are very few references in Empire Day promotional literature to Canada's "internal others" – whether they be Aboriginal, French-Canadian, or immigrant communities.[42] Because the nationalist vision attached to Empire Day was not the most inclusive, the study of the celebration's reception among the various segments of the Canadian population constitutes a promising avenue for inquiry. Similar studies have been published on Empire Day's reception in Australia and Britain. In Australia, many groups, including Catholics, labour activists, and the labour movement in general, did not show strong enthusiasm for the day's observance. Labour publications would use "satire and ridicule" as means to deride Empire Day, referring to it as "Vampire Day," "Day of Dupes," or "All Fools Day."[43] In Britain,

4.2 The cover of *Empire Day in the Schools of Ontario, May 22 1931* (Toronto: Ontario Department of Education, 1931).

appreciation of Empire Day seems to have been more nuanced, including within the labour movement. Using working-class biographies, Jim English argues that Empire Day crossed class lines and "establish[ed] an imperial consciousness in the minds of working-class children," at least before the First World War.[44] The authors of some of these biographies wrote that what they remembered were the songs that young people sang because of their "emotive effect on the participants."[45] English establishes that, after the First World War, Empire Day in Britain became more politicized, and Conservatives would frequently attack groups who were critical of it.

The Fate of Empire Day in Canada

What of Empire Day in Canada? Did the appreciation for this celebration vary through the years, as in Britain? Did specific groups reject it outright, such as labour in Australia? French Canadians, perhaps? And what of immigrant communities – did they respond positively to the changes in rhetoric described above? Very little is known about these questions.[46] The following two chapters begin to explore such issues. The first, by Joel Belliveau and Marcel Martel, deals with French Canadians' evolving attitudes towards Empire Day. It argues that francophones' attitudes towards the celebration are much more nuanced than one might have expected in the years prior to 1917, and shows how the subsequent emergence and promotion of the Fête de Dollard des Ormeaux constituted a powerful means to neutralize Empire Day's influence. The second, by Brittney Bos and Allison Ward, examines what activities the government prescribed for commemorating Empire Day and how it was observed in practice in Ontario. Using a local case study of Hamilton, Ontario, which had a rich history of British cultural attachments but also incoming waves of non-British immigration, it demonstrates the ways in which the public and of education fought to keep the day relevant for the province's growing population.

NOTES

1 *Empire Day in the Schools of Ontario, May 23, 1929* (Toronto Ontario Department of Education, 1929).
2 *Empire Day, Circular to Inspectors* (Toronto: Ontario Department of Education, March 1899).

3 Matthew Hayday, "Fireworks, Folk-dancing, and Fostering a National Identity: The Politics of Canada Day," *Canadian Historical Review* 91, no. 2 (June 2010): 287–314.

4 André Larané, "Symboles nationaux: Les fêtes nationales dans le monde," *Hérodote.net*, 15 July 2014 http://www.herodote.net/Symboles_nationaux-synthese-1928.php.

5 For an early history of Victoria Day and how it was informally celebrated, see Nancy Bouchier, "The 24th of May Is the Queen's Birthday," *International Review of the History of Sport* 10 (August 1993): 164–85.

6 Molly Pulver Ungar, "Clementina Fessenden Trenholme," *Dictionary of Canadian Biography*, http://www.biographi.ca/en/bio/trenholme_clementina_14E.html.

7 Maurice French, "The Ambiguity of Empire Day in New South Wales, 1901–21: Imperial Consensus or National Division," *Australian Journal of Politics and History*, 24, no. 1 (April 1978): 62; Reginald Fessenden, *The Founding of Empire Day* (Hamilton, 1931).

8 Fessenden, *The Founding of Empire Day*.

9 "Hamilton Makes Plans for Centennial," *Eaton's Hamilton Bi-Weekly*, no. 240 (13 May 1946): 1–4, F 229–141, Eaton's Employee Magazine Fonds, Archives of Ontario.

10 Robert M. Stamp, "Empire Day in the Schools of Ontario: The Training of Young Imperialists," *Journal of Canadian Studies* 8, no. 3 (1973): 32–42.

11 Ungar, "Clementina Fessenden Trenholme."

12 See Peter Price's chapter in *Celebrating Canada*, vol. 2 (forthcoming) about the 1895 flag debate.

13 Carl Berger, *The Sense of Power: Studies in the Ideas of Canadian Imperialism, 1867–1914* (Toronto: University of Toronto Press, 1970); Robert M. Stamp, *The Schools of Ontario, 1876–1976* (Toronto: University of Toronto Press, 1982), 33–5; Stamp, "Empire Day."

14 J.R. Miller, "Unity/Diversity: The Canadian Experience, from Confederation to the First World War," *Dalhousie Review* 55, no. 1 (spring 1975): 65.

15 Ibid., 73–4.

16 Berger, *The Sense of Power*, 103.

17 Ibid., 104.

18 Ibid., 105.

19 Ibid., 105.

20 *Empire Day, Circular.*

21 "Empire Day," *Toronto Globe*, 12 August 1898.

22 In the booklets produced by the Ontario Department of Education, the creation of Empire Day was attributed to a "movement" from the Maritimes. *Empire Day in Ontario, Thursday May 23rd 1912* (Toronto: Ontario Department of Education, 1912). A few years later, the Department of Education would acknowledge the role played by Ross. It was only in 1924 that Trenholme was officially acknowledged for her leadership role. *Empire Day in the Schools of Ontario, Friday May 23rd 1924* (Toronto: Ontario Department of Education, 1924).

23 Ungar, "Clementina Fessenden Trenholme"; Stamp, "Empire Day."

24 Fessenden, *The Founding of Empire Day*.

25 Ibid.; Ungar, "Clementina Fessenden Trenholme."

26 *Empire Day in Ontario, Thursday May 23rd 1912* (Toronto: Ontario Department of Education, 1912).

27 Jim English, "Empire Day in Britain, 1904–1958," *Historical Journal* 49, no. 1 (March 2006): 248.

28 French, "The Ambiguity of Empire Day," 62.

29 *Empire Day in the Schools of Ontario, May 23rd 1929* (Ontario: Department of Education, 1929), 14.

30 *Empire Day, Circular*, 1.

31 Ibid.

32 French, "The Ambiguity of Empire Day"; English, "Empire Day."

33 *Empire Day in the Schools of Ontario* (Toronto: Ontario Department of Education, 1923).

34 *Empire Day, Circular to Inspectors* (Toronto: Ontario Department of Education, 1902).

35 J. Castell Hopkins, F.S.S., *The Origin and History of Empire Day* (Toronto: Ontario Department of Education, 1910), 4–5.

36 *Empire Day in Canada, Friday May 19th, 1911: The Story of the British Empire in a Nutshell* (Toronto: Department of Education for Ontario, 1911).

37 *Canada's Part in the Present War: Empire Day, Thursday May 23rd 1918* (Toronto: Department of Education for Ontario, 1918).

38 Ibid., 12–14.

39 *Empire Day in the Schools of Ontario, May 23rd 1928* (Toronto: Ontario Department of Education, 1928).

40 Ibid.

41 Ibid.

42 For a description of the space afforded to French Canadians in Ontario's promotional booklets, see the chapter by Belliveau and Martel in the present volume.

43 French, "The Ambiguity of Empire Day," 68.

44 English, "Empire Day," 248.
45 Ibid., 251.
46 One exception is that of the "Irish" Catholics of Toronto. In a recent book, William Jenkins shows that, despite their sour relations with Britain, Irish Catholics took part in the annual celebrations of Empire Day in Toronto. See William Jenkins, *Between Raid and Rebellions: The Irish in Buffalo and Toronto, 1867–1916* (Montreal: McGill-Queen's University Press, 2013), 320.

5 "One Flag, One Throne, One Empire"? Espousing and Replacing Empire Day in French Canada, 1899–1952

JOEL BELLIVEAU AND MARCEL MARTEL

In the previous chapter, we saw how Empire Day was created amid a flurry of imperialistic political and cultural activity in Canada at the twilight of the nineteenth century, and how, along with a now permanently enshrined Victoria Day, it constituted a kind of proto-national day for Canada.[1] In this chapter, we will examine the reception Empire Day was given by French Canadians, from its early years to the 1950s.

In a superb article, Arthur Silver has shown how the rise of imperialism as a form of ethnocultural nationalism, during the last two decades of the nineteenth century, was followed by French-Canadian disaffection with the idea of empire.[2] Contrary to popular belief, French Canadians had no particular aversion to British imperialism prior to the 1890s. Young French Canadians had participated in military campaigns in India, Egypt, and the Sudan, among others, with the backing of both French Canada's elite and its public opinion. Moreover, imperial campaigns and the British Empire itself were integrated in the dominant French-Canadian political discourse. British colonialism was presented as an important part of a larger European and Christian mission to civilize the world, while the empire itself was presented as a space of great liberty, united by the Crown, in which multiple "nationalities" could co-exist and work together.

During the last decade and a half of the nineteenth century, however, the new cultural definition of "Britishness" that circulated in Canada, and the ways in which this new Britishness transformed the meaning of empire, had an abrasive effect on French Canadians everywhere. They became known for their lukewarm support or outright opposition to imperialism. This was, of course, the backdrop to the rise of Henri Bourassa, the largely undisputed representative of French Canadians, and of his brand of Canadian bicultural nationalism, which became French Canada's preferred option in terms of national identity. During the first decade of the twentieth century *bourassisme* was regarded both as an alternative to imperialism and a way out of it.[3] Wilfrid Laurier's government, for its part, was truly stuck between a rock and a hard place.

It is in this polarizing context that Empire Day was created, with the explicit aim of promoting "civic spirit" and a "sound patriotic feeling" among all Canadian subjects.[4] In hindsight, this appears to have been a lofty and likely unattainable goal. After all, British imperialism in general, as well as the host of organizations it inspired, enjoyed very little support in French Canada, among the working classes, or among the nation's farmers.[5]

Yet we believe that dismissing this ambition from the outset would be anachronistic. Imperial sentiment was a powerful force in early twentieth-century Canada. For this reason, it is worthwhile exploring how various segments of the population responded to the call of Empire Day. It is likely that the ways in which various groups, including French Canadians, Aboriginal peoples, and ethnic minorities, chose to celebrate and create a collective memory differed. We will see here that, surprisingly, French Canadians "gave a chance" to Empire Day in its early years, using the festivities as an opportunity to negotiate the meaning of empire and of Canada. After the conscription crisis, however, nationalist French-Canadian leaders opted to develop a different national celebration, the Fête de Dollard, as a strategy of resistance and to promote national characteristics based on elements of their own past. The symbols and aspects of history selected for these celebrations suggest what types of values promoters hoped to instil in their "imagined communities,"[6] and the roles given to English- and French-speaking people, Aboriginal people, and other ethnic communities shed light on the relationships between these cultural communities. Before we examine French Canada's relationship to the celebration, however, we will reflect on the means that are at our disposal to measure a population segment's response to public festivities.

The Historiography of National Celebrations and Commemorations in Early Twentieth-century Canada

Studies on national commemorations and celebrations of the early twentieth century have revealed how their organizers conceived of the nation and the act of commemoration itself. Although the influential people (including politicians and businessmen) who organized these festivities mostly shared an upper-middle-class background and world view, their planning was fraught with intense rivalry. Viv Nelles's analysis of Quebec City's 1908 tercentenary, for instance, explored both the event's elaborate pageantry and the less visible competition among various state and non-state actors to advance their own particular narrative.[7] In his study of bilingual and bicultural Montreal, Alan Gordon showed how "public memory is the product of competitions and ideas about the past that are fashioned in a public sphere and speak primarily about structures of power."[8] Finally, Ronald Rudin expanded on the case of Quebec City by analysing the commemorations of three distinct events over a thirty-year period. He was able to show how national celebrations at the end of the nineteenth century were influenced by the ambient fears and apprehensions brought about by industrialization and the changing social, political, and economic environments that accompanied it.[9]

These studies focused on the people who conceived these national celebrations, pageants, and other events. They analysed these people's divergent goals and motivations, and strove to understand the ability of certain actors to shape, and to impose their understanding of, how the past should be remembered, celebrated, and staged.

The spectators and others who consumed these festivities, however, including those who read news articles and commemorative booklets, are most often beyond the reach of the historian. They have become part of a vast but anonymous and inaccessible crowd. Who were they? Where did they come from? What were their motivations and expectations? What was their understanding of the festivities unfolding before their eyes, and, above all, what did they remember? Some spectators of these festivities kept diaries and letters, documents that offer researchers the tantalizing opportunity to delve into the motivations of some who attended these celebrations. Although Nelles employed some of them in his study, these scattered testimonies are few and far between, and their inclusion always raises the issue of their representativeness.

On this theme of how the public in general consumes and gives meaning to these festivities and national celebrations, we believe that one avenue has been underutilized: the analysis of the dominant representations of the celebration as depicted in the media, as well as the evolution of coverage in time and space. After all, organizers' actions, politicians' and elites' attitudes, and spectators' behaviours are filtered by the newspapers' ideologies and interests. Dailies and weeklies had a dual role, as they observed and reported on the annual celebration of Empire Day while also serving as producers of meaning. They gave significance to what they witnessed and selected what they chose to report. While the coverage afforded to the events in *one* town in *one* given year is likely to seem banal, a comparison of the celebration's coverage to its treatment elsewhere in the country or at other moments in time is likely to reveal many trends and countertrends.

This chapter therefore looks at media coverage of Empire Day in many French-Canadian communities, over a long period of time and a wide area, in the hopes of better understanding French Canadians' rapport with the celebration. How did people celebrate? What did they celebrate? What was written about the celebrations? And which narratives did the media develop? Did they focus on what community leaders said? Did they comment on the crowd, its behaviour, and its reactions? In analysing this coverage, we consider both the media's choice of words and its revealing silences, in addition to how coverage differed across the country.

Empire Day in French-Language Newspapers

Michihisa Hosokawa proposed, in a 2007article, a very nuanced and well-documented picture of Empire Day in Canada. He spent little time, however, exploring French Canadians' rapport with the day of celebration, suggesting that, for them, Empire Day was "une fête pour les Anglais" and "a threat to enforce imperial conditions upon them." However, he admits that, "among the newspapers examined," only one "implicitly criticized Empire Day."[10] This chapter aims to examine this topic further.

In our attempt to identify how French Canadians took part in Empire Day celebrations, we turn to a variety of French-language newspapers. Were there any references to Empire Day therein? Did French-Canadian communities have any affinity with this holiday and how did this rapport evolve over time? As a state-sponsored event, did Empire Day serve up a moderate kind of imperial pride, capable of attracting sympathy even from within French Canada?

In order to answer these questions, we examined the content of French-language newspapers in four cities: Montreal (*La Presse, Le Devoir*), Ottawa (*Le Temps, Le Droit*), Moncton (*L'Évangéline*), and Winnipeg (*Le Manitoba, La Liberté, La Liberté et le Patriote*). We examined the issues around Victoria Day and Empire Day for the years 1902, 1907, 1912, 1917, 1922, 1932, 1942, 1952, and 1962.

We know that the promotional material prepared for Empire Day did little to be inclusive,[11] including with regards to French Canadians. There are remarkably few references to French-speaking people (and none to Aboriginals) in the booklets prepared by the Ontario Department of Education, for instance, although those few are positive. The 1912 booklet insisted that French- and English-speaking people shared the ability to live together according to their religious beliefs without fear of persecution in Canada. In addition, it reminded readers that these linguistic groups participated in the empire's defence when it was threatened in North America, notably during the American Revolution and the War of 1812.[12] In the documents prepared for Confederation's fiftieth and sixtieth anniversaries, in 1917 and 1927, respectively, there was a particular reference to French Canadians: the author, ignoring the Acadians, wrote that French-speaking people in Quebec and the West "cling tenaciously to their religion, their language, and their customs."[13] In addition, in the 1928 booklet, there was a single sentence about French-speaking people meant to reassure those who doubted their sense of loyalty.[14] Surely, a project whose proponents afforded so little attention to French Canadians had no chance of having even moderate success in Francophone communities. Yet, as we will see, the situation on the ground was, surprisingly, far from unequivocal.

1899–1917: Empire Day Is Given a Chance

French-Canadian newspapers were not altogether indifferent to the appeals to celebrate Empire Day. Although coverage of the celebrations varied from year to year and from region to region, it must be said that, in general, French-language newspapers dutifully reported on these activities on a regular basis. The one exception, in terms of regions, is the Maritimes. Despite many efforts, we have been able to find only three references to Empire Day in Acadian newspapers.[15] This singularity would be an interesting topic of inquiry, but will not be the focus of this chapter.

Elsewhere, the coverage afforded to Empire Day pales in comparison to that of "indigenous" French-Canadian national holidays – which corresponded to the French Canadians' and Acadians' patron saints' feast days, those of St John the Baptist (24 June) and the Virgin Mary (the feast of the Assumption, 15 August). Events associated with these days received far greater treatment, in terms of the amount of coverage extended (usually reporting every detail, including meetings, masses, speeches, and programs as well as publishing reflective pieces), the time spent in the news cycle (which could be more than a month in the early twentieth century),[16] and the geographic extent of the events described. Reports on Empire Day, in contrast, were usually limited to brief articles, a high percentage of which related to local school activities, and the news cycle was shorter.

However, although Empire Day was given little media coverage, the tone of what was reported was nevertheless positive. Moreover, from its inception in 1899 to the Great War and the 1917 conscription crisis, many articles had an emotional content and feeling. It is not obvious, in reading French-language newspapers, that Empire Day was "doomed to fail" in francophone Canada from the outset. Could Empire Day also be for French Canadians?

From the beginning, French-language newspapers in Quebec would dutifully report on the activities organized by the English-language schools of the Protestant education commission.[17] The authors seemed to hesitate as to the ownership of this day of celebration: although they frequently presented these as the "Other's" activities, they would rejoice when French Canada was symbolically included. One 1907 *La Presse* article reported that "Last night, six thousand people gathered at the arena to hear the Empire Day concert given by 1200 English schools' pupils... French Canadians were not forgotten, since they sang 'Vive la Canadienne,' which provoked an indescribable enthusiasm."[18]

The "othering" of the holiday was even less pronounced in the French-language communities and newspapers from other provinces, where all schools were mandated to participate. In those communities, it was not a case of an "English" institution carefully including, symbolically, its francophone neighbours. Rather, it was the carefully crafted work of public, culturally shared institutions trying to make the holiday inclusive. In one event in St Boniface, Manitoba, for example, the evening was launched with patriotic French-Canadian songs such as "Vive la France" and "Partout le canon gronde," which were reportedly very much appreciated by the public. The "English programme" followed suit, with British classics such as "Nearer My God to Thee" (sung by all students), "It's a Long Way to Tipperary," and, of course, "God Save the King."[19] It is worth noting that the program seems to have avoided the more pungently imperialistic anthems such as "Land of Hope and Glory" and "Rule Britannia."

Articles pertaining to Empire Day were not limited to polite descriptions of school activities. One may easily find, in the early twentieth century, many earnest proclamations of fidelity to the empire in French-Canadian newspapers.[20]

On 22 May 1907, for example, *Le Manitoba* would report that "May twenty-fourth's celebrations are our homage to the British Crown. They represent the positive affirmation of a people who are satisfied with their political status. We can indeed congratulate ourselves for the regime under which we live."[21] The article continues with a relatively classic ode to British liberties, before giving one warning: "Should London restrain this liberty through imperial excess, the situation will become more complicated, for everyone."[22] In other words, British imperialism was becoming, ironically, a menace to British liberties. This warning was followed up with one caveat pertaining to the liberty currently enjoyed by British subjects: "We cannot write these lines on the liberty of the English citizen without one very precise hesitation: we, Manitoba Catholics, ruled over by British institutions, are the victims of legal injustices."[23] These reservations are, however, immediately followed with an affirmation of optimism: it was hoped that French Canadians of Manitoba would soon be placed on an equal footing to that of "other elements living under the British flag."

This article could be interpreted as simply an attempt by the linguistic group to profit from Empire Day, but it can also be argued that such a dialogue with (and adaptation of) the discourse of British political values shows that French Canadians were still considering Empire Day as something that might become a legitimate shared day of celebration for all Canadians – if only the definition of empire could be adapted to be more inclusive.

Articles that demonstrate some attachment to the empire are numerous; some emphasize the fact that French Canadians found their liberty in the empire,[24] while others excitedly describe the Empire Day activities awaiting the public.[25] During the years leading up to the First World War, even the more nationalistic French-Canadian newspapers had something positive to say about Empire Day. In 1912, for example, a *Le Devoir* article lauded a "superb children's event … at the arena, on the occasion of Empire Day," noting that more than 6,000 people participated. What the paper approved of most was the celebration's goal of instilling patriotism in young generations: "Now there's a nice way to develop the idea of patriotism within our children, and it is our wish that this be repeated everywhere, especially in French-Canadian contexts."[26]

Until early 1917, despite the tensions occasioned by Ontario's infamous Regulation 17 on the language of instruction and by the prospect of conscription, many French-language newspapers continued to show support for both the Empire and its annual celebration:

> Let's hope, for the greater glory of this Empire and of the British flag that protects us, that all of George V's subjects will continue to show themselves united, strong and determined to defeat the Germanic colossus... Canada is able to fulfil its duty to the end. On this ... important anniversary ... we hasten to cry out: "long live the British Empire! Long live, also, the other members of the Quadruple Entente!"[27]

This last statement, made by the liberal-leaning *La Presse*, should not be taken as an isolated, disconnected act. On the contrary, it echoed similar statements made by many members of francophone civil society, including representatives of the patriotic Société Saint-Jean-Baptiste. In this time of crisis, representatives of "practically every patriotic or national society of Montreal" met in Victoria Square on the occasion of Empire Day in order to lay wreaths of flowers at the foot of the late queen's statue.[28] Thus, on the eve of the conscription crisis, Empire Day maintained an ecumenical aura about it.

Despite the polarizing context of the Boer Wars, the 1905 Alberta and Saskatchewan schools question, the 1910 Naval Service bill, and Henri Bourassa's Ligue nationaliste canadienne, Empire Day was "given a chance" in French Canada, both inside and outside Quebec. The celebration was observed, albeit not as much as in English-speaking Canada. What is significant is that the holiday – and indeed the empire – was still valued in terms of identity by a significant portion of the discourse producers. French Canadians were still willing participants in the discussion around the empire and were prepared to try to negotiate the meaning of the empire as well as to define their place in it. For a time, then, it seemed that Empire Day had an opportunity to rally majorities of both English- and French-speaking Canadians. That possibility disappeared with the conscription crisis.

1917–1952: The Demise of Empire Day and the Rise of the Fête de Dollard in French Canada

French-Canadian newspapers were generally supportive of Empire Day until 1917 and were particularly enthusiastic about the idea of putting aside a day in order to instil sound patriotic feeling in youth. There was certainly much hesitation with regards to the symbolism of empire, with some political actors rejecting it out of hand, but there were also attempts to negotiate the meaning of empire, as well as French Canada's place in it. In any case, identification with the empire was certainly not seen as encapsulating French Canada's "total" identity, and so Empire Day was presented as a complement to other holidays such as Saint-Jean-Baptiste Day. For all of the hesitation and nuances, however, Empire Day could still claim legitimacy in national life.

This claim would be very seriously put into question in the context of the late war years. The conscription crisis fanned the flames already lit by the Ontario schools crisis and resulted in a Conservative-led "Union" government that essentially put all of French Canada in the opposition. In this environment, both the options of imperial allegiance and of pan-Canadian nationalism à la Bourassa fell out of favour, particularly among francophones in Quebec.[29] These developments encouraged the burgeoning organizations and symbols that were devoted wholly and unequivocally to the French-Canadian nation. Naturally, patriotic celebrations were part of this trend, and thus the Fête de Dollard des Ormeaux became a yearly celebration as of 1919.

Dollard, as he was commonly known, had been a French soldier stationed in Ville-Marie (Montreal) in the middle of the seventeenth century. He was killed during an expedition in 1660 when his party – comprising seventeen Frenchmen and a group of allied Wendat – was attacked by a large Haudenosaunee[30] force at the Long Sault on the Ottawa River (near present-day Carillon, Quebec). Long forgotten, he was "rediscovered" by the nationalist, but liberal, historian François-Xavier Garneau in the 1840s and popularized by romantic historian Étienne-Michel Faillon in the 1860s. The latter crafted a narrative that made him into an archetype of Christian values and a hero who saved Ville-Marie. This narrative was consolidated between the 1860s and 1910 by multiple historians, including the American Francis Parkman.[31] At that point, however, Dollard was not yet depicted as a "national" French-Canadian hero.

The work of these historians and the polarizing context of the First World War set the stage for the intense popularization of Dollard, his companions, and their story in the late war years. Nationalist leaders and historians, most notably Abbé Lionel Groulx, shone a spotlight on the battle and made two key modifications to its narrative. Thereafter, from 1919 until well into the 1950s, it would be circulated yearly, in abbreviated but archetypical form, in newspapers across the country. First, Dollard and his men were transformed into purely French-Canadian and Catholic heroes – that is to say, into *national* heroes – who willingly sacrificed their lives for *la Patrie et la foi*.[32]

> Dollard and his companions left Montreal and went ahead of the Iroquois. They did not consider the fact that they were but sixteen to resist many hundreds of enemies. They knew they were young and that the young French colony needed their sacrifice. They needed no more: they walked straight towards their goal, towards their heroic duty. Without an afterthought, without compromise, without half-measures: they went to be sacrificed with joy in their hearts, conscious of their responsibilities. The love of God and of the homeland kept them going; ... they saved the homeland.[33]

Second – and this was Groulx's most important contribution – the myth became prescriptive: Dollard's abnegation and his devotion to *la Patrie et l'Église* became models for contemporary French Canadians.[34]

> Dollard's courage was that of a warrior. In 1922, when we need to shield ourselves not from tomahawk blows, but from the moral menace of Anglicization and Protestantism, Dollard's courage will be ardour, generosity, confidence in our race and in life... Let us remain what we have been.[35]
>
> By their act of heroism, Dollard and his companions rank [as] heroes ...; they especially gave the French Canadian youth ... a splendid example. What Dollard has accomplished, we must accomplish today, each of us in our field.[36]

The elevation of Dollard went beyond discourse. Important commemorative events were organized for 1919, including a pilgrimage to the site of the battle at Carillon and large demonstrations and festivities in Montreal and dozens of other cities and towns across Quebec and the rest of Canada.[37] The celebrations would be repeated yearly thereafter, well into the 1950s.

Was the creation of this mythology and the instauration of this celebration a deliberate attempt to minimize or overshadow Empire Day? We have not yet been able to establish this with absolute certainty, but there is enough circumstantial evidence to argue that it is all but certain.

The meteoric rise of the Fête de Dollard occurred precisely at the time when Empire Day lost the space it had in the French-Canadian public sphere. Never again, after 1917, would newspapers cover Empire Day events with the same regularity as they had prior to the conscription crisis. Meanwhile, coverage of Dollard – in multiple forms – increased exponentially. As early as 1922, *La Presse* reported – with perhaps a bit of exaggeration – that "Dollard des Ormeaux day is celebrated in all of Canada's French centres of population."[38] That same year, *Le Devoir* marvelled at the day's "sudden popularity," which the paper attributed to the fact that "the entire race recognized, in it, its highest aspirations, a superior form of its ideals."[39]

What is more, a few quotes from members of the nationalist elite strongly suggest that replacing Empire Day was a priority. Lionel Groulx wished, for example, that the new holiday "become universal, that it enter into our habits and traditions so completely to the point where May 24th becomes known only as 'la fête de Dollard.'"[40] In 1922, Father Rodrigue Villeneuve, a professor of theology at the University of Ottawa and future Archbishop of Quebec, remarked to Groulx in a letter that Dollard's day had "entered the mores" of the French Canadians of Ottawa, and "that Empire Day [is] dead here."[41]

There is also the timing of the celebrations. Initially, Dollard's exploits had been commemorated on 21 May, the supposed day of the attack; but by 1919 it became a tradition to commemorate the Battle of Long Sault precisely on Queen Victoria's birthday, which is, of course, a holiday and was celebrated close to Empire Day. Was this for practicality's sake? Perhaps in part. But it is difficult to ignore the powerful symbolism of this juxtaposition.

The Fête de Dollard, much like Empire Day, was from the outset presented as being of particular importance to youth. This manifested in many ways. On the day prior – that is, on Empire Day – schools organized activities relating to Dollard's heroism. "In schools – from the most modest to the most renowned – [Dollard's] illustrious memory is evoked."[42] Moreover, on the day of the celebration itself, local processions traditionally gave pride of place to schoolchildren.[43] In many locales, the organization of the wider festivities was actually coordinated by youth groups. Most often, including in Montreal, Quebec City, and Ottawa, this role was bequeathed to the Association catholique de la jeunesse canadienne-française (ACJC), a prominent nationalist youth organization.[44] In other cases, such as in Saint-Boniface in 1922, they were coordinated by "les jeunes de l'Union Canadienne,"[45] that is to say, the youth wing of a French-Canadian fraternal society. In Hawkesbury, Ontario, in 1932 and in other smaller communities, local school commissions or schools organized historical re-enactments, which were open to the wider public but intended to "provide a living lesson of Canadian history to all the French Canadian children in [their] schools."[46] Significantly, Dollard was most often portrayed as "youth's hero"[47] and as a symbol of "French Canada's heroic youth, which spills its blood for the salvation of a Christian and French civilization."[48] For this reason, youth were encouraged to wear "la rose de Dollard," a pin sold to French-Canadian organizations everywhere in North America by the ACJC and, occasionally, by the network of Sociétés Saint-Jean-Baptiste. This tradition of a "memorial flower" allowing youth to "show their pride" spanned the decades between the early 1920s and the 1950s.[49]

This focus on youth was justified by the ideas that youth represented the future of the nation and that its survival depended on their actions: "We would like for the spirit that animated Dollard to pass, at least a little, into the soul of our [Franco] Manitoban youth. It has an important mission to fill ... and too many difficulties are accumulating in its path for it to succeed without an ideal moved by faith. Our faith and our language are under attack."[50]

Elites seemed to consider this pedagogical aspect of the festivities a success. As early as 1922, *Le Devoir* asserted that "youth in particular has become enamoured of the glorious victims."[51] Twenty years later, its rival *La Presse* was still happy to report that "it is a great comfort to see youth so active on such a day... Youth remembers."[52]

Finally, just like Empire Day, the Fête de Dollard, while having a predominantly pedagogical intent, also unofficially played the role of a proto-national holiday. In other words, while it was supposedly about instilling civic virtues, it was in fact as much about extolling national identity. This "national identity" dimension manifested itself in numerous ways: in the multiplicity of activities organized (including masses, rallies, cadet marches, poetry and singing recitals, concerts, athletic tournaments, theatrical plays, fireworks, and ceremonies),[53] in the very symbolic locales that were used for the celebrations (in Montreal, for example, the main celebrations were held in Parc Lafontaine, next to a monument to Dollard commissioned in 1920),[54] in the important media coverage (including broadcasts by Radio-Canada),[55] and in the great number of diverse associations, groups, and governments that sponsored the events (including chambers of commerce, scout and guide clubs, municipalities, professional associations, benevolent societies, the Alliance française, workers unions, local Société Saint-Jean-Baptiste chapters, and so on).[56]

Even more tellingly, this dimension of the Fête de Dollard is underscored by its commemoration by French Canadians across Quebec,

Ontario, Manitoba, and New England, and the proud and fawning coverage this geographical reach received from newspapers in Montreal, Quebec City, and Ottawa, as in this 1922 *Le Devoir* article:

> Tomorrow, from one end to the other of French America, people will sing to the glory of the hero... Programmes and plans for the celebration are being sent to us from the Western plains and from the United States, from French Ontario and Acadia. All are accompanied by [local] articles that communicate the reasons and the deep meaning behind our homage to yesterday's martyrs.[57]

After quoting Ontario and Manitoba newspapers as proof, the author goes on to say that, "For all of us, [Dollard] could be a principle of a greater unity, a connection transcending borders and local differences,."[58]

But ultimately, the best proof of Dollard's day becoming a national day of sorts is the fact that people said it was. As early as 1922, *Le Devoir* matter-of-factly referred to "Dollard day, henceforth [a] national holiday,"[59] noting, a couple of days later, that "Dollard day has definitely taken on all of the attributes of a truly national celebration."[60] In Ottawa, ten years later, *Le Droit* reminded readers that "Dollard day is not only a celebration for youth; it is that of the entire race, of all classes, of all ages."[61] And as late as 1952, politicians and officials could be heard saying in speeches that "the celebrations of May 24th are perhaps the most important in terms of national action."[62]

The importance of the Fête de Dollard did not wane until the 1950s. Even when McGill history professor E.R. Adair publicly refuted the veracity of the Dollard myth in 1932,[63] organizers throughout the country protested to protect the holiday's sanctity. As *Le Droit* stated, we must "accord this day of celebration [much] solemnity, if only to avenge the memory of this national hero against the attacks that it has endured of late."[64] The paper argued that Dollard "is not a legendary adventurer, as claim certain professors of an English university, but in fact a historical figure who is one of our national glories."[65]

To say that Empire Day was completely supplanted by the Fête de Dollard in French Canada would be an overstatement, but not a big one. One can still find the odd reference to Empire Day in certain liberal-leaning newspapers such as *La Presse* from the 1920s to the 1950s. Some of these references take the well-rehearsed form of odes to British liberties and to the British political system. However, these odes are *always* composed within a frame that is shared with the Fête de Dollard. In other words, for a few liberal French-Canadian papers, Empire Day is, at best, represented as but one head of a bicephalous holiday. Below are a few examples of these typical – if surprising – juxtapositions of the virtues of the queen and those of Dollard. Note that the crossover goes so far as to affirm that without Dollard, Canada might have been lost even to the British Empire:

> Today is the British Empire's day, that of our motherland ..., the longevity and strength of which continues to surprise the world. Canadians, without distinction of nationality or religion, are uniting in a shared sentiment of joy and prayer with the British people... For us, French Canadians, Empire Day is also a celebration of Dollard des Ormeaux and of his [illegible] valiant companions... If Canada constitutes one of the British Crown's most exquisite jewels, it is thanks to Dollard and his brave men's dedication and heroism [who saved New France] from barbarians.[66]
>
> There was fine weather, yesterday, for Empire Day and, for us, Dollard's day too.[67]
>
> It has become customary to associate in a single national tribute, on May 24th, the memory of the august Queen Victoria ... and, in our country, that of Dollard des Ormeaux and his companions... There is ample matter in these commemorations to feed our patriotism and our devotion to the commonweal.[68]
>
> Homage to Victoria and to Dollard! The future will appear more certain as long as the virtues and qualities that they embodied impregnate the nation and support its initiatives.[69]

Despite their interest, the importance of these statements should not be overstated, for two reasons. First, statements of this hybrid type appear only in a handful of liberal newspapers and only once a year at best. Second, while Dollard was celebrated with multiple activities, Empire Day and Victoria Day were seen, at best, as public holidays with no corresponding public events.

For the average French-Canadian newspaper reader during the interwar years, the only reminders of the existence of either Empire Day or Victoria Days were the advertisements of multiple businesses wanting to profit from the long weekend and informing their customers of their closing in order to conform to "la fête Victoria" or "the Queen's birthday."[70] The May long weekend thus became synonymous with the beginning of summer, a perfect time for a first summer outing.[71]

Surprisingly, the surest sign that Empire Day was becoming completely irrelevant in French Canada came from the actions of none other than the Canadian military during the Second World War. At this time, in order to drum up support and find recruits in Quebec, the armed forces employed Dollard des Ormeaux as a recruiting tool, eschewing the symbolism and heritage of the empire. In des Ormeaux, they found a symbol that was not only martial but that also appealed to French Canada's imaginary.[72]

In 1941, the armed forces were content to sponsor the ACJC's annual celebrations of the Fête de Dollard and to be included in the celebrations. This interest in Dollard was well received by the clergy: "The religious authorities hastened to approve the army's decision, which signifies a desire to pay a splendid homage to this young, Christian soldier, for today, youth takes its turn to combat barbarism, always the same despite changes in name and in form."[73]

In 1942, as the exigencies of war mounted, the military attempted to become the principal organizer of the event, to which it wanted to give a more martial tone by including "a vast military deployment" and "a call to the brave."[74] Finally, after a robust and very public protestation from the ACJC,[75] it was decided that there would be two distinct celebrations in honour of Dollard that year in Montreal and Quebec. In Montreal, the two rallies took turns occupying the grounds next to "le monument à Dollard" in Parc Lafontaine. Dollard was also celebrated "in every training centre of the province."[76]

Not certain what to do, most newspapers simply informed readers of their options, and Catholic school commissions did the same.[77] For more nationalistic elements, the military's actions smacked of opportunism and consequently its celebrations were dismissed by *Le Devoir* and marred by protests as well as by bickering among the invited speakers.[78] Meanwhile, the ACJC considered its 1942 celebration to have been one of the best of their twenty-three-year history.

Despite lingering doubts about the historical veracity of the story of the battle at Long Sault, the Fête de Dollard was still very much observed in 1942. The celebrations were even resuscitated in Saint-Boniface, after a hiatus of a few years.[79] Ten years later, "grandiose celebrations" were once again carried out in Montreal, and the Quebec government even organized the first "Dollard Day in Paris."[80] In contrast, Empire Day was dead and buried in French Canada, seemingly irrelevant even to Canada's armed forces. However divergent these two celebrations' paths might have been from the 1920s to the 1950s, they led to the same destination: by 1962, one hardly found mention of either one in French-Canadian newspapers around the country.

Conclusion

Although Empire Day was initially celebrated among French Canadians, simmering tensions within French Canada boiled over during the First World War conscription crisis, and thereafter French-Canadian nationalists created their own competing holiday, the Fête de Dollard, which successfully superseded "la fête de l'Empire."

The elites chose Dollard, an individual who had lived during the French colonial period, and elected him to be commemorated on the same day that the rest of the country celebrated their belonging to the British Empire. The choice of Dollard, elevated to the rank of "national hero," was part of a strategy for reasserting the distinctiveness of French-Canadian nationality by insisting upon its supposedly intrinsic "noble virtues," such as courage, loyalty, selflessness, and determination. According to the archetypical discourse that was circulated by French-language newspapers for forty years, despite having lost his life with his companions, Dollard's sacrifice was not in vain as it guaranteed the survival of French Canada. In the aftermath of the First World War, the choice of Dollard as a new "hero" for French-Canadian nationalists reflected a strong will to reaffirm "la survivance" of French Canada.

Thus, as a strategy of resistance to the celebration of the British Empire, French-Canadian nationalists were able to develop a counter-narrative destined to remind themselves and others that they would and should stay distinct. However, this counter-celebration was not conceived to trigger negative feelings towards English Canadians and the British Empire. Although the annual celebration of Dollard – both in Quebec and among French-speaking minority communities – bears witness to a will to remain different, it did not go so far as to advocate disloyalty to Canada or the empire.

Although both holidays diminished in importance by the 1960s, an examination of the narratives developed by each day's proponents tells us much about the nature of national identities and national celebrations. In particular, it allows us to revisit a question we evoked while discussing the historiography of commemoration. Historians often wonder to what extent the general population gives meaning to such events. Are people and crowds really attending events out of patriotism? Or are they simply out for a good time? Since there is undoubtedly some element of truth in the second hypothesis, historians wonder if they can learn anything at all from the existence of national celebrations. At best, they often conclude, the content of such celebrations reflects the priorities of elites.

The examples of Empire Day and the Fête de Dollard demonstrate both the very real influence that elites have, on the one hand, and the limits of their powers, on the other. The reception of Empire Day in French Canada during its early days points to the flexibility of national celebrations. Despite the lackluster effort on the part of its proponents with regards to the inclusion of French Canadians, the celebration was adapted successfully by a variety of social actors in French-Canadian communities, and was celebrated and noticed, albeit with a certain restraint. As the post–First World War events relating to Empire Day revealed, however, that elasticity and flexibility could only go so far. Once a holiday truly fails to resonate within a population, it will cease to be celebrated. Inversely, the example of the Fête de Dollard shows that, if a unified elite *does* manage to present the case for a national day that is coherent and has affinities with the population's sensibilities, such a "tradition" can be created in a few short years.[81]

NOTES

We thank our research assistants, Elizabeth Labrie, Caroline Vandergoten, Mike Rowan, and Dave Leonard. A SSHRC Insight Grant (2013–18) has made this research project possible. Thank you also to our colleagues David Leeson and Matthew Hayday for having revised an earlier version of this text.

1 For a longer discussion of the shifting meanings of empire and Confederation at this time, refer to the preceding chapter by Martel, Ward, Belliveau, and Bos.

2 Arthur Silver, "Quelques considérations sur les rapports du Canada français avec l'impérialisme britannique au XIXe siècle," *Canadian Journal of African Studies* 15, no. 1 (1981): 55–75.

3 Sylvie Lacombe, *La rencontre de deux peuples élus: comparaison des ambitions nationale et impériale au Canada entre 1896 et 1929* (Sainte-Foy, QC: Les Presses de l'Université Laval, 2002); Joseph Levitt, "La perspective nationaliste d'Henri Bourassa, 1896–1914," *Revue d'histoire de l'Amérique française* 22, no. 4 (March 1969): 567–582.

4 *Empire Day, Circular to Inspectors* (Toronto: Ontario Department of Education, 1899).

5 Carl Berger, *The Sense of Power: Studies in the Ideas of Canadian Imperialism, 1867–1914* (Toronto: University of Toronto Press, 1970), 104.

6 Benedict Anderson, *Imagined Communities: Reflections on the Origin and Spread of Nationalism* (London: Verso, 1983, 1991).

7 H.V. Nelles, *The Art of Nation-Building: Pageantry and Spectacle at Quebec's Tercentenary* (Toronto: University of Toronto Press, 2000).

8 Alan Gordon, *Making Public Pasts: The Contested Terrain of Montreal's Public Memories, 1891–1930* (Montreal: McGill-Queen's University Press, 2001), i.

9 Ronald Rudin, *Founding Fathers: The Celebrations of Champlain and Laval in the Streets of Quebec, 1878–1908* (Toronto: University of Toronto Press, 2003).

10 Michihisa Hosokawa, "Making Imperial Citizens: Empire Day in Canada," *Journal of American and Canadian Studies* 25 (2007): 64–5.

11 See the preceding chapter by Martel, Ward, Belliveau, and Bos on the origins and evolution of Empire Day.

12 *Empire Day in Ontario, Thursday May 23rd, 1912* (Toronto: Ontario Department of Education, 1912).

13 *Jubilee of Confederation, 1867–1917, Empire Day, May 23rd, 1917* (Toronto: Ontario Department of Education, 1917), 44. The historical description of how Canada had evolved was identical in both booklets.

14 *Empire Day in the Schools of Ontario, May 23rd, 1928* (Toronto: Ontario Department of Education, 1928).

15 "Empire Day," *Le Courrier des provinces maritimes* (Bathurst), 30 May 1901, 3; "'Empire Day' célébrée avec éclat à South River, Caraquet et Shippagan, N.-B.," *L'Évangéline* (Moncton), 19 June 1902, 3; Charles-D. Hébert, "La fête de l'Empire," *L'Évangéline*, 4 May 1916, 8.

16 For example, one can find articles on the upcoming Saint-Jean-Baptiste celebrations in the 22 May 1907 edition of *Le Temps* (Ottawa) and in the 16 May 1907 edition of *Le Courrier de l'Ouest* (Edmonton).

17 "La plupart des écoles anglaises de cette ville célébreront avec éclat 'Empire Day' demain," *La Presse* (Montreal), 21 May 1902.

18 *La Presse* (Montreal), 24 May 1907, 1 ("Hier soir, six milles personnes se réunissaient à l'Arena pour entendre le concert 'Empire Day' donné par les élèves des écoles anglaises au nombre de 1200… Les Canadiens-Français [sic] ne furent pas oubliés et on chanta au milieu d'un enthousiasme indescriptible 'Vive la Canadienne.'").

19 *La Liberté* (Winnipeg), 30 May 1917, 5. For a similar event in Ontario, see for example *Le Temps* (Ottawa), 21 May 1907.

20 It should be said, however, that there was significant confusion with regards to Empire Day and Victoria Day. Consequently, it was not always possible to distinguish the discussion of the two in the newspapers. For example, *Le Temps* (Ottawa) states on 25 May 1912, "l'anniversaire de la reine Victoria et comme on l'appelle aujourd'hui, la fête de l'Empire" (4).

21 "Le chômage et les réjouissances du 24 mai sont de notre part un hommage à la couronne britannique. C'est l'affirmation positive d'un peuple satisfait

de son status [sic] politique. Nous pouvons en effet nous féliciter du régime sous lequel nous vivons."

22 "Le jour où Londres voudra restreindre cette liberté par excès d'impérialisme, la situation se compliquera pour tout le monde."

23 "Nous ne pouvons terminer ces lignes sur la liberté du citoyen anglais sans une réserve très précise: nous, catholiques du Manitoba, régis par des institutions britanniques, nous sommes les victimes d'injustices légales."

24 *Le Temps* (Ottawa), 23 May 1912, 1.

25 *Le Droit* (Ottawa), 18 May 1917, 2.

26 *Le Devoir* (Montreal), 1912 ("superbe manifestation enfantine … à l'Aréna, à l'occasion de la Fête de l'Empire"; "Voilà une belle manière de développer chez les enfants l'idée du patriotisme et il est à souhaiter que ceci soit répété un peu partout, surtout dans les milieux canadiens-français.").

27 *La Presse* (Montreal), 24 May 1917, 5 ("Espérons, pour la plus grande gloire de cet Empire et du drapeau britannique qui nous protège, que tous les sujets de Georges V continueront à se montrer unis, forts et déterminés à vaincre le colosse germanique… Le Canada est capable de faire son devoir jusqu'au bout. Comme l'important anniversaire que nous célébrons aujourd'hui nous invite tout naturellement à faire des vœux, nous nous empressons de crier: vive l'Empire britannique! Vivent aussi les autres membres de la Quadruple Entente.").

28 *La Presse* (Montreal), 25 May 1917, 14.

29 Patrice Groulx, *Pièges de la mémoire: Dollard des Ormeaux, les Amérindiens et nous* (Hull, QC: Éditions Vents d'Ouest, 1998), 207.

30 Europeans called them Hurons and Iroquois, respectively.

31 Groulx, *Pièges de la mémoire*, 90–173.

32 Ibid., 210.

33 "Le geste de Dollard," *Le Droit* (Ottawa), 23 May 1932, 3 ("Dollard et ses compagnons quittent Montréal et s'en vont au-devant des Iroquois. Ils ne songent pas qu'ils ne sont que seize pour résister à plusieurs centaines d'ennemis. Ils savent qu'ils sont jeunes et que la jeune colonie française a besoin de leur sacrifice; il ne leur en faut pas plus: ils marchent droit vers leur but, vers ce qui est pour eux l'héroïque devoir. Point d'arrière-pensée, point de compromis, point de demi-mesure: ils vont au sacrifice de gaieté et de cœur, conscients de leurs responsabilités. L'amour de Dieu et de la patrie les animait; … ils ont sauvé la patrie." It should be noted that their ability to save Ville-Marie depended not on strength, but on will and courage. "Les Iroquois stupéfaits de la résistance opiniâtre de ces quelques

hommes, ayant perdu le tiers de leur armée, regagnent honteusement leurs parages en renonçant au désir d'attaquer Ville-Marie."). *Le Droit* (Ottawa), 30 May 1932, 2.

34 Groulx, *Pièges de la mémoire*, 210.

35 *La Liberté* (Winnipeg), 16 May 1922, 3 ("La bravoure de Dollard était guerrière; en 1922, où nous avons à parer non pas les coups physiques des tomahawks, mais la menace morale de l'anglicisation et du protestantisme, la bravoure de Dollard sera ardeur, générosité, confiance en la race et en la vie... Restons ce que nous avons été.").

36 "Dollard modèle de fierté, d'initiative, de désintéressement," *Le Droit* (Ottawa), 23 May 1942, 5 ("Par leur acte d'héroïsme, Dollard et ses compagnons se sont classés [comme] héros ...; ils ont surtout donné à la jeunesse canadienne-française ... un magnifique exemple. Ce que Dollard a accompli, nous devons l'accomplir aujourd'hui, chacun dans notre domaine.").

37 On the occasion of the 250th anniversary Dollard's death, in 1910, the "battle at Long Sault" had even been commemorated a few times. Interestingly, the idea had first been put forward by an English-language newspaper, the *Montreal Daily Herald*, 26 March 1910. Groulx, *Pièges de la mémoire*, 201. However, interest in Dollard had petered out during the following years.

38 *La Presse* (Montreal), 24 May 1922, 11, 21. "La fête de Dollard des Ormeaux est célébrée dans tous les centres français [du Canada]."

39 *Le Devoir* (Montreal), 23 May 1922, 1 ("Popularité presque foudroyante ... la race entière [y] a reconnu ses plus hautes aspirations, l'une des formes supérieures de son idéal.").

40 Lionel Groulx, "La fête de Dollard," *L'Action française*, April 1920, 168, quoted in Michel Bock, *Quand la nation débordait des frontières: Les minorités françaises dans la pensée de Lionel Groulx* (Montreal: Hurtubise HMH, 2004), 202 ("Groulx désirait que la fête du héros du Long-Sault dev[înt] universelle, qu'elle entr[ât] si bien dans nos habitudes et dans nos traditions que le 24 mai ne s'appel[ât] *plus*, dans l'Amérique française, *que* 'la fête de Dollard'" [our emphasis]).

41 Bock, *Quand la nation débordait des frontières*, 204. ("En 1922, Rodrigue Villeneuve indiqua à Groulx que la fête de Dollard était 'entrée dans les mœurs' et 'que l'*Empire Day* [était] mort chez-nous.'").

42 *Le Devoir* (Montreal), 23 May 1922, 1 ("Dans les écoles – des plus modestes aux plus renommées – on évoquera la mémoire illustre [de Dollard]."). For other examples in various schools and colleges, see *Le Devoir* (Montreal), 26 May 1922, 2; *La Presse* (Montreal), 24 May 1922, 21, and 21 May 1942, 11.

43 For example, see *La Presse* (Montreal), 24 May 1922, 11, 21.

44 For a good idea of the ACJC's role, see *Le Devoir* (Montreal), 25 May 1932, 8; *Le Droit* (Ottawa), 30 May 1932, 2.

45 *La Liberté* (Winnipeg), 16 May 1922, 1, 7.

46 *Le Droit* (Ottawa), 12 May 1932, 12 ("Fournir une leçon vivante d'histoire du Canada à tous les enfants canadiens-français de ses écoles."). See also *La Liberté et le Patriote*, 9 May 1952, 9.

47 For a good example, see *La Presse* (Montreal), 25 May 1942, 3.

48 "La jeunesse héroïque … de la jeunesse française qui verse son sang pour le salut d'une civilisation chrétienne et française." *Le Devoir*, 23 May 1922, 3; see also *La Presse* (Montreal), 23 May 1942, 36.

49 *La Liberté et le Patriote* (Winnipeg), 13 May 1942, 5; ibid., 3 June 1942, 7.

50 *La Liberté* (Winnipeg), 16 May 1922, 1, 7 ("Nous voudrions que l'esprit qui animait Dollard passe, au moins un peu, dans l'âme de notre jeunesse manitobaine. Elle a une grande mission à remplir … et trop de difficultés s'amoncellent sur sa route pour qu'elle puisse la remplir sans le souffle de l'idéal animé par la foi. C'est à sa foi comme à sa langue qu'on s'attaque.").

51 *Le Devoir* (Montreal), 23 May 1922, 1 ("la jeunesse particulièrement s'est prise d'amour pour les glorieuses victimes").

52 *La Presse* (Montreal), 23 May 1942, 36 ("il est éminemment consolant de voir la jeunesse aussi active en un jour pareil [la fête de Dollard]… Elle se souvient").

53 *La Presse* (Montreal), 22 May 1942, 11; ibid., 23 May 23, 1942, 43; ibid., 25 May 1942, 6, 7; *La Liberté et le Patriote* (Winnipeg), 20 May 1942, 1.

54 Groulx, *Pièges de la mémoire*, 208.

55 *Le Devoir* (Montreal), 21 May 1942, 12.

56 *La Presse* (Montreal), 21 May 1942, 18, and 25 May 1942, 6 and 7; *Le Devoir* (Montreal), 26 May 1922, 2.

57 *Le Devoir* (Montreal), 23 May 1922, 1. Signed by Omer Héroux, Henri Bourassa's trusted ally. ("Demain, d'un bout à l'autre de l'Amérique française, on chantera la gloire du héro… Des plaines de l'Ouest comme des États-Unis, de l'Ontario français et jusque de l'Acadie, nous arrivent les programmes et les projets de fête, avec les appels et les articles qui disent la raison et la signification profonde de l'hommage aux sacrifiés de jadis."). This type of reminder of the geographical extent of the celebration becomes common in the following years and decades. See, for example, *La Presse* (Montreal), 25 May 1922, 11, 21 and 23 May 1942, 36.

58 "Pour nous tous, [Dollard] peut être, par-dessus les frontières, par-dessus les divergences locales, un lien, un principe d'unité supérieure." See also *Le Devoir*, 26 May 1922, 1. It is interesting to observe that despite these claims,

"la fête de Dollard" was never actually talked about in *L'Évangéline*, Acadian New Brunswick's most important newspaper during the years observed here. In a striking parallel, *L'Évangéline* also did not publish a single article on Empire Day during the whole period. One might say that Acadians seemed to be living in "splendid isolation" as far as patriotic celebrations went.

59 It should be noted that the French formulation is ambiguous as to whether it is "a" national holiday or "the" national holiday. *Le Devoir* (Montreal), 24 May 1922, 3 ("La fête de Dollard, désormais fête nationale").

60 Ibid., 26 May 1922, 2 ("La fête de Dollard a définitivement pris tous les caractères d'une fête véritablement nationale.").

61 *Le Droit* (Ottawa), 19 May 1932, 19 ("La fête de Dollard n'est pas seulement la fête de la jeunesse, elle est celle de toute la race, de toutes les classes, de tous les âges.").

62 *La Presse* (Montreal), 26 May 1952, 24. In this particular case, it was Gérard Thibault, MNA for Montréal-Mercier and "representative for the provincial authorities" for the day ("la fête du 24 mai est peut-être la plus importante au point de vue de l'action nationale").

63 On this episode, see Groulx, *Pièges de la mémoire*, 249–57.

64 Published in both *Le Droit* (Ottawa), 16 May 1932, 3 and *La Liberté*, 18 May 1932, 3 ("[il faut] accorder à cette fête [beaucoup] de solennité, ne serait-ce que pour venger la mémoire de ce héros national des attaques dont elle a été en butte, en ces derniers temps").

65 *Le Droit* (Ottawa), 30 May 1932, 2 ("[Dollard] n'est pas un aventurier légendaire comme certains professeurs d'une Université [sic] anglaise le prétend, mais bien un personnage historique qui est l'une de nos gloires nationales.").

66 *La Presse* (Montreal), 24 May 1922, 4 ("C'est aujourd'hui la fête de l'Empire britannique, celle de notre mère patrie … dont la durée et la force continuent d'étonner l'univers. Les Canadiens, sans distinction de nationalités ou de religions, s'associent dans un même sentiment de joie et de prière avec la masse du peuple britannique… Pour nous, Canadiens-français, la fête de l'Empire est encore la fête de Dollard des Ormeaux et de ses [illegible] vaillants camarades du Long Sault… Si le Canada constitue aujourd'hui l'un des plus beaux fleurons de la Couronne britannique, cela est dû au dévouement et à l'héroïsme de Dollard et de ses braves … qui ont sauvé la Nouvelle France] des barbares.").

67 *Le Droit* (Ottawa), 25 May 1932, 2 ("Il a fait beau hier en la fête de l'Empire et pour nous, de Dollard aussi.").

68 *La Presse* (Montreal), 23 May 1942 ("C'est devenu la coutume d'associer dans un même tribut national, le 24 mai, la mémoire de l'auguste reine

Victoria ... et, dans notre pays, la mémoire de Dollard des Ormeaux et de ses compagnons... Il y a en effet dans ces deux commémorations de quoi nourrir largement notre patriotisme et notre dévouement à la chose publique.").

69 Ibid., 24 May 1952, 32 ("Hommage à Victoria et à Dollard! L'avenir paraîtra plus sûr aussi longtemps que les vertus et les qualités qu'ils ont incarnées imprègneront la nation et l'appuieront dans ses initiatives.").

70 The expression "la fête de la Reine" is a very common way to denominate May 24th in francophone Canada.

71 Throughout the first three quarters of the century, one can find advertisements for outings by boat or train (see, for example, *La Presse* (Montreal), 10 May 1902; *Le Temps d'Ottawa*, 10 May 1902, 3), *Le Manitoba* (St Boniface), 7 May 1902, 3; 22 May 1922, 4; *La Presse*, 21 May 1952, 26; *Le Devoir* (Montreal), 21 May 1952, 7. One can also find multiple ads for "Tout ce qu'il faut pour rendre la fin de semaine plus agréable, que vous restiez chez vous ou que vous alliez en dehors de la ville" (promised by Chez Ogilvy in *La Presse*, 22 May 1942, 19), mostly sportswear (for example, see *Le Temps*, 24 May 1902, 1; 21 May 1907, 4); *La Presse*, 23 May 1922, 20; *Le Droit* (Ottawa), 22 May 1922, 6; *La Presse*, 22 May 1942, 2), and easy-to-carry meal items (for example, see *La Presse*, 21 May 1942, 12; 18 May 1962, 3).

72 Dollard was also used in First World War recruitment posters, but did not figure nearly so prominently in the army's symbolic arsenal.

73 *Le Devoir* (Montreal), 20 May 1942, 9 ("Les autorités religieuses ont approuvé avec empressement le geste des autorités militaires qui désirent rendre un hommages [sic] guerrier splendide à ce jeune soldat chrétien; car la jeunesse d'aujourd'hui combat à son tour la barbarie, toujours identique sous les changements de nom et de forme.").

74 *La Presse* (Montreal), 20 May 1942, 17; *La Presse*, 23 May 1942, 39 ("un vaste déploiement militaire" and "un appel aux braves").

75 "Déclaration de l'ACJC," *Le Devoir* (Montreal), 22 May 1942, 10. Here is an excerpt: "Never, until last year, did federal authorities consider it useful to do something to honour Dollard's memory or to cite him as an example for youth... This year ..., rather than offer its collaboration to the ACJC, the minister of National Defence asked the ACJC to collaborate with his organization... French Canadians do not accept all of the injustices that they encounter in all of the departments in Ottawa... French Canadian youth does not reach the same conclusions as the Canadian army when pondering Dollard's heroic act. Neither is it convinced by the willingness of the English element to celebrate the memory of this hero." ("Jamais, jusqu'à l'an dernier, les autorités fédérales se sont-elles avisées de faire

quelque chose pour honorer la mémoire de Dollard en le citant en
exemple à la jeunesse... Cette année ..., plutôt que d'offrir sa collaboration
à l'ACJC, le ministre de la Défense nationale demandait à l'ACJC de
collaborer avec son organisation... Les Canadiens français n'admettent pas
les injustices dont ils sont l'objet dans tous les départements à Ottawa...
La jeunesse canadienne-française ne tire pas les mêmes conclusions que
l'armée canadienne de ce fait héroïque. Et elle n'est pas *convaincue* non plus
du désir de l'élément anglais de célébrer la mémoire de ce héros.")

76 *Le Devoir* (Montreal), 20 May 1942, 9.

77 *La Presse* (Montreal), 23 May 1942, 27; *Le Devoir* (Montreal), 22 May 1942, 10.

78 *Le Devoir* (Montreal), 25 May 1942, 6. The squabbling speakers were
Brigadier-General Panet and Senator Athanase David.

79 *La Liberté et le Patriote* (Winnipeg), 20 May 1942, 3, 4; ibid., 27 May 1942, 5.

80 *La Presse* (Montreal), 21 May 1952, 37; 26 May 1952, 5.

81 Eric Hobsbawm, "Introduction: Inventing Traditions," in *The Invention of
Tradition*, ed. Eric Hobsbawm and Terence Ranger (Cambridge: Cambridge
University Press, 1983), 1–14.

6 Love the Empire, Love Yourself? Empire Day, Immigration, and the Role of Britishness in Anglo-Canadian Identity, 1920–1955

BRITTNEY ANNE BOS AND ALLISON MARIE WARD

A family of four huddles together for strength, eyes set forward on their new land. A girl clutches her father, while a boy carries an axe, face determinately set ahead. The father urges the group on, new land ordnance in hand; the mother clings to her waist and almost hesitates. The family is dishevelled, having faced expulsion from their previous home and arriving on uncultivated land. Despite the hardships left behind and those in front of them, the father hurries everyone along, insisting that their land, given by the generous Crown, is just ahead. An embodiment of settlement, together this group of four was intended to represent the United Empire Loyalists (UEL) and their determination in the face of hardship as they arrived in Upper Canada. Unveiled in 1929 as a part of Empire Day celebrations in Hamilton, Ontario, the monument was a piece of public education on imperial greatness and the strength of the empire and its subjects. With this portrayal of both hardships and determined strength, imperial subjects of the twentieth century were educated on the British values embodied by these builders of Upper Canada. Thus, the unveiling of this monument on Empire Day was fitting and was representative of the intent of the holiday in educating all Canadians about not only the greatness of the empire but about the continuing role of Canadians in fostering its future strength.

As discussed in chapter 4, Empire Day blossomed from a civic, to a national, and finally to an inter-Commonwealth observance, intended to instruct young people on the values of the British Empire. Taking Hamilton, the birthplace of Empire Day, as a case study, this chapter examines the educational campaigns directed at the public and how these were intended to shape young Canadians' conceptions of themselves. In the preceding chapter, Joel Belliveau and Marcel Martel demonstrate the importance of the local context of Empire Day, with reference to French Canada. In contrast, Hamilton's strong British cultural connections and rapidly diversifying population provides an excellent example of the changes that Empire Day underwent as the relationship of empire to Canadian identity changed. The largely British city of Hamilton had based its culture and identity around its UEL heritage, which was held up proudly by its growing middle-class population from supposed founding families. For these people, Empire Day served as a touchstone and celebration of their own heritage and connection to the greater British past. However, as a result of business and industrial expansion, as well as a national push for immigration, by 1931 one fifth of the city's population was non-British. By this time, Empire Day began to be viewed by its main propagators as an important instructive opportunity for indoctrinating the children of recent immigrants in the British way of life celebrated in Canada, from its culture to its governmental structures, through play and active participation in preserving the symbolism of empire.

Previous studies of Empire Day have suggested that these celebrations had meaning only "as long as the majority of English-speaking Canadians could equate Canadian nationalism and British Imperialism."[1] However, our examination argues that the meaning of Empire Day was more flexible than has been previously supposed. By considering the connections between changing demographics and social conditions, in conjunction with the commemorative ceremonies of Empire Day, this chapter interrogates how this local holiday took on national importance. By considering the commemorative activities that promoted collective memory, but also those that fed counter-memory, this chapter examines the complex relationship between changing populations that is revealed in the celebration of this holiday. These tangled memories and commemorations mirror the social changes of the Canadian nation and reflect shifting notions of Canadian identity.

Including the Immigrant "Other" in the Age of Empire

Beginning with the new century, Canada welcomed unprecedented numbers of immigrants from outside the British Empire, and immigration increased over the interwar period.[2] Within its social, legal, and political landscape, Canada had traditionally shaped its ideas of respectability and acceptability around a strong culture of white, British heritage.[3] As Daniel Coleman discusses in *White Civility: The Literary Project of English Canada*, by the mid-twentieth-century, "popular images of cooperative, pan-ethnic Britishness [informed] the Canadian concept of White civility: [including] 'Britishness' – as a form of government, as a union of formerly hostile peoples, as a civilization."[4] The growing immigrant population presented a challenge to this dominant notion of how Canada should function, and, as this study of Empire Day demonstrates, Canada's educational leaders were confronted with how to incorporate this group into their commemorations and learning opportunities.

Hamilton was certainly growing as well. Its population increased by 55.7% in 1901–11, by 39.3% in 1911–21, and by 36.3% in 1921–31.[5] This growth was owing to rural-to-urban migration fed by the city's growing industries and to an increasing number of immigrants choosing the city because of that same promise of employment. As a result of this immigration boom, Hamilton was becoming more diverse. By 1931, statistically significant numbers of immigrants called the city home. In a population of 155,547 were, according to the 1931 census, 5,217 Italians, 4,356 Germans, and 4,326 Poles.[6] The Hungarians, French (including both French Canadians and recent French immigrants), Dutch, and "Hebrews" all had populations of over 2,000, and there were over 1,000 of both Ukrainians and Rumanians.[7] These populations made a visible mark on Hamilton's landscape, settling in consolidated neighbourhoods that spread from the centre to the east of the north end of the city.[8] Given this diverse and constantly growing and changing population, the commemoration of Empire Day became an important tool for reinforcing British power structures in the city. Empire Day celebrations in Hamilton were a method by which to instil particular social values within a changing demographic, and these values to the physical space of Hamilton. The popular press made frequent reference in the interwar years to the pride Hamiltonians should take in the origins of Empire Day and the continued grand celebration put on in the city.[9] In 1929, a local paper stated that "Hamilton more than any other city has reason for showing its enthusiasm on this occasion."[10] Empire Day and Hamilton went hand in hand; therefore, to be connected with the physical space of Hamilton meant a connection with the values of Empire Day.

Although public memory is often constructed and reproduced by those in power, subordinate groups do not always simply buy into nationalist rhetoric. As demonstrated by two case studies from the early twentieth century in diverse North American cities, foreign-born populations often used public spectacles to promote their own communities. Writing about the Diamond Jubilee of Confederation celebration in Winnipeg, Robert Cupido considers the participation of large immigrant communities in pageants, parades, and other nationalist displays. By specifically targeting young foreign-born residents, the Diamond Jubilee was intended to create "true Canadians."[11] However, many immigrant groups were able to challenge official meanings and hegemonic Anglo-conformity by displaying their own cultural traditions in a public setting.[12] Similarly, in his consideration of public memory in Cleveland, John Bodnar explores the relationship between commemorations of the past and the large immigrant communities of that midwestern American city. Bodnar argues that ethnic leaders sought a middle ground from where they could recognize the cultural traditions of their community members while still appealing to their American peers.[13] Based on the source materials considered for this chapter, it is unclear to what extent non-British communities in Hamilton were able to assert their independence within the festivities of Empire Day. Nonetheless, given the striking population changes in the city during the first few decades of the twentieth century, "foreign values" were certainly evident in the city's celebration of Empire Day, and targeting these non-British values became one of the primary functions of this national holiday in Hamilton.

Educating the Public on the Changing Importance of Empire Day

Empire Day was primarily intended for the education of youth through the city's school system; however, the general public was also a target of imperial rhetoric.[14] Nearly every year in the interwar period, the *Hamilton Herald* and *Hamilton Spectator* published at least one informative editorial on the importance of Empire Day.[15] Notably, the coverage of this holiday dramatically decreased during the Second World War and then nearly disappeared in the postwar period.[16] Yet, between the wars, the extensive newspaper coverage served three functions. First, it was an important method of social education that primarily targeted adults outside the formal school system (although many editorials were titled "for young people"). Based on their discourse, these newspapers were intended largely for the British-origin population of Hamilton, but they also served as an educational tool for immigrants who could read English. Second, these articles covered the changing importance of Empire Day within both the imperial context and the local context of Hamilton. Articles from the early 1920s stressed the importance of continued allegiance and military drills by local students to demonstrate their discipline, while those from the late 1920s focused on linking consumerism to support for the empire. The 1930s promoted a stronger connection with past traditions and the glory of the future, while clear references were made to the escalating crisis in the motherland. Articles from the Second World War emphasized the importance of patriotism and of being united by imperial values, while the postwar period briefly reaffirmed the victory of Britishness over opposing forces. Finally, the articles reveal the links between specific social values and the British Empire that were promoted through the celebration of Empire Day and suggest, as well, the suppression of any dissent. The coverage of Empire Day, and specifically the coverage intended to educate the public about the importance of the holiday, reveal the significance of public memory in reinforcing social values.

Empire Day celebrations immediately following the First World War recognized the importance of imperial solidarity but also the continued conditioning of younger generations for defence. From 1925 to 1933, both the *Hamilton Herald* and the *Hamilton Spectator* reported on the public school cadet parades through the streets.[17] Thousands of cadets would file through the streets and place wreaths at the First World War cenotaph and often at the statue to Queen Victoria. In 1925, the *Spectator* observed: "Young and old were thrilled at the scene at the cenotaph where 2,200 cadets gave the salute. None could have failed to be impressed by the scene of animation, of marching and counter-marching... In their khaki uniforms the cadets made a fine sight."[18] This symbolic recognition of the Great War and the British Empire by the younger generation confirmed their future role in preserving imperial glory. In addition, the military drills themselves, often performed with a precision noted by the press, were a method of controlling and disciplining the youth and steeping them not only in militarism but also in British values. In 1928, an article in the *Herald* remarked on the marchers, calling them "young Canadians proud of their heritage of British blood and tradition."[19] In 1932, they were described as making "a brave showing at the review, well trained and smart appearing."[20] As remarked in the popular press, these drills were a link between past and future and served to confine public memory within the empire.

In the late 1920s, both newspapers wrote about a "buy empire" campaign that coincided with the national holiday. Through advertisements and editorials, Hamiltonians were encouraged to use their purchasing power to help support the empire by the strengthening its economy.[21] Specifically targeted at American manufacturers, this campaign sought to educate the public on the role of individuals within the empire.[22] Similar to school curriculum that emphasized the importance of individual actions by future citizens, the "buy empire" campaign encouraged participation through economic action. Individual action was emphasized in a *Spectator* editorial: "To buy Canadian and imperial goods is to contribute in a direct way to the welfare of our country and the Empire, and so to increase our own prosperity."[23] While it did not differentiate between British and foreign-born Canadians, the article encouraged every shopper to contribute to imperial success. In 1929, the movement picked up additional momentum when the governor general was named its patron.[24] In a response to "Empire Shopping Week," publicized in the *Herald* in the same year, a "Canadian shopper" appealed to the connection between patriotic spirit and economic action: "I don't want to take up too much of your space, but buying Canadian and empire goods is of such vast importance to everyone, not only for one week, but for all times, that no true Canadian would miss the opportunity of keeping her money within the empire."[25] As the writer captured in her letter, buying within the empire meant being part of the empire, and it was something all people could or should do, even if their values were not represented in Empire Day.

One of the last acts associated with the celebration of Empire Day in the 1920s was the unveiling of the UEL monument (see figure 6.1). Donated by the Mills family, prominent Hamilton business owners and UEL descendants, this monument stood as a permanent reminder of the significance of Empire Day and its interwar rhetoric in Hamilton. Representative of the vast numbers of British migrants fleeing the United States after the American Revolution, the monument to the Loyalists embodied the British values promoted during Empire Day. Brian Osborne, who argues that monuments focus attention of citizens on a particular place and event in order to convey dominant values, recognizes the power of monuments as nationalist symbols.[26] These values were summed up in the *Spectator*'s coverage of the unveiling, in which the monument was described as "the wonderful work of sculptural art, symbolic of hope, faith and determination."[27] In his main address, prominent Hamilton politician and UEL member Colonel Charles R. McCullough captured the common purpose of Empire Day and the erection of the monument – to promote shared values of the past, present, and future: "We assemble on a day set apart to celebrate the great fact of a united Empire (the preservation of which long ago possessed the minds and animated the private and public acts of the UEL), to

6.1 The United Empire Loyalists monument, designed by Sydney March, unveiled May 23 1929 in Hamilton, Ontario, Canada. Photo by Brittney Anne Bos, 2011.

vindicate their character, to extol their principles, to praise their patriotism and to unveil and dedicate this imperishable memorial in testimony of their devotion to King and constitution."[28] In describing the story of the Loyalists in an "Editorial for Young People," the *Spectator* remarked that "it is necessary to think of them as enduring great hardships and making tremendous sacrifices for their principles, if we are to get a proper conception of the supreme service they rendered the Empire."[29] The UEL story, filled with hardship and self-sacrifice, and embodied in the monument, was the perfect one to tell future generations in order to educate them on the virtues expected of a citizen of the empire.

The transition from the 1920s to 1930s witnessed a slight shift in imperial rhetoric, while nonetheless maintaining the promotion of the same shared values across the empire. By the mid-1930s, the cadets program was phased out of public schools. Despite the lack of a military-style parade, students still gathered to demonstrate the discipline they learned at school through a demonstration of sports. Newspaper coverage was quick to point out that this new spectacle was similar to its predecessor. The first year after the abolition of the cadets program, the *Spectator* reported that "this athletic program was indicative of the measures taken by the Board of education to develop the youth of the city in bodily perfection and discipline since the abolition of cadet training in city schools."[30] The next year, a similar article stated that the physical demonstration "was a thrilling sight, a patriotic demonstration which proved that the abolition of the cadet corps had not dealt the death blow to the fostering of a love of country."[31] Despite the disappearance of military parades, physical demonstrations were still understood as part of disciplining the imperial body and proving patriotism. Yearly celebrations throughout the interwar period were also accompanied by the singing of patriotic hymns and anthems. The "Maple Leaf Forever," "O Canada," and "God Save the King" appeared on the program for every celebration covered in the popular press. The singing of these anthems, usually by a chorus of 3,000 children's voices, confirmed the patriotic purpose of the physical displays.

In the 1930s, informative editorials on Empire Day began to reflect the changing world. In some ways they were similar to their 1920s counterparts, promoting the continued glory of the empire through individual actions. In 1935, readers of the *Spectator* were reminded that "the patriotic spirit thus instilled into the minds and breasts of the young is a most valuable factor in the fostering of common ideals and in strengthening allegiance to the flag and to the throne."[32] As in the 1920s, readers were told that their individual actions and thoughts had an impact on the future of the empire. The *Herald* reminded the (assumed British-origin) public that it was their duty to spread imperial values to foreign-born communities: "We are constantly in danger of forgetting these things and our forgetfulness leads our immigrating brethren to grow up in ignorance of the spirit and fashion of our national life."[33] While this rhetoric was similar to that in editorials printed in the previous decade, the 1930s brought new challenges for the empire, and these were reflected in the press. The public was increasingly reminded to remain loyal to the British Empire and the important values that it stood for:

> What the Union Jack stands for is not warlike aggression, but justice and the maintenance of peace. It represents the highest ideals of democratic progress; there is no danger that to instil into young minds a proper respect and love of the flag will breed a martial imperialism, however much its history may foster the virtues of courage, of endurance and fidelity to what is noblest in human relationships.[34]

In another case, history was recalled in order to explain present circumstances, while the unity of the empire was promoted:

> The world has had much too much of warfare to become enthusiastic over vainglorious boasts of military aggrandisement, and what the British people are celebrating in the Mother Country and throughout the dominions to-day is something entirely different from that concept of imperialism. In these troublous times the British Empire is regarded rather as the chief hope of international peace and understanding.[35]

As the 1930s progressed, it was made clear to readers of the popular press that conforming to British values was significant not only for them as individuals but also for the threatened empire as a whole.

When the Second World War broke out, this rhetoric was further amplified. Coverage of Empire Day throughout the war emphasized the important duty of Canadians, as members of the empire, in defending not only its physical territory but also the values the empire represented. Despite a similarity in the message, the Empire Day coverage does subtly shift as the war progresses. In the 1940 coverage, the coming attack on Britain is anticipated and strong language is employed to contrast the "good" of the empire and the "evil" of the Axis powers:

> A formidable foe, who as sworn to destroy British hegemony, and is employing every devilish device at this command to accomplish that end, has succeeded in overrunning western Europe and is now preparing to launch a desperate assault on the Motherland, whose sons and daughters stand, firm and undismayed, ready to deal with the intruder and whatever he may send.[36]

That same year, Colonel George A. Drew (later premier of Ontario) spoke confidently at an Empire Day event of the empire's coming victory. He predicted that the war would serve to unite the empire and that, out of the devastation, an even greater empire would emerge.[37] The coverage in the following year was still decidedly patriotic and uplifting in tone, with editorials continuing to rally people of the empire and herald the coming victory.[38] By 1942, as the war continued to drag on, the mood had become more sombre, with fewer striking adverbs and adjectives. There were no rousing speeches or discussions of virtue or victory; in fact, only one short editorial appeared for Empire Day in 1942, which primarily covered the history of the holiday. While 1943 contained a single rousing and patriotic piece, there was no coverage whatsoever in 1944.

As with prewar coverage, the editorials and articles on Empire Day during the Second World War emphasized the values of the British Empire and the need to impart these virtues on the leaders of tomorrow. These virtues are laid out in an editorial for young people in 1940: "They can be roughly summed up as the graces of life. We are told that the old courtesy and politeness, the high code of honour, which is best defined by the French phrase 'noblesse oblige' are out of place to-day. That people have neither the time nor the inclination to practice them. The more's the pity, if this be so."[39] In the coverage of Empire Day during the Second World War, emphasis is placed on the peace-loving ways of the British Empire compared to the tyranny and aggression of the Axis powers. It becomes clear to readers that the war is a result of German aggression and British defence, and eventually will result in the triumph of "good," which is tied to the natural qualities of the British race.

> The young should take heed at the inspiring examples of unselfish sacrifice and courage which these cruel tests are producing, not only in the fighting forces, but in the civilian population as well, giving emphatic denial to the taunts of jealous rivals that the virility of the Empire had gone, that its citizens were a decadent race unworthy of their rich inheritances, and incapable of maintaining it.[40]

The importance of imparting these values to the youth of the empire is consistently emphasized in wartime Empire Day coverage, but youth were also imbued with the special task of securing the empire's future, something hinted at during the interwar years. While the values from the interwar period remain consistent through the outbreak of war, the juxtapositions of good and evil, the virtues of the British race, and the importance of developing leaders of the future gain increased importance, particularly at the beginning and end of the war.

After the Allies secured victory in Europe in early May 1945, the mood was once again victorious and celebratory on Empire Day. The primary article of the year cited this Empire Day as particularly significant, owing to the recent victory: "Empire Day and Victoria Day come this year with a significance that is perhaps deeper than usual and stirs a sense of pride in what the British Empire has achieved in the long struggle against tyranny."[41] The triumph of good over evil was once again emphasized in 1946. With an eye to the future, editorialists called on the youth of the nation to continue spreading the values of the empire: "The fight has been won, but it is more essential than ever that the grand ideals which inspired the effort and brought it through to a successful conclusions should be kept clearly before the minds of our youth."[42] While these "grand ideals" are not named in the article, it is clear that the education of youth is considered a primary method of achieving future world peace. The triumph of British values also implicitly reminds the immigrant populations of Hamilton of the importance of educating their children in the "Canadian" way, a primary purpose of Empire Day that is re-emphasized following the war.

After the Second World War, coverage of Empire Day nearly disappeared from the *Hamilton Spectator*. Between 1947 and 1954, only a single article appeared in that paper regarding Empire Day. This 1949 article recounts the history of Empire Day, including the leadership of Clementina Fessenden Trenholme, but contains no rousing patriotic speeches, nor does it discuss the virtues of the British Empire that were so prominent in previous coverage.

Despite its short history as an educational holiday, Empire Day was covered in the popular press as an opportunity to emphasize British values and shape public memory. However, the interwar period and the years of the Second World War witnessed a shift in how this rhetoric was framed for the public in both the press and educational materials produced by the board of education. This shift in opinion changed how Empire Day was celebrated. The coverage in the *Herald* and the *Spectator* demonstrated that, while the promotion of British values and the continued glory of the empire remained paramount goals, changing social situations (locally, nationally, and internationally) required that Empire Day celebrations in schools, and the educational materials used for those purposes, to adapt. Youth were continually encouraged to participate in Empire Day activities in the hopes of becoming more productive citizens, while the general (English-reading) public was also expected to promote similar "British" values. While the coming of the Second World War re-ignited the need for such patriotism, particularly within an increasingly ethnically diverse population, the war also eventually saw the decline of the holiday in the popular press.

Educating Immigrant Children for the Betterment of Themselves and the Empire

Beginning on 16 August 1930, Hamilton was the host of the first British Empire Games, the predecessor of the modern Commonwealth Games. "To-day," waxed the *Spectator*, "is the day for which not only Hamilton but all parts of the world where flutters the Union Jack have been waiting."[43] This event was intended to bring together all of the countries in the empire for a week of sports and friendly competition, in what "has been best described as a 'great family party.'"[44] The event was explicitly advertised as being open to any citizen of any dominion or former dominion who shared a dedication to British ideals. The *Spectator* highlighted the diversity of the attendants: "From all corners of the world, competitors have come, eager, of course, to reflect credit on their respective colonies, but proud of the blood ties that bind them in a great entity."[45] Discussions of the games in the press focused on bringing these diverse peoples together in shared values of good sportsmanship, honesty, and athletic skill, all things that would bring pride to the empire. These characteristics reflected ideals surrounding imperial unity. One did not have to be British by birth so long as one shared in the common goals of the empire and was willing to work towards furthering its greatness.

The Ontario Department of Education recognized that, in order to keep Empire Day relevant, it must seek to include and incorporate the growing group of immigrants and their second-generation families. In this, the department diverged significantly from an exclusionary view, which considered that immigrant groups had a "racial" inability to integrate. Instead, it viewed these people, especially children in English-language schools, as viable future citizens of the empire, ready for instruction. Prior to 1930, educational booklets prepared by the department for Empire Day had emphasized British heritage, but newer programs sought to inculcate students who were new residents of Canada into the imperial order. These practices were emphasized in province-wide curriculum, which was whole-heartedly embraced in Hamilton. By 1931, Department of Education policy, as described by R.J. Wright, a Hamilton principal, "stress[ed] the matter of the Empire, its ideals and standards in the training of children, of whom between 35 and 40 per cent attending this school are of foreign parentage."[46]

In the latter part of the 1920s, this change began to creep slowly into curriculum. The 1928 program still alluded to British heritage and stock, but it made explicit references to French Canadians and immigrants as potential British subjects, and spoke more of good behaviour than of a single good heritage. "An Eminent French Canadian" was quoted as saying, "I am ... proud to be a sharer in that great work of advancing peace and progress throughout the world, for which the British Empire stands."[47] This message of inclusion suggested that immigrants could overcome their former ethnic identities and, through working together, could become good citizens of the British Empire. These more inclusive lessons, accompanied by instructive examples, became common features in Empire Day teaching aids, adding immigrant stories to the British one.

It is apparent from popular press coverage in the interwar years that immigrant children were special targets of Empire Day observance. If their stories were integrated within the programs in later years, it was also assumed that they would be included within the broader empire-building project. A method to encourage this integration was reverence for the flag and national anthems. According to the *Hamilton Spectator* in 1921, "the flag will be a special object of veneration in the schools to-day ... the board of education being strongly impressed with the value of Empire Day exercises as being helpful in transforming the very considerable number of foreign-born pupils into good Canadians."[48] As the years progressed, the title "British subject" came to represent those that adhered to particular values, regardless of whether they were Canadian born: "No naturalized Canadian, no matter how far back he can trace his origin to native soil, could object to being called a British subject... But the definition of a 'British subject' is of much broader significance, signallizing ideals and a tradition which reach far beyond the confines of any national spirit, genuine or bogus."[49]

George S. Henry, who was the provincial minister of education in 1931, made it clear that a more inclusive Empire Day should communicate the importance of shared responsibilities of imperial citizenship. Like many leading politicians of the day, he was concerned that immigrants be inculcated with both the benefits and the responsibilities associated with being a British subject and member of the empire:

> Under the British Flag lives one-fifth of the world's population. These peoples are joint heirs of traditions of justice and freedom that have "slowly broadened down from precedent to precedent." Varied in Race and Creed they enjoy in common the universal prestige and protection of the British Crown. Sometimes, I fear, they are apt to forget the responsibilities that go with great privileges.[50]

The rhetoric of that year's publication also reflected the changed audience that Henry and Principal R.J. Wright observed in Hamilton classrooms and those across Ontario. "Love of Country" replaced notions about shared heritage and kinship connections to the "motherland." Learned virtues, such as patriotic citizenship, replaced inborn ideals of Britishness.

One of the closing stories in the Department of Education's 1931 publication for Empire Day explicitly included non-Anglo and non-Franco Canadians in the narrative of Canada's upwards progress. "The Remarkable Story of an Immigrant Family" told the story of the Crolls, a Russian-Jewish couple who had moved from Moscow to Windsor in 1906 with their six children. The eldest son became mayor of Windsor, and the family also included a doctor, two dentists, and a lawyer; even the only daughter enjoyed a successful career as a dental hygienist. In the midst of the Great Depression, the moral, that an immigrant family could succeed as a result of self-determination and hard work, was intended to serve as a broader lesson outside the immigrant community: "The record of that family is one which should inspire not only their own thrifty and industrial race, but all other Canadians who face adversity and mean to conquer it."[51] This message, while still clearly separating the immigrant "other" from the Canadian-born, suggested that even these outsiders could become imperial citizens. It would be repeated in later years, especially during the Second World War, when countries from across the empire were once again called to serve the cultural motherland. The idea of being able to *learn* to be an imperial citizen, instead of being born into it, remained an important goal for Empire Day in the schools until specific educational programming for the day was phased out. Such goals reflected the changing population landscape and a desire to aid immigrant "others" in becoming productive Canadian citizens like the Croll Family.

Despite the inclusion of diverse groups in Empire Day lessons, it was clear that these groups needed to conform to British values and that these values would connect them with the virtues of the British race. Depictions in the popular press promoted the superiority of such values and the importance of carrying them into the future. In 1933, in a period of increased economic and political strain, the *Hamilton Spectator* stated, "Unquestionably, the Anglo-Saxon races are destined to play a crucial part in world re-establishment on a saner and happier foundation of human relationships."[52] Two years before, in the *Herald*, the annual editorial on Empire Day reminded future generations of their responsibilities in fostering British values: "'Let him that is greatest among you be the servant of all' was the injunction that made civilization what it is in grace and blessing."[53] Although imperial loyalty was important, spreading the values and taking on responsibilities of empire was also an important component passed on to the youth of Hamilton.[54]

An Empire Comes Together: Diversity in the Second World War

A diverse empire was a symbolic virtue in the interwar years. However, when the Second World War broke out in 1939, this wealth of peoples was a necessary asset to the war effort. Imperial subjects became foot soldiers in the fight to protect democracy and the British way of life that they all supposedly cherished. In this changed atmosphere, even the most remote members of the British Empire were cast as part of the imperial family. Any self-governing dominion was cast as a "cousin," who shared a common ancestor in Britain. Again, any person or country that respected British democracy could be a part of this circle. This family included both the rich and the poor, as adherence to political values was more significant than material resources. The minister of education, Duncan MacArthur, advised teachers that "more important than its material resources has been the fidelity of the Empire to the practices of democracy. That has been the real and effective cement of Empire."[55] This message was echoed in a reprint of George VI's Empire Day speech from 1939, which was circulated to Ontario students during the war: "It is not in power or wealth alone, nor in dominion over other peoples that the true greatness of an Empire consists… The end is freedom, justice, and peace in equal measure for all, secure against attack from without and from within."[56]

The wartime promotion of the image of a more culturally and racially varied empire extended to educational materials sent to Ontario's classrooms for Empire Day. The 1942 booklet prepared by the provincial Department of Education gave the dominions colonized by white, British settlers a place of primacy, with references to New Zealand, Australia, and South Africa receiving two-page spreads. However, in a marked change from earlier materials, it made room for other countries as well. "East Africans, Jews, and Arabs have fought bravely in Africa and the Middle East; colonials from Nigeria, the Gold Coast, Sierra Leone, Aden, Malta, Barbados, and Malaya are manning British ships," the Department of Education advised readers, "and from the West Indies and West Africa have come volunteers to serve in the R.A.F."[57] This passing mention was not, the writers noted, out of a lack of respect for these contributions: "Space alone imposes restrictions on the listing of the aid of all those areas which are coloured red on the map of the world."[58] The image on the back cover of the booklet demonstrated the importance of these contributions, with the inclusion of the face of a darker-skinned soldier in a turban alongside a white soldier, sailor, nurse, and airman.[59] Implicit in this booklet was the idea not only that British virtues were attainable but also that school children should attain them in order, ultimately, to serve the British Empire, including by boosting military numbers.

Postwar educational materials continued to place Canadian contributions to the empire at the forefront while reminding students of the diversity of the group of nations that Canada was connected to. This message spread from the youngest students to the oldest, with the Department of Education suggesting the following as a discussion topic for third graders in 1949:

> The people of the Commonwealth and Empire live in many lands, hot or cold, wet or dry, flat or hilly, some like ours, some very different. They wear many different kinds of clothes and eat many different foods; they go to different churches and have different complexions. To make our Empire a happy family we should know what things are important about a person and try to see that it doesn't matter what his colour may be, what kind of clothes or house he has, or whether he travels by car or cart or camel. It does matter whether he is kind, honest, unselfish, helpful to others. We can be good citizens of Commonwealth and Empire by liking and helping all worthy people.[60]

This international focus was prevalent in postwar educational materials for Empire Day in Ontario. It had replaced curriculum materials that only described the benefits that colonies received from the mother country. For example, a play in the schoolbook entitled *The Changing Empire* featured "Inspector Co-operation," overseeing students dressed as Great Britain, Canada, Australia, New Zealand, South Africa, Muslim and Hindu India, Ceylon, Burma, Newfoundland, and "Others."[61] Such an approach matched the increasingly accepting tone of the Canadian government towards immigrants from outside of the British Empire and reflected attempts to harmonize relationships with many discontented former colonies. In an age where empire seemed increasingly irrelevant, the Department of Education worked to make it an appealing concept to Canada's growing population of children who had no British ancestors.

Conclusion

The monument depicting the determined and loyal family of four, crouched together in their defensive unit, was intended to make a permanent mark on the Hamilton landscape. The Loyalist monument, as conceived by Sydney March, was meant to be a final statement, a stone marker of the values of the United Empire Loyalists, standing the test of time from 1929 to eternity. It was not long, however, before the monument was moved to make way for the demolition of the old courthouse and the construction of the new in the early 1960s. The monument, like the empire itself, needed to adapt to modernity. The monument still stands, like the Commonwealth and the ever-present position of the monarchy in Hamilton, but in a new position, divorced from its original context, a fitting second chapter to a monument that was meant to embody the spirit of Empire Day.

By 1958, the sun was setting on the British Empire. As that institution collapsed and was reimagined as the British Commonwealth, Empire Day was renamed Commonwealth Day and lost much of the serious tone its early founders had felt was so important. One of the final Department of Education Empire Day booklets reflected the continued importance of immigrants and non-British Canadians to the nation's future. The message of the minister of education, J.W. Dunlop, to Ontario's teachers spoke of the lessons now open, thanks to the province's Anti-Discrimination Act, to all Ontarians: "Empire is really made up of a great family of strong independent nations along with colonies and dependencies of various kinds and sizes":

> Canadian citizenship is a great boon to all who enjoy its advantages and this is something which may properly be emphasized in our schools. It

might be well, as occasion presents itself, to remind our boys and girls that
in Canada there are no second-class citizens, since, at the 1954 session of
the Legislature of Ontario the Government passed an Anti-Discrimination
Act which ensures to all citizens of this Province the same rights no matter
what their colour, creed, or race may be.[62]

Clementina Fessenden Trenholme may not have recognized the
Ontario citizens of 1955, but it is clear that, until it ceased to exist,
Empire Day, as it was idealized in the province's curriculum, was still
meant to uphold, and to instil in the province's youth, the virtue of patriotism and knowledge of their national heritage – the very goals that
she had so idealized.

National celebrations serve as critical opportunities for residents and
citizens to imagine themselves as part of a larger community. They also
serve as opportunities for governments at all levels to provide instructive information about how they believe this image formation should
work. This instruction can occur by promoting the day as an official
holiday, through curriculum development, and through local program
planning. In the case of Empire Day in Hamilton, educational opportunities gradually expanded beyond the traditional crowd of British
nationalists and imperial descendants in an attempt to shape the children of a growing group of non-British immigrant into proper British subjects. These programs did not grant these subjects equality but
rather were promoted as a way to provide immigrant groups a passage
towards social, political, and cultural inclusion, often at the expense of
their own heritage. As Hamilton's ethnic make-up changed, these programs became increasingly important ways to reach out to a new group
of residents and shape how they imagined their investment in their
community. Drawing on the city's strong UEL connections, immigrant
groups were pulled into the ideal of imperial citizenship through the
games, songs, skits, and parades of Empire Day.

NOTES

1 Robert M. Stamp, "Empire Day in the Schools of Ontario: The Training of
   Young Imperialists," *Journal of Canadian Studies* 8, no. 3 (1973): 32.
2 Dominion Bureau of Statistics, *Census of Canada, 1951: Population, General
   Characteristics*, vol. 1 (Ottawa: Dominion Bureau of Statistics, 1953),
   table 52.

3 Constance Backhouse, *Colour-Coded: A Legal History of Racism in Canada, 1900–1950* (Toronto: Osgoode Society for Canadian Legal History, 1999), 9–11, 13; Ian McKay and Robin Bates, *In the Province of History: The Making of the Public Past in Twentieth-Century Nova Scotia* (Montreal: McGill-Queen's University Press, 2010), 8–16, 33–6.

4 Daniel Coleman, *White Civility: The Literary Project of English Canada* (Toronto: University of Toronto Press, 2006), 18–20.

5 Dominion Bureau of Statistics, *Census of Canada, 1941: Population by Local Subdivisions*, vol. 2 (Ottawa: Dominion Bureau of Statistics, 1944), table 17. Like cities across Canada, Hamilton's population growth was stymied by the Great Depression but would explode during the Second World War, when its industries drew in workers, swelling the city's population above 200,000.

6 W. Burton Hurd for the Dominion Bureau of Statistics, *Census of Canada, 1931: Racial Origins and Nativity of the Canadian People*, Monograph No. 4 (Ottawa: Dominion Bureau of Statistics, 1937), 204–5.

7 Ibid., 32–4.

8 J.W. Watson, "Urban Developments in the Niagara Peninsula," *Canadian Journal of Economics and Political Science* 9, no. 4 (November 1943): 485.

9 "School Cadets Pay Tribute to Empire Day," *Hamilton Herald*, 22 May 1926; "British Empire Celebrates Festival Started Here," ibid., 23 May 1931; "Thousands of Children Celebrate," ibid., 23 May 1933; "Empire Day Was Observed in Schools To-day," *Hamilton Spectator*, 23 May 1923; "Empire Day," ibid., 23 May 1929; "Empire Day Is Celebrated in Local Schools," ibid., 22 May 1931; "Honor Memory of Founder of Empire Day," ibid., 26 May 1931; "Empire Day," ibid., 22 May 1933; "Empire Day," ibid., 23 May 1934; "Empire Festivals," ibid., 22 May 1936.

10 "Empire Day," *Hamilton Spectator*, 23 May 1929.

11 Robert Cupido "Appropriating the Past: Pageants, Politics, and the Diamond Jubilee of Confederation" *Journal of the Canadian Historical Association* 9 (1998): 67

12 Ibid., 64.

13 John Bodnar, "Public Memory in an American City: Commemoration in Cleveland," in *Commemorations: The Politics of National Identity*, ed. John R. Gillis (Princeton, NJ: Princeton University Press, 1994), 83.

14 This chapter focuses its analysis on the two largest Hamilton newspapers of the period, the *Hamilton Spectator* and the *Hamilton Herald*. Despite a growing population, no significant ethnic presses existed in Hamilton during the period of study and therefore only the "popular press" is considered.

15 Due to archival limitations, 1921–24 was not covered in the *Hamilton Herald*, and thus the presence of editorials for these dates is unknown. The paper closed in 1936, and thus coverage ended. In the *Hamilton Spectator*, every year between 1920 and 1939 (except for 1938) featured at least one informative editorial on the meaning of Empire Day.

16 The *Hamilton Spectator* did not provide any coverage for Empire Day in 1944, although the other war years are covered (albeit very sparsely). Between 1946 and 1956, only 1947 and 1949 feature short articles on Empire Day.

17 It appears that cadet marches started in 1925 and were last covered in 1933. "School Cadets Pay Tribute to Empire Day," *Hamilton Herald*, 22 May 1926; "Cadets March Past Cenotaph on Empire Day," ibid., 25 May 1928; "Schools Feature Empire Exercises," ibid., 23 May 1930; "Four Thousand Cadets, Girls on Review," ibid., 25 May 1932; "Thousands of Children Celebrate," ibid., 23 May 1933; "Two Thousand Cadets March through City," *Hamilton Spectator*, 23 May 1925; "Empire Day Held in City Schools," ibid., 23 May 1927; "Impressive Parade by School Cadets," ibid., 23 May 1928; "Empire Day Is Celebrated in Public Schools," ibid., 23 May 1930; "Six Thousand Children Walk in Big Parade," ibid., 23 May 1932.

18 "Two Thousand Cadets March through City," *Hamilton Spectator*, 23 May 1925.

19 "Cadets March Past Cenotaph on Empire Day," *Hamilton Herald*, 25 May 1928.

20 "Four Thousand Cadets, Girls on Review," *Hamilton Herald*, 25 May 1932.

21 Both prior to and throughout the depression, the Hamilton-based labour papers the *Canadian Labor World* and the *Labor News* ran several issues with "Buy Empire"–themed banners and ran similar content. See, for example, the following articles in *Canadian Labor World*: "Cheap Labor Is a Menace to Industry," 31 January 1929; "Patronize Canadian Made Goods," 31 January 1929; "Hamilton's Annual 'Made in Canada' Exhibition," 28 February 1929; "Steady Employment," 29 May 1930; "Unemployment," 30 October 1930.

22 Hamilton manufacturers faced significant competition from the importation of American goods. The advent of cheaper travel also made cross-border excursions more popular. 'Buy Empire' was part of a larger campaign to encourage Canadians to keep their money within Canada and "buy local."

23 "Buy Empire Goods," *Hamilton Spectator*, 23 May 1929.

24 "Governor-General and Empire Day," *Hamilton Spectator*, 22 May 1929.

25 Letter to the editor, "Buy Empire Goods," *Hamilton Herald*, 27 May 1929.

26 Brian Osborne, "Constructing Landscapes of Power: The George-Etienne Cartier Monument," *Journal of Historical Geography* 24 (1998): 433

27 "Great Spirit Lives Again in Hamilton," *Hamilton Spectator*, 25 May 1929.

28 Ibid.

29 "U.E. Loyalists," *Hamilton Spectator*, 25 May 1929.

30 "Pageant of Youth Seen from Stadium," *Hamilton Spectator*, 23 May 1934.

31 "Young Canadians Reveal True Empire Spirit," ibid., 23 May 1935.

32 "Empire Day," ibid., 23 May 1935.

33 "The Empire Mission," *Hamilton Herald*, 23 May 1933.

34 "Empire Day," *Hamilton Spectator*, 22 May 1931.

35 "Empire Day," ibid., 23 May 1932.

36 "Empire Day," ibid., 23 May 1940.

37 "Drew Asserts British Navy Will Again Save the Empire," ibid., 24 May 1940.

38 "The Empire Stands as the Stronghold of Humanity," ibid., 23 May 1941; "Our Glorious Empire," ibid., 23 May 1941.

39 "The Victorian Spirit," ibid., 25 May 1940

40 "Our Glorious Empire," ibid., 23 May 1941

41 "The British Empire," ibid., 23 May 1945

42 "Empire Day," ibid., 23 May 1946

43 "To-day's the Day," ibid., 16 August 1930.

44 Ibid.

45 Ibid.

46 "Refuses to Sing National Anthem," ibid., 19 May 1931.

47 Department of Education, *Empire Day in the Schools of Ontario, Wednesday May 23rd 1928* (Toronto: Department of Education for Ontario, 1928).

48 "Empire Day," ibid., 23 May 1921.

49 "A British Subject," ibid., 21 May 1937.

50 Department of Education, *Empire Day in the Schools of Ontario, May 22, 1931* (Toronto: Department of Education, 1931), 13. During some years in the Depression and the Second World War, the Department of Education cut back on its elaborate publications (1931's had stretched across over fifty pages). It instead sent out two-page reminders on card stock that recommended that teachers reuse past year's publications for their instruction. See Department of Education, *Empire Day May 23rd, 1935: Greetings from the Minister of Education* (Toronto: Department of Education, 1935).

51 Department of Education, *Empire Day in the Schools of Ontario, May 22, 1931*, 48.

52 "Empire Day," *Hamilton Spectator*, 22 May 1933.

53 "Victoria Day," *Hamilton Herald*, 23 May 1931.

54 "Empire Day Was Observed in Schools To-day," *Hamilton Spectator*, 23 May 1923; "Empire Day Is Celebrated in Local Schools," ibid., 21 May 1931.

55 Department of Education, *Empire Day in the Schools of Ontario, May 22, 1942* (Toronto: Department of Education, 1942), 7.
56 Department of Education, *Empire Day in the Schools of Ontario, May 23, 1940* (Toronto: Department of Education, 1940).
57 Department of Education, *Empire Day in the Schools of Ontario, May 22, 1942*, 16.
58 Ibid.
59 Ibid., back cover.
60 Department of Education, *Empire Day in the Schools of Ontario, May 23, 1949* (Toronto: Department of Education, 1949), 5.
61 Ibid., 26.
62 Department of Education, *Empire Day in the Schools of Ontario, May 20, 1955* (Toronto: Department of Education, 1955), 2.

7 From Armistice to Remembrance: The Continuing Evolution of Remembrance Day in Canada

TERESA IACOBELLI

The eleventh hour of the eleventh day of the eleventh month is a time and date poetic in its symmetry. It is also a time and date enshrined in the national consciousness of Canadians. That this date, marking the end of the First World War, provides a natural point to pause for a few minutes of silence each year in order to remember Canada's war dead is today generally seen as appropriate by most Canadians. However, the acceptance of this date and the rituals associated with it has not always been universally agreed upon. Since 1918, the meaning and practice of Remembrance Day has evolved, and it has been shaped and reimagined by the forces of politics, culture, and special interests. As such, Remembrance Day provides a lens with which to examine a number of facets of Canada's past, including its military history, its social memory, and its policies towards veterans over the past one hundred years.

Several Canadian authors have touched on the evolution of Remembrance Day in wider works on war and remembrance. Foremost among these works has been Jonathan Vance's *Death So Noble*, published in 1997. Even with the passage of two decades, this book remains a definitive work on Canadian memory and the First World War. Vance explores a number of issues related to myth making and nation building, including the observance of Remembrance Day during the interwar period. He discusses the ways in which the day was observed and used by various groups, including business leaders, politicians, pacifists, and veterans, and concludes that, rather than being a day of peace, the day was used to honour those who had fought and also to reaffirm existing myths of war.[1] More recently, in *Warrior Nation*, authors Ian McKay and Jamie Swift argue that what they term "new warriors," whose members include conservative politicians, as well as a number of military historians and members of the media, have used familiar national symbols, including the rituals associated with the observance of Remembrance Day, to glorify militarism and rebrand Canada as a "warrior nation" rather than a "'peacekeeping nation." McKay and Swift point to the overtly militaristic rhetoric of many Remembrance Day speeches as an example of how Remembrance Day, and our national history more generally, has in recent years been co-opted for political purposes, including as a justification for Canada's participation in the recent war in Afghanistan.[2] In addition to works dealing specifically with Canadian military history, a body of literature on holidays more generally helps to draw interesting parallels between Remembrance Day and other holidays. For example, in Craig Heron and Steve Penfold's *The Workers' Festival: A History of Labour Day in Canada*, the authors show that Labour Day, like Remembrance Day, had its meaning change significantly over time in accordance with cultural and political contexts and owing to the power of specific interest groups, including business leaders, who played an important role in effecting those changes.[3]

On the fields of battle and on the home front, the armistice of 1918 was met with a combination of shock, sorrow for those lost, and, among the Allied nations, widespread relief and celebration. George Walter Adams, a young soldier from Toronto serving in the 7th Canadian Battalion, Canadian Railway Troops, noted the cessation of hostilities at 1100 hours in his 11 November diary entry, writing that, "Needless to say we are all tickled to death and there's been all sorts of celebrations during the day. Whale of a blow out in the officers [sic] mess last night. The next question is when will we get home." Back in Canada, Adam's mother, Emily, described the joy that overtook Toronto with the announcement of peace. Writing to her son four days after the news of the armistice broke, Emily Adams described the people of Toronto banging pots and pans at 4:30 a.m. in impromptu street parades and burning an effigy of the kaiser in a large bonfire.[4] The joy in Toronto was no doubt matched or surpassed by the citizens of Allied European nations. While on leave in Paris, Robert Shortreed observed that Parisians, depleted by four years of war on their soil, erupted in jubilation. In correspondence with his mother on 12 November 1918, Shortreed wrote, "Yesterday Paris was crazy with joy and streets were impassable for people. Today is going to be almost as bad. Flags are to be seen everywhere. The French way of showing their joy is to kiss everyone and few people escaped it yesterday. Of course the soldiers came in for their share."[5]

7.1 Crowds gather at the Toronto Star Building, 18 King Street West, to watch for bulletins announcing the Armistice. City of Toronto Archives, Item #1558, Fonds 1244, William James family fonds, 11 November 1918.

One year later, with the celebrations long over and mourning deeply entrenched in countless families, ideas on how to more permanently and appropriately mark the anniversary of the armistice were beginning to take shape across nations. Surprisingly, in Great Britain, a nation so deeply affected and scarred by the war, plans were somewhat haphazard and initially left to the discretion of individuals and families rather than to the state. While plans were well underway in 1919 to construct a cenotaph in London, little to no thought was initially given about a public ceremony of remembrance on 11 November. Evidencing this fact, Adrian Gregory, author of *The Silence of Memory*, a comprehensive study of the evolution of Armistice Day in England, cites cabinet minutes from 15 October 1919 in which Alfred Mond, who headed the

Board of Works and oversaw the construction of the official cenotaph, complained of the public practice of placing flowers and wreaths at the foot of the temporary memorial. Mond noted that "a mass of decaying flowers needs almost daily attention besides tending to attract crowds in a crowded thoroughfare." Mond asked that, once the permanent structure was built, the public be relegated to placing their memorials at set times. Towards this end, Mond suggested the dates of 19 July, a date that had been set aside to celebrate the signing of peace treaties in France, and, alternatively, Easter Monday. Less than one month before the anniversary of the armistice, Mond made no suggestion that 11 November might serve as an appropriate date for an annual public ceremony at the memorial.[6]

In fact plans were so haphazard in England that the now commonplace two minutes of silence was set in place only days before the anniversary of the armistice. The plan was first proposed by Sir Percy Fitzpatrick, who had observed the practice while serving as high commissioner in South Africa, where a daily silence to remember the war's fallen was adopted in May 1918. Borrowing from this convention, Fitzpatrick proposed to the British War Cabinet that the ritual might be adopted in an annual observance of the armistice. The War Cabinet quickly approved Fitzpatrick's idea.[7] Following the approval of the practice in England, King George V sent out a request that this ritual be adopted throughout the British Empire. On 6 November 1919 the king's message was read aloud by the governor general of Canada to the Canadian Parliament. Labelled as urgent, the King's message read:

> To all of my people:
> Tuesday next, November 11th, is the first anniversary of the armistice which stayed the world-wide carnage of the four preceding years and marked the victory of right and freedom. I believe that my people in every part of the Empire fervently wish to perpetuate the memory of that great deliverance and of those who laid down their lives to achieve it. To afford an opportunity for the universal expression of this feeling it is my desire and hope that at the hour when the armistice came into force, the eleventh hour of the eleventh day of the eleventh month, there may be for the brief space of two minutes a complete suspension of all our normal activities. During that time, except in the rare cases where this might be impracticable, all work, all sound and all locomotion should cease, so that in perfect stillness the thoughts of every one may be concentrated on reverent remembrance of the glorious dead.

No elaborate organization appears to be necessary. At a given signal, which can easily be arranged to suit the circumstances of each locality, I believe that we shall gladly interrupt our business and pleasure whatever it may be and unite in this simple service of silence and remembrance.[8]

While British plans to observe the armistice were quickly being put together that November, in Canada debate on creating an official day of remembrance linked to the anniversary of the armistice dominated parliamentary sessions during the autumn of 1919. Initially, Parliament considered modifying the Thanksgiving Day holiday to accommodate this remembrance. A bill titled the Thanksgiving Day Act was introduced on 9 April 1919 by member of Parliament Isaac E. Pedlow to "set aside Armistice day, the second Monday in November each year, as a perpetual memorial of the victorious conclusion of the recent war."[9] After its initial reading, the bill was brought up for debate in the House of Commons in September 1919. During this time, Pedlow argued that a permanent day of the week should be settled upon "so that the commercial life of the country will not be unduly disturbed by the uncertainty of the date."[10]

Business interests proved no small consideration when choosing an appropriate date to commemorate those who served and died in the First World War. In fact much of the 1919 discussions centred on the concerns of the Commercial Travellers' Association, which lobbied for a long weekend in November. The Retail Merchants' Association of Canada and provincial boards of trade were also at the forefront in calling for a holiday to be set on a Monday, rather than on 11 November, which would intermittently fall on a Saturday or Sunday. A holiday on 11 November would, in their view, inconvenience not only the general public, but also Canadian retailers, who did their briskest business on weekends.[11] American businesses also weighed in on the debate. In a letter addressed to Isaac Pedlow, an unnamed "editor of one of the most important trade journals published on the American Continent, if not in the world," wrote to concur with Pedlow's suggestion that Canada and the United States should link their days of thanksgiving so as not to disrupt two days of banking, stockbroking, and commercial business.[12] (Consideration of business interests when setting the holiday calendar was not unprecedented. For example, as Chris Tait notes in chapter 3, in 1897 some members of Parliament voted against the creation of Victoria Day in order to protect Canadian merchants and manufacturers, arguing that economic disruption would be the inevitable result of another holiday.)[13]

Pedlow's choice of date met with some resistance. Some MPs rose to suggest that 11 November, the actual date of the armistice, should be formally recognized as Armistice Day. Included among these members was William Foster Cockshutt of Brantford, who noted, "The 11th of November was Armistice Day. The second Monday in November may or may not be Armistice Day. It certainly cannot be Armistice Day at all times. It is true that it was on a Monday that the Armistice was signed, but the second Monday in November will not always fall on the 11th."[14] At the end of the debate, the motion was passed to recognize Armistice Day on the second Monday in November regardless of the date on which it would fall; however, only two years later, in 1921, a new Armistice Day Bill was passed that created a formal holiday on the first Monday during the week of 11 November, a move that combined Armistice Day with the already existing Thanksgiving Day.[15]

This change resulted in a variance of observance practices across the country. While some communities observed combined Thanksgiving and Armistice Day services on the Sunday before 11 November, in other locations, including Ottawa, official observance of the armistice continued to be held on 11 November. Ceremonies held on 11 November satisfied the desire of many veterans to honour the armistice on its true date but, without a formal holiday on that date, many of these veterans were precluded by their work schedules from attending these ceremonies in those years when 11 November fell upon a weekday.[16] The tradition of a combined Thanksgiving and Armistice Day remained in place for ten years, until 1928, when a series of changes began to take place that challenged business interests and introduced a resurgence of interest in memorializing the First World War.

First among the reasons for the renewed interest was the ten-year anniversary of the armistice, which naturally prompted reflection on the war and its meaning. In light of the anniversary, activities were undertaken to promote a national program of remembrance. For example, the Armistice Ceremonial Committee of Canada (ACCC) was created by a number of prominent Canadians to encourage the observance of Armistice Day in a meaningful way by fellow citizens. As part of its efforts, the ACCC issued 17,000 pamphlets to churches and clergy across Canada and created a newspaper supplement of four memorial pages, which made its way into 600,000 homes across Canada on 10 November 1928.[17] Encouraged by the ACCC's efforts, in that year

40,000 people gathered together in the shadow of the Peace Tower at Parliament Hill, where a temporary cenotaph had been erected for the event.[18]

The resurgent interest in the war during the late 1920s and early 1930s was also influenced in part by the publication of a number of important literary works. These works, which included poetry, drama, and memoirs, often challenged the dominant narrative of the war that had previously framed the conflict in nationalist terms and as a fight between good and evil in which good had ultimately prevailed. In Canada, this new narrative was represented by works like Charles Yale Harrison's *Generals Die in Bed*, published in 1930, while internationally, the poems of Wilfrid Owen, Erich Maria Remarque's novel *All Quiet on the Western Front*, and R.C. Sheriff's play *Journey's End* were all works representative of this trend. These new narratives were influenced as much by the postwar decade as by the war itself. In this period, veterans were struggling to overcome unemployment and to gain benefits, including pensions and long-term care for disabilities. Furthermore, the onset of a global economic depression and the rising political instability in Europe all contributed to a pervading sense of disillusionment with the war and its costs as well as the inability of the state to solve present-day problems.

Eventually, the new narrative moved beyond the pages of novels and poetry and inched into official Armistice Day ceremonies. By the late 1920s, ceremonies that had once promoted militarism and nationalism now focused more on the maintenance of global peace and on the terrible costs of war. Adrian Gregory writes that, by the early 1930s, the main focus of Armistice Day ceremonies became the bereaved. He notes that, while the actual ceremony changed very little during the interwar years, the language underwent a significant shift: "The bereaved were to be given the central emphasis in Armistice Day, yet at the same time denied the traditional comfort of being told that their loved ones had died for King, Country and Empire. Such rhetoric was clearly going to sound hollow in the wake of the new writing on the war."[19] Gregory goes on to note that some purpose would still need to be derived from death on such a massive scale and, to this end, a new meaning evolved – that the war had been fought for lasting peace.

In giving the bereaved a central emphasis, Armistice Day ceremonies gave a special prominence to women, especially mothers. Memorials constructed throughout the 1920s often reflected this emphasis. Both national and local memorials often relied on symbols of mourning,

7.2 War widows attend 1927 Armistice Day ceremonies in Toronto. City of Toronto Archives, Item #12118, Fonds 1266, Globe and Mail fonds, Box 158828, Folio 94, 11 November 1927.

grief, and loss, including images of weeping maternal figures. For Canada, there is no better representation of this trend than the Vimy Memorial in France and its dominant sculpture, "Canada Bereft" – a female figure with head bowed in mourning. Memorials like Vimy, and the countless other local memorials across Canada, depicted the losses symbolically in their imagery but also literally in the etched names of dead soldiers, which identified those families and mothers who grieved the loss of a son.[20]

While these popular literary works and new understanding of the war were certainly influential among a segment of Canadians, they also inspired a conservative backlash and prompted some to retreat to the more traditional rhetoric of honour, courage, valour, and nationalism that had originally been used to give meaning to the war and its unprecedented scale of death. For example, in a speech to the Westmount Women's Club of Montreal on 10 November 1933, Sir Andrew Macphail, a prominent physician who has served during the First World War and had gone on to write the official history of the Canadian Medical Services during that time, acknowledged the sorrow of women who had sent their sons to war in 1914, but also spoke to them regarding what he saw as a troubling move towards pacifism, especially on the part of young men. Speaking of those vowing to never go to war again, Macphail asked:

> Do these people ever ask themselves what would have happened to them had we been defeated in the last war? Those who profess themselves dissatisfied with our present situation would do well to ask themselves that question. For such persons you women have your own method; and I suggest to you the words of old Chaucer:
>
> Now have ye lost my heart and all my love;
> I cannot love a coward, by my faith.

Macphail went on to add, "In the world's code, cowardice is the one deadly sin."[21] Two years later, bemoaning the changing tone of Remembrance Day ceremonies in Canada, *Saturday Night* magazine published an editorial on 16 November 1935, titled "Armistice Oratory," that read:

> The whole tone of Armistice Day celebration in this country and the United States is becoming unsatisfying and unedifying. Little honor is done to the memory of those who died in the conflict which ended seventeen years ago, or of those who risked their lives in it but are still in our midst, by the constant reiteration of the thought that their sacrifice was in vain and mistaken, and that no such sacrifice should ever have to be repeated… That statement that all war is futile is irritating enough at any time, but peculiarly so on the anniversary of the day which marked the saving of Europe from the possibility – at any rate for a generation or so – of complete domination by one of the least humane, least tolerant, and least freedom-loving of its races.[22]

Although the ten-year anniversary, anxieties about forgetting the war, and postwar disillusionment all contributed in some way to a resurgence of interest in Armistice Day, and the First World War more generally, the most influential factor in reigniting interest in Armistice Day and working to secure its holiday status was the efforts of veterans themselves. The creation of Armistice Day as a stand-alone holiday can be attributed to the lobbying efforts of an increasingly powerful group of veterans newly united under the banner of the Royal Canadian Legion. While the government debated and set legislation, it was veterans who initially organized and pushed for the change.

Both during and in the immediate aftermath of the war, veterans sought out the company of others like them and formed a number of organizations united by identities based around former battalion affiliations, military branches, or region. By 1916, there were fourteen national veterans' organizations, as well as a number of local organizations. Just one year later, thirty-five organizations joined to form the Great War Veterans Association (GWVA), which, while the largest organization up to that point, still existed alongside fourteen other national veterans' organizations.[23] The GWVA was expressly non-political in its mandate, and other groups were for the most part too small and scattered to have any real political power.

Veterans' status, and their political power, began to change with a visit by the former commander of the British Expeditionary Force, Sir Douglas Haig, to Canada in 1925. Haig, who remained popular among the majority of veterans in the postwar period, travelled to Canada while president of the British Empire Service League, an organization devoted to uniting veterans from across the British Empire. Clearly understanding the fragmentation that existed among Canada's veterans' organizations, Haig made an attempt to promote unity and a singularity of vision. He achieved success quickly. Within days of his visit to Ottawa, Canada's main veterans' organizations had surrendered their charters and resolved to place their resources, including members and assets, at Haig's disposal for the purpose of creating a Canadian organization similar to the British Legion.[24] By November 1925, the Canadian Legion of the British Empire Services had been founded. This amalgamation ultimately helped Canadian veterans concentrate their power and act as a unified voice in order to further their agenda, an agenda that included a number of issues, including a greater recognition of Armistice Day.

For veterans of the First World War, a greater recognition of Armistice Day could be achieved only when it was granted a holiday separate from Thanksgiving. Only by this separation could the special status of the day be truly recognized. Furthermore, veterans' desire for the creation of a public holiday came from their wish to attend Armistice Day ceremonies, an activity that proved prohibitive to many working-class veterans when the day fell during the working week.[25] To address this situation, the newly organized legion members passed a general resolution in 1929 calling for the sacredness of the date to be recognized annually on 11 November. The resolution went on ask the Parliament of Canada to make November 11th an annual holiday. The general resolution was circulated among local legion branches in order to be voted upon by their members and then communicated to their local MPs.[26]

It was because of this lobbying by veterans that Canadian parliamentarians eventually took up the cause of establishing a separate Armistice Day in 1930. Leading the fight was member of Parliament A.W. Neil of British Columbia, who introduced a bill to repeal the existing Armistice Day Act in favour of recognizing Armistice Day each year on 11 November.[27] In so doing, Neil deferred to the wishes of ex-servicemen, noting that:

> The old act has been the law for ten years, and no one would have supposed that what opposition there might have been to it originally would have died out, but on the contrary it has been increasing year after year. The reason why this opposition did not come to a head sooner is, I believe, that a great many soldiers did not know that that was the law. Many of them simply went ahead and celebrated Armistice Day on November 11 regardless of what day was fixed by law. They are beginning to find out what is the law and there is a general feeling throughout the country that Armistice Day should be celebrated on November 11 and on no other day. The only people who object to this proposal are commercial travellers who desire to be able to come home on a Friday or Saturday night and have a holiday on Monday. Perhaps there are a few others who would like to go to their homes and have a holiday on Monday, but I would point out that this day was never intended to be a public holiday in the sense of bank holidays and so on; it was intended as a remembrance day for the soldiers, and they are entitled to have it on that day... This matter is solely and entirely the concern of the returned men and we as a government body ought to respect their wishes. It has nothing to do with what other people want, and the soldiers should surely have the right to decide.[28]

Neil's bill passed in 1931, with the only amendment being that 11 November would henceforth be known as Remembrance Day instead of Armistice Day. The change in terminology was no small matter, but a move heavy with symbolism and intent. The change in name came at the request of the Royal Canadian Legion. It was meant to take the focus away from the political event of the 1918 armistice and to place it squarely on the act of remembering the ordinary men and women who fell in service to the nation.[29] This change also clearly reflected the fear that the importance of the day would disappear once the armistice itself faded from memory. As stated by member of Parliament C.H. Dickie to the House of Commons, "Remembrance Day sounds very well, and implies all that we wish to remember and perpetuate. We know it commemorates the cessation of hostilities, but, as I say, the word 'armistice' will be forgotten when the sad memories associated with the day still live among those who on that day foregather in sacred remembrance of those who gave of their best for this empire of ours."[30]

Immediately following the passing of the 1931 bill, J.R. Bowler, general secretary of the Royal Canadian Legion, sent out a circular to every Legion branch, calling on members to remember and reinforce the sanctity of the day, so as to set the tone for all subsequent Remembrance Days. Writing to members, Bowler reiterated the fears of some that, by having a separate holiday, the day "might degenerate into a public holiday." To avoid this possibility, Bowler asked every member and branch "to make adequate preparations to insure that the celebrating of Remembrance Day this year shall be such as to emphasize the sacred nature of the day." Bowler went on to state that, "this suggestion does not necessarily preclude the arranging on the evening of this day of social re-unions of our Comrades but it is felt that these functions should not be the outstanding feature of the day and that its sacred nature should be stressed above everything else."[31]

Having worked to establish the day, veterans came to feel a special sense of ownership over it. As Denise Thomson notes in her article "National Sorrow, National Pride: Commemoration of War in Canada, 1918–1945," "ultimately, making the veterans' day into a national day placed veterans in the position of being custodians of the history of Canada's participation in the Great War, elevating their perception of the Canadian wartime experience above that of any other group."[32]

The tension between celebration and solemn observance that Bowler alluded to was one that was common throughout the British Empire and was acknowledged early on. Adrian Gregory reports that this debate played out annually in British newspapers throughout the 1920s. Some saw celebratory activities as crass and as the exclusive domain of war profiteers or non-combatants. In an attempt to settle this debate on how

Armistice Day should be spent, in 1925 the *Daily Express* sought out an opinion of no less of authority than Sir Douglas Haig on the matter. In a well-measured answer to the question, Haig stated, "I recommend that Armistice Day be observed throughout the Empire as a day of remembrance. In the forenoon all ages should attend a thanksgiving service with a parade of veterans at the local war memorial. In the afternoon games suited to the climate should be played, in the evening people should rejoice according to taste."[33]

The debate over observance would play out in Canada throughout the 1930s and beyond. Was Remembrance Day meant to be a solemn observance, and if so, was a public holiday the proper way to recognize it? While veterans certainly felt a holiday was appropriate, others were less sure and cited a number of reasons, including, once again, its impact on business as well as the concern that a public holiday might be abused and lead to activities that did not necessarily reflect the solemn intention of the day. Citing the concerns of the business community, on 14 November 1931, just three days after the first Remembrance Day, the *Financial Post* published an editorial stating that:

> Even Parliament cannot create a holiday where the business public does not want it. The unfortunate fiasco of Armistice Day calls for the repeal, at the next session of Parliament, of the act declaring November 11 a public holiday. *The Financial Post* and many boards of trade opposed the bill but Parliamentarians slipped it through practically without discussion. Another holiday was not needed and if it had been, it should have been fixed on a Monday. We already have too many holidays that float around in the middle of the week to the annoyance and discomfort of the people generally.[34]

In the days following Remembrance Day, *Saturday Night* magazine also published a piece that, while acknowledging and approving of the solemnity of the 1931 services, questioned the motivations of the politicians who worked to secure its place on the calendar. In an essay titled "The Fallen and the Politicians," the writer noted that "the sincerity of certain politicians in various parts of Canada who piously held up their hands in horror as the disinclination of business concerns to observe the renamed Armistice Day as a public holiday is open to grave doubts. The threats to 'compel' observance were nauseating, and we do not believe that the public men who urged this course were moved by any real sentiment with regard to the fallen. They were merely making a bid for the soldier votes."[35] The author went on to cynically note that those most interested in the recognition of Remembrance Day were likely owners of movie theatres and sporting event venues who would see an uptick in business by those who would forgo solemn observance in favour of a day of leisure provided to them by the federal government.[36]

This debate over Remembrance Day continued into the next year. In February 1932 a circular was sent to all legion branches warning them that despite overall general public support for the Remembrance Day Act, encouraged by lobbying from certain business interests new attempts would be made in Parliament to secure a repeal. The circular asked that all legion branches communicate their support of Remembrance Day to their local MPs in an effort to ensure that the holiday be maintained.[37]

While Remembrance Day has remained in place since 1932, debates on its status as a holiday and on the proper way to observe it have continued to this day. Currently, the status of the day differs across provinces. British Columbia, Alberta, Saskatchewan, New Brunswick, Prince Edward Island, Newfoundland, and all three territories recognize 11 November as a statutory or a general holiday. Ontario, Manitoba, Quebec, and Nova Scotia do not, although Manitoba and Nova Scotia both have legislation curbing business hours on that day. Each year, debate on the status of the day is renewed. While some argue that the day should be a statutory holiday across Canada, the argument persists that a statutory holiday carries the risk of creating just another day off and consequently lessening Remembrance Day's importance among not only adults but also among children, who learn about the day's significance in class.

Concerns over youth forgetting the meaning of Remembrance Day can be traced as far back as 1919. In that year, as parliamentarians debated how to recognize the very first anniversary of the armistice, member of Parliament Robert Lorne Richardson of Manitoba argued that celebrating Armistice Day on any day other than 11 November would eventually cause people, especially children, to lose sight of the day's intended meaning.[38] Today, fears over children forgetting the meaning of the date have been used to justify arguments both for and against making Remembrance Day a federal holiday. While some argue that a federal holiday stresses the importance of the day, others argue that, by creating a holiday children will see November 11th as just another day off of school and lose sight of its meaning. Proponents of this argument believe that school curricula and ceremonies are essential to reinforcing the importance of Remembrance Day with the next generation. In Ontario, these beliefs and concerns resulted in 2004 amendments to provincial legislation. Amendments to the Ontario Education Act mandate that schools must hold Remembrance Day ceremonies on 11 November or on the nearest school day if Remembrance Day should fall on a weekend. The 2004 amendments focus on protocols for this observance, mandating that Remembrance Day ceremonies should include the playing of the last post, the cessation of all other school activities, and the observance of two minutes of silence to allow for reflection.[39] School activities typically combine symbols of nationalism and militarism, such as the national anthem and the last post, while also trying to provide a basic knowledge of Canadian military history. In addition to these symbols, common at most Remembrance Day ceremonies, these activities also often rely on language that reiterates the wish for global peace. This stands in stark contrast to school activities during the era of the First World War, which often blatantly promoted nationalism and militarism among students. For example, during the war years, children in English-speaking Canada celebrated Empire Day, an occasion meant to promote imperialism and patriotism among children. As noted in chapter 4 in the present volume, during the war years, "curriculum programming [for Empire day] focused heavily on great generals, great battles, and brave Canadian soldiers fighting for the motherland."

Today the status of Remembrance Day remains an ongoing question. As recently as May 2014, a private member's bill was introduced by Dan Harris, an MP from Ontario, to clarify the meaning of Remembrance Day within the existing Holidays Act. This would have given each province the opportunity to revisit the question of whether November 11th should be a statutory holiday. The House of Commons approved Bill C-597 – "an Act to Amend the Holidays Act" – on 5 November 2014. The bill was then reviewed by a parliamentary heritage committee that included members of the Royal Canadian Legion as well as other veterans' organizations. In June 2015 the bill was sent back to Parliament for a third reading, but it failed to pass before the end of the session.[40] Yet, it may be that a call for a federal Remembrance Day holiday might be repeated in the future.

This call to change legislation reflects the renewed national interest in remembering Canada's military history. This heightened interest has been reflected in the increased interest in and attendance at Remembrance Day ceremonies. Since the 1990s, the national Remembrance

Day ceremony in Ottawa has seen rising attendance, and the CBC, which broadcasts the ceremony live every year, has seen an uptick in viewership.[41] There may be several reasons for this increased interest. First, since the 1990s, there has been an increasing awareness that we are rapidly losing our links to the living past as veterans of the two world wars diminish rapidly in number. On 18 February 2010, Canada's last living veteran of the First World War, John Babcock, passed away at the age of 109, and veterans of the Second World War are disappearing at a quickening pace.[42] The increasing interest can also be linked to the anniversary boom. Since the 1990s, attention has been given to a number of important anniversaries in Canada's military history, including the fiftieth anniversary of the end of the Second World War in 1995 and, more recently, the centenary of the First World War. Interest in these events has also been encouraged by the federal government, which has provided funding for initiatives to mark these occasions. For example, in 2007, to mark the ninetieth anniversary of the Battle of Vimy Ridge, a commemorative coin was issued by the Royal Canadian Mint. In addition, a Vimy Vigil took place at the National War Memorial in Ottawa, where the names of 3,598 Canadians who died during the battle were projected onto the memorial from dusk to dawn on 8 April 2007. In 2014, the government of Canada announced a special commemorative period from 2014 to 2020 that will recognize the centenary of the First World War and the seventy-fifth anniversary of the end of the Second World War. During this period, the government has committed to funding a number of national and local ceremonies and projects in order to educate and create awareness among Canadians of their military legacy. These initiatives include the digitization of military records held by Library and Archives Canada, as well as the construction of a new education centre at the Vimy Memorial in France.[43]

It has been argued that the funding for such events has come with a purpose deeper than recognizing history and that the government of Stephen Harper used this military history to justify current military policy and military spending and to recast Canadian history as that of a warrior nation. Ian McKay and Jamie Swift have argued that Remembrance Day has been one more tool in this recasting and that the former Conservative government used Remembrance Day ceremonies to promote their intended image of Canada as a warrior nation. However, they note that this use of Remembrance Day, and commemoration in general, has always had "other dimensions":

For some, commemoration has been about protesting against the governments and corporations that create wars. For some, it has been about reconciliation and, ultimately, the search for peace. For others – and today they have the upper hand – it is about the glorification of war itself. They have a strong interest in transforming Canada's image, into that of a "warrior nation."[44]

Without a doubt, Remembrance Day will continue to be used and co-opted by special interest groups and shaped by political and cultural climates. Beyond remembering the fallen, the day provides the opportunity to reevaluate our historical understanding of ourselves as well as our current foreign policy. The day has never simply been about mourning; it has been about business interests, veterans' interests, national myth making, and social policy. It has come to be understood differently in times of war and in times of peace. The rhetoric surrounding Remembrance Day has often reflected current political climates. For example, in times of war, including most recently, during Canada's years-long involvement in Afghanistan, Remembrance Day ceremonies have been used by politicians as a platform to promote nationalism and expand Canada's financial commitment to its armed forces. In times of peace, including during the interwar period of the 1920s and 1930s, Remembrance Day offered opportunities to recognize the cost of war and to demand recognition for those who gave, both veterans as well as the wives and mothers of the fallen. The evolving narrative of Remembrance Day continues to this day. It is a day heavy with old symbols, but still open to new interpretations almost a century after its beginning.

NOTES

1 Jonathan Vance, *Death So Noble: Memory, Meaning, and the First World War* (Vancouver: UBC Press, 1997).
2 Ian McKay and Jamie Swift, *Warrior Nation: Rebranding Canada in an Age of Anxiety* (Toronto: Between the Lines, 2012).
3 Craig Heron and Steve Penfold, *The Workers' Festival: A History of Labour Day in Canada* (Toronto: University of Toronto Press, 2005).
4 Diary entry from George Walter Adams, 11 November 1918 and letter from Emily Adams to George Walter Adams, 15 November 1918, the Canadian Letters and Images Project, www.canadianletters.ca.

5 Letter from Robert Shortreed to Mother, 12 November 1918, ibid.

6 Alfred Mond, 15 October 1919, Public Record Office (hereafter PRO), CAB 24/GT 8335, quoted in Adrian Gregory, *The Silence of Memory: Armistice Day, 1919–1946* (Providence, RI: Berg, 1994), 8.

7 Gregory, *The Silence of Memory*, 9–10.

8 Canada, House of Commons, *Debates*, 13th Parliament, 3rd session, vol. 2, 6 November 1919, 1835.

9 Ibid., 2nd session, vol. 2, 9 April 1919, 1306.

10 Ibid., 3rd session, vol. 1, 4 September 1919, 25.

11 Ibid., 18 September 1919, 433.

12 Ibid., 434.

13 For more on the debate surrounding the creation of Victoria Day, see the chapter by Chris Tait in the present volume.

14 Canada, House of Commons, *Debates*, 13th Parliament, 3rd session, vol., 1, 18 September 1919, 436.

15 Ibid., 5th session, vol. 4, 23 May 1921.

16 Denise Thomson, "National Sorrow, National Pride: Commemoration of War in Canada, 1918–1945," *Journal of Canadian Studies* 30, no. 4 (Winter 1995/96) http://search.proquest.com.proxy.queensu.ca/docview/203519299/fulltext/CAF1E2F31E864A09PQ/2?accountid=6180.

17 *Armistice Day Ceremonial* (Toronto: Armistice Ceremonial Committee of Canada), 45.

18 Ibid., 27. The National War Memorial in Ottawa did not open until 1939.

19 Gregory, *The Silence of Memory*, 122.

20 While the role of women as widows and grieving mothers was given prominence in early Armistice Day ceremonies, recognition of the service of nurses was largely absent.

21 Sir Andrew Macphail papers, Library and Archives Canada (hereafter LAC), MG 30, vol. 6, series D 150, folder "Armistice Day Address," address to Westmount Women's Club, 10 November 1933.

22 "Armistice Oratory," *Saturday Night* 51, no. 2 (16 November 1935).

23 John Scott, "Three Cheers for Earl Haig: Canadian Veterans and the Visit of Field Marshal Sir Douglas Haig to Canada in the Summer of 1925," *Canadian Military History* 5, no. 1 (spring 1996): 35–6.

24 Ibid., 35–38, and Graham Wootton, *The Official History of the British Legion* (London: MacDonald & Evans, 1956), 71.

25 One would be wrong to assume, based on this desire to have its working-class members attend Armistice Day ceremonies, that the Royal Canadian Legion was an organization that fought for the rights of working-class veterans more generally or that the organization had

"left-wing" or "socialist" leanings during this period. While the Legion did incorporate other working-class issues into its mandate, including fighting for veterans' pensions, the organization also lobbied hard to preserve what might be considered conservative or traditional Canadian (British) values, including stances against non-British immigrants (in an effort to preserve their own job prospects) and a roll-back on social changes brought on by the war, including the greater inclusion of women in the workforce. The Legion did not represent what might be described as "radical" working-class interests. This was true of Legion members in Great Britain as well. For example, during a 1929 general strike, the official Legion policy in Great Britain was to remain neutral. The Legion called on its members to support the state and the police forces in the name of security as well as "justice, freedom and democracy … [and it called] upon all ex-service men who saved the country in war, to come forward once more and offer their services in any way that may be needed by the authorities." Wootton, *Official History*, 325. Also see Desmond Morton and Glenn Wright, *Winning the Second Battle: Canadian Veterans and the Return to Civilian Life, 1915–1930* (Toronto: University of Toronto Press, 1987).

26 Thomson, "National Sorrow, National Pride."
27 Canada, House of Commons, *Debates*, 17th Parliament, 2nd session, vol. 1, 18 March 1931, 104–5.
28 Ibid., 27 April 1931, 1033.
29 Thomson, "National Sorrow, National Pride."
30 Canada, House of Commons, *Debates*, 17th Parliament, 2nd session, vol. 1, 28 April 1931, 1068.
31 Royal Canadian Legion (hereafter RCL) Papers, LAC, MG 28, vol. 7, series I 298, file "Master Circulars, January to August 1931," Legion Circular no. 31/2/9, 2 June 1931.
32 Thomson, "National Sorrow, National Pride."
33 Gregory, *The Silence of Memory*, 71.
34 RCL Papers, LAC, MG 28, vol. 7, series I 298, file "Master Circulars, September to December 1931," Legion Circular no. 31/2/62, 10 December 1931.
35 "The Fallen and the Politicians," *Saturday Night* 47, 2 (21 November 1931).
36 Ibid.
37 RCL Papers, LAC, MG 28, vol. 7, series I 298, file "Master Circulars, January to June 1932," Legion Circular no. 32/2, 3 February 1932.
38 *Canada*, House of Commons, *Debates*, 13th Parliament, 3rd session, vol. 1, 22 September 1919, 478.

39 Legislative Assembly of Ontario, Bill 139, Remembrance Day Observance Act, 2004, http://www.ontla.on.ca/web/bills/bills_detail.do?locale= en&BillID=330&isCurrent=false&detailPage=bills_detail_the_bill.

40 Parliament of Canada, Hansard, 41st Parliament, Second Session, 19 June 2015, accessed May 2016, http://www.parl.gc.ca/HousePublications/ Publication.aspx?Language=E&Mode=1&Parl=41&Ses=2&DocId=8058128

41 Suzanne Evans, *Mothers of Heroes, Mothers of Martyrs: World War One and the Politics of Grief* (Montreal: McGill-Queen's University Press, 2007), 119.

42 Richard Goldstein, "John Babcock, Last Canadian World War One Veteran, Dies at 109," *New York Times*, 24 February 2010. As of March 2014, Veterans Affairs Canada estimates that, of an estimated one million Canadian veterans in 1945, about 88,400 remain alive. Their average age in 2014 is ninety years old. Veterans Affairs Canada, General Statistics, accessed January 2015, http://www.veterans.gc.ca/eng/news/general-statistics.

43 "Commemorating and Honouring a Legacy of Service and Sacrifice," Canadian Heritage, accessed January 2015, http://www.prnewswire.com/ news-releases/commemorating-and-honouring-a-legacy-of-service-and-sacrifice-239960281.html.

44 Jamie Swift and Ian McKay, "Politics Shapes How We Commemorate Canada's Wars," *Toronto Star*, 5 November 2012, http://www.thestar. com/opinion/editorialopinion/2012/11/05/politics_shapes_how_we_ commemorate_canadas_wars.html.

8 Dominion Day and the Rites of Regionalism in British Columbia, 1867–1937

FORREST D. PASS

Frank Kitto loved the Canadian West. Each summer, the surveyor and engineer with the federal Natural Resources Intelligence Branch was anxious to leave the drudgery of Ottawa office work for the freedom of "camp life." However, even the keenest outdoorsman enjoys a day in town, and on Dominion Day 1919 Kitto found himself in the rough-and-tumble rail and lumber centre of Prince George, British Columbia. There he found that the boisterous manner in which the locals celebrated the national holiday was markedly different from the more staid traditions of the east:

> Dominion day ... was right royally celebrated in true western fashion. Streamers were stretched at frequent intervals across the main street and innumerable gaily decorated booths lined the walks. Foot and horse races were run on this thoroughfare. I believe there was quite a programme of sports but the people interested me more than the games. Rough frontier men of every stamp there were, lumbermen, trappers, miners, farmers, ranchers and railroad builders, Indians with Shiks [sic], and Shiks with Chinamen. The town was evidently "wide-open" for the occasion and liquor flowed freely. As may be surmised the day ended in boisterous revelry but, western like, with much noise and little damage.

Kitto's account noted several distinctive features of a frontier Dominion Day. The presence of Sikh and Chinese Canadians and Aboriginal people was one aspect that distinguished the holiday in rural British Columbia from that in some other centres. So, too, did the liberal consumption of alcohol. Dominion Day celebrations in the rural Ontario of Kitto's youth had been sober affairs; in 1895, when Kitto was fifteen, a highlight of the festivities in his hometown of Brampton had been the unveiling of a public drinking fountain by the Woman's Christian Temperance Union. By contrast, in Prince George booze was freely available – in defiance of the province's prohibition laws – yet the day passed without serious incident. The diversity of celebrants and their boisterous but harmless conviviality contributed to an atmosphere Kitto twice described as typically western. To Kitto, there was an exoticism in this regional celebration of the national holiday among "rough frontier men," but the frontier atmosphere was amusing and exciting rather than menacing.[1]

Dominion Day, the anniversary of the proclamation of the British North America Act on 1 July 1867, has been a de facto Canadian national holiday since Confederation, but, as Kitto's account illustrates, Dominion Day traditions have varied considerably from region to region, reflecting local social, cultural, and economic circumstances and practices. Only since the Second World War have observances of the holiday become institutionalized, as ties with Great Britain weakened and federal authorities confronted the challenge of resurgent Quebec nationalism. As Matthew Hayday has observed, Dominion Day before the 1960s lacked the set of clearly defined and ubiquitously replicated traditions that might have made it a unifying force. At first glance, this variation would seem to undermine the unifying power of a "national holiday." However, a close reading of the popularity and adaptation of Dominion Day in one region, British Columbia, suggests that the flexibility of the holiday during its informal early years was a strength rather than a weakness. British Columbians, like other Canadians, experienced nationalism locally, and the national holiday and regional politics benefited from mutual reinforcement.[2]

In the six decades between Confederation and the Great Depression, Dominion Day in British Columbia evolved from an emulation of an American national holiday through a grand Victorian patriotic spectacle and into a celebration of western distinctiveness. Before British Columbia entered Confederation in 1871, Dominion Day celebrations in the colony melded partisan agitation for responsible government with rituals borrowed from Fourth of July observances; given the pre-existing tradition of celebrating the Fourth, it is not surprising that many British Columbians conceived of Dominion Day as their own Independence Day, an association rarely made in eastern Canada. The two holidays continued to be celebrated side by side for over two decades, a phenomenon consistent with the province's cosmopolitan character. With the completion of the Canadian Pacific Railway, the Fourth of July waned, and Dominion Day took on more overtly patriotic characteristics. In the development of parades and celebratory newspaper editorials, the celebration of the national holiday in British Columbia came to resemble observances elsewhere in Canada, especially in Ontario. After the First World War, as Kitto discovered, Dominion Day in the British Columbia hinterland remained a lively celebration of frontier culture, and urban British Columbians made concerted efforts to replicate this frontier spirit. Particularly important in this process of replication was the ongoing and increasingly ritualized participation of First Nations people. The elaboration of regional Dominion Day rituals occurred in the context of British Columbia's occasionally tumultuous relationship with Ottawa, and newspaper editors did not shy away from addressing federal-provincial disagreements in their Dominion Day editorials. However, the choice of Dominion Day as an occasion for regional or sectional discourse indicates an acknowledgment of nationalism's power and suggests that British Columbia regionalism was not a centrifugal ideology, but the result of an ongoing dialogue over precisely what it meant, and means, to be Canadian. This conclusion echoes the work of American scholars on the regionalization of the Fourth of July, which argues that national holidays have drawn their vitality from the perpetual contestation, including regional reformulations, of their meaning.[3]

The parallel with the evolution of the Fourth of July was not coincidental, for in colonial British Columbia the Fourth preceded the First. When British Columbians considered the institution of a patriotic summer holiday, or a ritual vocabulary to express their displeasure at the autocracy of the existing colonial regime and their anticipated connection with Canada, they had a ready-made model in the Fourth of July, which had been celebrated annually since the first settlement of the colony. W.B. Cameron, a veteran of the Overland trek of 1862, recalled that it was the only holiday observed in the Cariboo during the gold rush, and Charles Hayward, the future mayor of Victoria, noted that the Fourth of July was generally kept as a holiday in that city during the 1860s. At Yale in 1867, the national salute concluded with "a big 'Tiger' for Alaska," a surprising gesture given British Columbians' well-documented anxiety at William Seward's purchase of the Russian-American territory three months earlier. At Barkerville in 1870, a federal salute at sunrise and a national salute at noon preceded a reading of the Declaration of Independence and an oration. At New Westminster the following year, the Fourth featured federal and national salutes, sports, and free strawberries and ice cream.[4]

Given the record of American expansionist filibustering, colonial authorities were uneasy about American patriotic celebrations. Dr. J.S. Helmcken noted in his reminiscences that the colonial government tolerated such observances, provided they did not threaten public order. However, American festivities that verged on insult to the British flag prompted anxiety. Governor James Douglas refused to permit the firing of a salute for George Washington's birthday in February 1859, ostensibly because the firing was to be undertaken by private citizens. For the Fourth of July 1866, the American consul at Victoria deliberately defied a prohibition on saluting by chartering a scow, whence he fired the thirty-six-gun national salute at sunrise and again at sunset. A furious Governor Arthur Kennedy complained to London, and much discussion ensued within the Colonial and Foreign Offices. In the end, Lord Granville advised that American agents and citizens in Victoria ought to enjoy the same latitude in celebrating the Fourth as was extended to expatriates of European countries for royal birthdays. In this decision, Whitehall recognized the limits of imperial power.[5]

Yet the Fourth was more than just a celebration for expatriate American citizens; prominent Canadians also patronized the festivities. Alongside orations and patriotic salutes, the organizers usually included a toast or cheers to the queen as a concession to local sentiment. The Methodist missionary Edward White, an eager promoter of eastern British North American immigration to British Columbia, attended a Sunday school picnic on the Fourth of July 1865, and made no objection to the date selected. In New Westminster in 1868, the local militia fired the national salute, and various local dignitaries responded to toasts at the evening's banquet. In 1871, Dr Israel Powell, a staunch pro-Confederate, served as one of Victoria's representatives on the Committee of Invitation for a Fourth of July celebration in Port Townsend, Washington, an event regularly attended by Victoria excursionists. That the other Victoria representative was David Eckstein, the American consul and annexation proponent, indicates the non-partisan nature of the celebration. Amor de Cosmos, editor of the *Victoria Daily Standard* and a peripheral member of the colonial elite, was a great admirer of the United States and sensationally proclaimed on the Fourth of July 1870 that the American Declaration of Independence was the greatest event in human history since the birth of Jesus of Nazareth. With each recurrence, the Fourth of July became less a cause for official anxiety and more an accepted feature of the local calendar.[6]

When Canadian patriotic celebrations became more common, it was not surprising that they adopted many of the conventions of the American observance. At Moodyville (now North Vancouver) on 20 July 1871, Ontario-born Josiah Clarke Hughes marked British Columbia's admission to Confederation with a speech that owed much to American patriotic oratory. He began with a profession of inadequacy, a common elocutionary conceit, as was the familiar narrative of a nation's establishment and discord, couched in metaphors from the natural world, such as his description of Canada having "rizen [sic] on the horizon of nations." Turning to the promised Canadian transcontinental railway, Hughes foresaw "Mountains ... hurled down and Cast into the valleys," alluding to Christ's exhortation to build a highway in the wilderness for the Lord and mimicking American orators' practice of juxtaposing biblical precedent and current political circumstances. It is noteworthy that the oration followed a "Dominion Salute," apparently a Canadianization of the Fourth's federal and national salutes.[7]

Like its American archetype, Dominion Day in pre-Confederation British Columbia was a partisan celebration. The impulse for the first celebrations, in 1868, came from Canadian settlers on the mainland who desired both responsible government and union with Canada. Canadians in Barkerville marked the First of July 1868 with a salute – the traditional twenty-one-gun variety – and speeches on the benefits of Confederation that recalled the American tradition of Fourth of July oratory. Celebrants were then asked to vote on two resolutions calling for British Columbia's immediate admission to the dominion and a third authorizing the formation of a "league" to press for Confederation. John Robson's pro-Confederation organ, New Westminster's *British Columbian*, saw in such observances evidence that the colonists had come to recognize "the advantages that Confederation will bring in its train," and the paper expressed hope that Dominion Day 1869 might have a greater significance for British Columbians.[8]

The adaptation of Fourth of July traditions indicated not only a familiarity and comfort with the American holiday but also a prevailing conception of Confederation as a revolutionary event. Hughes briefly alluded to this revolutionary interpretation, identifying "the great principle of Self Government" as "one of the accompanying benefits of Confederation." Pro-Confederation newspaper editors dwelt at length on the colony's coming "independence" from Downing Street misrule. Robson acknowledged that Canada's progress towards self-government was a more peaceful process than that which had transpired in the United States. Nevertheless, he looked for a Canadian equivalent to the American Revolution and found one in the Rebellions of 1837, when "the freedom of Canada was purchased with the blood of some of her most promising sons." For D.W. Higgins, editor of the *Victoria Daily Colonist*, the colony's entry into Confederation marked "the Birth of Liberty." The more radical de Cosmos rejoiced that "the moment the [Confederation] compact is agreed to and signed by the high contracting parties that moment will we as a people become politically free – be emancipated from the condition of semi-serfdom under which we have so long fretted and protested." Israel Powell, addressing the Victoria Fire Department on 1 July 1871, hoped that, through the imminent union with Canada, British Columbians would "obtain a lasting freedom [and] establish our independence among the nations of the earth." If union with Canada was a revolutionary moment, it followed that British Columbians should view the Canadian national holiday as analogous to the glorious Fourth.[9]

Although not entirely unheard of elsewhere in British North America, this interpretation of Dominion Day was uncommon in the east. There, politicians and journalists went to great lengths to distance their national holiday from the disorderly republican observance south of the border. The year before Hughes delivered his Confederation Day oration, the London, Ontario, *Advertiser* noted that "the stump orator is not quite such an institution with us as it is over the lines," and in 1875, politician Matthew Crooks Cameron delivered a "public address" to a Dominion Day gathering in Toronto, eschewing "the oration" as an American institution "imperilling to ... fidelity to the Mother country." Other Ontario commentators poked fun at the boisterous and intemperate nature of celebrations south of the line, delighting in the enumeration of sensational riots, fires, pyrotechnic accidents, and even deaths that characterized the Fourth. The defining differences between the two holidays were to be found not only in the traditions associated with their observance but also in the events they commemorated. Confederation may have been a revolutionary moment for British Columbians, but for the *Toronto Globe* it had "none of the traditional associations of the Declaration of Independence, and is, to most people, only a piece of very dry, practical legislation." The challenges facing the Canadian people as they worked to build a nation were, therefore, "impelling to sober thought rather than enthusiasm or excitement." In 1880, the

Globe's Conservative competitor, the *Toronto Daily Mail*, remarked that, while the national holidays of Canada and the United States might coincide on the calendar, there were "essential points of difference between the two anniversaries," foremost among these being Canada's "wiser policy" of choosing constitutional over revolutionary change. In Ontario, Dominion Day was emphatically not a Canadian Independence Day. [10]

Yet in British Columbia the anniversaries of American independence and Canadian Confederation were celebrated together long after 1871. De Cosmos's *Standard* observed, on 5 July 1872, that "a stranger visiting the city yesterday would almost be led to believe that Victoria was under the 'Stars and Stripes,' so unanimous were our citizens in keeping it [a] holiday." William Barneby, an Englishman who visited British Columbia just before the completion of the railway, found that the Fourth was celebrated in British Columbia almost as much as across the line, which he attributed to good neighbourliness. An American journalist visiting the province in the 1890s also approved of the friendly sentiment towards the United States evident in the "informal but general" celebration of the Fourth in most centres. Press opinion continued to support the American holiday's observance alongside Canadian celebrations. Reporting on the 1872 festivities, the New Westminster paper, the *Mainland Guardian*, remarked that "patriotism is always creditable, but nothing is more praiseworthy than marking the anniversary of the greatest republic the world ever saw." Similarly, de Cosmos hoped that the First and Fourth would be celebrated together in perpetuity as evidence of the friendly relations between the two countries. Although the idea was never expressed in print, the Fourth may have continued to serve a political purpose after 1871, as a reminder to Ottawa that annexation to the United States remained an option for a province dissatisfied with its treatment.[11]

Given that, by the early 1870s, Americans had spent almost a century refining Fourth of July rituals, their festivities included slightly more patriotic symbolism than those on the First. After the factionalism of the colonial period, the post-Confederation holiday was largely non-partisan, unlike in eastern Canada, where Dominion Day editorials lambasted political opponents for disloyalty and the Nova Scotia government banned public observances of the First of July to express its dissatisfaction with Ottawa. The absence of overtly patriotic rituals or decorations did not necessarily imply a lack of interest in the Canadian connection. Reporting on an 1876 Dominion Day celebration at

Langley, which had consisted of sports and a "sumptuous lunch," the editor of the *Mainland Guardian* was "convinced that the people of this part of the Province, are nowise lacking in their loyalty, to their Canadian relationship." Federal-provincial relations had reached their nadir during the summer of 1876, and the comment was a deliberate gibe at the provincial political class in Victoria from a staunch ally of the federal government. The same year, the Liberal-aligned *Colonist* predicted that British Columbians would celebrate the holiday in "their usual happy manner" because, "although some of the greatest hopes of the people in connection with Confederation have not yet been realized, still it is admitted on all sides that the Province has materially increased in prosperity since the date of the union." The paper had changed its tune slightly by 1884, when it predicted that Dominion Day would not be observed "with that enthusiasm with which it would have been had the various promises of the Dominion with the province been faithfully carried out." Though generally lacking in blatant political content, the very act of celebrating – or not celebrating – a national holiday could be a political act. [12]

The political potential of patriotic celebrations clearly animated elites, but it is difficult to determine from newspaper coverage and the occasional traveller's account the motivations of ordinary participants or the breadth and depth of the appeal of national holidays. However, one remarkable document does give some sense of the level of popular participation in Dominion Day and Independence Day festivities in the province's hinterland. The source is a subscription book for Dominion Day and Fourth of July horse races in the Cariboo around 1880, preserved in the papers of John Boyd, the proprietor of Cottonwood House, a way station on the road between Quesnel and Barkerville. The subscription lists are a unique record of meaningful participation, for they identify members of the community who were willing not only to attend celebrations, but also to invest their own money in ensuring the success of those festivities. According to his accounts, Boyd and his associates collected over $1300 from about 160 residents of the mining district to support a program of races for the First of July; individual subscriptions ranged from one dollar to one hundred. The population of the mining frontier was notoriously transient, so linking the subscription lists to the 1881 census is imperfect. However, it does suggest that the celebration appealed to miners, farmers, labourers, tradesmen, merchants, and civil servants from a variety of national and ethnic backgrounds. Of particular interest is the number of Chinese subscribers: at least fifteen, or about 10 per cent of the total subscribers, have Chinese names, and each subscribed at least one dollar to the purse. In a frontier region like the Cariboo mines, the population was likely too small to justify segregation along class lines, and even racial divisions could be set aside in preparing for annual holidays.[13]

The appeal of the Fourth of July was more limited. Only ninety-nine subscribers came forward, and the total collected was a little more than a third of that subscribed for the Dominion Day races. There is no discernable difference in the occupational and ethnic profile of the subscribers on the two lists; in fact, those who can be definitively identified as American-born are slightly more prevalent among the Dominion Day supporters. Although there is some overlap in the lists, generally those who subscribed to both were less generous in their contributions to the Independence Day races. The fur-trapping Favel brothers contributed to the American celebration exactly half what they had subscribed for Dominion Day, while Sam Wha, the only definitely Chinese subscriber on the Fourth of July list, offered eight dollars for that celebration and twenty for Dominion Day. Perhaps some residents refused to contribute for patriotic reasons. A more probable explanation is that the market for celebratory horse races was saturated: having contributed to the Dominion Day stakes, residents may have felt that the Independence Day event was superfluous. In the provincial interior, both American and Canadian national holidays were community-building events, appealing to people from a variety of class and ethnic backgrounds. Whether for sentimental or economic reasons, however, the First was clearly surpassing the Fourth in popularity.

The response to Boyd's appeal points to a wider decline in the observance of Independence Day. The change was neither immediate nor absolute. In districts such as the Kootenays, where American settlers and migrant workers preponderated, residents celebrated the Fourth of July well into the 1890s; in some border communities an excursion to a Fourth of July celebration across the line was an enduring ritual into the twentieth century. By 1900, however, formal observances within British Columbia were uncommon. Small private parties for expatriate Americans replaced the public Independence Day celebrations of the 1860s and 1870s, and the British Columbia press came to view the American holiday with hostility. When an Independence Day celebration was proposed in Rossland in 1903, the editor of the *Kamloops Inland Sentinel* wondered "just why that day should be made the occasion for a celebration in a Canadian city," and found in the decision to abandon the proposal "ample proof that the majority of the people of Rossland were not in favour of it." Out of respect for American miners, Rossland's mines did close on the Fourth that year, but there does not appear to have been a public celebration. The *Colonist* hoped that the American citizens who had organized a 1910 Independence Day picnic in Sidney would seek naturalization and take a greater interest in Canadian public affairs and progress. In language increasingly reminiscent of its eastern counterparts, the *Vancouver Sun's* Dominion Day editorial for 1915 drew a strong distinction between Dominion Day and Independence Day. Later that week, the display of the Stars and Stripes on the Fourth without accompanying British flags irritated the *Sun's* editor: "If the occurrence had been as glaring as in former years it would not have been tolerated," the paper warned.[14]

Newspapers were not impartial recorders of nationalist rituals; they were themselves participants, giving national significance to local observances. The Dominion Day editorial, an essay on the significance of the holiday, was the press's most significant contribution to Dominion Day discourse. Editorials on the meaning of Dominion Day had appeared in British Columbia newspapers during the Confederation campaign but had largely disappeared after 1871. They re-emerged in the late 1880s, and the tropes of fatherly foresight, setbacks overcome, freedom and prosperity, the imperial connection, the steady decline of sectionalism, and the annual intensification of national spirit were defining features of the genre over the next three decades. The *Colonist's* 1890 Dominion Day editorial expressed faith that railway and telegraph networks would unite the country, and pointed to changes in local self-identification as evidence of a growing national spirit. "In Nova Scotia and British Columbia," the paper observed, "the natives, particularly those who are past middle age, speak of 'Canada' as of some foreign country... But this state of things is passing away, and the inhabitants of the Dominion of Canada, east, west and middle, are beginning to realize that they are one people." Ten years later, the *Colonist* again summarized the early obstacles faced by the confederated provinces, reaffirmed the wisdom of the Fathers of Confederation, and concluded that "the people have only just succeeded in realizing what the Dominion of Canada really is."[15]

Perhaps the most important addition to the vocabulary of nationalist celebration in urban British Columbia was the parade. By the 1870s, Dominion Day parades were common in eastern Canadian cities. The practice reached British Columbia later, and became particularly popular in Vancouver. In 1892, the city's Dominion Day Celebration Committee sponsored a grand patriotic parade choreographed by Professor J.W. Trendall, a local music teacher. A "Grand Procession of school children, with flags and banners" was to be followed by "two cars in pyramidal shape on which are placed young ladies representing Canada, the Provinces, mineral and vegetable products, [and] Flora, the goddess of flowers, with her attendant children representing the various flowers." Coinciding as it did with the George Vancouver centenary celebrations in the United States, Trendall's procession was perhaps a one-time attempt to match the displays in Seattle, Washington, and Astoria, Oregon. The parade accounted for over one quarter of the committee's expenditure, and the expense entailed may explain future committees' reluctance to mount such grand patriotic pageants. Nevertheless, Vancouver did continue to organize more modest Dominion Day parades. In 1900, the parade opened with military contingents, followed by municipal dignitaries, allegorical floats, representatives of various friendly societies, merchants' displays, First Nations marching bands, and school children, as well as "illuminated bicycles." As Robert A.J. McDonald has suggested, Dominion Day parades in turn-of-the-century Vancouver ritualized social relationships as well as patriotism: they were conscious performances of respectability, in contrast with less-status-conscious celebrations in remote areas, such as Boyd's Cariboo horse races. Sporting events also took on symbolic significance, reflecting the city's multiple contexts. The "national sport" – lacrosse – typically pitted a Vancouver team against a representative of its cross-strait rival, Victoria. In the imperial game of cricket, a local "eleven" took on a Royal Navy crew, and a baseball match between Vancouver and a Washington State team rounded out the day's athletic events. Explicit in these pairings was an association of particular sports with particular nations: lacrosse with Canada, cricket with Great Britain, and baseball with the United States. A Vancouver team's participation in each suggested that the city was equally proud of its Canadian, imperial, and western North American heritage.[16]

The degree of Aboriginal participation differentiated British Columbia Dominion Day pageantry from that of the rest of Canada. During the first quarter-century after Confederation, Aboriginal peoples were conspicuous in Ontario Dominion Day events. In Toronto, for example, a highlight of the day was a lacrosse match between a city team and a visiting team from an outlying reserve. However, references to Aboriginal participation in urban Ontario Dominion Days decrease

after the 1880s. By contrast, contingents of First Nations people in traditional costume, as well as sports for "Indians" and "Klootchmen,"
were almost obligatory features of British Columbia celebrations. Aboriginal groups had their own reasons for observing settler holidays; for
example, crest poles honouring coronations and royal anniversaries
reminded viewers of the special relationship between First Nations and
the Crown. Holding potlatches on national holidays served a similarly
paradoxical function: the choice of occasion suggested loyalty, but the
choice of ceremony – banned by the federal government in 1884 – was
an act of defiance. In 1892, when First Nations around Vancouver held
a potlatch on the Queen's Birthday and again on Dominion Day, civic
authorities seized the opportunity to secure Aboriginal participation
in a seaside illumination. This adaptation of a very popular European
celebratory ritual featured Aboriginal canoes adorned with Chinese
lanterns and proved so successful that it became a regular tradition. In
addition to the illumination, bands of Aboriginal musicians regularly
provided musical entertainment, and 200 Tsimshian people from Fort
Simpson travelled over 500 miles to participate, in traditional costume,
in the 1900 Vancouver Dominion Day parade. First Nations marching
bands from the North Coast also performed in celebrations closer to
home, in the communities of Prince Rupert and Anyox. At first glance
a colonial institution, the Aboriginal brass band took on a variety of
cultural and political meanings, from the adaptation and perpetuation
of the musical tradition of the Potlatch to the demonstration of loyalty to Crown and country. Aboriginal people exercised considerable
agency in their participation in Dominion Day festivities: marching
bands actively sought opportunities to perform and negotiated their
own terms and fees.[17]

Regardless of the meanings that Aboriginal musicians themselves
ascribed to their involvement, white organizers had their own motives
for insisting on Aboriginal participation. On one level, white British
Columbians perceived Aboriginal participants as living proof of successful assimilation; the marching bands were, for example, formed at
the instigation of missionaries, who sometimes served as intermediar-
ies in discussions with Dominion Day organizers. In smaller frontier
communities like Prince Rupert or Anyox, where interaction between
Aboriginal people and other residents was a fact of everyday life, it
stood to reason that local Aboriginal groups, especially those deemed
"civilized," would be invited to participate in national holidays. More
problematic is the involvement of the "uncivilized" – that is, Aboriginal

people who marched in parades in traditional costume. For white citizens of Vancouver, a self-consciously modern city where authorities sought to erase most evidence of the Aboriginal past, costumed Aboriginal marchers were an exotic anachronism. Moreover, some urban British Columbians considered their First Nations neighbours admirable markers of regional distinctiveness. In Kamloops' 1897 Calithumpian parade, First Nations involvement was a matter of local pride. "The Indians really formed the backbone of the procession," boasted the *Inland Sentinel*, "and it is doubtful if there was another town in Canada that could have produced such an imposing array of red-skinned warriors." Marching in parades amid merchants' floats, bicycles, and other representations of urban progress, Aboriginal peoples suggested that, for all its integration into modernity, British Columbia remained a romantic last frontier where "Indians" continued to roam.[18]

The importance ascribed to First Nations involvement suggested the new, regionally specific meaning for Dominion Day that would develop during the 1920s, as British Columbians increasingly used the national holiday to celebrate local experiences of frontier life. The notion that hinterland celebrations of national holidays were singularly authentic was well established by the time Frank Kitto found himself in Prince George in 1919. As early as 1911, the editor of the *Fort George Herald* had opined that frontier towns exhibited a particular "vim and éclat" in their observances of Dominion Day, in contrast with "large and congested cities," where community events vied with private excursions for residents' attention. That year, Aboriginal canoeists tested their mettle in the turbulent waters of the Fraser River, and a tug-of-war pitted Aboriginal visitors against white settlers. Eight years later, the *Prince George Citizen* interpreted the multitude of Aboriginal attendees that Kitto had observed as a testament to the success of the festivities. "The Indian is the best judge of a proper celebration," affirmed the paper in 1919, "and the visiting red brothers were unanimous in declaring this year's blowout 'one hyu good time.'" Six years later, the *Citizen* explicitly associated frontier identity with indigeneity, reporting on the success of the Dominion Day stampede that, "when it comes to horses most of the people of the west are as much Indians as the red men."[19]

Regionalism was even more explicitly expressed in the paper's Dominion Day editorials. The editorial in the *Citizen* for Dominion Day 1920 resembled those elsewhere in the country in its optimistic tone; however, its optimism focused on local, rather than national, progress. Past Dominion Days in Prince George had given rival factions an occasion to bury their differences, and now all sides were united in building the city and its hinterland. With the imminent completion of a rail link to Vancouver in the south and Peace River in the north, Prince George was poised to become "the natural distributing centre for the whole interior country." Moreover, the *Citizen*'s editor could not resist a shot at naysayers from outside the region. "While this and other towns along the line of the G.T.P. [Grand Trunk Pacific] may appear crude and unimportant to the superficial observation of an occasional Easterner in the observation car, yet the signs are all plain for the man who has followed the trend of western development to read, which point to the promise of big future development." Perhaps with the regional aspect of earlier Dominion Days in mind, the newly formed Native Sons of Canada assembly in Prince George announced in 1924 that they would play an active role in the organization of Dominion Day celebrations, in the hope that the celebration might exhibit "a more national character than it has borne in the past." Little appears to have changed, however, for in 1928, the program of sports still featured lumbermen's competitions, "Indian" sports, and the obligatory horse races, with names – the Prince George Derby and the Cariboo, Vanderhoof, and Telkwa Stakes – that defined the town's hinterland. Kitto's boisterous, multicultural, frontier celebration was not a contrived performance, but it did reinforce the boosterist press's conception of regional distinction.[20]

Frontier imagery became a popular Dominion Day motif elsewhere in the province, but in the large cities of the south it lacked the spontaneous authenticity of the Prince George example. Rather, it was a manufactured marker of regional identity. The most explicit example was the Vancouver Tyee Potlatch, a week-long Dominion Day festival first held in Stanley Park in 1922 and repeated in 1924. If the insistence of Vancouverites of an earlier generation on Aboriginal participation had suggested a tension between assimilation and exoticism, the organizers of the 1922 "potlatch" clearly favoured the latter. Spearheaded by the city's Gyro Club as a fundraiser for children's playgrounds, the event took as its inspiration a similar festival held annually in Seattle before the First World War. As in its American prototype, "playing Indian" was the underlying theme of the potlatch; for the organizers, indigeneity and regional identity were interchangeable, and white participants enthusiastically assumed Aboriginal personas. The patrons and organizers of the potlatch adopted chiefly titles – Lieutenant-Governor W.C. Nichol served as "the Great White Chief," presiding over a "War

Council" – and Miss Isobel Morrison donned the regal robes of an Indian "Princess of the Potlatch" to inspect her subjects from a sylvan bower erected on a flatbed truck. In the evening, she presided over the Tyee Potlatch "Powwow," a fancy dress ball at which a prize was offered for the best Indian costume; an "authentic Indian," Squamish leader and activist Andrew Paull, served as adjudicator.

Aboriginal sports featured prominently in the spectacle and, like its Prince George contemporaries, the *Vancouver Sun* imbued the First Nations with newcomer notions of masculinity, transforming them into exemplars of frontier virtue: "Bending their stout cedar paddles, as they shot their hand-carved dugouts through the water in keenest competition and cheered by their fellow tribesmen and whitemen [sic] alike, the descendants of B.C.'s aboriginal populace were stirred again into the spirit of tribal battle, matching skill and strength in sportsmanlike fight." Romantic indicators of a frontier landscape, British Columbia's indigenous people were called upon to demonstrate the ancient virtues of their race in the name of region building.[21]

The romantically contrived Tyee Potlatch obfuscated very real tensions between Aboriginal and non-Aboriginal British Columbians; the "potlatch" took place just months after the mass arrests and seizure of Kwakwaka'wakw ceremonial regalia at Alert Bay that followed Dan Cranmer's more authentic – and illegal – potlatch on Christmas Day 1921. Such apparent contradictions abounded in British Columbia and throughout the Pacific Northwest during the interwar period. Yet beyond the gimmicky appropriation of First Nations imagery to turn a profit for the organizers, the inclusion of Aboriginal sports, costumes, and symbols in this particular Dominion Day celebration spoke to Vancouverites' visions of their city and province, which emphasized both the modern and the anti-modern. The organizers played on nostalgia, offering "the one-time good old-fashioned First of July celebration that we ourselves knew and cherished, but which our children have never enjoyed." In the *Sun*'s estimation, the presence of Aboriginal people "lent an air to the celebration that made it really Western." Truly western, perhaps, but not truly British Columbian, for it blended Prairie and coastal First Nations symbols and costumes with no apparent concern for authenticity: totem poles and Chinook Jargon slogans mingled with feathered head dresses, teepees, and calumets on potlatch parade floats, in promotional materials, and in the costumes of participants. They evoked a generalized "West" or "frontier" rather than the specific location in which the celebration took place.[22]

8.1 Vancouver Mayor W.R. Owen, wearing buckskin and a feathered headdress, poses with the city's float for the 1924 Vancouver Tyee Potlatch. Note the float's totem poles and British and American flags. City of Vancouver Archives, AM54-S4-: Fl P3.2.

In Vancouver, as in Prince George and elsewhere, Dominion Day was an exercise in defining a hinterland. The metropolitan influence of regional centres could be measured by the distances that visitors travelled to attend the festivities, and the unifying potential of the day on a local and provincial level did not go unnoticed. For the *Victoria Colonist*, a successful excursion to Vancouver for its 1895 Dominion Day festivities reminded Victorians that "we are British Columbians and that we are becoming a united people in a united province, each city proud of the other cities as part of our own province." Conversely, in 1905 the *Kamloops Inland Sentinel* criticized the Canadian Pacific Railway for its failure to offer excursion fares for Kamloopsians travelling to Armstrong for another July holiday, the Orange Order's festivities on the "Glorious Twelfth," the anniversary of the Battle of the Boyne. The *Sentinel* was a consistent critic of the railway, whose rates, schedules, and policies frustrated the efforts of Kamloops's city fathers to consolidate their influence over the interior region. As Dominion Day pageantry became more elaborate, it came to epitomize the metropolitan aspirations of the cities. Kamloops's Dominion Day celebrations in the early 1920s celebrated the history of the entire interior region, with a midway called the "Cariboo Trail" and stagecoaches and other frontier elements prominently displayed in the parade. Meanwhile, Vancouver's celebrations melded the regional, the national, and the global. The Native Sons of Canada entered a float in Vancouver's Calithumpian Parade of 1925, incorporating Miss Canada and her provincial princesses, as well as a fire evocative of the "spreading flames of national spirit." The use of allegorical female figures recalled Professor Trendall's 1892 float and anticipated the imagery of the Diamond Jubilee of Confederation celebrations in 1927. However, the Native Sons' float shared the parade with a Hudson's Bay Company bastion, Cariboo sourdoughs, and cowboys, as well as a giant silkworm representing Vancouver's place in Pacific trade. As at the turn of the century, multiple contexts underpinned local pride: Vancouver was at once the metropolis of a vast provincial hinterland and Canada's Pacific gateway.[23]

For some celebration organizers, the participation of Canadians of Asian descent could evoke this Pacific context, just as the presence of Aboriginal people suggested the frontier. As with Aboriginal participation, the presence of Asian Canadians at British Columbia Dominion Day celebrations was probably commonplace, even unremarkable – except to eastern visitors. Chinese names among the subscribers to John Boyd's horse races in the 1880s may suggest a grudging racial equality among frontier celebrants, as seems also to be the case in Frank Kitto's account of Dominion Day in Prince George. On other occasions, Chinese- or Japanese-Canadian involvement was part of an orchestrated program. A Chinese Carnival Village figured in Mayor Gerald Gatten McGeer's celebration of Vancouver's Pacific connections for the Golden Jubilee of the city's incorporation in 1936. McGeer opposed Asian immigration, but he happily worked with existing Asian immigrant communities to evoke transpacific economic ties and to entice tourists hungry for the exotic; promotional materials for the Vancouver Golden Jubilee invited visitors to "savour the tangy cooking of

Nippon" and experience "a riot of colour and pungent ... odours of ancient China" in the city's Oriental enclaves. Conversely, Asian Canadians used their participation in patriotic celebrations to protest their exclusion from mainstream Canadian society and to assert their claims to citizenship. During the 1920s and 1930s, some Chinese Canadians in Vancouver subverted Dominion Day with their own Chinese Humiliation Day, as discussed in Lianbi Zhu and Timothy Baycroft's chapter in this volume. Similarly, the Vancouver Golden Jubilee parade organized by the Chinese Benevolent Association featured a float honouring "the Chinese pioneers of British Columbia." This bid for the inclusion of Chinese railway navvies among the province's founding fathers paralleled the enthusiastic involvement of Japanese Canadians in local Dominion Day festivities, particularly during the Diamond Jubilee in 1927. In Prince Rupert, the Japanese community contributed a float to the jubilee Dominion Day parade, while the Japanese Canadians of the Cowichan Valley raised almost seventy dollars for the jubilee festivities in Duncan. In Vancouver, the Canadian Japanese Association sponsored the Diamond Jubilee fireworks. This desire to participate in patriotic celebrations was consistent with the movement for political integration and enfranchisement that animated Asian-Canadian communities, especially Japanese Canadians, during the 1920s and 1930s. Their involvement in Dominion Day celebrations signified not only regional demographic realities and white organizers' thirst for the exotic, but also the aspirations of immigrant communities themselves.[24]

The province's continental context also returned to the fore. Brandon Dimmel has documented the generally cordial relations between Canadians and Americans during and after the First World War, as reflected in efforts to commemorate the 1914 centenary of the end of the War of 1812. Dominion Day iconography from the period evoked a spirit of good-natured competition, in place of the hostility that had typified pre–First World War commentary on American holidays. The program for the 1923 Dominion Day celebration in Vancouver, featured "Jack," the typical Canadian, reminding Uncle Sam that, with more territory than the United States, Canada would soon boast a population of over fifty million. In Kamloops that year, "John Bull" and "Uncle Sam" marched side by side as part of a Rotary Club contingent in the Dominion Day parade. John Bull taunted his teetotalling companion with a whiskey bottle throughout the parade, and the caption to their portrait, "No 12 Mile Limit Here," (see figure 8.2) playfully alluded to the dispute between Great Britain and the United States over American

8.2 "No 12 Mile Limit Here, Dominion Day, Kamloops BC 1923." Kamloops Museum and Archives #3049.

enforcement of prohibition at sea. The economic relationship with the neighbouring American states was strengthened by the rise of automobile tourism, and the July national holidays coincided nicely with the opening of tourist season. The Vancouver Tyee Potlatch, as a week-long spectacle, included an "American Day" on the Fourth of July; Old Glory wafted among the Union Jacks and Red Ensigns, and Washington State licence plates were reportedly as prevalent as British Columbia ones on Vancouver streets.[25]

Recognition of the value of tourism – American and domestic alike – to the local economy accounts for this more accommodating attitude, as economic benefit was never far from the minds of celebration organizers, particularly after the onset of the Depression. In 1931, the organizing committee for the Diamond Jubilee of British Columbia's provincehood hesitated about asking the provincial government to proclaim the day of the jubilee – 20 July – a public holiday out of concern that requiring local businesses to close would deny them the benefit of the anticipated tourist trade. Instead, the committee recommended that civil servants be given the day off and private businesses be encouraged to close only for the afternoon, during the jubilee pageant. Moreover, when asking businesses to sponsor jubilee festivities, the organizers emphasized the aggressive tourism advertising campaign that they had undertaken in western Canada and the United States. Patriotic celebrations toed the line between fostering national and local pride and attracting almighty tourist dollars.[26]

Such economic imperatives notwithstanding, Dominion Day remained an occasion for considering British Columbia's place within Confederation, and, in general, celebration organizers were content with the Canadian connection. During the 1927 jubilee, for example, local organizing committees in British Columbia faithfully adhered to the programming suggestions of the national committee in Ottawa. The secretary of the local committee on Hornby Island, near Comox, was proud to report that she and her fellow islanders were "endeavoring as far as possible to carry out the programme suggested by the National Committee... Although a small community we hope to take just as important a part." Observances in other parts of the province suggest a similar commitment to participation and uniformity; the linguistic, sectarian, and sectional controversies that accompanied Diamond Jubilee celebrations elsewhere in Canada had little resonance in British Columbia. Celebrating a national anniversary in tandem with the rest of the country was a source of local pride, and organizers were also keen to send a message of national solidarity in their procurement policies. Both the Duncan organizing committee for the Diamond Jubilee of Confederation in 1927 and the Victoria committee for the British Columbia Diamond Jubilee of 1931 opted to purchase their fireworks from the F.W. Hand Company of Hamilton rather than the Hitt Company of Seattle, which typically supplied the British Columbia market and had hoped to capitalize on the Canadian celebration. Ordering from Ontario was both less convenient and more costly than ordering from Washington State; thus, organizers' preference for Canadian products suggested a patriotism that went beyond the pocketbook.[27]

Amid organizers' attempts to balance national dreams with continental realities, Dominion Day editorials of the 1920s and 1930s reprised frontier themes, regional particularity, and, increasingly, regional discontent. Correcting the misconception that the frontier was no more, the *Vancouver Sun*'s 1915 editorial noted that British Columbia still offered much virgin land where, with hard work and moral fortitude, modern-day pioneers would prosper and achieve independence. The *Colonist*'s Dominion Day editorial for 1920 noted the fiftieth anniversary of British Columbia's Confederation negotiations. In the 1870s, some eastern politicians had derided British Columbia as a "sea of mountains," but more recent commentators confirmed that, even if the province was not "a country literally 'flowing with milk and honey'," it certainly possessed resources that would ensure its prominence, and even pre-eminence, within Confederation. By the mid-1920s, with the resurrection of resentment over the Crow Rate and the Railway Belt, overt acknowledgment of sectional differences became a trope of Dominion Day editorials throughout the province. While his 1925 Dominion Day editorial did not itself express specific grievances, the editor of the *Nanaimo Free Press* nevertheless feared that sectional and factional divisions were inevitable; this gloomy acknowledgment in an otherwise optimistic editorial stood in contrast with the rosy projections of national and cross-partisan unity that had typified Dominion Day editorials in the 1890s. The *Colonist*'s 1925 editorial put a positive gloss on the existence of sectional tension, which, alongside contested discussions of a national flag and the abolition of appeals to the Privy Council, was proof of Canada's growing "virility." More pessimistic was the editorial published that year in the *Kamloops Sentinel*. The Dominion Day "panegyrics" of yesteryear had done nothing to ease the nation's economic distress, and the Kamloops editor saw no disloyalty in pointing out the problems with Confederation, especially British Columbia's long-standing irritant, the tariff. Tariff reform, rather than hopeful platitudes and promises so long deferred, would make for "a Dominion Day worth remembering." By 1937, the *Sentinel*'s pre–Dominion Day editorial concluded that Confederation had not been an unqualified success. Its five "great divisions" had not yet been integrated, and central Canadian neglect of British Columbia was particularly egregious. "Despite the steel rails," the editorial ran, "despite the advances of modern transportation and communication the Rocky Mountains still rise like an inseparable [sic] barrier between British Columbia and the rest of the dominion of Canada. British Columbia feels, at times, like the country cousin who, though every fibre may strain toward the blood relations with whom he lives, has the idea that he is only permitted by sufferance and for what his relations can make out of him." In spite of the east-west axes of tradition and technology, the editor concluded that "still the propinquity of the peoples of Washington, Oregon and California pull [sic] us to the south."[28]

In addition to attributing new regionally specific meanings to Dominion Day, some British Columbians proposed a new provincial holiday. The idea was not new: as early as 1872, a correspondent of the *Victoria Daily Standard* had suggested the consecration of 20 July, the day the Terms of Union came into effect, as the birthday of British Columbia and a day to measure the value of Confederation to the province. That date still had its adherents during the interwar period. During the 1920s, the British Columbia Historical Association and the Native Sons of British Columbia, a regional fraternal organization and rival of the nationalist Native Sons of Canada, suggested the observance of "Douglas Day," the anniversary of the proclamation of the mainland colony on 19 November 1858, as a local complement to holidays of national and imperial significance. However, the new holiday itself was threatened by sectional rivalry. Vancouver Island members of the historical association instead selected the anniversary of the proclamation of the colony of Vancouver Island, and observed it as "Blanshard Day" until well into the 1930s. Undeterred by the controversy, the Native Sons of British Columbia endeavoured to popularize Douglas Day by scheduling their public activities on the day and wearing sprigs of native evergreen in their lapels. However, the celebration achieved lasting popularity only in Fort Langley and New Westminster, both communities being associated directly with the proclamation of the colony. Whether because of the controversies surrounding its emergence, or because a holiday in late November was less conducive to picnics, fireworks, and outdoor games than a holiday in early July, Douglas Day never enjoyed a significant following.[29]

A third factor perhaps accounts for the failure of Douglas Day – or any other provincial holiday – to present a serious challenge to Dominion Day: over seven decades, the national holiday had proven itself flexible enough to accommodate regional rituals and meanings. The British Columbian experience of Dominion Day parallels the "geopolitical" pattern David Waldstreicher has identified in patriotic celebrations in the early American republic. Waldstreicher's research suggests that the nationalist rituals and rhetoric varied considerably from region to region, as local elites commandeered the symbolic potential of the national holiday to advance local interests. In New England and the South, Fourth of July toasts, orations, and newspaper editorials cast the authors' regions as heartlands of true Americanism, juxtaposed with other regions lacking in republican virtue. In the West, celebratory rituals tended to underline local grievances and demands, such as free navigation of the Mississippi River and, later, statehood. Early exposure to American patriotic practices, especially when they attracted the attention of irresponsible colonial authorities, made British Columbians keenly aware of the political potential of a national holiday. Therefore, Dominion Day initially became the occasion for political agitation in favour of responsible government and Confederation; its emulation of the Fourth of July reinforced local perceptions of union with Canada as a revolutionary event. In the 1880s and 1890s, British Columbia Dominion Day traditions converged somewhat with those of eastern Canada, especially Ontario: parades and other patriotic pageantry became more common, and the rhetorical conventions of the Dominion Day editorial became well established. After the First World War, these rituals themselves became media for the expression of regional identities and grievances. To eastern Canadian nationalists, the rhetoric of the *Kamloops Sentinel*'s 1937 Dominion Day editorial might be alarming, but the regionalization of Dominion Day did not necessarily imply dissatisfaction with Confederation. Rather, as in the United States, the process was indicative of the strength of nationalism: British Columbians could redefine Dominion Day because they viewed national identity as a participatory process rather than a received ideology. The elaboration of familiar Canadian and American traditions into "rites of regionalism" strengthened national sentiment as it legitimized regional identities.[30]

NOTES

1 Frank Hugh Kitto, "Season of 1919: Mainly Central British Columbia," 4,
   British Columbia Archives (hereafter BCA), Frank Hugh Kitto fonds, G/
   B77/K65; "Dominion Day Doings," *Brampton Conservator*, 4 July 1895.
2 José Eduardo Igartua, *The Other Quiet Revolution: National Identities in
   English Canada, 1945–71* (Vancouver: UBC Press, 2006), 96–107; Matthew
   Hayday, "Fireworks, Folk-dancing, and Fostering a National Identity: The
   Politics of Canada Day," *Canadian Historical Review* 91, no. 2 (2010): 287–314.
   See also Hayday's chapter in the present volume.
3 David Waldstreicher, *In the Midst of Perpetual Fetes: The Making of American
   Nationalism, 1776–1820* (Chapel Hill: University of North Carolina Press, 1997);
   Len Travers, *Celebrating the Fourth: Independence Day and the Rites of Nationalism
   in the Early Republic* (Amherst: University of Massachusetts Press, 1997).
4 "Life of the Late W.B. Cameron, an Overlander of '62," 3, BCA, R.W.
   Gardiner fonds, MS 2438; Charles Hayward Diary, entry for 4 July 1862,
   29, City of Victoria Archives (hereafter VICA), Charles Hayward fonds, PR
   118, Loc. 27-D-4, file 3; "The Fourth of July at Yale," *New Westminster British
   Columbian*, 6 July 1867; Richard E. Neunherz, "'Hemmed In': Reactions in
   British Columbia to the Purchase of Russian America," *Pacific Northwest
   Quarterly* 80, no. 3 (1989): 101–11; "Fourth of July Celebration," *Cariboo
   Sentinel* (Barkerville), 9 July 1870; "Independence Day," *New Westminster
   Mainland Guardian*, 5 July 1871. A "federal salute" consists of thirteen guns,
   to honour the original Thirteen Colonies. A "national salute" consists of one
   gun for each contemporary state (i.e., between thirty-two and thirty-seven
   during the period 1858–71). In nineteenth-century American slang, a "tiger"
   was a "shriek or howl ... terminating a prolonged and enthusiastic cheer"
   (*OED Online*, accessed 24 December 2014. www.oed.com).
5 J.S. Helmcken, *The Reminiscences of Dr. John Sebastian Helmcken*, ed. Dorothy
   Blakey Smith (Vancouver: UBC Press, 1975), 186; "Vancouver and British
   Columbia," *Toronto Globe*, 2 April 1859; "Letters from British Columbian
   Missionaries," *Christian Guardian* (Toronto), 6 April 1859; Kennedy to Cardwell,
   5 July 1866, 2, and [Illegible] to Under-Secretary of State, 20 September 1866,
   114, Library and Archives Canada, MG 11, CO 305/29, reel B-251.
6 Edward White Diary, 1859–66, entry for 4 July 1865, United Church of
   Canada British Columbia Conference Archives, Edward White fonds,
   file 2; "The Celebration," *New Westminster British Columbian*, 8 July 1868;
   "Independence Day," *British Columbian*, 4 July 1868; "Grand Celebration of
   the Fourth of July at Port Townsend," *Victoria Colonist*, 30 June 1871; "The
   Greatest Event of Modern Times," *Victoria Standard*, 4 July 1870.

7 "Speech Delivered at Moodyville, 20 July 1871," BCA, Josiah Charles Hughes fonds, E/B/H87.3. Compare Hughes's depiction of railway construction with Luke 3:4–6: "Prepare ye the way of the Lord, make his paths straight. Every valley shall be filled, and every mountain and hill shall be brought low; and the crooked shall be made straight, and the rough ways shall be made smooth. And all flesh shall see the salvation of God." On the formula of American patriotic oratory, see Barnett Baskerville, "19th Century Burlesque of Oratory," *American Quarterly* 20, no. 4 (1968): 731.

8 "Dominion Day," *Cariboo Sentinel* (Barkerville), 2 July 1868; "Dominion Day," *New Westminster British Columbian*, 1 July 1868.

9 "Dominion Day," *New Westminster British Columbian*, 1 July 1868; "The Birth of Liberty," *Victoria Colonist*, 20 July 1871"; Our Future," *Victoria Standard*, 5 July 1870; "Dominion Day: Firemen's Parade and Picnic," *Victoria Colonist*, 2 July 1871.

10 "Dominion Day," *Toronto Globe*, 4 June 1875; "Fourth of July," *London Daily Advertiser*, 4 July 1870; "Independence Day in the States," *Sarnia Observer*, 10 July 1874; "Dominion Day," *Toronto Mail*, 1 July 1880.

11 "Fourth of July," *Victoria Standard*, 5 July 1872; William Henry Barneby, *Life and Labour in the Far, Far West: Being Notes of a Tour in the Western States, British Columbia, Manitoba, and the North-West Territory* (London: Cassell, 1884), 136, 150; Julian Ralph, "Canada's El Dorado," *Harper's New Monthly Magazine* 84 (1891): 172; "The Fourth of July," *Mainland Guardian*, 6 July 1872; "The Two Anniversaries," *Victoria Standard*, 6 July 1872.

12 "Dominion Day," *London Daily Advertiser*, 30 June 1870; "The Nova Scotia Grits and Confederation," *Toronto Mail*, 1 July 1875; "Welcome to a Secessionist," *Toronto Mail and Empire*, 3 July 1900; "Dominion Day at Langley," *New Westminster Mainland Guardian*, 5 July 1876; "Dominion Day," *Victoria Colonist*, 1 July 1876; "Dominion Day," *Victoria Colonist*, 1 July 1884.

13 "Dominion Day Subscriptions," BCA, John Boyd fonds, MS 1588, Reel A01029, item 1.

14 "Monday's Celebration," *Yale Inland Sentinel*, 7 July 1881; "Fourth of July," *Nanaimo Free Press*, 4 July 1885; "The Glorious Fourth," *New Westminster Mainland Guardian*, 8 July 1885; "Fourth of July at Peck's," *Nanaimo Free Press*, 4 July 1890; "Dominion Day and the Fourth of July," *Nelson Daily Miner*, 5 July 1890; "Cariboo Notes," *Kamloops Inland Sentinel*, 11 July 1899; "4th July at Port Angeles [advertisement]," *Victoria Colonist*, 30 June 1895; "Keeping the Fourth," *Nelson Daily News*, 5 July 1905; "Rossland has Dropped ...," *Kamloops Inland Sentinel*, 30 June 1903; "The Fourth a

Holiday," *Rossland Miner*, 3 July 1903; "The Gathering at Sidney," *Victoria Colonist*, 5 July 1910; "Dominion Day," *Vancouver Sun*, 1 July 1915; "Our Flag," *Vancouver Sun*, 5 July 1915.

15 Waldstreicher, *In the Midst of Perpetual Fetes*, 11; Igartua, *The Other Quiet Revolution*, 96–107; "Dominion Day," *Victoria Colonist*, 1 July 1887; "Dominion Day," *Victoria Colonist*, 1 July 1888; "Dominion Day," *Kamloops Inland Sentinel*, 3 July 1906; "Throughout the Length and Breadth of Canada ..." *Inland Sentinel*, 2 July 1907; "The Day We Celebrate," *Inland Sentinel*, 3 July 1908; "Dominion Day and Incorporation," *North Vancouver Express*, 28 June 1907; "Dominion Day," *Nelson Daily News*, 1 July 1910; "Dominion Day," *Victoria Colonist*, 2 July 1890; "Dominion Day," *Victoria Colonist*, 2 July 1900.

16 "The Speeches Yesterday," *Globe*, 2 July 1875; *Inaugural Celebration Held in the Village of Deseronto, Dominion Day, 1881* (Napanee: Templeton & Beeman, 1881), 24; "A Great Celebration," *Toronto Mail*, 2 July 1890; Minutes, 10 May 1892 and 15 June 1900, City of Vancouver Archives (hereafter CVA), Dominion Day Celebration Committee, Add. MSS. 47, Loc. 502-F-4, files 1 and 2"; Puget Sound's Discoverer: Capt. Vancouver's Voyages a Century Ago," *New York Times*, 11 May 1892; Robert A.J. McDonald, *Making Vancouver: Class, Status and Social Boundaries, 1863–1913* (Vancouver: UBC Press, 1996), 33–5, 60; "In Honor of Canada," *Vancouver World*, 2 July 1895; *Committee Program: Dominion Day and Coronation Celebration* (Vancouver: Dominion Day Celebration Committee, 1902), 4–5.

17 "Dominion Day," *London Daily Advertiser*, 10 July 1868; "'Canada First' Ought Now..." *Toronto Mail*, 2 July 1875; *Inaugural Celebration Held in Deseronto*," 24; Ronald William Hawker, *Tales of Ghosts: First Nations Art in British Columbia, 1922–61* (Vancouver: UBC Press, 2003), 100–11; "A Potlatch: The Siwashes Intend Holding a First Family Affair," *Quebec Morning Chronicle*, 8 March 1892; Minutes, 10 May 1892, 20 June 1893, 24 June 1893, 30 May 1894, 5 June 1895, 15 June 1897, 28 June 1900, and Minutes of Sub-Committee on Programme, 2 June 1897, CVA, Add. MSS 47, Loc. 502-F-4, files 1–2; *Dominion Day: Programme of Sports* (Prince Rupert, BC: Empire Print, 1909); Anyox Community League, *Dominion Day Celebration, Friday, July 1st, 1921: Programme of Events* (Anyox: Author, 1921); Susan Neylan and Melissa Meyer, "'Here Come the Band!' Cultural Collaboration, Connective Traditions, and Aboriginal Brass Bands on British Columbia's North Coast, 1875–1964," *BC Studies* 152 (2006): 35–66. "Klootchman," the Chinook Jargon word for woman, was initially not derogatory, but eventually took on much the same connotation as "squaw" in eastern North America.

18 Minutes, 27 and 28 June 1894, CVA, Add. MSS 47, Loc. 502-F-4, file 1; Jean
   Barman, "Erasing Indigenous Indigeneity in Vancouver," *BC Studies* 155
   (2007): 3–30; "Kamloops Celebration," *Kamloops Inland Sentinel*, 25 June
   1897.

19 "Dominion Day Celebration a Huge Success," *Fort George Herald*, 8 July
   1911; "Canada's National Holiday Was Fittingly Celebrated," *Prince George
   Citizen*, 3 July 1919; "Three Thousand People Cheer When Prince George
   Stampede Was Formally Opened," *Prince George Citizen*, 2 July 1925. "Hyu"
   is likely a variant spelling of the Chinook Jargon superlative, "hiyu."

20 "Welcome!" *Prince George Citizen*, 30 June 1920; "Prince George Assembly
   Native Sons of Canada Elected Officers for Year," *Prince George Citizen*,
   27 March 1924; Prince George Agricultural and Industrial Association,
   Prince George: Fourth Annual Dominion Day Celebration and Race Meet (Prince
   George: Author, 1928).

21 "'Seattle Spirit' Soars on Hype," *Seattle Times*, 10 March 1996; "'Princess
   Isobel' Leads Her Subjects in Imposing Procession through Crowds
   Thronging Streets," *Vancouver Sun*, 2 July 1922; "Potlatch Will Enhance Big
   Celebration," *Vancouver Sun*, 1 July 1922; "Parade Miles Long Viewed by
   Thousands," *Vancouver Sun*, 2 July 1922.

22 Tina Loo, "Dan Cranmer's Potlatch: Law as Coercion, Symbol, and
   Rhetoric in British Columbia, 1884–1951," *Canadian Historical Review* 73, no.
   2 (1992): 125–6; Paige Raibmon, *Authentic Indians: Episodes of Encounter from
   the Late-Nineteenth-Century Northwest Coast* (Durham, NC: Duke University
   Press, 2005); *Official Programme: Vancouver Tyee Potlatch, June 30 to July 5,
   1922* (Vancouver: Sun Publishing, 1922), 9; "Parade Miles Long Viewed by
   Thousands," *Vancouver Sun*, 2 July 1922; "Vancouver Tyee Potlatch: Hi-Yu
   Tillicum! [advertisement]," *Vancouver Sun*, 1 July 1922; "'Hi-Yu Tillicum':
   Vancouver Tyee Potlatch Swings on the New Successes [advertisement],"
   Vancouver Sun, 3 July 1922.

23 "News of the Province," *Victoria Colonist*, 3 July 1895; *Kamloops Inland
   Sentinel*, 7 July 1905; "Celebration Was Great Success," *Kamloops Sentinel*,
   4 July 1922; "Kamloops' Dominion Day Celebration Starts Sunday,"
   Kamloops Sentinel, 30 June 1923; "Parade Amazes Citizens," *Vancouver Sun*,
   2 July 1925.

24 Vancouver Golden Jubilee Committee, *Vancouver's Golden Jubilee Official
   Pictorial Souvenir Programme, 1886–1936* (Vancouver: Author, 1936), 70;
   "Glamorous Night of Chinese Festival," *Vancouver Sun*, 17 July 1936;
   "Chinatown on Parade," *Vancouver Sun*, 20 July 1936; Canada, National
   Diamond Jubilee Executive Committee, *Report of Executive Committee,
   National Diamond Jubilee of Confederation* (Ottawa: F.A. Acland, King's

Printer, 1928), 18; Duncan District Japanese Shinwa-Kwai to Committee, undated [1927], and Subscription Lists, 30 June 1927, Cowichan Valley Museum and Archives (hereafter CVMA), Committee for Canada's Diamond Jubilee Celebration fonds, Acc. 981.4.2.1; "Fine Display of Fireworks," *Vancouver Sun*, 2 July 1927. On early campaigns for Japanese-Canadian integration and enfranchisement, see Patricia Roy, *The Oriental Question: Consolidating a White Man's Province, 1914–41* (Vancouver: UBC Press, 2003), 153–65.

25 Brandon Dimmel, "Children of a Common Mother: The Rise and Fall of the Anglo-American Peace Centenary", in *Celebrating Canada*, vol. 2, ed. Matthew Hayday and Raymond Blake (forthcoming); Native Sons of Canada, *Program: Dominion Day Celebration, July 2 1923* (Vancouver: Native Sons of Canada, 1923), 4–5; "Pageant Proves Feature Dominion Day Attraction," *Kamloops Sentinel*, 3 July 1923; "Playgrounds Made Reality by Potlatch," *Vancouver Sun*, 5 July 1922. On the importance of American automobile tourism in British Columbia, see Michael Dawson, *Selling British Columbia: Tourism and Consumer Culture, 1890–1970* (Vancouver: UBC Press, 2004), chap. 2.

26 Reginald Hayward to Harry Maynard, 30 May 1931, and Hayward to P. Walker, 4 July 1931, BCA, Native Sons of British Columbia fonds, MS 503, file 145–3.

27 Mary A. Cleasley to John Hosie, 18 June 1927, BCA, British Columbia Provincial Library records, GR 523, box 1, file 2; James M. Pitsula, "Muscular Saskatchewan: Provincial Self-Identity in the 1920s," *Saskatchewan History* 54, no. 2 (2002): 13; Robert Cupido, "Appropriating the Past: Pageants, Politics and the Diamond Jubilee of Confederation," *Journal of the Canadian Historical Association* 9 (1998): 155–86. CVMA, Committee for Canada's Diamond Jubilee Celebration fonds, Acc. 981.4.2.1: Thomas Hitt to Committee Secretary, 25 February and 11 March 1927; John Greig to John Hosie, 25 April 1927; Hosie to Greig, 27 April 1927; Greig to Toronto Fireworks Co. and F.W. Hand Fireworks Co., 28 April 1927; and Greig to Hand Co., 28 May 1927. BCA, Native Sons of British Columbia fonds, M/D55: Minutes, 26 May 1931, J. Baxter to R.H. Hiscocks, 15 June 1931, Hiscocks to Baxter, 17 June 1931.

28 "Dominion Day," *Vancouver Sun*, 1 July 1915; "Canada's Natal Day," *Victoria Colonist*, 1 July 1920; "Canada's Birthday," *Nanaimo Free Press*, 2 July 1925; "Dominion Day," *Victoria Colonist*, 1 July 1925; "Dominion Day," *Kamloops Sentinel*, 30 June 1925; "Dominion Day," *Kamloops Sentinel*, 1 July 1937.

29 An Old Fifty-Eighter, "The Twentieth," *Victoria Standard*, 3 July 1872; "Wrong Date Honored, July 20 Actually Dominion Day in BC, Clubmen

Told," *Vancouver Sun*, 19 August 1938; Executive Minutes, 12 September 1925, Nanaimo Community Archives, Native Sons of British Columbia Grand Post fonds, Minutes series; Chad Reimer, "'Provincial in Name Only': The Great Birthday Debate of 1926 and the Early Years of the British Columbia Historical Association," *British Columbia Historical News* 35, no. 1 (2001/2): 2; "Native Sons Hold Douglas Day," *Ubyssey* (University of British Columbia, Vancouver), 16 November 1926; Minutes, 13 October 1927 and 17 November 1927 and Grand Post Minutes, 26–7 April 1929 and 25–6 April 1930, VICA, Native Sons of British Columbia fonds, PR 87, Loc. 29-B-6, files 5–6; Frederic William Howay, *Douglas Day: The Birthday of British Columbia* (New Westminster: Jackson Printing, 1941).

30 Waldstreicher, *In the Midst of Perpetual Fetes*, chap. 5.

9 Dominion Day in Britain, 1900–1919

MIKE BENBOUGH-JACKSON

National days are not confined by national boundaries. "Symbolic regimes," events, or figures that are particular to a nation's history are often exported, so "the nation is performed outside of the territorial nation state."[1] In new settings, national days take on additional meanings. Sometimes national identity is heightened by a foreign environment. In other locations, traditions may be dampened as migrants attempt to fit into their new environment. Imported celebrations also acquire a new audience, who may be welcoming, hostile, inquisitive, or indifferent; and in those instances it is not just members of the community who imagine their nation – outsiders do too. Given the public nature of most national celebrations, imported national days are noticeable and provide a platform for dialogue with and interpretation and assessment of the newcomers. When, as is the case in this study, nations share an imperial and cultural heritage and are allies during war, the relationship between host and outsider is all the closer.

The following examination of the symbolic components and reception of Dominion Day in Britain during the Edwardian era and the First World War contributes to the history of Canadian identity in two ways. First, a focus on activities in Britain and on the British home front during the war helps rebalance the emphasis that has been placed on the importance of the battlefield in the formation and projection of Canadian identity during the early twentieth century.[2] This is not to say that the battlefront did not play a crucial role in the development of Canadian identity, but the emphasis that has been placed on this aspect means that other related expressions are often overlooked, although they, too, contribute to the "perpetually mutating repository" that figures in the process of identity formation.[3] Some of these expressions of Canadian identity were in evidence in Britain before the war, such as the Dominion Day celebrations that played a role in the export of "Canadian-ness" during the Edwardian era as well as during the war. These manifestations of Canada in Britain did not portray a "grand national ideal" but presented "more tangible practices, encounters, and stories" that paid particular attention to the symbols, qualities, and traditions associated with Canada and sometimes a broader North American identity.[4] They included the dominion's flag, the presence and behaviour of Canadian soldiers, and qualities revealed on the sports field and in beliefs about the nation's relationship to nature. They were also revealed in the response of Canadians in Britain to Independence Day and Dominion Day and the relationship between them.

Second, this chapter considers how the British responded to manifestations of Canadian identity, with specific reference to how they received and perceived Dominion Day. After all, identity needs to be validated by others. While scholars, including Forrest Pass and Matthew Hayday in this volume, have used Dominion Day and Canada Day celebrations to gauge changes in how Canadians saw the relationship between Canada and Britain, Canada and the empire, and between different parts of Canada, the place of Dominion Day celebrations beyond the North American continent has rarely garnered attention.[5] It is difficult to acquire evidence of how Canadians celebrated in Britain, let alone what Britons felt about Dominion Day. Although the national and local press reported on Dominion Day celebrations, they offered only patchy coverage and were unlikely to have reported on all opinions about the celebration. Despite these limitations, the press provides an outline of the extent of the celebrations and what those celebrations involved, and, occasionally, it offers comments about the character of the occasion and the celebrants, sometimes diffusing or delimiting the symbols associated with Canada. To capture an overview of the British experience with Dominion Day, the present study uses local newspapers to identify Dominion Day celebrations in parts of Britain beyond the capital as well as newspapers that were more national in scope. The press provides some indication of how the British interacted, in both a physical and emotional sense, with the celebrations. Moreover, newspapers record the "national pride" that was expressed by Canadians in Britain.[6] Together with the existing work on the Canadian presence in Britain, these newspaper accounts help to provide a more comprehensive understanding of Canada's national day in the United Kingdom.

Jonathan F. Vance offers the most comprehensive assessment of Canada's relationship with Britain during the First World War. Awareness of Canadian identity was, Vance suggests, enhanced by contact with a British "other" that was at once familiar and strange. A shared language and imperial heritage could bring out the narcissism of small differences. Such differences would have been all the more apparent to the many soldiers not born in Britain who arrived as part of the second Canadian contingent during the summer of 1915.[7] In all, some 400,000 Canadians passed through Britain during the First World War, and Vance's reference to a "Canadian Empire in Britain" captures the energy and prominence of these visitors.[8] There was no single set image of the Canadian in the British national imagination. In some circumstances, the rough-around-the-edges colonial took centre stage; in others, particularly after notable military success or displays of sporting prowess, the Canadian assumed the praiseworthy status of being a "hardy colonial." With their explicit statement of Canadian identity, Dominion Day celebrations provided an occasion that drew out such comments. Vance's study also provides a starting point for considerations about the impression of Canadians held by Britons during the Edwardian era. By noting the British "stereotype of the Canadian militia men" during the Second Boer War, Vance underscores the importance of war in the construction of positive images of the Canadian male who was loyal to the empire. In the First World War, the ideal type – and the less than ideal type – of colonial was more familiar to Britons than it had been during the South African conflict.[9]

Other studies of Canadians in Britain during the First World War focus on both the cultivation of Canadian identity and British relations with Canadian troops. Luke Flanagan examined the Canadian presence in Bexhill-on-Sea in East Sussex, the location from 1917 of the Canadian Training School, the Canadian Trench Warfare School, and Princess Patricia's Canadian Red Cross Hospital. Drawing on local newspapers and camp records, Flanagan argues that the cultural and organizational features of camp life fostered "a greater attachment to Canada" among Canadian soldiers.[10] Diana Beaupré utilized the local press in her study of the relationship between Canadians and Britons at Shorncliffe in Kent, the site of a second Canadian Training School.[11] Like Vance, Beaupré notes that the relationship was not entirely amicable, as some British commentators observed that crime increased after the Canadians had arrived.[12] But she concludes that, on the whole, the Britons got along well with their colonial cousins. Vance, Flanagan, and Beaupré do not concentrate on Dominion Day, a time when notions of Canadian identity were condensed and magnified. Their studies were not, however, primarily concerned with the ways in which national identities have been portrayed and interpreted during national celebrations.

As Jane Nicholas and Allana C. Lindgren have shown, national celebrations contain symbols that stimulate the senses and evoke emotion.[13] Both scholars have explored the nature of such celebrations and their potential meaning, particularly in the context of the presentation of Canada during the diamond jubilee of Confederation. Nicholas noted how official souvenirs provided the "public with a vision of the nation."[14] Of course, even the largest Dominion Day celebrations in Britain during the Edwardian era and the First World War were on a smaller scale than the Canadian celebration of 1927. Still, symbols are a component of even the smallest celebration, and a comparison of Dominion Day celebrations from a variety of locations sheds light on the role of symbols, including their gendered presentation. During Canada's transformation from colony to nation, national symbols were "charged with the difficult task of *creating a nation*."[15] Yet, any attempt to examine national symbols faces the problem of not only determining their presence but also of understanding how they were perceived. Even on those occasions when symbols are mentioned by contemporary commentators, there are few traces of "the meaning of the symbol to the collective, their usage of the symbol, or the collective's level of attachment to the symbol."[16] Symbols, although abstract and open to different interpretations, constitute a tangible part of the social fabric and are a crucial element in "the style in which they [nations] are imagined."[17] In order to establish the potential meanings conveyed by symbols, attention needs to be paid to the contemporary and historical context, as reactions to symbols are influenced by circumstances.[18]

Dominion Day in Edwardian Britain was a rather sedate affair that tended to be celebrated indoors. Unlike the celebrations in Canada, where fetes and racing meets took place, in Britain the day was marked by more formal events.[19] In Canada, the authorities were less inclined to mark the day in an official manner: before the middle of the twentieth century, there were only two state-organized, centralized Dominion Day celebrations – the Golden and Diamond Jubilees of 1917 and 1927.[20] In Britain, the high commissioner to the United Kingdom played an important part in the official celebration of the day, which generally took the form of a dinner. The speeches at these gatherings articulated how relations between the mother country and the dominion were perceived and emphasized certain characteristics thought to typify Canada. At the Hotel Cecil in 1902, for instance, High Commissioner Donald Alexander Smith, Lord Strathcona and Mount Royal, presided over a banquet where toasts were made in praise of the Canadian contribution to the Boer War.[21] Four years after the Anglo-French Entente of 1904, Dominion Day provided an opportunity to reference the tercentenary of the establishment of Quebec and how Canada as a whole illustrated the benefits of Franco-British cooperation.[22] Other Dominion Day events, such as the reception and dinner at the Imperial Institute in 1911, demonstrated Canada's place in the empire at a time when English and French Canadians were debating whether the dominion ought to be freed from what Henri Bourassa, who later opposed Canada's role in the First World War, called "the absolute supremacy of England." [23] On the eve of the First World War, the official Dominion Day celebrations in London were held in the Connaught Rooms, which opened in 1908 on the site of the former Freemasons' Tavern and had been named after the Masonic Grand Master the First Duke of Connaught, the governor general of Canada from 1911 to 1916. The comments at the meeting held on Dominion Day 1914, chaired by the New Hampshire–born Canadian high commissioner to the United Kingdom and lumber magnate Sir George H. Perley, contained assumptions about the role of the dominion and its fundamental character. By this time, Canada's contribution to the Second Boer War was no longer a prominent feature of Dominion Day speeches. After mentioning how Canada had progressed during the nineteenth century, Perley observed that, although Canada had a wealth of natural resources, investors needed to be careful during this period of financial dislocation.[24] Prince Alexander of Teck, who was due to succeed the Duke of Connaught as governor general, acknowledged that there was an economic depression but noted that Canadian exports were increasing and imports had declined. For these influential men, Canada was an investment opportunity, a source of material or a place to be filled. From the speeches on Dominion Day 1914, Canada appears to have been viewed as a space rather than as a place. Given such views, it is little wonder that Prime Minister Robert Borden felt the need to stress that "Canada would not fulfil her mission if she simply raised wheat, built railways, and increased in prosperity. Her duty was to uphold the principles of democracy and British liberty."[25]

The prominent coverage given to these formal dinners was accompanied by shorter items, some no longer than a sentence, that referred to smaller, though still exclusive, occasions. An afternoon party at Queen's

Gate Gardens and an evening party at the Royal Institute of Painters in Water Colours and were held in 1902, for example.[26] There were also a "number of special private gatherings" in London during 1909 that were thought to be the consequence of more Canadians settling in the city and forming what one British national paper termed a "colony."[27] Such meetings in the imperial capital underscored Canada's contribution to the empire, thereby reinforcing the celebrants' dual Canadian-imperial identities. As an advertisement to encourage migration to Canada put it, Canada was "Britain's nearest overseas dominion," which accounted for the presence of the Edwardian Canadian colonies.[28] Responses to the Dominion Day celebration organized in 1909 by the London management of the Grand Trunk Railway of Canada on the opening of its new premises in Cockspur Street show how the day compelled some inhabitants of the mother country to reassess their own sense of imperial identity. Newspapers praised the friezes in the building that depicted the taming of Canada. The imperially minded *Daily Mail* noted how "we in this country are at last coming to realise the value and significance of such national festivals. It was from Canada that we borrowed Empire Day and all its inspiring rites."[29]

Canadian identity was articulated in other places besides London. In the summer of 1914, a "Canadian flag" was hoisted above Exeter's guildhall. The handiwork of schoolchildren from Exeter, Ontario, this gift to the English of Exeter was part of a transatlantic project entitled "Hands across the Sea" organized by Manitoba's chief secretary of education, Frederick J. Ney. With many immigrants from central and eastern Europe settling on the western plains, Ney stressed that these newcomers needed to be "welded into one race (a British race)." He noted the fundamental role of teachers in forging this single "British race" of Canadians and argued that teachers would be aided in this work if they visited the "Old Land."[30] There had been four earlier visits by Canadian teachers to the mother country, but this was the first time a delegation had visited Devon. On 10 July 1914, a party of 130 Canadian teachers arrived at Plymouth, where, just three months later, the first contingent of Canadian troops would disembark. Later, the visitors received an official welcome at Exeter. Their arrival may not have coincided exactly with Dominion Day, but reports in the local press highlighted the distinctiveness of the Canadian visitors.[31] Of course, members of the delegation had their own vision of Canada's place in the world and, as Ney himself noted, that vision did not appeal to all Canadians.

In their speeches, Ney and the mayor of Exeter used symbols and stories to link their respective nations. In his welcoming speech, the mayor referred to Britain as having been home to the majority of the visitors' ancestors and remarked that some of their forebears may have sat in the guildhall, which had been built in the fifteenth century. Yet, the speeches also included references to what Nicholas has called "potentially disrupting elements," an indication of how celebrations of Canadian identity are often partial and contested.[32] During their speeches, both the mayor and Ney turned to differences between Britain and the dominion as well as questions of Canadian identity. The mayor praised Canada for having established an educational system without the layers of complexity that bedevilled that in the mother country. In his remarks, Ney defined "real unselfish imperialism" before turning to critics who labelled his efforts to foster closer relations between the Canada and Britain as "jingoistic." "Certainly there were small Union Jacks [at the gathering], but there was nothing 'Jingoistic' about the Union Jack, although some people made it so." Ney reckoned that there were "very few" people in Canada who were not fond of Britain. The Canadian flag, a Red Ensign that included a Union Jack, "expressed better than words their common purpose and common hope in their own future." After the start of the war, Nye would have felt less need to be so defensive about the Union Jack. In the context of the conflict, Canada's ties with the British Empire and Britain took on a martial aspect and it would be unlikely that an educational delegation with a fondness for the Union Jack would be deemed "jingoistic." By the same token, the dominion's flag acquired further resonance on the outbreak of war.

The act of hoisting a flag in a public place is a simple, yet noticeable, way to display a national symbol. As "visual symbols, flags can be apprehended in a split second; they do not require performance or staging as is typical to anthems. Rapid apprehension and ease of display are key to the international arena where nations are competing for attention."[33] Canada did not have an official flag of its own at this time.[34] Officially the dominion's flag was in fact the same as that of Britain, although the Red Ensign with the coat of arms of Canada was a widely used unofficial banner until 1965, when the Maple Leaf flag was adopted. Canada's Red Ensign joined an array of flags, images, and national identities that came together and gained heightened meaning throughout the war and its aftermath. During a victory procession through London on 3 May 1919 by troops from the dominions, a colourful tapestry of flags lined the streets of the capital. Among these banners were a "surprising number of large new Union Jacks." Of "the symbols of the Dominions the starred banner of the Commonwealth of Australia was conspicuous."[35] In large part, the prominence of the Australian flag was put down to the convenient location of Australia House, which had been opened the previous year, and the fact that the building was easy to decorate.

As the author of the first volume of *Canada in Flanders*, Max Aitken, a Canadian-born newspaper tycoon who became Lord Beaverbrook in 1917, contributed to the idea, reiterated since by Pierre Berton among others, that the development of Canada's identity owed much to the experience of the First World War.[36] However, the war also provided the opportunity for the British to read or hear about their valorous Canadian cousins. A lengthy report on Canadian troops, written a month after Aitken had taken up his position as records officer of the Canadian War Records Office and published in a number of British national and local newspapers, related Dominion Day to the Canadians' martial achievements: "This is the first Dominion Day that Canada has spent with the red sword in her hand."[37] The day itself encouraged soldiers to think of themselves as Canadians and, perhaps more importantly, representatives of Canada: "When Dominion Day came they remembered with pride that they were the army of a nation, and those who were in the trenches displayed the Dominion flag, decorated with the flowers of France, to the annoyance of the barbarians who riddled it with bullets." Paradoxically, these bullet marks brought the flag to life. It did not matter if this image was the result of an over-imaginative reporter and that the flag was by no means ubiquitous on the front, the report brought the Canadian banner and Dominion Day to breakfast tables and reading rooms across the British Isles.[38]

Identity formation involves both an awareness and acknowledgment of difference.[39] The process was particularly notable at Folkestone in Kent, where, from early 1915, Canadian forces were based in camps such as Shorncliffe.[40] In Folkestone, Dominion Day and the Canadian banner took on a tangible form. The "Our Note Book" column of a Folkestone newspaper contained some reflections on the extent to which the residents of the town were aware of Dominion Day. When people were informed of a concert to observe the occasion, "most people asked 'What is Dominion Day?' Even in some usually well-informed circles there existed only a vague idea on the subject, and cautious people, when asked for information, gave an indefinite and non-committal reply. They did not like to confess their ignorance."[41] Aside from indicating a lack of awareness about Dominion Day, this extract shows how some individuals, such as the journalist who wrote the column, were interested in the degree to which people were aware of various national days and flags. Such observations were not limited to Canadian symbols. Soon after the start of the war, commentators noted the relative dearth of Russian flags vis-à-vis those of other Allied nations.[42] There was a heightened awareness of national days and symbols during the conflict, as Britons acknowledged the efforts of their allies. An advertisement in the *Folkestone Herald* indicates how the Canadian flag was introduced into the symbolic landscape of the Kentish port town on 1 July 1915. Before the anniversary, a draper in one of the main streets ordered "a large number of combined Union Jacks and Canadian flags of various sizes." These flags decorated properties during Dominion Day, "and Canadian brethren were pleased at the sight."[43] The combination of two flags on a single banner indicated parity and Canada's status as a nation. This symbolic balance, and even merging, was particularly significant when viewed in the context of contemporary Canadian debates. During the Edwardian era, the relative status of the Union Jack and the Red Ensign with the badge of Canada had resulted in confusion and consequent discussion about which of the banners should represent the dominion.[44] An article in a paper from southwest England suggested that Canada displayed greater affection for the British Empire than Britain itself did. "In Canada, for instance, we think a great deal of the Union Jack." Few people would fly a foreign flag in Canada "unless the Union Jack is flown with and above it." Examples cited included Winnipeg, where a by-law required two British flags to be flown for every foreign flag of an equal size, and Windsor, Ontario, where each foreign flag had to be accompanied by a Union Jack of the same size.[45] Such regulations, though, were not popular among all Canadians, some of whom favoured the Red Ensign. In 1909, it was noted that "some of the provinces, in complete ignorance of 'the recognised flag' have directed the Union Jack to be hoisted upon their school houses."[46] Although these matters were of little concern to the residents of British towns, the Canadians' hosts would have deemed a display composed entirely of Union Jacks as being impolite and a failure to acknowledge their allies.

The Dominion Day celebrations in Folkestone brought together a significant number of Canadian military personnel as well as Britons who were particularly close to the conflict in continental Europe. As such, the occasion was hardly typical of all Dominion Day celebrations in Britain. Yet, as will be seen below, some features of Folkestone's Dominion Day were similar to celebrations elsewhere. In Folkestone, the flags provided the backdrop to a lively occasion that seeded symbols associated with Canada through the streets of the port. Canadian "bugle and drum" bands paraded the main thoroughfares in the morning, and in the evening a concert was held in Radnor Park before a "very large crowd," who listened to humorous and patriotic pieces, one of which, "United Empire," evoked an association between Canada and Britain that stretched back to the late eighteenth century.[47] The event encouraged one councillor to request "if it was possible to get a band in the park a little oftener."[48] This association of the Canadians with entertainment was a common theme in the press and indicates the importance of the sensory dimensions of Dominion Day in Britain.

National days are notable for their sensory qualities. Sights, sounds, smells, and tastes are etched in the memory of those who observed or participated in the events that marked the day. Early Edwardian Dominion Day celebrations in Britain contained such elements, including those in response to foods, music, and decoration, but they were held indoors and were restricted to a small number of celebrants, many of whom were Canadian. During the war, however, events were held in environments such as Radnor Park, and the liveliness of the occasion was seen as an embodiment of the Canadian spirit. Prewar views of Canadians as optimistic and self-confident, sturdy and energetic, such as those related by John Foster Fraser in his 1905 book *Canada As It Is*, were reinforced by lively Dominion Day celebrations.[49] While it may be an exaggeration to say that these occasions were carnivalesque, in the sense of temporarily subverting authority, celebrations that included boxing nine-year-olds, "fat lady's and fat men's races," and catching a greased pig were certainly more akin to fairs than state-like occasions.[50] Events that were not explicitly related to Dominion Day but fell on 1 July could become proxy Dominion Day celebrations. This was the case at an event at the Opera House in Tunbridge Wells, where "Canada's sons attended in great numbers" and "the enthusiasm prevailing was positively infectious."[51]

One area that was singled out for particular commentary in the press was sports. Such physical activities can serve as a frame upon which were hung representations of Canada and its population. The body can be a significant site for the transmission and reception of behaviours that are, or become, associated with specific nationalities.[52] This transmission was by no means restricted to national days but, as the reports in the British press reveal, physical activity was given special attention by the British press in Dominion Day reportage.

Studies of sports among Canadian forces during the First World War have focused on baseball and its relation to a Canadian or North American identity. These studies are concerned with the part played by the sports in the military and even comment on practical aspects such as the dearth of baseballs in France.[53] At the same time as troops from North America were playing the game, other nationalities were interpreting the men who ran around the diamond or, less frequently, those who wielded a *crosse*. Newspapers often contained photographs of baseball or lacrosse players in reports about Dominion Day, and in 1916 the Pathé Gazette included footage entitled "Canadian troops in Bath hold sports and a baseball match."[54] While it is possible to establish where baseball was played, it is not as easy to deduce how Britons responded to the game and how the sport was incorporated into their understanding of Canada. Even so, the coalescence of a number of features contained in reports from across Britain suggests some ways in which Britons interpreted baseball.

The "Dominion Day Sports" hosted by the Canadian Red Cross Hospital at the Cliveden estate, Berkshire, in 1917 contained activities usually associated with an Edwardian hospital fund-raising event, such as bun-eating contests and "a parade of clowns and other comic people." Following an expression of thanks from Lady Perley, the wife of the high commissioner of Canada, "three hearty cheers and a 'tiger' were returned by the men in acknowledgment."[55] The "tiger" – a yell at the end of the cheers – is significant, as it is thought to be of North American origin, and "not British."[56] (Indeed, the "tiger" featured in British Columbia's celebrations of Dominion Day, as Forrest Pass notes in the previous chapter.) This "tiger," seen as an expression of manly enthusiasm, illustrates the resonance between masculine virtues and sports such as baseball as well as the association between sports and war. Cricket shared a similar, if less boisterous, reputation for cultivating the qualities that would be of value on the battlefield.[57] Comparisons between baseball and cricket were all the more likely to be made because some of the more well-attended baseball games were played at cricket grounds.[58] The differences between the two games were captured in one paper's account of the widely reported sports at the Cliveden estate on Dominion Day during the final year of the war: "The ground had every surrounding that could remind one of an English village gathering for traditional English games. The smoothly-shaven turf, the belt of noble trees, the haymakers only a few yards away, would have led a casual visitor to expect a cricket match." Subsequently, differences emerged, including the flags of the Allies and an "American band." These contrasts were "widened by the tones and the slang of the majority of the spectators." Finally, when the American Navy team arrived dressed in "blue and crimson" – the contrast with cricket whites would have been apparent to readers – "the likeness to a village cricket field vanished." This transformation was gradual, and neither abrupt nor harsh. The images and sounds emerge from an archetypal English setting and do not suddenly displace the backdrop. The effect of this transition is to render the arrivals less alien: an English idyll metamorphoses into a "breath of Canada."[59]

A less poetic account of a sporting occasion, and the departure of the Canadian troops from Bath, suggests the importance of baseball in Anglo-Canadian relations. The celebration of Dominion Day in Bath during 1916 included a baseball match to raise money for the French Red Cross fund.[60] Here, Dominion Day was integrated into a pre-existing celebratory framework: "a new celebration was added to those historical annual events already recognised and observed by the people of Bath."[61] The pageant included a troop of Boy Scouts with banners representing "the arms of the Canadian provinces."[62] Three months later, the discharge depot in Bath at Prior Park was closed and the Canadians were relocated to Shoreham on the south coast, much to the "surprise and regret" of Bath's residents.[63] The account of the Canadians' departure focused on the "Colonial cheers" of the men as they boarded the trains and reflected on the baseball match on Dominion Day: "It was through them that many Bath people received their initiation into the mysteries of baseball, and they [would] have been glad if circumstances had permitted the Canadians to add to the education of citizens as regards the peculiarities of the great game of the North American Continent." The events at Bath, and similar sporting occasions in Cumbria and Aberdeenshire, not only "showed what good athletes" the Canadians were, but they also provided an opportunity for people with two related but different cultures to contemplate how they differed from one another.[64]

A further illustration of Canadian vigour, and Canadians' difference not only from the British but the Germans, was provided by symbols derived from nature.[65] Dominion Day celebrations that took place in an arboreal environment included activities that evoked the Canadian relationship with nature and brought to mind the romance of the Canadian North.[66] Canada's association with nature facilitated a contrast with the German "highly scienced barbarian," whose technological aptitude resulted in "infamous barbarity." This distinction between the adversaries was made by Charles William Gordon (Ralph Connor) while he was chaplain of the 43rd Cameron Highlanders Battalion. Gordon described "English fields and these sweet English lanes" that Canadian troops marched along on Dominion Day, "5,000 miles from our Western Canada." In his emotional account, Gordon combined two rural idylls and, in so doing, intimated that, in their own ways, both Canada and Britain represented a force that was natural and life affirming.[67] At other times, the association between Canada and nature assumed a physical form. As part of the Dominion Day celebration at Oldmill Military Hospital in Aberdeen, a hall was decorated with various Canadian emblems, along with "specimens of Canadian grasses and grain lent by the Canadian government."[68]

Yet it was not so much nature that embodied Canada as the relationship between Canadians and their environment and its implications for the British countryside. Aitken's soldiers, with their trunk-like "lumberjack backs," echoed the work of those who rendered nature useful, who provided material that was used to build rather than destroy.[69] At Stover Park, Newton Abbot, Devon, Britons watched an "exhibition of Canadian lumbering methods" by the Canadian Forestry Battalion. What the local people, who included the mayor of Exeter among their number, made of the tree felling and the log sawing, rolling, and loading, as well as the canoe races on Stover Lake, is likely to have been framed by their conceptions, if any, of Canada and by the prevailing atmosphere at the event. Most of those who attended were enjoying time away from work, as businesses had agreed to close on the afternoon when the sports were held. Their enjoyment would have been accompanied by a feeling of having done something for the war effort, as the occasion raised money for the Red Cross. Looking back, a reporter thought that the crowd resembled "the scenes to be witnessed at the old-time Devonshire regattas."[70] According to this interpretation of the occasion, the Canadians rejuvenated a part of England that had experienced out-migration since the last quarter of the nineteenth century. During a visit to a Canadian forestry operation in Aviemore, Scotland, on Dominion Day 1917, the British prime minister, David Lloyd George, spoke of the rejuvenating effects of the Canadian loggers: "You bring to us from Canada a skill in this work that we here have almost lost. We have in the past paid too little attention to afforestation. You have come to teach us one part of the work, the cutting down of timber."[71] The prime minister's words reflected a feeling that, unlike Canada, Britain had loosened its ties with the natural world.

Wartime Dominion Day celebrations often featured martial music, sports, and other physical activities. To some extent these activities resembled those that many Canadians enjoyed at home. Yet they differed in the sense that the celebrants were, in the main, male and in the military. The celebrations were described as demonstrations of vim and high spirits. This form of masculinity differed from the more patriarchal and visionary variety promoted during the Diamond Jubilee of 1927. While both emphasized an active masculine principle, the activities that took place in Britain during the war were more physical than cerebral – at Abergavenny in Monmouthshire the Dominion Day sports included men with daubed faces racing to get washed and dressed for a military inspection.[72] Another difference was that there was no indication during celebrations in Britain of concerns about men becoming so civilized that they would lose the attributes that had defined previous generations.[73] It is possible that the concerns about a decline in masculinity during the interwar years owed their origins to the contrast between wartime and peacetime. The reputation of the Canadian citizen-soldier during the war, which often came to the fore during reports about Dominion Day, may have cast a shadow over civilian life after the war. Official celebrations of the Diamond Jubilee placed emphasis on the North, or "New North." Like the war in the previous decade, this virgin land presented opportunities for the display and cultivation of masculine qualities such as bravery and tenacity.

The Canadian soldier personified diffuse symbols and themes associated with Canada. Despite or perhaps because of their simplicity, personifications shape interaction and rapidly gain currency when they are confirmed or fulfilled. In his Dominion Day address in 1917, Borden defined the nation in terms of the "character of its people," their "ideals" and "sacrifice."[74] Like notions of the North, the war enhanced an extant sense of "Canadian-ness." Borden also contrasted Canada and Prussia. In an allusion to the Austro-Prussian War of 1866, he commented that, a year before Confederation, Prussia had started on the road to military aggression.[75] He was implying that the German soldier served a nation that was founded on acts of aggression, whereas Canadians fought to defend the values of a land that had less bloody origins. The condensation of the Canadian into a fiercely loyal but freedom-loving citizen may have generated some dissonance, as not all Canadians necessarily matched this characterization of the typical Canadian. Those, for example, who opposed the Military Service Act, which became law a month after Borden's speech, would have fallen short of this ideal type. For the most part, however, the disputes over conscription were not played out in front of Britons' eyes, whereas the presence of loyal Canadian soldiers was something that many had seen and more had read about in the press. These modern symbols of Canada were not simply new versions of past heroes: they were the representatives of an egalitarian nation. After referring to the attendance of numerous dignitaries at the Dominion Day Golden Jubilee service held in Westminster Abbey, the London correspondent for the *Montreal Star* and *Saturday Night*, Mary Macleod Moore, contended that the nation was truly represented by the soldiers in khaki and the wounded troops in "hospital blue," as there were "none greater in spirit" than these servicemen.[76] In a later article, published on Dominion Day 1918, Moore mentioned how Canada was free of the militarism that defined Germany.[77] Moreover, Canada's army was largely a volunteer force, conscription having been introduced only in the latter half of 1917, over a year after it had been launched in Britain.

On occasion, British identity was bound up in depictions of Canada. With Germany as a shared "other," the less palatable characteristics of the British were easily displaced onto the militaristic Hun. On Dominion Day in 1916 a piece by "W.H." in the *Daily Mirror* explored Anglo-Canadian relations through the medium of the ruminations of a Canadian private at a crowded railway station. This Canadian everyman undergoes a transformation. At first the trooper tells a friend about "how the old country needed improvement and what he would do if he had the running of it."[78] He especially disliked the "social distinctions" that he saw in Britain. His colleague's comment about the English being far less bound by such distinctions than the Germans had no effect on the opinionated colonial. For "W.H.," and doubtless some readers of the *Daily Mirror*, the Canadian was an embodiment of the colonial who had failed to grasp how the mother country had changed during the Edwardian era. A year later, however, not only has the soldier tempered his views about the British but he was engaged to an English woman. His understanding of Germany had made him reassess Britain. Although the editorial is ostensibly about the Canadian's volte-face, it also registers an increased awareness of Canada. In fact, "W.H." hints that there has been a readjustment in the relationship between Britain and Canada during the war. Highlighting the performance of the colonial military, "W.H." noted that the "Canadian exploits in the war are amongst the eternally memorable incidents of it." This, in turn, led to a redefinition of Dominion Day in Britain. The occasion came to mean more because it was based on contact, shared endeavour, and lived experience. "Dominion Day to-day need no longer be celebrated as a partial or coldly imperial function which you know vaguely is going on but don't care much about. To-day the occasion comes with a new concrete appeal."[79]

So far, this study has focused on coverage of Dominion Day and symbols associated with the day in a British context. It is important to bear in mind, though, that national days of various peoples are related (in both senses of the word) to one another. Such relationships present another transnational aspect to the study of national days. If the national days of different countries are close to one another on the calendar, there may be a struggle for recognition. For the Allies, the first half of July was particularly congested, with Dominion Day followed by Independence Day (4 July), the Irish Unionists' celebration of the anniversary of the Battle of the Boyne (12 July) and France's Bastille Day (14 July). British commentators paid attention to the proximity of Dominion Day and Independence Day and expressed concerns about the relative attention given to them. Comments in the French press about the United States' national day overshadowing its Canadian counterpart were supported by an English national daily. After acknowledging the importance of Independence Day, the paper noted that the "one, however, must not efface the other in our minds, and the Fourth of July must not make us forget the anniversary of the foundation of the Canadian Confederation."[80]

After the United States entered the war, Independence Day assumed a greater significance in Britain and France. An event that was previously outside, or on the edge, of their respective national cultures now took centre stage. One English local newspaper observed that "never until now was Independence Day celebrated with real affection in Britain."[81] There was no ideological conflict between the values signified by the national days of Canada and the United States. They were allies in war and they shared democratic values. The problem was not so much one of competing values as jockeying for recognition. Sometimes the proximity of the events could work in Canada's favour. For example, a Scottish paper compared the national days as follows: Dominion Day "differs usually from the American Day of Independence, three days later, in one way, in that it is not a fireworks day, for young Canada does not seem to have any special day for letting off fire crackers." From points made later on in the article, it seems that this aversion to fireworks fit in with the notion of Canada as "the Scotland of America." Canadians are depicted as a "hardier, more determined race than the country to the south on the whole produces."[82] When it came to the amount of space dedicated to the two days, Dominion Day may well have been dwarfed, but the way in which the celebrations were perceived could reinforce notions of a masculine, strong, undemonstrative northern people.

Nonetheless, even when Dominion Day was acknowledged, reporters could not overcome the temptation to dwell on Independence Day, as in the following commentary from 1918: "We do not forget Canada, which always leads the favourite July festivals of the free democracies. As it happens, Dominion Day comes to-morrow. But our eldest Dominion was in the war from the beginning. Her most thrilling and solemn occasion came nearly three years ago. It is otherwise with the United States."[83] After this acknowledgment, the article focused on the Fourth of July. Another piece that paid due attention to Canadian sensibilities contained a frank statement about the relative emphasis placed on the adjacent celebrations: "If on our side of the Atlantic the celebration of the latter [Independence Day] overshadows the recognition of the former [Dominion Day], as it assuredly does, our Canadian fellow-citizens will not misunderstand; indeed, they will be ready to approve and to sympathise with the motive that prompts our action." Whereas Canada had always been attached to the mother country, the United States was a prodigal son.[84]

These ruminations about the relationship between the two days in the British national and local press do not tell us anything about what Canadians in Britain thought about Independence Day. There is some indication that the Canadians in Britain during the First World War did not see July 4th as a rival celebration. Like the British Columbians of the late nineteenth century that Forest Pass discusses in this volume, at least some were not indifferent to Independence Day. The following account also suggests that Canadian and American forces had a better relationship with one another than was to be the case in the Second World War.[85] The aforementioned baseball matches between teams from the two countries on Dominion Day indicate the permeability of national celebrations. It should come as no surprise, therefore, that Canadian troops were just as likely to mark Independence Day as Dominion Day:

One of the significant features of the London celebrations of Independence Day has been the heartiness with which Canadians have participated in the anniversary ... Many soldiers from Canadian rest camps postponed the leave granted them for Monday, which was Dominion Day, to get to London for Independence Day, and attend the great meeting at the Central Hall. So great is the feeling of comradeship between Canadians and Americans that there is talk of an effort to combine in future Dominion Day and Independence Day in one holiday throughout the entire Continent of North America.[86]

It appears that, while some British commentators were concerned about upsetting Canadian sensibilities, at least some Canadians were prepared to partake in their neighbour's national day and even considered conflating the two national birthdays. Talk of a "North American" celebration was in all likelihood a consequence of an increased sense of difference from the "old world." Canadians and Americans shared an experience of Europe that enhanced the pre-existing links between the two nations.[87] Apart from a common language and cultural similarities, the Canadian involvement in Independence Day celebrations may also have owed something to the presence of some 35,612 U.S. citizens who joined the Canadian Expeditionary Force.[88]

The war had a significant effect on relations between states and the ways in which they perceived themselves and one another. In the first Dominion Day meeting held after the war at the Connaught Rooms in London, the topics under discussion differed from those that had been raised before the war. Canada's natural resources and economy still figured in the high commissioner's speech, but there was a clearer sense of Canada as a nation. Whereas previous definitions of Canada "accentuated the material, not the spiritual," the war gave the nation a clearer sense of mission.[89] A key role on the world stage was that of an intermediary between Britain and the United States. According to the High Commissioner Sir George Perley, Canada would be able to help "interpret" Britain to the United States and vice versa.[90] Norman Hillmer and Adam Chapnick have argued that "Canada shares much more, both in terms of values and interests, with its North Atlantic partners than nationalist accounts, preoccupied with distinctiveness, would suggest."[91] This distinctiveness need not be seen as the opposite of commonality. Indeed, Canada's distinctiveness came to the fore as a result of its relationship with the other nations.

Dominion Day celebrations were not simply transplanted from Canada to Britain. There were various ways in which Dominion Day was celebrated both before and during the war. This survey of the national and local press suggests that Edwardian Dominion Day celebrations were limited to official and private events in London. These gatherings were widely reported occasions that articulated Canadian identity and influenced perceptions of the dominion. With the advent of the First World War, more public, informal, and recreational modes of celebrating Canada's day appeared. Dominion Day celebrations reinforced the heroic image of the Canadian soldier, yet there was more to the celebrations than simply a display of Canadian martial prowess. Nevertheless, the events offered a virile, youthful energetic representation of Canada and Canadians that complemented the actions of a largely volunteer force with "red sword" in hand.[92] Wartime Dominion Day celebrations were not limited to certain buildings or cities, and the shared imperial war effort meant that British and Canadian celebrants often mingled with one another. While victories on the battlefield were a source of Canadian pride and garnered plaudits from Britons, Dominion Day was a hub for the expression and reception of messages about Canada and what it meant to be Canadian.

Others have demonstrated that there were numerous encounters between Canadians and Britons on the British home front in the First World War and that these helped foster both a Canadian and imperial identity.[93] This chapter has scrutinized the way in which Dominion Day celebrations expressed the *idea* of Canada and how these celebrations were related in both the national and local press. It is possible to detect in the coverage the symbols and activities that were associated with Canada and permeated the cultural awareness of many Britons. The result was not so much the recognition of a clear-cut Canadian nation as an increased clarity with respect to Canadian values and characteristics among Britons from Aberdeen to Exeter. Moreover, the presence of Canadians and their symbols was not simply seen as a manifestation of Canadian identity or difference. Rather, becoming more familiar with Canadians often spurred British observers to reflect on their own nation.

NOTES

1 Gabriella Elgenius, *Symbols of Nations and Nationalism: Celebrating Nationhood* (London: Palgrave Macmillan, 2011), 136; Danielle Hemple, "Introduction: Forging the Nation through Performance and Ritual," *Studies in Ethnicity and Nationalism* 21, no. 1 (2012): 3.

2 John Pierce, "Constructing Memory: The Vimy Memorial," *Canadian Military History* 1, no. 2 (1992): 5–8; Frank K. Stanzel, "'In Flanders Fields the Poppies Blow': Canada and the Great War," in *Difference and Community: Canadian and European Cultural Perspectives*, ed. Peter Easingwood, Konrad Gross, and Lynette Hunter (Amsterdam: Rodopi, 1994), 213–26.

3 Duncan S.A. Bell, "Mythscapes: Memory, Mythology and National Identity," *British Journal of Sociology* 54, no. 1 (2003): 65.

4 Barbara Lorenzkowski and Stephen High, "Culture, Canada, and the Nation," *Histoire sociale / Social History* 39, no. 77 (2006): 10.

5 See also Robert Cupido, "Public Commemoration and Ethnocultural Assertion: Winnipeg Celebrates the Diamond Jubilee of Confederation," *Urban History Review* 38, no. 2 (2010): 64–74; Lianbi Zhu, "National Holidays and Minority Festivals in Canadian Nation-Building" (PhD diss., Sheffield University, 2012), 39.

6 Desmond Morton, *When Your Number's Up: The Canadian Soldier in the First World War* (Toronto: Random House, 1993), 174.

7 Jonathan F. Vance, *Maple Leaf Empire: Canada, Britain and Two World Wars* (Oxford: Oxford University Press, 2011), 65.

8 Ibid., 38, 167.

9 Ibid., 27.

10 Luke Flanagan, "Canadians in Bexhill-on-Sea during the First World War: A Reflection of Canadian Nationhood?" *British Journal of Canadian Studies* 27, no. 2 (2014): 140.

11 Diana Beaupré, "En Route to Flanders Fields: The Canadians at Shorncliffe during the Great War," *London Journal of Canadian Studies* 23 (2007/8): 45–66.

12 Ibid., 54.

13 Jane Nicholas, "Gendering the Jubilee: Gender and Modernity in the Diamond Jubilee of the Confederation Celebrations, 1927," *Canadian Historical Review* 90, no. 2 (2009): 247–74; Allana C. Lindgren, "Amy Sternberg's Historical Pageant (1927): The Performance of IODE Ideology during Canada's Diamond Jubilee," *Theatre Research in Canada* 32, no. 1 (2011): 1–29.

14 Nicholas, "Gendering the Jubilee," 257.

15 Michael E. Geisler, "Introduction: What Are National Symbols – and What Do They Do to Us," in *National Symbols, Fractured Identities: Contesting the National Narrative*, ed. Michael E. Geisler (Lebanon, NH: University Press of New England, 2005), xv.

16 K. Cerulo, "Sociopolitical Control and the Structure of National Symbols: An Empirical Analysis of National Anthems," *Social Forces* 68, no. 1 (1989): 95.

17 Benedict Anderson, *Imagined Communities: Reflections on the Origins and Spread of Nationalism* (London: Verso, 1983), 6.

18 Anatol Rapoport, *Conflict in Man-Made Environment* (Harmondsworth: Penguin, 1974), 53.

19 "Dominion Day," *Daily Mail* (London), 18 June 1909.

20 See Matthew Hayday's chapter on Canada's Day in the present volume.

21 "Dominion Day," *Daily Mail* (London), 2 July 1902.

22 "Dominion Day," *London Daily News*, 1 July 1908.

23 "Dominion Day," *Manchester Courier*, 13 June 1911; David Clark MacKenzie and Patrice A. Dutil, *Canada 1911: The Decisive Election that Shaped the Country* (Toronto: Dundurn Press, 2011), 149.

24 "Dominion Day," *Times* (London), 2 July 1914.

25 "Dominion Day Speeches at Sea," *Western Daily Press* (Bristol), 5 July 1912.

26 "Court and Society," *Daily Mail* (London), 18 June 1902.

27 "Canada's Birthday," *Daily Mail* (London), 1 July 1909; "Dominion Day," *Daily Mail* (London), 2 July 1909.

28 "The Land of Opportunity," *Daily Telegraph* (London), 1 July 1909.

29 "Dominion Day," *Manchester Guardian*, 2 July 1909; "British Apathy at the Toronto Exhibition," *Daily Mail* (London), 1 July 1909.

30 Frederick J. Ney, "Prelude," in *Britishers in Britain: Being the Record of the Official Visit of Teachers from Manitoba to the Old Country, Summer, 1910*, ed. Frederick J. Ney (London: Times Book Club, 1911), 5.

31 "Canadians Visit Exeter," *Devon and Exeter Gazette*, 16 July 1914; "Canadian Teachers," 16 *Western Times* (Exeter), July 1914.

32 Nicholas, "Gendering the Jubilee," 267.

33 Karen A. Cerulo, *Identity Designs: The Sights and Sounds of a Nation* (New Brunswick, NJ: Rutgers University Press, 1995), 114.

34 A new flag had been proposed in 1895, which gave rise to a heated debate in the Canadian media, as Peter Price's chapter in *Celebrating Canada*, vol. 2 (forthcoming) discusses.

35 "Dominion Troops' Day," *Times* (London), 5 May 1919.

36 Tim Cook, *Clio's Warriors: Canadian Historians and the Writing of the World Wars* (Vancouver: UBC Press, 2006), 33; Pierre Berton, *Vimy* (Toronto: McClelland and Stewart, 1986).

37 "Glory of the Canadians," *Daily Express* (London), 13 July 1915.

38 C.P. Champion, *The Strange Demise of British Canada: The Liberals and Canadian Nationalism, 1964–68* (Montreal: McGill-Queen's University Press, 2010), 174.

39 Rogers Brubaker and Frederick Cooper, "Beyond 'Identity'," *Theory and Society* 29, no. 1 (2000): 18.

40 Michael and Christine George, *Dover and Folkestone during the Great War* (Barnsley: Pen and Sword, 2008), 29.

41 "Our Note Book," *Folkestone, Hythe, Sandgate and Cheriton Herald*, 3 July 1915.

42 "More Russian Flags," *Daily Mail* (London), 8 September 1914.

43 "The Canadian Colours," *Folkestone, Hythe, Sandgate and Cheriton Herald*, 3 July 1915.

44 *Canadian Magazine of Politics, Science, Art and Literature* 30 (1907): 333–4; John Skirving Ewart, *The Kingdom of Canada, Imperial Federation, the Colonial Conferences, the Alaska Boundary and Other Essays* (Toronto: Morang, 1908), 70; Forrest D. Pass, "'Something Occult in the Science of Flag-flying': School Flags and Educational Authority in Early Twentieth-century Canada," *Canadian Historical Review* 95, no. 3 (2014): 321–51.

45 "Notes about Canada," *Devon and Exeter Gazette*, 11 August 1916.

46 *Canadian Magazine of Politics, Science, Art and Literature* 32 (1909), 528.

47 "Dominion Day," *Folkestone, Hythe, Sandgate and Cheriton Herald*, 3 July 1915.

48 "Folkestone Town Council," *Folkestone, Hythe, Sandgate and Cheriton Herald*, 10 July 1915.

49 John Foster Fraser, *Canada As It Is* (London: Cassell, 1905), 103.

50 "Canada's Dominion Day," *Kent and Sussex Courier* (Tunbridge Wells), 6 July 1917.

51 "War Notes," ibid., 6 July 1917.

52 Catherine Palmer, "From Theory to Practice: Experiencing the Nation in Everyday Life," *Journal of Material Culture* 3, no. 2 (1998): 183–7.

53 Craig Greenham, "On the Battlefront: Canadian Soldiers, an Imperial War, and America's National Pastime," *American Review of Canadian Studies* 42, no. 1 (2012): 44; Andrew Horrall, "'Keep-A-Fighting! Play the Game!' Baseball and the Canadian Forces during the First World War," *Canadian Military History* 10, no. 2 (2001): 27–40.

54 "Canadian Sports on Dominion Day," *Daily Mirror* (London), 2 July 1918; Advertisement, *Tamworth Herald*, 8 July 1916.

55 "Dominion Day Sports at Cliveden," *Observer* (Manchester), 1 July 1917.

56 Isabella L. Bird, *The Hawaiian Archipelago: Six Months among the Palm Groves, Coral Reefs, and Volcanoes of the Sandwich Islands* (London: John Murray, 1875), 202.

57 Jack Williams, *Cricket and England: A Cultural and Social History of the Inter-war Years* (London: Taylor and Francis, 1999), 6.

58 "Dominion Day," *Hastings and St Leonards Observer*, 7 July 1917; "Yesterday's Sport," *Sunday Times* (London), 1 July 1917.

59 "Dominion Day," *Times* (London), 2 July 1918.

60 "Untitled," *Bath Chronicle*, 15 July 1916.

61 "Arm-Chair Musings," ibid., 1 July 1916.

62 "Dominion Day in Bath," ibid., 8 July 1916.

63 "Canadians' Farewell," ibid., 21 October 1916.

64 "Dominion Day," *Times* (London), 3 July 1916; "Canadians' Baseball Match at Penrith," *Yorkshire Post and Leeds Intelligencer*, 3 July 1918; "Bon-accord Gossip," *Aberdeen Evening Express*, 29 June 1918.

65 "Dominion Day at Nairn," *Aberdeen Journal*, 4 July 1918.

66 George Altmeyer, "The Ideas of Nature in Canada, 1893–1914," in *Consuming Canada: Readings in Environmental History*, ed. Chad Gaffield and Pam Gaffield (Toronto: Copp Clark, 1995), 96–118; Sherrill E. Grace, *Canada and the Idea of the North* (Montreal: McGill-Queen's University Press, 2007), 74.

67 "Why the Canadians Have Left Their Homes," *Folkestone, Hythe, Sandgate and Cheriton Herald*, 17 July 1915.

68 "Wounded Canadians in Aberdeen," *Aberdeen Journal*, 3 July 1916.

69 "Glory of the Canadians," *Daily Express* (London), 13 July 1915.

70 "Dominion Day," *Western Times* (Exeter), 3 July 1917.

71 "Premier's Address to Lumbermen," *Aberdeen Journal*, 3 July 1917.

72 "Canadian Soldiers' Celebrations at Abergavenny," *Abergavenny Chronicle*, 6 July 1917.

73 Nicholas, "Gendering the Jubilee," 263.

74 "50 Years a Dominion," *Times* (London), 30 June 1917.

75 "Canadian Notes and News," *Newcastle Journal*, 1 August 1917.

76 "Canada's Day," *Sunday Times* (London), 1 July 1917.

77 "Dominion Day," ibid., 30 June 1918.

78 "Dominion Day," *Daily Mirror* (London), 1 July 1916.

79 Ibid.

80 "July 4," *Daily Mail* (London), July 2, 1918.

81 "Commemoration Days," *Cheltenham Looker-on*, 7 July 1917.

82 "Canada's Birthday," *Dundee Courier*, 1 July 1915.

83 "The Greatest Fourth of July," *Observer* (Manchester), 30 June 1918.

84 "Independence Day," *Lancashire Evening Post* (Preston), 4 July 1918.

85 Vance, *Maple Leaf*, 181.

86 "Allies Celebrate Independence Day," *Yorkshire Post and Leeds Intelligencer*, 5 July 1918.

87 Also see Brandon Dimmel, "Bats along the Border: Sport, Festivals, and Culture in an International Community during the First World War," *American Review of Canadian Studies* 40, no. 3 (2010): 326–37.

88 Fred Gaffen, *Cross-Border Warriors: Canadians in American Forces, Americans in Canadian Forces* (Toronto: Dundurn Press, 1996), 14.

89 Norman Hillmer and Adam Chapnick, "Introduction: An Abundance of Nationalisms," in *The Making and Unmaking of Canadian Nationalisms in the Twentieth Century*, ed. Norman Hillmer and Adam Chapnick (Montreal: McGill-Queen's University Press, 2007), 5.

90 "Canada's Imperial Task," *Times* (London), 2 July 1919.

91 Hillmer and Chapnick, "Introduction," 8.

92 "Glory of the Canadians," *Daily Express* (London), 13 July 1915.

93 Vance, *Maple Leaf*; Beaupré, "En Route"; Flanagan, "Canadians in Bexhill-on-Sea."

10 A Chinese Counterpart to Dominion Day: Chinese Humiliation Day in Interwar Canada, 1924–1930

LIANBI ZHU AND TIMOTHY BAYCROFT

As early as 1881, some Chinese joined in and donated to celebrations of Dominion Day in British Columbia. As Forrest Pass notes in his chapter in this volume, local authorities in Vancouver used Chinese lanterns to decorate Dominion Day pageantry. Indeed, Chinese participation in British Columbia's Dominion Day pageantry became one of its established traditions during the last ten years of the nineteenth century. By the time of the Diamond Jubilee of Confederation in 1927, however, the active engagement of the Chinese minority group in Dominion Day activities had entirely disappeared. Not only did it not participate in the national celebration, but the Chinese had by that time created a rival commemoration, explicitly designed to contrast with Dominion Day, named Chinese Humiliation Day. On this sixtieth anniversary of Confederation, the federal government played a leading role in encouraging celebrations, attempting to use the day to foster national unity, but the Chinese community clearly and deliberately excluded themselves from such a project.[1]

Dominion Day has been subject to widespread interpretation across the years by non-dominant groups entrenched in their own past; at the same time the efforts of these groups enriched the meaning of the national day and reflected their sense and understanding of their national identity. Ethnic perspectives on national holidays – the view "from below," in other words – can help us understand the full complexity of national day commemorations both as an instrument of nation building and as a means of identity formation more broadly.[2] This chapter will describe and analyse the commemorations of the Chinese community on Chinese Humiliation Day in interwar Canada as a case study. It aims at exploring the complex relationship between Canadian and other identities among ethnic minorities, focusing particularly on the jubilee celebrations on 1 July 1927, but with a view to understanding something of the longer-term place of holidays in Canada with respect to ethnic and cultural minorities. It will do so primarily through an examination of Chinese and English newspapers in Vancouver and Victoria between 1924 and 1930. We argue that Chinese Humiliation Day commemorations can be understood as part of a framework of what we call "competitive coordination" with the celebrations of Dominion Day, especially after the Diamond Jubilee of Confederation, and that such a model also reflects of the process of identity negotiation for the minority groups in Canada.

Created in 1924, Chinese Humiliation Day aimed to commemorate and spread awareness of the humiliations that the Chinese had suffered as a direct result of Canadian immigration regulations, especially the Chinese Immigration Act, 1923. Coming into effect on 1 July 1923, the act both restricted and controlled Chinese immigration to Canada and forced all Chinese already in the country, not just the newly arrived but also the native born, to register with local authorities.[3] By juxtaposing this act with Dominion Day, the Chinese community hoped to gain maximum attention and publicity for their cause, and hoped to renegotiate their relationship to and within Canada, not only legally but also in terms of their perception and identity as an ethnic group. When the federal government abolished the act in 1947, Chinese Humiliation Day vanished simultaneously and almost without a trace.

More than thirty years ago, the volume *From China to Canada: A History of the Chinese Communities in Canada* pointed out that the Chinese had used Chinese Humiliation Day to compete with celebrations of Dominion Day in the mid-1920s, but few others have paid attention to this subject.[4] Although nothing has been written specifically about Chinese Humiliation Day, several studies have begun to take an interest in the wider topic of competing or overlapping celebrations and commemorations, following from Robert Cupido's analysis of the meticulous preparation for and celebration of the Diamond Jubilee of Confederation.[5] João Leal discusses the history of celebrating another counterpart to Dominion Day, Portugal Day, asserting "the need of a more balanced study of the role of national identity in diasporic contexts," because certain ethnic groups are better "able to articulate different layers of collective selfhood and belonging."[6] Elsewhere in this volume, two chapters analyse counterparts to Canadian national holidays: Marcel Martel and Joel Belliveau's work details the reaction in

French Canada to Empire Day and the establishment of the Fête de Dollard, and Marc-André Gagnon's chapter focuses on Saint-Jean-Baptiste Day in Montreal as a rival to Dominion Day. Unsurprisingly perhaps, Canadian historiography is much more familiar with the Fête de Dollard and Saint-Jean-Baptiste Day than with Chinese Humiliation Day.

A Precedent for Competitive Coordination: The Case of Saint-Jean-Baptiste Day Celebrations

The Chinese community in British Columbia is not the only instance of a group that engaged in competitive coordination with Canada's national holiday. A brief look at Saint-Jean-Baptiste Day in 1917 and 1927 will help to contextualize the concept of competitive coordination.

On 31 May 1917, Minister of Trade and Commerce George Foster presented the arrangements for the Golden Jubilee of Confederation made by the special committee appointed for the celebration of this major anniversary by the House of Commons. Plans included coordinating local activities with the provincial governments as well as publishing commemorative pamphlets and postcards and constructing new commemorative structures.[7] Although the First World War had initially stimulated francophone Canadians' attachment to the nation, the conscription crisis in 1917 had led to a nationwide debate on the lack of patriotism among francophones. It was in these circumstances that some leading Québécois highlighted their identity as North Americans by celebrating the 275th anniversary of the establishment of Montreal in the Golden Jubilee year. Claiming their rights and combating assimilation were the main concerns of this group.[8] Saint-Jean-Baptiste Day (24 June) festivities that year included parades, religious services in Catholic churches, and individual celebrations in Montreal, and even in Chicago, which highlighted the identity and rights of French Canadians, just one week before the celebration of the Golden Jubilee.[9]

One day before the official and civic ceremonies marking Dominion Day, religious services for the Golden Jubilee were held in both Canada and England, following the plan outlined by George Foster. On 1 July 1917, Canadian nurses and soldiers joined in services in Westminster Abbey, London, which opened with "O Canada," the future national anthem, and drew together religious and civic, as well as francophone and anglophone, aspects of nation.[10] Two French Canadians, Calixa Lavallée and Adolphe-Basile Routhier, had composed the first version of "O Canada" in French. The anthem was first performed in the ceremony of the second national convention of the Société Saint-Jean-Baptiste (SSJB), the major association arranging Saint-Jean-Baptiste Day celebrations, in 1880. It had been part of the jubilee ceremonies in both England and Canada in 1917, symbolizing a bridge between the two national days. In the official ceremony of the Golden Jubilee on Parliament Hill, Ottawa, which started at 12 noon, on 2 July, a special choir sang "O Canada" before following it up with "The Maple Leaf Forever" and "God Save the King."[11] These civic and political ceremonies physically occupied the political centre of the capital city, just as celebrations of Saint-Jean-Baptiste Day had made political use of the centre of Montreal.[12]

A decade later, in 1927, the SSJB arranged celebrations for the Diamond Jubilee of Confederation in Montreal, combining them with those of Saint-Jean-Baptiste Day with the permission and financial support of the federal government.[13] This cooperation and combination, however, faced criticism and raised controversy. Organizers failed to clarify the intended role of national identity for francophone Canadians in the events.[14] The theme for Saint-Jean-Baptiste Day was "Quatre cents ans d'histoire," thus commemorating the establishment of French Canada rather than the major anniversary of Canadian Confederation. References to the separate origin of francophone Canadians led to some confusion among both the political elites and the mainstream participants in the celebrations about the national identity the organizers sought to recognize and to promote.[15] So the relationship between Saint-Jean-Baptiste Day and Dominion Day was competitive, yet coordinated, in this case even more closely than with Chinese Humiliation Day, as the SSJB was overtly involved, at least for the Jubilee year, in the organization of both events. Francophone Canadians were able to make effective use of these major national commemorative events to assert their own identity, raise concerns about their current status within the national framework, and stake a claim to their role within the broader Canadian identity. And yet, the legal status of French Canadians within the national framework was not challenged to nearly the same extent of that of the Chinese community of British Columbia. It is to how this community sought to make similar use of Canada's national day that we now turn.

The Chinese Community in Early Twentieth-century Canada

Before examining Chinese Humiliation Day in the interwar period, some background about the state of the Chinese community in Canada at the time will be helpful. Far from being a homogeneous community, the Chinese who invented, arranged, and participated in Chinese Humiliation Day had a wide range of social and political backgrounds. Although they shared a Chinese identity, it was neither "Chinese Canadian" nor "Canadian." To prevent the possible conflation of their identity with that of today's Chinese Canadians, this chapter will use the term *Chinese* or *Chinese immigrants* to refer to those Chinese in Canada in this period. Until the 1920s, most Chinese came to Canada for financial and educational purposes, rather than with the overt aim of becoming Canadian, and there was a great deal of coming and going (both legally and illegally). According to the Dominion censuses, the number of Chinese who paid head taxes for entering Canada between 1910 and 1920 was 32,244 and the number deported was 38,899. During the decade following the 1923 act, the total number of Chinese residents decreased by 53,285.[16] In British Columbia in 1921, the male-to-female ratio in the Chinese population was thirteen to one, and only 0.7 per cent of the whole Chinese population was born in that province.[17] Very few Chinese could establish a family in Canada. Acquiring citizenship was also difficult for the Chinese at this time. In spite of the fact that the acquisition of citizenship was made slightly easier after the act, more than 83.9 per cent of Chinese were still not British subjects by birth or naturalization in 1931.[18]

The Chinese in Canada remained highly focused on what was happening in their home country. Partly because many were destined to return and also because families were not being founded in Canada, their press and letters indicated a significant fixation with affairs at home. Furthermore, even for those hoping to stay, many deeply believed that their living conditions in a foreign country were directly linked to the fate and relative international position of China. Only if China were stronger and more respected by other nations would Chinese immigrants' living conditions be improved.

Focus on the home country did not prevent the establishment of several societies aimed at promoting the welfare of the Chinese in Canada. Before the first two Chinese consulates were established in Ottawa and Vancouver (cities located in the provinces with the largest Chinese communities) in 1908, the Chinese consulate in San Francisco had helped to form the Chinese Consolidated Benevolent Association of Victoria (CCBA) in 1884, an institution that aimed to struggle against discriminatory acts against the Chinese in Canada.[19] In the same year, the CCBA appealed to the Chinese to donate two dollars per person to found additional branches, known as the Chinese Benevolent Association (CBA), in other cities. Although they shared a name and goals, the CCBA and the CBAs were independent of one another in their day-to-day operations. They were also not affiliated with, nor did they have supervision or control over, political entities such as the Chinese Freemasons (Cheekung Tang, CKT, founded in 1886, whose Canadian headquarters were in Victoria), the Chinese Nationalist Party (Kuoming Tang, KMT, founded in 1919, whose Canadian headquarters were in Vancouver), or other clan or professional societies in Canada.[20] Even if independent of each other, most of the Chinese societies contributed to the fight to repeal a variety of discriminatory legislative acts in the first two decades of the twentieth century. They would go on to be significant in the fight against the 1923 act, alongside the Chinese newspapers that reported on their activities.

The Chinese community had a well-established press in Canada by the interwar period. Chinese newspapers reported on the activities of the Chinese associations and consulates, and published editorials about affairs in the Chinese homeland as well as immigrant issues. They also translated information and notices circulated by the local and federal governments and in Canadian newspapers for the convenience of their Chinese immigrant readership. These polyphonic media, however, failed to follow consistent translations of English terms.[21] Most Chinese news articles in the period used the official translations, especially those in the *Chinese Times*, a widely circulated daily newspaper in the Chinese-Canadian community, even if they were less strict or rigorous compared to that of today. Examining the translation of geographical terms allows us to gain insights into the backgrounds of the authors of different news and editorial items in the Chinese press, and to unpack some of the forces at work behind the creation of and the specific activities on Chinese Humiliation Day.

Although Chinese Humiliation Day lasted from 1924 to 1947, this chapter will concentrate on its history from 1924 to 1930 for two reasons. First, the first six years of Chinese Humiliation Day included its full development and climax, and in particular its conjunction with the Diamond Jubilee of Confederation in 1927. Second, changing demographic and political conditions among the Chinese in Vancouver and Victoria reduced the importance of political associations in the two cities, which had been at the very centre of the political life of the Chinese community in Canada. The Chinese population dramatically shrunk in Vancouver during the 1930s, and the *Chinese Times* was no longer the most significant publication among the Chinese media to explore local Chinese identity.[22] Politically speaking, after 1927, factions among and within the political associations also weakened the power and homogeneity of major societies such as the KMT, which was divided into left and right wings based on members' attitudes towards communism. From that time onwards, the Vancouver CBA lost its primacy over other political societies and was no longer able to arrange the ceremonies for Chinese Humiliation Day. Furthermore, from the mid-1930s most societies turned their attention to supporting the anti-Japanese war in China and stopped focusing on discriminatory acts and organizing Chinese Humiliation Day ceremonies in Canada. Finally, after the KMT took power in mainland China, it established an Overseas Chinese Affairs Commission in Ottawa in 1931, which moved the political centre of the Chinese community from western to eastern Canada.[23] British Columbia thereafter lost its position as the best place in which to analyse Chinese identities in Canada.

The final important element in understanding the background of Chinese Humiliation Day is the place of the wider concept of "humiliation," which the Chinese chose to put at the core of their day of commemoration and protest. Humiliation was a common idea among the Chinese political elites in the early twentieth century. It was based on the Chinese philosophical idea, drawn from the teachings of Confucius, that commemorating a humiliating past is about introspection and self-training. After the First Opium War (1840–42), when the kingdom was confronting the great powers and their expansionist colonial policies, the idea of humiliation spread extensively in Chinese discourse.[24] Educated in the home country, the Chinese elites in Canada seized upon this idea to describe their miserable conditions in the host nation because Canada, as one dominion of the British Empire, could be seen in this context as one of the colonialist powers. Moreover, designating a humiliation day was not a grand new invention. After Chinese president Shikai Yuan signed the Twenty-one Demands with Japan on 9 May 1915 – a treaty that expanded Japan's control in China and threatened China's sovereignty – the Chinese government named that day as a nationwide humiliation day. For several years, the Chinese in Canada also commemorated this humiliation day.[25] Therefore, although they did openly discuss links between the two humiliation days, the concept and vocabulary were already well established and were present in the minds of the Chinese in Canada.

The Chinese Counterpart to Dominion Day

To clarify how Chinese Humiliation Day was competitively coordinated with Dominion Day, this section will explain Chinese understandings of Dominion Day before 1924 and examine how Chinese Humiliation Day was developed in 1924. Although the Chinese had been appealing against the restrictive immigration acts and policies of the Canadian government since the 1880s, their attitudes towards Dominion Day had previously been unrelated to these lobbying efforts. In 1915, the *Chinese Times* announced that there would be no paper published on Dominion Day, in compliance with federal legislation, and explained to its readership that taking a day off was not unreasonable, for the national day was "a day to celebrate the self-governance of the Confederation of Canada." Its reports on the celebrations in Vancouver confirmed that these events aimed to promote Canadian patriotism, and the paper recognized the value of both the recreational and commemorative functions of Dominion Day.[26]

Persuading the Chinese to comply with local legislation and rituals was a common theme in Chinese newspapers in Canada. In 1916, the *Chinese Times* warned Chinese restaurants that Vancouver's local regulations required all restaurants and shops to remain closed on 1 July, and that that police had recorded the non-compliance of those that had remained open.[27] This story also indicated that some Chinese intellectuals accepted the national day of the host nation, while businesses rejected it out of their concern for their profits. On the fiftieth anniversary celebration of Confederation in 1917, the *Chinese Times* reported the planned activities in detail (including times and places) to facilitate the participation of its readership in the festivities and to help them make their choices about which to attend. The paper included information on military parade routes, venues for speeches, and events featuring patriotic songs, as well as the names of local politicians who would attend.[28]

Between 1919 and 1923, the *Chinese Times* clearly presented Dominion Day as Canada's national day, explaining that there would be no newspaper circulation and detailing the levels of holiday services at post offices.[29] In the year of the passage of the 1923 act, more news of Vancouver's celebrations for Dominion Day occupied this newspaper than earlier. Although veterans of the First World War played a major role in excluding Chinese from jobs in Canada in the early 1920s, the *Chinese Times* positively reported on Dominion Day events organized for veterans and praised their contributions in the Great War.[30] The paper's news reports for Dominion Day contained hardly any grievances directed at the federal government and devoted little space to presenting divisions between Chinese and Canadians.

On 20 April 1924, Mianchen Li, a merchant from Taishan, held a banquet in Victoria and invited about ten members from six major Chinese political societies: the CKT, the KMT, the Bureau for the Repeal of the Chinese Immigration Act (BRCIA), the Chinese Canadian Club, Shi Shi Xuan, and the Constitutional Party (Xianzheng Dang, or XZD). At this banquet, Li asked the participants to draft a plan for the CCBA to organize "a ceremony for overseas Chinese in Canada to commemorate the enforcement of the harsh regulations" – a reference to the 1923 act. He also wanted the CCBA to arrange a general meeting of the Chinese to decide the final plan and then to spread it throughout Canada and China, to demonstrate the fortitude of the Chinese immigrants.[31]

On 22 April, the *Chinese Times* reprinted the draft plan, which included the seed of what would become Chinese Humiliation Day:

> In spite of our great efforts to have the 1923 Act repealed using diplomatic and international political means, it came into force on 1 July 1923. The overseas Chinese in Canada can only powerlessly bear such humiliation and suffering... The only thing we can do is to commemorate such humiliation, and to wait for help in the future. This is why we established an annual commemoration on 1 July.[32]

It also explained why the Chinese had the right to stay in Canada, provided an overview of the act, and clarified the strategy and proposed content of the new commemoration. It highlighted that, in the late nineteenth century, the Chinese came to Canada and built the national railways and new towns with great effort and hardship. In return, the Canadian government showed no respect to the Chinese and treated them as livestock. To the Chinese, these humiliations were unforgettable, because only when one "knows of humiliation, one person can be brave" – a saying from *Zhong Yong*, one of China's ancient classics.[33] The key narrative that would back up Chinese Humiliation Day thus appeared, including the Chinese contribution to Canadian nation building, the unfair immigration regulations of the federal government, and the necessity for a commemoration of humiliation, to be brave and to fight for the repeal of the regulations.

On the day after Mianchen Li's meeting, the new consul-general, Chang Luo, arrived in Victoria en route to taking up office in Ottawa. Luo gave a speech in Victoria's Chinatown, briefly mentioning that the Chinese government was fully aware of the unfairness of the 1923 act, but strongly encouraging Chinese merchants to devote themselves to encouraging China-Canada trade.[34] Compared to his predecessors Shuwen Yang and Qilian Zhou, Luo showed little interest in helping the Chinese have the act repealed. Yang and Zhou had continuously sent documents to Beijing to ask for governmental negotiations on this issue. The total number of documents was no less than thirty, including petitions of various societies in Canada, transcripts from the House of Commons in Ottawa, and English newspaper clippings with their letters in English (to the Canadian government) and Chinese reports.[35] Luo sent only one telegram to Beijing, in July 1924, with less than one hundred characters, and attached the full translation of the 1923 act.[36] In the following two years, two successive consuls in Vancouver sent two documents in total, which were almost identical to those sent by Luo.[37] In other words, after 1924, the Chinese lobby that sought to repeal the act had lost most of its support from the Chinese government.

In the week following Li's meeting, one of the *Chinese Times*'s editorials criticized the act on its cover page and engaged in open debate with the new consul-general. In Luo's view, the 1923 Act merely protected the residents in Canadian ports; in contrast, the editorialist believed it was harsh regulations aimed at all Chinese.[38] In Luo's welcoming event in Ottawa, arranged by the local CKT, Guangzu Liu (the head of the CKT) presented a plan for a Chinese Humiliation Day but did not receive any comments from Luo.[39] Luo's attitude reflected that of the representatives of China throughout this time, and it was therefore not surprising that Chinese officers rarely participated in Chinese Humiliation Day ceremonies between 1924 and 1947:[40] they were representatives of the Chinese government, not politicians aiming to help the Chinese claim rights in the host nation.

On 4 May 1924, the CCBA held a meeting in Victoria, inviting representatives of other societies to discuss how to organize the proposed ceremonies on 1 July. They agreed that the CCBA and CBAs would be the organizers of local events, and that the key ceremony was to be a public speech of mourning. Other activities included the following:

First, sending telegrams to China about this ceremony to various societies and associations; second, writing Chinese articles for publication in newspapers in China, and leaflets in Canada, as well as writing English-language articles for English newspapers in Canada; third, compiling the narrative history for the 1 July ceremony; fourth, nominating 1 July as "Humiliation Day" on calendars published or used by Chinese shops and in the press; fifth, all Chinese should pin a badge, written "Remember the Humiliation" on 1 July; sixth, electing a committee to organize these events, each political society electing two members.[41]

These organizational arrangements, led by the CCBA and CBAs, lasted only for the first two years. On 19 May 1924, Chaoran Luo, the secretary in charge of the CKT in Canada, as well as chairman of the CCBA, wrote an open letter to all CKT members. He asked them to join Chinese Humiliation Day activities and to cooperate with the CCBA to organize these activities.[42] Two days later, the CCBA published a similar open letter in the *Chinese Times* to CBAs, CKTs, and KMTs, as well as all Chinese in Canada, in an attempt to lead all the ceremonies throughout Canada.[43]

On 22 May, a seventeen-member committee was elected in the hall of the CCBA, led by Chaoran Luo and Mianchen Li, who were asked to go to Vancouver as soon as possible to visit societies, schools, and the press to promote the ceremony on 1 July. Other members were asked to visit the local opera house to request financial support. All of the members of the committee were to write articles for leaflets to distribute in Vancouver and Victoria every week to attract greater numbers of Chinese to take part in the planned ceremony.[44] The *Chinese Times* promoted the Chinese Humiliation Day ceremonies in an article with similar content to Chaoran Luo's open letter. It added that if all the Chinese joined the ceremony, without flying any flag – either the Chinese national flag or the Union Jack – their call to repeal the 1923 act would be noticed by the Canadian authorities but would not contravene local legislation.[45]

Unsurprisingly, given what has already been said, Chinese diplomats disagreed with the CCBA's plan. The Chinese consul in Vancouver, Baoheng Lin, believed that

> It is unwise to organize the commemoration for humiliation on 1 July, the most important national day of Canada. If the Chinese fly flags and join celebrations of Dominion Day, they have to smile to others and weep at home; Canadians might tease us. If the Chinese reject the celebrations, it would reduce the profit of Chinese owners of restaurants and lead to chaos between Chinese and Canadians. As the 1923 act was signed on 30 June 1923, it is better to change Chinese Humiliation Day to 30 June.[46]

Hongxiang Liao, a member of the Chinese Canadian Club who had gained citizenship, agreed with Lin's suggestion to change the date, and sent an open letter to the CCBA. He noted that many Chinese might be attracted by celebrations of Dominion Day as a means to promote their social integration. Moreover, as everyone had a day off on 1 July, according to local legislation, if the Chinese attempt to demonstrate their grievances by closing their shops, no Canadians would notice.[47] The CCBA's next meeting about Chinese Humiliation Day rejected Lin and Liao's suggestion, emphasizing that the ceremonies aimed overtly to compete with celebrations of Dominion Day and clarifying that the role of Chinese Humiliation Day was to be a direct counterpart to Dominion Day. Leaders of the CCBA invoked the Jewish refusal to join in national day activities in host nations; instead, they mourned, and neither used fire nor flew the flag, and this resistance was met without interference from the host nation.[48] The CCBA thereafter became estranged from the Chinese consulate, particularly once the group rejected the consul-general's invitation to a meeting in Ottawa to discuss strategies to bring about the repeal of the 1923 act.[49] Symptomatic of this split was the fact that the *Chinese Times*'s news about Chinese Humiliation Day mainly used the southern translation of Canada (Jianada) for the remainder of the year.[50]

The CCBA stuck to its original plan and continued to advocate in the print media for its version of Chinese Humiliation Day. Middle school students in Vancouver and Victoria were one of its target groups, and they wrote poems and prose texts for the *Chinese Times* to strengthen the support for Chinese Humiliation Day.[51] Local branches of various societies sent letters to the CCBA or the *Chinese Times* to show their willingness to organize and participate in ceremonies in their own towns and cities.[52] Several English newspapers in eastern and western Canada, and even some in the United States – the *Quebec Telegraph*, the *Lewiston Evening Journal*, the *Deseret News*, the *Washington Post*, the *Toronto Globe*, and the *Montreal Gazette* – reported on the Chinese plans in mid-June with articles of around four paragraphs.[53] Comparing the content of these English news reports, it seems that they contained sufficiently similar content as to probably have been all taken from a single source of information from the Chinese community. The reports from Victoria opened with a contrast:

While Canadian flags flutter gaily from the masthead in commemoration of Canada's birthday, July 1, Chinese flags in the city will fly at half-mast and Chinese homes will be festooned with wreaths of mourning, for, smarting under a deep sense of insult offered them by the recent immigration regulations, the Chinese residents here have designated July first as "Humiliation Day."[54]

It continued by describing the content of the 1923 act and why Chinese Humiliation Day was created, and highlighted that these commemorations would be annual events unless the regulations were changed. Obviously, the common source presented the key narrative of Chinese Humiliation Day created by the CCBA and underlined "humiliation." The *Ottawa Citizen*'s report, which appeared a bit later, quoted the viewpoint of Thomas Hamilton, "a local restaurant man and powerful tong official of local Chinese, [who] stated that while Ottawa Chinese felt their position no less keenly they are not going to manifest it outwardly."[55] It mistakenly believed that ceremonies related to Chinese Humiliation Day were private and did not aim to compete openly with celebrations of Dominion Day. A briefer version, which was published in *Shen Bao* in Shanghai, stated that the Chinese would fly their flags at half mast on that day.[56] Different newspapers, therefore, displayed their own views on Chinese Humiliation Day, in particular with respect to the key question of whether Chinese Humiliation Day was to be a public or private event.

Although the CCBA had clearly and overtly defined Chinese Humiliation Day as a rival to Dominion Day, the *Chinese Times* continued to inform its readership about the mainstream plans for celebrating Dominion Day in Vancouver, with even more details in the last week of June 1924 than there had been in 1923: decorations and routes of parades, post office holiday services, times for watching fireworks, schedules of bus services, and other arrangements.[57] On the same page, it updated the progress of preparations for ceremonies for Chinese Humiliation Day.

Parallel reports on Chinese Humiliation Day and Dominion Day stopped after 1 July 1924. From that time onwards, the *Chinese Times* focused only on ceremonies, poems, and prose about Chinese Humiliation Day, as well as on the Vancouver CBA's restricted plan for monitoring Chinese activities with the support of the Chinese political societies.[58] The actual plans for the day included wearing badges, sticking banners on windows, and not hanging any flag (and removing regular ones), as well as not watching or joining in with any of the mainstream Dominion Day recreational activities.[59] The Vancouver

CBA also set up a team to observe whether the Chinese followed its directives, and felt satisfied afterwards with the obedience of local Chinese. Such monitoring was similar to the Canadian police record for those who ignored local regulations about Dominion Day.

Meanwhile, the CCBA arranged more public activities in Victoria, including an outdoor demonstration. Five merchants donated cars covered with English-language banners saying "We Protest Unfair Immigration Acts," "Never Forget," and "The Cruelest Regulation in the World," to cite but a few, which were driven through the streets while honking. The *Chinese Times* said these parades were orderly and that Canadians showed surprise or shame, or simply blamed the protestors.[60] Other societies and schools in Vancouver, Victoria, Cumberland, Kaslo, Kamloops, Nanaimo, Port Hammond, Haney, New Westminster, Revelstoke, Calgary, Winnipeg, and Halifax arranged speeches to commemorate the day.[61] As noted, news stories reporting these events tended to use the southern or Taishan translation of geographical terms. The content of speeches repeated the key narrative of Chinese Humiliation Day constructed by the CCBA. Ceremonies in Victoria and Calgary ended with singing Chinese patriotic songs. The *Vancouver Sun* recorded Chinese activities, noting that there were three thousand participants who joined the ceremonies in Vancouver, about half of the Chinese population of the city.[62] Other English newspapers and those in China barely reported activities of the first Chinese Humiliation Day in 1924.[63]

Some organizers worried that Chinese immigrants would fail to maintain the events of Chinese Humiliation Day in the future, and that other Canadians might mock the brief enthusiasm of the Chinese to claim rights. Such concerns seemed to be particularly relevant in the second year. In early June 1925, a Chinese man named Huansheng Huang was kidnapped in Vancouver, and the Vancouver CBA devoted time and energy to rescuing him. In the meantime, the municipal government invited the association to join parades on Dominion Day. The members of the Vancouver CBA unanimously rejected this suggestion in favour of continuing to commemorate Chinese Humiliation Day.[64] The municipal government, however, continued to send invitations to the CBA, which left it with a dilemma: if it were to join the mainstream celebrations, it would break its own rules; but if it continued to reject these invitations, it could harm the relationship between China and Canada and worsen the living condition of Chinese immigrants. Members of the Vancouver CBA decided to privately donate to municipal celebrations of Dominion Day while continuing to organize Chinese Humiliation Day for the same day.[65]

The events for Chinese Humiliation Day in 1925 replicated those of 1924, though on a smaller scale. Chinese middle schools were asked to arrange speeches for the evening of 1 July.[66] The *Chinese Times* published new poems between 23 and 25 June as well as an editorial on 30 June to encourage Chinese participation in Chinese Humiliation Day.[67] Its published reason to have no issue appear on 1 July became Chinese Humiliation Day, not Dominion Day, repeating its approach from the year before.[68] The Vancouver CBA repeated its 1924 rules and guidelines in a leaflet distributed throughout the city.[69] Activities in the evening were more organized than they had been the previous year. They opened with bowing to the Chinese national flag, followed by speeches, and ending with calling out "Never Forget the Nation's Humiliation."[70] On 4 July, the *British Colonist* briefly reported on the ceremonies in Victoria; other newspapers mentioned nothing.[71] At the same time, the *Chinese Times* completely ignored any news about Dominion Day, and its only report on Chinese Humiliation Day ceremonies in other cities was that of Nanaimo (this lack of coverage may have been possibly owing to the fact that the Chinese in Vancouver were concentrating on rescuing Huansheng Huang).[72] The southern translation of geographical terms had disappeared in the 1925 reports, and would not be widely used until the end of the Second World War.

When Chinese Humiliation Day Met the Diamond Jubilee

When, in 1926, Vancouver's municipal government started to prepare for the Diamond Jubilee, the *Chinese Times* decided not to ignore the mainstream news reporting as it had done in 1925. In June 1926, therefore, it once again listed the plans and routes for the Dominion Day parades, the various activities in parks and ports, and the holiday services of post offices.[73] It also explained, in an objective tone, the municipal government's plans to build a monument for the Diamond Jubilee.[74] The *Chinese Times*'s notices for why there would be no issue on 1 July, however, still attributed the reason to Chinese Humiliation Day, not Dominion Day. It published an editorial that repeated the narrative of Chinese Humiliation Day and also blamed Chinese diplomats who were unable to help the Chinese get the 1923 act abolished.[75] This was the beginning of the pattern of competitive coordination, at least in terms of the conception and reporting of the events. Information about the two competing commemorations appeared in parallel. The paradox of seemingly promoting both at the same time, while still explaining clearly about how one (Chinese Humiliation Day) was in direct contrast to and conflicted with the other (Dominion Day) was simply left unresolved.

In preparation for the 1926 Chinese Humiliation Day, the Vancouver CBA again established a team for monitoring the activities of the Chinese for 1 July. In its preparatory meeting, it stated that any Chinese who watched the Dominion Day parades, joined in any recreational activities, or hung Canadian flags would be noticed by this team, and their actions would be regarded as offensive towards the "masses," not just the CBA. The names of such offenders would then be published in Chinese newspapers.[76] It also confirmed the rituals of Chinese Humiliation Day: the core of the ceremony was an indoor public speech, chaired by the CBA, to which all Chinese were welcome. Students and leaders of social groups were the key speakers, suggesting future plans for bringing about the repeal of the 1923 act, and encouraging the Chinese to fight with their own efforts and not rely on the Chinese government. Each ceremony opened with mourning (which ranged from thirty seconds to three minutes) and ended with the recitation of a motto, either to never forget the humiliation or in support of the Chinese Republic.[77]

Here, the *Chinese Times* encountered a paradoxical question: how to explain its recognition of and reporting on these two conflicting holidays and still satisfy the CBA's requirements. The paper rationalized this dilemma in its own way: the reason for translating English news reports of Dominion Day was to encourage the Chinese to fight for the repeal of the 1923 act. After they achieved this goal, they would then be able to join local celebrations of the national day and share happiness with Canadians.[78] Given this rationale, one single page of the *Chinese Times* included reports on the public speech of Chinese Humiliation Day in Nanaimo, the singing of Chinese patriotic songs, as well as the Dominion Day parades and evening events in Vancouver.

By 1926 it was becoming clear that monitoring Chinese behaviour on 1 July was a unique feature of the Vancouver CBA. This measure led to a conflict with a Chinese film company called New China. Two managers of New China, the Guan brothers, published an open letter to the chair of the Vancouver CBA, Rui Zeng, in the *Chinese Times* on 22 July 1926. They found that the newspaper *Xin Minguo Bao* (run by the KMT) had criticized their company because it had originally planned to screen their new film on 1 July (thereby breaking the Vancouver CBA's rules for commemorating Chinese Humiliation Day with non-activity), but had backed down after pressure from the CBA.[79] From the Guans' point of view, this criticism was unjust because they had not received notice from the CBA telling them that they should postpone their plans to screen the new film. On the contrary, they argued, they had spontaneously decided to cancel the showing of the film on 1 July. The next day, Rui Zeng sent an open letter to the *Chinese Times* to defend himself. He had reacted, he said, after a member of the Chinese community had reported the screening date to the CBA and after a journalist of *Xin Minguo Bao* – Rukun Liu – had contacted Zeng to ask for his personal intervention. Zeng met the man he believed to be the manager of New China, Angzhan Huang, and negotiated with him to change the date for the screening. Zeng personally felt this affair had occurred after (and because) Huang had agreed with his suggestion. He was therefore surprised by the Guan brothers' letter twenty days later, which claimed that they had spontaneously decided to postpone the film.[80] This conflict shows that the Vancouver CBA still carefully monitored Chinese behaviour on 1 July 1926, using members of the press and public to help keep pressure on those who ignored their rulings. At least in some cases the pressure was felt to be unfair and unreasonable by members of the business community, who protested that they voluntarily adhered to the principles of Chinese Humiliation Day.

In the jubilee year, the editorial board of the *Chinese Times* showed great interest in reporting local preparations for the Diamond Jubilee from early June to the end of the month.[81] Its editorial first suggesting that the Chinese should not fully reject celebrations of the Diamond Jubilee was as follows:

> We should divide two kinds of activities: the negotiations between the Chinese and Canadian diplomats on the 1923 act, and the contact between Chinese and Canadians here. Chinese immigrants should not stop joining local celebrations, especially mega events. After the U.S. government enforced legislation to exclude the Japanese, they still actively jointed celebrations on 4 July. We Chinese, therefore, should never forget our humiliation, and at the same time join the celebrations to show our wisdom and magnanimity. If it was possible, we should change the date of Chinese Humiliation Day to 30 June for the convenience of commemoration. I hope the board of CBA can consider this suggestion.[82]

Another editorial by the same author ended by highlighting Canada's progress in the previous sixty years, which reflected the official tone of the Diamond Jubilee.[83] A newspaper that normally used few pictures used visual content with English captions to introduce Canada's past and present: a photo of John A. Macdonald, "Canada's First Premier [sic]" (figure 10.1); a photo of the "Home of [the] Minister of the Dominion to the United States, Vincent Massey"; and an illustration of the Quebec Conference meetings that had led to Confederation (figure 10.2).[84] The same pictures were widely used in other Canadian newspapers to glorify the birth and the progress of the nation. Thus the *Chinese Times* maintained its paradoxical strategy of reporting and apparently promoting both Chinese Humiliation Day and Dominion Day, and enhancing the sense of competitive coordination within the Chinese community.

The Vancouver CBA, still chaired by Rui Zeng, discussed whether the Chinese should join in and donate to the Diamond Jubilee.[85] It concluded with a compromise: it would hold public speeches for Chinese Humiliation Day in the late evening of 1 July, but the Chinese were allowed to join the Dominion Day parades and decorate their shops.[86] It did not mention anything about flying flags at half mast or about a monitoring team. In the following days, the *Chinese Times* translated the official programs of the Diamond Jubilee into Chinese while also reporting on Chinese Humiliation Day ceremonies in Vancouver and Nanaimo.[87] The Chinese Humiliation Day public ceremony in Vancouver included making three respectful bows to the national flag of China, a three-minute silence for commemoration, the chair's declaration of the opening of the ceremony with an explanation of the reason for its organization, speeches by representatives, and a question time for students. This ceremony copied the rituals of a Chinese funeral ceremony (bows and silence) in a way that sharply contrasted with the joyful celebrations of the Diamond Jubilee outside the room. The Chinese Humiliation Day public speech in Nanaimo ended with calling out different mottos. These mottos covered the commitment to abolishing the 1923 act as well as content drawn from the national humiliation day of 9 May. From some viewpoints, the humiliation the Chinese suffered in China and in Canada shared the same origin.

Differences between diverse Chinese Humiliation Day public speeches suggest that different organizers adopted their own ways of commemorating the same event. Local arrangements for Chinese Humiliation Day led to a conflict between the CCBA and the Vancouver CBA as to what constituted the "proper attitude to the Diamond Jubilee." The CCBA noted that the Vancouver CBA wanted the Chinese

此為加拿大第一任首相麥當路氏像。伊添於坎國告統一後就職。迄今適為六十周年

SIR JOHN A. MACDONALD
Canada's First Premier, whose term of office began shortly after Confederation, the 60th anniversary of which is being observed this year.

10.1 "Canada's First Premier." *Chinese Times*, 28–30 June 1927. With thanks to the Simon Fraser University Library.

THE FATHERS OF CONFEDERATION

MEMBERS OF THE QUEBEC CONFERENCE, OCTOBER, 1864

10.2 "Members of the Quebec Conference, October 1864." *Chinese Times*, June 28 to 30, 1927. With thanks to the Simon Fraser University Library.

to join in the activities of the Diamond Jubilee, and the CCBA criticized the CBA in an article to that effect in *Xin Minguo Bao*. It argued that the CBA had forgotten the motto of the Republic of China, for only thus could it make such a compromise.[88] In response, one member of the CBA used the pseudonym Guanhai to send two letters to the *Chinese Times*. He argued that it was unwise to close down all Chinese restaurants in order to commemorate Chinese Humiliation Day, as it reduced the profits of their owners. He wrote that, although *Xin Minguo Bao* appealed to the Chinese to join Chinese Humiliation Day ceremonies, one of its editors in chief instead had gone on a date with a "young beauty" on 1 July, and was witnessed (and criticized) by other Chinese. He claimed, too, that the newspaper ignored other societies that did not fully follow the regulations of CCBA and suspend all recreational activities on 1 July. He concluded that *Xin Minguo Bao*'s criticism of the Vancouver CBA's compromise was primarily due to the political conflicts between the KMT and other political associations in Canada. According to the CBA's meeting minutes, the association branded the CCBA's article criticizing the CBA as a fake and ignored it.[89] This is just one example that year of the increasing conflict between the CBA in Vancouver and the CCBA, which in the long run contributed to the toning down of Chinese Humiliation Day, even if it did not stop its continuation.

From the time of the Diamond Jubilee onwards, the pattern of competitive coordination remained, with place given in the press and among the population to both Chinese Humiliation Day and Dominion Day. This can be seen both through the explanations given for not publishing the *Chinese Times* on 1 July and in how much coverage the press gave to each commemoration.[90] In the first couple of years after the jubilee, the press used Chinese Humiliation Day as the reason for suspending publication, but from 1930 onwards, that was not the only reason given. The *Chinese Times* regularly either referred to Chinese Humiliation Day and Dominion Day at the same time or used the reasoning that it suspended publication simply to "follow local regulations" (as had been the stated reason in the years before 1924).[91] From 1930 to the end of Chinese Humiliation Day in 1947, the *Chinese Times* continued to publish news about Dominion Day alongside its reporting on the organized events for Chinese Humiliation Day. Meanwhile, the Vancouver CBA lost its controlling power in organizing Chinese Humiliation Day activities, and the *Chinese Times* reported its appeals to the Chinese to stop all business and recreational activities on 1 July only in the context of its standard editorials bemoaning the 1923 act and its explanation of the main motivations for Chinese Humiliation Day.[92] In 1928 and 1929, the *Chinese Times* included reports on Chinese Humiliation Day ceremonies in Vancouver, Nanaimo, and Victoria, where Chinese students, the CKT, CBAs, and the CCBA played the leading role in the public speeches.[93] Ceremonies in other cities received dramatically decreased coverage in the *Chinese Times* in the years after 1930.[94]

The history of Chinese Humiliation Day reveals that the symbolic value of the centralized national day – Dominion Day – was accepted and used by the Chinese, although it recognized a group identity in partial distinction from this national one. When Canadian governments promoted and supported the Diamond Jubilee, the Chinese did not fully reject these celebrations. Diverse Chinese groups reacted differently to the conflicting events of Dominion Day and Chinese Humiliation Day. The Vancouver CBA and the *Chinese Times* both worked out a compromise to handle this dilemma, recognizing Dominion Day and Chinese Humiliation Day simultaneously. They legitimized this compromise as an approach to integrating the community into the Canadian nation, meanwhile expressing the specific concerns, and continuing to support the identity formation, of the Chinese community within it.

The other striking feature of Chinese Humiliation Day is the extent to which it is illustrative of nation building from below within a minority ethnic community. With little support (and in some cases hostility) from the official representatives of the Chinese government, Chinese Humiliation Day continued for over two decades simply because of the driving energy of individuals and local associations within the community itself. Even if it is debatable whether it contributed to bringing about the repeal of the 1923 act, it certainly had the effect of cementing the Chinese community within Canada and giving them a narrative, repeated annually, that promoted both their Chinese and Canadian identities.

Conclusion

In analysing the reactions of Chinese immigrants to Canada's national day on the occasion of a major anniversary of the Confederation, this chapter has argued that the relationship between a national day and its counterpart for a specific ethnic community occurred in an atmosphere of competitive coordination. The competitive aspect illustrates the modifications the ethnic community made in seeking to promote wider understandings of its specificity against the national identities promoted by the national day. Meanwhile, the coordination dimension shows that, for the most part, the Chinese did not want to reject Canada or national identity; rather, they were still loyal, potentially patriotic, and certainly cooperative members of society who, as a group, had not been given adequate recognition for their contribution to Canada and, in some ways, had been denied their rights. Similar processes were underway in how francophones responded to the Golden and Diamond

Jubilees of Confederation, as well as to Empire Day in the early decades of the twentieth century (as discussed in the chapter by Marcel Martel and Joel Belliveau). A much more explicitly competitive and less cooperative model emerged in the 1970s in Quebec, when the provincial government transformed Saint-Jean-Baptiste Day into the Fête nationale (as Marc-André Gagnon's chapter illustrates). The history, experiences, and claims of a group may determine how far the inventor of the rival day departs from national identity or from the official understanding of the national day. In the case studied here, the function of Canada's national day as an instrument for nation building was clearly accepted by the Chinese and had a significant importance within the community itself. It may be said that the notion of competitive coordination that has been revealed in this specific snapshot of celebrating and commemorating the national day is indicative of Canadian nation building in general and what would later become officially formulated as multiculturalism. Different ethnic communities would ultimately seek just what the Chinese were seeking in the interwar period through the creation of Chinese Humiliation Day: national acceptance, an end to discrimination, and recognition as a group within the national community.

NOTES

1 Robert Cupido, "'Sixty Years of Canadian Progress': The Diamond Jubilee and the Politics of Commemoration," in *Canadian Identity: Region/Country/Nation – Canadian Issues* vol. 20, ed. Caroline Andrew, Will Straw, and J.-Yvon Theriault (Montreal: Association for Canadian Studies, 1998), 19–33.
2 Jon E. Fox, "National Holiday Commemoration: The View from Below," in *The Cultural Politics of Nationalism and Nation-Building: Ritual and Performance in the Forging of Nations*, ed. Rachel Tsang and Eric Taylor Woods (London and New York: Routledge, 2014), 38–39, 42–45.
3 "The Chinese Immigration Act, 1923," 13–14 George V, chap. 38 (Ottawa: F.A. Acland, 1923), 301–15.
4 Harry Con, Ronald J. Con, Graham Johnson, Edgar Wickberg, and William E. Willmott, *From China to Canada: A History of the Chinese Communities in Canada*, ed. Edgar Wickberg (Toronto: McClelland and Stewart, 1982, 1988), 157–8. Hua Wu and Xueqing Xu, "The First of July for Humiliation Day: A Study on *Chinese Times*'s Construction of Chinese's Identity, 1923–1947," *Forum of Chinese Literature Worldwide* 2 (June 2010): 9–13. This is the only Chinese article about Chinese Humiliation Day.

5 Cupido, "'Sixty Years of Canadian Progress.'"

6 João Leal, "What's (not) in a Parade? Nationhood, Ethnicity and Regionalism in a Diasporic Context," *Nations and Nationalism* 20, no. 2 (2014): 200.

7 Canada, House of Commons, *Debates* (hereafter *Debates*), 31 May 1917, 12th Parliament, 7th session, vol. 2, 1865–66.

8 Alan Gordon, *Making Public Pasts: The Contested Terrain of Montreal's Public Memories, 1891–1930* (Montreal: McGill-Queen's University Press, 2001), 159–60.

9 "French-Canadian Fete Tomorrow: St. Jean Baptiste Day Will Be Observed by Processions and Services," *Montreal Gazette*, 23 June 1917.

10 "Confederation Commemorated in Motherland," *Montreal Gazette*, 2 July 1917.

11 "Celebration Will Be Memorable Event, Details for Commemoration of Fiftieth Anniversary of Confederation on Monday," *Ottawa Citizen*, 30 June 1917.

12 For example, "The Lesson of 1867," *Ottawa Citizen*, 30 June 1917; "Reviewed Event of Fifty Years Ago," *Montreal Gazette*, 2 July 1917.

13 *Debates*, 17 February 1927, 16th Parliament, 1st session, vol. 1, 412. Mason Wade, *The French Canadians, 1760–1945* (Toronto: Macmillan, 1956), 809.

14 Cupido, "'Sixty Years of Canadian Progress,'" 24.

15 Annie Gérin, "Les espaces multiples de la fête: la Saint-Jean-Baptiste 1968 à Montréal," *British Journal of Canadian Studies* 27, no. 1 (2014): 10.

16 David Chuenyan Lai, Ding Guo, and Bobbie Jia, *History of Chinese Migration to Canada, 1858–1966* (Beijing: People's Publishing House, 2013), 216.

17 "Province of British Columbia Report on Oriental Activities within the Province; Prepared for the Legislative Assembly" (Victoria: Charles F. Baffled, 1927), 9.

18 Dominion Bureau of Statistics, *The Canada Year Book 1945* (Ottawa: Edmond Cloutier, 1945), 123; Con et al., *From China to Canada*, 150–1.

19 Con et al., *From China to Canada,* table 5, 300–1, and 102.

20 Ibid., 37–40.

21 Take, for example, the most influential Chinese newspaper in Vancouver from the second decade of the twentieth century to the 1980s, the *Chinese Times* (hereafter *CT*), or *Dahan Gongbao*, one of the most significant sources for the period under study. When translating "Canada," it had two options. One (Kannada) was the same as the official translation used by the Chinese government until the end of the Second World War; the other (Jianada) was normally used by the members of CKT. Since the Chinese use the phonic element of a character to translate a foreign geographical

term, in this case *Kannada* used characters that reflected Mandarin pronunciation (or the northern dialect in general) and *Jianada* reflected Cantonese pronunciation. Moreover, the *Chinese Times*'s translation of most Canadian cities followed the pronunciation of the dialect of Taishan (a town in Guangdong Province from which the largest number of Canadian immigrants to Canada had come), a sub-division of Cantonese. Although the *Chinese Times* was not the only surviving Chinese newspaper to explore Chinese Humiliation Day, it was the most circulated newspaper in British Columbia and covered news from home and aboard. Founded and run by CKT, it circulated the propaganda of this association but with a wide coverage, and it reflected a rich context of that time. Another influential and long-published newspaper of KMT, *Shing Wah Daily News* in Toronto, did not cover the second decade of the century, and had a smaller readership than the *Chinese Times*.

22 Con et al., *From China to Canada*, 149. Few other English and Chinese sources, however, discussed or mentioned Chinese Humiliation Day. Taking the House *Debates* as an example, only Lise Bourgault mentioned Chinese Humiliation Day, and she mistakenly believed the first commemoration happened on 1 July 1923. See *Debates*, 14 June 1990, 34th Parliament, 2nd session, vol. 9, 12798.
23 Con et al., *From China to Canada*, 157–68.
24 William A. Callahan, *China: The Pessoptimist Nation* (Oxford: Oxford University Press, 2010), 23–26. Although this work focuses on the contemporary use of "humiliation" in the Chinese context, the mark of its long practice from the 1840s to date was consistency.
25 Zhiyan, "Editorial: Several Thoughts on Humiliation Day," *CT*, 8 and 10 May 1915. Chinese schools in Canada also organized ceremonies for May 9th Humiliation Days in the 1910s and 1920s. See, for example, "School Associations Commemorated the Humiliation of the Nation," *CT*, 8 May 1920.
26 "No Circulation for Tomorrow," *CT*, 30 June 1915; "Yesterday Was the Autonomy Day," *CT*, 3 July 1915.
27 "Several Businesses Rejected to Follow the Holiday Regulation Yesterday," *CT*, 3 July 1916.
28 "Military Parades on the National Day," *CT*, 30 June 1917.
29 *CT*, 30 June 1919; 29 June 1920; 30 June 1921; "This Afternoon Is Not a Public Holiday," *CT*, 28 June 1922; *CT*, 30 June 1922; 30 June 1923.
30 "Dressed Pageant Queen Paraded to Salute War Veteran," *CT*, 3 July 1923.
31 "Consul-General Luo Has Arrived Victoria," *CT*, 21 April 1924.
32 "Draft to Appeal the July First Gathering," *CT*, 22 April 1924.
33 Ibid.

34 Ibid.
35 Zhenghua Jiang comp., *Document Collections for Immigration Acts upon Chinese Workers in Canada, 1906–1928* (Taipei: Institute of Modern History, Academia Sinica, 1998), 286–393, 484–97.
36 Ibid., 499–545.
37 Ibid., 545–719.
38 Lijun, "Editorial: Several Thoughts on How the Great Powers Treated the Chinese Immigrants," *CT*, 23 April 1924; Jianwu, "Editorial: To Consul-General Luo," *CT*, 24 and 25 April 1924.
39 "Welcome Consul-General Luo," *CT*, 25 April 1924.
40 According to the *Chinese Times*, only Zuan He, then consul in Vancouver, joined the ceremony in 1926. See, "Details about Chinese Immigrants' Commemoration on July First Gathering," *CT*, 2 July 1926.
41 "Never Forget the Nation's Humiliation: The CCBA Agreed to Organize the July First Gathering," *CT*, 7 May 1924.
42 "An Open Letter to All CKTs," *CT*, 19 May 1924.
43 "A Mail from the CCBA in Victoria," *CT*, 21 May 1924.
44 "Chinese Immigrants in Victoria Are Preparing the July First Gathering, and the CCBA Has Established the Committee for the Event," *CT*, 23 May 1924. The opera house refused to give financial support to the CCBA for this purpose, and the CCBA decided to collect money from all societies and shop owners throughout Canada. Finally, the BRCIA distributed money to the CCBA for preparing the Chinese Humiliation Day ceremony because of their shared objectives. The head of the bureau also wrote a script for a new Cantonese Opera (banben) on one leaflet to be released in Victoria and Vancouver. See "Chinese Immigrants in Victoria Are Preparing the July First Gathering, and the CCBA Held Its Second Meeting," *CT*, 30 May 1924; "Chinese Immigrants in Victoria Are Preparing the July First Gathering, and the CCBA Sent the Leaflets for the Second Time," *CT*, 2 June 1924.
45 "Fellow Chinese in Victoria Will Commemorate Humiliation, and What Should Those in Vancouver Do?" *CT*, 31 May 1924.
46 Hongxiang Liao, "A Suggestion on the July First Commemoration," *CT*, 6 June 1924.
47 Ibid.
48 "Chinese Immigrants in Victoria Are Preparing the July First Gathering, and the CCBA Held Its Third Meeting," *CT*, 9 June 1924.
49 After the CBA in Vancouver decided to send Hongxiang Liao to join the meeting in Ottawa, the CCBA said it was unnecessary to send a second person from Victoria for the same purpose. See "News about Struggling," *CT*, 23 June 1924; "Details about Gathering in CCBA in Victoria," *CT*, 25 June 1924.

50 See *CT*'s articles from late June to the end of July.

51 See, for example, Guijue Zhou and Chunji Liang, "Poems: Remembering July First," and Kaishi Zhou, "Prose: Remembering July First," *CT*, 10 June 1924; Akong, "Song for July First," *CT*, 12 June 1924; Kaishi Zhou, "Poem: Thoughts on Humiliation," *CT*, 20 June 1924. These pieces repeated in the form of verse the objective confirmed by CCBA. A different type of Cantonese opera (yue'ou) was composed and published in *CT*. See Shaoying, "Yue'ou: Remembering July First," *CT*, 16, 17, 20 June 1924; Yin, "Yue'ou: Remembering July First," *CT*, 21 June 1924; Mr. Zhou, "Yue'ou: Remembering July First," *CT*, 23 June 1924; for other poems, see, Mr. Four, "Poems: Two Weeks before July First," *CT*, 21 June 1924, and Gongji Zhao, "Poem: Thoughts," *CT*, 27 June 1924.

52 Letters came from the following societies: CBAs in Nanaimo, Saskatoon, Toronto, Regina, New Westminster, Winnipeg, and Duncan (perhaps Whonnock); CKT branches in Port Hammond and Haney (today's Maple Ridge), Revelstoke, Toronto, Halifax, Winnipeg, and Saskatoon; KMT's headquarter in Vancouver; Reading Rooms in Victoria and Battleford; BRCIAs in Vancouver and Edmonton; clan societies in Vancouver; schools in Vancouver and Victoria; the Shon Yee Benevolent Association in Vancouver. See "News from Other Towns Agreed with July First Commemoration," *CT*, 6 June 1924; "Responses to July First Commemoration," *CT*, 12 June 1924; "Letter from Saskatchewan," *CT*, 16 June 1924; "Chinese Immigrants in Ottawa Agreed with July First Commemoration," *CT*, 18 June 1924; "Security Bureau Changed Its Date of Anniversary," *CT*, 21 June 1924; "BRCIA Will Arrange Meetings for July First," *CT*, 24 June 1924; "*Shing Wah Daily News* in Toronto Quoted Letters for Chinese Immigrants in Eastern China Who Agreed with July First Commemoration," *CT*, 25 June 1924; "Chinese Immigrants in Nanaimo Are Preparing the July First Commemoration," *CT*, 28 June 1924; "The Fifth Anniversary of Security Bureau," *CT*, 30 June 1924.

53 "Chinese in Canada to Observe 'Humiliation Day' on July First," *Quebec Daily Telegraph*, 14 June 1924; "Chinese in Canada Will Have 'Humiliation Day'," *Lewiston Evening Journal*, 14 June 1924; "Canadian Chinese to Keep 'Humiliation Day'," *Salt Lake City Desert News*, 14 June 1924; "'Humiliation Day' Set by Canadian Chinese," *Washington Post*, 15 June 1924; "Day of Humiliation Planned by Chinese: Will Use Canada's Birthday to Resent Regulation Regarding Registration Smarting under 'Insult'," *Toronto Globe*, 16 June 1924; "First of July as Humiliation Day," *Montreal Gazette*, 16 June 1924.

54 "Chinese in Canada to Observe 'Humiliation Day' on July First," *Quebec Daily Telegraph*, 14 June 1924.

55 "No Demonstration by Local Chinese: Will Not Join in Humiliation Day but Will Observe Registration Regulation," *Ottawa Citizen*, 18 June 1924.

56 "Chinese Immigrants in Canada Will Commemorate the Humiliation Day," *Shen Bao*, 16 June 1924.

57 "Preparing Flowers for the Parade," *CT*, 24 June 1924; "Notices for the Post Office" and "Fireworks to Welcome the Ships," *CT*, 25 June 1924; "Decoration for the Parades on National Day," *CT*, 28 June 1924; "Schedule for Parades on National Day," *CT*, 30 June 1924.

58 For poems and prose, see Jianwu, "Comments: Never Forget the Nation's Humiliation," *CT*, 2 July 1924; Hanyuan, "Comments: What Shall We Chinese Immigrants Do after July First," *CT*, 4 and 5 July 1924; Zhao Kong, "Literary Circles: Song to Commemorate Canadian Government's Harsh Restriction on Chinese Immigrants," *CT*, 5 and 7 July 1924; Cunliang Wu from Victoria, "Poems: Feeling as an Immigrant," *CT*, 12 July 1924. All this writing re-stated the contents of earlier publications using different rhetoric. The seven societies were CBA, CKT, KMT, XZD, the Chinese Canadian Club, BRCIA, and the Chinese Labour Association. See "CBA's Commission Minute," *CT*, 25 June 1924; "CBA Is Preparing for the Commemoration on July First," *CT*, 26 June 1924.

59 "Details about Chinese Immigrants' Commemoration on July First in Vancouver," *CT*, 2 July 1924.

60 "Details about Chinese Immigrants' Commemoration on July First in Victoria," *CT*, 3 and 4 July 1924.

61 "Choo Yee Society's Meeting for July First," *CT*, 2 July 1924; "Report on CKT's Meeting on July First in Duncan," "Report on Schools' Meeting on July First in Victoria," "Report on July First Commemoration in Victoria," and "News from Winnipeg," *CT*, 3 July 1924; "News Collection of Chinese Immigrants' Commemorations on July First from Cumberland, Kaslo, Kamloops," *CT*, 4 July 1924; "News Collection of Chinese Immigrants' Commemorations on July First from Nanaimo, Port Hammond and Haney, and Calgary," *CT*, 5 July 1924; "News Collection of Chinese Immigrants' Commemorations on July First from New Westminster and Revelstoke," *CT*, 7 July 1924; "News Collection of Chinese Immigrants' Commemorations on July First from Halifax," *CT*, 8 July 1924.

62 "The Westerner Recorded Our Commemoration on Humiliation," *CT*, 3 July 1924.

63 *Shen Bao* used only two lines to repeat the telegram it had received from the Overseas Chinese Associations, including the purposes of ceremonies and its appeal to home nation for support. "Telegram from Victoria, United Kingdom [sic]," *Shen Bao*, 3 July 1924.

64 "CBA's Commission Minutes," *CT*, 4 June 1925.
65 "Decisions of CBA's Commission," *CT*, 20 June 1925; "Report on Chinese Immigrants' Commemoration on Humiliation," *CT*, 2 July 1925.
66 "Students' Preparing for Commemoration on Humiliation," *CT*, 23 June 1925.
67 Yinlu, "Collection of Poems: For July First Commemoration," *CT*, 23 to 25 June 1925; Shuo, "Editorial: Raging Words for Commemorating Humiliation on July First," *CT*, 30 June 1925.
68 "Notice," *CT*, 30 June 1924 and 1925.
69 "CBA's Leaflet," *CT*, 29 June 1925.
70 "Report on Chinese Immigrants' Commemoration on Humiliation," *CT*, 2 July 1925.
71 "Chinese Held 'Humiliation Day' in Victoria," *British Colonist*, 4 July 1925.
72 "Report on Chinese Immigrants' Commemoration on Humiliation in Nanaimo," *CT*, 4 July 1925.
73 "Vancouver Council Is Preparing the Celebrations on July First," *CT*, 7 June 1926; "George Bridge on July First," *CT*, 12 June 1926; "City Council Is Preparing the Celebration for Canada's National Day," *CT*, 21 June 1926; "Boy Scouts' Service on July First" and "Canada's Preparation for the Diamond Jubilee," *CT*, 26 June 1926; "Westerners' Parade on July First," *CT*, 28 June 1926; "The Holiday Service of the Post Office" and "Citizen's Gathering," *CT*, 29 June 1926; "Student Orchestra from Victoria Will Come to Vancouver" and "Westerners' Routine on July First Celebration," *CT*, 30 June 1926.
74 "Canada's Preparation for the Diamond Jubilee," *CT*, 26 June 1926; "Citizen's Gathering," *CT*, 29 June 1926; "Calling Donations for Building the Monument," *CT*, 2 July 1926; "The Aboriginal People's Gathering," *CT*, 9 July 1926.
75 Jianwu, "Editorial: Commemorating Humiliation on July First," *CT*, 30 June 1926.
76 "Notice of the CBA," *CT*, 30 June 1926.
77 "Report on Commemorating Humiliation on July First," *CT*, 2 July 1926.
78 "Westerners' Activities on July First," *CT*, 3 July 1926.
79 "Defense," *CT*, 22 July 1926.
80 "Notice," *CT*, 27–29 July 1926.
81 "Appeal to Build a Highway to Celebrate the Confederation," *CT*, 7 June 1927; "Canadian National Holiday," *CT*, 10 June 1927; "Shops Will Open as Normal on July Second" and "Inviting a Famous Pilot to Celebrate the National Day," *CT*, 17 June 1927; "Students Will Celebrate the National Day," "An American Pilot Will Join the National Day Celebration in

Ottawa via Airplane," and "Caution: Possible Fire on National Day," *CT*, 25 June 1927; "Schedule of Celebrating Canada's National Day," *CT*, 30 June 1927.

82 Jianwu, "Comments: We Can Join Both of the Humiliation Ceremony and National Day Celebration in Canada," *CT*, 25 June 1927.

83 Jianwu, "Editorial: Thoughts on July First," *CT*, 30 June 1927.

84 *CT*, 28–30 June 1927.

85 "Chinese Immigrants Will Hold a Commission Tonight," *CT*, 25 June 1927; "Chinese Immigrants' Commission Minute," *CT*, 27 June 1927.

86 "Notice of the CBA," *CT*, 30 June 1927.

87 "Celebrations for Today and Tomorrow," *CT*, 2 July 1927; "End of Celebrations for Canada's National Day," *CT*, 5 July 1927; "New Mint for Commemoration," *CT*, 6 July 1927.

88 Guanhai, "Comments: What's Strange in Immigrants' Commemoration on Humiliation in Victoria," *CT*, 4 July 1927.

89 Guanhai, *CT*, 4 July 1927; Guanhai, "Comments: How Could This Happen?" *CT*, 13 July 1927.

90 "Notice," *CT*, 30 June 1927.

91 "Notice," *CT*, 30 June 1930, 1932–4, 1935–8, 1940–5, and 1947; 29 June 1935 and 1946.

92 "CBA's Gathering Tonight," *CT*, 28 June 1930; "Notice of the CBA," *CT*, 28 June 1932; "CBA's Reply to the Consul in Vancouver," *CT*, 24 June 1935; "Notice of the CBA in Vancouver," *CT*, 29 June and 2 July 1935; "Notice of the CBA," *CT*, 30 June 1936. During the Second World War, *CT* focused only on ceremonies for July 7, the date when Japan invaded China. News about Chinese Humiliation Day in Vancouver returned in 1942.

93 "CBA's Commemoration on Humiliation," *CT*, 29 June 1928; "Tomorrow Will Commemorate Humiliation," *CT*, 30 June 1928; "Commemorate Humiliation" and "CKT Commemorated Humiliation," *CT*, 3 July 1928; "Chinese Commemorated Humiliation in Two Towns," *CT*, 4 July 1928; "Commemorate Humiliation on July First," *CT*, 26 June 1929; "Notice of the CBA," *CT*, 29 July 1929; "Reports on Commemorating Humiliation," *CT*, 2 July 1929.

94 *CT* mentioned only ceremonies organized by CCBA and schools in Victoria in 1930. See "Jing'e School's Debates on Commemorating Humiliation on July First," *CT*, 3 July 1930; "CCBA's Commemoration in Victoria," *CT*, 4 July 1930. On CKT ceremonies in Victoria and Toronto in 1932, see "CKT's Commemoration in Victoria for July First," *CT*, 4 July 1932 and "CKT in Toronto Held a Meeting for Commemorating Humiliation," *CT*, 7 July 1932.

11 Canada's Day: Inventing a Tradition, Defining a Culture

MATTHEW HAYDAY

On 1 July 1977, ten million Canadians watched on television as gold lame–clad Acadian disco diva Patsy Gallant crooned "Besoin d'amour" from a stage on Parliament Hill. Two years later, Gallant sang her hit "Sugar Daddy" to recently elected Prime Minister Joe Clark before a crowd of tens of thousands of live spectators on Parliament Hill and an audience of millions on television. Many Canadians wondered, and several inquired of their government, what exactly Gallant's performance had to do with the founding of Canada. Some opined that her act was better suited to a nightclub than to an event commemorating Confederation.

The manner in which the anniversary of Confederation – 1 July 1867 – has been celebrated in an official capacity has varied widely over the years. Parliament Hill has hosted acts as disparate as Ukrainian Shumka dancers, world-renowned jazz pianist Oscar Peterson, a ballet pas-de-deux, the Calgary Safety Patrol Jamboree, and pop stars from René Simard to Anne Murray. In more recent years, the official celebrations have featured Canadian pop, country, and indie musical stars, including Metric, Carly Rae Jepsen, Marianas Trench, Marie-Mai, and Serena Ryder. The format of the official celebrations has ranged from displays of military pageantry to ethnic folk festivals to variety shows featuring big-name stars. In some years, the government sponsored extravaganzas on Parliament Hill that were televised across the nation. In others, the Ottawa celebrations were downsized and downplayed in favour of funding community-based celebrations. Yet amid this diversity of form and content, what perhaps is most surprising is the fact that, prior to 1958, the federal government had organized only two celebrations of the anniversary of Canada's founding – in 1917 and

1927, the fiftieth and sixtieth anniversaries of Confederation. Apart from these major events, July 1st passed practically unobserved at the national level. As the chapters in this volume by Forrest Pass, Gillian Leitch, Lianbi Zhu, and Timothy Baycroft demonstrate, there were a number of different ways that Dominion Day was observed in various communities across Canada in the decades following Confederation, but the federal government was absent from these events as either an organizer or funder.

Government-sponsored annual celebrations of July 1st were instituted when Canada was passing through a period of national re-examination. By the mid-1950s, many Canadians no longer took for granted that Canada had a well-defined national culture, primarily rooted in British traditions. Changing immigration patterns and increased discontent from francophone Quebec led to a questioning of Canadian identity. A declining British Empire and changing trade relations prompted some to call for a rethinking of Canada's role in international affairs and of its relations with the United States. In its 1951 report, the Royal Commission on National Development in the Arts, Letters, and Sciences (the Massey Commission) called on the federal government to assume a role in the promotion of Canadian culture. Many wondered what Canadian culture and identity would look like by the 1967 centennial.

While a host of different ethno-cultural groups, artists, authors, and lobbyists advanced various prescriptions for how Canadian identity and culture would and should develop, the federal government was also seeking to exert some direction over an "official" Canadian culture that it would sanction and support through various programs and policies. The celebrations that it sponsored for July 1st are a fascinating case study of the type of national identity and culture that it wanted to support. As the following discussion will demonstrate, these celebrations varied substantially from year to year, as different government ministers, bureaucrats, and interest groups tried to shape a tradition of national, state-sponsored celebrations of Canadian identity and culture. This was a highly contested process, which extended not only to the content of these state-sponsored celebrations, but also to their structure and form. An examination of the celebrations of what was variously termed Dominion Day, Canada Week, Canada's Birthday, and ultimately Canada Day provides a crucial window into the federal government's emergent cultural policy and how it was wedded to the broader political objectives of the day. These objectives and policies shifted substantially from when these celebrations were initially instituted in 1958 to the forms that they would assume by the late-1980s and beyond. These shifts were shaped by four major forces: changing conceptions of the meaning of the Canadian nation and the place of individuals and communities within it; divergent opinions of what elements of Canadian culture should be included in official celebrations; political and economic factors that defined the desirable formats of the festivities; and an evolving conception of what role the mass media could and should play in fostering mass participation in these events.

Imagined Communities and Invented Traditions: A Bit of Theory

Canada was led by six prime ministers between 1958, when official federally sponsored Dominion Day celebrations were launched, and the early 1990s, by which point a standard structure for Canada Day celebrations had been settled upon. Each prime minister had different ideas about the direction of the country, and each government approached the celebration of July 1st with a clear aim of fostering a sense of national community by inventing a nation-wide tradition. In this respect, these governments were engaging in processes of creating linkages between Canadians and crafting the ideology and identity of the Canadian "imagined community," to use political scientist Benedict Anderson's useful concept. Anderson explored the processes by which individuals came to think of themselves as members of communities, and ultimately nations, even though they lived great distances from each other and would likely never meet most of their fellow citizens in person – a geographic challenge that is particularly significant in a state as vast as Canada. Anderson argued that a number of different elements fostered a sense of commonality among members of national communities. The development of a national mass media through print capitalism was crucial to this process. Anderson posited that a diverse group of people reading a given newspaper, for example, albeit in different locations, would feel a sense of community because all these individuals were reading the same news, at the same time, about the same people whom the publishers had decided were important for their readership to learn about. This was a way of creating a sense of shared national experience for people who did not necessarily live in immediate proximity to each other.[1] As will become clear, organizers of Canadian celebrations sought to create similar shared experiences for citizens, whether in person or mediated by television, on their national day. This project relates to the argument of Maurice Charland, writing in a Canadian context, about how Canadian governments have attempted to deploy a form of "technological nationalism," first by building railways and transportation networks, and then by constructing radio and television communication systems to bind together a geographically vast country through a web of shared telecommunications.[2]

Historians Eric Hobsbawm and Terence Ranger's concept of "invented traditions" is also directly pertinent to this analysis.[3] Hobsbawm, Ranger, and their colleagues were among the first to seriously investigate the development of rituals and how they were tied into nation-building projects. Specifically, they argued that many so-called rituals and national traditions were in fact relatively recent inventions. These traditions – anthems, folk activities, and the like – were assumed to have ancient historic roots, yet many were in fact invented by governments and elites to provide cultural reinforcement for relatively new national political boundaries.[4] Although Canada's political boundaries were more or less well established by the 1950s, the nation's identity and culture were clearly in flux, and the state took an active interest in shaping the direction in which they would evolve. As Stuart Ward discusses in chapter 13 in this volume, such a phenomenon was common to many settler countries throughout the British Commonwealth, and they engaged in similar processes of state-directed efforts to craft new or modified national identities using commemorative and celebratory events.

The case of the celebration of July 1st appears to fit well into these theoretical models of nation building. In June 1868, Governor General Monck called for a celebration of the anniversary of the formation of the Dominion of Canada and "enjoin[ed] and call[ed] upon all Her Majesty's loving subjects throughout Canada to join in the due and proper celebration of the said Anniversary on the said FIRST day of JULY next."[5] There was uncertainty, however, as to whether this proclamation meant that 1 July was a legal holiday. A bill put forth the following year by Thomas McConkey, Liberal member of Parliament for Simcoe North, to make Dominion Day a legal holiday ran into stiff opposition from both Liberal and Conservative MPs, largely because of lingering hostile feelings towards Confederation from Nova Scotia. Indeed, William Chipman, an anti-Confederate-turned-Liberal MP from that province, argued that it would be a "day of lamentation" and further evidence of the powerlessness of Nova Scotians should the bill succeed. McConkey opted to withdraw the bill after second reading.[6]

It would be a further decade before a Senate bill introduced by Dr Robert Carrall of British Columbia led to Dominion Day being officially made a public holiday in 1879. In the Senate debates on the Dominion Day bill, it became clear that July 1st was being observed as a de facto holiday in Ontario, Quebec, and Nova Scotia, but not necessarily in the other four provinces. Moreover, representatives from Nova Scotia noted the lingering bad blood over Confederation in their province, while Conservative Senator Clement Cornwall of British Columbia objected to the bill because the Terms of Union of that province's admission to Confederation were as yet unfulfilled.[7] The bill was, however, adopted by the Senate and swiftly passed through the House of Commons that year.[8]

Although Dominion Day was legally a public holiday from 1879 onwards, very little was done by the federal government to officially observe the day over the first ninety years following Confederation. The fiftieth anniversary celebrations in 1917 were largely overshadowed by the First World War. The only major anniversary celebration was the Diamond Jubilee of Confederation in 1927, an event that included a national radio broadcast from Parliament Hill. Robert Cupido has considered how the radio broadcast might have reached many Canadians with the means to afford radio receivers, but contends that many others would have been excluded from these celebrations because of a lack of access to this technology.[9] Jane Nicholas has considered how the Diamond Jubilee celebrations served to reinforce particular conceptions of gender, shoring up a bourgeois masculinity threatened by the modern era.[10] As Robert Talbot points out, the Mackenzie King government saw the Diamond Jubilee as an opportunity to advance a bicultural conception of Canada through the festivities.

Apart from the jubilee, Dominion Day was primarily observed as a day off work, when Canadians would head to their cottages, host a barbecue, attend a sporting event, or otherwise enjoy the beginning of summer. As is evident from Forrest Pass's chapter, for example, many towns and cities organized community-based celebrations, but nothing was done at the national level to try to make July 1st a celebration of Canadian nationhood. As the chapters by Marcel Martel, Joel Belliveau, Brittney Anne Bos, and Allison Marie Ward demonstrate, Empire Day was the site of similar municipally organized parades and school-based activities, while Victoria Day, after it was adopted as a national holiday in 1901 (discussed in Chris Tait's chapter), was an occasion for picnics, leisure, and fireworks displays. One should be careful not to assume that these and other holidays that lacked federal state ceremonial events and pageantry were devoid of importance or meaning. The fact that they were holidays was itself of significance to Canadians, and indeed labour movement leaders could attest to the complicated nature of how individuals responded to holidays. While union organizers wanted workers to march in parades and attend formal picnics on Labour Day, many were happy to have the day off for rest and relaxation with family and friends.[11]

From 1958 onwards, each federal government attempted to develop or modify the tradition of celebrating July 1st. The manner in which this process unfolded was shaped by different conceptions of what sort of culture Canada should (or did) have, the extent to which organizers wanted to explicitly tie cultural celebrations to national unity, and varying conceptions of what form of celebration would best foster a sense of a common Canadian culture. In the first thirty years of these celebrations, various models were tested to foster new traditions. Yet, inconsistencies in approach and content appear to have delayed the implantation of a tradition of celebrating July 1st as a national holiday.

Part of the delay in settling on a format for these celebrations and determining their content can be accounted for by the heated debates about Canadian identity that were ongoing in the immediate postwar period. Such debates have been the subject of an important and growing body of scholarship. As authors in a series of volumes edited by Phillip Buckner and R. Douglas Francis have observed, these were decades in which Canada was rethinking its relationship to the British world.[12] It was also a period in which Canadians simultaneously embraced economic, defence, and cultural ties to the United States while also worrying that Canada would lose its distinctive identity. It was these fears, in part, that prompted the creation of the Massey Commission in 1949. This commission recommended steps to bolster Canadian culture, but its vision was clearly rooted in "high culture" institutions such as literature, dance, theatre, and universities – all elements that were closely tied to Canada's British heritage. The Massey approach largely ignored, when it was not overtly disdainful of, the more "popular" forms of culture from the United States, including radio, popular music, popular fiction, and the emergence of television.[13] It would not be until the 1960s that the Canadian government began to try more actively to champion a "Canadian" popular culture.[14] This ambivalence about "high" versus "popular" culture would play out in significant ways in how July 1st was celebrated.

If Canada were to move away from its traditional, British-oriented cultural identity, there was active debate over what direction this move might take, to what extent it should occur, and whether all Canadians would embrace it. José Igartua and Bryan Palmer have both argued that, by the 1960s, the traditional model of Canadian identity had broken down. Palmer contends that no new culture had replaced it, while Igartua contends a bilingual, multicultural identity was emerging as its replacement.[15] Chris Champion, on the other hand, sees a British influence even in the new symbols that were emerging, such as the new Maple Leaf flag, while Gary Miedema argues that public religion persisted in Canada's public commemorations.[16] Canada's First Nations occupied an uncertain place in this evolving Canadian identity, although their presence and contributions were increasingly seen as important. How they were conceived as "fitting in" changed over time and fluctuated between assimilationist messages and ones that were more open to cultural preservation.[17] Such challenges to traditional British cultural identity have been and continue to be present throughout post-Confederation history in both national and provincial celebrations, but a new discourse on multiculturalism was emerging, however tenuously, by the 1960s. That other ethno-cultural communities would seek to be included in a redefined Canadian identity is not surprising, given how extensively many ethnic communities had been excluded from full participation in Canadian society, as Lianbi Zhu and Timothy Baycroft's chapter on Chinese-Canadian protest activity on Dominion Day shows. While many French-Canadian and Acadian minority communities welcomed this new openness, Québécois nationalists often failed to see themselves in these new models of Canada.[18] Indeed, Marc-André Gagnon's chapter clearly shows how Québécois leaders explicitly observed a celebration that was a rival to its English-Canadian counterpart. Also, as Eva Mackey points out, even if, by the time of Canada's 125th birthday celebrations in 1992 the federal government were articulating a new model of a bilingual, multicultural Canada that showed increased openness to First Nations, there was still a mass of white, unmarked "Canadian-Canadians" who neither accepted this new identity nor saw themselves reflected in it.[19] Even if many Canadians did accept this new national identity, some were more interested in how their local and regional identities were articulated and addressed. Certainly the process of defining, articulating, and promoting new conceptions of Canadian identity was hotly contested, which helps explain the tumultuous process of inventing a tradition of celebrating Canada's national holiday, to which we now turn.

Inventing a Canadian Tradition Rooted in British Tradition: The Early Diefenbaker Years, 1958–1960

John Diefenbaker's government was elected too late in 1957 to have time to organize any substantial event to celebrate July 1st. However, Dominion Day held a great deal of importance for Diefenbaker and his Progressive Conservative colleagues, at least partly because of its official name. During his years in on the opposition benches, Diefenbaker had been dismayed at what he considered to be a Liberal plot to gradually eliminate any official recognition of Canada's ties to the United Kingdom and its British heritage. He was a vocal critic of Lester Pearson's decision to side with the United States, rather than the United Kingdom, during the Suez crisis of 1956, and he was equally hostile to what he saw as a pernicious trend of eliminating the term "Dominion" from national institutions such as the archives and the post office. The fact that Louis St. Laurent's Liberal government refused to have Parliament adjourn for the Dominion Day holiday – unless, by the "fortunate coincidence,"[20] it was already in recess – had been the source of much consternation and many questions in the House of Commons in the 1950s from Conservative MPs, including George Drew, Diefenbaker's predecessor as party leader, and Donald Fleming.[21] It is therefore not surprising that Diefenbaker's cabinet authorized Secretary of State Ellen Fairclough's request to organize a formal event for Dominion Day 1958.[22]

In both form and content, the celebrations organized by the secretary of state reflected the federal government's desire to celebrate proud traditions of the past, in particular those that invoked Canada's British heritage. The central elements of the ceremonies were a nation-wide televised address by Governor General Vincent Massey, a carillon concert from the Peace Tower, and a series of performances by military bands. Each of these elements could be considered to represent elements of the British tie: the Crown, Parliament, the military alliance. The day was a solemn, formal affair. It is somewhat ironic that, in an internal memo written for the Department of the Secretary of State concerning the pros and cons of instituting an annual tradition of celebrating Dominion Day, one of Fairclough's officials noted that such celebrations of national days

> are unusual in British countries. Some people regard them as an evidence of national immaturity. Canada is now a mature nation and does not need

to make annual self-assuring gestures of adult nationhood. Unlike USA and republics on the American continents, which celebrate their heroic exploits in freeing themselves from cruel European oppressors, Canada does not celebrate her achievement of freedom. Annual government ceremonies are contrary to Canadian and Commonwealth tradition.[23]

Other arguments raised in the memo, including the suggestion that such a celebration could drive home a sense of Canadian history for children as well as new Canadians, were clearly viewed as sufficient reasons to override this break with Commonwealth tradition, particularly as the content of the ceremonies clearly stressed these ties to the Commonwealth.

The 1958 celebrations of Dominion Day proved to be a false start in getting this tradition off the ground. In 1959, Queen Elizabeth II's royal tour of Canada overlapped with July 1st. Rather than incorporating the queen into the 1959 Dominion Day celebrations, while using the template from the 1958 ceremonies, the government chose instead to focus exclusively on her visit. Her tour, ironically, featured the opening of the St Lawrence Seaway, a symbol of the burgeoning Canada-U.S. partnership. The queen's televised address to the country was timed to occur on 1 July. Like the governor general's Dominion Day address the previous year, the use of television created a shared national viewing experience for Canadians. While the decision to forgo Dominion Day ceremonies did not help foster the infant tradition of July 1st celebrations in Ottawa, it reflects a significant preoccupation of the Diefenbaker government: the reinforcement of Canada's British heritage and ongoing connections. Elizabeth II herself, as queen of Canada and Queen of the United Kingdom (as well as of many other Commonwealth states), was a living, physical embodiment of these shared connections. The government returned to its military-oriented approach to Dominion Day celebrations in 1960, with an event featuring an artillery salute, a trooping of the colour by a regiment of the military, and a naval sunset ceremony followed by fireworks.

Fostering Citizenship, Incorporating Folk Traditions, 1961–1966

After an abortive start, the federal government continued to sponsor Dominion Day celebrations throughout the 1960s. However, it substantially changed the format and content of these events. The process of reorienting them began in 1961. In contrast to the exclusively military format

11.1 The Canadian Guards in khaki uniforms, on parade, 1 July 1961. Military Pageantry was particularly prominent in the Dominion Day ceremonies on Parliament Hill of the 1950s and early 1960s. It continues to play a signifi-cant role in the noon-day ceremonies on Canada Day. Library and Archives Canada/National Film Board fonds/e010976060.

of the early celebrations, Ellen Fairclough, by then minister of citizenship and immigration, suggested that civilians should actively participate in the program. Her department indicated to Secretary of State Noël Dorion that she wanted "as broad a public participation as possible, and [she] would be willing through the Citizenship Council to supplement any official observance in Ottawa if the government would be prepared to consider other types of ceremonies, rather than a formal ceremony."[24]

Specifically, Fairclough's department proposed the inclusion of polished performances by amateur folk groups that would be suitable for inclusion in a television broadcast, but not so high calibre as to discourage emulation at the community level. As for the specific content, "the program should be so composed as to enable Canadians generally to identify themselves with it. It should have strong appeal to them as an expression of the historical evolution of our country. This principle should govern the extent to which the program would include New Canadian participants."[25] Fairclough's suggestions were driven by her ministerial mandate to integrate new Canadian citizens. Her directives suggested a celebration format whereby older folk traditions of immigrant communities could be inserted into a ceremony that stressed the dominance of the "founding" English and French communities.

For the remainder of the Conservatives' term in office, Fairclough's suggestions were addressed by adding a multicultural folk performance component to the proceedings. Each year, between one and three choirs and dance troupes were bussed to Ottawa from Ontario and Quebec to perform a program of songs and dances that included traditional French-Canadian and English-Canadian material, while also mixing in folk dances and songs from other countries such as Italy, Hungary, Israel, and Ukraine.[26] These groups, which included the Feux-Follets and the Travellers, also made a point of including dances from Canada's Aboriginal communities, such as the Abenaki. The military components continued to be central to the overall program, which had a modest budget of less than $10,000. By 1963, parts of the folk program were televised on CBC television and Radio-Canada.

The transition to a Liberal government under Lester Pearson did not lead to the cancellation of the Dominion Day celebrations for 1964. Indeed, with Canada's centennial fast approaching, the federal government decided to expand the scope and budget of these festivities for every year leading up to 1967. Organizers hoped that such celebrations would increase the enthusiasm of Canadians for nation-wide celebrations in the centennial year. Central to the effort to get Canadians to celebrate on July 1st was the decision to collaborate with CBC television and Radio-Canada on the production of a one-hour special broadcast from Parliament Hill, which would air from coast to coast.[27]

The change in government did signal some significant changes in the approach to the festivities. One key departure was an increased focus on regional representation. While the modestly funded celebrations of the early 1960s brought in folk groups that could drive to Ottawa, organizers during the Pearson years tried to have at least one performance from each province. Organizers maintained the general focus on amateur folk performers and drew on the regional networks of the Canadian Folk Arts Council to audition prospective talent. But rather than having predominantly British-Canadian and French-Canadian groups perform "ethnic" musical and dance numbers, the mid-1960s shows directly incorporated performers from Canada's multicultural and Aboriginal communities. It must be noted, however, that the Aboriginal performances subtly conveyed a culture of assimilation to Euro-Canadian cultural practices – unless one considers Scottish bagpipe playing and the twirling of flaming batons to be traditional folk performances of the Shuswap and Cree peoples.[28]

The Pearson-era celebrations placed a premium on reinforcing a conception of a bilingual and bicultural framework to Canadian culture, reviving the process begun in the King years. This echoed the work of the Royal Commission on Bilingualism and Biculturalism, launched by the government in 1963. Masters of ceremonies, such as Henri Bergeron and Alex Trebek, were selected partly on the basis of their ability to speak both English and French (and also to make bilingual jokes about the sometimes fractious nature of the country). The same Parliament Hill show was broadcast to both English- and French-speaking Canadians, which made bilingualism imperative. The selection of performers further served to reinforce the dual conception of Canadian culture. In any given year, about one-third of the performers were of francophone origin. Moreover, there was normally at least one francophone performer who came from a province other than Quebec – including Alberta, Manitoba, and New Brunswick.

While the build-up to the centennial was generally viewed as successful and the shows were well received by the press and those who wrote letters to the government, some concerns were raised. Perhaps most noteworthy were the comments about the structure of the show. The effort to incorporate all the provinces had led the shows' producers to adopt a variety show format. Some letter writers, bureaucrats, and media commentators suggested that such a format was creating an Ed Sullivan–esque approach to the celebrations. Canada, they felt, was veering too close to an American style of celebration.[29] In seeking to better reflect Canadian regionalism, some believed that the organizers were losing their distinctive Canadian (or British-Canadian, to be more precise) touch.

Post-Centennial Blahs, 1967–1975

Canada marked its first centennial with spectacular events, although the main tourist destination of the year was not Ottawa, but Montreal, host to Expo 67.[30] Millions of Canadians and foreign tourists flooded into Montreal throughout the spring and summer for the festivities. So too did dozens of heads of state and government leaders, the vast majority of whom also visited Ottawa and bid Canada congratulations on its first century as a country.[31] The federal government sponsored many events to celebrate the centennial, including a Confederation Train that travelled from coast to coast. July 1st was celebrated with great enthusiasm on Parliament Hill, where Secretary of State Judy LaMarsh played host to Canada's birthday "Hullaballoo" – a massive party where revellers were served birthday cake and entertained by a wide array of popular and folk entertainers.[32] The scope of the centennial was vast and manifested in many different ways in communities across the country, engaging a host of different actors and groups.

One might have thought that the success of the 1967 celebrations would have firmed up the tradition of celebrating the anniversary of Confederation. However, the next several years seemed to suffer from a hangover effect, lacking the enthusiasm and direction of their predecessors. It was as if, having celebrated the centennial with such excess, there was little energy left over for regular years. The elements of the celebrations from these years reflect some continuity with the Canadian culture being promoted in the mid-1960s. However, they also show some of the strains facing Canadian identity by the 1970s, and even echo concerns from the Massey Commission era about the fading of "high culture" in Canada.

Officials within the Department of the Secretary of State clearly thought that they would be able to develop the tradition started in 1958. They began planning early on to bring in performers from every province, with travel costs estimated at about $15,000. However, two key roadblocks fell in their path. The first problem was financial. Although the federal cabinet had been perfectly willing to sponsor the run-up to the centennial, it was much less willing to foot the bill for 1968. Instead, organizers had to scramble to find the funds needed for that year's performances, ultimately re-allocating money from another envelope when cabinet refused the secretary of state's request.[33]

More troublesome was the attitude of the CBC. In June 1968, CBC officials, who had earlier indicated willingness to participate in the annual festivities, suddenly announced that they were no longer planning on covering any of the evening celebrations, including the variety show that featured representatives from across the country. G.G.E. Steele, the undersecretary of state, was clearly stunned when the CBC cited financial concerns as an excuse not to cover the events. His director of state ceremonial events, C.J. Lochnan, was equally taken aback that the CBC considered its budget so meager as to render the network unable to cover the nation's birthday festivities.[34] The result was that the pan-Canadian, multi-ethnic variety show, hosted by six Ottawa-area youth, was not broadcast on television; it was viewed only by the live audience on Parliament Hill.

Following the disappointing events of 1968, federal officials attempted to reinvent their July 1st celebrations. A number of outdoor events were planned for Ottawa, including the annual carillon concert and changing of the guard, with new additions such as a horse show at Jacques Cartier Park. Such changes were part of what Secretary of State Gérard Pelletier's executive assistant, J. André Ouellette, termed a "Canadianization" of the event, which was supposed to put Canadian symbols, such as the anthem, in more prominent places, and downplay the role of the governor general.[35] The centerpiece for 1969 was a revamped gala show held at the new National Arts Centre (NAC), rather than outside on Parliament Hill. And yet this show, to be broadcast by the CBC, had a British inspiration. Officials planning the event noted: "It is hoped that this will be the beginning of a type of show comparable to the Royal Command Performance which will enable us to congregate well-known Canadian performers to perform on every July 1st."[36] There was thus a subtle tension between a desire to "Canadianize" the celebrations by moving away from the perceived American variety show format, and to embrace an explicitly British alternative model. The new show, "Bonjour Canada," was also intended to be a slicker production. Graham Glockling, a planner with the Secretary of State, observed that "we want to dispense with the 'ethnic' show of the past … and place the focus on Canadians."[37] There were clearly some tensions about how diversity might be incorporated in these celebrations, which predated the 1971 multiculturalism policy. In place of some of the amateur performers, bigger name stars such as Gordon Lightfoot would appear, alongside more professional folk dance troupes such as Les Feux-Follets. Some within the department went so far as to hope that if the "command performance" approach took root, it might reduce costs, particularly if top talent were willing to perform for free out of a sense of patriotism.

Following this gala, the events of the early 1970s did not go well for a variety of reasons. This was in part because of how the divided focus between Ottawa and the regions was handled in these years. The provinces of Manitoba, British Columbia and Prince Edward Island celebrated their centennials between 1970 and 1973, and the CBC broadcasts in 1970 and 1971 tried to split coverage between Ottawa and Winnipeg and Victoria. The year of the BC centennial was particularly bad, with Thom Benson, the CBC's director of entertainment programs noting that the "Dominion Day/Canada Today" show produced by Pierre Normandin had a host that stumbled all over the place, included "trite and meaningless" taped sequences, and overall "limped along in a rather tired an empty fashion and lacked imagination and ingenuity."[38] While Liston McIlhagga, the network's head of special events, tried to defend the show as the best that could be done on short notice, and argued that the overall concept was a good idea, he was told that "any such concept in the future will not be acceptable."[39] McIlhagga informed his team that they should be pitching ideas that "reflect a national birthday scene, and that regional emphasis can only be part of the total picture."[40]

The "Bonjour Canada" show continued to be part of the Ottawa-based festivities for the first half of the 1970s. Conceived in the early years of Pierre Trudeau's mandate, it bore some distinctive marks of his government's policies. Perhaps most noteworthy was the promotion of bilingualism, which extended right into the show's title. Hosts spoke in both languages. In 1970, a parade of guest MCs spoke in their second language, although often with mangled and awkward results, leading the Globe and Mail's critic to state that the show's ham-handed approach to bilingualism was undermining the government's efforts.[41] Most disastrous was the 1972 show, when host André Gagnon spoke exclusively in French. Translation was provided for the at-home television audience, but a bewildered audience of anglophones at the NAC was left frustrated. Only a handful of positive telephone callers to the CBC countered the 115 who expressed outrage, including comments that "Dominion Day should reflect all of Canada, not just one province," "Damn disgrace having this in French," "Not at all appropriate for Dominion Day."[42] Anti-bilingualism crusader Jock Andrew would later cite this incident as evidence of the Trudeau government's conspiracy to force French on the entire country.[43] Even organizers noted that, "to try to give equal representation to both languages is a pain and consequently the overall performance suffers."[44]

Broadcasting from the new, more formal venue of the National Arts Centre and employing a structure inspired by the command performance model, the CBC shows also included more "classical" cultural elements, such as ballet performances, piano recitals, and operatic arias, which shared the stage with rock and folk performances. These elements, arguably, represent a return to the Massey Commission's conception of how high culture should figure into Canada's cultural identity, although they complemented, rather than replaced, the more American-influenced popular culture elements. Amateur performers were largely replaced by professionals. Despite this effort to raise the tone of the July 1st celebrations and to more explicitly tailor the performances for a television audience, the event failed to catch on as a "command performance." It was often ignored or dismissed by media reports. Even a re-focused program in 1973, which moved back to Parliament Hill with a few key headliners – Moe Koffman, Ti-Jean Carignan, the Bells, and Jean-Pierre Ferland – attracted little enthusiasm. Senator Eugene Forsey observed that "there seemed nothing to remind people of the breadth and diversity of the country, of its history, of its many peoples and cultures."[45] Forsey bemoaned the loss of the colourful folk performances that used to be the highlight of the Parliament Hill events.

So too, apparently, did the CBC, which again declined to cover the show in 1974. It seems that this brief dabbling with a more British-inspired, if bilingual, structure for celebrating Canada's national day, featuring elements of "high" culture, had failed to catch on. The 1975 celebrations seemed like a throwback to the mid-1960s, with a return to the pan-Canadian, bilingual, multi-ethnic format. Graham Glocking observed that, of the nine acts, "one is of Chinese ethnic origin, one negro, two anglo-saxon, RCA band is representative of Canada as a whole, and three are French-Canadian."[46] Production problems, including a last-minute switch of producers, led even internal officials to deride what they deemed a "botched up" nationally broadcast show.[47] Few were shocked when the government cut all funding to these inconsistent July 1st celebrations as part of its 1976 austerity measures.

11.2 Dominion Day, 1974. Although the 1974 Parliament Hill concert was not televised on the CBC, it still attracted a large in-person crowd. © Government of Canada. Reproduced with the permission of Library and Archives Canada (2016). Library and Archives Canada/Department of Communications fonds/ e010937345.

Loving Canada during a National Unity Crisis, 1977–1979

Secretary of State officials were not pleased to see the end of the July 1st celebrations they had worked so hard to develop. As Graham Glockling observed, "cancelling a national day is like denying motherhood."[48] Some politicians expressed similar concerns. Joe Flynn, Liberal member of Parliament for Kitchener, Ontario, noted that "the money that would be saved by eliminating the festivities on this particular day, as announced by you [Secretary of State Hugh Faulkner] and your department, becomes rather disgraceful in view of the fact that we have been encouraging all Canadians to become more nationalistic. I feel that this is a saving that is going to cost us a lot of money in the end."[49]

More concerned with the nation's financial woes than nationalism, the Trudeau government stayed firm on this decision. The only federally sponsored event for 1 July 1976 was the presentation of citizenship certificates to forty new Canadians by the prime minister. Few predicted the event that led to the revival of these celebrations: the November 1976 election in Quebec of a Parti québécois majority government. The election of a separatist government sent shockwaves through the country, and Canadians clamoured for the federal government to address the national unity crisis.

By December 1976, memos were circulating within the Department of the Secretary of State concerning how to promote national unity. A revived July 1st celebration was central to these plans. The following February, cabinet considered a proposal for over $1.5 million to be spent on coast-to-coast festivities for the "Great Canadian Birthday Party." The budget would eventually be expanded to over $3.5 million – over fifty times the budget of the 1970 celebrations. Secretary of State John Roberts was explicit in his instructions to his officials about the government's plans to link Canadian culture to national unity. He wanted them to find as many opportunities as possible for Canadians to "wear their hearts on their sleeves." He outlined two explicit political objectives:

1) to convince French Canadians in Quebec that their cultural life in the narrower sense, and their "culture" in the broadest sense, has [sic] a better chance of survival and growth within Confederation;
2) to convince Canadians outside Quebec that their cultural life is already made richer by the presence of Quebec in Confederation and the answer to the question "what does Quebec want" is to be found in an understanding of Quebec's cultural life.

While these objectives were political in orientation, Roberts noted that, unless federal programs yielded cultural benefits, these objectives would not be attained. Overall, the federal government's approach was to try to make Canadian culture a force for political and national unity and for combating the separatist threat.[50]

The big questions facing the government were how this "Canadian culture" would be defined, and how it would be presented to Canadians, and particularly Quebeckers, via the July 1st celebrations. Certainly, such an approach to the celebrations was a much more massive undertaking than in the past. Well over one million dollars was allocated to the Canadian Folk Arts Council and the Council for Canadian Unity to sponsor community-based celebrations across the country. Organizers considered it essential that all publicity for these celebrations have a consistent message about Canada. Dropped in this effort was the official moniker for the day, because "Dominion Day" resonated poorly in Quebec and among multicultural groups, given its overtones of British colonialism. Instead, the celebrations went by the name of the "Great Canadian Birthday" in 1977, and "Canada's Birthday / Les Fêtes du Canada" or "Canada Week" in 1978 and 1979 (when the festivities were spread over the week 25 June–2 July). In 1978, the Canada Day Committee used the slogan "Canada: It's you and me / Canada: C'est toi et moi." This slogan shifted the emphasis on who defined Canada and its culture from governments back to citizens and promoted a more open-ended approach to Canadian identity. The new approach stressed an emotional appeal and sought to centre on individual Canadians coming together to celebrate their country. Consultants had suggested the explicit goal of de-emphasizing regional and linguistic differences, to "respect and reflect the regional and cultural diversity of Canada ... [but] transcend provincialism."[51] Organizers thought it was best to let individuals celebrate Canada in their own way and define Canadian culture as they saw fit. Switching from an emphasis on highlighting the provinces, cultural groups, and linguistic communities of Canada, the new approach was to downplay the explicit emphasis on these potentially divisive features and let individual Canadians reflect the nation's diversity by their mere presence in the celebrations.

To a certain extent, the effort to have a more populist approach to Canadian cultural identity and the celebration of July 1st was carried over into the centerpiece celebrations. In 1977, the program organizers, under the direction of Bernard Ostry, allocated over half a million dollars to a massive three-to-four-hour national television special to promote Canada's birthday. The show was carried on virtually all the television and radio stations in the country. Centred in Ottawa, it featured live satellite hook-ups from stages across the country, showcasing big-name Canadian stars in their communities. A more scaled-down version of this format was repeated in 1978, but the regional hook-ups were dropped in 1979. Particularly in 1977, program organizers wanted to depoliticize the celebrations and focus on Canadians celebrating on July 1st, expressing their love of the country. As the press release stated, "this spectacular will bring to Canadians the enthusiasm they share for their country, but in a way that is contemporary and relevant."[52] Politicians were not to be a significant part of these proceedings, which did not feature any speeches from government officials. A planning document for 1978 was similar in tone, proposing that the festivities "should be coordinated as a national love-feast, giving the people of each Province, or Territory, the feeling that on their particular day their fellow Canadians were thinking of them and wishing them well."[53] It would be hard to more pointedly capture the concept of Anderson's imagined community.

The rhetoric of the late-1970s celebrations stressed an open-ended, populist approach to defining what it meant to be a Canadian and how to celebrate the nation. One can nevertheless detect certain themes reflecting how organizers of the televised broadcasts conceived of Canadian identity and culture. Their broadcasts were designed to appeal to a mass audience, and it was with this in mind that the shows' producers opted for big-name stars, as opposed to the amateur acts that had predominated in the mid-1960s. With star quality as the top selection criteria, organizers then turned to filling out the program with individuals who would represent the vision of Canada that they had in mind. The live satellite hook-ups allowed for regional diversity to be showcased as never before. From the comfort of their couches, viewers were taken into Anne Murray's Springhill, Nova Scotia home, to see Buffy Sainte-Marie perform at the Broken Head Reserve in Manitoba, to hear the Cape Dorset Throat Singers at Frobisher Bay in the Northwest Territories, and to listen to Bruce Cockburn from Wascana Park in Regina, Saskatchewan, among a host of other locations. With Quebec separatism a major concern, a linguistic balance was central to the organizers' vision – hence Patsy Gallant's bilingual performances on Parliament Hill, coupled with other francophone stars, including Ginette Reno in Montreal, Calixte Duguay in Moncton, and René Simard in Ottawa. Aboriginal performers were included each year, including a mix of popular crossover artists such as Buffy Sainte-Marie and Métis singer Tom Jackson, plus more traditional groups such as the Prairie Intertribal Dancers and the Pang Story Singers. A limited level of multicultural diversity was also incorporated through acts such as the Ukrainian Shumka dancers and blues/jazz singer Salome Bey. Although a ballet performance by Karen Kain in Ottawa had to be cancelled at the last minute due to a downpour in 1977, she was invited back the following year. Between her pas-de-deux, opera singer Maureen Forrester's performance of "Oh Canada," and classical music from the Canadian Brass, elements of the "high culture" approach persisted in these late-1970s celebrations.

But how might one define the Canada that all these diverse performers claimed to love? While the celebrations of the late-1970s were filled with glitz and fervent patriotism, they did not make clear which political and social values bound the country together. The national unity fears that drove these spectacular celebrations had made organizers timid about explicitly highlighting the political dimensions of the country they sought to protect. Regional diversity, multiculturalism, and linguistic duality were implicitly present in these celebrations, but organizers seemed not to want to draw too much overt attention to these facets, and they definitely didn't want politics marring the party. One exception to this general rule was a spoken-word piece performed by Keath Barrie at Ontario Place in 1977. According to Barrie, "if all Canadians open their eyes, they would see that there has been no nation in the history of the world that has enjoyed more of the things that we consider most precious to humanity. Therein lies our greatest strength and our greatest weakness, because history tells us unerringly that any nation who became fat and complacent about its worth soon lost it all." Although Barrie's piece referred to aspects of different components of Canada's British, French, and other ethnic communities' heritage, the overall message was that Canadians should be "citizens not of a part, but of the whole, not living in the past. Put ethnic culture in its place, second to that which you must first embrace, Canadians to be."[54]

Over half of Canada's population watched all or part of the 1977 broadcast. Polling data showed that most of those who viewed the show enjoyed it, and a majority of citizens in all regions except for the Prairies thought that the show made it more likely that the country would remain united and considered it to be federal dollars well spent.[55] Fewer people watched the 1978 or 1979 broadcasts, but these events still drew audiences comparable to the Grey Cup or the Stanley Cup playoffs. However, by 1979, Canadians were less convinced that this was a good use of taxpayer's money.[56]

More troubling was the fact that Les Fêtes du Canada had not been terribly well received in Quebec. Participation rates in July 1st events were lower in that province than in the rest of the country, and the francophone media was quite critical of the content of the programming. Despite the best intentions of the federal organizers, many Quebeckers, particularly those leaning towards separatism, were quick to say that the participants in the July 1st events were not representative of the culture of contemporary Quebec.[57] Many artists had outright refused to participate in these events. As for those who agreed to take part, both Ginette Reno and René Simard were criticized as poor choices because they spent most of their time in the United States rather than in Quebec.

Patsy Gallant, meanwhile, was Acadian, not Québécoise, and was seen as an outsider (and vulgar to boot, in the eyes of those who derided her disco act). In a curious comment, *Le Devoir's* Lise Bissonnette criticized the celebrations for being too American, derisively referring to "tous les gadgets de music hall empruntés sans adaptation à nos voisins du sud."[58] Canada's Birthday celebrations were viewed as a poor second cousin to the thriving Fête nationale events heavily subsidized by the Lévesque government on 24 June, as discussed in detail in chapter 14, by Marc-André Gagnon. Faced with the declining popularity of the celebrations, some public criticism of the $3.5–4 million price tag, and hostility from the Quebec media, Joe Clark's newly elected Progressive Conservative government put a hold on plans for another media spectacular for 1980.[59]

Celebrating Canada in the Community: Local Culture and National Symbols in the 1980s and Beyond

In the minds of newly elected Progressive Conservative MPs and their advisers, the July 1st and Canada Week spectacles were too closely tied in the public eye to the Liberal Party and were inappropriate for a period of economic restraint. They also believed that the events were overly top-down, driven by the federal government, and centralized in the national capital region. With these concerns in mind, the new secretary of state, David MacDonald, sent his officials to consult provincial government representatives on how Canada's birthday should be celebrated and to determine what role the provinces would like to play.[60] This approach of consulting with the provinces was very much in keeping with Joe Clark's vision of Canada as a "community of communities" and the Progressive Conservative impulse to decentralize power in the Canadian federation. MacDonald submitted a proposal to cabinet in January 1980 that suggested that most of the funding for July 1st celebrations should be doled out to community celebrations, under the auspices of provincial committees. A much smaller amount of money would be reserved for a celebration in the national capital. In effect, what was suggested was a return to the community-based focus of the Dominion Day celebrations of the pre-1958 period, but with federal financial support. Ottawa allocated $2 million for these events, a substantial scaling back from the $3.6 million spent in 1979.[61]

Clark's government lost the February 1980 election after a mere nine months in power and thus was not able to implement its plans.

However, Trudeau's Liberals, who won the election, were faced with a dilemma. Should they completely reverse the course taken by the Conservatives, reinstate the $1.6 million in cut funding, and revive the major variety show in Ottawa? In the view of Secretary of State Francis Fox, this was not advisable. To reverse course would make the federal government appear to be rejecting the outcome of provincial consultations and would make it seem extravagant with money. Worse still, it might seem insensitive to the feelings of Quebeckers if Ottawa were to hold a massive nationalist celebration in a tense post-referendum atmosphere. Accordingly, the government decided to continue with the plans already in motion, evaluate their success afterwards, and blame the previous Conservative government if anything went wrong.[62] There was no national variety show broadcast from Parliament Hill by the CBC, which instead ran a show featuring clips from various events that had taken place across the country. The 1980 celebrations were also noteworthy for the fact that "O Canada," long considered Canada's national anthem, was officially designated as such by legislation that year. Communities across the country marked the new status with a noonday singing of the anthem. This simultaneous singing of the anthem is reminiscent of the communal reading of the newspaper noted by Anderson in *Imagined Communities*: an experience shared by millions of Canadians, even though they were separated by thousands of kilometers.

In the fall of 1980, with the referendum threat past, the federal cabinet announced a new social policy directive that would stress "the development of a cultural thrust related to the understanding and enhancement of national identity and symbols."[63] This directive set the tone for the July 1st celebrations organized by the government throughout the early and mid-1980s. The decision to abandon the televised variety show format was maintained until 1988. In its place, the community-based celebration elements introduced in 1977 were augmented and formalized. A National Committee for the Celebration of Canada's Birthday was created in 1981. Provincial committees were set up the following year, replacing the Canadian Folk Arts Council and Council for Canadian Unity as the main granting agencies for local celebrations. Funding to local communities was be provided for a maximum of three years, with the intention that this would be seed funding to begin a local tradition of celebrations, which could then become self-sufficient.[64]

The celebrations of the early to mid-1980s did maintain some key national elements. Although the Ottawa-based festivities were no longer televised, the Secretary of State continued to hold a formal noonday ceremony featuring the governor general and a more festive evening concert in the nation's capital for local residents and tourists. The government encouraged Canadians to visit Parliament Hill on July 1st as part of its promotional efforts for the day, and so this infrastructure for organizing a major event in the national capital was maintained. More importantly, Secretary of State officials attempted to build recognition and use of national symbols. In addition to the Maple Leaf flag (adopted in 1965) and national anthem (formally adopted in 1980), the Liberal Party had attempted several times since the Second World War to change the official designation of July 1st from Dominion Day to Canada Day. A 1980 attempt died on the order paper, but a private member's bill from Vaudreuil MP Hal Herbert finally achieved, in early July 1982, what the government could not. From that year forward, the Canada Day Committees and the Canada Day Secretariat (a new division within the Department of the Secretary of State) attempted to build recognition and observance of "Canada Day" as a national symbol and holiday.

Despite their emphasis on community-based celebrations, the National Canada Day Committee and its various affiliated groups also believed that some degree of national coherence to Canada Day celebrations would serve to unite these cultural events. Thus, in addition to organizing the noonday singing of the anthem and distributing pins, buttons, and stickers with the Maple Leaf flag, the committees began to develop annual themes around which communities could organize their celebrations. The first such theme, "Explorers," was launched in 1984 to coincide with the 350th anniversary of Jacques Cartier's voyage to Canada, which was being celebrated in Quebec.[65] The themes continued in 1985, with "Salute to Canada's Youth" – a tie-in to the United Nations' International Youth Year – and 1986's "En Route Together," a transportation and communications theme linked to Expo 86 events in Vancouver.[66] Each year, the national committee produced materials for local celebrations, such as colouring books, activity books, and suggestion lists of themed activities for community events. The books themselves included a balance of regional achievers, with a clear effort to maintain a balance of genders, linguistic groups, and ethnic communities while also ensuring representation from Aboriginal communities and various provinces. It was, however, an approach that put the emphasis on individuals, rather than the communities they represented. For a supposedly locally focused era of celebrations, there was significant coherency to the nationally coordinated events, which were increasingly oriented around key Canadian symbols and national themes that could be tied to all regions, ethnic communities, linguistic groups, and genders.

In 1988, following the advice of the National Capital Region Canada Day Committee, the Secretary of State revived its partnership with the CBC for a televised Canada Day celebration. Going forward, most years featured two centrepiece events every July 1st, both of which were usually televised.[67] The first was a more formal affair at noon, featuring speeches from the governor general (or queen, in some years), the prime minister, and other dignitaries, an inspection of the troops, and sometimes awards for "Canadian Achievers." These formal elements were interspersed with musical performances. The evening was dedicated to pure festivities, with a major popular music concert on Parliament Hill, followed by fireworks. This structure has been largely been maintained ever since, although the content of the speeches and the elements of Canadian identity that they emphasized have certainly reflected the changing agendas of the governments of the day. Ottawa itself has become a major destination for Canada Day, with major concerts, firework displays, and events throughout the day to entertain the throngs of tourists who flood the capital. The downtown core is blocked off to traffic to accommodate the massive crowds of red-and-white-clad revellers.

Conclusion

The process of establishing an annual tradition of Canadian celebrations on July 1st was far from straightforward. With so many abortive starts, cancellations, and format changes, it is remarkable that government-organized celebrations of Canada Day have not only survived to the present day but continue to be observed in a format that has been quite stable since the late 1980s.

The Canadian identity celebrated on Canada Day has changed dramatically from how it was originally envisioned in 1958. What began as a celebration of a British-Canadian identity with an emphasis on military tradition and formality quickly shifted form and content according to the dictates of successive governments. An emphasis on region, language, and ethnicity became the central focus of the Ottawa-based televised celebrations in the 1960s. In the early 1970s, concerns that this format was too American, despite its emphasis on bilingualism, led to some experimentation with British-inspired structures and high culture elements. This too gave way to a politician-free, hyper-patriotic televised extravaganza, as Canadian culture was pressed into the service of defending national unity in the late 1970s. That approach was just as quickly abandoned in the 1980s as government officials began to question the effectiveness of television as a means of engendering active celebration of the nation, and officials decided to press for more participatory celebrations at the community level. Finally, in the late 1980s, the proverbial pendulum stopped swinging so wildly, as planners in Ottawa decided to try to incorporate a balance of all of these elements. Thereafter, televised popular events centred in Ottawa, with some formal and high culture performances as part of the National Capital ceremonies and celebrations, were complemented by funding for community-based celebrations across the country.

Throughout all of these changes, there are some clear trends in how government officials came to conceive of and present Canadian culture and identity. Although they were not always highlighted as the central features of Canada in the format of the celebrations, organizers always took pains to ensure that there was a balance of elements from all of Canada's regions, from both major linguistic groups and from multicultural and Aboriginal communities.[68] They also attempted to foster popular recognition of national symbols that could serve as universal rallying points for Canadians, including a new flag, a new anthem, and a new official name – Canada Day.[69] Moreover, organizers tried to incorporate elements in the official celebrations that would recognize the accomplishments of the individual Canadians who made up the country, whether through highlighting them in television broadcasts, featuring them in activity books for children, or giving them awards on Parliament Hill. There was a distinctive move towards a broader conception of which elements of Canadian culture should be featured in the celebratory events, as the event grew from their military roots to encompass folk acts, pop, classical, and jazz elements, sports, and even scientific accomplishments. As Canada Day moved from an emphasis on the British past to the diversified present, one can also discern a parallel changing of official conceptions of the Canadian nation, which shifted from a Canada rooted in a colonial heritage to one in which the component ethnic, linguistic, and provincial communities were emphasized, ultimately trending towards a more postmodern identity rooted in the ongoing achievements of its individual citizens. That being said, the British heritage never completely disappeared from these events, although concern with an overly Americanized approach to celebrating

Canada's national day seems to have faded over time. While a precise definition of Canadian identity and its various cultural components may continue to bedevil both academics and ordinary Canadians alike, the tradition of annual celebrations of the founding of the country has slowly but surely taken root in many parts of the country, and the federal government's policy of celebrating Canada on July 1st remains firmly entrenched.

NOTES

1 Benedict Anderson, *Imagined Communities: Reflections on the Origins and Spread of Nationalism* (London: Verso, 1983, 2006).
2 Maurice Charland, "Technological Nationalism," *Canadian Journal of Political and Social Theory* 10, nos. 1–2 (1986): 196–220. I apply Charland's theories directly to the media-related aspects of Dominion and Canada Day celebrations in Matthew Hayday, "Variety Show as National Identity: CBC Television and Dominion Day Celebrations, 1958–1980," in *Communicating in Canada's Past: Essays in Media History*, ed. Gene Allen and Daniel J. Robinson (Toronto: University of Toronto Press, 2009), 168–93.
3 Eric Hobsbawm and Terence Ranger, eds. *The Invention of Tradition* (Cambridge: Cambridge University Press, 1983).
4 This in turn has spawned an extensive literature in Canada and around the world. Len Travers, *Celebrating the Fourth: Independence Day and the Rites of Nationalism in the Early Republic* (Amherst: University of Massachusetts Press, 1997); Lyn Spillman, *Nation and Commemoration: Creating National Identities in the United States and Australia* (Cambridge: Cambridge University Press, 1997); Linda K. Fuller, *National Days / National Ways: Historical, Political, and Religious Celebrations around the World* (Westport, CT: Praeger, 2004); David McCrone and Gayle McPherson, eds., *National Days: Constructing and Mobilising National Identity* (Basingstoke, UK: Palgrave Macmillan, 2009); H.V. Nelles, *The Art of Nation-Building: Pageantry and Spectacle at Quebec's Tercentenary* (Toronto: University of Toronto Press, 1999); Ronald Rudin, *Founding Fathers: The Celebration of Champlain and Laval in the Streets of Quebec, 1878–1908* (Toronto: University of Toronto Press, 2003); Robert Stamp, "Empire Day in the Schools of Ontario: The Training of Young Imperialists," *Journal of Canadian Studies* 8, no. 3 (1973): 32–42; Mary Vipond, "The Mass Media in Canadian History: The Empire Day Broadcast of 1939," *Journal of the Canadian Historical Association* 14 (2003): 1–22; and Jonathan Vance, *Death So Noble: Memory, Meaning, and the First World War* (Vancouver: UBC Press, 1997).

5 *Canada Gazette*, 20 June 1868, 504.

6 Canada, House of Commons, *Debates,* 3 May 1869, 163–4 (Thomas McConkey, MP) and 10 May 1869, 242–4 (Thomas McConkey, MP, Isaac Le Vesconte, MP, William Chipman, MP).

7 Canada, Senate, *Debates,* 26 March 1879, 123 (Robert Carrall, Senator) and 2 April 1879, 201–7 (Robert Carrall, Clement Cornwall, Laurence Power, senators).

8 Ibid., 7 April 1879), 253. Canada, House of Commons, *Debates*, 9 April 1879, 1123; 17 April 1879, 1286–7; 28 April 1879, 1575.

9 Robert Cupido, "The Medium, the Message and the Modern: The Jubilee Broadcast of 1927," *International Journal of Canadian Studies* 26 (fall 2002): 101–23.

10 Jane Nicholas, "Gendering the Jubilee: Gender and Modernity in the Diamond Jubilee of Confederation Celebrations, 1927," *Canadian Historical Review* 90, no. 2 (June 2009): 247–74.

11 Craig Heron and Steve Penfold, *The Workers' Festival: A History of Labour Day in Canada* (Toronto: University of Toronto Press, 2005), xvi, 27–29, 193–269.

12 Phillip Buckner, ed. *Canada and the End of Empire* (Vancouver: UBC Press, 2004); Phillip Buckner, ed. *Canada and the British Empire* (New York: Oxford University Press, 2008); Phillip Buckner and R. Douglas Francis, eds. *Canada and the British World: Culture, Migration, and Identity* (Vancouver: UBC Press, 2006).

13 Paul Litt, "The Massey Commission, Americanization, and Canadian Cultural Nationalism," *Queen's Quarterly* 98, no. 2 (1991): 375–87; Paul Litt, *The Muses, the Masses, and the Massey Commission* (Toronto: University of Toronto Press, 1992).

14 Ryan Edwardson, *Canadian Content: Culture and the Quest for Nationhood* (Toronto: University of Toronto Press, 2008).

15 José E. Igartua, *The Other Quiet Revolution: National Identities in English Canada, 1945–1971* (Vancouver: UBC Press, 2006); Bryan Palmer, *Canada's 1960s: The Ironies of Identity in a Rebellious Era* (Toronto: University of Toronto Press, 2009).

16 C.P. Champion, *The Strange Demise of British Canada: The Liberals and Canadian Nationalism, 1964–68* (Montreal: McGill-Queen's University Press, 2010); Gary Miedema, *For Canada's Sake: Public Religion, Centennial Celebrations and the Re-Making of Canada in the 1960s* (Montreal: McGill-Queen's University Press, 2005).

17 Myra Rutherdale and J.R. Miller "It's Our Country: First Nations' Participation in the Indian Pavilion at Expo '67," *Journal of the Canadian*

Historical Association 17, no. 2 (spring 2006): 148–73; Matthew Hayday, "Fireworks, Folk-dancing and Fostering a National Identity: The Politics of Canada Day," *Canadian Historical Review* 91, no. 2 (June 2010): 287–314.

18 Matthew Hayday, "La francophonie canadienne, le bilinguisme et l'identité canadienne dans les celebrations de la fête du Canada," in *Entre lieux et mémoire: L'inscription de la francophonie dans la durée,* ed. Anne Gilbert, Michel Bock, and Joseph Yvon Thériault (Ottawa: Presses de l'Université d'Ottawa, 2009).

19 Eva Mackey, *The House of Difference: Cultural Politics and National Identity in Canada* (Toronto: University of Toronto Press, 2002).

20 Canada, House of Commons, *Debates*, 30 June 1951, 5037 (Louis St-Laurent, Prime Minister).

21 Ibid., 27 February 1951, 739–40 (Howard Green, MP); 28 June 1952, 3958 (George Drew, MP; Donald Fleming, MP); 27 June 1956, 5427 (George Drew, MP).

22 Library and Archives Canada (LAC), RG 2, Privy Council Office, series A-5-a, vol. 1898, Cabinet Conclusions, 20 May 1958, 5–6.

23 LAC, RG 6, Secretary of State, Acc. 2002–01308-X, box 24, file 7215–1, vol. 1, Ceremonies and Celebrations – July 1st – General, memorandum from W.H. Measures, director, Special Division, to the undersecretary of state, 11 March 1958.

24 Ibid., letter from Noël Dorion, secretary of state, to Ellen Fairclough, minister of citizenship and immigration, 24 January 1961.

25 Ibid., letter from Ellen Fairclough to Noël Dorion, 8 February 1961.

26 LAC, RG 6, Acc. 1986–87/419, box 15, file 1–7-4/1–1 pt. 1962, National Celebrations – Dominion Day – Parliament Hill – 1962, press release from the Department of Citizenship and Immigration, 20 June 1962.

27 Ibid., file 1–7-4/1–1 pt. 1964, National Celebrations – Dominion Day – Parliament Hill – 1964, letter from acting director of Citizenship and Immigration to H. Measures, 20 April 1964.

28 See Rutherdale and Miller, "It's Our Country," and Hayday, "Fireworks, Folk-dancing" for further discussion of the Cariboo Indian Girls Pipe Band, who performed at both the 1965 Dominion Day celebrations in Ottawa and the Indian Pavilion at Expo 67 in Montreal.

29 LAC, RG 6, Acc. 1986–87/419, box 15, file 1–7-4/1–1 pt. 1965, National Celebrations – Dominion Day – Parliament Hill – 1965, memo from Paul Kellner, Citizenship Branch, Department of the Secretary of State, 30 July 1965.

30 John Lownsbrough, *The Best Place to Be: Expo 67 and Its Time* (Toronto: Allen Lane, 2012).

31 A notable exception was French president Charles de Gaulle, who took his
    visit to Quebec as an opportunity to fan the flames of separatism, leading
    to a harsh condemnation by Prime Minister Pearson. De Gaulle returned to
    Paris, cancelling his planned visit to Ottawa.

32 LAC, RG 69, Centennial Commission, vol. 453, file Dominion Day 1967,
    Centennial Birthday Party directive for the Hill on 1 July.

33 LAC, RG 6, BAN 2002–01308-X, box 26, file 7215–68–2 pt. 1, Ceremonies
    and Celebrations – 1 July 1968 – Programme, memo from G.G.E. Steele,
    undersecretary of state to secretary of state, 31 May 1968.

34 Ibid., box 27, file 7215–68–4 pt. 1, Ceremonies and Celebrations – 1 July
    1968 – Publicity and Photographs, letter from G.G.E. Steele, undersecretary
    of state to George Davidson, president of the CBC, 14 June 1968, and memo
    from C.J. Lochman to G.G.E. Steele, 24 June 1968.

35 Ibid., box 26, file 7215–68 pt. 1, letter from J. André Ouellette to G.G.E.
    Steele, 18 July 1968.

36 Ibid., box 27, file 7215–69–2, Ceremonies and Celebrations – 1 July 1969 –
    Programme, minutes, 16 May 1969.

37 Ibid., minutes, 20 May 1969,

38 LAC, RG 41, CBC, vol. 939, file 823: Production Book, Dominion Today, 25
    June 1971; RG 41, series B-1-5, volume 821, file 31, Canada Day 1969–1972,
    memo from Thom Benson to Liston McIlhagga, 9 July 1971.

39 Ibid., McIlhagga to Benson, 13 July 1971; Benson to McIlhagga, 15 July
    1971.

40 Ibid., McIlhagga to regional staff, 20 July 1971.

41 Blaik Kirby, "CBC's Holiday Concert Marred by Its Clumsy Bi-Bi Flaws,"
    Globe and Mail, 2 July 1970.

42 LAC, RG 41, series B-1-5, vol. 821, file 31, Canada Day 1969–1972,
    Telephone Reaction Report, 3 July 1971.

43 J.V. Andrew, *Bilingual Today, French Tomorrow: Trudeau's Master Plan and
    How It Can Be Stopped* (Richmond Hill, ON: BMG Publishing, 1977), 69–70.

44 LAC, RG 6, BAN 2002–01308-X, box 28, file 7215–71, Ceremonies and
    Celebrations – 1 July 1971 – General, Memo from Graham Glockling to
    Carl Lochnan, 9 December 1970.

45 Ibid., box 28, file 7215–73, Ceremonies and Celebrations – 1 July 1973 –
    General, Letter from Eugene Forsey to Hugh Faulkner, Secretary of State, 3
    July 1973.

46 Ibid., box 28, file 7215–75, Ceremonies and Celebrations – 1 July 1975 –
    General, memo from Graham Glockling to Pierre Forget, 21 April 1975.

47 Ibid., box 28, file 7215–75, Ceremonies and Celebrations – 1 July 1975 –
    General, memo from Graham Glockling to Pierre Forget, 23 July 1975.

48 Ibid., box 24, file 7215–1, vol. 3, Ceremonies and Celebrations – 1 July 1977 – General, Confidential Report on July 1st and Festival Canada by Graham Glockling, chief of special events, 11 July 1977.

49 Ibid., box 29, file 7215–76, pt. 1, Ceremonies and Celebrations – 1 July 1976, letter from Hugh Faulkner to Joe Flynn MP, 24 February 1976.

50 Ibid., box 29, file 7215–77, vol. 1, Ceremonies and Celebrations – 1 July 1977, memo from Peter Roberts to Secretary of State officials, 21 March 1977.

51 Ibid., box 29, file 7215–78, pt. 1, Byward Consultants, Recommendation for a Federal Government July 1st Program 1978 – Summary, 14 October 1977.

52 LAC, RG 41, CBC, vol. 917, series A-V-2, file PG 18–21, Special Events Programs, Dominion Day, 1938–1979, part 3, 1976–1979, press release "Celebrate Canada – A Three-Hour Entertainment Spectacular Live on CBC Television on July 1st."

53 Ibid., Special Events Programs, Dominion Day, 1938–1979, part 3, 1976–1979, Festival Canada 1978, 5th Revision, 24 October 1977.

54 Canadian Broadcasting Corporation, "Celebrate Canada" videorecording, 1 July 1977.

55 LAC, RG 6, BAN 2002–01308-X, box 29, file 7215–77, vol. 4, Ceremonies and Celebrations – July 1 1977, "A Study to Measure the Impact of the July 1st National Celebration," prepared by Complan Research Associates, July 1977.

56 Ibid., box 30, file 7215–79, vol. 4, Ceremonies and Celebrations – 1 July 1979, memo from Guy Lefebvre to Pierre Juneau, undersecretary of state, and Festival Canada – Rapport sommaire de l'évaluation, 6 November 1979.

57 LAC, MG 31, D230, G. Hamilton Southam, vol. 22, file 36, Festival Canada Report on Program Evaluation, November 1979.

58 "These music hall gadgets, borrowed without adaptation from our southern neighbours." Lise Bisonnette, "Pitié pour l'année prochaine," Le Devoir (Montreal), 4 July 1979.

59 LAC, RG 6, BAN 2002–01308-X, box 30, file 7215–80, vol. 1, Ceremonies and Celebrations – 1 July 1980, Proposals for a medium-profile celebration of Canada's Birthday in 1980, from Ann Chudleigh, administrator, 24 September 1979.

60 Ibid., Notes on conversations with provincial/territorial governments.

61 Ibid., Memorandum to cabinet from the Secretary of State re: Festival Canada, 22 January 1980.

62 Ibid., Memorandum to cabinet from the Secretary of State, 9 April 1980.

63 LAC, RG 6, BAN 2002–01308-X, box 31, file 7215–81, vol. 1, Ceremonies and Celebrations – 1 July 1981, memorandum to cabinet from the Secretary of State, 15 January 1981.

64 Ibid., memorandum to cabinet, "The Celebration of Canada's Birthday, July 1st," submitted by Hon. Gerald A. Regan, secretary of state, 30 November 1981.

65 LAC, RG 6, Acc. 2002–01223–7, box 16, file 7215–86–4, vol. 1, 1986 – Finance, briefing note for the minister, 1985.

66 Ibid., box 15, file 7215–86–1, vol. 4, General, press release "En Route Together – En Route Ensemble," 1986.

67 LAC, RG 6, BAN 2002-01223–7, box 23, file 7215–88–8-1 pt. 1, Harris Boyd to Secretary of State, 23 December 1988.

68 I go into further detail on how these various communities were incorporated into these celebrations in "Fireworks, Folk-dancing."

69 For more on how the widespread display and distribution of these symbols contributes to nationalism and national identity, see Michael Billig, *Banal Nationalism* (London: Sage, 1995).

12 Dreams of a National Identity: Pierre Trudeau, Citizenship, and Canada Day

RAYMOND B. BLAKE AND BAILEY ANTONISHYN

Although the Fathers of Confederation were largely silent on notions of national identity in 1867, George-Etienne Cartier, one of the important politicians engaged in constructing Confederation and a long-time political ally of Sir John A. Macdonald, promoted Canada as a new political nationality that embraced the ethnic diversity that existed in British North America at the time. "In our own federation we should have Catholics and Protestant, French, English, Irish and Scotch," Cartier declared during the Confederation debates. "Each by his efforts and his success would increase the prosperity and glory of the new confederacy." Although, Cartier said, "the idea of unity of races was utopian – it was impossible. Distinction of this kind would always appear," Canada would create a new political nationality with which "neither the national origin, nor the religion of any individual, would interfere."[1] The strength of Canada was its pluralism, and the new political order made possible a common citizenship without citizens having to surrender their particularistic and distinctive identities. The Canadian nation existed, and all Canadians could identify with the new nationality even though they did not share common origins or a common race.

Cartier had a clear design for Canada's national identity, but the country has faced challenges since then with the emergence of economic, social, and political dynamics that have had Canadians wrestling, almost continuously, with questions of identity. For much of that history, Canada failed to include all political communities and all citizens in various notions of identity. Although some political leaders and the state bureaucracy had at times promoted the duality of Canada, most notably during the entrance of Manitoba into Confederation in 1870 and in the 1960s when Lester Pearson reached out to French-speaking communities, there had been almost a determined effort to ignore the Cartier narrative on diversity, as most first ministers attempted to construct Canada as a British nation with a significant French factor. One could argue that, until the arrival of Pierre Trudeau as prime minister in 1968, Canada's first ministers had not sought to accommodate the goals and aspirations of various subnational groups within the parameters of the country's national identity as Cartier had hoped in 1867.[2]

Throughout his nearly fifteen years as prime minister, Trudeau praised Cartier and the other Fathers of Confederation as "joiners of extremes or extremities."[3] He often insisted – virtually paraphrasing Cartier – that Canada flourished because it had found "strength out of diversity."[4] When Trudeau became prime minister, Canada was very much a divided nation, however. Its national identity had been constructed without attempting to sustain a level of accommodation between the constituent parts, as Cartier had recognized was necessary, and he was determined to save the country from the particularisms that threatened to destroy it. Trudeau believed that Canada had to develop a workable politics of national identity, as it had become even more culturally diverse and regionalized after the Second World War than it had been in 1867. The challenge for Canada was still how to fashion its diversity into a national identity that could sustain the nation, minimizing the differences and accentuating points of commonality to achieve a degree of social cohesion that could keep the disparate elements united. This required more than imagination (to borrow from Benedict Anderson); for Trudeau the markers of a strong national identity and true national cohesion were based on constitutional patriation, national bilingualism, cultural pluralism, and entrenched human rights.[5] He regarded those measures as "good for Canadian patriotism because they [gave] Canadians a sense of belonging to one nation."[6] Together, they would create a common political citizenship for all and provide the basis for an identity that all citizens could support. In the hopes of restoring national unity, Trudeau initiated a series of policies to change the historic narrative from a French-English dichotomy to a new paradigm that he believed would transcend historical animosities and divisions and provide the political stability that Cartier had sought in 1867.

This chapter explores how Trudeau used Canada's national day – Dominion Day until it was renamed Canada Day in 1982 – to achieve his designs to construct a new national identity from 1968 to 1983. His approach was multifaceted and multidimensional, and this chapter focuses on several of them. It examines the speeches, language, and rhetoric that Trudeau used during Canada's birthday celebrations to show how he viewed the evolving and changing ideal of Canada and how he defined questions of nationalism and identity to accommodate Cartier's dreams of diversity in the modern reality of the 1970s and 1980s. It also shows how he developed his ideal of the national community to define not only Canada for Canadians but also Canada's place in the world. Trudeau attempted to achieve his objective by, first, embracing and then promoting the diversity of Canada and, second, through changing the name of Dominion Day to Canada Day. A new shared national day without any connections to its British and colonial past, he believed, would strengthen national unity and, hence, political stability in Canada.

As the introduction to this book demonstrates, national days, such as Dominion Day/Canada Day, provide an excellent opportunity to examine the rich and complex world of national identity and nationalism. Such days often signify and commemorate for settler societies, such as those in Canada, the United States, and Brazil, the anniversary of national independence; for older countries, like France and Ireland, they mark days of key historical significance. It is not unusual for countries to recast their national days to reflect new political, social, and/or cultural dynamics. In the post-Soviet era, Russia, for instance, attempted to reconstruct its traditional national day from one that had commemorated the October Revolution of 1917 to a Day of Reconciliation and Accord following the fall of Communism. When that attempted makeover failed, Russia created National Unity Day; that proved unsuccessful, and it now celebrates Russia Day on 12 June in an effort to captivate the attention of its citizens and strengthen national identity. Similarly, Australia has re-imagined its national day. Australia Day was long celebrated on 26 January to commemorate the landing of the British First Fleet in 1788, but Australia's Aboriginal peoples saw little to celebrate in British colonial rule. They took to calling it Invasion Day, eventually forcing the country to de-emphasize its heritage as a British colony and celebrate instead its emergence as an independent, postcolonial, multicultural, and diverse state.[7] Indeed, as the following chapter by Stuart Ward discusses, a re-imagining and reconfiguring of national days was underway throughout the settler states of the Commonwealth in the 1960s and 1970s.

National days are, then, a key part of nation-building strategies. They are often characterized by a continuous and ongoing search for an acceptable level of consensus, especially in countries that are ethnically diverse. National holidays are a vehicle used to reinforce national unity, while reminding citizens who they are, and who they are not. They also provide a window into the vast scholarship of national identity. As it emerged in the late nineteenth century, nationalism and national identity were seen as forms of social and cultural bonding designed to forge cultural and racial uniformity within the nation-state and to create an identity that separated one nation from another. This process of fostering the development of particular nationalisms and identity formation led to the creation of national myths, prompting Hans Kohn to consider nationalism "first and foremost a state of mind,"[8] an idea that Benedict Anderson extended into what he called an "imagined community." A nation is "imagined," Anderson contends, since "the members of even the smallest nation will never know most of their fellow members, meet them or ever hear of them, yet in the minds of each lives the image of their communion."[9] Successive generations of Canadian academics have examined the question of national identity, and, as historian Pierre Nora has pointed out, the present usually serves as an important reference for understanding a particular past.[10] The earliest studies into Canadian national identity focused on constitutional development, celebrating Canada's transition from colony to nation. Linguistic dualism was for several generations a staple in the study of national identity. Recently, the search has broadened considerably. Ryan Edwardson shows that Canada's national culture has been successively reinvented by the intelligentsia, the cultural elites, and state bureaucracies, noting in particular the emergence of cultural industrialism in the 1970s.[11] Philip Resnick shows the importance of Europe in the construction of Canadian identity,[12] and Keith Banting and Janine Brodie have linked social citizenship to national identity.[13] Will Kymlicka, Charles Taylor, Michael Ignatieff, and a variety of other scholars have shown how diversity, multiculturalism, and a rights-based political philosophy have come to define Canada.[14] Recent historiography contends that Canada embraced its own identity only when confronted with the assertiveness of French-speaking Canada. Then, the federal state and English-speaking Canadians abandoned vestiges of all things British in a process of "de-ethnicization" and "de-dominionization"[15] and began to re-imagine their country as a civic nation without ethnic particularities.[16] Matthew Hayday has attempted to move the analysis of national identity and commemoration out of the realm of social and cultural history to consider it as part of the public policy agenda that reflects the state's new policy objectives and new conceptions of national identity, presenting a vision of a multicultural and bilingual country with a strong Aboriginal component. The remaking of Canada's national day was led primarily by state bureaucrats responsible for the celebrations.[17]

National days can be used to foster a new national identity for countries, as older, more established identities are reshaped, re-imagined, and mobilized anew.[18] When this occurs, national leaders play a fundamental role in shaping national days, especially where states have a difficult time coming to terms with their pasts, as often happens in settler societies. As the design and reception of national days are changed to reflect new political, economic, and cultural circumstances within a nation-state, they provide a glimpse of how states and political leaders want citizens to imagine themselves as "being national" or, at least, how they would like citizens to imagine the national identity.

When Canada refashioned and transformed its national day, Pierre Trudeau played an important role. He praised Canada's traditions of accommodation, tolerance, and good will and its wisdom in allowing various diverse groups to make Canada their home, but he never shared the enthusiasm for the country's French and British history and traditions that had largely come to define Canada for many people.[19] The duality that Canadians seemed so proud of rarely found its way into the workings of the state, and Trudeau firmly believed that it was the primary responsibility of the federal state to deal with questions of national unity. He never equivocated on his political ambition to unite Canada, and he insisted in his first national election campaign as prime minister in 1968 that national unity was his primary goal.[20] He saw Quebec's disillusionment with the federation as a Canadian problem, not simply a Quebec one. After his election victory on 26 June, he said, "People who think I am going to put Quebec in its place should have voted for somebody else."[21] He entered federal politics, he claimed, to make bilingualism irreversible and to secure Quebec within Confederation, but he also fought the old notions of Canada as essentially a duality of French and English.[22] Canada's distinctiveness was to be defined as a civic and federalist nation that embraced the liberal ideals of diversity, multiculturalism, and individual rights.

This particular notion of Canadian identity and citizenship was necessary to unite citizens while at the same time undermining the sovereignist tendencies of Québécois nationalism.[23] Trudeau promoted a Canadian identity in which there was no single or dual ethnicity, only citizens who were bound together by their collective belief in the equality of all citizens through a set of shared rights. New Canadians – and, indeed, all Canadians – had to think about themselves, first and foremost, as rights-bearers, not as French, English, or Aboriginal citizens of a national community.[24] The rights philosophy, he maintained, created a new form of identity and attachment to the nation-state. Recognizing cultural differences became a matter of rights. Trudeau told Canadians that diversity was not a problem that had to be managed; like Cartier, he believed it was a strength to celebrate.

Pierre Trudeau's July 1st Speeches and the Crafting of a Canadian Identity for the Contemporary Era

The government of Trudeau, not surprisingly, embodied Trudeau's personal philosophy, and he demonstrated a commitment to those philosophical notions immediately upon his becoming prime minister. At the 1969 Dominion Day celebrations on Parliament Hill, he read a letter of Saint Paul to the Corinthians. Like Paul, who was addressing a people intensely divided, Trudeau urged those gathered to celebrate Canada's birthday to consider charity the greatest principle that a nation-state could embrace. In the sense used in the New Testament, he reminded Canadians, charity offers unconditional goodwill to all people. He praised Canada for its tolerance, telling the audience that it was their greatest attribute and a "basic part of the character of Canada."[25] This was a theme he reiterated each Dominion Day as he reminded Canadians that their diversity of languages, cultures, and outlooks "gives us a chance for mutual enrichment."[26] In a 1971 letter to the Canada Committee, a non-profit, non-political organization founded in Montreal in 1964 to promote Canadian unity, Trudeau wrote, "We [Canadians] have felt the deeply-rooted desire for community of spirit, of values and of ideas. We have sought to understand one another in a climate of tolerance and of mutual respect."[27] A similar idea was expressed a couple of years later when he wrote in 1973 that Canada's strength comes "from a value system which places first priorities on the quality of life for each individual person in our society, and which cherishes each person's uniqueness…We respect each other's differences." For him, Canada could flourish only if it embraced that ideal and could "build a society that has tolerance for others."[28] Shared Canadian citizenship was about respecting each other's differences, and the country's contribution to the world was measured in human, not military or economic, terms.[29]

Trudeau refused to use the term *Dominion Day* to refer to the celebrations on 1 July. Shortly after leading the Liberal Party to its first majority government since 1953, Trudeau pushed his cabinet to agree in November 1968 that July 1st should be designated as "Canada Day" regardless of the legislation designating the date as "Dominion Day."[30] The government did not introduce legislation in Parliament to formalize the change, however. Trudeau chose instead to speak of "our national holiday."[31] He insisted after he became prime minister that Canada was not "a northern extension of a foreign state, nor an historic accident ... but a homogeneous community, with a dynamic, social organization and a future of its own."[32] Many of the symbols and trappings of Canada's British heritage and its colonial past, such as British citizenship and the Red Ensign flag, had been erased, but the word "dominion" had remained, and it prevented French-speaking Canadians from embracing a pan-Canadian national identity. Having "Dominion Day" as the title of Canada's national day served to remind French-speaking Canada of the country's Britishness and its subservience to Britain. Trudeau maintained that unity could be restored only if the national identity was reconstituted and re-imagined to remove elements of Canada's British heritage. If the word "dominion" were removed from the title of Canada's national day, it would foster a sense of political cohesion and strengthen national unity. He spoke directly to the matter in his 1975 Dominion Day message. The name of Canada's national day should reflect the country's "maturity," he said, and he challenged Canadians to "look beyond narrow self-interest toward the common good of the family which is Canada."[33]

Trudeau's Dominion Day messages were also a reminder to Canadians of the necessity for self-reflection. Not only was the national birthday celebration an opportunity to reflect on the maturity of the nation, it was also a time for each Canadian to reflect on whether prejudice, ignorance, and self-interest were impeding Canada's "road to full adulthood" and the march to national sovereignty.[34] "We have learned," he had said in February 1974 during debate on the Throne speech, "that no society, no matter how democratic or politically mature, is guaranteed stability if elements in it become greedy or unmindful of the rights, dignity and needs of others." Where inequalities exist, it is the responsibility of the whole community to work together to exercise leadership and to "subordinate selfish interests to the cause of social justice."[35] Later that year, in his Dominion Day message, he called upon Canadians to test themselves to see if they were blinded by self-interest and if they demonstrated a fair balance between their own rights and privileges and those of other people. He singled out business interests, in one instance, and asked if their prices reflected a grab for excessive profits or a sense of responsibility and justice towards the consumer; to unions, he asked if they were interested in the highest possible wages only for their members or for all workers. He called upon all Canadians to take a close look at themselves.[36] A year later, he reminded Canadians that they all had a personal responsibility for the way of life in their community and in their country.[37] These pleas came during the time the federal government was considering wage and price controls to limit the increase in rampant inflation that then plagued Canada and much of the developed world.

It was common for Trudeau to challenge Canadians on Dominion Day to look beyond their own situation and self-interest. When Canada was a young country, Dominion Day was about celebrating the achievement of self-government, of steady economic and social growth, and the march to independence. By the 1970s, however, Canada had matured, and Dominion Day provided the opportunity for the nation to look outside itself and "think about its contribution to the development of a better life for the worldwide family of man." Although Canada continued in its struggle to achieve social and economic equity and justice at home during a period of high inflation and economic turmoil that marked much of the 1970s, Trudeau called upon Canadians to look beyond their narrow self-interest towards the common good on a global level. They had to fulfil their responsibility to do so in the less developed regions of the world. Canadians should not be happy when "millions in the developing countries ... are threatened with starvation, with stifled ambition, with a life of ceaseless struggle for survival and dignity." Canadians had to strengthen their sense of international commitment and renew their willingness to help others.[38]

Another theme that Trudeau pursued in his Dominion Day messages was the friction he saw in Canadian society and the optimism he had that Canada could successfully confront its challenges. For Trudeau, it was important that no Canadian feel isolated because of language, economic disparity, or age. In his second Dominion Day message, he pointed to the problems that would confront him for most of his political career. "There are frictions between our two major language groups," he reminded Canadians, adding that "the gap between the haves and the have-nots is still too wide; the varied interests of different regions create feelings of isolation; [and] misunderstanding damages

12.1 Trudeau in Toronto, 2 July 1972. Prime Minister Pierre Trudeau meets a little girl wearing a Dominion Day hat during festivities at Nathan Phillips Square in Toronto. Photo by Dennis Robinson / The Globe and Mail. © Copyright The Globe and Mail. Reproduced by permission of Canadian Press Images.

the relations between older and younger generations." Yet, Canada's traditions of freedom, good will, and tolerance, he optimistically said, will permit the country to overcome its problems and build a unified and progressive land where "brotherhood has replaced distrust, equity has triumphed over poverty, a feeling of unity has eliminated regional isolation, and mutual understanding has closed the generation gap."[39]

Although Trudeau declared on a number of occasions the importance of divorcing politics from Dominion Day activities, politics was often an integral part of many of his Dominion Day messages. In fact, it was only in 1972 – immediately before an election was called – and during the 1974 election campaign that Trudeau attended Dominion Day functions outside of Ottawa. Opposition party leaders accused him of playing politics with Dominion Day celebrations, but following the election of the Parti québécois (PQ) in 1976, he made no apology for confronting in his Dominion Day addresses those who threatened Canada.[40] After that pivotal election in Quebec, Trudeau took the national day more seriously, as the federal government more actively promoted national celebrations on July 1st and used the occasion to aggressively promote Canada and national unity, especially in Quebec.[41] In his formal message – as well as in his speech at the celebrations on Parliament Hill – Trudeau identified "separatists" in Quebec as the most serious threat to national unity and the survival of Canada that the nation had ever known. What they did not envision, he optimistically told Canadians, was that the sovereignist government stimulated a renewal of the Canadian spirit. You are here tonight, he told the gathering in Ottawa, "not only to be entertained, but also to stand up for the country you love, or re-affirm your pride and your faith in Canada and its people."[42] Trudeau returned to the "dark cloud" of separatism a year later and warned that a divided nation would destroy all that Canada had achieved since Confederation. If Canada were to come apart, it would see the re-emergence of an authoritarian regime in Quebec, a divided and balkanized English-speaking Canada, and the possible absorption of some provinces into the United States.[43] Thus, fear mongering was also a feature of Trudeau's Dominion Day addresses.

While many Canadians and the opposition parties, too, shared Trudeau's view of the dangers to Canada's survival posed by the PQ and other strong nationalists in Quebec, they did not agree with many of his initiatives on the national unity file. Nor did they endorse his approach to questions of cultural identity.[44] When the Canadian government began committing significant funds – most of which went to Quebec – to promote a greater sense of national identity, Senator Eugene Forsey complained that Ottawa's preoccupation with Quebec ignored Canada's multicultural and ethnic groups who, too, wished for state funds to celebrate Canada's birthday.[45] Press statements from the Department of the Secretary of State made it clear that the government was more concerned with instilling a sense of national identity in Quebec than in the rest of Canada. Government press releases noted that "Canada Day" was "an opportunity for Quebecers who believe in federalism to express their preference for a united Canada." When, in 1977, former prime minister and Conservative member of Parliament John Diefenbaker criticized Ottawa's prioritizing of spending for Dominion Day festivities in Quebec, Trudeau fumed that Ottawa would take advantage of the occasion "for Canadians to demonstrate their love for their country."[46]

There was greater objection, however, to the government and its various agencies calling 1 July "Canada Day" rather than "Dominion Day." Many vehemently disagreed with the federal government's belief that if it avoided such words as "dominion," it would go some distance to addressing Quebec's dissatisfaction with its place in Canada. The Conservatives particularly objected to the government using the term "Canada Day" without an amendment to the legislation that had created Dominion Day in 1879. Diefenbaker demanded that the House investigate the "whittling away through surreptitious means the traditional things of the heritage of our country and to put a stop to it."[47] The Liberals used their majority to defeat Diefenbaker's motion, but other Canadians complained too of the "prolific usage of Canada Day" when the act to change the name had not been passed.[48] Meanwhile, the Department of the Secretary of State prepared a report for the government in October 1979, recommending the name change. It also recommended that "Canada Day be an occasion for Canadians to enjoy themselves and have fun by participating in recreational, popular, cultural and community activities [and that] Canada Day be non-ideological and non-partisan and non-political."[49]

Despite his own government's insistence that Dominion Day celebrations be free of politics, Trudeau politicized Canada's birthday celebrations in the early 1980s more than at any time during his tenure as prime minister. Although he had lost power to the Joe Clark's Progressive Conservatives in 1979, he was returned to office in the federal election of 18 February 1980, believing that his nation-building plan had been unfairly and prematurely cut short. As he attempted to remake

Canada through constitutional renewal (a process that included a patriated constitution, with a Charter of Rights and Freedoms, and a stronger national economic union), he saw the premiers as the major obstacle preventing him from realizing his dream for the country. He used Dominion Day in 1980 to talk directly to Canadians, inviting them to participate with him in his fight with the premiers who, he believed, stood in the way of a united and cohesive Canada. In his Dominion Day message that year, after eight of the ten premiers had opposed his statement of principles as a preamble to a new constitution,[50] he asked Canadians to share their ideas on the constitution with him. In what might be considered the beginnings of his "people's package" on the constitution, promoted to bypass obstinate premiers, he told Canadians that he welcomed their comments and suggestions in revising his statement of principles. In essence, his appeal to citizens was an attempt to pressure the premiers, and he believed that Canadians agreed with his description of Canada that the premiers had rejected: "Born of a meeting of the English and French presence on North American soil, which had long been the home of our native peoples, and enriched by the contributions of millions of new Canadians from the four corners of the earth, we have chosen to create a life together which transcends the difference of blood relationships, language and religion and which willingly accepts the experience of sharing our wealth and cultures, while respecting diversity."[51] He hoped that Canadians' support for his views on the constitution would legitimize his efforts.

A year later, after failing to convince the provincial leaders to move forward with the patriation and renewal of Canada's constitution, he attacked the obstinate premiers again by calling upon Canadians to be vigilant "against our tendencies towards selfishness and mistrust." He dismissed the premiers for their selfishness and their determination to create in Canada "quasi-autonomous" states. In their demands for excessive decentralization, they threated to destroy the national community and all that had been achieved since 1867.[52] Because of its commitment to national solidarity and national tolerance, Canada has been able to overcome moments of pettiness, Trudeau said, to give the country official bilingualism, equalization payments to level provincial disparities, and a uniform oil pricing policy. Quebec's rejection of separation in 1980 and Parliament's vote to entrench a charter of rights in the constitution had been achieved because Canada was "built deliberately on the principles of economic sharing and cultural diversity." Canada had an "almost heroic ideal of sharing and tolerance" that had

318 Raymond B. Blake and Bailey Antonishyn

supported equalization payments to reduced economic disparity, transfer payments to guarantee comparable health care and social services throughout the country, a uniform domestic price for oil, and a federal bilingualism program.[53] Yet, ambitious provincial premiers could not be allowed to usurp the powers of the central government, he admonished. "How far can you go in dismantling the economic role of the national government before you cease to have an economic union, let alone a country in the political and cultural sense of the term," Trudeau wrote in challenge to those who did not share his view of Canada.[54] Within months of his appeal to Canadians in his Dominion Day message, Trudeau and the premiers found a compromise on the constitution.

What's in a Name? Dominion Day, Canada Day, and the Terminological Battles around Canada's National Day

There would be a resolution to the lingering issue of the official title for Canada's national day before Trudeau retired in 1984, though the debate over the name was well underway when he became prime minister in 1968. In fact, the official designation for Canada's birthday celebration had emerged as an important issue in the postwar period after a bitter battle over conscription had divided Quebec and much of the rest of Canada during the Second World War. By the 1960s, many French- and English-speaking Canadians believed that the promotion of the British connection and of Canada's British heritage presented the greatest threat to national unity, and Trudeau agreed. His contempt for the title of Dominion Day was well known. He contributed to the debate by ignoring the official name of Canada's national day: he never once used "Dominion Day" in his annual July 1st message to Canadians. He thus "consciously set [himself] against tradition and for radical innovation"[55] and agreed with those who had argued that the word "dominion" signified colonial status – a concept that, by the 1960s, no longer applied to Canada. The political and constitutional changes embodied in the Statute of Westminster in 1931 had recognized Canada as an autonomous state, an equal of Great Britain. In that paradigm, "dominion" was an artefact of the past.

Trudeau paid little attention to those who insisted that Canada had given "dominion" and "dominion status" considerable prestige in the march to national independence and full sovereignty and that the words did not signify anything demeaning or limiting. In 1865, when British officials helped put the Quebec Resolutions negotiated by political leaders in British North America into a legal document that would eventually become the British North America Act, they had used the word "colony" to refer to Canada. However, the Canadian delegates at the London Conference removed that word from the document entirely, showing that they saw Canada as something more than a colony. They eventually agreed that their new country would be known as a dominion, from the Latin root *dominus*, meaning master, and from Psalm 72 which spoke of "Dominion from sea to sea." Being a dominion gave Canada a rank above colonial status, and over time, the term came to describe states that had achieved autonomy within the Commonwealth. In arguing for greater Canadian independence from London in 1878, Edward Blake, a key figure in Alexander Mackenzie's Liberal government, claimed that "Canada is not merely a colony or a province: she is ... a Dominion."[56] Canada, as the leading member of the Commonwealth, had shown dominion status to be a badge of independence and autonomy; it was dominion status that was sought by South Africa in 1909 and by India in the interwar years. With the Balfour Report of 1926 and then the Statute of Westminster in 1931, Canada achieved the equal status with the United Kingdom that the delegates in London in 1865 had envisioned. By then, "dominion" had clearly come to mean a self-governing entity, equal in constitutional status to the United Kingdom itself.[57] Despite those arguments, many in the postwar period continued to see "dominion" as suggesting a subordinate role for their country, especially in such areas as foreign policy, where Canada had usually followed the British. For them, "dominion" could never signify anything more than subservience.

The first attempt to replace "Dominion Day" with "Canada Day" occurred in 1946; more than twenty other attempts were made before Canada Day was officially proclaimed in 1982. An analysis of the disputes over the attempts to change the holiday's name reveals that it was not a contest between those who wanted to keep Canada British and those who wanted Canada to have its own unique "Canadian" identity. Rather, it was a debate over the role that Canada's past should play in shaping national symbols. For many who wanted to retain "Dominion Day," the term was seen as an integral part of Canada's history and heritage, and they believed that this history and heritage – both French and British – should be a part of the national narrative. As C.P. Champion has shown with reference to arguments over a new flag, the debate over Dominion Day was not between "British and Canadian, but between rival interpretations of Canadianism."[58] Those who fought to retain the name Dominion Day maintained that Canada's national identity could not ignore its past. Trudeau's designs for strengthening the national community, many believed, were an assault on their cultural distinctiveness and threatened to erode their particularistic identities.

For Trudeau, history played little role in Canada's national identity as he strived to manufacture and invent a new one. In his first Throne speech, he promised to consider changing Canada's national symbols as a means to strengthen national unity.[59] In the 1970 "Reply to the Speech from the Throne," he remarked: "I personally do not share with any acuteness the sense of regret expressed by some commentators that Canadians pay insufficient heed to their past... It must be understood but it is not to be worshipped." He praised Pearson's plan to change many of Canada's symbols to create a new national identity: the past was of "relatively little consequence."[60] This perspective was reflected in the adoption in 1965 of the Maple Leaf flag, which Pearson had presented as "exclusively Canadian," necessary to imbue Confederation with "a greater feeling of national identity and unity."[61] Despite Trudeau's belief that Canada "is in a continuous process of invention," he chose not to introduce legislation to officially change Dominion Day,[62] even as he embarked in 1970 on a new and aggressive federal identity program designed to heighten awareness among Canadians of the federal presence across the country. That policy came from a recommendation from a 1969 study of government information services to create a "dynamic, imaginative, contemporary public image, immediately recognizable by any citizen." Trudeau's government eventually produced short new department and agency names, such as Environment/Environnement Canada and Postes Canada/Canada Post that would be similar in English and French.[63]

The word "dominion" also disappeared from official use, completing the process that former Liberal prime minister Louis St Laurent had begun in the early 1950s. Although he promoted "Canada Day" as the national day, and polls showed that this new designation was winning favour with many, Trudeau worried about a determined counter-campaign by those who argued that the government was disregarding Canada's heritage in favour of creating something new and modern. [64] In the 1970s, he relied on a series of private members' bills to achieve his objective rather than introducing his own legislation. When a private member's bill was introduced in 1970, it passed second reading and was referred to the Standing Committee on Justice and Legal Affairs, but, like most other attempts, it did not come to a vote in the

Commons.[65] Despite the failed attempt to change the official name for the 1970 Dominion Day celebration, the head of CBC News said that, it used the term "Canada Day" on the specific orders of Colin Gibson, the minister of the Department of the Secretary of State.[66] Such a directive was in keeping with the earlier cabinet decision to designate 1 July as Canada Day.

The government ultimately introduced Bill C-37 to change the name of Dominion Day to Canada Day on 19 June 1980, only days after Quebec voted against sovereignty in the May 1980 referendum but, still, more than a decade after Trudeau became prime minister. At the same time, Parliament passed legislation to make "O Canada" the national anthem, with the bill receiving Royal Assent on Dominion Day.[67] Trudeau proceeded much more cautiously with Bill C-37, however, despite occasional pleas from Liberal backbenchers to move more aggressively.[68] Although only a few Liberals remained committed to the term "dominion," the government did not wish to further the perception that it was simply catering to Quebec, where there was little celebration of Dominion Day, nor did it wish to create a backlash against French-speaking Quebec. Bill C-37 came up for second reading on 29 June 1981, just two days before Dominion Day and more than a year after it had been introduced. After promoting Canada Day in all of the government advertising, Francis Fox, the secretary of state and minister of communications, attempted to have the legislation passed (and the name changed) in time for the celebrations on July 1st. In this, he had the support of the New Democrats. He used the arguments that had been tried previously, adding that the change was designed to be more "modern" and offer a more "accurate description of our national self." He appealed to the Progressive Conservatives by insisting that the bill was not motivated by a "rejection of our heritage." Canadians saw themselves, he said, "not as citizens of a dominion – with its suggestion of control, dominance, and colonialism – but as citizens of a proud and independent nation, Canada." Moreover, he said, there was no French translation for "dominion," and millions of Canadians were already using the words Canada Day to refer to July 1st. It was time to retire "Dominion Day" in favour of a name that "no one can find objectionable."[69] The Conservative opposition held a different view on what the erasure of Dominion Day said about the role of heritage, traditions, and history in Canada's national symbols. It accused the Liberals of destroying all traditions within Canada and refused to fast-track the legislation.[70]

A different approach was necessary, then, if the Liberal government were to make the name change without causing an uproar in Parliament. That new approach was one of stealth – the notorious practice within governments to act when they are least likely to attract attention to policies that are certain to be controversial and often unpopular. After more than twenty legislative attempts since 1946 to rename Canada's national day – including seven from Hal Herbert, an anglophone Liberal from Quebec – the supporters of Canada Day seized an opportunity with the support of the Trudeau government and passed Herbert's private member's bill, Bill C-201, "An Act to Amend the Holiday Act" in the span of a few minutes, late on Friday afternoon, 9 July 1982, just weeks after the patriation of the Canadian constitution.[71] Ironically, the new constitution retained the word "dominion," but its essential feature, the Charter of Rights and Freedoms, was a plan to create a new Canadian identity based on citizenship rights.

First elected to the House of Commons in 1972, Herbert believed that the name change would placate French-speaking Canadians and stop "the divisiveness" that he believed was sweeping the country.[72] He and his supporters believed that removing one of the last British symbols in Canada would strengthen national unity. Because Herbert was an Anglo-Quebecker, it was hoped that the bill might garner more support than one coming from a francophone, who might be seen as trying to get rid of any reference to Canada's "British Roots."[73] When the bill was introduced on 6 May, it received little support and had gone to the "bottom of the list"; it was on the nineteenth page of the list of private members' business on the morning of 9 July but had moved ahead of the other 170 bills to the top of the list by mid-afternoon.[74] The New Democratic house leader and the Conservative whip received notice of the debate on Bill C-201 only an hour before it was introduced for second reading. Leaders of the major parties had agreed to move Herbert's bill to the top of the order paper and passed the measure when the Commons was all but empty.[75] Ed Broadbent, the NDP leader, had long agreed that "Dominion Day" was an "anachronistic" and entirely inappropriate term with which to designate Canada's birthday. It reminded Canadians, he lamented, of a particular and close relationship with Great Britain; Canadians needed a change, and Canada Day "would add a small, perhaps, but hopefully relevant impetus to a legitimate sense of national identity."[76]

Only twelve members were present with Deputy Speaker Lloyd Francis when Herbert's bill was introduced. Walter Baker, the Conservative house leader who had earlier opposed the change, is recorded as asking, somewhat disingenuously, "What is going on?"[77] Regardless, the bill immediately received second reading. David Smith, the parliamentary secretary to the president of the Privy Council and a powerful Liberal organizer with close ties to Trudeau, asked for and received unanimous consent for the House to move immediately into Committee of the Whole. No questions were asked, nor was there any debate during the committee stage; the bill was quickly reported back to the House, where it received third and final reading. The proceedings were concluded in five minutes. A member asked for unanimous consent that the hour set aside for private members' bill had lapsed. All three parties were represented in the House, including Baker and Vancouver South Tory MP John Fraser. Baker later told the press that he supported the bill because a poll taken in his riding had indicated a clear and large majority favoured the change, though he personally preferred the old name.[78] When some Conservative MPs later complained of the process, Conservative leader Joe Clark, who supported the bill, told them that individual members were responsible for keeping track of which private member's bills were up for debate.[79] Although the House of Commons' rules required a quorum of at least twenty MPs to conduct its business, Speaker Jeanne Sauvé later ruled that, despite the procedural irregularity, no rules had been violated because none of the members in the House had called for a quorum count.

The bill passed because the leadership of the New Democrats and the Progressive Conservatives cooperated with the Liberal government. Moreover, Trudeau was determined to give the country an independent identity. All the participants fully understood that the name change would stir controversy in the House of Commons and had the potential to rekindle the emotions and divisions that had accompanied the introduction of the new flag and the Official Languages Act. None of the party leaders wanted to revive any of those emotions or even allow a divisive parliamentary debate on the matter, given the anger in Quebec over the recent patriation process. A debate had the potential to heighten the tensions between English- and French-speaking Canada and exacerbate the national unity crisis. It was for those reasons that the government's own legislation (Bill C-37) to rename Dominion Day had not been moved forward. The major party leaders had succeeded in moving Herbert's bill through the House of Commons with as little fanfare as possible. Such tactics only strengthened the resolve of some senators and other interested parties to ensure a vigorous defence of

"Dominion Day" when the bill reached the Senate, where it required passage to become law. Columnist Michael Valpy, for example, could not control his anger: "Dominion Day got wiped out in five minutes in the House of Commons yesterday afternoon. It got wiped out by one of the sneakiest, dumbest, most politically cheap acts in the history of Canada's parliament."[80] Another newspaper called Bill C-201 "one of the sleaziest, politically cheap Acts ever passed."[81]

There was strong support for preserving the name "Dominion Day" when the bill moved to the Canadian Senate. However, the leadership of both major political parties supported the legislation: Bud Olsen, the government Senate leader, and Jacques Flynn, the opposition Senate leader, had been instructed to have the legislation passed without amendment. The Liberal government saw the bill as part of a process of recasting the national identity to make it truly Canadian as it struggled with the national unity issue and the attitude in Quebec towards Canada. It argued that a consensus had emerged among Canadians that the time had come to use the proper vocabulary and designate Canada Day as the title of the nation's birthday celebrations. After all, Canada was a fully sovereign country, and exorcizing the word "dominion" from the official Canadian lexicon could only strengthen national unity and build cohesion between Quebec and the rest of Canada.[82] Ethnic organizations such as the Council of National Ethnocultural Organizations of Canada (CNEOC) and the Canadian Consultative Council on Multiculturalism, an advisory group to the federal government, favoured the removal of all symbolism of Canada's association with most things considered British and encouraged the Senate to pass the Canada Day legislation. Representatives of ethnic groups saw the adoption of "Canada Day" as a positive step towards stimulating the growth of national self-awareness, noting that "precious little had been done [by Government] to enhance a truly Canadian national identity." Dr Laureano Leone, national chair of CNEOC, told the Senate committee appointed to review the legislation that he supported the change because substituting "Canada" for "Dominion" would "stimulate the growth of our national self-awareness and bring us closer to the long-sought Canadian national unity."[83] Public opinion surveys showed that most Canadians had little affinity with "Dominion Day"; yet, only 41 per cent of English-speaking Canadians, 44 per cent of French-speaking Canadians, and 33 per cent of other language groups favoured "Canada Day" – many did not seem to care what the day celebrating Canada's birthday was called.[84]

Those opposed to the change focused on three major points: first, the procedure used to pass Bill C-201 in the House of Commons; second, the disregard the change had for the role of Canada's heritage and history in the creation of national symbols; and third, the contradiction created by the belief that English-speaking Canadians were forced to ignore their British heritage to foster national unity while French-speaking Quebec celebrated and strengthened its French heritage. Although the Liberal government would have preferred a simple vote in the Senate, a number of Conservative and Liberal senators threatened to withhold support for the legislation to control public sector wages (which required unanimous support to fast-track it through the Red Chamber) unless the Senate held public hearings on the Canada Day bill. The government relented and agreed on 4 August to refer the legislation to the Standing Committee on Legal and Constitutional Affairs, which could hold public hearings.[85] That concession was by no means an indication of the government's willingness to retreat. Trudeau had made it abundantly clear since he assumed office that Canada's culture policy would not be tied to its British and French origins: "There is no official culture, nor does any ethnic group take precedence over any other," he had said.[86] Trudeau, who cared little for history and tradition, was delighted to see the word "dominion" condemned to the wastebasket of history.

The Senate committee hearings began on 13 October 1982. There was no formal advertising of the dates of the hearings, even though it was customary in such cases to publicize the dates. The committee also decided to hear representatives of only four "umbrella" groups.[87] The Senate, like the House of Commons, wanted to limit debate on Bill C-201, and supporters of "Dominion Day" saw such an approach as another attempt by the Trudeau government to ignore Canada's heritage and its history as a way to deal with national unity and win support for Canada in Quebec, although only a few of the supporters of the old name linked the legislation to an attempt to appease Quebec sovereignists. Bob Coates, PC member for Cumberland-Colchester, Nova Scotia, was one of them, and he described the legislation as "another sop to the ultranationalists in the province of Quebec." Yet, even he saw the bill primarily as another attempt by the Trudeau government to rid Canada of its history and traditions.[88]

In fact most of the opposition to the demise of "Dominion Day" was not about Quebec but rather focused on the complete disregard for Canada's past in the construction of a new Canadian identity. While maintaining that Canada had been defined by both its British and

French heritage, Quebec Senator Hartland Molson said during the Senate debate that Bill C-201 was "another very small step in the process, which has continued over the last few years, of downgrading tradition and obscuring our heritage."[89] The fleur-de-lis, which traced its origins to the early kings of France, had been proclaimed as the flag and symbol of Quebec, a clear recognition of the province's French heritage. Forsey noted that, while many wanted to ignore the reality of Canada's British heritage, it was, nonetheless, an important part of its past. "A country which assaults its history as this bill does," he said, "impairs its future."[90] Laura Sabia, vice-chair of the Toronto Branch of the Royal Commonwealth Society, agreed, noting that the change was a sad commentary on the poor teaching of history in Canada's schools and universities. We are simply exchanging "our cherished Dominion Day," long a symbol of Canada's maturation as a sovereign nation, for a "bland Canada Day," she suggested, to "placate Quebec and [the] multicultural aspects of our country... We give up our historic traditions and our heritage so easily." She wondered to the committee why Canada was "so insecure, so adolescent and so immature that we cannot take pride in our traditions, our loyalties and nourish them and enrich them. Is it not time that English-speaking Canadians stand up and be counted?"[91] The Monarchist League of Canada, the Baptist Joint Committee on Public Life in Canada, and the National Chapter of the Imperial Order Daughters of the Empire echoed similar sentiments. The *Halifax Chronicle* asked if parliamentarians "so enthusiastically join in ridding us of one of our most precious symbols" because they "know so little of our history and are reluctant to honour our past?"[92]

Despite the opposition to Bill C-201 and the nearly 1,700 submissions to the Senate committee supporting the retention of "Dominion Day," the committee recommended that the legislation be passed into law unchanged. Bowing to the pressure of the Trudeau government, the Senate passed Bill C-201 on 25 October 1982. It received Royal assent two days later. After twenty-three attempts, which first began in 1946, the supporters of "Canada Day" delighted in the removal of what they considered one of the last vestiges of British Canada. Trudeau was among them. When he tabled in Parliament the fourth volume of the Royal Commission on Bilingualism and Biculturalism on 8 October 1971, he said that there could not be one cultural policy for Canadians of British and French origin and another for all others. He lamented the past practice of the federal government's privileging the culture of English-speaking Canadian against all others, and he was pleased with the removal of "Dominion Day" as the official title of Canada's found-ing day. The change finally removed any sense of Canada as a British nation, and it finally gave Canadians, Trudeau believed, the freedom to interpret July 1st "in a deeply personal sense," thus strengthening national unity in the process.[93] The change was also a signal to others that Canada was, finally, an independent, sovereign country.

Conclusion

On 1 July 1983, Canadians celebrated their first official Canada Day, hoping perhaps, as had those who had lobbied to rid the country of the word "dominion" in 1946, that the new designation for Canada's birthday would, indeed, foster a new sense of national identity, greater unity, and greater social cohesion. That year also marked the first time that Trudeau used the official name for Canada's birthday: the official message was titled "The Prime Minister's Canada Day Message"; all previous messages for the occasion were simply titled "July 1 Message to Canadians." In his speech, Trudeau reminded Canadians that 1983 marked the "first" Canada Day.[94] As with the new flag almost two dec-ades earlier, English-speaking Canadians, especially, have embraced Canada Day as they had Dominion Day.[95]

All attempts to strengthen national identity and citizenship, includ-ing the change from "Dominion Day" to "Canada Day," were driven by a desire for political stability. They represent one of the normative anchors that political leaders hope will bind citizens to the common purpose of sustaining a political community. At the time of Confed-eration, there had been no attempt to unite Canadians around a single national loyalty, but Cartier realized that, if Canada were to become a stable nation, it had to embrace a political identity rather than a cultural or ethnic one. The objective then had been to unite an array of commu-nities, the members of which would become Canadians, a single united people under a national government.[96] Trudeau embraced this notion in 1968 and believed that Canada's national identity could be recon-structed to privilege cultural and ethnographic pluralism and foster a reconciliation of Canada's diverse peoples. His identity was based not on ethnic particularisms but on the rights of individuals.[97] Like Cartier, he believed that an identity that recognized and celebrated diversity and pluralism within a rights-based nation might sustain the Canadian political community and avoid the resentment and political splintering that the dual nation model had created. He believed that Canada could

328 Raymond B. Blake and Bailey Antonishyn

build national political solidarity by building a national identity that made space for, and accepted the legitimacy and diversity of, the members of the communities that existed within a bilingual country. This message was at the core of the speeches Trudeau delivered on Canada's national day, as he attempted to convince Canadians of the merits of this approach. National identity, for Trudeau, was based on diversity and was simply a means of legitimizing Canada as a stable, unified, and progressive state. Associated with that paradigm was a constant search for a set of core "national" values to identify the nation and foster social cohesion, thus preventing Canada from becoming a weak and divided plurality of separate and distinct groups. That search left no space for a Dominion Day, which many Canadians –Trudeau included – saw as one of the last remnants of Canada's British and colonial past.

NOTES

1 Peter Waite, *The Confederation Debates in the Province of Canada, 1865* (Toronto: McClelland and Stewart, 1997), 53–62.
2 See Library and Archives Canada (hereafter LAC), Pierre E. Trudeau Fonds, MG26, series 011, vol. 67, file Prime Minister's Speeches, Prime Minister's July 1st Message at Kirkland Lake, 1972.
3 "Canada's Strength Lies in Unity," *Saskatoon Star Phoenix*, 3 July 1973.
4 LAC, Trudeau Fonds, series O11, vol. 67, file Prime Minister's Speeches 1972, 67–4, Notes for Remarks by Prime Minister, Kirkland Lake, 1 July 1972.
5 Roy Romanow, John Whyte, and Howard Leeson, *Canada ... Notwithstanding: The Making of the Constitution, 1976–1982*, 25th anniversary ed. (Toronto: Thomson Carswell, 2007).
6 Quoted in Samuel V. LaSelva, *The Moral Foundations of Canadian Federalism: Paradoxes, Achievements, and Tragedies of Nationhood* (Montreal: McGill-Queen's University Press, 1996), 168.
7 Michael E. Geisler, ed., *National Symbols, Fractured Identities: Contesting the National Narrative* (Hanover, NH: University Press of New England, 2005); Michael E. Geisler, "The Calendar Conundrum: National Days as Unstable Signifiers," in *National Days: Constructing and Mobilising National Identity*, ed. David McCrone and Gayle McPherson (Basingstoke, UK: Palgrave Macmillan, 2009), 10–14.
8 Hans Kohn, *The Idea of Nationalism: A Study in Its Origins and Background* (New York: Collier Books, 1944).

9 Benedict Anderson, *Imagined Communities: Reflections on the Origins and Spread of Nationalism* (London: Verso, 1991).

10 Pierre Nora, *Realms of Memory: Rethinking the French Past*, trans. Arthur Goldhammer, ed. Lawrence D. Kritzman, (New York: Columbia University Press, 1996).

11 Ryan Edwardson, *Canadian Content: Culture and the Quest for Nationhood* (Toronto: University of Toronto Press, 2008).

12 Philip Resnick, *The European Roots of Canadian Identity* (Peterborough, ON: Broadview Press, 2005).

13 Keith Banting, "Social Citizenship and the Multicultural State," in *Citizenship, Diversity, and Pluralism*, ed. Alan C. Cairns et al. (Montreal: McGill-Queen's University Press, 1999); Janine Brodie, "Citizenship and Solidarity: Reflections on the Canadian Way," *Citizenship Studies* 6, no. 4 (2002): 377–94.

14 Will Kymlicka, *Politics in the Vernacular: Nationalism, Multiculturalism, and Citizenship* (Oxford: Oxford University Press, 2001); Charles Taylor, *Reconciling the Solitudes: Essays on Canadian Federalism and Nationalism* (Montreal: McGill-Queen's University Press, 1993); and Michael Ignatieff, *The Rights Revolution* (Toronto: House of Anansi Press, 2000).

15 Phillip Buckner, ed., *Canada and the British Empire* (New York: Oxford University Press, 2008), 7, 18.

16 José E. Igartua, *The Other Quiet Revolution: National Identities in English Canada, 1945–1971* (Vancouver: UBC Press, 2006), 191, 222. Other academics have made similar arguments. See Raymond Breton, "From Ethnic to Civic Nationalism," *Ethnic and Racial Studies* 11, no. 1 (1988): 92–93. Breton argues that the change was a response to "a profound crisis of legitimacy," as Canada's institutions and public symbols failed throughout the 1950s and 1960s to resonate with Canada's increasingly pluralistic society. In Australia, this phenomenon has been called the "process of de-dominionization," or the removal of all evidence that the country was ever a dominion. See Jim Davidson, "Dominionization Revisted," *Australian Journal of Politics and History* 51 (2005): 108–13, and James Curran and Stuart Ward, *The Unknown Nation: Australia after Empire* (Carlton: Melbourne University Press, 2010).

17 Matthew Hayday, "Fireworks, Folk-dancing, and Fostering a National Identity: The Politics of Canada Day," *Canadian Historical Review* 91, no. 2 (June 2010): 287–314.

18 See Geisler, *National Symbols*.

19 LAC, Trudeau Fonds, MG26, series O11, vol. 67, file Prime Minister's Speeches 1972 67–4, Prime Minister's July 1st Message, 1972.

20 Canada, House of Commons, *Debates*, 26 January 1970, 2813.
21 *Saskatoon Star-Phoenix*, 27 June 1968, 13. This is a point that Trudeau made repeatedly early in his tenure as prime minister. See Canada, House of Commons, *Debates*, 18 February 1972, 39.
22 See Pierre Elliott Trudeau, "The Practice and Theory of Federalism," in Pierre Elliott Trudeau, *Federalism and the French Canadians* (Toronto: Macmillan, 1968), 124.
23 On this point, see Kenneth McRoberts, *Misconceiving Canada: The Struggle for National Unity* (Toronto: Oxford University Press, 1997), 55–6.
24 Michael Ignatieff, *Blood and Belonging: Journeys into the New Nationalism* (Toronto: Penguin, 1993), 6.
25 LAC, Trudeau Fonds, MG26, series O11, vol. 63, file Prime Minister's Speeches, 1/7/1969 63–26, Prime Minister's July 1st Message, 1969; "Epistle to Canadians," *Globe and Mail*, 3 July 1969, 6; and *Le Devoir* (Montreal), 2 July 1969, 1–2.
26 "Dominion Day Is No Holiday for Thousands in Ontario," *Globe and Mail*, 30 June 1970, 1; Trudeau Fonds, MG26, series O11, vol. 67, file Prime Minister's Speeches, Prime Minister's July 1st Message, 1972.
27 "Canada Week Gets National Support," *Regina Leader-Post*, 28 June 1971, 14.
28 "PM Sees Canada Coming of Age Now," *Regina Leader-Post*, 30 June 1973, 13.
29 LAC, Trudeau Fonds, MG26, series O11, vol. 67, file Prime Minister's Speeches, Prime Minister's July 1st Message, Toronto, 1972.
30 LAC, Privy Council Office, RG2, series A-5-a, vol. 6338, Cabinet Conclusions, 11 November 1968.
31 "On Our Hundred and Third … er … Day," *Globe and Mail*, 1 July 1970, 6; "Dominion Day not Mentioned in July 1 Text," ibid., 30 June 1971, 4.
32 Canada, House of Commons, *Debates*, 24 October 1969, 35.
33 LAC, Trudeau Fonds, MG 26, Series O14, file Original Speeches, Statements and Messages, Prime Minister's Message, 1 July 1975.
34 Ibid.
35 LAC, Trudeau Fonds, MG26, series O14, vol. 2, Original Speeches, Statements and Messages, 1974, Notes for Prime Minister's Remarks to the Throne Speech Debate, House of Commons, 28 February 1974.
36 Ibid., series O13, vol. 47, file Speeches/Discours, 1 July 1975, Prime Minister's Message, 1 July 1975.
37 Ibid., series O13, vol. 47, file Speeches/Discours, 1 July 1976, Prime Minister's Message, 1 July 1976.
38 Ibid., series O13, vol. 46, file Speeches/Discours, 1 July 1974, Prime Minister's 1974, Prime Minister's Message, 1 July 1974; ibid., series O14,

vol. 1, file Original Speeches, Statements and Messages, Prime Minister's Message, 1 July 1975.

39 Ibid., series O13, vol. 43, file Speech/Discours, 1 July 1970, Prime Minister's Message, 1 July 1970; and ibid., series O11, vol. 65, file Prime Minister's Speeches 1/7/1971 65–29, Message by the Prime Minister, 1 July 1971.

40 See "PM Willing to Share Canada Day Limelight," *Globe and Mail*, 30 June 1977, 9.

41 For a good summary of federal bilingual policy and national unity during the Trudeau period, see, *A National Understanding: The Official Languages of Canada, Statement of the Government of Canada on Official Language Policy* (Ottawa: Minister of Supply and Services, 1977).

42 LAC, Trudeau Fonds, MG26, series O14, vol. 2, file Original Speeches, Statements and Messages, Prime Minister's Speech, 1 July 1977, and Memorandum to the Prime Minister, 28 June 1977.

43 Ibid., series O13. vol. 49, file Speeches/Discours, 1 July 1978, Prime Minister's Message, 1 July 1978.

44 McRoberts, *Misconceiving Canada*, 72.

45 This is discussed in Hayday, "Fireworks, Folk-dancing."

46 Canada, House of Commons, *Debates*, 2 May 1977. Diefenbaker referred to the press statements during the debate.

47 Ibid., 3 June 1977, 6259 and 6264.

48 "Dominion Day," *Winnipeg Free Press*, 3 July 1981, 6.

49 Quoted by Hal Herbert in Canada, House of Commons, *Debates*, 29 June 1981.

50 Stephen Clarkson and Christina McCall, *Trudeau and Our Times*, vol. 1, *The Magnificent Obsession* (Toronto: McClelland and Stewart, 1990), 285.

51 *Regina Leader Post*, 30 June 1980, 12.

52 See David Milne, *Tug of War: Ottawa and the Provinces under Trudeau and Mulroney* (Toronto: Lorimer, 1986), 5.

53 "July 1 Time to Reflect on What We Have: PM," *Globe and Mail*, 1 July 1981, 9; LAC, Trudeau Fonds, MG26, series O14, vol. 6, file Original Speeches, Statements, and Messages, Prime Minister's July 1st Message, 1981.

54 Quoted in "Offshore Ownership Ruling Hinges on 1832 Mandate," *Globe and Mail*, 15 March 1982; Tom Axworthy, "After 1984: A Liberal Revival," *Canadian Forum* (November 1984).

55 Quoted in Eric Hobsbawm and Terrance Ranger, *The Invention of Tradition* (Cambridge: Canto, 1983), 8.

56 Quoted in "Dominion Day," *Globe and Mail*, 1 July 1983, 6.

57 See F.R. Scott, "Political Nationalism and Confederation," *Canadian Journal of Economics and Political Science* 8, no. 3 (August 1942): 386–415.
58 C.P Champion, "A Very British Coup: Canadianism, Quebec and Ethnicity in the Flag Debate, 1964–1965," *Journal of Canadian Studies/Revue d'études canadiennes* 40, no. 3 (2006): 68–99.
59 Canada, House of Commons, *Debates*, Speech from the Throne, 12 September 1968.
60 Canada, House of Commons, *Debates*, 9 October 1970, 31.
61 Quoted in Champion, "A Very British Coup," 70.
62 Canada, House of Commons, Debates, 9 October 1970, 32.
63 LAC, Trudeau Fonds, MG 26, series O7, file 912.01.2 Pers & Conf, 1969–70. "Memorandum for the Prime Minister," 8 September 1969. The memo noted that Trudeau had authorized work to begin immediately to sharply improve the visual aspects of the federal presence everywhere in Canada.
64 Ibid., Cabinet Conclusions, 14 November 1968; Canada, House of Commons, *Debates*, 24 April 1970.
65 Canada, House of Commons, *Debates*, 17 February 1970, 3698–703; 24 April 1970, 6269–78; 12 May 1970, 6872–81.
66 Ibid., 26 June 1970.
67 LAC, Trudeau Fonds, MG 26, series O13, vol. 51, file Speeches/Discours, 1 July 1980, Transcription of the Prime Minister's Speech on the Occasion of the Proclamation of Canada's National Anthem, 1 July 1980.
68 Canada, House of Commons, *Debates*, 12 March 1981 and 26 June 1981, 10988.
69 Ibid., 29 June 1981, 11036–68; "Le dominion," *Winnipeg Free Press*, 30 June 1981, 4.
70 *Vancouver Sun*, 30 June 1981; "Latest Liberal Pitch for 'Canada Day' Turned Back by PCs," *Globe and Mail*, 30 June 1981.
71 *Halifax Chronicle*, 19 July 1982.
72 See "The Man Who Gave us Canada Day," *Globe and Mail*, 20 August 2003, for Herbert's obituary. When Herbert introduced his bill for the name change in 1980, he said that the pending referendum in Quebec should have been sufficient to convince all Canadians that they needed one particular day as Canada Day, when all citizens should "make a special and public commitment to Canada." House of Commons, *Debates*, 6 May 1980, 764–70.
73 Correspondence with Senator Serge Joyal, 4 March 2010.
74 LAC, Carl Goldenberg Fonds, MG 32, C55, vol. 1, file Canada Day, Submission to Senate Committee from Donald W. Munro, 15 September 1982.

75 Correspondence with Senator Serge Joyal, 4 March 2010.
76 Canada, House of Commons, *Debates*, 17 February 1970, 3699.
77 Ibid., 9 July 1982, 19201–2.
78 "Sleight of Hand Deal Killed Dominion Day," *Vancouver Sun*, 13 July 1982.
79 "Canada Day anti-Biblical, anti-Anglo Saxon, MP Says," *Winnipeg Free Press*, 13 July 1982, 13.
80 "There'll Be Hell to Pay," *Globe and Mail*, 10 July 1982, 6.
81 "Dominion Day Now Canada Day," *Winnipeg Free Press*, 16 July 1982, 6.
82 Canada, Senate, *Debates*, 3 August 1982, 4741–51 and 4763–7.
83 LAC, Carl Goldenberg Fonds, MG 32, vol. 1, file Canada Day, Vladimir Bubrin to Senator Joan Neiman, 20 September 1982, and Canada, *Proceedings of the Standing Committee on Legal and Constitutional Affairs*, no. 26, 13 October 1982.
84 LAC, Carl Goldenberg Fonds, MG 32, vol. 1, file Canada Day, Canada, *Proceedings of the Standing Committee on Legal and Constitutional Affairs*, no. 26, 13 October 1982. The results of the survey are included in the file.
85 "Senate Plans Public Hearings on Dominion Day Legislation," *Globe and Mail*, 6 August 1982, 8.
86 Canada, House of Commons, *Debates*, 8 October 1971, 8545–6.
87 See *Victoria Times-Colonist*, 29 August 1982.
88 "Truly Significant Part of Symbolism Will Be Erased," *Halifax Chronicle*, 19 July 1982, 7.
89 Quoted in "The Death of Dominion Day," *Ottawa Citizen*, 1 September 2006; LAC, Carl Goldenberg Fonds, MG 32, vol. 1, file Canada Day Bill C-201, Eugene Forsey submission to Senate Committee; LAC, MG 32 C55, vol. 1, file Canada Day.
90 "Dominion Day Becomes Canada Day," CBC Digital Archives, 16 October 1982, http://www.cbc.ca/player/play/1539501448
91 Canada, *Proceedings of the Standing Committee on Legal and Constitutional Affairs*, no. 26, 13 October 1982, 27–8; *Globe and Mail*, 14 October 1982, 14.
92 LAC, Carl Goldenberg Fonds, MG 32, vol. 1, file Canada Day, "A Brief Submitted to the Senate Committee on Legal and Constitutional Affairs by the Monarchist League of Canada," 17 September 1982; "Coates Wants Senate to Block Canada Day Bill," *Halifax Chronicle*, 19 July 1982, 5.
93 Canada, House of Commons, *Debates*, 8 October 1971, 8545–46.
94 LAC, Trudeau Fonds, MG 26, series O14, vol. 7, file Original Speeches Statements and Message, 1 July 1983 – Canada Day, Prime Minister's Canada Day Message, 1 July 1983.
95 Chantal Hébert, "Quebecers Have Become More Detached than Ever," *Toronto Star*, 19 January 2011. In a recent survey, 24% of francophone

Quebeckers expressed a strong attachment to Canada; only 18% of those
between the ages of 18–24 reported strong attachment, http://www.
thestar.com/opinion/columnists/2011/01/19/hbert_quebecers_have_
become_more_detached_than_ever.html.

96 Robert C. Vipond, *Liberty and Community: Canadian Federalism and the
Failure of the Constitution* (Albany: State University of New York Press,
1991), 4.

97 This history is explored in David Robertson Cameron, "An Evolutionary
Story," in Janice Gross Stein et al., *Uneasy Partners: Multiculturalism and
Rights in Canada* (Waterloo, ON: Wilfrid Laurier University Press, 2007),
71–94.

13 The Redundant "Dominion": Refitting the National Fabric at Empire's End

STUART WARD

In April 1946, a private member's bill was passed in the Canadian House of Commons to change the name of the 1 July national holiday from Dominion Day to Canada Day. Prime Minister Mackenzie King had given the bill his tacit support, noting with satisfaction in his diary that the bill formed "part of what has been achieved in rounding out Canada in the years of my administration."[1] His choice of metaphor was deliberately subtle. "Rounding out" referred, not to a radical program of national renewal, brazenly repudiating the colonial connotations of "dominion status." Rather, it conveyed a more delicate process of redefining Canada's ties to Britain and the Commonwealth in an emergent post-imperial world. The delicacy lay in finding an appropriate rhetorical and symbolic balance between national distinction and the British fraternity to which many English-speaking Canadians remained deeply attached. On this issue, King misjudged the temper of opinion. The proposal to drop "Dominion" prompted a spontaneous chorus of contempt from the English-language press, interpreting the move as a Quebec-inspired assault on Canada's British heritage.[2] Scorn was abundantly poured on the "ultra-nationalists" for "confusing love of Canada with dislike of everything British."[3] Taken aback by the furore, Mackenzie King allowed the bill to be quashed in the Senate. As Raymond Blake and Bailey Antonishyn have shown in the previous chapter, it would take more than thirty-five years, and twenty subsequent attempts, before "Dominion" would receive its quietus with the formal name change of October 1982.[4]

The Dominion Day uproar was an early harbinger of the often bitter debates that would accompany the overhaul of Canadian civic culture from the 1940s to the 1980s. It established a pattern that would be repeated in response to reforms to Canadian citizenship, the appointment of a Canadian-born governor general, the replacement of the Red Ensign with the Maple Leaf flag, and the adoption of "O Canada" as the national anthem. What was at stake was not merely the cherished symbolism of Canada's ties to Britain, but something that struck deeper for those who could not separate their idea of Canada from its loyalist beginnings. The *Globe and Mail* captured the dilemma in the heat of the 1946 Dominion Day debate: "A Nation without a past is an anomaly. It is as imperfect an entity as a person who has lost his memory. To attempt a deliberate erasure of historical fact is to injure, not augment, national consciousness." The *Hamilton Spectator* protested along similar lines, decrying the substitution of "Dominion" for "a term without meaning, without tradition or force," while the *Vancouver Sun* voiced astonishment that "a great and historic designation is close to oblivion."[5] The *Family Herald* turned its ire on the advocates of a name change, whose "inferiority complex is so deep that they are afraid of their own history."[6] For these vocal opponents, the issue went far beyond the constitutional niceties of Canada's Commonwealth ties, stoking deeper anxieties about the obliteration of the nation itself. Nearly twenty years later, John Diefenbaker would articulate the same fears about the removal of the Union Jack from the national flag:

> In what way does the design now proposed embody our history? ... There is nothing in this design for memorial, sorrow or old renown. There is nothing for those who with sword and crucifix went into the wilderness where they left their names and often their bones as sacred heritage for us all... Are we as Canadians to have a flag which treats our memories, our past sacrifices, all the milestones of greatness as irrelevancies? ... Is it beyond the realm of possibility that, should this new design become our flag in a few months hence, Canadians as a whole will feel their past has been forgotten?[7]

The spectre haunting all of these reactions was erasure – a foreboding sense that the people were being corralled into a debilitating collective amnesia. This was the other side of the coin of the "New Nationalism" of the Pearson–Trudeau era, the fraught process of "de-dominionziation."[8]

This chapter sets out to place the transition from Dominion Day to Canada Day in the context of global changes to the civic fabric of former British "dominions" in the end-of-empire era. Mathew Hayday's work has convincingly shown how Dominion Day was essentially co-opted by the Canadian government in the late 1950s and subjected to a process of official tinkering that continues to this day. He quotes one member of the bureaucratic team charged with the task of initiating government-sponsored celebrations of Dominion Day in 1958 who claimed that government ceremonies to celebrate national days were "unusual in British countries. Some people regard them as an evidence of national immaturity. . . Annual government ceremonies are contrary to Canadian and Commonwealth tradition."[9] This may have been true for the years prior to the 1950s. But even the most casual glance at wider Commonwealth practice from the 1950s onwards suggests the very opposite – that this was a time of rapidly expanding government intervention and innovation in the politics of national commemoration. Canada was by no means alone in the search for new commemorative practices for a national holiday languishing in outmoded British moorings. Three intriguing parallels in other Commonwealth realms will be considered here: the attempt to elevate Australia Day to the status of a "truly national" day; the official upgrade of Waitangi Day to a nation-wide holiday in New Zealand; and the (short-lived) search for a unifying alternative to the Queen's Birthday in the white rebel enclave of Rhodesia in the 1960s and 1970s. Although played out in profoundly divergent political contexts, these experiences clearly echoed the recurring difficulties in Canada in attuning imperial rites to the needs of a post-imperial world.

In this chapter, two broad areas of convergence will be identified. First, the spur to civic renewal was driven, not by any particularly coherent or consensual ideas about what the emergent nation-in-waiting should be, but by shared perceptions of a hackneyed civic cultural tradition in need of re-invention in the wake of empire. Second, official attempts to respond to these imperatives met deep pockets of resistance from conservative elements within the community, producing a climate of contestation and general rancour. The fault lines that emerged fuelled an enduring sense of doubt and discord about the precise meaning and purpose to be attributed to national holidays, which in turn generated never-ending debates about the appropriate rituals of national observance. It remains doubtful whether these attempts to engineer a new post-imperial patriotism, shorn of its British or loyalist dimensions, struck any kind of chord with its popular constituency. By the 1970s, evidence abounds of a pervasive popular cynicism when it came to officially orchestrated programs of ritualized civic pride and virtue.

I will touch only briefly on Canadian experience by way of counter-point, leaving the intricacies of the annual Dominion Day celebration in Canada to the preceding chapters. Instead my aim is to place the over-riding themes of this volume in their wider transnational context, fore-grounding the shared tensions and contradictions that shaped events and attitudes across all of the imperial dominions.

Festivals "in Search of a Meaning": The Case for Civic Renewal

The 26th of January, which marks the landing of the First Fleet of British ships in New South Wales in 1788, has been commemorated in differ-ent eras and under diverse names in various places across Australia since the early nineteenth century. But it was not until 1935 when all states and territories agreed to hold a long weekend under the ban-ner of Australia Day. It was a further decade before, in 1946, the first Australia Day Committees, consisting of volunteers from a variety of community organizations, were formed in the state capitals. To the extent that the day had acquired any consistent or shared connotations, it was regarded as much as an imperial as a national occasion. In the words of one 1938 pageant, the anniversary of the landing of the First Fleet of convicts represented the planting of a "fresh sprig of empire" in a strange new land. Responsibility for commemorating the event lay overwhelmingly with volunteer organizations in the states, with no coordination at the national level whatsoever. For Western Australia (founded decades after the first settlement of New South Wales) and South Australia (colonized by free settlers with no "convict stain") the relevance of 26 January seemed particularly remote. Meanwhile government agencies tended to avoid any direct involvement in the scarcely visible popular observance of Australia Day, with the excep-tion of the New South Wales sesquicentenary in 1938. Both the Chifley and Menzies governments in the 1940s and 1950s consistently refused requests for federal financial support for the activities of the Australia Day committees, confident that they risked no public backlash on the issue.[10]

In New Zealand, 6 February had been marked each year as Wait-angi Day since the early 1930s, but as with Australia Day it had never acquired the status of a national holiday. The anniversary of the signing of the Treaty of Waitangi between the British government and a coali-tion of Maori peoples in the Bay of Islands had become a prominent event on the calendar of the Northland region, but it had never really caught on in other parts of the country where its relevance seemed less immediate. This was borne out by attempts in the early 1960s to enhance the status of Waitangi Day as a national holiday. The Waitangi Day Act of 1960, one of the last initiatives of Walter Nash's Labour government, sought to substitute a single national holiday for the holidays marking various provincial anniversaries. But in order not to offend provincial sensibilities (or add an additional day off to the working calendar), Nash left it to each province to decide whether to make the switch or not. In the event, only Northland opted to replace Auckland Anniversary Day with Waitangi Day, while the rest of the country continued to honour the provincial holidays. As the Christchurch *Press* commented, the idea of "upsetting local arrangements" to mark the Treaty of Waitangi was "greeted with a national yawn."[11]

The case of the rebel Rhodesian state that illegally declared independence from Britain under Ian Smith in November 1965 is in many ways sui generis – and certainly a far cry from the issues debated in Australia, New Zealand, and Canada in these years. Rhodesia never formally acquired dominion status, despite long-standing aspirations and quasi-dominion entitlements at Commonwealth prime ministers' meetings and other such occasions. But the business of wrenching Rhodesia *symbolically* from its imperial foundations – of refashioning civic rites and rituals in a post-British guise – raised much the same dilemmas. The story of the Rhodesian Front's Unilateral Declaration of Independence (UDI) has been recounted many times and need not delay us here; suffice it to say that growing fears of the encroaching "winds of change" of African nationalism predisposed white Rhodesians to embrace their British heritage with a determination and zeal that was unmatched virtually anywhere else in the imperial world, including Britain.[12] In terms of identity politics, the moment of the UDI was counterintuitive, breaking faith with the very idea that gave depth and substance to being Rhodesian. Initially, Smith persisted in proclaiming his loyalty to the Sovereign and the Queen's Birthday continued to be the pre-eminent date on the commemorative calendar in the early years of the rebellion.[13] Thus, in the immediate post-UDI period, the question of refitting the symbolic fabric of the Rhodesian state did not arise. It was only with the British government's repeated refusal to support their "kith and kin" that the question of finding alternative, republican symbols of white Rhodesia arose.

At the same time that this drama was playing out in an era of increasing African nationalism, more subtle demands were being placed on the loyal British rites and rituals that had prevailed in Australasia for generations. The 1960s were generally unkind to the loyalist strain in the commemorative calendar. It was in this decade that Empire Day (24 May) was finally laid to rest, having survived the 1950s in stubborn defiance of an ever-declining empire. As in Canada, Empire Day in Australia and New Zealand had been observed from the early years of the twentieth century with greater fervour than in Britain itself, with the focus of activity primarily in the schools.[14] In the years after the Second World War, however, the language of imperialism acquired increasingly pejorative connotations. Initially, in 1958, the day was renamed Commonwealth Day, in an effort to dispel the increasingly dubious associations with "empire" – albeit with some residual controversy over whether it ought properly to be termed *British* Commonwealth Day.[15] When this failed to strike a popular chord, the occasion became increasingly known in Australia as "cracker night," with little if any reference to its imperial origins.[16] Finally in 1965, the British government, recognizing the anachronism, deftly moved the official date of Commonwealth Day to coincide with the Queen's birthday celebrations in early June, thereby quietly (and deliberately) ushering the occasion into oblivion.

Anzac Day, a day of remembrance in both Australia and New Zealand, also became increasingly marginalized in these years, as the younger generation felt increasingly alienated by the exclusiveness and perceived militarism of the occasion. The failed invasion of the Australian and New Zealand Army Corps at Gallipoli on 25 April 1915 had long provided a dual civic function – as a more local and hence intimate supplement to Remembrance Day but also, and more significantly, as a foundational myth of nationhood. In this latter sense, the Australian and New Zealand display of loyalty and self-sacrifice on the Gallipoli battlefields was said to have elevated these dominions to the status of fully fledged nations worthy of the British tradition from which they were struck. The notion of "Better Britons" was a recurring motif in Australian and New Zealand political culture from the late nineteenth century down to the Second World War and beyond,[17] but it became increasingly difficult to sustain in an era of global decolonization. This was reinforced by reports of declining attendances at Anzac Day marches throughout the 1960s, with headlines such as "Marchers Outnumber Spectators – Anzac Day Crowd Stays at Home"; "It Just Didn't Seem to Be Anzac Day";[18] "Thinner Crowds as Fewer Veterans Marched";[19] and "Anzac March May Be on the Way Out."[20] At a time of growing popular unrest over involvement in Vietnam, and the unfashionable connotations of blind loyalty that became associated with Gallipoli, the decline and even the ultimate disappearance of Anzac Day were frequently mooted.[21] Certainly there were few who predicted the spectacular resurgence of the 25 April anniversary in the 1990s.

The attendant void in the commemorative calendar prompted widespread calls for renewal, looking beyond the established rituals of Empire Day and Anzac Day and inaugurating instead a "truly national" holiday. Significantly, the case for innovation rested, not on any clear-sighted vision of the form such an occasion might take, but more on the perceived shortcomings of the existing state of affairs. Thus in 1959 the *Sydney Morning Herald* bemoaned the lack of progress in elevating the status of Australia Day, concluding that "pageantry and parades and orations are but the outward show; the spirit to give them real meaning still seems to be lacking."[22] The following year, the Melbourne *Age* lamented that "for all the past efforts of the Australia Day Council, there will be neither the solemn appraisal nor the joy which the occasion deserves."[23] Four years later, the verdict was the same: "Today is a public holiday to celebrate Australia Day … [It] produces little evidence of having much real meaning for most people."[24]

Similarly in New Zealand, the arguments for upgrading Waitangi Day to become New Zealand Day were informed by perceptions of what a national day *shouldn't be*, rather than what it might become. One might be forgiven for assuming that the process that enshrined 6 February as a national holiday in 1974 reflected a greater public awareness of issues relating to indigenous rights, and the need to address the legacies of colonization. And there can be no doubt that the 1960s and 1970s witnessed far greater attention to Maori grievances, heavily influenced by the civil rights movement in the United States and Australia, and the rapid processes of decolonization in Africa. But a closer examination of the priorities and motives of the Kirk Labour government that came to office in November 1972 indicates that a focus on Maori issues was by no means the decisive factor in the establishment of New Zealand Day. On the contrary, the holiday was originally conceived as the very opposite; an event that might distract attention from internal distinctions and divisions.

While it is true that Kirk's minister for Maori affairs, Matiu Rata, played a leading hand in placing the New Zealand Day proposal on the Labour Party's 1972 election manifesto, his aims to promote better race relations were quickly superseded by the new nationalist enthusiasms of the prime minister and by the minister for internal affairs, Henry May. In introducing the New Zealand Day Bill to Parliament in August 1973, May devoted almost the entirety of his speech to the theme that "all nations feel a need to express their independence and nationhood, and the event which Waitangi Day commemorates is very clearly connected with New Zealand's first step towards nationhood." The bill, he declared, reflected "the growing awareness among New Zealanders of the need to have a national day that we can observe in an appropriate manner." He underlined that, in changing the name from "Waitangi Day," the government was seeking to ensure that the message of maturity, independence, and national unity was not lost in the detail of the Treaty of Waitangi. He freely conceded the government's concerns that "keeping the name Waitangi Day could have led to the day being associated much more with one particular event."[25] Opposition spokesman (and former internal affairs minister) Allan Highet was in full agreement: "I prefer to call our national day New Zealand Day because, unfortunately, Waitangi Day has over recent years become an occasion for airing Maori discontents, and therefore I think ... it is far better we should call it New Zealand Day and try to come together and live as one people."[26]

Similar arguments arose in the deliberations of the organizing committee for the inaugural New Zealand Day celebrations. The prime minister had given verbal instructions that "the celebrations should desirably differ from those marking Waitangi Day." The emphasis should be placed on "New Zealand as one country of many people," drawing in the wider participation of the many nationalities that made up contemporary New Zealand. The committee discussed various ways in which this could be achieved – recruiting the many nationalities represented to participate in a New Zealand Day pageant in Auckland, featuring the varieties of national dress and national flags. The committee chair, A.J. Faulkner, fully supported Kirk's "multicultural" theme and emphasized that New Zealand Day "was really the total concept, not just Maori and British Pakeha."[27] Playing down the imperial dimensions of New Zealand's past, therefore, also meant a watering down of the Maori dimensions of Waitangi.

The case for civic renewal in white Rhodesia, which emerged towards the end of the 1960s, was similarly linked to a perceived need to make a break with the past. It was perhaps only a matter of time before the anomalies inherent in a "loyal rebellion" were bound to emerge, and it was the occasion of the Queen's Birthday in June 1966 that first brought them to light. The first Saturday in June had long been marked by a public holiday, but divisions emerged over precisely where and how the queen's subjects should register their fealty to the sovereign in an era of open defiance of the British government. The governor of Rhodesia, Sir Humphrey Gibbs (an English-born Rhodesian farmer), continued to occupy Government House in Salisbury (at the express request of the queen on the advice of the Wilson government) in the hope that he might play a constructive role in a negotiated settlement. But his function as head of state had been entirely usurped by Sir Clifford Dupont – himself a former member of Ian Smith's Rhodesian Front cabinet – now elevated to a higher station by the exigencies of UDI. Smith had initially approached Buckingham Palace with a request that Dupont be styled governor general. When this request was (inevitably) rebuffed, he was hastily adorned with the unpromising title of "officer administering the government." The title in itself evoked precisely the no man's land the Rhodesians had sallied into – too loyal to embrace Republican conventions, but beyond the pale of the royal blessing.

This coexistence of two nominal heads of state in Salisbury's sedate, country-town setting was one of the more incongruous aspects of the early UDI era, reaching the peak of absurdity at the annual duel for the hearts and minds of loyal Rhodesians on the official Queen's birthday. Each year, the two rival figureheads opened the gates of their official residences to welcome Her Majesty's devoted subjects to sign their respective visitors' books, staging impromptu tea parties to mingle among the faithful. And each naturally sought to make political capital out of the crowds thronging in their gardens. As Dupont recalled: "Nearly a thousand invitations were issued and well over seven hundred people attended. By 11.30, when the reception started, guests were still queuing down the entire length of the drive and for about two hundred metres along the road outside the grounds."[28] Both sides had a vested interest in massaging the figures, but Gibbs seems to have had a clear crowd advantage.[29] The diary of Gibbs's comptroller, John Pestell, underlines the political messages that were implicit in attendance at one or the other event: "A beautiful sunny day, and some 2100 people signed the book and there were letters with 600 signatures... There is some political significance in this of course, as only people who are loyal to Her Majesty and want a settlement would sign the book."[30] Whereas Dupont's Queen's Birthday celebration was understood as a manifestation of "widespread distrust of the British Government," the Gibbs tea party became a symbol of popular desire for a settlement with Harold Wilson. Some individuals contrived a visit to *both* events (the distance could be walked in fifteen minutes) much to the chagrin of the governor. Pestell's diary indicates that Gibbs kept close tabs on "waverers," voicing mounting concern at the annual defections to the Dupont party.[31]

This annual charade might have continued indefinitely were it not for developments in 1968 that altered the situation dramatically. In early March of that year, the Rhodesian high court heard an appeal from three African defendants who in 1964 had been sentenced to hang. Capital punishment had been abolished in Britain in 1965 but was still a mandatory sentence in Rhodesia for certain categories of murder. What distinguished this 1968 case was the eleventh-hour intervention of Queen Elizabeth herself who, on the advice of her UK ministers, issued a royal pardon to the three offenders. The move was a deliberate ploy to embarrass Smith and test his government's royalist rhetoric; but it also raised the legal question of whether the Rhodesian courts were in any way bound by Her Majesty's pleasure. The judges found that the queen's pardon could be legally binding only if given on the advice of her Rhodesian ministers, and the defendants were promptly despatched to the gallows in a move that shocked world opinion. It also had the effect of focusing the minds of Dupont, Smith, and the Rhodesian cabinet on the efficacy of governing in Her Majesty's name. Dupont would later confide to a journalist that the move to inaugurate a Rhodesian republic was effectively prompted by the "hanging case" of 1968, and Smith himself went on television to explain the complexities of the case, voicing for the first time the possibility of a change to a republican constitution.

Within weeks, the effects of these dramatic events were being subtly registered. Dupont's "speech from the throne" to officially open Parliament in May was edited to remove the words "in Her Majesty's name."[32] In April, the Queen's Birthday was officially defrocked as a public holiday; ostensibly because allowing the nation "to relax in the enjoyment of a public holiday ... would be quite inappropriate while this country is involved with terrorists on our northern frontier and member of our Security Forces are risking life and limb."[33] Thus it was officially announced that it would be "better for Rhodesians to devote this day, while Britain and other Commonwealth countries celebrate the official birthday of our Queen with colourful ceremonies, festivities or a holiday, to redoubling their efforts to consolidate Rhodesia in its place among nations."[34] By the end of the year, a new Rhodesian flag had been raised on the anniversary of the UDI to replace the Union Jack, and in June 1969 a whites-only referendum overwhelmingly voted for the inauguration of a Rhodesian republic. Gibbs was duly ousted from Government House and Dupont installed as the first president of Rhodesia. It remained only to enshrine a new national holiday and national anthem to complete the break with Britain.

While it is easy to point to the many striking differences between Australia, New Zealand, and Rhodesia in the circumstances surrounding these changes to the trappings of nationhood, there remains a common denominator in the creeping obsolescence of imperial observance. This not only accounts for the broad similarities in the timing of these deliberations but also underlines the shared dilemmas about relinquishing a long-nurtured narrative. As in Rhodesia, to the extent that Australians and New Zealanders felt the need for a more elaborate and meaningful commemorative tradition, it was invariably for the sake of leaving the past behind. Thus the imperative of stepping out of the shadow of empire and Britishness loomed particularly large, as in the plea of one leading newspaper for a "new identikit for an Australian" on Australia Day 1969:

> My generation ... finds it difficult to realise that economic security, the British Empire, white Australia, and European colonialism are no longer the ground over which rival armies will clash... What is needed is a myth more in line with present-day realities. A myth that will recognise the changed power patterns abroad and the social and industrial revolution at home.[35]

An editorial in the *Age* concurred – Australia Day remained "a festival in search of a meaning," and this served "only to demonstrate our uncertainty as to what we stand for and where we are going." This uncertainty, it was argued, had not mattered in the past, due to the protective umbrella of empire but, with the dismantling of Britain's military bases on the Malayan peninsular and the escalating conflict in Vietnam, Australia was confronted with a transformed geo-political outlook: "Suddenly we are confronted with a need to define an independent role for ourselves in the troubled area to our north."[36] It was as much the external pressure of a world "which is changing faster than most of us had dreamed possible" than any internal social dynamics that forced Australians to "Wake up ... [and] take a look at ourselves, at where we have been and where we are going."[37]

"Imaginative Pageantry or Tasteless Vulgarity?"
Devising Alternatives

By the early 1970s, a broad consensus had been reached in Australia, New Zealand, and Rhodesia that the traditional totems of civic observance on national holidays were in need of a major overhaul. But this in itself did not permit easy or readymade solutions that would strike a spontaneous chord with the general public. Sydney's mayor, Emmett McDermott, conceded as much in his feeble appeal to a Martin Place crowd on Australia Day 1971: "If the present function does not suit the needs of our times, would you please let us know what you suggest?"[38]

The election of the Whitlam Labor government in 1972 brought a more confident note to the demand for changes to the national civic fabric. The new prime minister chose Australia Day 1973 as the occasion to announce his national anthem competition, in a move that signalled the first concerted federal initiative to invest Australia Day with the significance and appeal that it was generally deemed to be lacking. Indeed within days of this announcement, Whitlam's flamboyant immigration minister, Al Grassby, launched a major public relations offensive to shore up the flagging patriotism of the Australian people. Borrowing freely from the language of Labor's election victory, he was reported as saying: "It is time to encourage a new awareness in our national heritage and to involve the apathetic suburban Australian in a recapturing of the spirit of national independence which flowed at the turn of the century." He added that Australia was "insulted rather than exulted" by the lack of observance of Australia Day, and announced his determination to explore new avenues for celebrating the nation.[39] The clear implication of his rhetoric was that he was starting from scratch, and that, fundamentally, was the problem.

Grassby's grand design was to make Canberra the focal point of a "truly national" occasion. He announced an ambitious scheme to stage an annual "national pageant" in the capital, enlisting the combined efforts of "artists, poets, trade-unionists, industry, Government and the Armed Forces." His reference to "poets," however, was widely misquoted as "pets," prompting the *Sydney Morning Herald*'s scathing judgment that Grassby "would need considerable skill to disentangle the Afghan hounds from the Siamese cats, the galahs from the goldfish and the blue-tongued lizards from the budgerigars. The occasion, in fact, might well be more of a shambles than a pageant. No; let the pets stay at home, as the vast majority of Australians do on Australia

Day."[40] The pageantry of nationalism seemed somehow old-fashioned and inappropriate for a newly emergent Australia, stripped of its British and imperial origins. By Australia Day the following year, Grassby had failed to come up with a single new commemorative innovation. His public incantations ran aground on the now familiar problems that dogged Australia Day – low levels of public enthusiasm and a shortage of ideas for appropriate commemoration. Added to this was the burgeoning era of indigenous rights, which made the anniversary of colonization a decidedly awkward historical symbol from which to construct a national-cultural renaissance.

Similarly across the Tasman Sea, the public row that emerged over New Zealand Day became bound up in the contested meanings of colonization for an indigenous community that had become increasingly outspoken in its demands for reform. Somewhat ironically, the implementation of the new holiday was carried out in such a way as to invite the very social tensions and divisions it was designed to transcend. New Zealand Day became caught up in widespread controversy over the date, the name, and the commemorative practices designed to mark the occasion. This exposed the government to several problems that were typical of the post-imperial dilemmas encountered elsewhere. First, imperial memories of the meaning of Waitangi could not be erased overnight. Organizations like the Maori Women's Welfare League lobbied continuously for the retention of the original label, protesting that "for over one hundred years it has been known as 'Waitangi Day' and to give a Pakeha name at this stage, to a day which is for both Maori and Pakeha, causes concern to the minority group who needs to identify themselves to this particular day."[41] And it was not only Maori who felt that something had gone missing in the name change. The Auckland Historical Society lobbied the minister for a reversion to the original, arguing that "the former name has some significance and interest, referring to the picturesque occasion of the signing of the Treaty by which New Zealand became British."[42] Even Prime Minister Kirk, when pressed on the subject, conceded that "in my heart I will probably still call it Waitangi Day."[43] The Wellington branch of the New Zealand Labour Party offered a novel solution to the naming problem in February 1974, proposing that the relevant legislation should be amended to include the words: "the 6th day of February each year shall continue to be known as Waitangi Day and shall henceforth be New Zealand Day." The formulation was deliberately vague and inconclusive, and merely underlined the intractability of the dilemma. As the branch secretary, David Walker, explained to the minister for Maori affairs: "Those who wanted to refer to the day as Waitangi Day would not be officially wrong, while those who followed the more general usage of New Zealand Day would also be officially correct."[44] Needless to say, this proposal hardly served to clarify matters and was politely ignored.

Others felt that the problem was not so much the use of the name New Zealand Day, as the date that had been chosen to celebrate it. Newspaper editorial opinion reveals a stark regional divide, with Northland endorsing the choice of 6 February to the hilt, and enthusiasm waning steadily southwards. South Island newspapers seemed particularly puzzled by the "nationalisation" of Waitangi Day. In Christchurch, the *Press* argued that at least two other dates had claims as valid – Anzac Day and Dominion Day (26 September). While the former was already a holiday, the latter seemed to hold real potential. "If a new national holiday – a 'New Zealand Day' – must be found, the occasion in 1907 when New Zealand received the title of 'Dominion' might have the best claim of all. By that time New Zealand was a country with a rugged sense of individuality, well aware of its separateness from Britain."[45] Here we see a direct parallel with the politicization of the redundant "Dominion" in Canada, but with the exact opposite implications. Whereas "Dominion" was widely perceived by Canadian Liberals to suggest subordination to Britain, in New Zealand there term was seen to hold the key to celebrating a distinctive national identity – far more so than the ambiguous resonances of Waitangi Day.

The lack of consensus about the date was compounded by a more fundamental problem faced by Labour in breathing life into the occasion – finding a coherent set of meanings for a "new" New Zealand nationalism around which the annual festivities might be constructed. The inaugural New Zealand Day pageant, performed in the presence of Her Majesty the Queen at Waitangi in February 1974 and featuring a heady mixture of song, ceremony, cabaret, sketch comedy, Maori ritual, and multicultural spectacle, received a mixed reaction from a record television-viewing audience. The *New Zealand Herald* summed up the diversity of opinion in a single headline: "Imaginative Pageantry or Tasteless Vulgarity?"[46] Either way, it was clear that nobody had the stomach to see the performance repeated annually. Thereafter, the government made it clear that it would not take the lead in staging the event and that it would rely on community leaders to come up with appropriate forms of commemorative practice. As Henry May put it in a press release, "Each town in New Zealand has its own history and its own present day composition which makes it unique. This diversity forms a colourful patchwork of both the Nation's history and of its present identity. It is appropriate that these particular features of any area be commemorated."[47] This was an extraordinary admission of creative and imaginative bankruptcy. By devolving responsibility for commemorative innovation to the "colourful patchwork" of regional diversity, the government undermined one of its key arguments in creating New Zealand Day in the first place – the need for a single occasion that would emphasize the burgeoning spirit of New Zealanders as "one people." New Zealanders had long enjoyed a holiday for every region. What purpose, then, would be served by a single national holiday with a regional emphasis?

Not surprisingly, the regions failed to respond to May's challenge, and New Zealand Day 1975 proved to be a phenomenal fizzer. Editorials around the country (with the exception of Northland) proclaimed the day a singular non-event, with headlines such as "Do-it-yourself New Zealand Day," "Just Another Day," "Another Holiday," and "Just Another Day Off."[48] If the Kirk Government had promoted New Zealand Day to help fill the post-imperial void, in the final analysis they merely succeeded in accentuating it.

In the event, the New Zealand Day initiative was partially revoked by the conservatives when they were returned to power in 1975. The precise reasons for this remain obscure but, on New Zealand Day 1976, Prime Minister Robert Muldoon announced that henceforth the occasion would be referred to by its original name, Waitangi Day. He stopped short, however, of revoking the nationwide holiday. Apart from some muffled cries of complaint in the *New Zealand Herald* ("Is this nationhood?"[49]) there were few who identified any great national setback in these measures. On the whole there seemed general agreement with the verdict of the *Oamaru Mail* that "efforts to make it a day of national significance and a rallying point for nationhood appear to have failed."[50] And Maori community leaders were invariably gratified that the real significance of the occasion would no longer be airbrushed for the sake of some nebulous national spirit.

Meanwhile in Rhodesia, the question of finding a serviceable replacement for the Queen's Birthday on the commemorative calendar was never properly resolved – not for the want of an alternative but rather the jostling for attention of too many contenders. Rhodes Day (Cecil Rhodes's birthday) and Founders' Day (celebrated, with

Rhodes Day, over a four-day weekend in July) had been observed from the earliest years of the colony but carried few resonances for a people turning their back on their British colonial origins. Pioneers' Day (established in the 1920s) commemorated the arrival of Pioneer Column at Forth Salisbury on 12 September 1890 and was similarly steeped in imperial imagery and rhetoric. These public holidays had been more recently joined by Independence Day (the anniversary of the UDI, on 11 November) and would later be augmented by Republic Day (honouring the declaration of a republic in March 1970 but celebrated in October to coincide with the school spring break). The Rhodesian external affairs minister, Angus Graham, raised the issue in cabinet in August 1967:

> The national day of most countries is celebrated on a date commemorating a significant occasion in the history of that country. In many sophisticated countries this date commemorates an important change in political status... Until recently pride of place has been given within Rhodesia to Pioneer Day, 12th September. The assumption of democratic rights on 11th November, 1965, was a decision of the utmost significance for Rhodesia... As it seems likely that the evaluation of Rhodesia and Rhodesians by others will be conditioned by our own evaluation of ourselves, it is important now that we determine for ourselves which date we regard as our National Day.[51]

Graham's preference was that 11 November be elevated to pre-eminence on the Rhodesian calendar. But, as in Australia and New Zealand, the problem of devising appropriate commemorative practices for these new departures was by no means straightforward. The official military parade to mark the Independence Day celebrations was abolished in 1971 because "the annual staging of such an event tended to distract from its significance."[52] But in reality the ritualized display of military hardware had evidently failed to connect with popular feeling. Indeed, the spontaneous public observance of time-honoured ritual was not something that could easily be conjured out of new-fangled anniversaries, particularly in relation to events that had been the source of enduring political controversy. As if to acknowledge the muted public response, the Rhodesian cabinet never came up with a substitute for the military parade, agreeing that the annual 11 November celebrations should "be kept in a low key" – a euphemism for doing nothing.[53]

"Knowing Ourselves"

The semi-rural street scenes of khaki-clad Rhodesian militancy were, to be sure, a world away from the Canada of the 1960s. Yet the same material and ideological pressures that rendered obsolete the rituals and observances of "greater Britain" in Rhodesia, Australia, and New Zealand made themselves felt on Canada's national holiday. As the debate about the official name continued to ebb and flow, the increasing irrelevance of empire and Britishness to Canadian civic culture raised deeper questions about the quality of a Canadian nationhood stripped of this historical baggage. The simultaneous rumblings of Quebec separatism only gave the issue added urgency. Dominion Day thus became the focal point for an almost ritualized annual navel gazing among newspaper editors, as witnessed by the following flourish from the *Globe and Mail* on 1 July 1961: "Three basic tasks face Canada in the years ahead. First, to recover a sense of national identity and purpose, to be less imitative of other countries, to set our own standards – in short to be a real nation."[54] And again three years later: "Ninety-seven years ago some frock-coated gentlemen created a political entity called Canada. But it was not then and it is not now a nation, and what has begun to trouble a lot of Canadians is the thought that it may never become a nation. Yet it is in this thought, perhaps, that our greatest hope of eventual nationhood lies."[55]

The tension between a redundant dominionhood and an elusive future was fundamental to the problem of "real" nationhood. Were Canadians to strive to "recover a sense of identity and purpose" that they had somehow discarded, or were they to look ahead to a species of nationhood that had hitherto escaped them? It was within this prevailing climate of self-doubt that the organizing committee for the Canadian pavilion at the 1967 World Expo in Montreal opted for the theme "knowing ourselves."

Fundamentally, the business of "knowing ourselves" presupposes a measure of confidence about naming. The decades-long debate over the designation of "Dominion" or "Canada" in the official title of the 1 July holiday, and the regular reinvention of how the day was observed (as discussed in Matthew Hayday's chapter), suggests a pervasive uncertainty about the contours of collective belonging in post–Second World War Canada. Mackenzie King's 1948 suggestion in the House of Commons that "in the circumstances it would perhaps be only proper to allow every member to call it by what ever name he prefers"[56] presaged the

New Zealand proposal to allow two names for the 6 February holiday to circulate freely in the 1970s. In both cases, the suggestion was essentially an admission of discord and disunity, a concession to the very divisions and disputes that a more "truly national" holiday was meant to overcome. What the four case studies considered here had in common was a shared settler colonial history that bequeathed certain values, symbols, and commemorative practices tied up in an obsolete relationship with Britain that no longer held sufficient symbolic purchase. Added to this were the political and ideological upheavals of an era of global decolonization and civil rights that made alternative, credible, and above all, consensual renderings of the imperial past inherently elusive.

Arriving in Ottawa for the first time on the eve of Canada Day 2003, I was driven into the city by an old Canadian friend who gestured to the extravagant bunting festooning every building and lamppost. "I think we tend to overdo the flag on Canada Day," he noted apologetically. "I mean … we know where we are." This entirely spontaneous remark captures neatly what was at stake for the redundant dominions in the years after the Second World War in their efforts to refit the national civic fabric. The historic landmarks of empire and dominionhood that had once served to orient offshore Britons in a British world had become a poor guide to the future. The task of "knowing ourselves" was fundamentally caught up in the new political geographies of the post-1945 era – about making sense of "where we are" at a time of unprecedented change. While it remains crucial to attend to the unique contextual factors that rendered these many pathways out of empire so profoundly divergent in their immediate social and political implications, there is surely more than a mere coincidence in the timing and ambivalent tenor of the debates that redefined these national holidays.

NOTES

1 Library and Archives Canada, Mackenzie King Diaries, 4 April 1946.
2 A useful overview is provided by Jose Igartua, *The Other Quiet Revolution: National Identities in English Canada, 1945–71* (Vancouver: UBC Press, 2006), 30–33. For a slightly different emphasis, see Raymond B. Blake, "From Dominion Day to Canada Day, 1946–82: History, Heritage and National Identity," *Asian Journal of Canadian Studies* 17, no. 2 (2001): 1–32. See also chapter 12 by Blake and Antonishyn, chapter 11 by Hayday, and chapter 8 by Pass in the present volume.

3 *Ottawa Journal*, quoted in Igartua, *Other Quiet Revolution*, 31.

4 See Blake, "From Dominion Day."

5 All quotations are from Igartua, *Other Quiet Revolution*, 30–2.

6 Quoted in Blake, "From Dominion Day," 11.

7 Quoted in John Ross Matheson, *Canada's Flag: A Search for a Country* (Belleville, ON: Mika Publishing, 1986), 159–60.

8 The term *New Nationalism* was first coined by Claude Ryan in 1964, but was also later used in other "dominion" contexts. See James Curran and Stuart Ward, *The Unknown Nation: Australia after Empire* (Melbourne: Melbourne University Press, 2010), 7–8. For "de-dominionization," see Jim Davidson, "The De-Dominionisation of Australia," *Meanjin* 38, no. 2 (July 1979): 139–53.

9 Matthew Hayday, "Fireworks, Folk-dancing and Fostering a National Identity: The Politics of Canada Day," *Canadian Historical Review* 9, no. 2 (June 2010): 294.

10 Curran and Ward, *Unknown Nation*, 194–7.

11 Editorial, *Press* (Christchurch), 2 January 1973.

12 Carl Watts, *Rhodesia's Unilateral Declaration of Independence: An International History* (London: Palgrave Macmillan, 2012); Alice Ritscherle, "Disturbing the People's Peace: Patriotism and Respectable Racism in British Responses to Rhodesian Independence," in *Gender, Labour, War and Empire*, ed. Philippa Levine and Susan Grayzel (London: Palgrave Macmillan, 2008).

13 See also chapter 3 by Chris Tait in the present volume.

14 See chapter 6 by Bos and Ward and chapter 5 by Belliveau and Martel in the present volume.

15 R.J. Heffron (acting premier, NSW) to Menzies, 8 July 1958, National Archives of Australia (hereafter NAA), A1209 1958/1608.

16 Stewart Firth and Jeanette Hoorn, "From Empire Day to Cracker Night," in *Australian Popular Culture*, ed. Peter Spearritt and David Walker (Sydney: Allen and Unwin, 1979), 17–38.

17 See Neville Meaney, "Britishness and Australian Identity: The Problem of Nationalism in Australian History and Historiography," *Australian Historical Studies* 116 (April 2001): 76–90; James Belich, "The Rise and Fall of Greater Britain," in *Replenishing the Earth: The Settler Revolution and the Rise of the Anglo-World, 1783–1939* (Oxford: Oxford University Press, 2009).

18 *Courier Mail* (Brisbane), 26 April, 1967 and 26 April 1968.

19 *Australian* (Canberra), 26 April 1973.

20 *Courier Mail* (Brisbane), 26 April 1973.

21 See, for example, K.S. Inglis, "Anzac: The Substitute Religion," *Nation* (Sydney), 23 April 1960.

22 *Sydney Morning Herald*, 26 January 1959, quoted in K.S. Inglis, "Australia Day" in *Observing Australia, 1959–99*, ed. Craig Wilcox (Melbourne: Melbourne University Press, 1999), 110.

23 Editorial, *Age* (Melbourne), 26 January 1960.

24 Ibid., 26 January 1964.

25 *New Zealand Parliamentary Debates*, Representatives, vol. 385, 1 August 1973, 2886–7. As a concession to Rata, who clearly preferred retention of the original name, the full text of the Treaty of Waitangi was included as a schedule to the bill.

26 Ibid., 2898.

27 Notes of discussion: Meeting of New Zealand Day Celebrations Steering Committee, 2 October 1973, Archives New Zealand (hereafter ANZ), AAAC/7536 W5084, bBox 231 CON/9/3/14.

28 Dupont, *The Reluctant President* (Bulawayo: Books of Rhodesia, 1978), 180.

29 It is clear, given the blank columns whose text had been excised by the government censor, that the coverage of the governor's garden party was deemed unfit for publication in the *Rhodesian Herald*.

30 Pestell diary entry, 8 June 1968, Pestell Papers 2208 1/4, Bodleian Library, Oxford.

31 Ibid., 4 November 1967.

32 Rhodesian Cabinet Memorandum, "Speech from the Throne," RC(s) (68)94, 8 May 1968, Smith Papers, 2/007(A), Cory Library (hereafter CL), Grahamstown.

33 Rhodesian Cabinet Memorandum, "Queen's Birthday," RC(s) (68) 75, 8 April 1968, Smith Papers, ibid.

34 Official Statement: "The Queen's Birthday," April 1968, Smith Papers, ibid.

35 W.F. Broderick, "Wanted: A New Identikit for an Australian," *Age* (Melbourne), 26 January 1969.

36 Editorial, *Age* (Melbourne), 24 January 1969.

37 Editorial, *Sunday Australian* (Canberra), 30 January 1972.

38 "Lord Mayor Asks Us for Aust Day Ideas," *Sydney Morning Herald*, 27 January 1971.

39 Editorial, *Age* (Melbourne), 30 January 1973.

40 Editorial, *Sydney Morning Herald*, 31 January 1973.

41 Submission by Maori Women's Welfare League to the Maori Affairs Committee, undated 1973, AAAC/7536, W5084, box 231 CON/9/1/5, ANZ.

42 Margaret R. McCormick, honorary secretary of the Auckland Historical Society, to Henry May, 21 March 21, 1975, ibid., Box 227 CON/9/2/3.

43 Quoted in *The Dominion* (Wellington), 7 February 1974.

44 David Walker to Matiu Rata, 6 February 1974, AAAC/7536 W5084, box 227 CON/9/2/3, ANZ.

45 Editorial, *Press* (Christchurch), 2 January 1973. Two years later the *Christchurch Star* described the occasion as an "ill-timed holiday," and asked "how many spared a thought today for the reason for the holiday – the signing of the Treaty of Waitangi 135 years ago? How many of those who did cared?" 6 February 1975.

46 Editorial, *New Zealand Herald* (Auckland), 7 February 1974.

47 David Walker to Matiu Rata, 6 February 1974, AAAC/7536 W5084, box 227 CON/9/2/3, ANZ.

48 See *Te Awamutu Courier*, 30 January 1975; *Greymouth Evening Star*, 1 March 1975; *Marlborough Express*, 5 February 1975; *Evening Post* (Wellington), 6 February 1975 respectively.

49 Editorial, *New Zealand Herald* (Auckland), 9 February 1976.

50 Editorial, *Oamaru Mail*, 16 February 1976.

51 Rhodesian Cabinet Memorandum, "Celebration of National Day," RC(s) (67) 159, 5 August 1967, 2/013(A), Smith Papers, CL.

52 Minutes of the Rhodesian Cabinet, RC(s) 71, 32nd meeting, 31 August 1971, ibid.

53 Minutes of the Rhodesian Cabinet, RC(s) 75, 21st meeting, 17 June 1975, 2/107, ibid.

54 Editorial, *Globe and Mail*, 1 July 1961.

55 Ibid., 1 July 1964.

56 Quoted in Blake, "From Dominion Day," 16.

14 "Adieu le mouton, salut les Québécois!" The Lévesque Government and Saint-Jean-Baptiste Day/Fête Nationale Celebrations, 1976–1984

MARC-ANDRÉ GAGNON

The date of 7 April 1984 marked an important milestone in the history of Quebec's national holiday. On that date, a protocol was signed between the Mouvement national des Québécois (MNQ) and the provincial government with respect to the coordination of 24 June, the Fête nationale du Québec (see figure 14.1). At a press conference to announce the agreement, Guy Chevrette, the minister responsible for the holiday, admitted that he was not willing to relive the drama of the last few years: "I would not say that it was ... an error: there has been a lot of goodwill."[1] He then laid out his plans to reinstate a central organizing structure for 24 June celebrations, bringing local and regional events together under a single promotional campaign. Acknowledging the expertise of the MNQ, he emphasized that it was natural to give the management of the holiday back to the patriotic association, especially as 1984 marked the 150th anniversary of the first national holiday banquet, which was organized by a forerunner of the Société Saint-Jean-Baptiste. He also noted that the agreement would benefit the taxpayers, reducing the cost of organizing the celebrations to half of what it had been in recent years. Clearly, there were significant concerns about how this national holiday had been managed by the government between 1977 and 1984.

This chapter explores the public policies related to Quebec's national holiday from the perspectives of politicians and nationalist movement. In a period when Quebec's constitutional status was the major focal point of Canada's political life, 24 June celebrations took on an important role for the Parti québécois (PQ) administration. Seeking to build support for the PQ's vision of civic nationalism, provincial authorities elaborated a strategy to promote these celebrations and foster public participation. René Lévesque's government issued a decree in May 1977

14.1 Protocol-signing between the Mouvement national des Québécois and the Government of Quebec, 7 April 1984. From left to right: Paulette-Michèle Hétu, Treasurer; Guy Chevrette, Minister of Leisure, Hunting and Fishing; Gilles Rhéaume, President; Bruno Roy, Secretary. Photographer: Jacques Lavallé. Courtesy of the Mouvement national des Québécoises et Québécois.

stating that the traditional Saint-Jean-Baptiste Day would thereafter be known as the Fête nationale du Québec. His government also decided to take control over these events by institutionalizing the organization and funding of celebrations through the creation of the Comité organisateur de la fête nationale and the Programme d'aide technique et financière for local events. Through these actions, the Lévesque government hoped not only to increase celebration of the Fête nationale and bolster support for its sovereignist agenda, but also to keep at bay the federal government and its attempts to promote national unity. However, as the state increased its participation, friction increased between the PQ and the Movement national des Québécois over how these celebrations should be organized. Once central to the coordination of 24 June events, the MNQ found itself marginalized for political reasons during the Lévesque years, and sought to regain control over the holiday.

Saint-Jean-Baptiste Day had been established by French-Canadian nationalist elites in the mid-nineteenth century to highlight the existence of a distinct French and Catholic society through the use of public dem-onstrations. These demonstrations spread from Quebec across North America. The Société Saint-Jean-Baptiste (SSJB), a patriotic association founded in Montreal from the remains of Aide-toi et le ciel t'aidera in 1842–3, used the celebration as a moment to reflect on the unique challenges posed by the Anglo-dominant society and as a reminder to French Canadians of their duty to maintain their language, traditions, and faith. By the end of the 1960s, some began to contest this long-time symbol of solidarity among members of the "French-Canadian family." With the changing nature of French-Canadian nationalism, the rise of the sovereignist movement in Quebec, and the greater secularization of society, organizers were forced to rethink the celebration.[2]

Based in part on new archival material from the Mouvement national des Québécois fonds, National Assembly debates, and newspapers, this chapter provides a descriptive analysis of the PQ's policies regarding the Fête nationale, their consequences for Quebec's political debates, and ultimately the party's withdrawal from this sector in 1984. Up to now, historians have primarily used cultural analysis to trace the con-tours of the new traditions established around these celebrations and have spent less time exploring the crafting of public policies.[3] National holidays matter, Matthew Hayday reminds us, as they are fundamen-tal in the construction of national identities, shaping representations of the past and incorporating visions of the future.[4] As objects of public debate, they convey a variety of meanings or explicitly contest those of other actors. In addition, their recurring character allows us to trace changes as individual organizers, resources, and objectives evolved over time. This is common to many holidays, as is demonstrated in the chapters in this volume by Matthew Hayday (on Canada Day), Marcel Martel and Joel Belliveau (on Empire Day), and Michael Poplyansky (on the Acadian national holiday).

"Adieu le mouton, salut les Québécois": The Genesis of State Intervention

Taken from the jingle originally produced in 1975 to promote 24 June festivities, the phrase "Adieu le mouton, salut les Québécois" evokes the liberating spirit that organizers wanted to convey in the celebrations. Referring to bonfires, fireworks, and the joy of life, the song depicts Quebec as a mature society, free of two of Saint-Jean-Baptiste Day's traditional symbols: the lamb and its inseparable master in the person of John the Baptist. Elected in November 1976, the Parti québécois adopted a proactive attitude vis-à-vis the national holiday, which was partly a reaction to the federal government's use of Dominion Day (which became Canada Day in 1982) to promote Canadian unity.[5] In response, René Lévesque's cabinet strategy was to clarify the status of 24 June and foster public participation through a series of initiatives reflective of the larger socio-political context of Quebec at that time.

Until the mid-1970s, state sponsorship of 24 June celebrations was sporadic, was usually only for major events in Quebec City and Montreal, and came mainly from the discretionary funds of ministers' offices. The burden of financing the festivities was borne by the SSJB, which appealed to municipalities or private corporations to sponsor its parades.[6] However, the SSJB started to lobby the provincial government to have specific funds attached to these celebrations and, at the beginning of the 1970s, during the Liberal government of Robert Bourassa, the Ministry of Cultural Affairs was put in charge of the dossier. In order to effectively meet the growing demands of the organizers, the ministry in 1973 recognized the Mouvement national des Québécois as its primary interlocutor for 24 June. With its dedicated budget, the ministry used its regional offices to distribute subsidies to MNQ affiliates. However, this operating system was problematic, as the ministry did not have managers across the province.[7] In addition, as the festivities became more popular, new actors outside the SSJB network, such as leisure committees or municipalities, tried to access these funds, creating confusion and sometimes conflicts among them.[8]

It was not only to resolve these conflicts and streamline the organization of these celebrations that the government of René Lévesque decided to intervene. After the election of the PQ in November 1976, the federal government, via its Secretary of State, injected $4 million to sponsor Canada Day activities, with the clear intention of fostering francophones' sense of Canadian national unity.[9] To deal with this offensive, Lévesque's cabinet pursued the objective of officializing the June 24th celebrations and establishing them as a civic event throughout the province. First, in February 1977, the government adopted an order-in-council, which laid out the provisions for funding celebrations, an act that also created a national organizing committee and placed the dossier under the responsibility of the premier's office.[10] However, this aid was conditional on the inclusion of representatives of the premier's office and the Ministry of Cultural Affairs on the provincial organizing committee. In addition, the government allocated $250,000 to repay the deficit from the 1976 events.[11]

Second, in May 1977, the government adopted another decree, which declared that Saint-Jean-Baptiste Day would also be known as Quebec's National Holiday.[12] According to Katia Malausséna, this change can be understood as the Lévesque government's attempt to confirm its commitment to civic nationalism and move away from ethnocentric nationalism.[13] This commitment is particularly evident when one looks at the parliamentary debates. Ministers expressed a desire to make the National Holiday a celebration for all Quebeckers, including immigrants and non–Roman Catholics. It was seen as a powerful integration tool that could unite the nation. As Robert Burns, the government house leader, said, "On behalf of the Government, I am pleased to wish a happy birthday ... to all true Quebeckers. When I say all true Quebeckers, to avoid any ambiguity that could arise in some minds, I do not mean only francophones, I mean all true Quebeckers of whatever origin, whether they be anglophones or of another ethnic origin."[14] Although Burns was mingling linguistic communities and ethnicities here, his statement expresses the government's desire to make the 24th a celebration for everyone. Citing René Lévesque's address to the people of Quebec where he invited them to celebrate their culture "rooted in the strength of its identity," Marc Ouimet notes that there was a perceptible tension between this desire for an inclusive political project and that of an affirmation of the memory and heritage of the francophone majority. This tension can be explained by the debates surrounding "convergence culturelle," a concept that influenced the Parti québécois's legislation on language and culture. Elaborated in the *Politique québécoise de développement culturelle*, this concept viewed the French-Canadian language and heritage as the linchpin or bonding point in the relationship between the Québécois and the province's various minorities.[15]

In 1977, the government gave control over organizing the Fête nationale events to the MNQ. Formerly known as the Fédération des Sociétés Saint-Jean-Baptiste, the MNQ was a nonpartisan nationalist organization advocating for Quebec's sovereignty. In awarding this mandate, the government made the practical decision to reward those who had traditionally given life to the festivities on June 24th.[16] It also ensured regional collaboration, as local societies affiliated with the MNQ would organize celebrations throughout the province. As outlined in the first order-in-council from February 1977, a pan-Québécois committee was set up, composed of the MNQ, its affiliates, and the committee for Montreal, each with three representatives. With the help of two government officials, the "Committee of Eleven" (Comité des onze) was responsible for programming, advertising, and public relations surrounding the celebrations. It would also work to ensure links with various regional partners and to see that the budget was shared among regional organizers. It also adopted a project-selection policy.[17] The presidency was entrusted to Alain Généreux, who was also president of MNQ.

The 1977 celebrations were oriented around the theme of memory and heritage, as the government saw an opportunity to attach them to another sponsored event in June, the Semaine du patrimoine (Heritage Week). In a memo sent to the organizers, coordinator Jean-Pierre Guay invited them to rethink earlier approach, replacing the more passive television-oriented mega-concerts with "genuine popular festivities naturally integrated into all of our daily life."[18] Over the preceding decade, important changes had occurred in the way people participated in the Fête nationale after violent protests during the Montreal parades in 1968, 1969, and 1971. Moving away from its traditional form, the holiday had embraced a new image, especially among the younger generation, with popular gatherings and music shows such as the festivities on Mount Royal in 1975 and 1976. It was estimated that 1.25 million people participated in the holiday over five days in 1975. Among the most memorable moments of this event was singer-songwriter Gilles Vigneault singing "Gens du pays," which became an instant hit and a recognizable symbol of the national holiday.

In 1977, Montreal once again played host to the largest celebrations in the province. The Montreal organizing committee got the largest share of funding, with over 50 per cent of the budget.[19] Part of the city's funding was for a major television-oriented extravaganza hosted at the Olympic stadium. The rest of the province-wide budget of $1,226,185.85 was distributed to nineteen regional committees, leaving a budget of only $92,000 for the central office. This situation annoyed Quebec City MPs, who questioned the regional distribution of funds.[20] The active participation of the government in the funding of the holiday was also widely criticized by opposition party members. The Union nationale took a dim view of the PQ government's decision to repay part of the 1976 celebrations' deficit and to increase spending authorizations, raising particular questions about artist fees.[21]

Some members of the National Assembly (MNAs) also suggested that there was collusion between the PQ and the organizing committee. The Mouvement national des Québécois and the Parti québécois were viewed as having close ties, no doubt due to their affinity regarding the national question. Several activists in the MNQ network were also members of the PQ. The government was placed on the defensive when allegations arose in *La Presse* about the misuse of funds by the committee in Montreal.[22] Lévesque agreed to call for an inquiry by the auditor general if necessary.[23]

The organizers and the government were also monitored by federal authorities, who were careful not to directly compete with provincial activities.[24] However, the National Battlefields Commission, which is responsible for the maintenance of the Plains of Abraham, gave organizers in Quebec City a hard time, prohibiting them from producing their traditional fireworks show on the site. This triggered a debate in the National Assembly, which condemned this decision.[25] Despite these glitches, the 1977 edition of the Fête nationale was considered a success on many levels. It was celebrated in 250 municipalities, and the organizers were able to collaborate with the Semaine du patrimoine.[26] More than one million people participated in the various events, despite some criticism of the music show at the Olympic stadium in Montreal, which was organized mainly for the television broadcast. Several activities were held around the theme of memory, including the dedication of a plaque at Lionel Groulx's house in Montreal by Lévesque on 24 June.

In its attempts to build a national consensus, the 1977 celebrations were a success on many levels, and served as the foundations for government policy with respect to this holiday. However, the official opposition accused the government of partisanship, which could have significantly damaged the image of the premier's office.

Democratization, Decentralization, and Depoliticization

Lévesque's cabinet made a number of key adjustments after 1977. The event was transferred to the jurisdiction of the Ministry for Youth, Sport, and Leisure under Claude Charron. There were two reasons for this move. First, the government wanted to distance the premier's office from any appearance of partisanship, thereby ensuring his protection in case of any allegations from the press or the official opposition. The cabinet also sought to depoliticize the celebrations, to decentralize their organization, and to expand their popularity by partnering with recreational and community groups. In this context, it created a financial and technical assistance program to promote local projects and passed a law about the statutory observance of the national holiday.

Invited to submit recommendations at the end of the 1977 festivities, the president of the Committee of Eleven, Alain Généreux, proposed the creation of a permanent structure dedicated to the celebration. This recommendation, along with others in his report, would have ultimately confirmed the ascendency of the MNQ as the main non-governmental actor involved.[27] However, Claude Charron, fearing the appearance of partisanship in the granting of subsidies, ignored Généreux's report.

Charron decided to adopt a different approach. A new structure was put in place based on democratically elected regional committees. Hoping to take advantage of the growing popularity of the celebration and the enthusiasm of the many volunteers devoted to its organization (around 16,000 in 1978), he toured the province, explaining his plan and the initiatives his government was taking to finance these celebrations. This led to the creation of fifteen *comités organisateurs de la fête nationale du Québec* (COFNQ), each composed of eleven members, who were selected following a general meeting convened by the Regional Council on Leisure.[28] Then, an assembly of representatives of each COFNQ was asked to elect five members to the national organizing committee. Another five members were appointed by the minister, who could choose from a list of fifteen names submitted by the COFNQ.[29]

Opposed to this new structure, the MNQ denounced the bureaucratization of the holiday, fearing it could open the door to nepotism through the minister's involvement in selecting committee members.[30] In addition, the group resented being left out after organizing the 1977 celebrations.[31] Despite the highly political nature of these events, the government sought to project a neutral image and tried not to exacerbate the constitutional question. One public servant declared to the press that the MNQ was too political: "We want neighborhood parties, not complaints and lamentations," referring to the MNQ as the kind of nationalists who rant about "the humiliations of French Canada."[32] However, not all members of the cabinet were happy about this shift of attitudes regarding the MNQ. "It's dumb," said Jacques Parizeau, the minister of finance, who publicly questioned the choice of his colleague, especially as the government was actively seeking support for its constitutional option.[33] Charron had to defend his actions, given the tensions they created within the nationalist movement. He believed that a truly decentralized and depoliticized event could not be organized by a single group. [34] As the minister said:

> We have held fifteen regional assemblies where, from the regional councils of leisure, all organizations interested in the organization of the national holiday could attend the meetings, where people on site chose, in their regions, an organizing committee for the National Day of Quebec. I specify, to be very clear, that I have been blamed for not having given the organization of the national holiday in its totality to Quebec nationalist movements, which are closely identified with the constitutional option of the current government. This got me into trouble. This has caused me problems. But I wanted to give the national holiday back to the people of Quebec. When the premier gave me this job, on January 13, asking me to take on this dossier that he could not hold anymore, this was my condition. He accepted it, and my cabinet colleagues have also accepted my approach. [35]

An effort to create a veneer of non-partisanship could be a logical explanation for this change of strategy. However, other clues indicate why Charron was pushing for the involvement of regional actors. In 1978, national holiday festivities turned into a bidding war between Ottawa and Quebec, and the two governments had different approaches about how they would spend their funds. Charron's office was aware that the federal Secretary of State's focus was almost entirely on the Parliament Hill television show, leaving only "pocket money" to federalist organizations in Quebec, such as the Council for Canadian Unity. "Ottawa won't rally Quebeckers with military marches, Royal Canadian Mountain Police parades, and a majorettes show," commented Daniel Drolet, the director of the provincial organizing committee. [36] One employee of Charron's office also commented that Ottawa's strategy was inefficient. He argued that the Quebec strategy was better in the long term, as it was expanding its network in the province's regions. For him, the national holiday was the foundation from which the government could demonstrate that Quebeckers supported the same cause. [37]

For its part, the MNQ was discussing how to respond to the minister's decision and sought to present a united front of its regional members. During the winter of 1977–78, the MNQ attempted an ultimately unsuccessful lobbying campaign to reverse the government's decision and to convince the cabinet to adopt the Committee of Eleven's report recommendations.[38] In February 1978, during a meeting with its regional constituents, the MNQ leaders heard different opinions: some wanted to influence regional committees while others were leaning towards boycotting the celebrations. However, the meeting concluded with the sense that they needed to rally behind a common position in order to support the MNQ and maintain its influence. This position was made public in March, when Alain Généreux announced that the MNQ would refrain from participating in the celebrations.[39] While almost all of the 1977 organizers followed the MNQ's lead, the organization in Montreal took a different stance. In a heated exchange with Généreux, Montreal representative Luc Lamy regretted that the Committee of Eleven did not consult him before drafting its recommendations. His organization accepted a later offer from Claude Charron to join the new structure.[40] In addition, two other branches of the MNQ (Saguenay–Lac-St-Jean and Est-du-Québec) would join the ranks of the provincial organizing committee.[41] The minister was thus able to temporarily calm the nationalist lobby by showing signs of good will, and he avoided an escalation of his public confrontation with the MNQ.

Besides the new governing structure, new resources were devoted to the festivities. A permanent secretariat was established under the direction of Daniel Drolet. It employed five people, including two secretaries. No employees from the ministry worked directly for the organization. In addition, the regional committees could hire employees on a seasonal basis to prepare for the festivities. The national organizing committee was placed under the presidency of Marcel Couture, a Hydro-Québec public servant and president of the Fête nationale organization in Montreal since 1975. It had a budget of $2,550,000, of which $1,883,235 was paid directly to local projects through the financial and technical assistance program.[42] The approach was not entirely new, as the 1977 celebration organizers had set up guidelines and developed a similar structure for the allocation of subsidies to each region. However, the program's creation indicated the government's willingness to formalize its decentralization and popular participation objectives and to officialize the terms under which projects were selected. The objective of boosting public participation in local, smaller events was also reached. In 1978, the secretariat subsidized 781 projects in more than 600 municipalities.[43] Opinions about local and neighbourhood-based festivities were mixed. Jean-Paul Champagne of the Société Saint-Jean-Baptiste of Montreal believed that these smaller projects were less suitable in his city because "neighborhood life does not exist everywhere."[44] Others found this focus too restrictive in terms of program planning and thought that it interfered with the natural festive ambience.[45]

The program had other goals as well. It aimed to shift the balance of funding between Montreal and Quebec City. It also sought to empower COFNQ, which was responsible for awarding funding grants. In addition, the program was used to connect with non-traditional participant groups, such as ethnic communities. In this regard, the 1977 and 1978 celebrations demonstrate some interesting contrasts. Despite the desire to regionalize the celebrations and develop popular participation in various events in 1977, no specific mention was made about ethnic communities in the Committee of Eleven's report and its other administrative papers. In contrast, the 1978 report mentioned that thirty-one projects were subsidized because they targeted ethnic communities.[46] In 1979, when the theme was Le Québec au monde (Quebec in the world), Lévesque placed special emphasis on minorities in his national holiday message:

> Our fellow citizens from ethnic communities will also be widely participating in the cultural activities, which will highlight this year's event with more splendour than ever. This June 24, is it necessary to say, must be a celebration of all Quebeckers, from all groups as from all different backgrounds, and from all faiths, and from all origins, and of all political stripes. A celebration of all, and the celebration for all.[47]

In his address, the premier also emphasized that the celebration should be one for everyone without regard to religious affiliation. Religious discourse as a vector for the definition of the celebrations was gradually losing its influence in the sixties. Although they retained the expression "la Saint-Jean" to refer to the day, nationalists were reluctant to use all the symbols associated with the traditional celebrations. However, this did not prevent the Catholic dimension of the celebrations from persisting in certain forms. The 1978 report, for example, noted that 2000 Saint-Jean masses were held in different regions of Quebec. In addition, the organizers had planned a "national mass" celebrated by Bishop Paul Gregory, archbishop of Montreal. The mass was broadcast live by Radio-Canada and was followed by a "tribute to the founders by the civil and religious authorities" at the Place d'Armes in Montreal. The 1978 report also contained photos featuring Deputy Premier Jacques-Yvan Morin with clergy members (the premier was in Quebec City where he presided over the reception of the consular corps). In addition, the technical and financial assistance program considered parish councils (*les fabriques*) to be eligible for government subsidies.[48] Religious references were even included in the organizers' speeches. Traditionally, St John the Baptist is seen as a forerunner, one who proclaims the coming of Christ. This notion was used by nationalists to symbolize the forefront of patriotic interests of French Canadians.[49] A brochure from the organizing committee published in 1980 updated the idea to stress the theme of inclusiveness: "we will be forerunners in the world, building in harmony a new race, a race of more human humans."[50]

This desire to democratize the Fête nationale's structures and popularize neighbourhood celebrations was combined with another element of government policy: to make the festival a statutory holiday and a day off for Quebeckers. In 1977, the ministerial decree contained no clause on this point, but the cabinet had proposed to the Minimum Wage Board that it might adopt an ordinance to allow a greater number of Quebeckers to celebrate with a day off. This ordinance was limited in time and could have been challenged in court. To give this decision permanent status, the government chose to go ahead with a bill.[51]

Debate on the Loi sur la fête nationale began on 25 May 1978, and the government expected quick and easy passage. The bill was sponsored by the minister of labour, Pierre-Marc Johnson, who recalled the Catholic origin of the festivities and drew on the heritage of the Patriotes and the 1834 Saint-Jean-Baptiste banquet to emphasize inclusiveness: "We truly affirm that Quebeckers, whether they be of Irish origin, even British, and, of course, French, will be recognized, historically, in the celebration of June 24."[52] The opposition parties were not opposed to the principle of the bill, but they used the parliamentary debates to criticize the government for its management of the holiday itself. For Claude Forget, Liberal MNA for Saint-Laurent, the Parti québécois had used the holiday to boost its sovereignist agenda.[53] In committee, the wording of the first section of the bill gave rise to the most important partisan exchanges. Forget said that there was confusion between the ethnic and religious origins of the celebrations and the policy of proclaiming 24 June a national holiday. He feared that the reference to Quebec as a nation would limit the participation of ethnocultural communities.[54] This argument was quickly countered by Lise Payette, who drew on her own experience as an organizer in Montreal to respond to this criticism, highlighting the growing contribution of these communities in the celebrations. The bill was passed unanimously on third reading on 8 June. The act contains provisions to enforce the statutory public holiday for all employees in Quebec. It established the conditions of employee leaves, the calculation of monetary compensation, and the applicable penalties. However, the legislation excluded some employers, particularly those operating under a federal charter.

For its part, the MNQ continued to lobby to retrieve its mandate to organize Fête nationale festivities. At the request of the MNQ, a meeting was held in Montreal in February 1979 that included René Lévesque, Claude Charron, François-Albert Angers (president of the Montreal SSJB), and Claude Rochon (president of the MNQ). "We quickly understood from the words of introduction by Mr. Lévesque that we had not been invited to submit a project, but to receive one. The premier, indeed, had in hand the text of the Order in Council that the cabinet would adopt in the coming days," reported Rochon in a circular letter sent to the MNQ's regional members. He had hoped to use this opportunity to assert the need to return to a structure similar to that of 1977. Instead, Lévesque announced plans to increase the number of regions to eighteen and to keep the 1978 structure, including the method of appointment of members of the national organizing committee. However, the government proposed that the MNQ could provide the names of twelve of the eighteen members of the list from which the minister would choose. The government also announced that the budget would be increased to $4 million to absorb losses from 1978.[55] Visibly disappointed, the MNQ executive made no alternative recommendations, in order to avoid a public confrontation with the government.[56]

On the eve of the referendum debate, the government had clarified its policy on the national holiday. However, the political situation following the referendum's defeat and the budgetary context of the province would test this newly adopted model, and the Parti québécois would have to deal with a situation that could affect its credibility.

Nationalists Are Back in the Game

The political context of the early 1980s, including the sovereignty referendum, the patriation of the constitution, and an extended recession, resulted in tensions, and popular participation in Quebec's national holiday tended to reflect that. As the recession peaked and the fiscal situation of the provincial government declined, operational budgets were significantly reduced. The organizational model was increasingly questioned, and the intervention of the auditor general in 1981 tarnished the general image of the national holiday.

The year 1981 marked another turning point in the management of Quebec's national holiday. René Lévesque was aware of the difficulties his government faced with respect to that issue. He was the first to recognize that "it was a disaster from the administrative point of view, the budgetary point of view. If this shows us anything, it's that we cannot continue like this, we need a cleansing, and there must be very strict controls."[57] He and his ministers faced a barrage of questions from the opposition, and the cabinet had to deal with the publication of allegations in the press. Although not all were true, they put the government and organizers on the defensive.

A first set of allegations concerned the relationship between the employees of the national organizing committee and the Parti québécois. The opposition revealed that employees of various ministries had pocketed salaries from the committee, in particular members of Claude Charron's office in Montreal. An advertising firm close to the PQ also pocketed $180,000 in contracts.[58] In addition, staff from the minister of justice's office were rumoured to have been involved in granting money to the COFNQ in Saguenay–Lac-Saint-Jean after pressuring the national committee.[59] The new minister for leisure, Lucien Lessard, was forced to investigate the Saguenay–Lac-Saint-Jean and Montreal cases, although the former, at least, proved to be baseless.[60] As for his predecessor, Claude Charron denied being involved in such affairs:

> I affirm that I never recommended anyone to the Board of Directors. I was in no way involved with those who were hired at the regional level or at the level of the national administration. Yes, it is true that some members of my party and the riding association of Saint-Jacques was given these positions, and were selected by a Board of Directors that I did not nominate and could not control. But I can't do anything about it.[61]

Because misfortune never comes alone, the minister of justice, Marc-André Bédard confirmed to the National Assembly that the Quebec Provincial Police were conducting an investigation about allegations of drug trafficking perpetrated by employees of the national organizing committee in Montreal. No charges were laid, owing to insufficient evidence, but these events were numerous enough for René Lévesque to ask his Lessard to conduct a "spring cleaning." [62]

Nationalists, such as those in the Société Saint-Jean-Baptiste in Montreal, were discouraged by these failures associated with the national holiday. They first tried to dissociate themselves from the government's management.[63] Then, they wrote to the premier to encourage him to give them back the responsibility for the management of the holiday.[64] While Lessard considered his options, the minister of state for economic development, Bernard Landry, favourably viewed the idea of entrusting responsibility for the holiday to the MNQ.[65] However, the prospect of seeing the MNQ regain this role displeased opposition leader Claude Ryan. He refused to let the Fête nationale fall into the hands of a "fanatical" organization, an "antechamber of political separatism."[66] While the MNQ continued lobbying to recover the mandate, it also met resistance from some in the PQ, especially from Lessard. Instead of bringing back the MNQ, the minister decided to hand over the organization to the Société des festivals populaires, a provincial federation of festivals.[67] To justify his choice, he prepared a memorandum to cabinet. The victim of a cabinet leak, the text contained negative opinions about the MNQ, which Lessard considered unable to fulfil the task. According to Lessard, the MNQ did not offer enough guarantees in terms of financial management, nor did it solve the problem of self-financing the celebration. He also stated that the MNQ could not offer any guarantee of its ability to solve the management problems. Furthermore, the minister emphasized his desire to associate the festival with a neutral, non-partisan society.[68] The text was compromising for the government, as it admitted the limitations of its management model and recognized that corruption charges and financial mismanagement were recurrent problems. Moreover, despite tight budgeting, the 1982 holiday was headed for a $300,000 deficit.[69]

During delays in the auditor general's report, the opposition capitalized on the Lessard memorandum to address the management of the holiday. Fernand Lalonde, Liberal MNA for Marguerite-Bourgeoys, believed that the problems lay in administrative practices. Citing the memorandum, he said:

> the same problems experienced last year are likely to recur in the short term, whether because of the high political visibility of some of these corporations – it probably means they are identified PQ – or because none of them – these are the MNQ, the SNQ [Société nationale des Québécoises et Québécois, and SSJB for the entire province – are immune to the same problems, lavish spending, corruption charges, waste of funds. How can the minister lay a serious accusation against all the national societies? Is the identification of national societies with the Parti Québécois, in the mind of the minister, such that they must bear the guilt of all the abuses of the Parti Québécois?[70]

This episode between the government and the MNQ could have proved fatal for the latter. Struggling to recover from the referendum defeat, the group was experiencing a period of decline in terms of both its organizational and financial capacities. However, its president, Gilles Rhéaume, managed to position the organization advantageously in the public debate over the Fête nationale as a rational observer of the situation. Rhéaume was able to use the MNQ's public positions since 1978 in order to demonstrate the continued interest of the group in the national holiday. In addition, it tried to refocus the discourse on the meaning of the celebration. In seeking to increase the number of participants, it asked, could it be that the government had forgotten the profound meaning of 24 June?[71]

When he became minister of leisure and sport in the fall of 1982, Guy Chevrette was aware of the precarious situation surrounding Quebec's national holiday. For the Société des festivals populaires (SFP), the 1982 celebrations were a success, and internal studies showed that 80 per cent of local organizers were satisfied with their management. Despite a small surplus, and the difficult economic environment, the SFP decided to pressure Chevrette's office for more money.[72] This move damaged the relationship between them. The situation became worse when the Société des festivals populaires threatened to file a lawsuit against the government for unpaid expenses between September 1982 and March 1983.[73] Other actors, such as the Regroupement des corporations régionales de la fête nationale, an umbrella association of the COFNQs in various regions, were also pressuring Chevrette to return the coordination mandate to the MNQ.[74] At the end of April 1983, Chevrette severed ties with the SFP, despite having a formal contract with them, in favour of the Regroupement des corporations régionales. The financial demands of the SFP had been too high.[75] A more decentralized and budget-friendly structure was quickly elaborated two months before 24 June. There was no central committee, but COFNQs decided to unite the celebrations under an umbrella theme: *Le 24 juin, tout le Québec se fête.* Despite the management problems, the public response was positive. More than 900 local projects applied for funding.[76] Because the COFNQ was not present in some regions, MNQ members took up the slack. This was the case in Montreal, the Outaouais, Lanaudière, and Saguenay–Lac-St-Jean. Montreal and Saguenay were particularly sensitive regions, as their deficits in 1981 were the source of the troubles with the COFNQ model of management. Nationalist groups were back in the game.

Chevrette knew that this hybrid situation was temporary. He wanted to keep the gains of recent years, which included increased regional influence in the organizational structure, improved budgeting for local projects, and increased involvement of civil society. After considering the opinion of his fellow caucus members, he entered into negotiations with the MNQ.[77] After three months of talks, a five-year protocol was signed between the two parties on 7 April 1984. The MNQ was recognized as the national representative for the Fête nationale and sole contact for the government of Quebec with respect to its organization. As for the government, the sociocultural branch of the Ministry of Leisure, Hunting, and Fishing remained responsible for the financial administration program to support local events. The 1984 protocol with the MNQ was the direct result of the various management policies explored by the Quebec government between 1977 and 1983.

Conclusion

This chapter has traced the evolution of public policy relating to Quebec's Fête nationale between 1977 and 1984. Once in power, the Parti québécois decided to assume proactive leadership in institutionalizing the organization and funding of the holiday at a time when conflict with Ottawa was the focal point of political life. However, the PQ had to adapt its policy because of the economic environment, the personal preferences of various ministers assigned to this dossier, and the lobbying efforts of the nationalist movement. The constitutional question and rivalries with the federally funded holiday of July 1st were central to this policy and its evolution. Ottawa and Quebec were waging a virtual cold war in terms of their national holidays. Both significantly increased state funding for various activities, with each level of government matching the other's funding levels. Both explored ways to decentralize the celebrations through the funding of regional committees. Both endorsed a similar range of activities, including the production of television shows involving celebrities. While Quebec adopted its local festival-related policies in 1978, the Canadian government launched the *Canada en fête* program at the beginning of the 1980s. Each government was clearly aware of and responding to the actions of the other.

This chapter explores how the lobbying activities of the MNQ shaped PQ policies. Thanks to its militancy, the Mouvement national des Québécois was able to regain its role in managing of the national holiday. The advent of more centralized financing and the greater emphasis on regional and community celebrations were key shifts that occurred over this period. What might be seen as a simple re-orientation was in fact a major one. At the same time, as it restored the oversight of the national holiday to the MNQ, the government also made sure to return to a simplified management structure, decreasing the number of players in the regional and provincial committees. It decided that the national holiday was not an event that could be organized by professional leisure corporations. It recognized the specificity of the holiday with regard to its history and its place within Quebec society and decided that the MNQ was more qualified to manage the day's events, given its expertise in these subjects. The protocol has had a lasting effect. Since 1984, the MNQ has been responsible for organizing the Fête nationale and has been the government's interlocutor for its organization. It also became the manager of the Programme d'aide technique et financière in 1995. Renewed by successive governments, the agreement between the public authorities and the MNQ has been beneficial for citizens. Management problems appear to be a thing of the past, and the objectives pursued by the government in 1984 have largely been achieved.

NOTES

1 "Le MNQ maitre d'œuvre: Retour probable du défilé," *Le Devoir* (Montreal), 10 April 1984; "Retour du défilé de la Saint-Jean?" *Le Droit* (Ottawa), 10 April 1984.
2 In the 1960s, Saint-Jean-Baptiste Day was undergoing an important shift. In a context of a redefinition of Quebec's identity, several commentators and organizers were questioning the need to celebrate it. Combined with the polarization of the political discourse, they criticized the symbols and the meanings traditionally associated with the celebration. The festivities became a contested terrain with the 1968 riots in Montreal and the decapitation, the following year, of the statue of St John the Baptist during the day's parade. These events cast doubt on the future of the celebrations and had implications outside the province, where the festivities continued to be celebrated in francophone communities in Canada. See Marc-André Gagnon, "Le Canada français vit par ses œuvres: La Saint-Jean-Baptiste vue par le journal *Le Droit*, 1950–1960," *Francophonies d'Amérique* 35 (spring 2013): 79–92.

3 See Marc Ouimet, "Le lys en fête, le lys en feu: la Saint-Jean-Baptiste au Québec de 1960 à 1990" (master's thesis, Université du Québec à Montréal, 2011); Katia Malausséna, "Essai d'archéologie comparée des commémorations nationales anglaises, françaises et québécoises (1980–2000)" (PhD diss., Université Laval, 2002); Katia Malausséna, "Commémoration et lien territorial: L'Angleterre et le Québec en comparaison," *Recherche sociographiques* 43, no. 1 (2002): 79–110; Louis-Robert Frégault and Ignace Olazabal, "La fête de la Saint-Jean-Baptiste dans le quartier du Mile-End de Montréal: nouvelle signification pour un lieu de mémoire?" *Revue européenne de migration internationale* 16, no. 2 (2000): 143–52; Ronald Rudin, "Marching and Memory in Early Twentieth-Century Quebec: La Fête-Dieu, la Saint-Jean-Baptiste, and le Monument Laval," *Journal of the Canadian Historical Association / Revue de la Société historique du Canada* 10, no. 1 (1999): 209–35; Eva-Marie Kröller, "Le Mouton de Troie: Changes in Quebec Cultural Symbolism," *American Review of Canadian Studies* 27, no. 4 (1997): 523–44.

4 Matthew Hayday, "La francophonie canadienne, le bilinguisme et l'identité canadienne dans les célébrations de la fête du Canada," in *Entre lieux et mémoire, l'inscription de la francophonie canadienne dans la durée*, ed. Anne Gilbert, Michel Bock, and Joseph Yvon Thériault (Ottawa: Presses de l'Université d'Ottawa, 2009), 93.

5 Matthew Hayday, "Fireworks, Folk-dancing, and Fostering a National Identity: The Politics of Canada Day," *Canadian Historical Review* 91, no. 2 (June 2010): 302–4.

6 Gagnon, "Le Canada français vit par ses œuvres," 87–89.

7 Mouvement national des Québécois (hereafter MNQ), *Procès-verbal*, 4 May 1974, Bibliothèque et Archives nationales du Québec (hereafter BAnQ), Fonds MNQ, P161, 1981/04/047\19; Jean-Baptiste Bouchard, "1973–1974, un an de réflexion, et un nouvel élan," 1974, BAnQ, Fonds MNQ, P161, 1981/04/047\19. The state also wanted to see organizations finance themselves through various means. The best-known case is that of the special lottery launched in 1975 by Lise Payette, then responsible for the celebrations in Montreal.

8 For example, in Quebec City the Saint-Jean-Baptiste Society would compete with another committee to get the subsidies.

9 Hayday, "La francophonie canadienne," 103.

10 Comité des onze, *Rapport du comité des onze relatif à la fête nationale du Québec: présenté au Premier ministre du Québec Monsieur René Lévesque*, 7 October 1977, BAnQ, Fonds de la Société Saint-Jean-Baptiste de Québec (here after SSJBQ), P412, 2011–09–02\39; Gouvernement du Québec, *Décision 77-51 du Conseil des ministres*, 17 February 1977.

11 Gouvernement du Québec, *Décision 77-51 du Conseil des ministres*, 17 February 1977.

12 Gouvernement du Québec, *Gazette du Québec*, Part 1, June 1977, 5213.

13 Malausséna, "Commémoration et lien territorial," 101.

14 " 31st Législature, *Journal des débats de l'Assemblée nationale*, 23 June 1977, 1630 ("Au nom du gouvernement, il me fait plaisir de souhaiter bonne fête … à tous les vrais Québécois. Lorsque je dis tous les vrais Québécois, pour éviter toute ambigüité qui pourrait s'installer dans l'esprit de certains, je ne veux pas dire seulement les francophones, je veux dire tous les vrais Québécois de quelque origine qu'ils soient anglophones ou d'une origine ethnique autre").

15 Quebec, *La politique québécoise de développement culturel*, vol. 1 (Quebec: Éditeur officiel, 1978), 43–60.

16 Cabinet du Premier ministre, "Texte de la conférence de presse du Premier Ministre," *Rapport du comité des onze relatif à la fête nationale du Québec.*

17 Comité des fêtes nationales de la Saint-Jean, *Procès-verbal*, 4 April 1977, 6.

18 Ibid., 18 March 1977, 1. In the volatile context of the sixties, a critique of the traditional Saint-Jean-Baptiste Society allowed new players to emerge. This included municipalities and their leisure divisions. With the development of recreation in Canada and the professionalization of the field around organizations such as Regroupement loisirs Québec (1974), the Société des Festivals Populaires du Québec (1975), and the Confédération des Loisirs du Québec (1969), attention was given to the national holiday and the nationalist actors had to deal with these groups.

19 Comité des onze, *Rapport du comité des onze relatif à la fête nationale du Québec.*

20 31ᵉ Législature, *Journal des débats de l'Assemblée nationale*, 2 June 1977, 1280–1.

21 31ᵉ Législature, *Commission permanente des engagements financiers*, 24 February 1977, pp. B-450–7and 28 April 1977, pp. B-1629–30.

22 31ᵉ Législature, *Journal des débats de l'Assemblée nationale*, 21 June 1977, 1529.

23 Ibid., 22 June 1977, 1579.

24 Cited in Ouimet, "Le lys en fête," 128–30.

25 The resolution (76–0–1) stated: "Les députés de l'Assemblée nationale du Québec dénoncent la décision de la Commission des champs de bataille nationaux de ne pas autoriser la tenue sur les plaines d'Abraham du feu d'artifice et du spectacle de la Saint-Jean pour le 24 juin et demandent au ministre fédéral, M. Warren Allmand, de prendre les mesures qui s'imposent pour que cette décision soit renversée. Que copie conforme de cette résolution soit transmise par le secrétaire général de l'Assemblée

nationale du Québec au ministre M. Warren Allmand." 31ᵉ Législature, *Journal des débats de l'Assemblée nationale*, 17 June 1977, 1493–1520.

26 In this regard, the organizers of the national holiday emphasized the confusion about the funding program for local organizations. Comité des onze, *Rapport du comité des onze relatif à la fête nationale du Québec.*

27 Ibid.

28 Comité organisateur de la fête nationale, *Les comités régionaux de la fête nationale du Québec,* 17 February 1978, BAnQ, Fonds SSJBQ, P412, 2011–09–02\23.

29 On this topic, see Marie Chicoine et al., *Lâchés lousses: les fêtes populaires au Québec, en Acadie et en Louisiane* (Montreal: VLB éditeur, 1982), 261–3.

30 "Le comité des onze dénonce la politisation de la fête nationale," *Journal de Québec,* 2 March 1978.

31 Comité des onze, Texte de la conférence de presse de M. Alain Généreux au sujet de la fête nationale du Québec, Montreal, 1 March 1978, BAnQ, SSJBQ, P412, 2011–09–02\23.

32 François Forest, "La Saint-Jean: 576 villes fêteront grâce à 16,000 bénévoles," *La Presse* (Montreal), 6 June 1978.

33 Angèle Dagenais, "Le Comité de la fête réplique durement à Parizeau et Vaugeois," *Le Devoir* (Montreal), 6 June 1978.

34 31ᵉ Législature, *Journal des débats de l'Assemblée nationale du Québec*, 8 March 1978, 335. ; Michèle Tremblay, "Québec veut faire fêter les Québécois en isolant les nationalistes," *Journal de Québec,* 28 March 1978.

35 31ᵉ Législature, *Journal des débats de l'Assemblée nationale du Québec*, 8 June 1978, 2099 ("Nous avons tenu quinze assemblées régionales où, à partir des conseils régionaux des loisirs, tous les organismes intéressés à l'organisation de la fête nationale pouvaient participer à cette assemblée, où les gens sur place se choisissaient, au niveau de leurs régions, un comité organisateur pour la fête nationale du Québec. Je précise, pour être très clair, que je me suis fait faire le reproche de ne pas avoir confié en bloc à des mouvements nationalistes québécois, très identifiés à l'option constitutionnelle du gouvernement actuel, l'organisation de la fête nationale. Cela m'a valu des ennuis. Cela m'a valu des problèmes. Mais j'ai voulu remettre la fête du Québec au monde du Québec. Quand le premier ministre m'a confié cette fonction, le 13 janvier dernier, en me demandant de prendre ce dossier qu'il ne pouvait plus assumer, c'était ma condition. Il l'a acceptée, mes collègues du Cabinet ont accepté ma formule aussi").

36 François Forest, "Les fêtes tournent en guerre de dollars," *La Presse* (Montreal), 10 June 1978 ("Ce n'est surement pas avec des défilés

militaires, des parades de la gendarmerie royale et des majorettes d'Ottawa qu'ils embarqueront les Québécois").

37 Ibid.

38 A meeting with the premier was held in December 1977. Alain Généreux, letter to Marcel Gauvreau, 28 November 1977, BAnQ, Fonds de la SSJBQ, P412, 2011–09–02\23.

39 Comité des onze, *Texte de la conférence de presse de M. Alain Généreux.*

40 Luc Lamy, correspondence with Alain Généreux, 31 October 1977; Nathalie Petrowski, "La corporation des fêtes de la Saint-Jean décide de jouer le jeu," *La Presse* (Montreal), [April 1978], BAnQ, Fonds SSJBQ, P412, 2011–09–02\23.

41 Comité organisateur de la fête nationale, *Rapport annuel 1978*, November 1978.

42 Ibid., 10.

43 Ibid., 5.

44 Cited in Chicoine et al., *Lâchés lousses*, 258.

45 Ibid., 260.

46 Ibid., 5.

47 Corporation des fêtes du 24 juin, *À la découverte de notre fête nationale* (Quebec : Éditeur officiel, 1980), 38 ("Aux activités culturelles qui vont donc cette année, avec plus d'éclats que jamais, souligner l'évènement, participeront très largement aussi nos concitoyens des communautés ethniques. Ce 24 juin, est-il besoin de le dire, doit être la fête de tous les québécois, de tous les groupes comme de tous les milieux et de toutes les confessions et, de toutes les origines comme de toutes les nuances politiques. La fête de tous et une fête pour tous").

48 Comité organisateur de la fête nationale, *Rapport annuel 1978*, November 1978.

49 Gagnon, "Le Canada français vit par ses œuvres."

50 Corporation des fêtes du 24 juin, *À la découverte de notre fête nationale,* 43.

51 31ᵉ Législature, *Journal des débats de l'Assemblée nationale,* 1 June 1978, 1820. The bill also aimed to indirectly pressure the federal government to ensure that its employees could have a day off on 24 June, especially in Hull, where the federal government kept its buildings open. 31ᵉ Législature, *Journal des débats de l'Assemblée nationale,* 22 June 1977, 1581; "Le fédéral fait volte-face: un choix entre la Saint-Jean et le 1ᵉʳ août," *Le Droit* (Ottawa), 21 June 1977; "La SNQ est très déçue," *Le Droit,* 21 june 1977; Gérard Desrochers, "Les employés du fédéral au Québec "oublieront" leur anglais vendredi," *Le Droit*, 22 June 1977; "Des fonctionnaires d'Ottawa réclament aussi le libre-choix," *Le Droit*, 23 June 1977.

52 31ᵉ Législature, *Journal des débats de l'Assemblée nationale*, 1 June 1978, 1816.
53 Ibid., 1817.
54 31ᵉ Législature, *Journal des débats de l'Assemblée nationale*, 8 June 1978, 2098.
55 On this point, the sources disagree. In the National Assembly, Claude Charron stated that the first deficit occurred in 1981.
56 Claude Rochon, "Aux présidents généraux des Sociétés nationales," 23 February 1979, BAnQ, Fonds MNQ, P161 1981/04/047\20.
57 32ᵉ Législature, *Journal des débats de l'Assemblée nationale*, 1 October 1981.
58 Ibid., 42.
59 Ibid., 10 November 1981, 28.
60 Ibid. An alleged theft of the financial documents at the offices of the organizing committee of the Fête nationale in Montreal delayed the inquiry. Ibid., 2 March 1982, 2133.
61 Ibid., 1 October 1981, 46 ("J'affirme de ma place que je n'ai jamais recommandé quiconque au conseil d'administration. Je ne me suis aucunement mêlé de ceux qui étaient embauchés, ni au niveau des régions, ni au niveau de l'administration nationale. Que certains des membres de mon parti et de l'association de comté de Saint-Jacques aient postulé ces postes et aient été retenus par le conseil d'administration que je n'avais pas nommé et que je ne contrôlais pas, oui, c'est vrai. Mais je n'y peux rien").
62 Ibid., 472.
63 Société Saint-Jean-Baptiste de Montréal, "Communiqué de presse: mise au point de la SSJB-M," 29 September 1981, BAnQ, Fonds SSJBQ, P412, 2011–09–02\23.
64 Benjamin Carry, letter from the Société Saint-Jean-Baptiste de Valleyfield to René Lévesque, 1 December 1981; Noel Giroux, letter from the Société Saint-Jean-Baptiste de Québec to René Lévesque, 10 November 1981, BAnQ, Fonds SSJBQ, P412, 2011–09–02\23.
65 32ᵉ Législature, *Journal des débats de l'Assemblée nationale*, 15 December 1981.
66 Claude Ryan, correspondence with M. Noël Giroux, director general of the Société Saint-Jean-Baptiste de Québec, 1 December 1981, BAnQ, Fonds de la SSJBQ (P412), 2011–09–02\23; 32ᵉ Législature, *Journal des débats de l'Assemblée nationale*, 15 December 1981. A few weeks earlier, the Saint-Jean-Baptiste Society of Montreal had published an advertisement in major newspapers calling all federalists agreeing with the constitutional repatriation "traitors."
67 32ᵉ Législature, *Journal des débats de l'Assemblée nationale*, 17 June 1982, 5026.
68 Normand Girard, "Le PQ a une bien mauvaise opinion des mouvements nationalistes!" *Journal de Québec*, 10 May 1982; "Pour les Sociétés nationales, Lucien Lessard a fait son nid," *Le Devoir* (Montreal),

20 May 1985. Lucien Lessard, correspondence with Gilles Rhéaume, président du MNQ, Quebec, 19 May 1982, BAnQ, Fonds Gérard Turcotte (CLG59), 2009–08–003\345.

69 32ᵉ Législature, *Journal des débats de l'Assemblée nationale*, 18 June 1982, 5135.

70 32ᵉ Législature, *Journal des débats de l'Assemblée nationale*, 11 May 1982, 3386 ("En effet, les mêmes problèmes vécus l'an dernier risquent de réapparaître à court terme, soit à cause de la forte visibilité politique de certaines de ces sociétés – il veut probablement dire qu'elles sont identifiées au Parti québécois – soit parce qu'aucune d'entre elles – ce sont le MNQ, la SNQ et la SSJB pour toute la province – n'est à l'abri des mêmes problèmes, dépenses somptuaires, accusations de corruption, gaspillage de fonds. Comment le ministre peut-il porter une accusation aussi grave à l'égard de toutes les sociétés nationales? Est-ce que l'identification des sociétés nationales avec le Parti québécois, dans l'esprit du ministre, est telle qu'elles doivent porter la culpabilité de tous les abus du Parti québécois?").

71 Jacques Bouchard, "Lévesque rencontrera Rhéaume," *La Presse*, 27 October 1982.

72 Georges Lamon, "La fête nationale a besoin de plus d'argent de Québec," *La Presse* (Montreal), 23 October 1982.

73 Conrad Bernier, "Le ministre Guy Chevrette ne respecte pas ses engagements" and Jacques Bouchard, "Un dossier qui continue de faire couler beaucoup d'encre," *La Presse*, 23 March 1983.

74 Jean-Paul Charbonneau, "Les corporations régionales veulent organiser la fête," *La Presse* (Montreal), 17 March 1983.

75 32ᵉ Législature, *Journal des débats de la Commission permanente de l'aménagement et des équipements: étude de crédits du ministère des Transports et du Ministère des Loisirs, Chasse et Pêche*, 12 April 1984, p. CAE-247.

76 Jacques Benoît, "Des fêtes dans 750 villes et villages," *La Presse* (Montreal), 14 May 1983.

77 32ᵉ Législature, *Journal des débats de la Commission permanente de l'aménagement et des équipements: étude de crédits du ministère des Transports et du Ministère des Loisirs, Chasse et Pêche*, 12 April 1984, p. CAE-247.

15 The Rootedness of Acadian Neo-nationalism: The Changing Meaning of le 15 août, 1968–1982

MICHAEL POPLYANSKY

From the late 1960s until the early 1980s, New Brunswick's Acadian community experienced enormous change. A new nationalism emerged, calling into question the old customs, symbols, and institutions.[1] This neo-nationalism represented a desire to control state structures for the purpose of ensuring Acadians' collective development. It took different forms, ranging from the struggle for an Acadian province to the desire for separate sub-state institutions.

Le 15 août[2] – Acadians' historic *fête nationale* – came in for its fair share of criticism in neo-nationalist circles. Yet, as this chapter seeks to demonstrate, the rejection of le 15 août among neo-nationalists was far from being as overwhelming as might appear at first sight. On the contrary, neo-nationalists' reappropriation of le 15 août speaks to their continued respect for their ancestors' achievements. By focusing on the national holiday, this chapter seeks to demonstrate "the persistence of the old in the guise of the new"[3] in contemporary *Acadie*.

First, we must provide a brief recapitulation of the origins of Acadia's *fête nationale* with reference to the relevant historiography. We will then describe the phenomenon known as Acadian neo-nationalism and the way in which it might be perceived as representing a clean break with Acadia's past.[4] We will, lastly, challenge this interpretation by closely analysing neo-nationalists' views of Acadia's national holiday. As other contributors to this volume have illustrated, the significance of recurrent national holidays may change over time. Yet, in contrast to other efforts to shape historic holidays – such as that of 1970s sovereigntist activists in the case of Saint-Jean Baptiste Day / the Fête nationale du Québec, as discussed by Marc-André Gagnon in chapter 14, or of Prime Minister Pierre Trudeau in the case of Dominion/Canada Day, as analysed by Matthew Hayday in chapter 11 and Raymond Blake and Bailey Antonishyn in chapter 12 – Acadian neo-nationalists ultimately sought to emphasize continuity with the origins of le 15 août.

The origins of le 15 août

Le 15 août was proclaimed at Acadians' first national convention, held in Memramcook, New Brunswick, in 1881. The convention brought together Acadia's professional and religious elites who had been invited to attend the first Congrès catholique des Canadiens français in Quebec City in 1880. There, the hundred or so Maritime delegates decided to hold a specifically Acadian convention the following year. At Memramcook, a heated debate ensued as to whether Acadians should partake in French Canada's Saint-Jean-Baptiste Day celebrations or have their own national holiday. Ultimately, led by Monsignor Marcel-François Richard, an ultramontane priest from Saint-Louis-de Kent, delegates chose the Virgin Mary as Acadians' national patron and le 15 août – Assumption Day – as Acadia's national holiday.[5]

The classic study of the 1881 convention was written in 1960 by one of Acadia's first academic sociologists, Camille-Antoine Richard. He described it as the beginning of Acadians' national consciousness. Noting a "separatist" sentiment among delegates, Richard demonstrated the Acadian elites' desire to avoid being absorbed into a larger French-Canadian community. He also illustrated the extent to which the *congressistes* were conscious of Acadians' perceived vulnerability. Monsignor Richard, himself, spoke of how Acadians were a weak people, requiring a "strong patron saint."[6] This weakness was, naturally, linked to the Deportation, a theme that Chantal Richard has recently analysed.[7] Indeed, one of the great defenders of le 15 août, Pascal Poirier, who would soon become a Canadian senator, explicitly presented it as an opportunity to commemorate the Deportation:

> Let us choose a celebration that belongs to us, gentlemen. We have our own history; we have an unfortunate past unique to us; our condition is humble; our future is not one of a powerful people, whether in terms of numbers or resources: let us have, only for ourselves, a national holiday where we will meet to speak of our forefathers; where we will remember the glories and the misfortunes of the past; where we will lament over the great holocaust of 1755; a day when we will dare to look to the future because we will be together, united, hand in hand.[8]

The rationale behind the desire to distinguish Acadia from French Canada and the accompanying emphasis on the Deportation was never fully elucidated. It may have been motivated by a revolt against the Quebec clergy for its lack of support during New Brunswick's 1871 school crisis and for its general indifference to Irish dominance over Maritime ecclesiastical institutions.[9] Overtly, however, delegates at the 1881 congress limited themselves to celebrating Acadians' unique historical experience and did not engage in strong anti-French-Canadian rhetoric. There were, for instance, regular references to "our French-Canadian brothers." Above all else, le 15 août was presented as an opportunity to celebrate the providential *survivance* of a people that had overcome, to use Poirier's words, a "great holocaust."[10]

Along with a national holiday, the Acadian conventions of the late nineteenth and early twentieth century led to the adoption of a distinct Acadian flag, the creation of the Société nationale de l'Assomption (SNA),[11] and the expansion of Acadia's network of classical colleges. Joel Belliveau has noted that, "between 1881 and 1960 Acadians could have been under the impression of having their own country."[12] It was this traditional nationalism – divorced from any idea of controlling state structures – that le 15 août was originally meant to symbolize.[13] Throughout the twentieth century, therefore, 15 août celebrations would begin with a religious service. Other activities were incorporated as well: parades, picnics, lobster festivals, and, eventually, beauty contests. Professional and political elites would also make speeches evoking Acadian history and encouraging the audience to remain true to their "language and faith."[14] These speeches were made in a spirit of *bonne entente*, however. Anglophone public figures were frequently present during Acadian festivities, secure in the knowledge that the parallel society that Acadians were constructing did not call into question anglophone political dominance. Indeed, in the late nineteenth and early twentieth century, anglophone and francophone elites believed that it was possible to reconcile competing cultural traditions within a single imperial framework, as demonstrated in chapter 5 by Joel Belliveau and Marcel Martel.[15]

The Rise of Neo-nationalism

Starting in the 1960s, the old markers of Acadian nationhood came under attack. A new nationalism would develop, whose central aim was access to political power. There is little scholarly literature analysing the way in which Acadian neo-nationalists reconciled themselves with traditional national symbols, such as the *fête nationale*. After a brief summary of the rise of neo-nationalism, it is to this issue that our attention will turn.

Given Acadian demographic realities, neo-nationalism found a particularly hospitable terrain in New Brunswick, a province where Acadians formed roughly a third of the population. Neo-nationalism expressed itself in many forms, ranging from attempts at gaining control over sub-state institutions – a cause taken up notably by the Société des Acadiens du Nouveau-Brunswick (SANB) – to the struggle for a separate Acadian province, the raison d'être of the short-lived Parti acadien (PA).[16] This chapter will focus on these two organizations' perceptions of le 15 août, as they represent perfectly the two main strands of neo-nationalist thought, the former being more moderate and the latter more radical. In contrast to the situation described in Marc-André Gagnon's chapter on Quebec's Fête nationale, neither group had a monopoly on the organization of 15 août celebrations; yet, they both sought to stimulate patriotic fervor among New Brunswick's Acadian population. Although the PA was quite marginal compared to the SANB, it still attracted significant support among Acadian intellectual elites. Considering its small size, the PA maintained a strong media presence, and its program was taken seriously, even by those who did not vote for it at election time.[17]

The ideas behind neo-nationalism – notably the notion that Acadians had to find ways to control political power in order to advance their community's collective interests – began to percolate in the mid-1960s, gaining momentum as the decade reached its end. Thanks notably to the SANB and the PA, neo-nationalists remained quite influential throughout the 1970s, before reaching a modus vivendi with the New Brunswick government in the early 1980s.[18] The years between 1968 and 1982 represent, therefore, the heyday of Acadian neo-nationalism, which explains this chapter's chronological markers.

Neo-nationalism was an outgrowth of what is known as New Brunswick's Quiet Revolution. During this period, the provincial state, under the leadership of Louis Robichaud, who was premier throughout the 1960s, became far more interventionist. Programs that had been managed at the local level were centralized in Fredericton.[19] Although his reforms were initially divorced from any nationalist rhetoric, Robichaud created institutions, such as the Université de Moncton, that would allow for the emergence of a new generation of Acadian nationalists. As historian Joel Belliveau has argued, in the early 1960s, young Acadians were generally liberal, seeking only to participate on an equal basis in New Brunswick society. Yet, as the decade progressed, they realized that the structural inequalities between francophone and anglophone New Brunswickers remained in place. It was only then that they turned to neo-nationalism.[20] Like their Québécois counterparts, they were members of what political scientist Kenneth McRoberts calls the "new middle class": social scientists, teachers, government employees.[21] Perhaps troubled by the fact that they were abandoning the liberal ideals of the early 1960s, neo-nationalists insisted that they had an entirely different understanding of nationalism from that of their elders. Rather than being anchored in ancient traditions, their nationalism was to be rooted in the modernity represented by the ever-expanding state.

This perspective had several implications. First, it appeared doubtful to some neo-nationalists that the francophone minority in Canada could ever exercise any real political power outside Quebec. Second, having called into question the old markers of Acadian nationhood, neo-nationalists were no longer sure what distinguished them from their Québécois cousins. Indeed, annexation or immigration to Quebec became a viable option in neo-nationalist circles.

The clearest illustration of this way of thinking may be found in essayist Michel Roy's *L'Acadie perdue*. Perhaps seeking to be deliberately provocative, Roy severely criticized the nineteenth-century elites who were behind traditional Acadian nationalism. The symbols they created, he argued, represented an exercise in myth making designed to cover up francophones' subordinate position vis-à-vis their English-speaking neighbours. Concluding that he did not "know whether we are, or ever have been, essentially different from the 'Québécois'," Roy implied that distinctions from Quebec – as evidenced by le 15 août – were artificial and ought to be abandoned.[22]

While not going quite so far as Roy, neo-nationalists set out to organize a *rapprochement* with the Québécois and to distance themselves from Acadian traditions throughout the late 1960s and early 1970s. At the time, neo-nationalism was not an organized movement but rather made itself felt in various spheres of civil society, particularly among students and young university professors.

The first "green shoots" of Acadian neo-nationalism emerged in 1966, with the Ralliement de la jeunesse acadienne (RJA). Organized by two Université de Moncton professors, philosopher Roger Savoie and sociologist Camille-Antoine Richard, this convention attracted roughly two hundred young people from across the Maritimes. Savoie and Richard hoped to re-examine traditional Acadian nationalism and develop a new collective project. Everything was to be called into question: Acadians had to ask themselves, Savoie wrote, "whether the patriotic symbols (flag, national anthem, patron saint, national holiday) have become irrelevant or whether they still hold some significance."[23] The participants at the RJA responded to Savoie's call, at least insofar as rejecting the symbols of Acadia's past was concerned.[24] Pierre Savoie – a former Université de Moncton student working in Chicoutimi – bluntly declared that he did not "know the words to our national anthem" nor was he "sure if the tricolor flag wore its star high to the right or the left." "To be honest," he continued, "that does not matter to me. What interests me is the future... We are not all museum curators, as far as I know."[25] Among the resolutions adopted by the RJA was a declaration that "patriotic symbols, such as the flag, the patron saint and the national holiday, may be conserved in the rich folklore of Acadia, but they shall not be invoked as signs of national identity."[26] Beyond a rejection of the past, however, the RJA did not produce a political action plan for Acadia's future.

This political project began to develop later in the 1960s. In 1968–69, the Université de Moncton was paralysed by a series of student revolts, the students demanding supplementary funding to make up for centuries' long *retard*. One of the students' mentors was none other than Roger Savoie, who had by then moved to Montreal. Before the beginning of student unrest, in February 1968, he had made a dramatic speech urging students to consider the possibility of annexation to Quebec. The speech also evoked the rebellious spirit that was so prevalent at the RJA. Calling Acadians a "faceless people," living "in a house of fools where we no longer know … our tasks, our leaders or our goals," his rhetoric represented a sharp critique of Acadia's traditional elite.[27]

Among the student leaders during the 1968 strike were Michel Blanchard and Bernard Gauvin, who would later become involved with the Parti acadien. Their actions were immortalized in Michel Brault and Pierre Perrault's classic documentary *Acadie, Acadie?!?* Therein, Gauvin is particularly blunt when he asserts that "there is no future outside of Quebec."[28] Acadians would be deluding themselves, therefore, if they remained true to their ancestral homeland and its customs; immigration to Quebec, and the rupture that it symbolized, was the only viable solution for North America's francophones, including Acadians.

Two years after the end of the students' strike, its former leaders defended the possibility of annexing northern New Brunswick to Quebec at a meeting of the Société nationale des Acadiens (SNA), a group that had always been at the heart of traditional Acadian nationalism. The groundwork for the SNA had been laid at the 1890 Acadian convention in Church Point, Nova Scotia; since then it had been the institution par excellence of Acadia's professional and religious elites from the three Maritime provinces. At the SNA's 1970 convention, however, Blanchard, Gauvin, together with Collège de Bathurst student Joseph-Yvon Thériault and Euclide Chiasson, a Collège de Bathurst professor who would become the first leader of the PA, called for it to seriously study the annexationist option. In the meantime, they suggested that the SNA give birth to a new association of francophone New Brunswickers, pointedly refusing to use the historic term "Acadian" to designate their proposed organization.[29] Although this group of neo-nationalists would not receive the support of a majority of SNA members, their demands reflect a broad-based calling into question of the historic foundations of Acadian nationhood.

Perhaps the most forceful plea for annexation came thanks to former Université de Moncton student-turned-poet, Raymond LeBlanc. In December 1970, in the student newspaper L'embryon, he published what he called a "political manifesto" based on a recently delivered public lecture at the Université de Moncton campus. "We must have a new beginning: the future," he wrote. Moreover, he called for "a collective suicide" that would allow Acadians to "'quebecisize' themselves … to join with our Québécois brothers who speak the same language as ourselves, to opt for Acadia to become a province within a strong and sovereign Quebec."[30] It would be difficult to find a more explicit call for the rejection of the trappings of traditional Acadian nationalism.

In such a context, one can imagine that celebrating le 15 août was not necessarily a popular idea in neo-nationalist circles in the late 1960s and early 1970s. Université de Moncton student Ronald Cormier, who identified with the neo-nationalist movement, could not have been blunter in an article published in L'Évangéline in 1968: "The national symbols, such as the flag, the national holiday, the national anthem, and the patron saint hinder an awareness on the part of the population, forcing them to focus on a sorrowful past,"[31] he wrote. In his manifesto, Raymond LeBlanc also evoked the general need to "to liberate ourselves from our fear, which is of religious origin."[32] Considering the religious roots of Acadia's national holiday, one cannot help but see an indirect attack on le 15 août. Such was the general hostility to le 15 août that an editor of *L'Évangéline*, presumably Claude Bourque, hesitated to refer to it in his newspaper. Speaking with anthropologist Louis Cimino he described the trepidation with which he wrote his 1971 editorial calling on Acadians to take pride in their national holiday.[33] His readers did not even wish to hear about Acadians, he said, "because the only ones talking about the Acadians were supposed to be the Old Establishment. You were supposed to be talking about francophones[;] that was the new word."[34]

Indeed, some neo-nationalists, such as Euclide Chiasson and Raymond LeBlanc, appeared to join with left-wing activists in suggesting that the term "Acadian" might be outdated.[35] Throughout 1971 and 1972, these individuals applied sustained pressure on the SNA to disband, in favour of a new provincial association of francophones, possibly called the Front commun des francophones.[36] On the surface at least, by rejecting the term "Acadian," neo-nationalists of the late 1960s and early 1970s seemed willing to abandon the old nationalism and join with the Québécois in building a new francophone nation, cut off from the symbols and institutions of the past.

A True Tabula Rasa?

Yet, reality was far from being this clear-cut. It is worth questioning whether neo-nationalists' rejection of the past and its symbols, including le 15 août, was as great as might at first appear. At the dawn of the neo-nationalist era, in 1966, Camille-Antoine Richard began a "Document préparatoire" distributed to all RJA participants by acknowledging that

> I must honour those who we have come to call, since 1881, our national elite: this bourgeois intelligentsia, trained for the most part in our classical colleges... I sincerely believe that, this elite, through the social organizations that it established, has played a seminal role ...[of] consciousness raising, as much among the anglophone majority as among the Acadians themselves.[37]

In his 1968 article in *L'Évangéline* vigourously critiquing the *fête nationale*, Ronald Cormier also wrote that traditional institutions such as the SNA "have succeeded in obtaining something for francophones."[38] Michel Blanchard, one of the leaders of the 1968 student strike, was also far from entirely rejecting the work of his ancestors. In the film *Acadie, Acadie?!?* Blanchard evoked the necessity of remaining true to his forefathers. "I do not understand how, being brought up by a father and a mother who gave their all to raise us, [we could], when we get a degree, tell them good-bye ... thank them, and then leave. I do not understand that! It might be sentimental, but I do not understand it," he declared. True, Blanchard portrayed Acadia's religious heritage in less than flattering terms. His parents had had to "endure the priests, all the wretched mess, instead of living in Montreal, with the big shots."[39] Yet, the general sentiment emerging from his statements seems to be one of gratitude. We can assume that the young Blanchard would have agreed with Quebec historian Eric Bédard, who recently wrote, in quite a different context, that, "while I do not deny that our ancestors were like us, imperfect, capable of the best and of the worst, they inspire in me, nonetheless, a great sense of gratitude. Without their tenacity, their sacrifices, their dreams and their ambitions, we would be nothing, or very little."[40] In sum, statements by neo-nationalists such as Richard, Cormier, and Blanchard allow us to anticipate le 15 août's continued importance in 1970s *Acadie*.

We should also question the significance of neo-nationalists' desire to identify themselves as "francophone" beginning in the late 1960s. It may have had more to do with involving the Brayons from the Madawaska than with a desire to negate a special "Acadian" heritage.[41] Likewise, neo-nationalists' openness to annexation may have been less a rejection of "Acadia" than a form of support for some type of association with Quebec in the event of the latter's separation from Canada. As Jean-Paul Hautecoeur has noted, annexationists such as Raymond LeBlanc could not help using the terms "Acadie" and "Acadiens" when describing the geographic region that would be annexed to Quebec and its future inhabitants. Annexationist professor Roger Savoie likewise lauded Acadia's "particular character" in his 1968 speech.[42] Therefore, by introducing the term "francophone" and in advocating a "rapprochement" with the Québécois, annexationists were not necessarily proposing a wholesale rejection of Acadia's unique character.

At any rate, the term "francophone" never really took hold among neo-nationalists in New Brunswick, as is evident in the evolution of the SANB. Those who had been pressuring the SNA to give birth to a provincial organization finally had their way with the 1972 Congrès de francophones du Nouveau-Brunswick (CFNB). Bringing together roughly 1000 delegates, mostly young neo-nationalists, the CFNB would ultimately give birth to the SANB, which was officially founded on 4 June 1973. Significantly, this neo-nationalist association would carry forward the Acadian identity and not be styled "le Front commun des francophones," as had been proposed at one point.[43] Delegates at the CFNB had insisted on the relevance of the term "Acadian" to distinguish francophone New Brunswickers – the terms "francophone New Brunswicker" and "Acadian" were used interchangeably – from "les Québécois." Moreover, the CFNB paid direct tribute to "the clergy that worked for the cause of francophone minorities."[44] Characterizing neo-nationalism as being in complete rupture with the nationalism of the past would be a very significant oversimplification.

The SANB and le 15 août

Once it was founded in 1973, the SANB itself turned out to be relatively moderate in tone. Led in its early years by Collège de Bathurst sociologist Pierre Poulin (1973–74) and then by lawyer Roger Savoie (1974–75), the SANB did not call for annexation to Quebec; instead it concentrated its efforts on bringing about reforms within New Brunswick so as to give Acadians the means of self-government through various sub-state institutions. Given the distance that it placed between itself and the Québécois, it is not at all surprising that the SANB wished to maintain signs of Acadian particularity and was fully engaged in celebrating le 15 août from its inception.

In 1974, the SANB board published a short text in *L'Évangéline* commemorating the early-twentieth-century *congressistes* and calling on Acadians and francophones – the terms were again used synonymously – to celebrate the *fête nationale* with pride.[45] The same reverential attitude towards *les ancêtres* would continue throughout the 1970s and into the 1980s. Le 15 août represented a noble tradition; it was "an Acadian holiday par excellence" and had to be celebrated as such.[46] Despite the fact that "for many years Acadians had had very little communication among themselves ... every year, for a hundred years, on le 15 août, the Acadians have striven to demonstrate that they will continue to exist against all odds." Le 15 août was therefore an opportunity to defy those who tried to "exaggerate the differences between Acadians in order to justify their refusal to recognize the Acadian people in New Brunswick." It was a way of proving that there existed within the province "another collectivity that is alive and well, which is not only different in terms of language, but also in terms of history, traditions, and culture."[47] To that end, the SANB organized letter-writing campaigns attempting to convince mayors across New Brunswick to fly the Acadian flag throughout the month of August, most especially on le 15 août.[48] Abandoning the national holiday was therefore never part of the SANB's agenda.

Le 15 août was not just an occasion to celebrate the past; it was also an opportunity to plan future action. In 1978, for instance, the SANB published a full-page ad in *L'Évangéline*, quoting annexationist Raymond LeBlanc's poem "Acadie-Québec." (see figure 15.1) LeBlanc wrote of changing "the slaves' misery / Into the reality of the new and the free."[49] Considering LeBlanc's ideas, the "slaves" to which he was referring were Acadians wedded to traditional nationalism. Yet, instead of promoting annexation to Quebec, as was LeBlanc's original intent, the SANB re-titled his poem "Bonne fête à tous les Acadiens" and included an image of an Acadian flag. It did not see the need to reject the past and its symbols in order to develop the new Acadian nationalism that LeBlanc was calling for.

The PA and le 15 août

The more radical neo-nationalists – those who had presented the annexationist motion at the 1970 SNA congress – formed their own organization in February 1972: the Parti acadien. Here, too, the name is significant. PA leaders were not interested in calling themselves only "francophones" – they enthusiastically embraced their *acadianité*. The party's first leader, Euclide Chiasson, clarified the PA's nationalism at the moment of its founding: it did not have an official position on annexation and was open to the possibility of an Acadian province.[50] Eventually, the latter option would become the party's official policy. The PA's "Objectif national," approved at its 1977 convention, stated that it would be an error of historic proportions "to choose an option dependent on the option chosen by another people: the Québécois, for example."[51] A clear distinction was therefore being made between Quebec and Acadia, something that was less than evident in 1960s neo-nationalist discourse.

The PA's ultimate rejection of a complete "fusion" with Quebec should come as no surprise, considering the ideas of the man who would become one the party's major intellectual leaders, University of Moncton history professor Léon Thériault. As far back as 1966, Thériault criticized RJA participants for having thrown opprobrium on the

15.1 SANB message for le 15e août in L'*Évangéline*, 15 August 1978.

"elites" who had declared le 15 août to be Acadia's national holiday in 1881. In choosing a date that was different from French Canadians' Saint-Jean-Baptiste Day, Thériault claimed, "Acadians did not want to risk losing our Acadian identity, and maybe even our capacity to solve our problems."[52] Once he became involved in the PA, Thériault published an article in L'Évangéline vaunting the *fête nationale*'s modernity. It was never meant to be an exclusively religious celebration, he claimed; le 15 août was rather an affirmation of Acadians' distinctiveness and a rejection of their "minority mentality."[53] The *fête nationale* was, therefore, not a symbol of an Acadian past to be abandoned, but an ever-relevant celebration of Acadia's future potential.

Such was the way in which the PA embraced le 15 août. True, its position changed slightly throughout the 1970s as the party's own policy orientations gradually evolved. At its founding in 1972, the PA was a heterogeneous group, involving not only nationalists but also individuals from the extreme left who had little interest in the trappings of Acadian nationhood.[54] Initially, the PA was wary of promoting the creation of a separate Acadian state, preferring to advance the less radical solutions proposed by the SANB coupled with a strong leftist discourse.[55] As a result, the party's early communiqués on le 15 août gave relatively short shrift to the "national" importance of Acadia's holiday, preferring to present it as an opportunity to reflect on Acadians' economic exploitation. On the 15th of August 1972, for instance, the PA's executive committee issued a statement highlighting a number of socio-economic issues affecting New Brunswick's francophone population: the struggle against the expropriation of land to create Kouchibouguac National Park as well as the economic impact of cooperatives and the Union des consommateurs occupied pride of place. Concluding that, while "hostile interests will not give up their powers without a fight,… the Acadian people are still stronger than a few exploiters," the PA's executive committee chose to emphasize "down-to-earth" struggles rather than dwell on the continuities between the party and earlier forms of Acadian nationalism.[56]

The PA's leaders – first Euclide Chiasson and then, especially, his successor, Bathurst physician Jean-Pierre Lanteigne[57] – were closer to the party's nationalist than its socialist wing. As the years passed, therefore, the nationalist connotation of le 15 août – its potential for allowing Acadians to reconnect with their ancestors as they developed a new political project – was never far removed from the PA's public discourse. In 1975, for instance, Lanteigne declared that le 15 août "may seem paradoxical when we have such a history of injustices and exploitations. However, it matters not. If one still speaks of the national holiday in *Acadie* ... it is because hope grows among us. The struggle taken up by our ancestors for our survival continues and becomes stronger."[58] Pointedly reminding Acadians' of their debts to their ancestors, Lanteigne evoked the century's long struggle for "survivance," which was finally culminating thanks to his party's political action.

By 1977, the extreme left would abandon the PA. The party could then continue appropriating le 15 août in support of its overtly nationalist agenda right up until the October 1978 provincial election. The election gave the PA its greatest triumph, when it came within two hundred votes of winning the Restigouche-Ouest constituency. The election also allowed the PA to present "a star recruit": the SANB's president Donatien Gaudet. Gaudet's vision of Acadian nationalism is especially important, for he would become PA leader in 1979. A parish priest from Memramcook, he was driven to the party by his conviction that the SANB's goal of reforming the New Brunswick state in order to grant Acadians meaningful self-government was unachievable.[59] Gaudet's nationalism was imbued with a profound gratitude to the nineteenth-century *congressistes*, whom he considered his political mentors. Moreover, he was categorical in differentiating Acadians from the Québécois. For instance, as president of the SANB, he had written in the Quebec magazine *L'Action nationale* that "Acadians are not glorified Québécois or second-rate French Canadians… Despite all the vicissitudes, past and present, Acadians are a completely and absolutely distinct people from the Québécois or other French Canadians."[60] In that context, le 15 août was not to be slighted. "Acadians' national holiday is, at once, a symbol and a reality," Gaudet had declared while at the SANB. It "takes on a special meaning: it reminds Acadians of their origins and sensitizes them to the reality of their life together today. Therefore, more than any other celebration, it is an occasion of both rejoicing and of reflection, as much on the past as on the present and on the future."[61] Gaudet would return to this theme as a PA candidate in the 1978 election. In his speeches, he reminded his electors that "it [was] at Memramcook and Miscouche where the Acadians first chose the symbols of a people that wished to be autonomous."[62] Now, he declared, "a hundred years after Memramcook, we will have the occasion to take the initiative, once again, in giving *Acadie*, not only symbols, but that which they signify concretely: power."[63] For Gaudet, therefore, le 15 août symbolized "unfinished business" to be completed with the creation of an Acadian province.

As PA leader, Gaudet maintained this attitude towards the *fête nationale*. Writing in *L'Évangéline* on 15 August 1979, he saluted the *congressistes* for having given Acadians symbols "that belong to a country" – first among which was the national holiday – but noted that Acadians did not yet have a country of their own. "That is why I cannot be satisfied with wishing my Acadian compatriots well on the national holiday without wishing them, with ardour, a concrete and real country... At that moment we could truly celebrate," he concluded. Until that day arrived, le 15 août would remain insufficient – "What would we celebrate?" he asked rhetorically.[64]

Once Gaudet left the PA leadership in June 1980 – over apparently personal issues – his successor, Louise Blanchard, maintained the ideological direction that he had set. Blanchard's brother was none other than the former Université de Moncton student leader Michel Blanchard. Both Blanchards, along with a third sibling, Jean-Pierre, closely collaborated on setting the party's direction in the early 1980s.[65] They remained committed to a separate Acadian province – even though, following the Quebec referendum defeat, it came to be seen as more of a "long-term project."[66] They also insisted on le 15 août as a celebration of Acadia's distinct nationhood. "Today, on le 15 août, the Acadians show their attachment to their customs, values, language, and religion," Louise Blanchard wrote in 1980.[67] In referring to Acadians' shared religion, Blanchard acknowledged that the defining features of the Acadian nation had not changed so dramatically over the course of the previous century. Indeed, although celebrations of 15 août in the 1970s and 1980s included a wide range of activities – frolics, concerts, and so on – the traditional mass still took place.[68] The Acadian celebrations, in this respect, were more explicitly religious than the rebranded Fête nationale celebrations of Quebec in this period, as discussed in the previous chapter by Marc-André Gagnon, although there was still a lingering religious element in the latter events as well. Moreover, Blanchard was explicit in drawing a parallel between those who proclaimed le 15 août – the *congressistes* of 1881 – and her own party.[69] Blanchard saw both as being ahead of their time: the *congressistes* dreamed of setting up a parallel Acadian system of education, an objective that had been achieved in New Brunswick nearly a century later. The PA's aim, she hoped, would also be realized in due course.

Le 15 août and the Hegemony of Moderate Neo-nationalism

In the interim, the PA did indeed prove itself to be, at the very least, ahead of its time. The party fared dismally in the 1982 provincial elections. In large part, this was because New Brunswick premier Richard Hatfield had taken stock of neo-nationalists' demands and had acted accordingly. In 1981, the Hatfield administration passed Bill 88, which guaranteed Acadians their own cultural, social, and educational institutions. The PA appeared to have lost its raison d'être and could not maintain a presence on the New Brunswick political scene.[70]

It was, therefore, the SANB's weaker brand of neo-nationalism that "carried the day" in the early 1980s. As the PA had linked le 15 août with the idea of an "Acadian province," so too did the SANB attempt to use the national holiday to justify its own political projects. On 15 August 1981, the SANB took the opportunity to draw a direct connection between its moderate neo-nationalism, which had culminated in the adoption of Bill 88, and the efforts of the *congressistes*. SANB president Denis Losier began his *fête nationale* statement by reminding Acadians that Monsignor Richard's 1881 speeches "still made as much, if not more, sense" a century later. In the year of Bill 88's passage, the SANB committed itself to the realization of what it interpreted as Richard's ultimate objective: "equality in every sphere of government activity affecting directly or indirectly our lives as Acadians."[71]

Losier reasserted the same message a year later. As he had done in 1981, he drew inspiration from a prominent nineteenth-century clergyman. This time, he quoted Stanislas Doucet in support of his contention that "apart from their mother tongue, that which best accentuates the national identity of a people is their national holiday."[72] In order for the dreams of the nineteenth-century nationalists to be fully realized, Losier asserted that the New Brunswick government had to respect the spirit of Bill 88 and make le 15 août a statutory holiday.[73] In a memo presented to Premier Richard Hatfield, the SANB affirmed that, "if one wants to recognize our right to separate institutions, one would have to start by accepting those that we have given ourselves. Consequently, if the government ... wants to be consistent with its declaration of principles, it should officially recognize le 15 août."[74] "Equality between the linguistic communities will not be recognized by the government as long as our national holiday is not officially accepted," SANB president Denis Losier concluded in

L'Évangéline.[75] Despite the support of several ministers,[76] the recognition that Losier sought remains illusory to this day. Nevertheless, as Losier himself had acknowledged, with the passage of Bill 88, the struggle that le 15 août commemorated – the century-long battle for Acadian autonomy – had a significant victory.

Conclusion

Acadia was not spared the upheavals that spread across the Western world in the 1960s. The growth of the state called into question the old approaches to preserving francophone culture in the Maritime provinces. Henceforth, Acadia became, in the eyes of some neo-nationalists, limited to New Brunswick, where it was theoretically possible to gain access to the levers of provincial power. The Société des Acadiens du Nouveau-Brunswick sought to reform the state so as to give Acadians control of some governmental institutions. The more radical neo-nationalists in political and intellectual circles dreamed of partitioning New Brunswick so that Acadians could at last live in a state where francophones would form the majority.

In the late 1960s and early 1970s, particularly among some neo-nationalists who would later gravitate towards the Parti acadien, it was possible to detect a sharp critique of Acadia's past efforts at self-preservation. To that end, symbols such as le 15 août came to be seen as deeply insufficient. Indeed, as a result of the enormous change brought on by New Brunswick's Quiet Revolution, Acadians from all walks of life were calling into question the old markers of their national identity. Such was the generalized disillusionment with traditional nationalism that editorials appeared in *L'Évangéline* lamenting Acadians' lack of patriotic fervor on le 15 août.[77] Yet, the neo-nationalist critique of le 15 août was far from representing a wholesale rejection of Acadia's past in general or of its national holiday in particular. As with contemporary nationalists in other corners of the globe, Acadian neo-nationalists were not aiming to create a new nation out of nothing; they were looking for ways to continue their ancestors' struggles, using the tools of the twentieth century. Even Quebec neo-nationalists – whose desire to construct a new civic nation is well illustrated by Marc-André Gagnon – were not entirely divorced from their collective past.[78] Undoubtedly, however, the importance of establishing continuity with traditional nationalism was even more important in Acadia. As a result, even the most radical neo-nationalists in the PA began to present themselves as heirs to Monsignor Richard, notably celebrating Acadia's catholic origins. Le 15 août, with all its traditional overtones, remained a hallmark of their vision of Acadian identity.

The explicit reappropriation of le 15 août by the SANB and the PA coincided with (or perhaps even contributed to) a renewed pride in traditional national symbols among New Brunswick's Acadians, which manifested itself as the 1970s progressed.[79] By emphasizing their connections to le 15 août and to those who had conceived the national holiday, members of the PA and the SANB sought to legitimize their respective political agendas in the eyes of their fellow citizens. They did not seem troubled by the fact that the nationalism that they espoused was, in many ways, different from the one that gave birth to le 15 août. Perhaps it is worth ending, therefore, with the words of sociologist Jean-Paul Hautecoeur who, when concluding his classic study *L'Acadie du discours*, illustrated the connection between old and new forms of nationalism. Quoting his mentor, the leading Quebec intellectual Fernand Dumont, Hautecoeur asked rhetorically "why the young, apparently so detached from traditional values, are those most determined to perpetuate them into the future."[80] A worthwhile question to consider when examining neo-nationalists' view of le 15 août.

NOTES

1 Over the past several decades, numerous works have analysed the various tenets of what scholars refer to as "Acadian neo-nationalism." They include Joel Belliveau, *Le "moment 68" et la réinvention de l'Acadie* (Ottawa: Presses de l'Université d'Ottawa, 2014); Joel Belliveau, "Tradition, libéralisme et communautarisme durant les trente glorieuses: les étudiants de Moncton et l'entrée dans la modernité avancée des francophones du Nouveau-Brunswick" (PhD diss., Université de Montréal, 2008); Jean-Paul Hautecoeur, *L'Acadie du discours* (Quebec, Presses de l'Université Laval, 1975); Louis Cimino, "Ethnic Nationalism among the Acadians of New Brunswick: An Analysis of Ethnic Political Development" (PhD diss., Duke University, 1977); Roger Ouellette, *Le Parti acadien de la fondation à la disparition* (Moncton: Centre d'études acadiennes, 1992).
2 I will refer to le 15 août by its French appellation. Since the decline of Catholicism in *Acadie*, such is the way in which Acadians refer to their national holiday, rather than by the traditional "Assumption Day."

3 Fernand Dumont, *Genèse de la société québécoise* (Montreal: Boréal, 1997), 332 (la persistence de l'ancien sous les revêtements du nouveau). My thanks to Cody Donaldson and Noé Bourque for their help with the translations.

4 Joseph-Yvon Thériault briefly deals with this theme in *Évangéline Contes d'Amérique* (Montreal: Québec-Amérique, 2013), 199–211.

5 Léon Thériault, "Synthèse historique," in *L'Acadie des maritimes,* ed. Jean Daigle (Moncton: Chaire des études acadiennes, 1993), 67.

6 Camille Richard, "L'idéologie de la première convention nationale" (MA thesis, Laval University, 1960), 61.

7 Chantal Richard, "Le récit de la Déportation comme mythe de creation dans l'idéologie des Conventions nationales acadiennes, 1881–1937," *Acadiensis* 36, no. 1 (2006): 69–81.

8 Quoted in ibid., 74 ("Choisissons-nous une fête qui nous soit propre, messieurs. Nous avons une histoire à nous; nous avons un passé malheureux qui nous est propre; notre condition est humble; notre avenir n'est pas celui d'un peuple puissant par le nombre et les ressources: ayons pour nous seuls un jour national, où nous nous réunirons pour parler de nos pères; où nous rappellerons les gloires et les malheurs du passé; où nous pleurerons ensemble sur ce grand holocauste de 1755; un jour où nous oserons regarder l'avenir en face parce que nous serons ensemble, unis, nous tenant par la main").

9 Joseph-Yvon Thériault, *Faire société* (Sudbury, ON: Prise de parole, 2007), 261–2.

10 Fernand Robidoux, *Conventions nationales des Acadiens: recueil des travaux et délibérations des six premières conventions,* vol. 1, *Memramcook, Miscouche, Pointe de l'Église, 1881, 1884, 1890* (Shediac, NB: Imprimerie du Moniteur acadien, 1907).

11 An elite organization, bringing together members of the clergy and of the professions, it would become the Société nationale des Acadiens in 1957.

12 Joel Belliveau, "Le père Clément Cormier et l'âge d'or du paradoxal «nationalisme libéral" en Acadie du Nouveau-Brunswick, 1945–1967," in *D'une nation à l'autre: discours nationaux au Canada,* ed. Frédéric Boily and Donald Ipperciel (Quebec: Presses de l'Université Laval, 2011), 214 (entre 1881 et 1960 les Acadiens pouvaient avoir l'impression d'avoir un pays à eux).

13 15 août celebrations were aterritorial, taking similar forms across the Maritime provinces. See, for example, "La messe de l'Assomption célébrée à minuit," *L'Évangéline* (Moncton), 15 August 1959. This chapter will focus on the way in which le 15 août was conceived in New Brunswick between 1968 and 1982. Owing in large part to Acadians' demographic

concentration, it was in this province that Acadian neo-nationalism was most developed.

14 There is a surprising lack of scholarly research on the nature of 15 août celebrations. The Société des Acadiens du Nouveau-Brunswick (SANB) provided a brief summary in its memorandum to New Brunswick premier Richard Hatfield requesting that he make it a statutory holiday. See "15 août institution distincte. Présentation au Premier ministre Richard Hatfield, 17 juin 1982," Centre d'études acadiennes (hereafter CEA), SANB fonds, file 42.168

15 For an example of an anglophone politician's involvement in early-twentieth-century 15 août celebration, see "Les Acadiens de Moncton célèbrent dignement leur fête nationale" *L'Évangéline* (Moncton), 17 August 1910.

16 Founded in 1973, the SANB is still in existence today. The PA was present on the New Brunswick political scene only from 1972 to 1982, running candidates in the 1974, 1978, and 1982 provincial elections.

17 Julien Massicotte and Philippe Volpé explain the historical importance of the PA in "Le quarantième anniversaire de la fondation du Parti acadien: que reste-t-il d'une Acadie prospective aujourd'hui," *Bulletin d'histoire politique* 22, no. 1 (2012): 180–90.

18 In particular, New Brunswick premier Richard Hatfield adopted Bill 88 in 1981, which guaranteed Acadians control of their own social, cultural, and educational institutions. Not unrelatedly, the PA would disappear a year later. See Monique Gauvin and Lizette Jalbert, "Percées et déboires du Parti acadien," *Revue parlementaire canadienne* 1, no. 3 (1987).

19 Joel Belliveau and Fréderic Boily "Deux révolutions tranquilles? Expériences néo-brunswickoise et québécoise comparées" *Recherches sociographiques* 46, no. 1 (2005):11–34.

20 Belliveau, "Tradition, libéralisme."

21 Kenneth McRoberts, *Quebec: Social Change and Political Crisis* (Toronto: McClelland and Stewart, 1988).

22 Michel Roy, *L'Acadie perdue* (Montreal: Québec-Amérique, 1978), 145 ("je ne sais pas si nous sommes par le fond différents de Québécois, même si nous l'avons jamais été").

23 "RJA: Document préparatoire: Roger Savoie, Néo-nationalisme acadien, 1966," CEA, SNA fonds, file 41.35.1 ("si les signes du patriotisme (drapeau, hymne, patronne, fête nationale), sont dégonflés ou s'ils tiennent encore une puissance de signification").

24 Joel Belliveau has illustrated an important difference between the thought of professors such as Richard and Savoie and the student participants

in the RJA. While the professors were intent on developing a new nationalism, the students were perhaps more intent on participating in the same institutions as anglophone New Brunswickers. These differences would narrow by 1968, when the students turned away from the doctrine of individual rights, and began insisting on a national project for New Brunswick's Acadian (francophone) citizens. See "Tradition, libéralisme," 163–228.

25 "Pierre Savoie: Néo-nationalisme acadien," in CEA, SNA fonds, file 41.35.5 ("je ne connais pas les mots de notre hymne national et je ne suis pas certain si le tricolore étoilé porte son étoile en haut à gauche ou à droite. Et pour tout dire, cela m'est profondément indifférent. Ce qui m'intéresse c'est l'avenir… Nous ne sommes pas tous conservateurs de musée que je sache").

26 Hautecoeur, *L'Acadie du discours*, 202–3 ("les signes patriotiques tels que le drapeau, la patronne, et la fête nationale soient conservés dans la richesse folklorique de l'Acadie, mais ne soient pas invoqués comme signes d'identité nationale").

27 "Un peuple improvisé," CEA, Roger Savoie fonds ("dans une maison de fous où on ne sait plus … quelles sont nos tâches, qui sont nos chefs, quels sont nos objectifs").

28 "Transcription de *Acadie, Acadie?!?*" Archives de l'Université Laval (hereafter AUL), Pierre Perrault fonds, file 8, 6 ("il n'y a pas d'avenir à l'extérieur du Québec").

29 "Procès-verbal: Assemblée annuelle 1970," CEA, SNA fonds, file 41.5.1.

30 Raymond LeBlanc, "Manifeste politique," *L'embryon*, December 1970 ("Il nous faut une nouvelle origine: l'avenir … un suicide collectif … se québéciser, rejoindre nos frères québécois qui parlent la même langue que nous, opter pour que la région Acadie devienne un comté au sein d'un Québec fort, souverain").

31 Ronald Cormier, "La jeunesse veut provoquer le progrès," *L'Évangéline* (Moncton), 15 August 1968, special edition ("Les signes nationaux tels que le drapeau, la fête nationale, l'hymne et la patronne entravent une prise de conscience de la part de la population en les obligeant à se pencher sur un passé larmoyant").

32 LeBlanc, "Manifeste politique" ("nous libérer de notre peur qui est d'origine religieuse").

33 Claude Bourque, "La fête nationale des Acadiens," *L'Évangéline* (Moncton), 13 August 1971.

34 Cimino, "Ethnic nationalism," 165.

35 Ibid., 164.

36 "Assemblée annuelle mai 1971, Annexe X: Atelier no. 6," CEA, SNA fonds, file 41.5.3; Paul-Émile Richard, "A-t-on compromis l'avenir de l'association provinciale?" *L'Évangéline* (Moncton), 30 October 1972.

37 "Document préparatoire: l'idéologie nationale face à la nouvelle société acadienne," CEA, SNA fonds, file 41.35.1 ("il me faut d'abord rendre hommage à ceux [qu'] il est convenu d'appeler depuis 1881 notre élite nationale, cette intelligentsia bourgeoise, formée pour la plupart sur les bancs de nos collèges… Cette élite, je le crois sincèrement, par l'organisation sociale qu'elle a mise sur pied, a joué un rôle d'avant-garde … d'éveilleur de conscience tant chez la majorité anglophone que chez les Acadiens eux-mêmes").

38 Cormier, "La jeunesse" ("ont réussi à obtenir des choses pour les francophones").

39 AUL, Pierre Perrault fonds, file 8,6 ("Moi je ne comprends comment on a pu être élevés par un père puis une mère qui ont chié toute leur vie eux autres nous élever, puis quand on a le baccalauréat leur dire bye-bye … leur dire merci puis s'en aller. Moi je ne comprends pas ça! C'est peut-être sentimental mais je ne le comprends pas"; "endurer les curés, toute la maudite pagaille, au lieu de vivre à Montréal, vivre avec les gros jupons").

40 Eric Bédard, *Recours aux sources* (Montreal: Boréal, 2010), 14 ("si je n'ignore pas que nos ancêtres étaient comme nous des êtres imparfaits, capables du meilleur et du pire, ils m'inspirent néanmoins un profond sentiment de gratitude. Sans leur ténacité, leurs sacrifices, leurs rêves et leurs ambitions, nous ne serions rien, ou si peu").

41 Jacques Paul Couturier explains how the francophone inhabitants of northwestern New Brunswick did not identify as "Acadians" in the late 1960s and early 1970s. See "La République du Madawaska et l'Acadie: la construction identitaire d'une région néo-brunswickoise au xxe siècle," in Maurice Basque and Jacques Paul Couturier, *Les territoires de l'identité: perspectives acadiennes et françaises, xviie-xxe siècles* (Moncton: Chaire d'études acadiennes, 2005), 25–54.

42 Hautecoeur, *L'Acadie du discours*, 302.

43 "Un an après le congrès des francophones la SANB est créée," *L'Évangéline* (Moncton), 4 June 1973.

44 "Rapport de discussion: Assimilation" CEA, fonds SNA, file 41.9.12a (le clergé qui a travaillé pour la cause des minorités francophones).

45 "Message du conseil d'administration de la Société des Acadiens du NB," *L'Évangéline* (Moncton), 15 August 1974.

46 Donatien Gaudet (president loaf the Société des Acadiens du Nouveau-Brunswick), "Nous ne sommes peut-être pas assez habitués à fêter," *L'Évangéline* (Moncton), 15 August 1975.

47 "15 août institution distincte: présentation au Premier ministre Richard Hatfield, 17 June 1982," CEA, SANB fonds, file 42.168 ("pendant de nombreuses années les Acadiens eurent très peu de communication entre eux ... chaque année depuis cent ans, lors du 15 août les Acadiens s'emploient à démontrer qu'ils continueront d'exister envers et contre tous ... amplifier les différences entre Acadiens pour justifier la non-reconnaissance du peuple Acadien au Nouveau-Brunswick ... une autre collectivité bien vivante qui n'est pas seulement différente par la langue, mais aussi par l'histoire, les traditions et la culture").

48 Letter to "Monsieur le maire," CEA, SANB fonds, file 42.168.

49 "Bonne fête à tous les Acadiens," *L'Évangéline* (Moncton), 15 August 1978; Catriona LeBlanc, "*Cri de terre*: A translation of Raymond Guy LeBlanc's *Cri de terre*" (MA thesis, Dalhousie University, 1998), 75.

50 Gérald LeBlanc, "Le Parti acadien se rendra-t-il au premier but?" *Le Devoir* (Montreal), 23 May 1972.

51 "Congrès 1977: objectif national," Société historique Nicolas-Denys (hereafter SHND), Parti acadien fonds, file 2–37 ("de choisir une option conditionnée par l'option que pourrait choisir un autre peuple, par exemple les Québécois").

52 Léon Thériault, "Le ralliement des jeunes francophones des Maritimes," *L'Évangéline* (Moncton), 3 December 1966 ("les Acadiens ne voulaient pas risquer de perdre notre identité acadienne, peut-être aussi notre efficacité pour régler nos problèmes").

53 Léon Thériault "Modernité de notre fête nationale," *L'Évangéline* (Moncton), 15 August 1975 (mentalité de minoritaires).

54 Ouellette, *Le Parti acadien.*

55 Euclide Chiasson, André Dumont, Jacques Fortin, Arthur William Landry, Donald Poirier, Armand Roy, and Lorio Roy, *Le Parti Acadien* (Montreal: Parti Pris, 1972).

56 "Vœux de la fête nationale: tout people vivant a besoin de se réjouir et de fêter son existence," *L'Évangéline* (Moncton), 15 August 1972 ("les intérêts opposés au peuple acadien ne cèderont pas leurs pouvoirs sans combat mais le peuple est toujours plus fort que quelques exploitants").

57 Following the 1974 provincial election – in which the PA failed to elect a single candidate – Chiasson resigned the party leadership and began humanitarian work in Bolivia.

58 "A l'occasion de la fête nationale le PA parle d'un espoir grandissant," *L'Évangéline* (Moncton), 15 August 1975 ("peut paraître paradoxal alors que nous avons tous les jours des situations d'injustices et d'exploitation. Pourtant il n'en est rien. Si l'on parle toujours de fête nationale en Acadie...

c'est que l'espoir grandit chez nous. La lutte entreprise par nos ancêtres pour la survivance se poursuit et s'accentue").

59 Jean Couturier, "Donatien Gaudet au Parti acadien," *L'Évangéline* (Moncton), 27 September 1978.

60 Donatien Gaudet, "Les Acadiens du Nouveau-Brunswick." *L'Action nationale* 67, nos. 3–4 (1977): 201–8 ("les Acadiens ne sont pas des Québécois glorifiés ou des Canadiens français diminués ... malgré toutes les vicissitudes passées et présentes les Acadiens sont un peuple nettement et absolument distinct des Québécois ou des autres Canadiens français").

61 "Donatien Gaudet, président de la SANB, 15 août," CEA, Donatien Gaudet fonds, file 70.48 ("La fête des Acadiens est à la fois symbole et réalité ... Elle revêt un caractère spécial: elle rappelle aux Acadiens leurs origines et les sensibilise à la réalité de leur vie ensemble aujourd'hui. Plus que tout autre fête donc, elle est une occasion à la fois de réjouissance et de réflexion, tant sur le passé que sur le présent et sur l'avenir").

62 "La Grande réunion, 1978," CEA, Donatien Gaudet fonds, file 70.41 ("c'est à Memramcook et à Miscouche où les Acadiens se sont choisi les symboles d'un peuple qui se veut autonome").

63 Ibid., ("Cent ans après Memramcook on aura l'occasion de prendre les devants encore une fois en donnant à l'Acadie, non seulement des symboles mais ce qu'ils signifient concrètement: le pouvoir"). "

64 Donatien Gaudet, "Un vrai pays pour les Acadiens," *L'Évangéline* (Moncton), 15 August 1979 ("qui sont propres à un pays ... Voilà pourquoi je ne puis me contenter de souhaiter bonne fête à mes compatriotes acadiennes et acadiens sans leur souhaiter avec ardeur un pays concret, réel... A ce moment-là nous pourrons faire la vraie fête ... nous fêterons quoi au juste?").

65 It was Jean-Pierre Blanchard who edited volume 67, no. 10 of *L'action nationale*, entitled "L'Acadie aux Acadiens!"

66 Paul-Arthur Landry, "Louise Blanchard élue chef du PA," *L'Évangéline* (Moncton), 4 May 1981.

67 Louise Blanchard, "L'union pour un futur meilleur," ibid., 15 August 1980 ("Aujourd'hui, le 15 août, les Acadiens montrent leur attachement à leurs coutumes, à leurs mœurs, à leur langue et à leur religion").

68 Jean-Claude Blanchard, "Regard sur l'Acadie ecclésiastique," ibid., 13 August 1982.

69 Louise Blanchard, "Animés d'un sentiment de fierté et d'effort," ibid., 15 August 1981.

70 Gauvin and Jalbert, "Percées et déboires du Parti acadien."

71 Denis Losier, "Un déploiement nationaliste en Acadie," *L'Évangéline* (Moncton), 15 August 1981 ("encore autant sinon plus de sens … l'égalité dans toutes les sphères d'activités gouvernementales touchant de près ou de loin notre vie comme acadiens ou acadiennes").

72 Denis Losier, "Un peuple distinct," ibid., 13 August 1982 ("après la langue maternelle ce qui accentue le mieux le caractère national d'un people c'est sa Fête nationale").

73 Although Premier Richard Hatfield issued statements on le 15 août, reprinted in *L'Évangéline*, the SANB did not acknowledge other formal provincial government commemorations. See "15 août institution distincte: présentation au Premier ministre Richard Hatfield, 17 juin 1982," CEA, SANB fonds, file 42.168.

74 Ibid. ("si l'on veut nous reconnaître notre droit à des institutions séparées, il faudrait commencer par accepter celles que nous nous sommes données. Par conséquent, si le gouvernement … veut être logique avec sa déclaration de principe, il devrait officiellement reconnaître le congé … du 15 août").

75 Denis Losier, "Un peuple distinct," *L'Évangéline* (Moncton), 13 August 1982 (L'égalité des communautés linguistiques reconnue par le gouvernement ne se réalisera pas tant et aussi longtemps que notre Fête nationale sera pas officiellement reconnue)..

76 Letter from Jean Gauvin to Richard Hatfied, 13 July 1982 and letter from Jean-Maurice Simard to Richard Hatfield, 14 July 1982," CEA, SANB fonds, file 42.168.

77 Claude Bourque, "La fête nationale des Acadiens," *L'Évangéline* (Moncton), 13 August 1971.

78 See, for example, Xavier Gélinas, "Notes sur René Lévesque et le traditionalisme canadien-français" in *René Lévesque: mythes et réalités*, ed. Alexandre Stefansecu (Montreal: VLB éditeur, 2008).

79 Paul-Émile Richard, "L'Acadie en fête," *L'Évangéline* (Moncton), 15 August 1977.

80 Hautecoeur, *Acadie du discours*, 306–7 ("pourquoi les jeunes apparemment si détachés des valeurs traditionnelles sont les plus soucieux de leur trouver un avenir").

16 Marketing the Maple Leaf: The Curious Case of National Flag of Canada Day

RICHARD NIMIJEAN AND L. PAULINE RANKIN

In a postreferendum environment – and some say prereferendum as well – the Maple Leaf and the word Canada have combined to become Ottawa's favourite communications tool. It is a brand, and the government is selling it.

Daniel Leblanc, *Globe and Mail*, 12 July 1999

Michael Geisler has argued that national flags are a key symbol of national identity and an important expression of patriotism.[1] National symbols connect the nation to the state: on the one hand, they help to create the state; on the other, they also facilitate the state's definition of the nation. Consequently, countries take great pride in celebrating their flags and even outlawing their desecration. Burning the American flag both inside and outside the United States is often seen as an attack on the country itself, and the 1989 U.S. Supreme Court decision allowing flag burning as a legal form of political protest was highly controversial.[2] Given their emotional power, Geisler argues that flags top the hierarchy of national symbols.[3] They are not only uncontested external and internal symbols of the nation: owing to their popularity, flags also embody power relations in a way not seen in other national symbols.

Although the introduction of a new Canadian flag in 1965 was quite divisive,[4] within a few short decades the flag became one of the most popular Canadian symbols. Celebration of the flag, as we explore, has been used to attempt to heal the country in periods of national unity crises. While Canadians were slow to adopt a "flag culture" in comparison to the United States[5] and often refer to their American neighbours as "flag wavers," Canadians remain just as enthusiastic about their own flag,[6] a sentiment increasingly encouraged by political leaders. Immediately before the 2010 Vancouver Winter Olympics, for example, Prime Minister Stephen Harper stated that the Maple Leaf was a symbol of immense national pride that can and should be displayed through a more visible patriotism.[7] Thus, it is not surprising that the decision was made to publicly acknowledge and honour the flag on a designated day.

Since its inception in 1996 in the wake of the 1995 Quebec referendum, successive federal governments have deployed National Flag of Canada Day[8] to shore up Canadian unity and identity, promote Canadian nationalism, and, more recently, justify certain aspects of Canadian foreign policy. For example, Prime Minister Stephen Harper's 2013 National Flag of Canada Day press release lauded the Canadian flag as a "symbol of peace, freedom, diversity and the strength of our nation."[9] Harper has linked the flag to the Canadian Armed Forces' presence in Afghanistan, Canada's role in NASA and the International Space Station, and even the Olympics.[10]

Nevertheless, the official relationship between Canadians, their federal government, and their national flag is complicated and contested. It took Canada nearly a century to adopt its own flag, and a further three decades to adopt a national day commemorating its existence. Perhaps not unsurprisingly, this commemorative holiday remains relatively unacknowledged and unobserved by most Canadians, in contrast to other more celebrated flag days elsewhere with much longer and very different histories. Prime ministers and members of Parliament have issued press releases and held small events, as have cities such as Kingston, Ontario, but the Canadian celebration of Flag Day pales in comparison to other countries. It seems that Flag Day in Canada is best known for either not actually being a statutory holiday[11] or as the day when Prime Minister Jean Chrétien grabbed anti-poverty protester William Clennett by the throat in what became known as the "Shawinigan handshake" at the first Flag Day celebration in Hull, Quebec.[12]

Katarzyna Rukszto correctly points to the creation of Flag Day by the Chrétien government as a manufactured commemorative holiday and an attempt to instil patriotism via the development of an artificial sense of tradition, a tactic reflective of politics in the Chrétien era (1993–2003).[13] As Richard Nimijean argues, the creation of the holiday aligned with the Chrétien government's celebration of patriotism rather than the promotion of values that inform a vision of Canada as socially and economically progressive.[14] Instead, the celebration of patriotism was intended to promote a neoliberal agenda, address national unity pressures, and associate Canadian values with the Liberal Party of Canada.

Although approaching governance from a decidedly different ideological stance, Prime Minister Harper, like Chrétien before him, employed patriotism as an important political tool, if for somewhat different strategic purposes. The Conservatives, who long regarded patriotism as the monopoly of the Liberal Party and thus were cognizant of the need to "reclaim patriotism" in order to win electorally, adopted a "Stand Up for Canada" theme in the 2006 federal election campaign.[15] After their election to power, the Conservatives consistently attempted to redefine Canadian values in terms of their own party's values, particularly through the promotion of "Brand Harper," in which the prime minister embodied and espoused a decidedly masculine northern vision of Canada that framed his government as a strong defender of the country and its citizens.[16]

This chapter explores the rather curious status of Flag Day in the Canadian political culture. Given the importance of celebrating flags as national symbols elsewhere, the popularity of the flag in Canada, and the fact that we live in a period in which governments rely on the politics of memory and commemoration as a lever to advance partisan political agendas, the question of why Canada's Flag Day retains such a low profile remains perplexing. This low profile is reflected, too, in scant academic analysis.[17] We begin by examining the nature of commemoration and make a case for drawing together insights from commemoration scholarship with work on political culture and nation branding to best account for the peculiar commemorative nature of Flag Day. We then consider the factors leading to the creation of Flag Day in 1996. We take a different approach than Rukszto, who stresses the importance of the holiday as symbolic of the conflictual relationship between national narratives and the counter-narratives of marginalized groups. This chapter situates Flag Day as an integral element of the Chrétien government's development of a "domestic brand state."[18] This development was designed to sell Canada both abroad, a move consistent with the emerging phenomenon of nation branding, and to its citizens, with national identity becoming an increasingly important strategic tool for politicians. We argue that, under Stephen Harper, Flag Day continued to fulfil a role in the Conservative's branding strategy, which articulated an equally powerful but distinctive vision of Canadian identity and deployed a range of national symbols to entrench that vision domestically.[19]

Beyond consideration of the domestic role of Flag Day, however, we illustrate how the perpetuation of celebrations that Canadians do not actually celebrate also can be understood by analysing the strategic role that such events play as part of nation branding internationally. On a theoretical level, the chapter revisits foundational work on Canadian political culture and the "the roots of disunity" associated with the failure to develop indigenous institutions and symbols.[20] Political culture is a useful referent for understanding Flag Day, for its explanatory power is drawn from linking institutions, politics, symbols, and identity. We meld this approach with the politics of nation branding to frame our analysis of this unique commemorative event. Our approach differs from the historical lens adopted by most chapters in this collection, but it is not simply based in political science. The approach reflects the interdisciplinary nature not only of Canadian studies but also of nation branding – which transcends narrow disciplinary outlooks by incorporating insights from both the social sciences and the humanities. Such an approach allows us to explain the complex nature of commemoration involving disparate topics such as symbolism, commemoration, and the politics involved in official national celebrations.

We make two major arguments. First, the peculiar nature of Flag Day is best explained by situating it within the nexus of Canadian political culture and national brand politics; Prime Ministers Chrétien, Martin, and Harper all turned to patriotism strategies to advance their different partisan goals. Such approaches reflect the political appeal of national symbols as integral to politicians' efforts to enhance their own personal status and agenda and also to brand Canada in specific ways. The chapter traces how Chrétien established Flag Day as a bulwark to national unity threats but shows that his government used Flag Day very minimally, owing to the exigencies of the political scandal that erupted around national unity efforts at the time. Arguably, Paul Martin Jr.'s short tenure as prime minister following Chrétien's resignation prevented his government from developing a strategy to exploit Flag Day fully. In contrast, the Conservatives deployed this commemoration systematically and deliberately to reinforce their vision of Canadian values and identity and lend symbolic support to particular policy orientations. Second, we argue more broadly that the study of memory and commemoration can be enhanced theoretically by integrating insights from both political culture and nation-branding literatures and by acknowledging the importance of analysing how celebrations – minor as well as major – are used by different regimes across time.

Commemoration, Political Culture, and Brand Politics

Our analysis of the distinctive character of Canada's Flag Day begins with Brian Osborne's observation that the orchestration of collective remembering underpins national state identities.[21] Osborne explains how the role of nationalizing states constantly develops and reinforces people's identification with specific social values through commemorations and celebrations. Certainly, states globally engage in identity formation through the manipulation of symbols and events; it is important to emphasize, however, that the contested nature of such commemorative exercises can result in unexpected identifications and allegiances among certain communities over time and across space. This requires states to recalibrate their commemorative strategies periodically, in what Alan Gordon describes as "the ongoing contest for hegemony."[22] Gordon advocates the interrogation of those who have control of the remembering agenda and the investigation of how the creation of public memory captures specific events and individuals, often quite ahistorically. This insight is particularly instructive in the case of Flag Day, given that this celebration marks a conflictual debate about the flag yet attempts to transform the flag into a shared symbol of cohesiveness and unity. The Harper government's attempts to link the flag to a more militaristic element in Canadian foreign policy reflected this orientation, and was not surprising, given the argument that national flags can be used to advance interests of statehood and mobilization for war.[23]

Nevertheless, strategies related to the use of commemorative symbols do not necessarily work. Hobsbawm agrees that the invention of traditions in order to promote identity and social cohesion is linked to "political purposes." Still, he maintains, "Official new holidays, ceremonies, heroes or symbols, which commanded the growing armies of the state's employees and the growing captive public of schoolchildren, might still fail to mobilize the citizen volunteers if they lacked genuine popular resonance."[24]

Arguably, such "genuine popular resonance" depends on the national context. Whatever the nature of the commemorative labour undertaken by governments, rituals of commemoration inevitably fall subject to the political culture in which those acts occur. Thus, while Rukszto's treatment of Flag Day's creation in 1996 offers an important baseline from which to trace the celebration's chronology, insights from political culture add an additional dimension to understanding the limited potential of Flag Day as a unifying national event. Political culture's value for examining commemorative events like Flag Day lies in its broader analysis of the connections between politics, institutions, and identity. Political culture is the language of politics, relating long-lasting individual and collective attitudes about politics to the evolving institutional frameworks of the political system.[25] Political culture helps us understand why and how people try to shape political systems and why people make choices, "but rather than focusing directly on political institutions and decision making, the approach is indirect."[26] As Elkins and Simeon note, political culture helps us understand agenda-setting issues and the range of political and policy options considered by political actors, given the cultural orientations of the polity.[27]

Domestic brand politics involves the intersection of ideology, values, national identity, politics, public opinion, and political institutions.[28] Political culture is therefore a useful starting point for examining the case of Flag Day, for it looks at "values assumed to be most sensitive to political actions" and "the legitimate identities people can assume in contending for power and the common identity which the polity provides for all."[29] David Bell, for example, argues that the ongoing crisis of Canadian unity is linked to the historic failure to adopt indigenous institutions and symbols that reflected the populations of a new country. Indeed, writing around the time of the Charlottetown Accord, well before the advent of Flag Day, Bell's work anticipated the recent emphasis on symbolic politics and the shortcomings of commemorative efforts such as Flag Day: "Canadians were just starting to change the most basic symbols of national self-image – flag, anthem, constitutions – in hopes of strengthening solidarity," but they were "a little too late, [and] a little too small," as this occurred a century after Confederation.[30] Bell maintained that Canada's political culture would inevitably remain fractured, given that such shows of symbolic politics failed to address the underlying challenges associated with a lack of institutions and programs that adequately promoted and sustained national sentiment.[31]

Nation-branding scholarship further contributes to understanding the contemporary manipulation of identities, symbols, and values in which governments engage in order to position a country's image internationally while selling that national "brand" to its domestic population. According to van Ham, "the brand state uses 'nationalism' in a superficial, playful manner where patriotic feelings no longer run deep. Flags turn into logos; anthems become opening tunes for festivities and sports events; and kings and castles are reworked into cute tourist attractions."[32] Although van Ham's comment accurately captures the superficiality of these branding exercises, brand politics, in fact, carefully privileges symbolism and identity as the primary currency of electoral political competition,[33] with the "logos of nation-states serv[ing] the dual purposes of acting as a commercial vehicle to compete in the marketplace of nation-states … and as a condensation symbol for the nation."[34] Thus, nation branding is potentially a very conservative force, privileging rhetoric over action,[35] leading to the presence of gaps between rhetoric and reality that symbolic communication seeks to cover rather than address.

Initiatives like Flag Day, therefore, form part of what O'Shaughnessy understands as the "symbolic state," which encompasses "the creation of symbolic images, symbolic actions and celebratory rhetoric" that has now "graduated into becoming its central organizing principle, absorbing, therefore, much of the energy of government."[36] O'Shaughnessy cautions that this principle translates into permanent campaigns by states that seek "to persuade through governing by narratives" and, therefore, requires "utter control" over all messaging.[37] However minor a celebration, therefore, the creation and continued commemoration of Flag Day confirms its strategic function as a tool of the domestic and global nation-branding strategies governments pursue.

Creating Flag Day

Flag Day commemorations regularly occur in different countries around the world to honour national flags, in some cases coinciding with celebrations to mark independence from colonial powers or other historic events. The use of histories as the basis for celebrations is complex, however, and reveals much about internal political struggles over symbols, national identities, and history. In the United States, for example, President Woodrow Wilson proclaimed Flag Day in 1916. It took until 1959, however, for Congress to formally recognize National Flag Day, 182 years after the adoption of the American flag in 1777, and Flag Day in the United States still is not an official federal holiday. Mexico's Día de la Bandera is a national holiday that has been celebrated annually since 1937 on 24 February to commemorate General Don Vicente Guerrero, the first Mexican military officer to swear allegiance to the flag in 1821. In Lebanon, National Flag Day was launched in 1979 and has, at least on one occasion, erupted in violence and even death, as was the case in 1985.[38] Australia adopted its Flag Day in 1996 to celebrate the Australian national flag that first flew in 1901. Echoing sentiments expressed by Prime Minister Chrétien when Canada's Flag Day was announced, Australian prime minister John Howard explained that his government had created Flag Day to celebrate the country's "foremost national symbol," as it wished to "re-enforce Australian values and to create a secure and stable environment for our national institutions and trust between Government and the people."[39]

National Flag Day of Canada was declared on 15 February 1996 to commemorate Queen Elizabeth II's proclamation of the national flag of Canada in January 1965 as well as the date – 15 February of the same year – when the Maple Leaf flag first was raised over Parliament Hill in Ottawa. The name selected for Canada's Flag Day evidences the complexity of defining national identities and symbolism in a Canadian context. Canada could not use the most obvious title for the commemoration, "National Flag Day," as its use would remind an already tense nation of the highly contested use of the word "nation" in a Canadian context, given substantive indigenous and Québécois populations claiming their own nationhood, the recent political struggles concerning the renegotiation of the Canadian constitution (the Meech Lake and Charlottetown Accords), and the 1995 Quebec referendum. Instead, the awkward moniker "National Flag of Canada Day" makes it unclear to which nation the name refers; in fact, it can also be read as implying that there is a national flag for July 1st, Canada Day. Interestingly, the official name of the commemoration is frequently misused, including by prime ministers themselves.[40]

To understand the creation of Canada's Flag Day necessitates a review of developments in the Canadian political culture over the preceding three decades. In the 1960s, when the Liberals first promised to introduce a new flag for Canada to replace the Red Ensign, Canadian identity was in flux. While British symbolism dominated the governmental landscape, this was, at best, an awkward fit for a country that was experiencing a "Canadianization" movement,[41] was debating "two nations," had a renascent indigenous peoples movement, and was becoming increasingly diverse, given the easing of racialized immigration policies. As Herschel Hardin has argued, Canada at the time was "a nation unaware."[42]

Prime Minister Pearson's goal was a distinctive flag that would distinguish Canada internationally from Britain and address national unity concerns at home.[43] As Liberal MP John Ross Matheson stated, "The search for a flag had a single objective, namely, Canadian symbolism in its purest form."[44] Pearson was responding to Canadian public opinion that, over the previous two decades, had increasingly wished for "specifically Canadian symbols," including a distinctly Canadian flag.[45] Conversely, the official leader of the opposition, Conservative John Diefenbaker, and other supporters of the Red Ensign argued that a new flag would divide the country by appealing to French Canada;[46] more cravenly, some in English Canada saw Pearson's proposal as a reflection of his being "soft on Quebec" and "yet another sop to French Canada."[47] It should be noted, however, that there was also opposition in Quebec to the possibility of adopting a new flag; in this view, the blue-and-white fleur-de-lis flag was the flag of the Québécois and French Canadians.[48] In the end, the Liberal-sponsored Maple Leaf flag was introduced. The Progressive Conservative opposition was fractured, as some Tory MPs also felt uncomfortable with the Red Ensign.[49] Thus, it is not surprising that discussions to introduce a new flag for the country were controversial and divisive, especially as support for a new flag was based on political affiliation, region, language, and religion.[50] A new flag would alter the nature of the political culture, posing a threat to those who believed in the old order.

Mackey argues that the flag debate was a symbolic battle that affected relations between the major elements that influenced Canadian society: Quebec, Britain, and the United States. Pearson was concerned primarily with national unity and Quebec, and he wanted the flag as a new symbol to which all Canadians could adhere and, according to Matheson, be "a symbol of Canada's will to survive." Conversely, partisans of the British Ensign flag believed that the Union Jack ensured Canada's survival against American Manifest Destiny. Mackey maintains that the introduction of a new Canadian flag and the subsequent introduction of a new national anthem "were instances of state intervention in cultural politics to ensure the survival of the nation."[51]

Ironically, such symbolic politics did not necessarily address the fractured nature of Canada's political culture, which was rooted in adopting symbolism that was not fully inclusive, especially for Québécois and indigenous peoples. Matheson seems to acknowledge this, stating, "It was popularly assumed in English Canada that a distinctive Canadian flag would enchant the French. Pearson knew better. Alienation of Quebec had reached the point where a Canadian or federal flag would serve only as an offence to many persons who by now envisaged Quebec's destiny as entirely independent. By hoisting the flag of Canada, the issue was being joined. It was not a flag of surrender, it was a flag of battle – battle for one Canada."[52]

Nevertheless, Canadians' rapid embrace of the new flag marked a turning point in the political culture. Whereas the flag debate clearly exposed the country's divisions, the flag gave Canadians, including some Québécois, something around which to rally. Despite the hard-fought nature of the flag debate, Granatstein notes: "The maple leaf flag quickly became *the* Canadian symbol, and the divisiveness of the debate that gave it birth was largely forgotten."[53] This new flag and the debate foreshadowed a shift in the political culture, from deference to increasing defiance.[54] The flag was a symbol that united Canadians against forces that threatened them, be they Americans or Québécois sovereignists. While Canadians still had their American neighbours who allowed them to think of themselves as humble and modest by comparison, the public opinion data revealed significant changes: Canadians were no longer unsure of their identity – they were becoming fiercely patriotic and increasingly anti-elitist.[55]

Yet, increasing displays of patriotism linked to a new unifying symbol did not suddenly heal the fractured roots of the political culture. In the 1990s, we witnessed the new "paradoxical nature of the Canadian identity,"[56] in which an increasingly boisterous Canada was simultaneously becoming less distinctive. Nimijean argues that this occurred as neoliberalism was making Canada's policies and institutions less distinctive; rallying around patriotism allowed elites to assuage a population that wanted to be different, especially from the United States.

The creation of Flag Day, therefore, recognized the shifting Canadian political culture and formed part of Prime Minister Chrétien's symbolic response to the national unity crisis engendered by the close results of the 1995 Quebec referendum. Whereas in the 1980 referendum, Prime Minister Trudeau promised a renewed federalism if the Québécois rejected sovereignty (which ultimately led to the patriation of the Constitution in 1982), Chrétien could promise no such thing: the country had grown weary of ongoing constitutional negotiations following debates over the Meech Lake and Charlottetown Accords. While Chrétien came to the view that Quebec could be recognized as a distinct society, meeting the demands of Québécois federalists,[57] he quickly discovered that there was little appetite outside of Ottawa to accommodate Quebec.[58]

In 1994, a Parti québécois (PQ) government was elected, led by Jacques Parizeau, who stressed sovereignty as part of his mandate. Bill 1, An Act Respecting the Future of Quebec, proclaimed the need for Quebec to become a sovereign country, following the offer of an economic and political partnership with Canada, and a second referendum was called for 30 October 1995. The referendum campaign started slowly. Initially, the low-key federalist approach led by Daniel Johnson had the *Non* side leading the polls, but the sudden emergence of Lucien Bouchard as leader of the *Oui* campaign turned things around. Chrétien's strategy for the referendum was to deliver and emphasize good government; this, plus emphasizing a "faith in Canada," he believed, would be sufficient to convince the Québécois to vote against the *Oui* side, and he would therefore not need to make concessions. Critics said he had sleep-walked his way into a national unity crisis.[59]

Chrétien hoped that an emphasis on "shared Canadian values" and shared symbols – notably the Canadian flag – in the name of promoting pan-Canadianism, combined with outlining clearly the consequences of separatism, would increase the attachment of Québécois to Canada. He decided to sell Canada to the Québécois, with the Maple Leaf flag featuring prominently in this effort. Much has been written about the deployment of the flag by the Chrétien government during and after the 1995 campaign. Antonia Maioni explains that the federal government's strategy to challenge Québec nationalist forces "was about flags: more flags, bigger flags, lots and lots of maple leaf flags. Fluttering in the wind. Waving at parades. Stuck to professional football players' helmets. Prominently displayed at sporting events, at trade shows, on men's ties, golf balls, and anything else worth imprinting with the distinctive Canada logo."[60]

In a cabinet shuffle at the time, the prime minister appointed Sheila Copps, the deputy prime minister, as minister of Canadian heritage, and she assumed much responsibility for the symbolic promotion of Canada though initiatives such as encouraging one million Canadians to fly the flag. As Greenspon and Wilson-Smith recount, the cabinet immediately began discussing a national unity strategy, listening to the work of the cabinet national unity committee headed by Marcel Massé. Cabinet also heard from Maurice Pinard, a veteran sociologist and analyst of Quebec public opinion, who argued that the province no longer manifested signs of economic colonialism, but that memories of historical humiliation remained strong.[61] Pollster Frank Graves of EKOS told cabinet that, for the federal government to make inroads into Quebec, it was necessary to get away from a debate on economics and politics, areas in which the federal government believed it was winning the debate. He argued that the federal government was vulnerable in the area of "symbols and culture," and that, despite strong economic and political arguments, many Québécois were swayed by the emotional appeal of Quebec nationalists.[62] In the end, although the federalist *Non* side won the legal and political battle with a very narrow victory, the *Oui* side won the emotional and symbolic battle.[63] This result provides the context for understanding the creation of Flag Day.

Flag Day under the Liberals

In the aftermath of the razor-thin referendum results, the Chrétien government embarked on a two-pronged strategy to deal with national unity, both options of which relied heavily on the idea of "one Canada." His government would expose the consequences of Quebec separation and would employ symbols, information, and emotion as part of a communications strategy to persuade Québécois to remain in Canada. "Plan A" would promote a "feel-goodism" dimension of Canada and "Plan B" would outline the consequence of sovereignty to Quebec nationalists.[64] Antonia Maioni refers to Plan A as "make them love Canada" and Plan B as "punish them if they won't."[65] Plan A was the federal government's attempt to sell Canada to the Québécois in order to create an emotional connection, to counter "separatist myths" by giving out information, to promote Canada, federal initiatives, and the federal flag in Quebec, and to celebrate core Canadian values. Plan B, by contrast, was devised to confirm that the federal government would deal firmly with Quebec and emphasized the importance of clear questions on the possible secession of Quebec from Canada via implementation of the federal Clarity Act.

Theses strategies also included a political dimension aimed not only at showcasing the federal government and ministers but also at building up the federal Liberal Party in Quebec.[66] The strategy was vintage Chrétien. According to his biographer Lawrence Martin, Chrétien had advocated for an emotional campaign for the federalist side during the 1980 referendum campaign: "He told organizers, 'We've got to sell Canada. Quebeckers are proud Canadians. There's an attachment to Canada.' He wanted a straight-out street fight in which he'd take the virtues of Canada into the ring and score a knockout."[67] In the aftermath of the 1995 referendum, therefore, Chrétien opined that Canada, even though a country in "perpetual crisis," could overcome its differences. The key was to let Canadians know how good their country was: "'The PQ did not win,' he said. 'Canada won. We have such a good product that, put it under the proper light, the people will buy it'."[68] Documents indicate that the cabinet was both rattled by the narrow defeat of the sovereigntist option and determined to counter the myths of separatism, as they saw it.[69] To implement Plan A, the federal government extended funding to institutions like the Canada Information Office, the Centre for Research and Information on Canada (CRIC), and the Canada Unity Council, and created the Federal Sponsorship Program.[70] Forensic audits later commissioned by the Gomery Commission inquiry into the "sponsorship scandal" revealed that $332 million was spent to promote Canada.[71] Federal money was used to fund artistic festivals, sporting events, films, and television series in Quebec, with promotion of the flag as a prominent element of these efforts.

The 1996 Throne speech emphasized national unity, acknowledging the close results of the referendum and signalling a desire of the federal government to address several of Quebec's historic demands, such as federal withdrawal from labour market training.[72] As Susan Delacourt recounts, the government became preoccupied with rebranding Canada in Quebec. Chrétien's chief of staff, Eddie Goldenberg, had noted earlier that not many Canadian flags were flying in Quebec so, with the support of cabinet ministers Sheila Copps and Brian Tobin, the idea for Flag Day was born.[73] When Flag Day was instituted in 1996, it was an integral part of a broader domestic branding strategy to promote Canada to Canadians, to "show the flag" via the Canada wordmark,[74] and to double signs of "Canada" on federal buildings to "affirm [the federal government's] presence in local communities and foster pride in the country."[75] Most importantly, Prime Minister Chrétien felt that he had not been used properly by the *Non* campaign, and he insisted that he would take charge in the post-referendum era.[76] The announcement of Flag Day in 1996, therefore, occurred against a backdrop of lingering anxiety over national unity that had climaxed the previous October with the referendum vote. The creation of Flag Day was accompanied by a campaign to distribute one million flags to Canadians (a plan that later would be dubbed "Flagscam"), which subsequently was estimated to cost between $16 million and $23 million.[77] Minister Copps claimed that "this is a good investment… One of the most visible ways to promote our country is with our flag."[78]

It is important to recall that the orientation of national unity activities in this era was not simply about national unity: there was also a deliberate partisan dimension that sought to promote the Liberal Party of Canada. This, to us, signifies the key feature of Chrétien's Flag Day: the effort to sell Canada to Canadians – an effort in which values are articulated and sold rather than emerge from actions, in part owing to a growing resistance in the "Rest of Canada" to accommodating Quebec. Although symbolic politics were central to the promotion of the Canadian flag, so were partisan considerations, and the example of Flag Day illustrates how politicians embed politics into commemoration activities. Chrétien's Flag Day attempted to reinforce his vision of Canada as Liberal, thus giving a Liberal glow to the flag.

Despite the furor around its initial creation, the second Flag Day, in 1997, was decidedly low key. The minister of Canadian heritage's spokesperson claimed, "It's not about huge fireworks, lots of noise and lah-dee-dah... The whole idea was not to concentrate on a single ceremony, but to have one million flags circulated coasts to coast."[79] Perhaps more accurate was Ottawa mayor Jacquelin Holzman's assessment that "this weather just isn't suited for flag-waving." Indeed by 1998, the *Globe and Mail* quipped that Flag Day was "a half-mast kind of holiday."[80] By 2003, the *Ottawa Citizen* reported that "federal finance officials have apparently dissuaded Heritage Minister Sheila Copps from supporting a new statutory holiday. They have estimated that an additional national holiday would cost the economy $3 billion and would be inconsistent with the government's message of fiscal restraint."[81]

Paul Martin's tenure as prime minister spanned only two National Flag of Canada Days. On 15 February 2004, there was little time for flag celebrations, as Martin chose that day to appear on CBC Radio's *Cross Country Checkup*, promising to resign if there was evidence he know about the federal sponsorship scandal. In 2005, however, the Martin government appeared anxious to re-establish the link between the Liberal Party and the Canadian flag. Martin celebrated the flag's fortieth anniversary in a more conventional fashion at a public ceremony in Kingston, Ontario, replete with a flag-shaped cake, a children's choir singing "The Maple Leaf Forever," and assorted dignitaries, including Judge John Matheson, Prime Minister Pearson's parliamentary secretary who had convened the committee that eventually came up with the flag design in 1964.[82] The following year, when the Conservatives defeated the Martin Liberals just days prior to Flag Day, Prime Minister Stephen Harper moved quickly to rebrand Flag Day with Conservative rather than Liberal values.

Flag Day and the Harper Government

Flag Day as a strategy of political opportunity continued under the Conservative government, with a more explicit focus on patriotism, militarism, and the promulgation of a particular set of Canadian values labelled by Ian McKay and Jamie Swift as promoting an image of Canada as a "warrior nation."[83] This approach emphasized a much more muscular foreign policy stance around issues such as Arctic sovereignty and Canada's place as a resource superpower.

Critics' concerns over militarism and creeping Americanization missed an important evolution in Stephen Harper – the emphasis on patriotism. Indeed, Marland and Flanagan argue that, even before the Canadian Alliance began merger discussions with the Progressive Conservatives, Harper planned to reclaim patriotism, given resentment over the Liberals' claiming of national symbols like the maple leaf.[84] This approach was targeted at effectively "de-branding" the Liberal Party.[85] As Billig notes, right-wing parties often play the "patriotic card," rooted in praise for the nation ("we"), or at least the nation that supports the articulated policies of the government.[86]

Kheiriddin and Daifallah, in their "blueprint for a conservative revolution," called on the Conservatives to adopt a more confident outlook as a way to return to power and to emulate Margaret Thatcher and Ronald Reagan in adopting a positive and patriotic vision. They note that Harper was often negative and pessimistic, summarizing his basic argument in 2005 as "vote for me or the country is finished."[87] By 2007, however, pundits noted that Harper had seemingly left behind his regionalist and continentalist orientations in favour of a "Canada-first policy."[88] The Throne speech of 16 October 2007, "Strong Leadership: A Better Canada," listed "strengthening Canada's sovereignty and place in the world" as its first core priority.[89]

Flag Day communications served as an ideal vehicle to connect the symbolic to a re-articulated national identity by reclaiming the flag and linking it to Conservatives' visions of Canada. In his first Flag Day remarks, delivered in 2006, the new prime minister emphasized the relationship between the flag and Canadian values, noting, "on this National Flag Day let us all celebrate the values symbolized by our flag. Let us re-dedicate ourselves to upholding these fundamental values that have made Canada the great nation it is today." For Harper, this meant celebrating a Canada that is "strong, united, independent and free." He further stressed that "it is our duty, as Canadian citizens, to ensure that this flag inspires just as much pride in future generations. Because soon, we will be asking them to carry it – and our country – farther and higher."[90]

Unlike his predecessor, Harper did not need Flag Day to counteract uncertainty over national unity. By 2006, the narrative of Canadian identity, which Rukszto argues Chrétien needed to stabilize through symbolic gestures like Flag Day, once again was more firmly intact, leaving Flag Day free to be deployed by the new Conservative government for different political purposes. The contestation and protest over the adoption of Flag Day witnessed ten years earlier and documented by Rukszto had largely dissipated by 2006 to the point that it could function unchallenged as a pillar of the Harper government's new branding strategy.

In 2007, Harper used the occasion of Flag Day and a celebration at an Ottawa high school to pay tribute to Canada's Second World War veterans and announce a contribution of $5 million to the Juno Beach Centre in Normandy, France. Speaking to an audience of more than 1,000 students and Canadian Forces veterans, including several veterans of the D-Day invasion, Mr. Harper said:

> A flag, whatever its design, is also a portal, a door that leads and connects us back to our history and our values, and that is why it is so appropriate to have the veterans with us here today, and why it's so appropriate on Flag Day to make an important announcement related to a seminal event in Canadian history. On D-Day, June 6, 1944, a massive allied force landed on the beaches of Normandy, France and began the invasion of fortress Europe that would reclaim the continent from the tyranny of fascism… It was a stunning military success, one that made Canadians as proud as they have been of the tremendous victory at Vimy Ridge 27 years before. The Canadians who took Juno Beach … deepened our worldwide reputation as a country that produces highly-skilled and courageous military personnel.[91]

Between 2008 and 2010, Flag Day elicited little attention, marked only by press releases such as the prime minister's message in 2010 that spoke of the Canadian flag as "recognized both at home and abroad as a symbol of peace, democracy, freedom and courage."[92] Flag Day festivities changed significantly in 2011, however, with the introduction of a new tradition that solidified Harper's personal prominence on Flag Day and concentrated on lauding outstanding Canadians who have "exemplified the values our country holds most dear" by presenting recipients with flags that had flown from the Peace Tower on Parliament Hill. Such a re-orientation of Flag Day as an opportunity to recognize worthy Canadians for patriotic acts, and to celebrate the individual, meshed seamlessly with the broader neoliberal emphasis

on individual achievement characteristic of the Conservative government. This new commemoration practice also was reflected in the visu-
als that accompanied the marking of Flag Day, with the photo history
narrowed to pictures of the prime minister presenting flags to the honoured individuals, a representation consistent with the consolidation
of the identification between Harper himself and Canada that has been
observed as a strong element of the Harper regime.[93]

The inaugural recipients on this rebranded Flag Day were Lisa Miller
and Karen Boire from Petawawa, Ontario, home of a Canadian Forces
Base. Miller and Boire received the recognition (and a neatly folded flag)
for spearheading a grassroots movement to support Canadian men and
women in uniform through the wearing of the colour red every Friday.
The two women organized the first Red Friday rally on Parliament Hill
in 2006, earning them the nickname "Red Friday Ladies." In his 2011
citation, Harper noted, "Our Canadian flag represents the ideals of freedom, democracy and justice – it's these values that are upheld each day
by the brave men and women of the Canadian Armed forces, and their
family members – like Lisa and Karen – who support them as they do
their heroic work."[94]

The recipients that followed included Pierre Lavoie (2012), a world-
class triathlete from Quebec and founding chair of the Grand défi Pierre
Lavoie, a health promotion program known for educating youth on the
benefits of physical activity and for its work on the health of children
and youth and helping improve their quality of life. In the citation for
Lavoie, whom he cited as "a perfect example of what it means to be
Canadian," Harper described the flag as "a symbol of honour, pride,
and Canadian identity."[95]

In 2013, the prime minister presented a Peace Tower flag to Canadian
astronaut Dr Dave Williams who, in turn, bestowed on Harper a flag
that had been to space. In his remarks that day, Harper stated: "The
Canadian flag is a symbol of peace, freedom, diversity and the strength
of our nation… It is worn proudly by our Canadian Armed Forces in
Afghanistan and around the world … and can even be found in outer
space." In perhaps the most optimistic statement of the potential of
the flag as a vehicle for exporting Canadian values, the prime minister
asserted, "our flag will continue to mean home and belonging for Canadians around the planet *and beyond.*"[96]

Other members of the Harper government also used the occasion of
Flag Day to celebrate Canada's military tradition. The MP and parliamentary secretary to the minister of national defence, Chris Alexander

used the occasion in 2013 to remind his constituents of the many symbols, historical events, and citizens to be proud of, among them

> our hard-working men and women of Canada's Armed forces, Veterans, and their families who, for the lifetime of the country of Canada, have been taking a stand and making sacrifices for the values that Canadians hold dear. On Flag Day, I urge you to take a moment and recognize the members of our military who are currently serving across our country, overseas, and all around the world … and forever remember the sacrifices and dedication of our brave men and women in uniform, Veterans, and their families, now and in the past.[97]

When Flag Day overlapped with the 2014 Winter Olympics in Sochi, Russia, the prime minister presented the Peace Tower flag to the family of the late freestyle skier Sarah Burke. In those remarks, Harper described Canada as a "peaceful and progressive country of enormous natural beauty, prosperity and generosity of spirit. At no time is national pride in our flag more evident than during the Olympic Games."[98]

Although the Conservatives did little else to promote Flag Day, Canadian Heritage did produce a National Flag Day of Canada video in 2014, enlisting the assistance of some prominent Canadians, including country singer Terri Clark, opera star Measha Brueggergosman, figure skaters Patrick Chan and Joannie Rochette, and curler Lisa Weagle to share testimonials about what the flag meant to them. Educational materials were also made available through Canadian Heritage on Flag Day for use in schools.

Flag Day in 2015 marked the fiftieth anniversary of the adoption of the Canadian flag. Given Harper's willingness to invest in historical commemoration – for example, the estimated $28 million spent celebrating the two hundredth anniversary of the War of 1812 and $4 million to mark the two hundredth birthday of the country's first prime minister, Sir John A. Macdonald – it was surprising that his government took a very low-key approach in 2015, committing only $50,000 directly and an additional $200,000 to be granted to the provinces and other organizations.[99] Instead, the government issued a press release recognizing the creation of the flag as a national historic event.[100] In his annual Flag Day statement, the prime minister downplayed the anniversary of the flag, instead noting that the symbol of the maple leaf had a long tradition in Canada (including the pre-Confederation era). Rather than splashy celebrations, Harper announced that fifty individuals and organizations "who have contributed significantly to the well-being of our citizens" (including Thornhill, Ontario, "Flag Lady" Marga Van den Hogan, cited for her role in spreading awareness of Flag Day throughout Greater Toronto) would receive flags to mark the anniversary.[101]

Popular Reception of Flag Day

The announcement of Flag Day in 1996 reflected the political environment of the time – namely, national unity concerns – combined with public recognition that Canadians did not celebrate the anniversary of the creation of an important national symbol.[102] Yet, political rhetoric aside, the holiday has failed to capture the public imagination. Despite Chrétien's claim, in announcing the celebration, that "our maple leaf is a symbol that unites Canadians" the response to Flag Day has been as much dissatisfaction and a lack of interest and awareness as isolated expressions of patriotism.

Elementary and secondary schools have been an important site for Flag Day celebrations, providing opportunities for students to learn more about the history of the flag and to express their patriotism. Schools provide outlets for the political narratives favoured by national governments – issues of national unity for the Liberals and militarism for the Conservatives. For example, at a 1996 school celebration, former Liberal Toronto-area MP Jesse Flis argued that public displays of celebration of the flag promoted national unity and nationalism.[103] Meanwhile, in 2013, speaking to Guelph-area students, the Conservative minister of national defence, Peter MacKay, explicitly linked celebration of the flag to members of the Canadian military: "The Canadian soldiers wear the flag each and every day… That flag is so recognized and admired around the world for what it represents, for what it's always represented – peace, democracy, freedom, the things that previous generations of soldiers fought and, in many cases, died for."[104]

However, when the spotlight briefly shines on Flag Day every February, it is noteworthy that popular reports of the day focus as much on non-patriotic elements as they do on nationalism. For example, some Toronto schools noted that Flag Day had been "overshadowed" by other events in the month – namely, Valentine's Day, Heritage Month, and Black History Month – making it difficult for civics classes to always focus on Flag Day.[105] This neglect is compounded by the fact that Flag Day is not a statutory holiday. The Ottawa-Carleton District School Board noted that Ontario's Ministry of Education has suggested that this is why Flag Day activities are optional for schools.[106]

Inevitably, public reaction to Flag Day also refers to the cold Canadian climate and the fact that it is not a national holiday. One response in 1997 reflected this: an Ottawa public servant "knew Flag Day was in the winter, but didn't realize it was today. 'I've got three feet of snow on my roof,' he said apologetically. 'I'm not going to climb out there and put it [the flag] up, sorry.'"[107]

Finally, for many Canadians, the flag is an awkward element of the political culture, reflecting Bell's assertion that Canadian political culture is rooted in disunity. Despite proclamations in English Canada, the Maple Leaf flag is not a symbol of unity for many Québécois. Reflective of this was the reaction of a federal public servant in the National Capital Region who, when asked how she would celebrate Flag Day, responded by asking, "Which flag?"[108] Despite a growing patriotism in Canada, many Canadians continue to associate flag waving with the United States. As a Moncton man stated, one day for expressive patriotism – that is, Canada Day – was enough: "We don't want to be like the Yanks, waving our flags every day."[109]

Conclusion

Hobsbawm suggests that the "theatrical" was an important factor for successful invented traditions,[110] yet there is little room for theatricality – either in terms of setting or performance – in the observance of Flag Day. Hobsbawm suggests, too, that new state-sponsored commemorations might not be successful if they lack "genuine popular resonance." In Canada – at least outside of Quebec – the Maple Leaf flag remains one of the most important symbols of national identity. Why, then, hasn't the holiday honouring it been a success?

Even at the height of their national unity promotional campaigns, the Liberals were concerned about costs associated with promoting the flag in poor economic times and about possible perceptions of state-funded federalist propaganda in Quebec.[111] The fact that Flag Day was announced by press release, and that the prime minister did not even attend the second annual celebration, shows how the day was caught up in the broader political environment of the time. The Harper government, however, was not shy about spending money on certain commemorative events. Whereas the Liberals could speak of the flag in glowing terms, confident that its creation was intimately linked to the former Liberal prime minister Lester B. Pearson, it is likely that the Conservatives saw Flag Day through a partisan lens, ultimately regarding it as a Liberal commemorative event. How else can one explain that a government that was not reluctant about promoting (and spending significant tax dollars on) commemorative events invested only $250,000 celebrating the fiftieth anniversary of the Canadian flag – an amount so small that many Canadians questioned this decision? Harper's response is reminiscent of the thirtieth anniversary of the Canadian Charter of Rights and Freedoms, which his government "celebrated" by issuing a terse press release.[112] Rather than highlight events that are, or can be, seen by Canadians as linked to the Liberal Party, it may be that the Conservatives decided to commemorate only those events that relate to its core constituencies.

Perhaps the Harper government recognized that there are drawbacks to commemoration, particularly in an election year like 2015. Widespread condemnation of the planned National Memorial to the Victims of Communism, panned by the Royal Architectural Institute of Canada, the editor of *Canadian Architect* magazine, and the mayor of Ottawa, among others, reminds us that people do feel ownership of history and will not be reluctant about criticizing governments that take a heavy hand in making that history too partisan.[113]

Flag Day remains a curious case of commemoration. Despite high levels of pride in the country and strong attachments to the flag as a symbol of national identity, neither Liberal nor Conservative governments have transformed the day into a high-profile event. Even at the municipal level, celebrations are unevenly held across the country. For example, in Montreal in 1997, the site of the large rally for national unity two years earlier, no official Flag Day events were planned.[114] In Ottawa, mayor Jim Watson, a Liberal, declared in 1999, "in Ottawa, our heritage buildings are more tangible to celebrate than the flag."[115]

Given such attitudes, not surprisingly there has been little movement on entrenching Flag Day as a national holiday;[116] while mayors, premiers, and MPs acknowledge it, and there is some media attention particularly around milestone anniversaries, it is far from entrenched in the national psyche. This is reflective of the state-driven nature of nationalism in the Canadian political culture. Philip Resnick argues that Flag Day is another example of "state-fostered nationalism" that fails to create strong national bonds, as such simple celebrations do not reflect the complex nature of Canadians and their binational and multicultural identities. Such an argument helps explain why the flag has been celebrated more in English Canada than in Quebec.[117]

In the end, Flag Days are perhaps best understood as part of the "brand politics toolkit" governments use to help create an alternative version of national identity, which can reflect a redefined sense of patriotism and, simultaneously, may reveal the contested nature of national identities.[118] In this sense, we can understand the criticism former Liberal Canadian heritage minister Sheila Copps directed at the Harper Conservatives and their low-key celebration of Flag Day, when she stated that "Flag Day passed with barely a whimper."[119] While she claimed that the Harper government focused on divisive wedge issues and not an "emphasis on positive symbols," it remains that her government's messaging on Flag Day also reflected its political priorities. The low-key nature of the day can be as much attributed to her government's refusal to make Flag Day a bigger event (including proclaiming it a national holiday), a decision continued by the Conservatives. For the Conservative government, symbols of state were one part of the effort to build a new narrative linking the Conservatives to the Canadian identity, even though many key symbols and institutions historically were identified with the Liberals. We thus understand Stephen Harper's usage of Flag Day as part of the evolving nature of domestic brand politics in Canada. As Nimijean explains, brand politics features the use of constructed senses of national identity for partisan political purposes, as a means of distinguishing one political party from its opposition, particularly in an era of increased policy homogeneity.[120]

Our examination of National Flag of Canada Day reinforces the necessity to integrate analyses of political culture and nation branding into the study of commemorations. Jonathan Rose observes that "politics – especially the emotionally laden politics of nationalism – seems to be more about wielding prominent symbols in popular culture than it does about choosing substantive policy alternatives."[121] Although we stand with Rose in arguing the centrality of nation branding insights to the study of national commemorations, the example of Canada's Flag Day reveals that such commemorations, regardless of their apparent minor significance, can assume important roles in reinforcing policy orientations. Indeed, the Conservatives focused very strategically on the flag in other ceremonies to confirm the government's foreign policy directions and celebrate patriotism and military service beyond the confines of Flag Day. The 9 May 2014 National Day of Honour commemorating Canada's mission in Afghanistan, for example, was preceded by a six-day relay through several Canadian cities with Canadians injured in Afghanistan carrying the last Canadian flag flown in that country as far as Ottawa, where the flag was presented to the prime minister.

Karen Cerulo's insights into the need to "emphasize the conscious efforts that link symbol and ruler" are also instructive in assessing the pivotal role of commemorations in contestations over political culture and definitions of domestic brand politics. As she notes, "leaders intentionally exploit the legitimating function of national symbols in an effort to solidify their control." The example of both Chrétien's and Harper's efforts to link their vision of the country and, indeed, tie the fortune of their parties (and their own leadership) to the country's flag confirm Cerulo's observation that "political leaders often attempt to merge their persona with these symbols... Combining leaders with symbols renders the leader the standard-bearer of all that the nation's citizens value and believe."[122] National Flag of Canada Day, therefore, is best understood as a symbolic form of celebration created to operate on multiple levels related to identity, values, culture, partisan politics, and even leadership, not simply as a perfunctory and somewhat muted day of commemoration.

Finally, this case study confirms the relevance of analysing the entire range of commemorative activities in which states engage. Although full-scale celebrations like Canada Day reveal much about how states use the pageantry of major holidays to frame and communicate messages about citizenship and belonging – as discussed in several chapters in this volume – and indeed the associated expenditures may signal much about the prioritization accorded such events, attention to smaller acts of commemoration is also instructive in understanding tensions and even shifts in a country's political culture. Tracking such commemorations over time allows for comparison of how governments of different political stripes utilize commemorations for similar or diverging priorities, but it also can reveal how a single government can craft its approach to commemorations in subtle ways designed to reinforce its branding messages around particular policy orientations.

NOTES

1 Michael E. Geisler, "What Are National Symbols – and What Do They Do to Us?" in *National Symbols, Fractured Identities: Contesting The National Narrative*, ed. Geisler (Middlebury, VT: University Press of New England, 2005), xv.

2 Robert Justin Goldstein, *Burning the Flag: The Great 1989–1990 American Flag Desecration Controversy* (Kent, OH: Kent State University Press, 1996).

3 Geisler, "What Are National Symbols," xxii.

4 Critics saw the new flag as abandoning Canadian heritage, while supporters saw it as part of the forging of a new Canadian identity. C.P. Champion argues that it actually was not so much of a break from the past as it was a continuation of "Britishness." C.P. Champion, "A Very British Coup: Canadianism, Quebec, and Ethnicity in the Flag Debate, 1964–1965," *Journal of Canadian Studies* 40, no. 3 (2006): 68–99. On the history of the 1964–65 flag debate, see Rick Archbold, *I Stand for Canada: The Story of the Maple Leaf Flag* (Toronto: Macfarlane Walter & Ross, 2002) and John Ross Matheson, *Canada's Flag: A Search for a Country* (Belleville, ON: Mika, 1986).

5 Forrest Pass, "'Something Occult in the Science of Flag-flying': School Flags and Educational Authority in Early Twentieth-Century Canada," *Canadian Historical Review* 95, no. 3 (2014): 327–9.

6 For example, in a 2010 Angus Reid poll 88% of Canadians stated that it was their greatest source of pride, topping the list of Canadian symbols. See https://www.angusreidforum.com/mediaserver/3/documents/20100630_CanadaDay_EN.pdf. A 2015 poll released right before Flag Day reported that 75% of Canadians were proud to fly the flag and almost 80% believed that Canada was the best country in the world. Brian Daly, "Most Canadians Proud to Fly Flag, Think Canada Is World's Best Country," *Toronto Sun*, 14 February 2015.

7 Stephen Harper, "PM Addresses British Columbia's Legislature on Eve of 2010 Winter Olympics," 2010, https://web.archive.org/web/20120808115051/http://pm.gc.ca/eng/media.asp?category=2&featureId=6&pageId=46&id=3105, accessed 13 May 2016.

8 This is the official title, in recognition that the Royal Proclamation of 28 January 1965, which stated that "there be designated, as the National Flag of Canada, the flag hereinafter described." See Matheson, *Canada's Flag*, 240. Throughout the chapter, we will use the more common shorthand of "Flag Day."

9 Stephen Harper, Statement by the Prime Minister of Canada on National Flag of Canada Day, 2013, http://nouvelles.gc.ca/web/article-en.do?crtr.sj1D=&crtr.mnthndVl=2&mthd=advSrch&crtr.dpt1D=&nid=720809&crtr.lc1D=&crtr.tp1D=&crtr.yrStrtVl=2013&crtr.kw=flag&crtr.dyStrtVl=9&crtr.aud1D=&crtr.mnthStrtVl=2&crtr.page=1&crtr.yrndVl=2013&crtr.dyndVl=16, accessed 12 May 2016.

10 This theme was also present in Prime Minister Harper's 2010 speech noted above.

11 In 2007, Peggy Nash of the NDP introduced a private member's bill to make Flag Day a federal statutory holiday. Provinces would be encouraged to follow suit. In 2013, NDP MP Peter Julian reintroduced the bill; however, it was not adopted by the House of Commons. A small organization, Canada Flag Holiday, attempted to mobilize Canadians to support Julian's bill (C-337). See http://canadaflagholiday.icancreateit.com/, accessed 19 December 2014.

12 The first Flag Day was celebrated at a park in the National Capital Region. The event was overshadowed, however, by protests against deep cuts to the federal budget. The incident can be viewed at http://www.cbc.ca/archives/categories/politics/federal-politics/chretien-extends-a-shawinigan-handshake.html. A still of the video clip with the "handshake" became the 1996 Canadian Press News Photo of the Year.

13 Katarzyna Rukszto, "National Encounters: Narrating Canada and the Plurality of Difference," *International Journal of Canadian Studies* 16 (1997): 149–62.

14 Richard Nimijean, "Articulating the 'Canadian Way': Canada™ and the Political Manipulation of the Canadian Identity," *British Journal of Canadian Studies* 18, no. 2 (2005): 26–52; Richard Nimijean, "The Politics of Branding Canada: The International-Domestic Nexus and the Rethinking of Canada's Place in the World," *Revista Mexicana de Estudios Canadienses* 11 (2006): 67–85.

15 Thomas Flanagan, *Harper's Team: Behind the Scenes in the Conservative Rise to Power* (Montreal: McGill-Queen's University Press, 2007), 209.

16 Richard Nimijean, "Domestic Brand Politics and the Modern Publicity State," in *Publicity and the Canadian State*, ed. Kirsten Kozolanka (Toronto: University of Toronto Press, 2014), 172–94; L. Pauline Rankin, "Gender and Nation Branding in 'The True North Strong and Free'," *Place Branding and Public Diplomacy* 8, no. 4 (2012): 257–67.

17 Rukszto's study remains, to this point, the primary scholarly analysis of Flag Day.

18 See Nimijean, "Articulating the 'Canadian Way'" and "Domestic Brand Politics."

19 Other elements of this strategy include rewriting the Canadian Citizenship Guide, questioning by the federal government of how and what history is taught in schools, renaming the Canadian Museum of Civilization to the Canadian Museum of History and reorienting its mandate, and re-emphasizing the monarchy in several Canadian institutions.

20 David V.J. Bell and Lorne Tepperman, *The Roots of Disunity: A Look at Canadian Political Culture* (Toronto: McClelland and Stewart, 1979); David

V.J. Bell, *The Roots of Disunity: A Study of Canadian Political Culture*, rev. ed. (Toronto: Oxford University Press, 1992).

21 Brian Osborne, "Landscapes, Memory, Monuments, and Commemoration: Putting Identity in Its Place," *Canadian Ethnic Studies* 33, no. 3 (2001): 39–77.

22 Alan Gordon, *Making Public Pasts: The Contested Terrain of Montreal's Public Memories, 1891–1930* (Montreal: McGill-Queen's University Press, 2001).

23 Michael Billig, *Banal Nationalism* (London: Sage, 1995), 1–4.

24 E.J. Hobsbawm, *Nations and Nationalism since 1780: Programme, Myth, Reality*, 2nd ed. (Cambridge: Cambridge University Press, 1992), 263–4.

25 Ian Stewart, "All the King's Horses: The Study of Canadian Political Culture," in *Canadian Politics*, ed. James P. Bickerton and Alain-G. Gagnon (Peterborough, ON: Broadview Press, 1994), 75.

26 Arthur Asa Berger, "Introduction," in *Political Culture and Public Opinion*, ed. Arthur Asa Berger (New Brunswick, NJ: Transaction Publishers, 1989), 3.

27 David J. Elkins and Richard E.B. Simeon, "A Cause in Search of Its Effect, or What Does Political Culture Explain?" *Comparative Politics* 11, no. 2 (1979): 139–42.

28 Nimijean, "Domestic Brand Politics."

29 Berger, "Introduction," 3.

30 Bell, *The Roots of Disunity*, 189.

31 Ibid., 190–1.

32 Peter van Ham, "Interview with the Author," *Foreign Affairs* 2001, https://www.foreignaffairs.com/articles/global-commons/2001-09-01/interview-author.

33 Nimijean, "Domestic Brand Politics."

34 Jonathan Rose, "The Branding of States: The Uneasy Marriage of Marketing to Politics," *Journal of Political Marketing* 9, no. 4 (2010): 262.

35 Ibid., 271.

36 Nicholas O'Shaughnessy, "The Symbolic State: A British Experience," *Journal of Public Affairs* 3, no. 4 (2007): 298.

37 Ibid., 299, 305.

38 "35 Dead as Brutal Fighting Halted by Truce in Beirut" *Ottawa Citizen*, 23 November 1985: A2.

39 John Howard, "Remarks on National Flag Day," 3 September 1996, http://www.australianflag.net.au/index.php?option=com_content&task=view&id=87&Itemid=69.

40 For example, in his 2006 Flag Day remarks, Harper refers incorrectly to "National Flag Day" instead of the correct "National Flag of Canada Day." In recent years, the NDP has proposed amending the Holidays Act to change the name to Flag Day (and also make it a statutory holiday).

41 Jeffrey Cormier, *The Canadianization Movement: Emergence, Survival, and Success* (Toronto: University of Toronto Press, 2004).

42 Herschel Hardin, *A Nation Unaware: The Canadian Economic Culture* (Vancouver: J.J. Douglas, 1974).

43 J.L. Granatstein, *Canada, 1957–1967: The Years of Uncertainty and Innovation* (Toronto: McClelland and Stewart, 1986), 201–2.

44 Matheson, *Canada's Flag*, 3.

45 Mildred A. Schwartz, *Public Opinion and Canadian Identity* (Scarborough, ON: Fitzhenry and Whiteside, 1967), 106–10.

46 Granatstein, *Canada, 1957–1967*, 201–2.

47 Peter C. Newman, *The Distemper of Our Times; Canadian Politics in Transition, 1963–1968* (Toronto: McClelland and Stewart, 1968). There was another view, namely that there was a need for a new flag, but this flag should recognize the symbols of the past. Supporters included notable historians Donald Creighton and W.L. Morton. See Granatstein, *Canada, 1957–1967*, 202.

48 See Jean Guy Genest, *Non au drapeau canadien* (Montreal: Éditions Actualité, 1962).

49 Granatstein, *Canada, 1957–1967*, 201–2.

50 Schwarz, *Public Opinion and Canadian Identity*, 106–10.

51 Eva Mackey, *The House of Difference: Cultural Politics and National Identity in Canada* (Toronto: University of Toronto Press, 2002), 56, 55–8.

52 Matheson, *Canada's Flag*, 229–30.

53 Granatstein, *Canada 1957–1967*, 205 (his emphasis).

54 Peter C. Newman, *The Canadian Revolution, 1985–1995: From Deference to Defiance* (Toronto: Viking, 1995).

55 Richard Nimijean, "The Paradoxical Nature of the Canadian Identity," *Teaching Canada* 23 (2005): 25–31.

56 Ibid.

57 Edward Greenspon and Anthony Wilson-Smith, *Double Vision: The Inside Story of the Liberals in Power* (Toronto: Doubleday, 1996), 323.

58 See ibid., chap. 21 for a detailed account.

59 Lawrence Martin, *Chrétien*, vol. 2, *Iron Man: The Defiant Reign of Jean Chrétien* (Toronto: Viking, 2003), 115, 97.

60 Antonia Maioni, "Showing the Flag: The Origins and Consequences of the Sponsorship Scandal," *Policy Options* (June 2005): 23.

61 Greenspon and Wilson-Smith, *Double Vision*, 357.

62 Rose notes that, in the 1995 referendum, proponents of the *Oui* side used popular 1960s symbols like the peace sign in their advertising, even though the link to their political option was not clear. Jonathan William

Rose, *Making "Pictures in Our Heads": Government Advertising in Canada* (Westport, CT: Praeger, 2000), 1.

63 Greenspon and Wilson-Smith, *Double Vision*, 358

64 Ibid.

65 Maioni, "Showing the Flag," 23.

66 Kathryn May, "Cabinet Panicked at '95 Vote," *Ottawa Citizen*, 29 September 2004.

67 Lawrence Martin, *Chrétien*, vol. 1, *The Will to Win* (Toronto: Lester Publishing, 1995), 284.

68 Cited in Tu Thanh Ha, "National Unity 'Perpetual Crisis' Chretien Believes," *Globe and Mail*, 19 December 1995.

69 May, "Cabinet Panicked."

70 Opinions on its origins vary, for while the program was funded by a special unity fund controlled by the prime minister since the mid-1990s, legally it was established only in 2001.

71 Canada, Commission of Inquiry into the Sponsorship Program and Advertising Activities, *Who Is Responsible? Phase 1 Report* (Ottawa: Commission of Inquiry into the Sponsorship Program and Advertising Activities, 2005).

72 Greenspon and Wilson-Smith, *Double Vision*, 365–6.

73 Susan Delacourt, *Juggernaut: Paul Martin's Campaign for Chretien's Crown* (Toronto: McClelland and Stewart, 2003), 99.

74 Paul Gessell, "Government Orders CBC, Other Agencies to Show Canada Logo," *Ottawa Citizen*, 23 May 1998.

75 Leblanc notes that this strategy was roundly condemned, both by the Reform Party, which saw it as "propaganda" and a waste of taxpayer funds, and the Bloc québécois, which saw it as federalist propaganda. In response to this unwillingness to spend relatively small sums of money on an important national symbol, Nolan wryly notes, "Only in Canada would the same people who declare the Canada flag the most important symbol of national identity also, with equal passion, blow a gasket over spending $23-million on something so trivial and stupid." Nicole Nolan, "Memo to Sheila Copps: Forget Those Flags – The Slickest New Nationalism Is in the Latest Wave of Beer Ads," in *Canadian Communications: Issues in Contemporary Media and Culture*, ed. Jeannette Sloniowski and Bohdan George Szuchewycz (Toronto: Prentice Hall Allyn and Bacon, 1999), 391.

76 Eddie Goldenberg, *The Way It Works: Inside Ottawa* (Toronto: McClelland and Stewart, 2006), 222.

77 Daniel Leblanc, "Liberals to Promote 'Canada' as a Brand," *Globe and Mail*, 12 July 1999. Ironically, not only did the funds not come out of the

Federal Sponsorship program, but also only 12.5% of the flags were sent to Québécois. Moreover, the initiative created a $13 million shortfall in the Department of Canadian Heritage, leading to program cuts. Kathryn May, "Top Bureaucrat Hints He'll Deny Files to Gomery," *Ottawa Citizen*, 7 December 2004, A1.

78 Nolan, "Memo to Sheila Copps," 389.

79 "National Capital too Busy for Flag Day: It's also Too Cold for Flag Waving, Ottawa Mayor Says," *Ottawa Citizen*, 16 February 1997.

80 "A Half-Mast Kind of Holiday," *Globe and Mail*, 13 February 1998, A22.

81 Randy Boswell, "Patriots Invited to Click for a New Holiday: Online Petition Calls for National Flag Day," *Ottawa Citizen*, 11 February 2003.

82 "Canada Wishes Its Flag a Happy 40th" CBC News, 15 February 2005.

83 Ian McKay and Jamie Swift, *Warrior Nation: Rebranding Canada in a Fearful Age* (Toronto: Between the Lines, 2012).

84 Alex Marland and Tom Flanagan, "Brand New Party: Political Branding and the Conservative Party of Canada," *Canadian Journal of Political Science* 46, no. 4 (2013): 958–9, 963–4.

85 Ibid., 965–6.

86 Billig, *Banal Nationalism*, 99–103.

87 Tasha Kheiriddin and Adam Daifallah, *Rescuing Canada's Right: Blueprint for a Revolution* (Mississauga, ON: J. Wiley & Sons, 2005), 196–9.

88 Lawrence Martin, "Can Harper Make Canadians Feel Good?" *Globe and Mail*, 16 July 2007.

89 Speech from the Throne to Open the Second Session – Thirty-Ninth Parliament of Canada, 2007, http://www.parl.gc.ca/Parlinfo/Documents/ThroneSpeech/39-2-e.html.

90 Stephen Harper, "Viewing the First Canadian Flag on National Flag of Canada Day," 2006, http://www.collectionscanada.gc.ca/webarchives/20071124192326/http://www.pm.gc.ca/eng/media.asp?category=2&id=1019, accessed 13 May 2016.

91 Stephen Harper, "Remarks on National Flag of Canada Day," 2007, http://www.collectionscanada.gc.ca/webarchives/20071119173956/http://pm.gc.ca/eng/media.asp?id=1539, accessed 13 May 2016.

92 Stephen Harper, Remarks on National Flag of Canada Day, 2010, http://news.gc.ca/web/article-en.do?crtr.sj1D=&crtr.mnthndVl=2&mthd=advSrch&crtr.dpt1D=&nid=512729&crtr.lc1D=&crtr.tp1D=&crtr.yrStrtVl=2010&crtr.kw=&crtr.dyStrtVl=15&crtr.aud1D=&crtr.mnthStrtVl=2&crtr.page=2&crtr.yrndVl=2010&crtr.dyndVl=15, accessed 13 May 2016.

93 Harper's strict control over photographs resulted in the most common backdrop of his pictures issued by the PMO in 2010 being the Canadian flag (35%) and the most common text backdrop being "Canada." See Susan Delacourt, "The Picture-book Harper Government," *Toronto Star*, 2 June 2012.

94 Stephen Harper, "Statement by the Prime Minister of Canada on National Flag of Canada Day," 2011, http://news.gc.ca/web/article-en.do?crtr. sj1D=&crtr.mnthndVl=2&mthd=advSrch&crtr.dpt1D=&nid=589219&crtr. lc1D=&crtr.tp1D=&crtr.yrStrtVl=2011&crtr.kw=&crtr.dyStrtVl=15&crtr. aud1D=&crtr.mnthStrtVl=2&crtr.page=2&crtr.yrndVl=2011&crtr. dyndVl=15, accessed 13 May 2016.

95 Stephen Harper, "Statement by the Prime Minister of Canada on National Flag of Canada Day," 2012, https://web.archive.org/ web/20130404014142/http://www.pm.gc.ca/eng/media.asp?category= 1&featureId=6&pageId=26&id=4655, accessed 13 May 2016.

96 Stephen Harper, Statement by the Prime Minister of Canada on National Flag of Canada Day, 2013, http://news.gc.ca/web/article-en.do?crtr. sj1D=&crtr.mnthndVl=2&mthd=advSrch&crtr.dpt1D=&nid=720809&crtr. lc1D=&crtr.tp1D=&crtr.yrStrtVl=2013&crtr.kw=&crtr.dyStrtVl=15&crtr. aud1D=&crtr.mnthStrtVl=2&crtr.page=1&crtr.yrndVl=2013&crtr. dyndVl=15, accessed 13 May 2016. Emphasis added.

97 www.chrisalexander.ca, accessed 10 April 2014.

98 Stephen Harper, "Statement by the Prime Minister of Canada on National Flag of Canada Day," 2014, https://web.archive. org/web/20140401031459/http://news.gc.ca/web/article-en. do?mthd=tp&crtr.page=10&nid=815899&crtr.tp1D=980, accessed 13 May 2016.

99 Meagan Fitzpatrick, "Conservatives Draw Fire for War of 1812 Spending," CBC News, 15 June 2012, http://www.cbc.ca/news/politics/ conservatives-draw-fire-for-war-of-1812-spending-1.1265851, accessed 15 January 2016; Lee-Anne Goodman, "Feds to Spend $50,000 for Flag's 50th Birthday Celebration," CBC News, 2015, 15 June 2012, http://www. cbc.ca/news/politics/feds-to-spend-50-000-for-flag-s-50th-birthday-celebration-1.2906890, accessed 21 February 2015.

100 "Harper Government Celebrates 50th Anniversary of the Canadian Flag," Canada Newswire, 15 February 2015, http://www.newswire.ca/en/ story/1487599/harper-government-celebrates-50th-anniversary-of-the-canadian-flag, accessed 17 February 2015.

101 Stephen Harper, "National Flag of Canada Day," 2015, https:// web.archive.org/web/20150218035917/http://pm.gc.ca/eng/

news/2015/02/15/statement-prime-minister-canada-national-flag-canada-day, accessed 13 May 2016.

102 See, for example, Catherine Ford, "Flag Waving Isn't Our Style," *Calgary Herald*, 11 February 1995, A1.

103 Trish Crawford, "Getting All in a Flap on Flag Day," *Toronto Star*, 15 February 1996, A1.

104 Rob O'Flanagan, "MacKay Lauds Soldiers in Patriotic Guelph Address: Defence Minister Visits Our Lady of Lourdes for National Flag Day," *Guelph Mercury*, 16 February 2013, A1.

105 Ian McMillan, "Flag Day Overshadowed by other Holidays: Valentine's Day, Black History Month Celebrations Garner More attention in February," *Scarborough Mirror*, 14 February 2004.

106 Dave Rogers, "'I Am So Proud to Be Canadian': Two Local Schools, One Government Office, Mark National Flag Day," *Ottawa Citizen*, 16 February 1999, D2.

107 Jacquie Miller and Catherine Lawson, "Flag Day? Which Flag, Which Day? New National Holiday Has an Image Problem," *Ottawa Citizen*, 15 February 1997, A3.

108 Ibid.

109 Charles Perry, "Do We Care That It's Flag Day? After 36 Years, Maple Leaf Stirs Pride in Citizens," *Moncton Times-Transcript*, 16 February 2001.

110 Hobsbawm, *Nations and Nationalism*, 304–5.

111 Hugh Winsor, "Ads Promoting Flag Could Backfire, Copps Warned," *Globe and Mail*, 25 September 1996, A5.

112 "Charter Anniversary Celebrations Show Partisan Tone," CBC News, 17 April 2012, http://www.cbc.ca/news/canada/charter-anniversary-celebrations-show-partisan-tone-1.1175002, accessed 15 February 2015.

113 Don Butler, "Architects Call for New Site: Memorial to Victims of Communism Should Move 300 Metres, Group Urges," *Ottawa Citizen*, 5 February 2015, A2; Elsa Lam, "The Monumental Mindset: Ottawa's Planned Memorial to Victims of Communism Is Both Misguided and Misplaced," *National Post*, 11 February 2015, A10; "Jim Watson Joins Critics of 'Victims of Communism' Monument Location," CBC News, 12 February 2015, http://www.cbc.ca/news/canada/ottawa/jim-watson-joins-critics-of-victims-of-communism-monument-location-1.2954861, Accessed 12 February 2015)

114 Terrance Wills, "Canadians Marking Flag Day Today: But There Are No Special Events Planned for Montreal," *Montreal Gazette*, 15 February 1997, A10.

115 Dave Rogers, "Flag Day Largely Ignored," *Ottawa Citizen*, 15 February 1999, D2.

116 Earlier in 2011, New Democrat MP Peter Julian (Burnaby New Westminster) re-tabled a private member's bill (Bill C-337) first introduced by the NDP in 2009 to designate every 15 February as Flag Day and make it a legal holiday throughout Canada.

117 Interviewed in Barbara Yaffe, "Flag Giveaway Effort Proves You Can't Legislate National Unity," *Vancouver Sun*, 13 February 1997, A3. Still, while much has been made of the powerful political symbolism of the fleur-de-lis flag, Quebec's announcement in late 1999 that the province would have its own flag day generated equal levels of lack of knowledge, even among provincial bureaucrats. See "Fleur-de-lis Flaps with Modest Fanfare: Flag Day? What Flag Day?" *National Post*, 22 January 2000, A4.

118 Thanks to Anne Trépanier for pointing out that the date chosen for Canada's Flag Day, 15 February, coincided with the date on which several *patriotes* were hanged for their role in the 1839 Rebellions.

119 Sheila Copps, "Flag Day Passed with Barely a Whimper," *Hill Times* (Ottawa), 20 February 2012.

120 Nimijean, "Domestic Brand Politics."

121 Jonathan William Rose, *Making "Pictures in Our Heads,"* 1.

122 Karen A. Cerulo, *Identity Designs: The Sights and Sounds of a Nation* (New Brunswick, NJ: Rutgers University Press, 1995), 27–8.

17 Conclusion

MATTHEW HAYDAY AND RAYMOND B. BLAKE

Most red-and-white-clad revellers on Parliament Hill on the evening of Canada Day, perhaps somewhat intoxicated from a few pints of beer, likely spare little *active* thought for politics as they await a spectacular fireworks display. But in all probability they have sung at least one or two boisterous renditions of "O Canada," waved or worn a Maple Leaf flag (and seen hundreds more throughout the day), and perhaps watched a concert on the Parliament Hill stage featuring carefully chosen performers representing Canada's linguistic, cultural, and regional diversity. By celebrating with their presence one of Canada's key founding events, they are actively participating in a construction of the nation and engaging with efforts to define their country's identity.

Politics are all around us on our national days. Governments and organizers try to craft narratives of identity. Speeches by dignitaries deliver specific messages about the nation. Flags, anthems, coats of arms, and even national colours create a symbol-laden backdrop of nationhood and shared community. Spectators and participants accept or contest the overarching conceptions of the day. The long-term success of a holiday or national day depends on getting the right mix of elements and, as the chapters in this book demonstrate, these holidays may change radically over time, or even fade away.

Over the five years since work on this book started, there has been ample evidence of the politicization of holidays and commemorations in contemporary politics. When we launched this project, Canada was in the midst of the intensely politicized commemoration of the War of 1812 orchestrated by the Conservative government of Stephen Harper. This commemoration, together with the government's plans to mark the First World War, its messaging on National Flag of Canada Day,

Canada Day, and Remembrance Day, and even its use of art and por-
traiture in Canadian embassies and high commissions, made it clear
that Harper's government intended to redirect official messaging
about Canadian identity towards a more pro-monarchy, militaristic orientation that it saw as a part of Canada's British and French heritage.
National holidays were a key element of this agenda, as was clear from
government spending and politicians' speeches on those days.

Suddenly, and surprisingly to many, in October 2015 a new Liberal
majority government headed by Justin Trudeau was elected. Although
at the time of writing we have yet to see what exactly this change will
mean in terms of messaging about Canadian identity, the new government has been crystal clear that it intends to promote Canada's diversity and multicultural heritage. In his first speech abroad, at Canada
House in London, Trudeau invoked the memory of George-Étienne
Cartier and said "Canadians understand that diversity is our strength.
We know that Canada has succeeded – culturally, politically, economically – because of our diversity, not in spite of it."[1] Shortly after her
appointment as minister of Canadian heritage, Mélanie Joly was quoted
as saying that "the past government didn't have the same vision and
values as Canadians, and to that extent some symbols were changed."
She considers it a key part of her job to have the government return to
promoting "symbols of progressiveness."[2] We can anticipate that this
view will lead to shifts in the celebration of national days, and likely a
radical alteration of the plans currently in motion to celebrate Canada's
150th anniversary in 2017.

Certainly, the essays in this collection demonstrate that national days
and holidays have a lively history and are rich sources for analysing
Canada's social, cultural, and political development. Because each one
occurs annually, and on a single date, national holidays have been focal
points for celebration and/or solemn observance and also for contestation and debate. Almost all of them were the subject of heated debate as
to what they would be called, and most have had their names changed
their name over the course of the past century: Dominion Day became
Canada Day; the Fête Saint-Jean-Baptiste became the Fête nationale;
Empire Day became Commonwealth Day; Armistice Day became
Remembrance Day. The same has been true of other national days and
holidays that did not get full-length treatments in this book, including
the Fête de Dollard, which was rebranded as la Journée nationale des
patriotes in 2003, celebrating the 1837 Patriote uprising. National Aboriginal Day, celebrated on 21 June since 1996, seems a likely candidate

for a renaming in the near future, in light of the recent shift of the related government ministry to using the term "Indigenous" in place of "Aboriginal."

We have seen how the dates of observance of these holidays and national days have often been shifted to accommodate various interests. Business and personal interests often militated in favour of statutory holidays having dates conducive to creating a long weekend. In other cases, business interests fought against creating mandatory statutory holidays, at least if this was perceived as cutting into their profits. For holidays with an educational mission, such as Remembrance Day and Empire Day, many thought it preferable not to have these as statutory holidays, to better allow for school-based programming that could reach young Canadians and inculcate them with desired values. Even the weather has played a role in determining the timing of national days. It is perhaps fortunate that Queen Victoria was born in late May, when most Canadian cities are finally feeling at least spring-like, rather than in the dead of winter, when there is less yearning for a holiday or possibility for outdoor celebration. The ultimate placement of Canadian Thanksgiving on the second Monday in October, after decades of being bounced around from October to December, is the result of a host of factors ranging from the religious to the commercial. But it also reflects the fact that a feast day honouring the Canadian harvest should perhaps be held when Canadian fields are not blanketed with snow.

As the authors in this collection have shown, national days and holidays have provided a vehicle for Canadians to consider their place in the world, their sense of how they compare to other nations (particularly the United States and the United Kingdom), and how they fit (or did not fit) within the national picture. It would be inaccurate to cast this history as a clear trajectory – from the orbit of the United Kingdom to that of the United States, for example, or from the integration of Quebec within a Canadian framework to a clear will for independence. Rather, these holidays have often demonstrated a state of creative tension, a back and forth between competing poles of attraction, sensitive to the political and cultural currents of given decades.

It is clear from the studies that make up this volume that the meaning and traditions of these holidays have never been completely fixed and concretized. Rather, they have been subject to a regular process of reinvention, albeit with periods of relative stability. Changes were sometimes rapid and abrupt, but other times more subtle and long-term. While some of the predominant traits of Canadian-ness from the era of Laurier, including Britishness and a public religious Christian identity, seemed to have largely faded away by the latter decades of the twentieth century, recent experience demonstrates that these facets could be revived by groups wishing to see them assume greater prominence. National identity, then, is clearly an ongoing process, subject to challenge, and requiring active engagement and participation.

While we hope that this collection has served as a solid introduction to the study of Canadian national days and holidays and their connections to nationalism, identity, and cultural and social change, we encourage other scholars to continue to pursue research in this field. Beyond extending the temporal scope of the holidays we have addressed in this volume, other national days and holidays, such as National Aboriginal Day, the Journée nationale des patriotes, and Louis Riel Day, are fertile territory for exploration. The observance of religious holidays (in ways both secular[3] and spiritual) and the marking of national days of other countries in Canada are also fertile ground for the exploration of issues such as hybridity, multiculturalism, and integration. Moreover, very little work has yet been done on how Canadians overseas celebrate their national days, and transmit conceptions of Canada to an international audience while also reinforcing particular conceptions of what it means to be a Canadian.

As authors in this collection have noted, the past few years have seen multiple attempts to create new national holidays, proposals to convert existing national days into statutory holidays, and the successful creation of new statutory holidays at the provincial level – with a particular clustering of these in the bleak mid-winter month of February. Recently, some Canadians have proposed the creation a new national holiday in January to honour the birth of Canada's first prime minister, Sir John A. Macdonald, much as the United States observes the birthdays of key political figures such as Martin Luther King and George Washington. In light of the intense controversies swirling around Macdonald's legacy, particularly regarding indigenous peoples and Chinese immigrants, it seems unlikely that this proposal will be accepted in the immediate future, although we will likely see private members' bills in Parliament to propose such a holiday.

Although the future of how Canada's many national days and holidays will be observed and celebrated remains to be seen, what is clear is that these days will continue to have significance beyond what is perceptible at a passing glance. Politicians, interest groups, public servants, religious leaders, and the general public will continue to engage with these celebrations in a variety of ways as they attempt to steer the future of their country, region, or community in the direction of the identity they prefer. If history is any guide, it is unlikely that any of these groups will ever be able to claim a definitive victory. If Canadian history tells us anything, it is that our country, with its diverse population made up of so many ethnic, linguistic, and religious communities, not to mention a wide array of ideological affiliations, is rarely able to agree over the long term to anything other than to continue an ongoing dialogue and process of change and accommodation. Such diversity perhaps does not produce as clear a national identity as we associate with our neighbour to the south, but nor does it prevent us from enjoying fireworks on our national holidays and celebrating our country and its diverse communities on various occasions throughout the year.

NOTES

1 Address by Prime Minister Justin Trudeau, "Diversity Is Canada's Strength," London, UK, 26 November 2015, http://pm.gc.ca/eng/news/2015/11/26/diversity-canadas-strength#sthash.N6jsJaVF.dpuf?
2 Robert Everett-Green, "Mélanie Joly to Reset 'Symbols of Progressiveness' as Heritage Minister," *Globe and Mail*, 6 November 2015.
3 Steve Penfold's work on the history of Santa Claus parades, for example, looks at some of the commercial dimensions of the celebration of Christmas. See Steve Penfold, *A Mile of Make-Believe: A History of the Eaton's Santa Claus Parade* (Toronto: University of Toronto Press, 2016).

Appendix – National Days and Holidays

The following list, roughly in calendar order, includes the major holidays discussed in this book, with some explanatory notes on when they were observed and, where relevant, their different names and legal status.

JANUARY
Australia Day (Australia) – 26 January

FEBRUARY
Waitangi Day (New Zealand) – 6 February: Officially renamed New Zealand Day from 1973 to 1976, then name reverted to Waitangi Day.

National Flag of Canada Day – 15 February: First proclaimed in 1996 by the federal government.

Family Day – Second or third Monday in February: Observed as a statutory holiday on the second Monday of February in British Columbia (since 2013), and the third Monday in February in Alberta (since 1990), Saskatchewan (since 2007), and Ontario (since 2008).

Islander Day – Third Monday in February: Observed as a statutory holiday in Prince Edward Island since 2009.

Louis Riel Day – Third Monday in February: Observed as a statutory holiday in Manitoba since 2008.

Nova Scotia Heritage Day – Third Monday in February: Observed as a statutory holiday in Nova Scotia since 2015.

MARCH
St David's Day (Wales) – 1 March
St Patrick's Day (Ireland) – 17 March

St George's Day (England) – 23 April

Anzac Day (Australia / New Zealand) – 25 April: Commemorates the failed invasion of Gallipoli by the Australian and New Zealand Army Corps in 1915.

MAY
Fête Dieu / Corpus Christi – 60 days after Easter: Catholic festival.

Empire Day – 23 May: Observed on the last school day before 24 May (Victoria Day), normally 23 May. First celebrated in Dundas, Ontario, 22 May 1898; observed in Ontario, Quebec, and Nova Scotia, 23 May 1899; observed nationally in Canada, from 1900; recognized throughout the British Empire, from 1903; renamed Commonwealth Day in 1958.

Commonwealth Day (Canada, Australia, New Zealand, United Kingdom) – May: Name changed from Empire Day in 1958; date moved to the second Monday in March in 1976.

Victoria Day – 24 May / last Monday in May before 25 May: Queen Victoria came to the throne in 1837, but the first recorded official observance of her birthday (24 May) as a holiday in any part of pre-Confederation Canada was in 1845. Until 1901, the Queen's Birthday was observed on 24 May, unless it fell on a Sunday, in which case it was observed on 25 May. After Queen Victoria's death in 1901, the Parliament of Canada made 24 May a perpetual statutory holiday known as Victoria Day. In 1952, Victoria Day became a floating holiday that was always attached to a weekend, to be observed on the last Monday before 25 May.

Queen's Birthday/King's Birthday – The formal date of the observance of the birthday of the reigning monarch of the United Kingdom and the Commonwealth, which may or may not coincide with his or her actual birthday. In Canada, the Queen's Birthday is observed on the last Monday in May before 25 May (Victoria Day). Queen Elizabeth II's birthday is actually 21 April but is officially celebrated in the United Kingdom, Australia, and New Zealand in June (on different dates).

Fête de Dollard des Ormeaux – May 24: Observed in Quebec and throughout French Canada on 24 May, starting in 1919; observances faded out after the 1950s.

Journée nationale des patriotes – Last Monday in May before 25 May: Observed in Quebec on the same Monday as Victoria Day, since 2003.

JUNE

Anniversary of the Battle of Waterloo – 18 June

National Aboriginal Day – 21 June: First proclaimed in 1996 by the government of Canada to celebrate the contributions of Aboriginal peoples to Canada.

Fête Saint-Jean-Baptiste / Fête nationale – 24 June: Observed in Quebec and French Canada; officially renamed la Fête nationale du Québec in 1977.

Discovery Day – 24 June: A public holiday in Newfoundland on the closest Monday to 24 June; celebrates John Cabot's arrival in Newfoundland.

JULY

Dominion Day / Canada Day – 1 July: Officially proclaimed by the governor general in 1879 to commemorate Confederation. Officially renamed Canada Day in 1982. In Newfoundland and Labrador, this day is also set aside to commemorate the losses from the Battle of Beaumont-Hamel (1915) during the First World War.

Chinese Humiliation Day – 1 July: Observed by Chinese communities in British Columbia to protest the Chinese Exclusion Act, which was in effect from 1923 to 1947.

Independence Day (United States) – 4 July

Orangemen's Day (Ireland and Newfoundland) – 12 July: "The Glorious Twelfth," marking the anniversary of the Battle of the Boyne, observed by the Irish Orange Order. A provincial holiday in Newfoundland and Labrador on the Monday closest to 12 July.

AUGUST

Anniversary of the Hanoverian Succession (Germany) – 1 August: Observed in Montreal during the nineteenth century.

Le 15 août / Fête de l'Assomption (Assumption Day) – 15 August: Feast of Mary, patron saint of Acadia, proclaimed as the Acadian national holiday by the first Acadian National Convention, 1881. The Parliament of Canada recognized 15 August as "National Acadian Day" in 2003, but it is not recognized as a federal or provincial statutory holiday.

SEPTEMBER

Labour Day – First Monday in September.

OCTOBER

Canadian Thanksgiving – First observed in 1859. From 1859 to 1913, date of observance ranged from late October to early December, on various days of the week; from 1914 to 1919, observed on the second Monday in October; from 1921 to 1930, combined with Armistice Day and held on Monday of the week of 11 November; from 1931 to 1956, observed on the second Monday in October. In 1957, the date was permanently fixed by law on the second Monday in October.

NOVEMBER

Remembrance Day / Armistice Day – 11 November: Recognizes the 11 November 1918 armistice ending the First World War. In 1919, Armistice Day was the 2nd Monday in November (floating). In 1921, Armistice Day was combined with Thanksgiving and celebrated on the 1st Monday during the week of 11 November (floating). In 1931, the day became Remembrance Day, observed on 11 November.

Douglas Day – 19 November: The anniversary of the 1858 proclamation of the Crown Colony of British Columbia; initiated by the Native Sons of British Columbia, in 1925; recognized by the provincial government, 1959 (Douglas Day Observance Act, S.B.C. 1959, c. 27) as a lasting legacy of the British Columbia Centennial, 1958.

St Andrew's Day (Scotland) – 30 November

DECEMBER

Feast of St John the Evangelist – 29 December: Observed by the Masonic Order.

Contributors

Bailey Antonishyn recently completed an MA in history at the University of Regina. Her interests include post–Second World War American history, with an emphasis on identity formation and American cinema.

Timothy Baycroft is a senior lecturer in history at the University of Sheffield. He specializes in the history of nation building, commemoration, and borders, particularly in comparative context. He has edited *What Is a Nation? Europe, 1789–1914* (2006) and *Folklore and Nationalism in Europe during the Long Nineteenth Century* (2012), and is the author of *France: Inventing the Nation* (2008).

Joel Belliveau is an associate professor in the Department of History at Laurentian University. His primary area of research is social and cultural movements within minority francophone communities. His first book, *Le "moment 68" et la réinvention de l'Acadie* (2014), deals with 1960s student movements in New Brunswick and their effects on the political culture of that province's French-speaking minority.

Mike Benbough-Jackson is a senior lecturer in history at Liverpool John Moores University. He is interested in the relationships between individual, local, regional, and national identities. His PhD thesis (published as *Cardiganshire and the Cardi, c. 1760–c. 2000: Locating a Place and Its People*, 2011) investigated the changing representation of a county in Wales. He has published articles and book chapters on a variety of celebrations.

Raymond B. Blake is a professor in and head of the Department of History at the University of Regina. He has authored or edited fifteen books on Canadian history and Canadian studies. His most recent book is *Lions or Jellyfish: Newfoundland-Ottawa Relations since 1957* (2015).

Brittney Anne Bos is a recent PhD graduate of Queen's University in the Department of History. Her dissertation focused on developing a methodology for the visual analysis of monuments in Ontario, particularly in relation to Canada's colonial and racial construction. She has published articles on the Underground Railroad monument in Windsor, Ontario, and on historical memory in Canada.

Marc-André Gagnon is a PhD candidate in the Department of History at the University of Guelph. His research focuses on identity and political movements in French Canada, primarily the Société Saint-Jean-Baptiste.

Matthew Hayday is associate professor of Canadian history at the University of Guelph. He is the author of *So They Want Us to Learn French: Promoting and Opposing Bilingualism in English-Speaking Canada* (2015) and *Bilingual Today, United Tomorrow: Official Languages in Education and Canadian Federalism* (2005). He has also published several articles, book chapters, and edited collections on topics related to language policy, Canadian identity, Canada Day, nationalism, social movements, Quebec history, and English-French relations in Canada.

Teresa Iacobelli is the author of *Death or Deliverance: Canadian Courts Martial in the Great War* (2013), which won the Charles P. Stacey Prize for distinguished work in twentieth-century Canadian military history. She received her PhD from the University of Western Ontario in 2010 and was a Social Sciences and Humanities Research Council Postdoctoral Fellow at Queen's University. She has curated several major exhibitions for museums and archives in the United States and Canada. Her current areas of interest lie in the fields of military history, social memory, commemoration, and media studies

Gillian I. Leitch completed her PhD dissertation about Montreal's British population ("The Importance of Being English? Identity and Social Organization in British Montreal, 1800–1850") at the Université de Montréal in 2007. After a year as a postdoctoral fellow at the University of Edinburgh, she joined Canadian Development Consultants International in Ottawa as a historical researcher. In addition to her work on Canadian history, she has also published three academic books on popular culture.

Marcel Martel is a professor of Canadian history at York University. He has published several journal articles and book chapters on public policy, minority rights, moral regulation, and identity. His most recent books include *Canada the Good? A Short History of Vice since 1500* (2014) and *Langue et politique au Canada et au Québec* (with Martin Pâquet, 2010), which was translated as *Speaking Up: A History of Language and Politics in Canada and Quebec*.

Richard Nimijean is a member of the School of Canadian Studies at Carleton University. He is co-editor of the *International Journal of Canadian Studies*. His most recent publication is "A Passport to Identity: The Decline of Duality and the Symbolic Appropriation of Quebec" (with Anne Trépanier) in *Études canadiennes / Canadian Studies*.

Forrest D. Pass is a historian at the Canadian Museum of History in Gatineau, Quebec. He holds a PhD from the University of Western Ontario, and has published widely on the history of British Columbia and of Canadian nationalism.

Michael Poplyansky is an instructor in the Department of French and Francophone Intercultural Studies at the Cité universitaire francophone (University of Regina). He has published several articles on Quebec and Acadian nationalisms in journals such as *Francophonies d'Amérique* and *Acadiensis*.

L. Pauline Rankin is associate vice-president (research and international) at Carleton University and a professor in the School of Canadian Studies. Her research interests focus on gender and politics, nation branding, and gender mainstreaming. She is co-editor (with Patrizia Gentile and Gary Kinsman) of the recently published volume *We Still Demand! Redefining Resistance in Sex and Gender Struggles* and frequently serves as a gender consultant on international development projects.

Peter A. Stevens has a PhD from York University, where he now teaches history and Canadian studies. His largest project to date, a history of family cottaging in postwar Ontario, has produced articles in the *Canadian Historical Review* and the *Journal of Canadian Studies*, among other journals.

Chris Tait earned his PhD in history from the University of Western Ontario in 2007, and now works as a senior policy analyst for the Canadian Department of Immigration, Refugees and Citizenship. His contribution to this volume is a personal project and does not necessarily reflect the views of the Government of Canada or the department.

Allison Marie Ward completed her PhD in history at Queen's University in 2014. Her dissertation, "Guarding the City Beautiful: Liberalism, Empire, Labour, and Civic Identity in Hamilton, Ontario, 1929–53," examines the political culture of Hamilton, Ontario.

Stuart Ward specializes in British imperial history at Copenhagen University, where he directs the "Embers of Empire" project. His most recent works are *The Unknown Nation: Australia after Empire* (co-authored with James Curran, 2010) and *Exhuming Passions: The Pressure of the Past in Ireland and Australia* (co-edited with Katie Holmes, 2011). He is currently completing a book on the eclipse of British identities around the world since the Second World War for Cambridge University Press.

Lianbi Zhu is lecturer in modern history at Fudan University, China. Her current research interests are the history of the British Empire in the nineteenth and twentieth century and how national holidays contribute to nation building. Her publications, mainly in Chinese, include studies on Remembrance Day and Empire Day from the perspective of global history.